By the People

A History of the United States

Volume 1 – To 1877

James W. Fraser
New York University

PEARSON

Boston   Columbus   Indianapolis   New York   San Francisco

Amsterdam   Cape Town   Dubai   London   Madrid   Milan   Munich   Paris   Montréal   Toronto

Delhi   Mexico City   São Paulo   Sydney   Hong Kong   Seoul   Singapore   Taipei   Tokyo

Dedication

To my children and grandchildren and all the students of their generations. May they find the American story in all its complexity as fascinating as I do.

Editor in Chief: Dickson Musslewhite
Publisher: Charlyce Jones Owen
Program Manager: Seanna Breen
Editorial Assistant: Maureen Diana
Project Manager: Emsal Hasan
Procurement Manager: Mary Fischer
Procurement Specialist: Mary Ann Gloriande
Associate Director of Design: Blair Brown
Cover Designer: Lumina Datamatics
Cover Art: Main photo: Joseph Fayadaneega, called the Brant, the Great Captain of the Six Nations by George Romney (Library of Congress Prints and Photographs Division/LC-DIG-ppmsca-15712); **Insert photos from left to right:** 1. Civil rights march on Washington, D.C., photograph by Warren K. Leffler (Library of Congress Prints and Photographs Division/LC-DIG-ppmsca-03130); 2. "His daughter! And he thought she was "just a little girl" by W.E. Hill. (Library of Congress Prints and Photographs Division/LC-USZC2-1205); 3. Two emigrants on the seashore, photograph by Underwood & Underwood (Library of Congress Prints and Photographs Division/LCUSZ62-35634); 4. "The first vote" by A.R. Waud. (Library of Congress Prints and Photographs Division/LC-USZ62-19234).
Digital Media Editor: Michael Halas
Media Project Manager: Elizabeth Roden Hall
Composition and Full-Service Project Management: GEX Publishing Services
Printer/Binder: RR Donnelly-Willard
Cover Printer: Phoenix Color-Hagerstown
Text Font: 10.5/13 Minion Pro-Regular

Acknowledgements of third party content appear on pages C2-C3, which constitute an extension of this copyright page.

Library of Congress Cataloging-in-Publication Data

Fraser, James W., 1944-
By the people : a history of the United States / James W. Fraser, New York University.
    volumes cm
Includes index.
ISBN 978-0-205-74309-4 (entire book)-- ISBN 978-0-205-74305-6 (volume 1)-- ISBN 978-0-205-74307-0 (volume 2) 1. United States--History--Textbooks. I. Title.
E178.1.F83 2014
973--dc23
                    2014026518

10 9 8 7 6 5 4 3 2 1

PEARSON

Contents

Maps

Tables

Special Features

REVEL™

Educational technology designed for the way today's students read, think, and learn

When students are engaged deeply, they learn more effectively and perform better in their courses. This simple fact inspired the creation of REVEL: an immersive learning experience designed for the way today's students read, think, and learn. Built in collaboration with educators and students nationwide, REVEL is the newest, fully digital way to deliver respected Pearson content.

REVEL enlivens course content with media interactives and assessments — integrated directly within the authors' narrative — that provide opportunities for students to read about and practice course material in tandem. This immersive educational technology boosts student engagement, which leads to better understanding of concepts and improved performance throughout the course.

Learn more about REVEL
<http://www.pearsonhighered.com/revel/>

To the Student

I hope you enjoy reading *By the People* and that you learn the value of the study of American history and historical thinking skills as a result of reading it.

The title of this book—*By the People*—describes one of my key goals. This is a history of the many different peoples who have shaped the United States as it is today. Whenever possible, I have focused on the stories of average everyday women and men who have created this country. In a survey of U.S. History it is essential to tell the stories of the leaders—the people from George Washington to Barack Obama and also from Benjamin Franklin to Andrew Carnegie to Jane Addams—who have had been the best known leaders of their generation. At the same time I believe it is equally important to tell the story of some of those whose names have been forgotten—women and men who fought in the Revolutionary army, enslaved people who ran away or found other ways to resist and ultimately gain freedom, women who worked for decades to win the right to vote, immigrants who came to the United States in the hope of building a better life, American Indians of many different tribes who found ways to maintain their cultures in spite of formidable obstacles. These and many other people are essential to the story that is told in this book.

In focusing on the stories of the diverse peoples of this country I have also sought to foster a sense of agency—as well as historical knowledge. When history becomes one thing after another, it gets boring. When history becomes only a celebration of the good and greats among us, it is unbelievable. And when history is only a story of the bad things that some Americans have done to others, it is just plain depressing. On the other hand, if American history can be the story of those who fought back against injustice, who organized to win new rights, who found ways to build a better society, then our students can ask, "why not me?" And, I believe that such a history of people who made a difference in the past can lead today's students to join the list of those who have helped build a better and more hopeful country.

Please let me know what your experience is like. Email me at jim.fraser@nyu.edu. I am anxious to hear and to learn.

Jim Fraser
New York City, December, 2013

Features of *By the People*

T he pedagogical approach of *By the People* is designed to provide numerous opportunities for students to engage in historical inquiry and to focus on historical analysis and interpretation. Each feature connects to the historical thinking skills that are an essential part of the study of history. They are intended to serve as points of discovery through which students learn and understand the past and its significance.

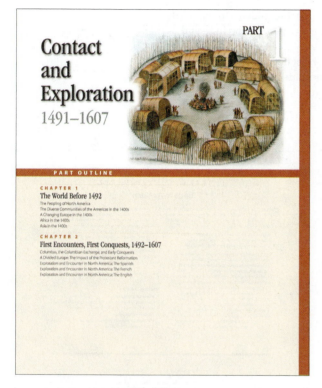

Part Opening Outlines

Each of the 5 parts opens with an outline of the text chapters covered in the Part.

Chapter Learning Objectives

Objectives for each main section of the chapter serve as a guide for the student learner to the chapter's main topics and themes.

Quick Review Questions

Questions that ask students to use historical thinking skills necessary for the practice and study of history conclude each main section of the chapter. These questions ask students to construct arguments, consider cause-and-effect, evaluate patterns of change, and evaluate comparisons and contrasts. Students are asked to use these skills as they relate to the content of the section.

American Voices

Primary source document excerpts bring history alive by introducing students to the words, thoughts, and ideas of people who lived and experienced the events of the time. Each document includes a brief head note and critical analysis questions to help students put the sources in their historical context.

Thinking Historically

This feature continues the emphasis of providing ample opportunity for the practice of historical thinking skills. The feature includes questions that connect to the skills.

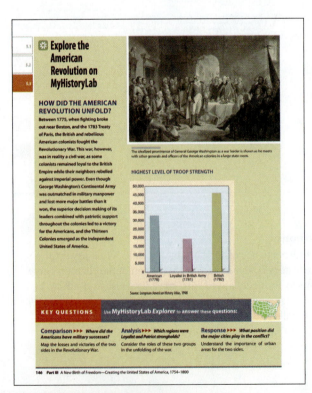

In-text Explorer Activities

There is an Explorer activity feature in each part that focuses students on exploring and analyzing maps and topics related to key events in history.

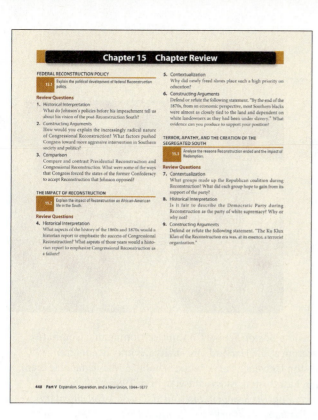

Chapter 15   Chapter Review

FEDERAL RECONSTRUCTION POLICY

15.1 Explain the political development of federal Reconstruction policy.

Review Questions

1. Historical Interpretation
What do Johnson's policies before his impeachment tell us about his vision of the post-Reconstruction South?

2. Constructing Arguments
How would you explain the increasingly radical nature of Congressional Reconstruction? What factors pushed Congress toward more aggressive intervention in Southern society and politics?

3. Comparison
Compare and contrast Presidential Reconstruction and Congressional Reconstruction. What were some of the ways that Congress forced the states of the former Confederacy to accept Reconstruction that Johnson opposed?

THE IMPACT OF RECONSTRUCTION

15.2 Explain the impact of Reconstruction on African-American life in the South.

Review Questions

4. Historical Interpretation
What aspects of the history of the 1860s and 1870s would a historian report to emphasize the success of Congressional Reconstruction? What aspects of those years would a historian report to emphasize Congressional Reconstruction as a failure?

5. Contextualization
Why did newly freed slaves place such a high priority on education?

6. Constructing Arguments
Defend or refute the following statement. "By the end of the 1870s, from an economic perspective, most Southern blacks were almost as closely tied to the land and dependent on white landowners as they had been under slavery." What evidence can you produce to support your position?

TERROR, APATHY, AND THE CREATION OF THE SEGREGATED SOUTH

15.3 Analyze the reasons Reconstruction ended and the impact of Redemption.

Review Questions

7. Contextualization
What groups made up the Republican coalition during Reconstruction? What did each group hope to gain from its support of the party?

8. Historical Interpretation
Is it fair to describe the Democratic Party during Reconstruction as the party of white supremacy? Why or why not?

9. Constructing Arguments
Defend or refute the following statement. "The Ku Klux Klan of the Reconstruction era was, at its essence, a terrorist organization."

448   **Part V** Expansion, Separation, and a New Union, 1844–1877

Chapter Review

An extensive set of review questions based on the chapter learning objectives and key concepts.

MAP 20-5 Europe in 1919. The Treaty of Versailles created a number of new nations in eastern Europe out of what had once been the Austria-Hungary and Ottoman empires as well as new nations in the Middle East.

people like himself who had been excluded from the treaty-making process and his personal animosity to the president. Nevertheless, Lodge insisted that the issues were beyond party, that the United States "is the world's best hope but if you fetter her in the interests and quarrels of other nations, if you tangle her in the intrigues of Europe, you will destroy her power for good and endanger her very existence."

592   **Part VII** War, Prosperity, and Depression, 1890–1945

Exceptional Art and Illustration Program

A full complement of maps, photographs, and illustrations support the discussions within the text and provide geographic context as well as many iconic images of the past.

About the Author

James W. Fraser is Professor of History and Education at the Steinhardt School of Culture, Education, and Human Development at New York University. His teaching includes a survey course in U.S. History for future Social Studies teachers and courses in the History of American Education, Religion & Public Education, and Inquiries into Teaching and Learning. He holds a Ph.D. from Columbia University. Dr. Fraser is the President of the History of Education Society and a former member of the Editorial Board of the *History of Education Quarterly*. He served as Senior Vice President for Programs at the Woodrow Wilson National Fellowship Foundation in Princeton, New Jersey, from 2008 to 2012. He has also served as NYU liaison to the New Design High School, a public high school in New York's Lower East Side, and to Facing History and Ourselves.

Before coming to New York University Dr. Fraser taught in the Department of History and the program in education at Northeastern University in Boston, where he was the founding dean of Northeastern's School of Education. He was also a member and chair of the Commonwealth of Massachusetts Education Deans Council, the Boston School Committee Nominating Committee, and other boards. He was a lecturer in the Program in Religion and Secondary Education at the Harvard University Divinity School from 1997 to 2004. He has taught at Lesley University; University of Massachusetts, Boston; Boston University; and Public School 76 Manhattan. He is an ordained minister in the United Church of Christ and was pastor of Grace Church in East Boston, Massachusetts, from 1986 to 2006.

In addition to *By the People*, Dr. Fraser is the author or editor of twelve books including *The School in the United States: A Documentary History*, a third edition of which will be published in 2014, and *Preparing America's Teachers: A History* (2007), and *A History of Hope: When Americans Have Dared to Dream of a Better Future* (2002). He lives in New York City with his wife Katherine Hanson and their dog, Pebble.

Contact and Exploration

1491–1607

PART OUTLINE

1 The World Before 1492

CHAPTER OBJECTIVE

Demonstrate an understanding of the life and culture among the first North Americans and, later, the independent development of cultures among Native Americans, Europeans, and Africans before the encounters of 1492.

Jacques Le Moyne, an early French explorer, recorded Native American women cultivating crops. Within the cultures of most North American tribes, women were, indeed, the prime cultivators of crops, while men hunted.

The Navajo people, or Dine as they prefer to be called, tell a story of their coming into this world. The story begins in a world of darkness (Nihodilhil):

> Because of the strife in the First World, First Man (Atse Hastin), First Woman (Atse Estsan), and the Coyote called First Angry, followed by all the others, climbed up from the World of Darkness and Dampness to the Second or Blue World.

From this dark or black world the people emerged through the blue and yellow worlds before finally making their way to the bright white world where they live today:

> The Locust was the first to reach the next world. He looked around, and saw that the world was covered with water that glittered and everything looked white. This is why they call it the Glittering World or White World (Nihalgai).
>
> Soon, First Man and First Woman began to make things the way they were supposed to be. The Holy People helped them. Their first job was to rebuild the mountains....Then, the people made a fire. To start it, they used flint....First Man and First Woman wanted a hogan....Talking God helped to build the first hogan....This was the place where the people lived and worked.
>
> By now First Man and First Woman had become human. They were like us.

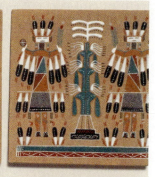

Navajo art regularly portrayed the many different gods that in Navajo tradition accompanied human beings in their emergence into the world. The Navajo believed that these gods could help, hinder, or occasionally play tricks on people in their daily lives.

Significant Dates

Approx. 30,000 years ago	Earliest signs of settlement in Western Alaska and California; Stone Age carvings dating to this era found in France and North Africa
c. 750	Mound-building cultures expand in the Mississippi River Valley
850–1100s	Rise and decline of the Anasazi in Chaco Canyon; founding of Acoma Pueblo
950–1400	Rise and decline of Cahokia
1101	Norse colony of Vineland established in North America
1142	Possible date for the founding of the Iroquois Confederacy
1324	Pilgrimage of Mansa Musa, Emperor of Mali, to Mecca
1325	Rise of Aztec Empire
	Founding of Tenochtitlán (Mexico City)
1348–1350s	Bubonic plague begins in Europe
1415	Portuguese begin exploration of the Atlantic coast of Africa
1421–1423	Chinese explore the Indian Ocean and East Africa
1453	Ottoman Turks capture Constantinople
	End of the Hundred Years' War between France and England
1458	Songhay Empire captures Timbuktu
1469	Marriage of Isabella of Castile and Ferdinand of Aragon
1485	King Henry VII ends the War of the Roses, unified England
1488	Bartolomeu Dias rounds Cape of Good Hope
1492	Granada falls to Christians ending Islamic rule in Spain
	Christopher Columbus sails from Spain to the Americas
1493–1528	Askia Muhammad rules Songhay Empire at its height
1498	Vasco da Gama reaches India from Portugal

1.1

1.2

1.3

1.4

1.5

After this, there were four seasons. In the spring, the plants came up from the ground. In the winter, the plants died and were hidden under the snow. Then in the spring they came up again. The plants grew into crops like corn, beans, and squash.

Source: There are many versions of the Navajo creation story. This account was provided by Harry Benally, a Navajo carver and silversmith from Sheep Springs, New Mexico, and Harold Carey, a Navajo historian from Malad City, Idaho. http://navajopeople.org/blog/navajo-creation-story-nihalgai-the-glittering-or-white-world/ downloaded February 14, 2013.

Other North American tribes had their own stories of how their people emerged onto the earth from a region below, or arrived through the water, or came down from the clouds. All believed that some ancient pilgrimage had brought them to the place where their tribe resided and would, with divine favor, reside forever.

Modern anthropologists tend to trace the path of early human immigration from Asia either on foot across what was sometimes dry land between what is now Russian Siberia and Alaska or by small boats that hugged the coast of the two continents beginning some 25,000 or even 35,000 years ago. Hunters from Siberia may have followed their animal prey across solid land and then fanned out across the Americas. Seafaring travelers might have followed the fish from Alaska down the coast of North and South America. Perhaps both forms of migration took place.

While the ancestors of modern American Indians were building their communities, establishing their culture, and engaging in extended trade with other Native Americans, other humans in other parts of the world were developing their own often quite different cultures. Carvings found in southern France and North Africa date from the same period as the earliest settlements of the Americas. Although contact between the rest of the world and the Americas was at best minimal, the people who lived in Africa, Asia, and Europe maintained some level of contact with one another over thousands of years, even as they developed their own languages as well as agricultural and social systems. The arrival of Europeans in the Americas after 1492 led to dramatic transformations of the cultures of all of these places. Peoples who had developed very different cultural norms as well as different ways of viewing the world suddenly came into contact with each other. Understanding the independent development of people and cultures on both sides of the Atlantic is essential to understanding how contact between them would significantly change them all.

THE PEOPLING OF NORTH AMERICA

1.1 Describe what the archeological record tells about the arrival, development, and cultures of the first peoples of North America.

While the Navajo told the stories of First Man and First Woman emerging after the long journey up through various worlds to find themselves in the place where the tribe lived, other Native Americans had their own creation stories. To the residents of the Jemez Pueblo in northern New Mexico, Fotease (chief of the War society) planned a journey to come to this world to test the people's power, and when they arrived at the site of their pueblo they knew they had found the right place saying, "This will be the place for us forever; from here we are not going to move the pueblo to any other place." For the Shasta of what is now the Northwest United States, their world began when Old Man Above bored a hole through the sky and came down to Earth to plant the first trees and to create birds and fish and all the animals, including the grizzly bear, and then continued to live in his tepee, Mount Shasta. In the Zuni story the sun was lonely, so he sent for the people who lived below the ground and invited them to come out and live in the sunlight and gave them corn.

While storytellers in every tribe keep these creation stories alive, modern anthropologists have a different explanation of the way the various tribes arrived in the places where they lived. During an ice age, more of the world's water is stored in glaciers. As a result, the oceans are lower, sometimes much lower. Geological evidence indicates that between 36,000 and 32,000 years ago and again between 25,000 and 14,000 years ago, substantial dry land existed between the northern tip of Asia in Siberia and North America (see Map 1-1).

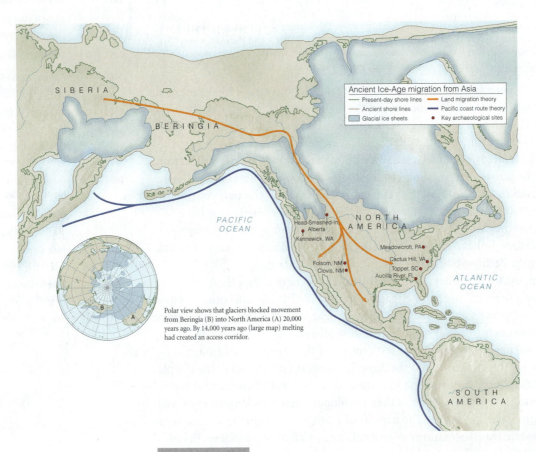

MAP 1-1 The Earliest Americans. While there is great debate about just when the first Americans migrated from Asia, there is strong evidence that ice made the trips possible. Since sea levels were much lower—because so much water was being held in glaciers—it was possible to walk from Siberia across what is now the Bering Sea into North America and then down through passage ways in the glaciers. It is also likely that migrants came by small boats down the Pacific coasts of North and South America.

This land was wide enough for animals, including mammoths and the human hunters who followed them, to cross. But when the glaciers melted, oceans rose, and what anthropologists now refer to as the **Bering Land Bridge** disappeared under what is now the Bering Sea. Any further human migration had to be by boat, which would explain the rapid expansion of human communities from Alaska to the southern tip of South America.

The Land Bridge, Clovis Culture, and Recent Discoveries

Most anthropologists used to believe that the first immigrants to the Americas were the **Clovis people** who might have come to North America around 13,000 years ago. The Clovis people took their name from a site near what is now Clovis, New Mexico, where a trove of 13,000-year-old arrow and spear points was found in 1929. The points, which were fluted so they could be attached to spears, were obvious signs of human activity and were the oldest human artifacts found in the Americas up to that time.

Recent excavations in central Texas, however, found primitive spear tips that are at least 15,500 years old, much older and less sophisticated than those found at Clovis. Archaeologists have discovered similar evidence at many sites elsewhere in the Americas. Because no Clovis-like spear tips have ever been found in Siberia, most anthropologists now believe that the Clovis spear point was an invention that early Americans developed long after they had lost contact with Asia.

Newer anthropological evidence also suggests that not all of the first peoples of the Americas walked to get there. Other peoples may have crossed the oceans thousands of years before the first Europeans ever set foot in the Western Hemisphere. Whenever and however the first inhabitants of the Americas came, their descendants adapted to their new lands, spread out across the Americas, and created a wide range of languages and civilizations. By 14,000 years ago, various peoples were living in every part of North and South America.

Bering Land Bridge
The name given to the land that connected Alaska and Siberia thousands of years ago, which is now under the current Bering Sea.

Clovis people
The name of early residents of North America whose spear points were found near what is now Clovis, New Mexico, in 1929.

Spear points found near Clovis, New Mexico. The human workmanship on these points is obvious, and though earlier spear points have now been found these show the development of Native American hunting skill at an early time.

American Voices

The Natchez Tradition, ca. 800

Many American Indian tribes moved often, seeking better hunting or farming or to escape more belligerent neighbors. The Natchez tribe of Louisiana is related linguistically and culturally to the pyramid builders of Mexico and Guatemala. They tell a story of their movement north to Louisiana that fits with the archeological evidence of such a movement around the year 800. A Keeper, or priest, of the Natchez told the following story to a Frenchman in Louisiana in the 1700s.

Before we came to this land we lived yonder under the sun [pointing with his finger nearly southwest, by which I understood that he meant Mexico]; we lived in a fine country where the earth is always pleasant; there our Suns [chiefs] had their abode, and our nation maintained itself for a long time against the ancients of the country, who conquered some of our villages in the plains but never could force us from the mountains. Our nation extended itself along the great water [the Gulf of Mexico] where this large river [the Mississippi] loses itself; but as our enemies were become very numerous, and very wicked, our Suns sent some of their subjects who lived near this river, to examine whether we could retire into the country through which it flowed. The country on the east side of the river being found extremely pleasant, the Great Sun, upon the return of those who had examined it, ordered all his subjects who lived in the plains, and who still defended themselves against the ancients of the country, to remove into this land, here to build a temple, and to preserve the eternal fire.

Source: From Judith Niles, *Native American History* (New York: Ballantine Books, 1996), p. 43.

Thinking Critically

1. **Documentary Analysis**
   How does the story teller explain the migration patterns of his people?

2. **Historical Interpretation**
   What light does the story shed on relations between American Indian peoples before the arrival of Columbus in the Americas?

Changing Climate and Cultures—Anasazi and Cahokia

Before the arrival of Columbus, the largest and most sophisticated civilizations in the Americas were found in Mexico and South America. Nevertheless, hundreds of years before Columbus crossed the ocean, complex communities could be found in the present-day United States—among the ancient residents of Chaco Canyon in New Mexico, known as the Anasazi, and among the Cahokia people of the Mississippi River Valley.

Anasazi

Anasazi, meaning "ancient ones," lived in modern day New Mexico, Arizona, and Colorado some 700 years before Columbus.

THE ANASAZI OF THE SOUTHWEST The **Anasazi**, or "ancient ones," began building communities in New Mexico and Arizona perhaps 700 years before the arrival of Columbus. They cultivated crops such as corn (or maize), beans, squash, and chilies that were needed to feed a settled, urbanized community. In time, the Anasazi began developing Chaco Canyon in northwest New Mexico as the hub of a widespread trade and ceremonial-religious network. Chaco Canyon was a large city built of logs and adobe (mud bricks) with buildings as high as five stories. It included more than a dozen pueblos (large buildings) in an area measuring 8 miles by 2 miles. Facing the main plaza, with its underground kivas where religious rites were conducted, Pueblo Bonito contained 800 rooms and may have housed 2,000 people. It was the largest "apartment" building in North America until the 1880s. Roads from Chaco Canyon allowed trade to develop in many directions. Turquoise and other valuable goods were traded, perhaps as far south as central Mexico.

After a prolonged drought in the early 1100s, the Anasazi abandoned Chaco Canyon. Their descendants created small farming communities across the Southwest. Some built the cliff dwellings that can still be seen at Mesa Verde in southwestern Colorado. While smaller than Chaco Canyon, Mesa Verde includes some 200 rooms. Built into the side of the canyon wall, the rooms offered protection

The Anasazi built housing or palaces into the cliffs to provide protection from the weather and from other tribes who might try to attack.

from enemies, since they could be reached only by ladders. By 1300, the Anasazi, faced with another great drought, also abandoned Mesa Verde and seem to have disappeared from history, though the founders of Acoma Pueblo may have been Anasazi. Acoma, not far from Albuquerque, New Mexico, was established some time in the 1100s. Still functioning today, it may be the oldest continuously inhabited city in the current United States.

Other peoples, known as the Hohokam, settled on lands further west near present-day Phoenix, Arizona. While the Hohokam communities existed for hundreds of years, the high point of their civilization is estimated to have been between 1150 and 1450. They developed an extensive agricultural system using canals to irrigate crops that included cotton, tobacco, corn, beans, and squash. But like the Anasazi, they slowly declined. Ruins of Hohokam communities may be seen in Casa Grande, Arizona. Slowly Hopi, Zuni, Pueblo, and Navajo peoples moved into the older Anasazi and Hohokam territory of New Mexico, Arizona, Utah, and Colorado and built the pueblos and villages that the first Spanish explorers encountered in the 1500s.

CAHOKIA AND THE MISSISSIPPI RIVER VALLEY   The Cahokia people of the Mississippi Valley, also known as the **Mound Builders**, created a flourishing culture between 900 and 1350. If one could go back 1,000 years and visit Cahokia, the center of this culture, one would find a city surrounded by strong wooden walls with thatch-covered houses that were home to 20,000 to 40,000 people, near what is now East St. Louis, Illinois. Cahokia was probably the largest settlement in what is now the United States, and 1,000 years ago, its "Mississippian culture" flourished throughout the Mississippi Valley and beyond. Archaeologists have found similar mound-building communities at Coosa and Etowah, Georgia; Moundville, Alabama; and Natchez, Mississippi.

Mound Builders
A name given to Native American tribes that built large burial and ceremonial mounds on which religious and sports activities took place.

This artist's rendition of ancient Cahokia shows the large city on the banks of the Mississippi River.

At the center of Cahokia, a series of wide earth mounds up to 100 feet high led to the people being called the Mound Builders. These mounds were used to bury the most prominent leaders. Atop the central mound was a temple and a wide plaza used for ceremonies centered on the seasons and the sun. The plaza was located on a perfect north-south axis, and a massive circle of wooden posts functioned as a kind of observatory to trace the sun's path.

Priests and chiefs at Cahokia tracked the sun, conducted rituals, and dispensed gifts that displayed their power, while nearby hamlets grew the food that fed the city's inhabitants. Such large, settled communities were possible because agricultural practices had replaced the earlier hunting and gathering economy and made a differentiated society possible. By about 900, a warming trend in the earth's climate had made new forms of agriculture possible. Instead of being limited to what they could find or hunt to eat, residents of Cahokia were thus able to begin farming. Like the Hohokam of the Southwest, they cultivated squash, corn, and beans, which they could grow on a seasonal basis, store as a surplus through the winter, and thereby support an urbanized culture. When eaten together, maize and beans form a complete protein, and as a result, the population could be well nourished.

In Cahokia, and in most settled Native American cultures, farming was women's work. Men hunted to add animal protein and flavor to the diet. Together, they produced a rich supply of food, enough to sustain not only themselves but a much larger community that included many—priests, chiefs, and the workers who built the mounds—who neither farmed nor hunted.

Aztec artists created this drawing of the cultivation of corn before the arrival of the first Europeans.

1.1 **Quick Review** Describe in what ways the Anasazi and Cahokia cultures changed over time. What unique features did each culture develop? What did they have in common?

THE DIVERSE COMMUNITIES OF THE AMERICAS IN THE 1400s

1.2 Describe the diversity of American Indian cultures in the United States on the eve of their encounter with Europeans.

The native peoples of North America were a remarkably diverse group.* They spoke many different languages, some more different from each other than English is from Chinese.

These languages were spread among 500 to 600 independent societies with different approaches to hunting and farming, different social structures, varying creation stories, and diverse understandings of the spiritual (see Map 1-2). Nevertheless, Native American tribes

MAP 1-2 North American Culture Areas, c. 1500. The lands that would become the United States include significantly different climate zones, and in the 1500s, when many Native American tribes had their first contact with Europeans, these different climates produced significantly different tribal cultures depending on where the people lived.

---

*There is considerable debate today about the terms *American Indian* and *Native American*. In fact, most of the descendants of the first peoples of North America prefer to be identified by their specific tribe—Navajo or Mohawk or Cherokee or whatever specific group—when possible. When speaking of larger groups of native peoples, some think that Native American is a more respectful term while many others prefer to be called American Indian or Indian. In Mexico most prefer "indigenous" while many Canadian tribes prefer "first nations." In keeping with that diversity of preferences, this book uses tribal names when relevant and otherwise uses the terms *American Indian* or *Indian* and *Native American* interchangeably.

also tended to share some things in common. They tended to live comfortably with nature and in harmony with the sacred, which they found in every aspect of life. They saw time as circular—not a steady line from creation to the present and future, but a reoccurring series of events to be celebrated in rituals that involved the retelling of ancient stories linked to the annual growth of the crops and to animal life. They honored shamans and priests who were considered visionaries and who were expected to have contact with the supernatural and keep the stories alive. These shamans and priests had the special responsibility of helping restore harmony when it was disrupted by disease, war, or climactic changes that brought famine. Most native North Americans saw the community and not the individual as the focus of life and labor. Community members won fame and respect by what they gave away more than by what they kept for themselves. The accumulative spirit of autonomous Europeans, gaining ever more possessions—especially land and the status in European society that came from land ownership—made no sense to most American Indians.

Although precise measurement is impossible, scholars estimate that approximately 7 million Indians lived in what is now the United States and Canada with much larger numbers in Mexico and Central and South America. The total population for all of the Americas was probably 50 to 70 million, perhaps as high as 100 million, when the first Europeans arrived. Europe's population at the time was approximately 70 to 90 million, and Africa's population was 50 to 70 million. If these numbers are correct, then although North America was relatively sparsely populated, the Americas as a whole had as many or more people than either Europe or Africa in 1492. Asia, it is worth noting, had a far larger population, perhaps in the range of 200 to 300 million people.

North American Indians also lived in a land of extraordinary physical diversity, from the tundra of Alaska to the forests of New England, from the prairies and grasslands of the Midwest to the lush Pacific Coast and the dry Southwest. In these diverse environments, climatic changes led to seasons of plenty and seasons of famine. Different environments also led to radically different ways of life. While the settled farmers of Cahokia and their descendants in the southeast and the pueblo peoples of the southwest left the clearest records, many nomadic tribes roamed the heart of the continent and the Pacific coast, depending much more on their skills as hunters and their ability to gather abundant plant foods than on settled agriculture. Success and failure in war or the spread of disease caused American Indian populations to ebb and flow long before the first European encounters.

The Pueblo People of the Southwest

Some of the largest American Indian settlements in what is now the United States were in the Southwest. In place of the abandoned Anasazi centers, Pueblo and Hopi people created thriving settlements in New Mexico and Arizona. Taos Pueblo in northern New Mexico, with its multistoried buildings for many families, is still inhabited as are many other Pueblo and Hopi communities in the region.

In the Pueblo and Hopi Southwest, an intricate maze of canals, dams, and terracing allowed agriculture to flourish in a dry climate. Like the Anasazi, the Pueblo and Hopi diet relied on corn, brown beans, and various forms of squash. They had domesticated turkeys and used dogs to hunt, so wild game, in addition to turkey, added animal protein to their diet.

In both Hopi and Pueblo communities, members of special societies wore ritual masks called kachinas and danced in ceremonies designed to connect the community with its ancestors while seeking their presence and blessing on the crops. The Pueblo people eventually spread out over Arizona and New Mexico, speaking different languages yet connected to each other by trade and common religious practices.

The Tribes of the Mississippi Valley

In the mid-1300s, Cahokia and the mound-building culture began to disappear. No one knows all of the reasons for this decline, but climate almost certainly had a role in it. Around 1350, a relatively rapid colder climate shift known as the "Little Ice Age" began and lasted until 1800. As the climate got colder, agriculture suffered. Europeans abandoned their settlements in places like Greenland. If the power of its priests and kings in Cahokia depended on their seeming control of the sun and the seasons, the Little Ice Age sapped that power. The change in weather drastically reduced the supply of food from outlying hamlets on which their large cities depended. Whatever all the reasons, by 1400, Cahokia was abandoned.

With the decline of Cahokia and the mound-building culture, the population of the Mississippi Valley shrank. The most direct descendants of Cahokia, the people later known as the Creeks, Choctaws, and Chickasaws, settled on the eastern side of the Mississippi River and the southern Appalachian Mountains.

Other tribes dominated other parts of Cahokia's former territory. The Cherokees and Tuscaroras settled in parts of Georgia, Tennessee, and North Carolina. They are connected linguistically with the Iroquois of the Great Lakes and New York more than with the Creeks and Choctaws. Yet other tribes dominated the Piedmont of what would be the Carolinas. Whatever their language or background, most of these tribes lived in small communities of 500 to 2,000 people. None lived in cities that were anything like Cahokia. Neighboring villages might exchange corn or meat. Longer-distance exchange—and there was considerable long-distance exchange—was generally limited to things that were rare and easy to carry: copper implements, beads and shells from the Atlantic Coast, or quartz from the Rocky Mountains. Artifacts uncovered in almost any native settlement in North America attest to the lively trade among all of the continent's tribes.

Archeological evidence also suggests that as Cahokia declined, smaller chiefdoms developed and often fought with each other and with other tribes. These communities, sometimes only a few families, built places of refuge throughout the Mississippi Valley. Mississippian villages in the 1400s included a half dozen to several dozen houses with a central field for games or ceremonies, all surrounded by a wooden wall that, if not strong enough to keep out a determined enemy, at least assured against surprise attacks. Several families often shared a single structure. Structures that housed a chief's family were somewhat larger but do not seem to have reflected a grander lifestyle. As weather and war made food scarcer, it was harder to cultivate crops and more dangerous to hunt game if human enemies were lurking nearby. The possibility of starvation increased. Still, the first European explorers who arrived in the 1540s reported finding large settlements in modern South Carolina, Georgia, Alabama, and Tennessee with rich well-tended fields and well-designed houses and villages.

The Pacific Coast—From the Shasta to the California Indians

In the Pacific Northwest, the Shasta and other tribes lived in towns of several hundred people, constructing houses as long as 60 feet built of cedar and richly decorated with painting and sculpture. These Pacific Coast Indians lived primarily on the abundant salmon in their rivers, which could be smoked or dried for year-round consumption. As a result of plentiful food and good housing, these tribes developed a settled community life with their own art and culture.

Farther down the Pacific Coast in California, the Yokut, Miwok, Maidu, and Pomo represented one of the largest concentrations of American Indians north of Mexico, perhaps 700,000 or 10 percent of the Indians north of the Rio Grande. These Native Americans lived in clans of extended families rather than larger tribal units. Their economy was based on gathering wild plants and on fishing and hunting. They did not engage in settled agriculture probably because the wild foods in California were so abundant and settled agriculture offered little improvement in their diet or way of life.

The Iroquois Confederacy and the Tribes of the Atlantic Coast

In the Northeast, the original five nations of the Iroquois (or the Haudenosaunee as they call themselves)—the Mohawks, Oneidas, Onondagas, Cayugas, and Senecas—developed

This drawing shows an Iroquois Onondaga village under an attack led by the French explorer Samuel de Champlain. It also shows the long houses that provided homes to several families, all surrounded by a stockade fence.

an alliance and a united front against other tribes, an approach that would also serve them well in their encounters with Europeans. The Iroquois Confederacy's central meeting place and council fire was near present-day Syracuse, New York. In Iroquois communities, several families would live in a single sturdy longhouse made of posts and poles covered with bark, but the house itself and the land around it belonged to the community. As many as 1,000 people lived in some Iroquois towns made up of many longhouses. Iroquois legends tell of a great peace-maker, Dekanawidah, who convinced the warring tribes to live together under the Great Law of Peace. An eclipse of the sun around the year 1142 supposedly strengthened his plea for unity. Clans led by women governed the five nations. The women leaders chose the sachems, male leaders who attended the council meetings and led in war but who were also accountable to the clans.

On the Atlantic Coast and the eastern slopes of the Appalachians were Algonquian-speaking tribes, the largest of which, the Powhatans, may have included 60,000 or more people. For these tribes—some of the first to encounter Europeans—hunting and fishing as well as farming corn, beans, and squash provided the major food sources. They lived in permanent towns and villages. Like other tribes, the Atlantic Coast Indians did not keep written records but even as late as the 1670s an English trader described an Indian town of many houses along crisscrossing streets, surrounded by a stockade 2-feet thick and 12-feet high. Social life centered in the ceremonies of the seasons that gave thanks for the gifts of food, especially the green corn dance held in late summer, which might attract several hundred Indians from surrounding villages, to give thanks for the harvest and to celebrate the start of a new year. Although the description came from the early 1600s, there is no reason to assume that Algonquian community life had changed much since the 1400s.

The Aztec, Mayan, and Inca Empires

Traveling south from the current United States in the mid-1400s, one came to the great Aztec city of Tenochtitlán. With a population of 200,000, it was as large as or larger than any contemporary city in Africa or Europe. The Aztecs founded Tenochtitlán

American Voices

Richard Hakluyt, The True Pictures and Fashions of the People in that Part of American Now Called Virginia, 1585

In 1585, the English adventurer Sir Walter Raleigh founded the short-lived colony of Roanoke on the coast of what is now North Carolina. Richard Hakluyt—who never left England—used stories of Raleigh's experiences in North America to create a "true picture" of the American Indians. Since the Indians themselves did not keep such records, Hakluyt's account provides some of the best examples of what Native American life was like at the time of their first contacts with Europeans.
Note: The Elizabethan English of the original is hard to follow. The text below has been rendered in contemporary English.

The Princes of Virginia…wear the hair of their heads long…. They wear a chain about their necks of pearls or beads of copper, which they much esteem, and they wear bracelets of the same material on their arms….They carry a quiver made of small rushes holding their bow ready bent in one hand, and an arrow in the other, ready to defend themselves. In this manner they go to war, or to their solemn feasts and banquets. They take much pleasure in hunting deer whereof there is great store in the country, for it is fruitful, pleasant, and full of good woods….The women…are of reasonably good proportion. In their going they carry their hands dangling down and wear a deer skin excellently well dressed, hanging down from their navel unto the middle of their thighs, which also cover their hinder parts. The rest of their bodies are all bare.…

At a certain time of the year they make a great, and solemn feast whereunto their neighbors of the towns adjoining repair from all parts, every man attired in the most strange fashion….Then being set in order they dance, sing, and use the strangest gestures….All this is done after the sun is set for avoiding of the heat….

The towns of this country…are compassed about with poles stuck fast in the ground, but they are not very strong. The entrance is very narrow. There are but few houses therein, save those which belong to the king and his nobles.

This people therefore void of all covetousness live cheerfully and at their hearts ease. But they solemnize their feasts in the night, and therefore they keep very great fires to avoid darkness and to testify their joy.

Source: Copyright 2004 by the University Library, The University of North Carolina at Chapel Hill.

Thinking Critically

1. **Documentary Analysis**
   Based on this document, what picture might an Elizabethan reader have formed about conditions in Virginia?

2. **Crafting an Argument**
   In your opinion, how useful is this document as evidence of the true nature of American Indian societies in Virginia? What argument can you make to support your opinion?

A map of the Aztec capital of Tenochtitlán on site of what is now Mexico City. The Aztec built Tenochtitlán on an island with only a few easy to defend causeways linking it to the mainland and built beautiful floating gardens along the waterways.

on an island in the middle of Lake Texcoco in 1325, connected it to the mainland by three broad causeways, and supplied the city with fresh drinking water through a carefully designed aqueduct. When the Aztecs first arrived in central Mexico, the people who then ruled the region, known as the Toltecs, looked down on them as barbarians. That soon changed. The Aztecs conquered the Toltecs and destroyed their capital. The Aztec's Tenochtitlán used Toltec designs, but was a new and grander capital. Led by their emperor, Aztec society was highly stratified; the emperor and priests at the top ruled a powerful empire with a population of 10 to 20 million that dominated subjugated tribes in surrounding areas.

The huge markets of Tenochtitlán in which 40,000 or 50,000 traders met to exchange gold and jewelry, pottery and baskets, meat, fish, fruit, and vegetables amazed the first Spaniards who described it as "thrice as large as the celebrated square in Salamanca [in Spain]." The Aztecs maintained an extensive trade network with other peoples but also made war on them to expand their empire and ensure a steady stream of prisoners for the human sacrifices they believed their gods demanded. While the Aztecs built their empire by making strategic alliances with other tribes, by the mid-1400s, they relied on their own large army and attacked former allies, creating enemies who would help the Spanish conquer the Aztecs in the early 1500s.

To the east and southeast of the Aztec Empire was the once great empire of the Maya. The Mayan Empire had been at its height long before the Aztecs emerged on the scene. Indeed, the Mayan culture had been developing for thousands of years when they first came into contact with Europeans. The high point of Mayan culture, known as the classical period, entered a period of decline hundreds of years before the rise of the Aztecs, probably due to an extended period of drought and overfarming of the land.

The Mayans dominated what is now the Yucatan Peninsula of Mexico and much of modern Honduras, Belize, and Guatemala. The Mayans were the only American culture to develop a fully functional written language. They also developed sophisticated systems of mathematics and a calendar that projected time far into the future. Like the Aztecs, they practiced human sacrifice and subjugated other nearby tribes in pursuit of people and goods. They had an extensive agricultural system producing not only food but also cotton, which was a source of trade and wealth.

While in decline, the Mayans, some 800,000 people divided into 16 to 18 independent kingdoms, were still a strong presence in western Mexico and Central America in the 1400s. The remains of their greatest architecture could be seen all around them. They still produced and traded cotton, and their trade routes connected them with the other empires of the Americas.

Further south, the Inca Empire was even larger than that of the Aztecs. It extended along the Pacific coast of South America from southern Colombia to northern Chile, and included almost all of what is today Peru, Ecuador, and Bolivia (see Map 1-3). The Incas ruled some 32 million people from their capital of Cuzco, another city of 200,000, in what is now Peru, and from the mountain fortress and religious center of Machu Picchu. The empire had a vast bureaucracy and army as well as 25,000 miles of roads and bridges rivaling those of ancient Rome, all supported by heavy taxes. Incan religion was centered on the sun and its seasons; human and animal sacrifice was common. The Inca emperor and his family were considered divine. Like the Aztecs, the Inca Empire was relatively new when Europeans encountered it in the early 1500s. The main Inca conquests had occurred only in the 1400s.

MAP 1-3 Inca Empire in 1500. The Inca Empire was perhaps the largest empire in the world stretching down nearly all of the Pacific coast of South America, connected by roads and reporting to a single centralized government based in modern-day Peru.

American Indian Cultures, Trade, and Initial Encounters with Europeans

While the peoples living in North and South America before 1492 were divided by significant language differences and great distances, they still knew quite a bit about each other and traded regularly with far distant communities. Trade networks stretched from the Aztec Empire across all parts of North America. The presence of sea shells in Native American communities a thousand miles from the ocean and copper implements hundreds of miles from the nearest copper mine attests to the trade in goods that was rich and varied by the 1400s (see Map 1-4).

Not all exchanges between tribes were friendly. There was certainly warfare also, sometimes to settle matters of honor and sometimes in the search for valuables. Hunting peoples seem to have raided farming communities, and farming communities fought with each other from time to time if one was thought to encroach on another's land. Bows and arrows were deadly weapons, and scalping an enemy to gain a trophy, and perhaps a part of the enemy's spirit, were well known before 1492.

Even though the native peoples of North and South America maintained their trade networks and fought with other tribes, each tribe saw itself as the center of its own world. Their different stories and cultures reflected that, although trade might be of value, trading partners were not seen as part of their community. To understand Indian responses to the arrival of the Europeans, it is essential first to understand that no Indians thought of themselves as being American Indians or Native Americans as opposed to white Europeans. Instead, they thought of themselves as Senecas or Creeks or Hopi or some other discrete population. This mindset prevented any unified resistance to the first European aggressions in the 1400s and, later, in the 1500s and even 1600s. If a particular tribe thought it made sense to ally with the Europeans against another tribe, or trade with the Europeans for new goods that would give them an advantage over another tribe, they saw no reason not to do so. If the Europeans could become part of well-established trade networks or allies in attacking long-standing enemies, so much the better. It took several hundred

MAP 1-4 Native North American Cultural Areas and Trade Networks, ca. 1400 CE. While the peoples of North America were divided by climate, customs, and languages, they established complex trade networks in which goods produced in one region were traded over significant distances and found in regions far from their origin.

years before most American Indians realized that the Europeans did not look on them as they looked on themselves and that any equality in trade or warfare was to be short lived.

While different tribes were happy to make alliances with different groups of Europeans, Native American culture tended to understand warfare in ways radically different from most Europeans. War among tribes was usually a way to settle specific issues or achieve honor and, most of all, to restore the balance that was essential to Indian life. The European model of total conquest was a concept that would have been foreign to most American Indian cultures. In this way as in so many other ways, the Europeans who began arriving in the 1490s could not have been more different.

At the same time, and unknown to the people of the Americas, other peoples, living in Europe, Africa, and Asia were developing their own societies, creation stories, and world views. The world was never the same once representatives from these diverse peoples—Spanish explorers, slaves and free servants from West Africa, and those who followed them across the Atlantic—met and mingled with the native peoples of the Americas. But to understand the mingling, one must understand the development of separate cultures in other parts of the world.

> **1.2** **Quick Review** What are three unique cultural developments among specific American Indian tribes that were influenced by the geography or climate in which their tribe lived?

A CHANGING EUROPE IN THE 1400s

> **1.3** Describe the changes in Europe that led to Columbus's voyages and that shaped European attitudes when encountering the peoples of the Americas.

Europeans had been sailing on the Atlantic long before Columbus was born. Norse sailors, commonly known as Vikings, came from modern-day Norway and Denmark and settled Iceland in the late 800s. In 980, they expanded their territory to Greenland where they interacted—not always peacefully—with the local Inuit people and exported lumber to Scandinavia while maintaining themselves with successful farms. In 1001, a Norse party led by Leif Erickson established a colony further west that they named Vineland. No one is sure where Vineland was, though tradition places it in North America. Modern excavations show the remains of a Norse colony in the modern Canadian province of Newfoundland. Some claim Norse settlements as far south as the modern state of Maine. But while Iceland maintained contact with Europe and the Greenland colony survived until the early 1400s when the same colder weather that undermined Cahokia also brought the Greenland colony to an end, Vineland was never permanent, and by the time Columbus was born, all earlier European contact with North America was long forgotten. In the hundred years before Columbus sailed across the Atlantic, Europe went through a series of extraordinary changes. Those changes not only set Columbus on his travels but shaped the beliefs and expectations with which the first Europeans arrived in the Americas.

If a time-traveler were to go back to the Europe of the 1400s—to London, England, or Seville, Spain, or Paris, France, or the rural countryside where most people lived—they would find a world that would seem strange and primitive. There were not a lot of people around. Europe was still recovering from the devastating **Black Death**, the bubonic plague that arrived in 1348 on rats carried by ships trading in the Black Sea. In a few years after it first arrived, the plague wiped out at least one-third, perhaps even one-half, of Europe's population. About 70 million people lived in Europe in 1300. By the late 1350s, the plague had reduced the population to perhaps 45 million. Whole families and villages disappeared. Through the late 1300s, there were empty fields or forests where people had once lived or farmed. The loss of so many people traumatized the survivors who looked for someone to blame for the disaster. Jews, religious nonconformists, and foreigners made good scapegoats, and there were massive persecutions across Europe.

Black Death
The bubonic plague that devastated Europe in the 1300s, reducing the population by as much as half.

A unified Roman Catholic Christian Church dominated the religious life of Europe in the 1400s. The Protestant Reformation was still a century in the future. Distance between cities, the difficulty of travel, and political divisions resulted in a Catholic Church that was far less centralized than it is today. Nevertheless, the church with its liturgy, creeds, and clergy—the pope, bishops, priests, monks, and nuns—was the strongest institution in Europe, unifying people who had different languages and leaders. Literacy, learning, and the preservation of culture rested mostly with the church. The church also provided what social services there were for the aged, sick, and poor. Jews lived in most parts of Europe, sometimes tolerated, sometimes savagely repressed, occasionally honored for their contributions to medicine, commerce, and scholarship, but they were a small minority. In the cities a great cathedral was the largest building, and everywhere church spires marked the center of both secular and religious life.

Life to modern eyes would seem primitive. Most people were dirty, poorly clothed, and illiterate. Life expectancy was in the 30s, especially because infant mortality and deaths from childbirth were high. Trade was limited because transporting most things was difficult and expensive. The church taught that seeking wealth, especially charging interest for loans, was sinful. People were encouraged to stay where they were—in the community and in social class where they were born, whether they were peasants or nobles.

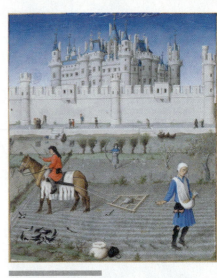

In the 1400s, the vast majority of the people of Europe were poor peasants who worked long days in the fields with little economic gain to show for their work. At the top of society were nobles who lived in grand castles, like the one pictured, and the clergy who reminded nobles and peasants of their responsibility to stay in the class to which they were born and not seek economic or social advancement.

The Ottoman Empire Changes Eastern Europe

In 1453, when Christopher Columbus was 2 years old, Muslim Ottoman Turks conquered the city of Constantinople, the most important city in Eastern Europe. From their new capital, renamed Istanbul, the Ottomans ruled an empire that stretched from Hungary to include the Balkans and most of the Middle East and North Africa. The Ottoman Empire controlled the eastern Mediterranean for the next 4 centuries.

The fall of Constantinople shocked Europe. Constantinople had been at the crossroads of the trade routes between Europe and Asia and was considered the equivalent of Rome as a religious and political center. The Ottomans encouraged trade within their empire, but restricted others from using the land and sea routes across the eastern Mediterranean. Suddenly Christian Europe was cut off from the lucrative land-based trade in spices and luxury goods with Asia that had existed since Italy's Marco Polo had traveled to China in the late 1200s. The Mediterranean, which had been the great unifying conduit of the Roman Empire, was now as divided as the lands surrounding it. The city states of Italy—Venice, Genoa, and Florence especially—which had dominated the Mediterranean and trade with Asia and grown wealthy from it, began a slow decline. Other Europeans on the Atlantic Coast, especially those in Portugal and Spain, began to seek new ways to reach Asia—without the need to deal with the Ottomans.

The Rise of Portuguese Exploration

The first and in many ways most adventurous European to seek a new way of connecting with Asia was Prince Henry of Portugal (1394–1460). Even before the Ottoman conquest of Constantinople, Henry, a younger son of the King of Portugal, decided that Portugal, with its strategic location on Europe's southern Atlantic Coast, should try to establish a new trade route to Asia by sailing around Africa.

Although he is known to history as "the Navigator," Henry's personal seagoing was modest. In 1415, he commanded a Portuguese fleet, but for the rest of his life, he stayed at his castle at Sagres on the Portuguese coast and commissioned others to make voyages and report back to him. These voyages generated not only geographical information about the African coast, but they also led to better navigational instruments and charts as well as better-designed ships that could travel greater distances in bad weather and good.

In 1424, Prince Henry organized a long series of expeditions—in which others did the actual travel—that sailed farther and farther south along the coast of Africa. Once they learned how to navigate the currents off the African coast, Portuguese explorers moved quickly. In 1444, Portuguese ships reached Senegal, long fabled as a source of

Prince Henry, a younger son of the king of Portugal, sponsored new developments in ship building and navigation and ordered a series of voyages that allowed Portuguese sailors to explore the west coast of Africa and eventually, after Henry's death, to sail around the continent and on to India where they developed lucrative trade.

gold, and established a slave-trading company in Lagos. They reached Sierra Leone around 1460 as well as claimed and settled the previously uninhabited Cape Verde Islands. Finally, in 1488, Bartolomeu Dias rounded the Cape of Good Hope on the southern tip of Africa. A decade later, in 1498, Vasco da Gama followed Dias's route and reached India. These successful expeditions led to flourishing trade with Asia and Africa by the early 1500s. The Portuguese not only established a string of trading colonies in India, Indonesia, and China, they also developed a massive new African trade. Portuguese merchants virtually reinvented slavery in Western Europe, and Portugal became the first and most significant player in the African slave trade as well as in the spice trade with Asia. By 1504 at least one ship a month sailed from Lisbon to Asia, and the wealth from Asian spices and other luxury goods and from African gold and slaves was making Portugal the richest nation in Europe.

Historians have argued about Henry's, and by extension Portugal's, motives. Henry certainly wanted to find a route that would put Portugal at the center of the trade with Asia. Asian goods—porcelain, silk, spices—had long been popular and profitable luxury goods in Europe. The nation that could secure access to these goods after the Ottomans restricted the eastern Mediterranean routes would become rich. Old animosity between Christian Europe and the Muslim world fueled the quest to defy Ottoman trade obstacles. Legends of a Christian presence in the heart of Africa also motivated expanded contact with that continent. If the Christians of Europe could ally with Christians who might be in Africa, their armies would surround the Muslim world and weaken its power. Perhaps most important to Henry, however, was the wealth to be made in Africa itself. Portugal could obtain African gold and slaves from every voyage whether or not it made discoveries or alliances with far-off Christians.

Slavery was an ancient institution. It was sanctioned in the Bible and other ancient texts thousands of years before the days of Prince Henry. The Roman Empire had slaves, including some from Africa. But while slavery had died out in most of Europe during the Middle Ages—although serfs in Russia were only semi-free—it persisted in the Middle East and Africa. Arab traders brought African slaves across the Sahara to sell in markets in the Middle East. In fact, various African peoples routinely captured and enslaved their rivals. And Muslim conquerors and pirates enslaved captured European Christians. Europeans developed new forms of slavery along with the exploration of Africa. As early as 1336, King Alfonso IV of Portugal reported, and probably sponsored, slave raiding in the Canary Islands off the coast of West Africa. Indeed, the Canary Islands would be an important base for further exploration of Africa, one often contested between Portugal and Spain. After 1500, slavery would transform European commerce, most of all in the trade with European colonies in the Americas, while also transforming and weakening the economies of Africa, and—in particular—utterly changing the lives of millions of Africans.

England and France

While Portugal was establishing its ocean routes to Asia and growing fabulously wealthy in the process, most of the rest of Europe remained poor and distracted with more immediate worries. France and England fought the Hundred Years' War (1337–1453) with each other, depleting both nations' resources. When the war ended, France was divided by a bitter civil war until 1477 as the royal government sought to assert its control of the kingdom. England was also torn by a civil war, the War of the Roses, as the Lancaster and York branches of the royal family fought until Henry VII defeated Richard III of York in 1485. The destruction wrought by war and plague left little time, money, or energy for either France or England to engage in exploration.

Despite all their troubles, England and France were relatively unified kingdoms. In contrast, other areas of Europe were not united at all during this period and, in fact, would not be until the mid-1800s. For centuries before its unification, most of what is now Germany was considered part of the Holy Roman Empire but the empire was actually a very loose confederation divided into a number of much smaller entities. No even nominally unified Italian state existed. Until the 1800s, what is now modern Italy was divided into many competing, independent free cities, principalities, and small kingdoms that spoke different and often mutually incomprehensible versions of Italian. These groups were also often at war with each other. As a result, these areas did not initiate much organized external exploration. Even though many sailors from what is now Italy were among the most important European explorers of the era, they worked for other governments.

The Unification and Rise of Spain

Unlike some other parts of Europe, Spain, however, achieved a dramatic new unity in the late 1400s, and this unified Spain would be a powerful force in the Americas. The political, cultural, and religious unification of Spain—known as the *Reconquista*, or "reconquest"—was an extraordinary development given the 7 centuries during which unity of any sort had seemed impossible. In 711, Muslim invaders from North Africa conquered most of the Iberian Peninsula (modern Spain and Portugal) and remained in control of parts of it for almost 800 years. While the rest of Europe remained Christian, much of Medieval Spain was in African Muslim (Moorish) hands.

Reconquista
The long struggle (ending in 1492) during which Spanish Christians reconquered the Iberian Peninsula from Muslim occupiers, who first invaded in the 8th century.

Christian monarchs gradually reconquered Portugal and most of Spain from the Muslims, but the struggle took centuries. While some areas were ruled by Christians, many others remained Muslim. Yet the very divisions of Spain resulted in some of the richest cultural developments in Europe. While armies fought, people mingled, producing new ideas and some of the scientific developments that would later enrich all of Europe. It was through Spain that the culture of Islam came into Europe, including Arabic numerals, algebra, paper, cotton, rice, and sugar. It was in Muslim Córdoba that Greek philosophy, Roman law, and eastern art and architecture mixed. It was also in Spain, far more than elsewhere in Europe, that Jews were treated with respect, even honor, as "peoples of the book" who shared sacred scriptures with Christians and Muslims. It was also on the border lands between Christianity and Islam that some of the great medieval cities of Spain—León, Zamora, Burgos, and Ávila—emerged, creating an independent class of citizens who were neither nobles nor serfs but free women and men. As the medieval saying went, "the air of the city makes you free."

Spain's long-standing divisions ended in the late 1400s. By 1400, the Iberian Peninsula was divided into four Christian kingdoms—Castile, Aragon, Portugal, and Navarre—and one Muslim kingdom in the south—Granada. In 1469, Isabella of Castile married Ferdinand of Aragon. This marriage united the two most powerful Spanish thrones. The joint monarchs then began a long campaign to finish the reconquest of Spain. In January 1492, their armies defeated Muslim Granada, adding its territory to their kingdom and ending the 800-year long Islamic presence in Spain. That same year, in the name of religious uniformity, Ferdinand and Isabella expelled all Jews from Spain, a move that cost them some of their most innovative citizens. But Isabella and Ferdinand wanted their nation to be unified, and like most Europeans at the time, they saw religious uniformity as key to that goal. And in that same eventful year, Isabella commissioned an Italian sailor named Christopher Columbus to try to find a route to Asia that would be different from the African one Portugal was exploring.

1.3 **Quick Review** How did changes in Europe in the 1400s determine European states' ability to launch expeditions of discovery in the Atlantic? How did the unification of Spain and the fall of Constantinople to the Ottomans affect this process?

AFRICA IN THE 1400s

1.4 Describe the political, cultural, and religious developments in Africa that would shape contact between Europeans and Africans in the Americas.

In the late 1400s, parts of Africa were also undergoing changes that would influence the cultural interactions that would take place in the "New World" in the 1500s. Just as in Europe and the Americas, none of the people in Africa knew that they were living on the edge of events that would turn their world upside down. Yet events were underway that would change the lives, economies, cultures, and worldviews of almost everyone.

Ancient Ties Between Africa and Europe

Contact between Africa and Europe did not begin with Prince Henry's voyages. North Africa had been part of Mediterranean civilization for at least 3,000 years. What are today the nations of Egypt, Libya, Algeria, Morocco, and Tunisia were some of the richest provinces of the Roman Empire. As Christianity spread throughout the Roman Empire, some of the strongest Christian centers were in North Africa. One of the most influential of all early Christian thinkers was St. Augustine (354–430), born in what is now Algeria, who served as bishop of the Algerian city of Hippo. Farther south, Christianity took root quickly in Ethiopia, and that part of east Africa has remained predominantly Christian for 2,000 years. In addition, southern Europe and parts of Africa south of the Sahara Desert shared a long history of trade (see Map 1-5). This trade was never entirely interrupted, even when Arab armies conquered North Africa in the 600s and Islam replaced Christianity as the dominant religion there.

The Empires of Ghana, Mali, and Songhay

Coastal areas of Africa south of the Sahara that the Portuguese encountered in the mid-1400s differed in customs, ethnicity, and economic life from Muslim North Africa. As these coastal Africans met Portuguese traders, they quickly took an interest in particular European goods, including iron and cloth, acquiring them through exchanges of hides, copper, ivory, and slaves. Trade produced a greater variety of goods on both continents and, for the African elite, added the prestige of owning goods from far away. The Africa that first began major economic and cultural contact with Europe in those years was a continent that met its northern neighbor on terms of equality in military, cultural, and technological terms, its population not yet decimated by the massive trade in slaves that was to come or by attacks by industrialized European colonial forces.

Just south of the Sahara, the kingdom of Ghana governed much of West Africa for hundreds of years. Ghana's power was based on trade and its mastery of metalworking to make weapons and tools. Ghana was at the northern end of African trade routes that brought gold, ivory, and slaves out of the African interior and at the southern end of the desert routes by which Muslim traders brought the slaves, gold, and ivory from south of the Sahara to North Africa, the Middle East, and Europe in exchange for salt, silk, and other goods. Control of that trade made Ghana rich. Royal and religious officials, soldiers, merchants, and iron workers dominated Ghana.

As early as 1050, King Barmandana of Mali began to extend his kingdom, and the empire of Mali slowly dominated and replaced Ghana as the leading power in the region. Barmandana converted to Islam and made a pilgrimage to Mecca, the Muslim holy city in Arabia. Some 200 years later, another Malian king, Sundiata, made Mali the master of West Africa. When one of Sundiata's successors, Mansa Musa, made his pilgrimage to Mecca in 1324, his lavish caravan and generous gifts spread gold so freely that "the value of Cairo's currency was depressed for many years." Mansa Musa built new mosques and schools and established an Islamic university at Timbuktu that was respected throughout the Muslim world for its scholarship.

MAP 1-5 African Trade Networks. Like American Indians, Africans traded over great distances and the major trade routes made trade centers like Timbuktu and Gao rich and powerful as goods—and often people being sold as slaves—were transported through these cities from one region to another.

This mosque in Djenne, Mali, was originally built in the 1300s of mud hardened by the sun and was restored in the early 1900s to look much as it did at the height of the Mali Empire.

To the east of Mali, another empire, Songhay, grew stronger, capturing Timbuktu in 1458 just as the Portuguese were exploring the African coast. In the late 1400s, under two of its greatest kings, Sunni Ali (r. 1464–1492)—who died in the year of Columbus's first voyage—and Askia Muhammad (r. 1493–1528), Songhay became the strongest military and economic power in West Africa. When Sunni Ali became king of Songhay in 1464, he quickly established himself as an effective military leader. Sunni Ali also understood the religious divisions of his lands. The urban inhabitants, who controlled trade, were mostly Muslim. But in the countryside, most people held to traditional beliefs, and they were the source of the agricultural wealth of the kingdom. Though himself a Muslim, Sunni Ali treated both groups with respect and brought stability and prosperity to his kingdom. When Sunni Ali died in 1492, his son and heir, Sunni Baru, rejected Islam but was overthrown, and a new leader, Askia Muhammad (r. 1493–1528), came to power. Askia Muhammad was a devout Muslim, but like Sunni Ali, he respected traditional customs.

As with Mali and Ghana, Songhay's power was based on trade. Gold, ivory, and slaves could be collected from the south and east. In exchange, silks and other fine goods were brought in caravans across the Sahara from Egypt, the Middle East, and Europe. Trade created wealth, which allowed both lavish lifestyles and military power that extended the empires. And trade also facilitated the exchange of ideas and scientific information. Askia Muhammad's control was such that he was able to make his own pilgrimage to Mecca in 1494–1497, trusting subordinates to maintain his rule in his absence.

Kongo, Benin, and Central Africa

South of Songhay, in the kingdoms of Kongo, Benin, and surrounding areas, government was powerful but far less structured than in the empires of Mali and Songhay. In the 1490s, Portuguese missionaries converted the king of Kongo to Catholicism. Close ties developed between Kongo and the papacy in Rome despite the enormous distances between them. More than a century later, slaves from Kongo would confuse English and Spanish authorities who did not expect their Christian beliefs and knowledge of the Catholic Mass.

While Kongo kings were Catholic, most other Central Africans practiced traditional religions that included belief in a world after death, ancestor worship, and a central role for priests and other intermediaries between divine and human affairs. The Africans who were taken across the Atlantic to the Americas as slaves brought these religious and cultural traditions with them.

Kongo kings generally inherited the throne from their father or brother, but a group of nobles or electors could choose a different ruler. A similar system was found in much of Central Africa. In Ndongo, election ratified succession within a reigning family. In Biguba, in what is now Guinea-Bissau, the king was elected from among a group of elite families. In Sierra Leone, the ruler was elected, but once in office could dismiss the electors, and a similar system was followed in Benin. Europeans reported that, to maintain their own power, nobles sometimes deliberately selected weak monarchs. In 1601, one European wrote, "a village mayor in our country has more authority than such a king." In these West African kingdoms, a person or family could cultivate land secure in the knowledge that they would truly "own" the crops or goods produced on the land and could sell or trade them, but they could never sell the land itself. Indeed, if the family stopped working the land, any claim they might have to it disappeared.

Centralized government and the wealth generated by trade also led to military power that allowed West Africans to resist not only the first Portuguese attempts at conquest but also many subsequent ones. In 1446 when Portuguese explorers, seeking slaves and gold, reached the Senegal River (which is now the northern border of the country of Senegal), African canoes attacked their ship, and nearly all of the European raiders were killed. A year later the same thing happened to another crew near the island of Goree. Similar types of resistance would continue for the next 2 centuries.

African boats were small compared to European ships. They tended to be canoes dug out of a single log, but their small size gave them power. They could navigate shallow areas where the Europeans could not go and could move quickly between rivers, estuaries, and the ocean. These canoes carried as many as 50 to 100 fighters each. Facing such effective resistance at sea, before they ever landed on unknown shores or attempted to travel up uncharted and hostile rivers, the earliest Portuguese travelers quickly decided that it was better to seek peaceful trade agreements with African kings than to do battle. The result was that as early as 1456, Diogo Gomes represented the Portuguese crown in negotiating treaties of peace and commerce with African rulers of several states.

Slavery in Africa

Slavery was a significant part of the African economy in the 1400s. It was important in the empires of Mali and Songhay and in Kongo long before the Portuguese arrived. In an economic system where the community, not an individual, owned land in common, as it did in West Africa, owning people who could work the land was a way to accumulate wealth.

When the Portuguese began their African trade in the 1400s, African slaves had been brought across the Sahara to Europe and the Middle East for over 1,000 years. Benin City had seen slaves parade through for centuries. The Portuguese simply shifted part of this trade to Europeans on the coast and away from the Arab-dominated overland routes across the Sahara. Although the voracious demand for enslaved Africans in the Americas would disrupt the African economy in the 1600s and 1700s, that was a later story. When the Portuguese first became involved in the slave trade they merely built on existing trade and cultural traditions. Far fewer people were involved than would be the case in the future, but for those who were enslaved the new patterns created huge dislocations.

An African could be enslaved for many reasons—as punishment for crime or as payment for debt—but most slaves were captured in war from other communities. Those who sold them considered the slaves aliens, not people like themselves. Like the American Indians, Africans did not think of themselves as Africans but as members of a specific tribe—Ashanti, Yoruba, Kru—and enslaving members of another tribe did not distress them. The economic advantages of capturing slaves in war and then selling them also made war itself a profitable commercial venture and exacerbated other tensions.

Nevertheless, just because slavery and the slave trade were already part of the economic systems of West Africa when the Portuguese arrived in the mid-1400s does not change the horror of the institution. Being captured in war, losing one's freedom, and then being sent away from home must always have been terrifying. It was even worse if one was forced to march across the terrible Sahara Desert or loaded onto a ship controlled by strange-looking people who spoke a totally different language and who considered slaves not merely aliens but subhuman. Although the earliest African and European slave traders did not recognize it—or probably care about it—a more terrible form of slavery was being born in the 1400s. For the first time, not only the slaves' freedom but also their language, culture, and identity were being destroyed. The Africans unlucky enough to become American slaves already knew about slavery as an institution, but they had never encountered conditions in which they were stripped of everything familiar to them.

Africans, as slaves or as free people hired for the work, would accompany some of the earliest Portuguese, Spanish, and English explorers of North and South America in the 1500s, helping explore Florida, Virginia, Texas, and New Mexico. Descendants of Europeans and Africans have lived together with American Indians in the land that would be the United States for 500 years.

 Quick Review How were empires like Mali and Songhay similar to or different from European kingdoms in the 1400s? How did the earliest European contact with Africa change, or not change, the nature of African slavery?

ASIA IN THE 1400s

1.5 Contrast developments in Asia with those in Europe at the time when Europeans first reached the Americas.

While the Americas, Africa, and Europe were all divided into many small tribes, cities, and nation-states in the 1400s, China was united in a single empire and had been for more than 2,000 years. When Columbus sailed from Spain to the Americas in 1492, Europe had some 500 independent states. A single emperor governed perhaps 150 to 200 million people in China. Of course, China is not all of Asia. The Indian subcontinent included 75 to 150 million people living in many independent principalities. Korea and Japan were independent kingdoms, while Tibet and Vietnam struggled to maintain their independence from China. But Asia was much more unified than elsewhere, and most of the peoples of Asia were in contact with one another and enriched each one another's cultures.

In 1421, the Chinese Emperor Zhu Di celebrated the completion of the Forbidden City, his new palace and temple complex in Beijing. Envoys from as far away as East Africa and Arabia were present. Twenty-six thousand guests feasted at a 10-course banquet. In the same month, England's King Henry V celebrated his wedding to a French princess with 600 guests. Zhu Di's army included 1 million soldiers armed with gunpowder while Henry had 5,000 soldiers armed with bows and arrows. But then, Zhu Di's new capital of Beijing had a population that was 50 times larger than Henry's London.

Zhu Di (r. 1402–1424) also commissioned Chinese fleets that sailed to South Asia, India, and East Africa. These treasure fleets mapped the Indian Ocean and brought back exotic animals, trade goods, and knowledge that made China a center of geographic studies in the early 1400s.

But Chinese oceanic exploration came at high cost. Huge forests in China and Vietnam were cleared to provide the teak to build the fleets' ships. Thousands of artisans labored to build the ships, and many more left as sailors, most of whom never returned. The expensive ocean voyages also distracted China's attention from its vulnerable land frontiers in the northwest. And the mandarins, China's professional, highly educated bureaucrats, despised and resented the naval officers who were in charge of the fleets.

In 1424, a new emperor, Zhu Gaozhi, issued an edict:

> All voyages of the treasure ships are to be stopped....Those officials who
> are currently abroad on business are ordered back to the capital imme-
> diately....The building and repair of all treasure ships is to be stopped
> immediately.

For the next 200 years, China became increasingly isolated from the rest of the
non-Asian world. As a result, China played no role in the initial creation of the
new world that came into being as people of the Americas, Europe, and Africa
interacted.

By the 1490s, China was prospering but quite inward looking. South Asia, espe-
cially India, was just beginning to be engaged in what would be a growing trade with
Europe through the new trade routes that Portuguese explorers were establishing.
Sub-Saharan Africa, dominated by the Songhay Empire and the kingdom of Kongo,
was also trading with Europeans via a newly established Atlantic trade route dominated by the Portuguese, as well as their long-established trade routes across the
Sahara that connected them with the Muslim world, increasingly dominated by the
Ottoman Empire. American Indians had their own long-distance trade relationships that spanned thousands of miles, even though they never contemplated trade
that might cross the oceans that bounded them. As all of this interaction was taking
place, the newly united kingdom of Spain took the lead in seeking yet another way to
expand trade in the world that they knew. At the beginning of the year 1492, no one
living anywhere on the planet knew how eventful that effort to seek new pathways for
trade would be.

1.5 **Quick Review** How did Asia differ from Europe? What effect did these differences have
on the continent?

CONCLUSION
The world that existed before the encounter that took place in 1492 was rich and
dynamic in cultures, civilizations, and diversity. The first peoples of North America
had discovered and settled the continent long before Columbus set sail in 1492. The
ancestors of today's American Indians began to people North American during the
Ice Age, when land routes existed between Siberia and Alaska. Whether they came by
land or water, these original groups of people established agrarian and hunter–gath-
erer cultures over the centuries, and usually lived in remarkable harmony with their
environment. This respect for harmony was a feature of their religions and worldview
that, in so many ways, would be different from the European mindset. Later North
American Indian cultures established sophisticated trading empires and founded cities
that rivaled those of medieval Europe. Their cultural heritage would be lost or changed
forever by the impact of European arrival and colonization.

While the first peoples of North America had been establishing their communities,
Europeans in the 1400s were on the move, recovering from the wars and the bubonic
plague that had decimated the continent in the late 1300s. European contact with
North America was motivated in part by the 1452 Muslim conquest of Constantinople,
which placed the Eastern Mediterranean under the control of the Ottoman Empire
and closed off traditional land and sea routes to India and other centers of trade in
Asia. The kingdom of Portugal led the way in exploring sailing routes around Africa.
Eventually, new trade relationships gradually developed between Europeans and the
many preexisting African empires and kingdoms that had also developed sophisticated
cultures and agricultural economies. The Portuguese adopted and exploited the institution of slavery and the slave trade, which had generally disappeared in Europe, and
brought African slaves back to Europe even before the first slaves were transported to
the Americas.

Over a quarter century before Portugal's Prince Henry the Navigator dispatched his sailors to explore the African coast, the Chinese emperor Zhu Di ordered the construction of the "treasure fleets," which explored and established trade routes in the Indian and Pacific oceans. His ships and sailors matched those of Europe; however, Zhu Di's successor ordered the end of the treasure fleets, which were seen as a drain on China's wealth. For this reason, Europeans had no serious rivals when they first encountered the Americas.

While Portuguese sailors sailed around Africa to reach Asia, an Italian sailor, Christopher Columbus, was commissioned by the king and queen of Spain to try a different route, sailing west across the Atlantic rather than south and east around Africa. The result was an encounter between civilizations in Europe, Africa, and the Americas that knew nothing of each other—a world-changing event for everyone involved.

CHAPTER REVIEW | What was life and culture like for Native Americans, Europeans, and Africans before the encounters of 1492?

Chapter 1   Chapter Review

THE PEOPLING OF NORTH AMERICA

1.1 Describe what the archeological record tells about the arrival, development, and cultures of the first peoples of North America.

Review Questions

1. **Historical Interpretation**
   How do most anthropologists explain the peopling of North America? What evidence do they use to support this explanation?

2. **Crafting an Argument**
   How did the adoption of settled agriculture shape the development of Cahokia society?

THE DIVERSE COMMUNITIES OF THE AMERICAS IN THE 1400s

1.2 Describe the diversity of American Indian cultures in the United States on the eve of their encounter with Europeans.

Review Questions

3. **Comparison**
   What similarities existed between the Aztec and Inca Empires?

4. **Crafting an Argument**
   How would you explain the fact that after the demise of Cahokia no urban center of similar size and sophistication emerged to take its place?

5. **Synthesis**
   What common features characterized the world view of most American Indian peoples?

A CHANGING EUROPE IN THE 1400s

1.3 Describe the changes in Europe that led to Columbus's voyages and that shaped European attitudes when encountering the peoples of the Americas.

Review Questions

6. **Chronological Reasoning**
   What were the long-term consequences for Europe of the fall of Constantinople to the Ottomans?

7. **Contextualization**
   What prompted Portuguese exploration in the 15th century?

8. **Comparison**
   Compare and contrast Spain, England, and France on the eve of the Age of Exploration. Why did Spain take the lead in westward expansion?

AFRICA IN THE 1400s

1.4 Describe the political, cultural, and religious developments in Africa that would shape contact between Europeans and Africans in the Americas.

Review Questions

9. **Comparison**
   How did trade affect the development of Ghana, Mali, and Songhay?

10. **Contextualization**
    What characterized the African slave trade in the 15th century?

11. **Crafting an Argument**
    Why were Europeans unable to dictate the terms of their economic relationships with West and Central African states?

ASIA IN THE 1400s

1.5 Contrast developments in Asia with those in Europe at the time when Europeans first reached the Americas.

Review Question

12. **Comparison**
    Compare and contrast Europe and Asia on the eve of European westward expansion. What is the significance of the differences you note?

First Encounters, First Conquests

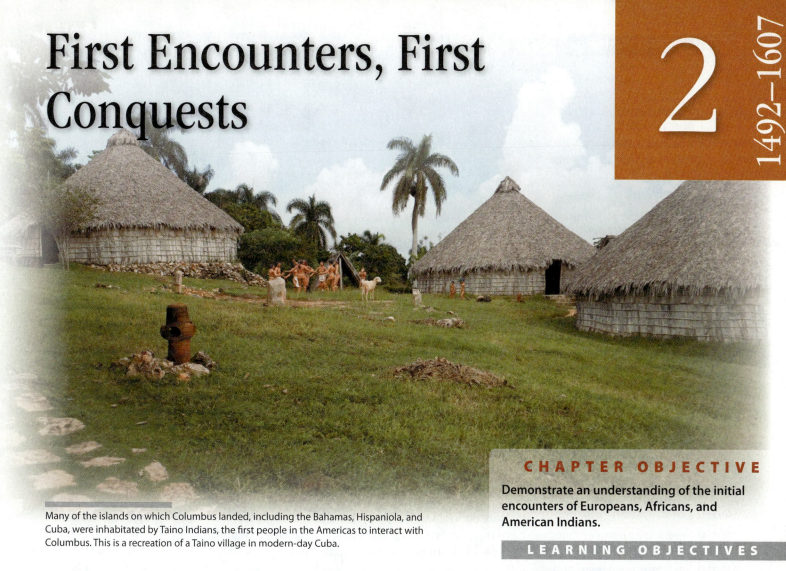

Many of the islands on which Columbus landed, including the Bahamas, Hispaniola, and Cuba, were inhabited by Taino Indians, the first people in the Americas to interact with Columbus. This is a recreation of a Taino village in modern-day Cuba.

CHAPTER OBJECTIVE

Demonstrate an understanding of the initial encounters of Europeans, Africans, and American Indians.

LEARNING OBJECTIVES

COLUMBUS, THE COLUMBIAN EXCHANGE, AND EARLY CONQUESTS

Explain the reasons behind the voyages of Columbus and early Spanish encounters with the peoples of the Caribbean, Mexico, and South America.
2.1

A DIVIDED EUROPE: THE IMPACT OF THE PROTESTANT REFORMATION

Explain how the Protestant Reformation and the development of the nation-state changed Europe and European ideas about how best to settle and govern America.
2.2

EXPLORATION AND ENCOUNTER IN NORTH AMERICA: THE SPANISH

Analyze early Spanish exploration of America north of Mexico.
2.3

EXPLORATION AND ENCOUNTER IN NORTH AMERICA: THE FRENCH

Analyze early French exploration and claims in North America.
2.4

EXPLORATION AND ENCOUNTER IN NORTH AMERICA: THE ENGLISH

Explain English explorers, privateers, and reasons for settlement.
2.5

After 66 days of sailing, the last half on uncharted open seas, an Italian sailor commissioned by Queen Isabella of Spain, Christopher Columbus, and his crew landed on a small Caribbean island on October 12, 1492. Columbus named the island San Salvador. No one is sure on which island in the Bahamas Columbus first landed. But there was a Taino village on the shore, and human contact came quickly. Columbus and his crew received a friendly greeting from the Tainos of whom Columbus said,

> I recognized that they were people who would be better freed [from error] and converted to our Holy Faith by love than by force—to some of them I gave red caps, and glass beads…and many other things of small value, in which they took so much pleasure and became so much our friends that it was a marvel. Later they came swimming to the ships' launches where we were and brought us parrots and cotton thread in balls and javelins….In sum, they took everything and gave of what they had very willingly….All of them go around as naked as their mothers bore them…

The world was never the same again.

Although Columbus did not know it, that encounter represented the beginning of an extraordinary change in worldwide human contact. Columbus claimed that he had achieved his mission to reach Asia. The Europeans who came after him quickly learned that they had encountered

This image of shows Columbus taking his leave from the King and Queen of Spain to journey across the Atlantic on the three ships in the background.

not Asia, but an unknown continent filled with people they had never imagined existed. The Columbian encounter led to unimagined power and wealth for many Europeans. It also led to the creation of new ethnic groups as children were born to American Indian-European couples. And it shifted the balance of trade and commerce around the world from land to the world's oceans.

For the American Indians, the encounter was even more of a surprise, and much more devastating. Suddenly, from across the ocean, unimagined people arrived, with a strange way of talking and dressing, a strange religion, and a different way of looking at the world. In part because of differences in technology, in part because of differences between European and indigenous people's understandings of war and conquest, and most of all, because of differences in the two groups' ability to withstand European diseases, the encounter led to conquest, disease, and death for many Indians.

Understanding what happened in the history of the United States over the next 500 years depends on understanding the differences between those who arrived from Europe—especially from Spain, France, and England—as well as from Africa and the diverse peoples who lived in the Americas when they arrived. With the arrival of Columbus and the many Europeans who followed him once news of his journey spread, something new in human history took place: a massive transit and mixing of peoples in North and South America.

COLUMBUS, THE COLUMBIAN EXCHANGE, AND EARLY CONQUESTS

2.1 Explain the reasons behind the voyages of Columbus and early Spanish encounters with the peoples of the Caribbean, Mexico, and South America.

As delighted as Columbus was by the Taino welcome and generosity and what seemed to him the easy opportunity to convert them to Christianity, Columbus also noted other things that would be more ominous for their future:

> They do not carry arms nor are they acquainted with them, because I showed them swords and they took them by the edge and through ignorance cut themselves. They have no iron. Their javelins are shafts without iron and some of them have at the end a fish tooth.

Conquest, Columbus came to believe, would be easy.

American Voices

The Dedication of Columbus's Log to the King and Queen of Spain, 1493

Returning from his first voyage in early 1493, Columbus understood how much his exploration was linked to Ferdinand and Isabella's efforts to unify Spain into a militant, single-minded nation. He spelled out these links when he dedicated his report to the rulers.

Whereas, Most Christian and Very Noble and Very Excellent and Very Powerful Princes, King and Queen of the Spain's and of the Islands of the Sea, our Lords: This present year of 1492, after your Highnesses had brought to an end the war with the Moors who ruled in Europe and had concluded the war in the very great city of Granada, where this present year on the second day of the month of January I saw the Royal Standards of Your Highnesses placed by force of arms on the towers of the Alhambra...and Your Highnesses, as Catholic Christians and Princes, lovers and promoters of the Holy Christian Faith, and enemies of the false doctrine of Mahomet and of all idolatries and heresies, you thought of sending me, Christóbal Colón, to the said regions of India to see the said princes and the peoples and the lands, and the characteristics of the lands and of everything, and to see how their conversion to our Holy Faith might be undertaken.... So, after having expelled all the Jews from all of your Kingdoms and Dominions, in the same month of January Your Highnesses commanded me to go, with a suitable fleet, to the said regions of India.

Source: Oliver Dunn and James E. Kelley, Jr., translators, *The Diario of Christopher Columbus's First Voyage to America, 1492–1493*, abstracted by Fray Bārtolomé de Las Casas (Norman: University of Oklahoma Press, 1988), pp. 17–19.

Thinking Critically

1. Documentary Analysis

What connection did Columbus make between Spain's defeat of Muslim Granada, the expulsion of the Jews from Spain, and his own voyage across the Atlantic?

2. Historical Interpretation

What does the document suggest about the role of religion in motivating Spain's efforts at overseas exploration and expansion?

Columbus described what would be the terms of much of the European contact with American Indians: "They should be good and intelligent servants, for I see that they say very quickly everything that is said to them." Columbus also looked closely at the ornaments and jewelry that some of the Indians were wearing and wrote, "I was attentive and labored to find out if there was any gold." The search for gold, and the effort to subjugate the Indians in its service, had begun.

The Four Voyages of Christopher Columbus

In spite of the friendly welcome he received, Columbus took some Tainos as captives. He wanted to teach them Spanish and show them to his sponsors in Spain. Columbus also wanted guides to the gold he was sure could be found since he had seen some Tainos wearing gold ornaments. Led by native guides, he sailed on to Cuba and sent a party inland to find the local chief (or *cacique* as the Taino called their leaders) who his guides said had access to gold. When Columbus did not find the leader or the gold, he sailed to another island he named Hispaniola (modern Haiti and the Dominican Republic). He built a fort and left part of his crew there with instructions to search for gold. In January 1493, Columbus, with six Taino prisoners, turned back to Spain.

Columbus never fully understood the importance of his voyage. He set out to discover a route across the Atlantic directly to Asia, and he thought he had indeed reached an unknown part of Asia, perhaps Japan or Korea. Thinking the people he met looked like those who came from the part of south Asia Europeans called "the Indies," he called them *Indians*. Of course, he did not really discover a new land because the *Indians* were already there. Columbus certainly discovered a new route across the Atlantic, but it led to a continent filled with people unknown to Europeans.

The rest of Columbus's life was a tragedy, for himself and for the peoples he had encountered. To impress the Spanish court, Columbus exaggerated what he had found, especially the gold. Isabella and Ferdinand gave him seventeen ships and 1,200 men for a second voyage to seek slaves and gold in this supposed part of Asia, just as the Portuguese were finding both in Africa.

When he arrived back on Hispaniola in 1494, Columbus found that the native residents had killed the sailors he had left behind in 1492. A local chief initially offered protection to the Europeans, but when the sailors sought to make the Tainos slaves, they rebelled. Columbus ordered retribution, and many Tainos were killed. As word spread of the harsh ways of the Europeans, the Indians became less friendly, and Columbus found himself "discovering" deserted villages. The Caribbean had little gold despite Columbus's desperate efforts to force the natives to find it, and many Tainos died from Spanish swords or from forced labor that the Spanish instituted.

Columbus himself was a better explorer than administrator and less vicious than many of his successors (see Map 2-1). During his third voyage to the Caribbean in 1498, he tried to set up a government on Hispaniola. But many Spaniards complained about hard lives there with little reward. A new governor sent Columbus back to Spain in chains. Although the Spanish monarchs forgave him and allowed him a fourth voyage in 1502, he never governed again.

Amerigo Vespucci Inspires a Continent's Name

Columbus was not the first European to reach the Americas. Archeologists have discovered evidence of a short-lived Norse settlement called L'Anse aux Meadows on Newfoundland somewhere between 900 and 1000, but the settlement was quickly forgotten on both sides of the Atlantic. If others crossed the Atlantic, or the Pacific, their voyages were also soon forgotten. What was different about the voyage of Columbus was that so much of Europe took interest and so many Europeans followed in his wake.

In the earliest exploration and conquest of the Americas, Spain was the unquestioned leader. Portugal focused primarily on its rich trade routes around Africa and

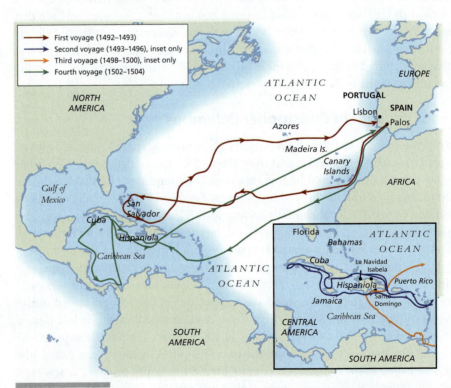

MAP 2-1 Columbus's Voyages. Columbus made a total of four voyages starting and ending in the Spanish port city of Palos and enabling him to see and describe the islands of Bahamas where he first landed, Hispaniola (modern day Dominican Republic and Haiti), Cuba, Jamaica, and much of the coast of Central America.

into the Indian Ocean. However, Portuguese explorers also quickly followed routes across the Atlantic similar to those of Columbus, exploring, and claiming much of South America. In 1494, Spain and Portugal agreed to the **Treaty of Tordesillas** in which a line drawn by the pope separated Spanish and Portuguese claims in South America. To this day, Brazil, east of the line, is a Portuguese speaking country while the rest of South America is Spanish speaking.

In April 1495, only two years after Columbus returned from his first voyage, Isabella and Ferdinand authorized other Spanish voyages across the Atlantic. A young Italian merchant, Amerigo Vespucci, made three or four trips—the historical record is not clear—between 1497 and 1504, some authorized by Spain, others by Portugal. Sailing along the coast of Brazil, much farther south than Columbus ever ventured, Vespucci concluded that the land mass on the other side of the Atlantic was much larger than the first reports indicated. Unlike Columbus, Vespucci was convinced that Europeans had reached a new continent, rather than Asia. As a result, a German publisher, Martin Waldseemüller, produced a new map of the world in 1507. He called the new continent that Vespucci described **America** in his honor.

The Impact of European Arms and Disease

The Spanish governors who came after Columbus were more efficient and more cruel. As they learned more about the lands and peoples that Columbus had claimed for them, Ferdinand and Isabella pressed harder for gold. They also ordered that the Indians be treated well and not enslaved. But Spanish governors focused on the gold and ignored the command to show kindness. Nicolás de Ovando who became governor on Hispaniola in 1502 set a pattern. He brought 2,500 Spanish settlers—families, not just male explorers—to build a permanent settlement. In the future, many Spanish explorers also married native women, creating new families of mixed ethnic heritage. Ovando attacked the Tainos ruthlessly. In 1502, he responded to a rebellion in Higüey by capturing 600–700 Indians and then ordering them all to be knifed to death and their bodies displayed. Later, in 1503, he convened an ostensibly friendly meeting of the caciques, the district chiefs, and when some 80 of them had assembled in one building, he ordered the doors locked and the building burned with them in it. With that act, the last independent chiefdoms of Hispaniola were ended.

However, the most devastating thing that Columbus and his successors did was unintentional. They brought European diseases. The Tainos, like all natives of the Americas, had no immunity to smallpox, measles, or other diseases they had never known. In Europe where these diseases were common and had been for hundreds of years, many people had developed immunity to them or at least to their worst effects. American Indians had no such immunity. As a result, while Indians died by the hundreds from Spanish swords, they died by the thousands from disease. There were probably 1 million people on Hispaniola when Columbus landed in 1492. By the early 1500s, only 1,000 Tainos were left. Within a century, all were gone. The European destruction of the first people of the Americas had begun.

From a total population of perhaps 70–80 million (no one really knows) when Columbus arrived, native peoples in both the Americas dropped to 4.5 million as a result of war and disease in the decades after the first encounter. However unintentional the introduction of European disease was, the staggering numbers of Indian deaths made their conquest easy, and many Europeans were happy to take advantage of their already cleared land. For the Indians, tragedy followed tragedy.

Soon, on the islands where Columbus first landed, the only Indian descendants were people of mixed races. A Spanish census of 1514 indicated that 40 percent of the Spanish men had native wives. The arrival of African slaves in the 1500s added African blood to the mix. Today, many of the peoples of the Americas are descendants of all three of the groups that met in the Columbian encounter.

2.1

2.2

2.3

2.4

2.5

Treaty of Tordesillas
Treaty confirmed by the pope in 1494 to resolve the claims of Spain and Portugal in the Americas.

America
The name given to the lands Europeans encountered across the Atlantic after 1492, in honor of the explorer Amerigo Vespucci.

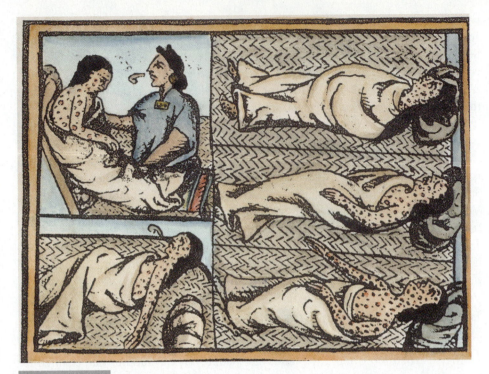

European diseases, especially smallpox, killed more of the original inhabitants of the Americas than any other cause. This illustration, originally done by Aztec scribes before their conquest, described "a great sickness" that came with sores "so terrible that the victims could not lie face down, nor on their backs, nor move from one side to the other."

The Making of an Ocean World—The Atlantic and Columbian Exchange

News of the new contact with the Americas changed the way many people looked at the world. Most educated Europeans already believed that the world was round and not flat. But until 1492, they were concerned primarily with the land. Traders had long gone over land on the **Silk Road** established between Venice and China by Marco Polo between 1271 and 1295 that brought luxury goods to Europe from Asia. Portuguese sailors stayed close to the coast of Africa as they sailed around that continent to Asia. Norse sailors had explored the far North Atlantic—hopping from Iceland to Greenland, and on to the nearest parts of North America—seeking new fishing opportunities. But Columbus and his successors did something different; they sailed directly across the ocean, with no landmarks to guide their journey. Soon after that journey, the oceans—the Atlantic, the Indian, and very soon the Pacific—became the primary trade routes for Europeans, Americans, and increasing numbers of unwilling Africans. Nations that had ports on the Atlantic, especially Spain, Portugal, and England, moved from the margins of a land-focused Europe to become the key points of contact with an ocean-focused world. The shift from primarily land-based, or near-shore sea trade, to trade spanning the world's oceans was a revolution in the way people thought, and it had winners and losers.

The trade and cultural exchanges across the interconnected continents of Europe, Asia, and Africa and did not end after 1492, but the relationships were different. Portugal and Spain replaced Genoa and Venice as the primary European links to Asia. Portuguese and Spanish ships dominated the Indian Ocean. Many other Spanish explorers followed Columbus in very short order. In addition to those who explored the Atlantic coast, Vasco Nunez de Balboa reached the Isthmus of Panama in 1513 and became the first European to view the Pacific. In 1519, five ships and their crews commanded by Ferdinand Magellan began a journey that led them around the tip of South America in 1520 and across the Pacific to the Philippines, where Magellan himself was killed. Three years after they had departed, a handful of the explorers, on one ship, became the first

Silk Road

The overland trading route first established by the Venetian trader Marco Polo in the late 1200s.

people to circumnavigate the globe, arriving back in Spain in 1522. Spanish galleons not only brought silver mined in the Americas across the Atlantic to Spain but soon also brought silver across the Pacific to Manila in the Philippines. (Manila itself was founded by Spanish traders in 1571.) The world of the 1500s was becoming an oceanic world including the Atlantic, the Indian Ocean, and the Pacific. The Atlantic Ocean that had been the great barrier on the western edge of Europe suddenly became the great highway connecting known and previously unknown continents. Portugal and Spain were the first European states to establish trading routes across the oceans, but during the 1500s, England, France, and Holland also assumed major roles in the new trade.

As Europeans came to terms with the Americas, the people of the Americas also had to come to terms with Europe. For each there were gains and losses. What became known as the **Columbian Exchange**—the interchange of diseases, plants, animals, and human cultures between New and Old Worlds after 1492—reflected some of these changes. The most tragic loss occurred with the transmission of disease-bearing microbes that devastated populations in the Americas. New populations began to emerge after 1492, when the peoples who met in the Americas produced offspring that carried the biological traits and the cultures of their ancestors from vastly different parts of the world.

The exchange also changed the eating habits of almost every person on the planet. In Europe, Asia, and Africa, foods such as corn, beans, peanuts, potatoes, cassava,

Columbian Exchange
The transatlantic exchange of plants, animals, and diseases that occurred after the first European contact with the Americas.

TABLE 2-1 The Columbian Exchange

	From the Americas to Europe, Africa, and Asia	From Europe, Africa, and Asia to the Americas		From the Americas to Europe, Africa, and Asia	From Europe, Africa, and Asia to the Americas
Plants	Corn (maize)	Wheat	**Animals**	Turkeys	Chickens
	Potatoes	Barley		Llamas	Donkeys
	Sweet potatoes	Rye			Cattle
	Peanuts	Oats			Goats
	Pumpkins	Apples			Horses
	Pineapples	Peaches			Pigs
	Guava	Pears			Sheep
	Squash	Plums			Cats
	Tomatoes	Apricots			
	Peppers	Cherries	**Disease**	Syphilis	Smallpox (the single most deadly disease among American Indians)
	Papayas	Bananas		(Syphilis was also known in the ancient Eurasian world and has been found in Egyptian mummies but a new and virulent form of the disease was brought to Europe from the Americas.)	Measles
	Avocados	Coffee			
	Beans	Tea			Influenza
	Cassava	Sugar cane			Yellow fever
	Blueberries	Melons			Typhus
	Tobacco	Lemons			Scarlet fever
	Cocoa	Oranges			Diphtheria
	Vanilla	Cabbage			(Sometimes multiple diseases from this list affected an American Indian community at the same time.)
		Carrots			
		Grapes			
		Lettuce			
		Onions			
		Garlic			

sweet potatoes, avocados, pineapples, tomatoes, chilies, vanilla, and cocoa from the Americas enriched people's diets. Rice, wheat, barley, oats and many new fruits and vegetables from Europe, Africa, and Asia fed the American Indians as did chickens, cattle, sheep, and pigs (see Table 2–1). Horses changed the way many American Indians lived. A world without this variety is unimaginable today.

The Conquest of the Aztec and Inca Empires

Besides European diseases, the peoples of the Americas faced another threat: armed conquest. Hernán Cortés sailed from Cuba to Mexico with 600 soldiers in 1519. Within 2 years, he conquered Tenochtitlán, the Aztec capital, and renamed it Mexico City. When he first arrived, some of the Aztecs may have thought Cortés might be their lost god Quetzalcoatl, who was said to have vanished from the place where Cortés landed. In their initial encounter, the Aztec Emperor Motecuhzoma (often written as Montezuma) welcomed Cortés. They exchanged gifts, which Cortés saw as a sign of submission to Spain. The relationship soured quickly. Cortés took the emperor prisoner but allowed him to maintain a façade of rule.

In July 1520, the Aztecs turned on Cortés, and he and his soldiers fled the capital. But they did not go far. With support from thousands of non-Aztec tribes—people who hated Aztec dominance and who hated having their people being used for the human sacrifices that Aztec religion demanded—the Spanish army regrouped and began a long, bloody siege of Tenochtitlán. Motecuhzoma himself was killed, probably by his own people, and Cortés completed his conquest of the city in August 1521.

With Tenochtitlán destroyed, Cortés set about building a new and grander city on the same spot. On the site of the main Aztec temple, he ordered the building of a massive new Catholic cathedral modeled on the one at Granada, which had recently been built in the former Muslim stronghold in southern Spain. In both cases, the religious architecture symbolized the defeat of the "infidels." Within a generation, a thriving new Mexico City, filled with great churches and government palaces, had become the home of the Spanish viceroy—the king's representative—and the capital of **New Spain**, as the Spanish called their empire in Mexico and Central America.

New Spain
The name of Spain's first empire in the Americas.

One of the earliest images of Hernán Cortés, on horseback, fighting with Aztec warriors.

In 1532, in Peru, Francisco Pizarro and his army of 168 Spanish soldiers defeated the Inca Emperor Atahuallpa and his army of 80,000 soldiers. Within a few years, the Inca Empire of 32 million people, much larger than the Aztec Empire, had become the Viceroyalty of Peru, a second major outpost of distant Spain. Its primary purpose was to supply gold and silver to finance Spain's European ambitions. At Potosí in Bolivia, 45,000 slaves—at first Indians then also Africans—worked the mines that created the wealth that made King Charles V and his son Philip II the richest and most powerful rulers in Europe.

The swiftness of the Spanish conquest of the Aztec and Inca Empires was possible for many reasons. Aztec resistance was undermined by a sense of fatalism fueled by early visions of their own defeat. Many non-Aztecs joined with Cortés, more than happy to be rid of the Aztecs. The Incas could not imagine, and therefore did not fear, Pizarro's initial surprise attack since he claimed to come in the name of friendship. Pizarro's dishonesty in announcing that he was coming in friendship followed by his surprise attack was simply inconceivable to people reared in the long history of Inca civilization. And both empires found Spanish horses, swords, and armor terrifying. The ruthless military skill of Cortés and Pizarro and the Spanish mastery of guns, steel swords, and horses created an enemy who was simply unimaginable to Aztec and Inca armies and therefore very difficult to resist. The Aztecs and the Incas could not match the Spanish strategies and tools of war.

Perhaps the most significant Spanish advantage was smallpox. The Aztecs may have lost half of their population to smallpox during the 2 years of attack by Cortés on their capital, and the Incas faced the same terrifying losses. An Inca emperor had died from smallpox shortly before Pizarro arrived. The disease traveled at a far faster pace than even Spanish armies could march and often preceded them. For people used to living in harmony with nature, the terrible ravishing of the disease that occurred along with the arrival of these frightening white-skinned, bearded, and horse-mounted soldiers tore apart their world—militarily, culturally, and spiritually—all in a very short time.

THINKING HISTORICALLY
Pizarro and Atahuallpa

In his popular book, *Guns, Germs, and Steel: The Fate of Human Societies*, Jared Diamond traces the unequal competition between different groups of humans from the beginning of recorded history to the present. His core question is why people of European origin came to dominate the planet despite the many advances Asians, Africans, and the peoples of the Americas made. In one chapter, he focuses on the early encounter of Europeans and Americans describing, "why the Inca Emperor Atahuallpa did not capture King Charles I of Spain." The analysis focuses on the development of ideas, technology, and disease before 1492 that allowed Atahuallpa and some 80,000 followers to be defeated by just 168 Spaniards led by Pizarro. This kind of questioning is an important part of accurately understanding historical events.

Source: Jared Diamond, *Guns, Germs, and Steel: The Fates of Human Societies* (New York, W. W. Norton, 1997, 2005).

Thinking Critically
1. **Chronological Reasoning**
   What ideas in Inca society prior to 1492 contributed to their defeat? What developments in European society contributed to Spanish victory?

2. **Crafting an Argument**
   In trying to explain the rapid European conquest of the Americas, how much emphasis would you place on advanced technology? What about disease? How about cultural differences? Since the Inca Empire was much larger than that of Spain in the 1530s, why did Atahuallpa not consider sailing across the Atlantic to conquer Spain?

This statue of Bartolomé de Las Casas stands in a prominent place in modern Mexico City as recognition of the respect in which he is held by many of the indigenous people of Mexico and the Americas.

encomienda
In the Spanish colonies, the grant to a Spanish settler of a certain number of American Indian subjects, who would pay him tribute in goods and labor.

conquistadores
The name given to the early Spanish conquerors of Mexico and Peru.

Bartolomé de Las Casas and the Voices of Protest

Spain's treatment of the American Indians did not occur without protest. On Hispaniola, it was denounced within less than 20 years. In 1511, on a Sunday before Christmas, Antonio de Montesinos, a Dominican priest, asked his Spanish congregation, "Tell me, by what right do you keep these Indians in cruel servitude?…You are in mortal sin for the cruelty and tyranny you deal out to these innocent people."

Bartolomé de Las Casas (1484–1566) may have heard Montesinos's sermon. Certainly he had heard *of* it. Las Casas edited the log of Columbus's journey and moved to Hispaniola to make his own fortune in 1502. Although he became a priest in 1510, he participated in the conquest of Cuba in 1512 and was rewarded with a large ranch, or **encomienda**, worked by Indian slaves. But his conscience bothered him. In 1514, he gave up the land and the slaves and began preaching and writing against the oppression of the Indians, which he continued to do for the next 50 years. Las Casas documented in detail the cruelty of the Spanish conquerors, begging the Spanish crown to stop the **conquistadores**, the soldiers who were creating the Spanish Empire in the Americas.

Las Casas also left an important record of the life and customs of the first peoples of the Americas. He wrote that among them, "marriage laws are nonexistent: men and women alike choose their mates and leave them as they please, without offense, jealousy, or anger." They live, he wrote, in

> large communal bell-shaped buildings, housing up to 600 people at one time… made of very strong wood and roofed with palm leaves.…They prize bird feathers of various colors, beads made of fish bones, and green and white stones with which they adorn their ears and lips, but they put no value on gold and other precious things.…They are extremely generous with their possessions and by the same token covet the possessions of their friends and expect the same degree of liberality.

If they worshipped at all, it was not in a form that this Catholic priest recognized.

Nevertheless, the key purpose of all of Las Casas's writings was to ask the Spanish authorities to intervene to protect the Indians. He described seeing native people worked

Although he never left Europe, Theodore de Bry (1528–1598) spent many years drawing illustrations of European-Indian encounters based on first-hand reports, including this one showing the attack by Spanish soldiers on an Indian village.

to death in the mines when "'moderate labor' turned into labor fit only for iron men: mountains are stripped from top to bottom and bottom to top a thousand times; they dig, split rocks, move stones and carry dirt on their backs to wash it in rivers, while those who wash gold stay in the water all the time with their backs bent so constantly it breaks them."

Las Casas always believed, or at least hoped, that if the Spanish monarchs only knew the truth, Spain's rulers would intercede. At times, the distant monarchs seemed to heed him. Shortly before her death, Isabella ordered that the Indians must be treated "as freemen and not as slaves, they must be given wages, they must be treated well [Christians should receive better treatment than non-Christians]." Las Casas was determined to show just how far reality departed from these orders.

While Las Casas may have led the Spanish authorities to make a few reforms, the biggest effect of his work was not what he expected. He was writing during the Protestant Reformation, and Protestants, far more than Catholics, republished his words, creating what came to be known as the "Black Legend" (for the color of the priest's robes) of unique Spanish cruelty. History would show that the Spanish were not unique in their treatment of American Indians, but the legend of their special cruelty persisted even as other Europeans adopted the same techniques and attitudes.

2.1 **Quick Review** Which factor do you believe was most responsible for the destruction of native populations? Justify your answer with evidence from the chapter.

American Voices
Bartolomé de Las Casas, *The History of the Indies*, 1550

The publication of The History of the Indies, along with the many speeches and other writings from priests like Las Casas had multiple results. Las Casas clearly documented for all time just how cruel the first Europeans were in their treatment of the indigenous people of the Americas. On a few occasions, it led Spanish authorities to end some abuses or replace vicious officials, but such steps were rare and seldom had lasting effect. In the hands of enemies of Catholic Spain, the documents were used to create a long-lasting story of unique Spanish cruelty. Ultimately, the careful documentation created one of the best reports—even if a romanticized one—on the experience of American Indians at the time of their first encounter with Europeans. The following is an excerpt from Las Casas's History:

The men were sent out to the mines as far as 80 leagues away while their wives remained to work the soil, not with hoes or plowshares drawn by oxen, but with their own sweat and sharpened poles that were far from equaling the equipment used for similar work in Castile. They had to make silo-like heaps for cassava plants, by digging 12 square feet 4 palms deep and 10,000 or 12,000 of such hills—a giant's work—next to one another had to be made, and they had other tasks of the same magnitude of whatever nature the Spaniards saw as fittest to make more money. Thus husbands and wives were together only once every 8 or 10 months, and when they met they were so exhausted and depressed on both sides that they had no mind for marital communication and in this way they ceased to procreate. As for the

newly born, they died early because their mothers, overworked and famished, had no milk to nurse them, and for this reason, while I was in Cuba, 7,000 children died in 3 months. Some mothers even drowned their babies from sheer desperation, while others caused themselves to abort with certain herbs that produced stillborn children. In this way husbands died in the mines, wives died at work, and children died from lack of milk, while others had not time or energy for procreation, and in a short time this land, which was so great, so powerful and fertile, though so unfortunate, was depopulated. If this concatenation of events had occurred all over the world, the human race would have been wiped out in no time.

Source: Bartolomé de Las Casas, *History of the Indies*. 1550.

Thinking Critically
1. **Documentary Analysis**
   What kinds of abuses did Las Casas identify? What motives did he imply were behind Spanish brutality?
2. **Contextualization**
   Who might Las Casas have been hoping to influence by publicizing Spanish abuses in the New World? What allies might he have found for his cause within Spanish society? How might the Protestant focus on his work have unintended consequences for Las Casas?

Martin Luther's challenge to Catholic teachings and practices in his day led to a decisive split in the unity among Christians that had been known in western Europe for centuries. Soon thereafter, John Calvin also challenged some of Luther's teachings leading to a three way split between Catholics, Lutherans, and Calvinists—followed by further splits among Protestants.

Ninety-Five Theses
A document with 95 debating points that a young monk, Martin Luther, hoped would lead to a series of reforms within the Catholic Church.

Protestant Reformation
The process that began with Martin Luther's efforts to reform the Catholic Church's practices in the early 1500s and that eventually led followers of Luther, Calvin, and others to completely break from the Catholic Church.

nation-state
A relatively new development in Europe during the 1300s and 1400s in which nations became the major political organizations, replacing both the smaller kingdoms and city-states.

A DIVIDED EUROPE: THE IMPACT OF THE PROTESTANT REFORMATION

 2.2   Explain how the Protestant Reformation and the development of the nation-state changed Europe and European ideas about how best to settle and govern America.

When Columbus sailed in 1492, he did so with a commission from the rulers of a newly unified Spain. Spanish explorers and conquerors brought the same quest for unity to the Americas. They sought to convert all native peoples to Catholic Christianity as part of the expansion of Spain's realm. In 1492, few Western Europeans would disagree with that mission. Soon, however, Europe's religious unity would disappear.

Less than 30 years after Columbus made his voyage across the Atlantic, the Protestant Reformation changed the way Europeans thought about the world, whether they became Protestant or remained Catholic. The initial European encounter with the Americas was led by representatives of a religiously united Europe. But nearly all of the subsequent exploration and settlement of North America was conducted by Europeans who represented particular groups from a continent deeply divided by religious hostility. That divide shaped the way they understood their efforts on both sides of the Atlantic.

The Birth of Protestantism

In 1517, before Hernán Cortés began his conquest of Mexico, a young German monk, Martin Luther (1483–1546), asked for a debate about religious doctrine by posting his **Ninety-Five Theses** on the door of a church in Wittenberg in the small independent German-speaking state of Saxony. At this time, some within the Roman Catholic Church began to challenge some of the church's practices, prompted partly by new translations of the Bible and by new attention to the writings of Saint Augustine, a theologian of the early church. The challenges questioned the Catholic Church's insistence that bishops and not everyday Christians should interpret the Bible and the idea that one could reach salvation through "good works." In particular, the challenge that Luther posted questioned the Catholic practice of using indulgences that granted forgiveness to sinners to raise money. His action quickly led to a religious split, first in Germany, and then across Europe. That split, known as the **Protestant Reformation**, would shape the cultural and political development of the future United States.

As word of Luther's protests spread, many Germans, including significant members of the nobility who controlled many of the small independent states of Germany, were drawn to the Lutheran cause. In the century that followed, other Protestants developed their own religious ideas, including followers of the French-Swiss reformer, John Calvin (1509–1564), who were known as Calvinists, while other Protestants went in other directions.

Part of what fueled the extraordinary response to Luther's challenge was the cumulating effect that the technology of printing had produced during the previous 62 years. Johannes Gutenberg's creation of a printing press that used moveable type in 1455 and the subsequent rapid spread of printing hugely expanded literacy beyond a small educated elite, mostly clergy, who had monopolized literacy in the medieval world. By 1500, at least 10 million individual books had been printed, and many people learned to read; thus, new ideas could spread with a rapidity not known before. Sermons and pamphlets by Catholics, Lutherans, and Calvinists circulated rapidly. The printing press prompted a free flow of ideas that most people in Europe had not experienced before.

Religion and the Nation-State

The idea of the **nation-state** developed more or less at the same time as the Protestant–Catholic split. The modern idea that the world should be governed by independent nations, or nation-states, was new in the Europe of the 1500s. Indeed, a world divided into separate independent nations clashed with a long-standing ideal, held by many, of a unified Europe—unified in religion and government. In reality, the Europe of the 1400s was not united at

MAP 2-2 **Europe on the Eve of the Columbian Encounter.** In the years before Columbus made his 1492 voyage across the Atlantic, western Europe was being divided into nation states including England, France, and Spain. Central Europe remained a series of separate states loosely united in the Holy Roman Empire.

all. Real power rested in very local territories. Frederick, Elector (or Duke) of Saxony, was Luther's protector and had enough power to ensure Luther's safety in spite of hostility from the Holy Roman emperor, the pope, and the kings of nearby France. But most of Europe's modern nations did not exist. Even within the church, distance and the difficulty of travel gave local Catholic bishops great independence from papal authorities in Rome.

By the late 1400s, however, something new was emerging in European views of the best forms of government. Ferdinand and Isabella united Spain by 1492. Kings in France, Sweden, Scotland, and England had done the same earlier in the 1400s. The idea of being part of a nation was taking on new importance (see Map 2-2).

Virtually no one argued in favor of religious freedom for the citizens of these nations. Instead, different religious parties, Catholics and assorted Protestants—Lutherans, Calvinists, and others—sought to impose their religious beliefs on as many others as possible. Each party argued that it was defending truth and saw no reason to tolerate those they believed were defending error. This belief in the absolute rightness of one's cause led to more than a century of bloody persecution and religious wars from Ireland and Scotland to France, Germany, and Hungary. The **Peace of Augsburg in 1555** that addressed divisions between Lutherans and Catholics and the **Treaty of Westphalia** that concluded the Thirty Years' War between Catholics and Protestants in Central Europe in 1648 each provided that, in each nation covered by the treaty, the ruler would decide the faith of the people and that foreign armies would no longer intervene in the religious affairs of another state. It was a long way from religious freedom, but it brought an end to the worst religious bloodshed while linking national unity and religious uniformity more tightly together than ever.

The Protestant Reformation and the divisions that followed had a huge impact on European settlement in the Americas. Different nations from a divided Europe battled with each other for control of those new lands. In addition, the wars and divisions in Europe led many to seek asylum in a new place, preferably as far away from the old as possible.

Peace of Augsburg in 1555
An agreement among different smaller kingdoms in Germany that no ruler would attack the kingdom of another on religious grounds.

Treaty of Westphalia
A 1648 peace treaty between a number of European powers that significantly extended the ideas of the Peace of Augsburg.

2.2 **Quick Review** Why might religious changes inspire people in Europe to look outward to the rest of the world? How would the link of religious and national unity in Spain and other parts of Europe affect the behavior of Europeans when they conquered other people?

EXPLORATION AND ENCOUNTER IN NORTH AMERICA: THE SPANISH

2.3 Analyze early Spanish exploration of America north of Mexico.

Conquests of the Aztec and Inca Empires produced extraordinary wealth for Spain. Exploration further north in the Americas—in the future United States—was secondary for the conquistadores and much less lucrative for Spain. In spite of the wealth being generated from the empires in Mexico and Peru, for more than a century, most Europeans showed more interest in getting through or around North America and on to Asia than in exploring the lands north of New Spain. Nevertheless, the unknown lands north of Mexico beckoned to some Spaniards in the 1500s, even if they were not considered as exciting as Central and South America (see Map 2-3).

Ponce de León in Florida, 1513–1521

Juan Ponce de León, who had been part of the Spanish army that conquered Muslim Granada in 1492, led the first known European expeditions to Puerto Rico and Florida. In 1508–1509 he founded the first Spanish community near what would become San Juan and was named Governor of Puerto Rico. In 1513, he led an expedition from Puerto Rico that arrived in what he thought was another island, which he named La Florida. Legend says he was seeking a "Fountain of Youth" that would keep him forever young. Certainly he was seeking an expansion of Spain's empire in the Americas and greater wealth for himself. Ponce de León was accompanied by free Africans whose families were slaves in Spain. Europeans, Africans, and the native peoples of the Americas first met on the soil of the future United States when Ponce de León landed.

In 1521, Ponce de León returned to Florida with some 200 followers—Europeans, Africans, and Indians from Puerto Rico. The Native Americans in Florida did not welcome them. Ponce de León was wounded by a poisoned arrow and died soon thereafter. But the first of many contacts between native peoples and travelers from Europe and Africa in what are now the 50 United States had been made in Florida.

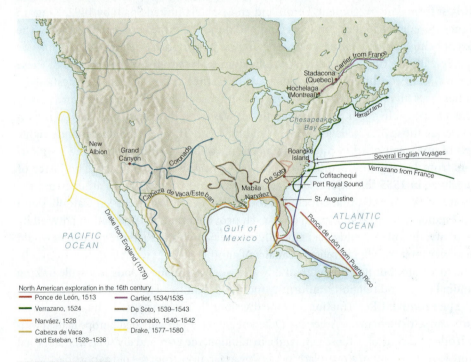

North American exploration in the 16th century

- Ponce de León, 1513
- Verrazano, 1524
- Narváez, 1528
- Cabeza de Vaca and Esteban, 1528–1536
- Cartier, 1534/1535
- De Soto, 1539–1543
- Coronado, 1540–1542
- Drake, 1577–1580

MAP 2-3 North American Exploration. In the first one hundred years after Columbus, European explorers traveled along both the Atlantic and Pacific coasts and through much of the interior of what almost two hundred years later would become the United States. By 1592, however, most Europeans had concluded that there was no easy route through North America to Asia and little gold to be found so they lost interest in the regions north of Mexico.

Exploring Texas by Accident: Cabeza de Vaca, 1528–1536

In 1528, there was another ill-fated effort to colonize Florida. Pánfilo de Narváez sailed to Tampa Bay with about 400 men—Europeans and a few Africans. The Narváez expedition was a disaster. Leaving the ships in Tampa Bay, about 300 men spent months tramping through swamps seeking gold and, soon, merely food and water. Along the way, American Indians attacked them, shooting arrows that penetrated their heavy Spanish armor. The attackers quickly vanished into the forests and swamps while the surviving Spaniards tramped on wearing 50 to 60 pounds of heavy armor.

Finally, ill, under attack, and starving, the survivors decided to build new boats and leave. Years later, one of them remembered:

> This seemed impossible to all, because we did not know how to build them, nor were there…one of all the things that are necessary, nor anyone who would know any way to apply ingenuity. And above all there was nothing to eat.

Nevertheless, they built five barges, and 250 men set out for what they hoped would be home. Instead, the currents, winds, and a hurricane took them west. Two or three of the five barges survived the storm and came ashore near what is now Galveston, Texas.

American Indians gave the survivors food, water, and shelter. Of the 80 explorers who survived the journey across the Gulf of Mexico, only 15 lived through the first winter on the Texas coast (see Map 2-2). The others died of cold and disease. Many of the American Indian hosts also died of European diseases that the Spanish brought with them, and the surviving Indians grew hostile to these intruders who had brought so much disease and trouble.

While others from the Narváez expedition may have lived out their lives among the American Indians of the Texas coast, only four of them, three Spaniards—Alvar Núñez Cabeza de Vaca, Andres Dorantes, Alonso del Castillo Maldonado—and an African Muslim slave from North Africa, named Esteban, decided to literally walk home to Mexico City. Thus, like Florida, Texas was explored by Europeans and Africans together, providing the Indians there with their first exposure to both. The foursome's 8-year adventure took them through southern Texas, the northern states of Mexico, and eventually to the Pacific coast and on to Mexico City.

The four travelers found villages, developed a reputation as healers and traders, and collected a trove of information about American Indians who lived in permanent houses and had a good supply of corn and beans. Later Cabeza de Vaca described the ways of the people he met:

> When Indian men get into an argument in their villages, they fist-fight until exhausted, then separate. Sometimes the women will go between and part them, but men never interfere. No matter what the disaffection, they do not resort to bows and arrows.…
>
> All these [plains] tribes are warlike, and have as much strategy for protection against enemies as if they had been reared in Italy in continual feuds.…Whoever fights them must show no fear and no desire for anything that is theirs.…
>
> I believe these people see and hear better and have keener sense in general than any in the world. They know great hunger, thirst, and cold, as if they were made for enduring these more than other men, by habit and nature.

Cabeza de Vaca also described "a big copper rattle" that was given to them:

> It had a face represented on it, and the natives prized it highly.…It had been brought from the north, where there was a lot of it, replied the natives, who considered copper very valuable. Wherever it came from, we concluded the place must have a foundry to have cast the copper in hollow form.

The American Indians refused to believe these men were of the same race as the Spaniards they had previously known. As Cabeza de Vaca wrote, the four explorers appeared to be distinct from earlier Spanish invaders because, "we cured the sick and they killed those who were healthy, and that we came naked and barefoot and they were clothed and on horseback and with lances, and…had no other purpose but to steal everything they found."

When the four explorers finally reached Mexico City in 1536, their story inspired further exploration. The expeditions that followed, however, did not heed the four explorers' peaceful approach to interactions but were, instead, motivated by suggestions of astounding riches.

Exploring the Southwest: Esteban, de Niza, and Coronado, 1539–1542

The four Texas explorers found great interest as they told their story in Mexico City. In their 8 years living with American Indians, the Spaniards heard stories of seven wealthy and powerful cities with buildings of four or five stories and copper, silver, and gold everywhere, upriver on the Rio Grande. For the Spaniards, stories of fabulous wealth were alluring.

A Spanish legend seemed to further validate what the four Texas explorers shared. The legend told about seven Christian bishops who had fled from the Muslim invasion of Spain in the 700s and established seven wealthy cities far to the west. As the Spanish community in Mexico City heard the stories brought from Texas, many of them remembered both the wealth that Cortés had found and the ancient stories of the fleeing bishops. The Texas survivors showed the copper rattle they had been given, which added to the allure. Many in Mexico City now wanted to explore the territory to their north.

In 1539, a Franciscan brother Marcos de Niza, led an expedition to find the fabled cities. De Niza asked Esteban, the African who had walked across Texas, to scout for them. Thus an African was the first non-Indian many of the Pueblo peoples met. Esteban knew that the Native Americans had never seen a black person. From his years in Texas, he also thought he knew what would impress them: he wore feathers, bells, and turquoise and took on aspects of a god. He sent messages back to de Niza indicating that he had come to wealthy towns. Esteban enjoyed his role until he came to the Zuni Pueblo of Hawikuh. The Zuni told Esteban to leave. When he threatened them, they killed him. De Niza came far enough north to see Hawikuh from a distance, but he did not want to risk Esteban's fate. He returned to Mexico City and reported to the viceroy that the city "is better seated than any I have seen in these parts," and he said "I was told that there is much gold there, and the natives make it into vessels and jewels for their ears, and into little blades with which they wipe away their sweat." De Niza was careful not to claim more than he had seen. He had *seen* irrigated fields, buffalo hides, and—from a distance—populous towns, and he had only *heard* reports of gold and great wealth. Nevertheless, such a report was enough to launch further expeditions. De Niza had also heard a name for the region—Cibola. From then on, the search for the **Seven Cities of Cibola** became the stuff of legend.

Seven Cities of Cibola
The name given by early Spanish explorers to a number of Native American pueblos.

In 1540, Francisco Vázquez de Coronado led a large expedition across what is now the U.S.-Mexican border into modern Arizona. At the Zuni pueblo of Hawikuh, in the confederation of Cibola, they had their first battle with the American Indians of the Southwest. The Zunis did not take kindly to the demand that they submit to previously unheard of Spanish authority. Coronado's men had gone without adequate food for quite some time by this point, and they attacked the village, primarily to gain access to food. The Coronado expedition then turned east to central New Mexico. Although the Spanish found many communities along the Rio Grande, the Pueblo Indians of the area were no more enthusiastic about submitting to Spanish power or supplying the Spanish with food and provisions than the Zuni had been. The Pueblos quickly found that, rather than fight, the best solution seemed to be to keep the Spanish moving by assuring them that the real wealth was just over the horizon.

In 1541, the expedition set off into what are now northern Texas, Oklahoma, and Kansas. The Spaniards met Teya Indians, seminomadic peoples who had found ways to live well in a harsh countryside far better than the Spaniards could. Coronado and his men did not, however, find gold or European-style cities. Finally, discouraged and with their supplies gone, they returned to Mexico City in 1542 with little to show for their efforts. It was decades before Spanish authorities would try again to settle in Arizona or New Mexico.

Exploring the Mississippi River Valley: The De Soto Expedition, 1539–1542

While Coronado was roaming the Southwest, another Spanish adventurer, Hernando de Soto, was exploring even more of the future United States. De Soto had won fame and gold through military exploits in Panama in the 1520s, and had been a part of Pizarro's conquest of the Inca Empire in the 1530s. He was then given a royal charter to settle La Florida and the lands beyond. He would try again where Ponce de León and De Narváez had failed. In 1539, he sailed to Florida with some 500 to 600 Spaniards and about 100 captive American Indians and Africans. The expedition also brought blacksmiths to make chains for the new slaves they expected to capture.

In northern Florida, near modern-day Tampa, they saw fields of corn and large towns led by powerful rulers. In 1540, the expedition moved into Georgia and the Carolinas. In a place they called Cofitachiqui, probably a Creek Indian village, the ruler, a young woman, greeted De Soto and "presented unto him great store of clothes of the country… and took from her own neck a great cordon of pearls, and cast it about the neck of the governor, entertaining him with very gracious speeches of love and courtesy." De Soto responded by taking the princess prisoner and demanding that she guide his expedition over the Appalachian mountains to the gold he sought. She did lead them over the mountains, but then escaped, taking the pearls that she had given De Soto home with her. Other Indians who happened to be in De Soto's path would not be so fortunate.

As the expedition crossed the Appalachian Mountains into Tennessee, and on into Alabama and Mississippi, they were met by Native Americans bringing gifts; the Spaniards quickly tried to make the natives into guides and slaves. But as word of the Spaniards spread, they found fewer gifts and more hostility. De Soto reported well-populated lands. Later European explorers, however, found far fewer Indians, most likely because of diseases unintentionally brought by De Soto's expedition.

In 1541, De Soto crossed the Mississippi River and explored what is now Arkansas and probably modern-day Texas. When they turned back to the Mississippi River, De Soto demanded that a nearby Native American town provide supplies and porters to help with the river crossing. When the village chief refused, De Soto ordered his soldiers to destroy the town; his journal reports that "the cries of the women and children were such as to deafen those who pursued them."

Jacques Le Moyne, an early French colonist in Florida, drew this picture of an Indian queen being carried by high-ranking men. While the picture is from the later 1500s in Florida, the princess that the de Soto expedition met a few years earlier may well have been treated with similar respect.

De Soto himself died of fever on June 20, 1542. His fellow explorers sunk his body in the Mississippi River so the now-hostile Indians would not know their leader was gone. Then they built rafts and drifted down the river. After considerable hardship, 311 survivors—about half the original group—reached Mexico. They had not found much in North America that interested them.

Exploring California: The Cabrillo Voyage, 1542–1543

While Coronado was exploring New Mexico and De Soto the Mississippi Valley, the Spanish authorities commissioned Juan Rodriguez Cabrillo to investigate the Pacific Coast. Cabrillo had come to New Spain as a young man and amassed a fortune, which he was prepared to use to outfit his own expedition in hopes of great returns. In 1542, Cabrillo sailed north from Mexico along the Pacific Coast with three ships "to discover the coast of New Spain" and continue until he reached China, which was assumed to be not far distant. Cabrillo's three ships left Navidad, Mexico, in June 1542, and by September had reached San Diego Bay in California. They exchanged gifts with friendly American Indians and reported seeing a beautiful land of valleys, savannas, high mountains, and smoke that indicated a large native population. Cabrillo called California a "good country where you can make a settlement."

He continued north along the Pacific Coast as far as the Russian River in northern California. Like many after him, Cabrillo overlooked the area of what is now San Francisco because of the heavy fog. He did, however, realize that in Monterey Bay— the future capital of Spanish and Mexican California—there was a fine harbor. After Cabrillo died of an injury while trying to rescue some of his men from an attack, the expedition returned to Mexico. They had found neither China nor the gold they sought.

Early Settlements in Florida: Fort Caroline and St. Augustine, 1562–1565

After all these failed efforts, Spanish interest in the lands north of Mexico waned. The first actual European settlements in North America reflected the growing divisions in Europe itself. Catholic Spain now had to compete with France—a nation divided between Catholicism and Protestantism—and with Protestant England and Holland. Only when these other European powers showed an interest in North America did Spain set up permanent settlements there.

No nation was more deeply split by the Protestant-Catholic divide than France, which had a large Protestant minority and a strong Catholic majority. It was from the French Protestants that the first settlers in Florida were recruited. In 1562, Gaspard de Coligny, a French Protestant nobleman and admiral, commissioned expeditions to Florida. Although there was no European settlement in Florida, it seemed to be a strategic location on the sea lanes between Spain's empire in Mexico and South America and Spain itself. As a loyal subject of the French king, Coligny wanted to secure lands for France. He also wanted to create a safe haven for his fellow Protestants. In 1562, Coligny commissioned Jean Ribault to make an initial trip to Florida, and then commissioned a larger French expedition, including many families with their livestock, supplies, and tools, which sailed in 1564. The settlers moved to the mouth of the St. Johns River where Jacksonville, Florida, is today and built a town they named Fort Caroline after King Charles IX of France. They meant to stay and build their lives there. It would be a useful outpost for France, yet far enough away to avoid the political and religious turmoil of their homeland.

The Spanish, however, considered this colony a major religious, political, and commercial threat to Spain's control of the Americas. Pedro Menéndez de Avilés was given jurisdiction of a new Spanish colony to reach from Florida to Newfoundland and told to establish cities in Florida and oust the French Protestants. He did both.

In 1565, Menéndez de Avilés founded St. Augustine, today the oldest city of European origin in the United States. All the lands north and west of it, he declared, now belonged to the king of Spain. He began a friendly trade with the Timuca Indians

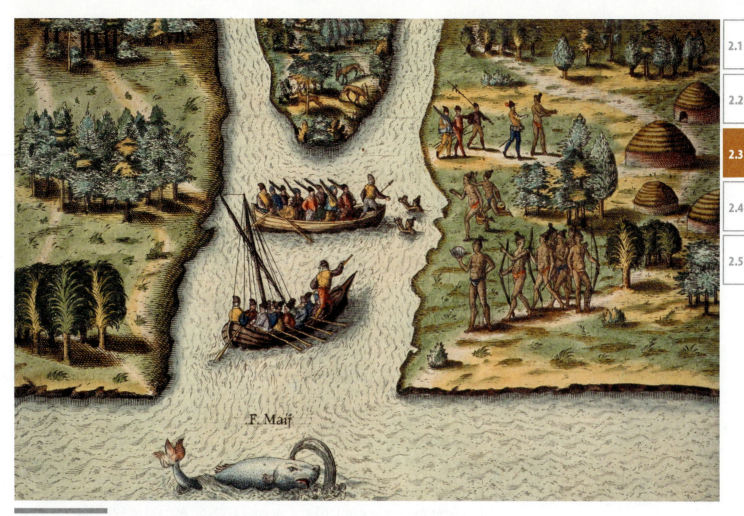

This illustration by Jacques Le Moyne shows the French, led by Jean Ribault, landing at the St. Johns River in Florida in May 1562 and being greeted by friendly Timuca Indians.

who lived in northern Florida and sought to convert them to Catholicism. The Timucas valued Spanish goods and provided the colony with food, root vegetables, wild fruit, fish, oysters, game, and corn, but they resisted religious conversion. Having established St. Augustine, De Avilés attacked Fort Caroline, killing all its inhabitants. When the French fleet coming to aid Fort Caroline was shipwrecked along the coast by a hurricane, De Avilés killed the survivors, too. Florida would remain in Spanish hands for centuries, and its bloody European beginnings mirrored Europe's divisions.

The founders of Spain's first colonies in North America, like those who settled in Latin America, reflected the spirit of the *Reconquista*, or "reconquest," of Spain itself when both Muslims and Jews were driven out of the country and religious and national unity were seen as one and the same. For hundreds of years, soldiers of Christian Spain fought against Muslims, whom they considered infidels, seeking to win military glory, wealth, and spiritual honor on the battlefield. It was a worldview in which religious fervor and military bravery were united in the service of the nation. After the victory over the last Muslim stronghold in Spain in 1492, the next generation of Spanish men could not hope for the success of their fathers, grandfathers, and great-grandfathers in Spain itself, but they brought the same mixture of military heroics and religious fervor to the Americas. In the 1500s, a way of looking at the world and especially at conquest that had been reshaping Spain itself for hundreds of years became the key to creating an ever-expanding empire in the Americas.

Cultural practices in Spain and other parts of Europe at the time may have also played a role in how ruthless the early Europeans were. Under a system of primogeniture, land was typically passed on to the oldest son. Younger sons, then, would not have the same opportunities to acquire land and the wealth that went with it. Some would opt to spend their lives in the church, but many would opt to spend their lives as soldiers where, through conquest of new lands, they might be rewarded.

Unlike Mexico and Peru, the Spanish colonies in Florida were settled by soldiers who did not want to create a vast empire but valued the independence that distance from imperial authorities gave them and by families of artisans and farmers who meant to build a richer life than they could have in Spain. As citizens on the border between European settlement and American Indian territory, these settlers wanted to enjoy the municipal liberties that the free cities of Castile had enjoyed when they had represented the border between Christian and Muslim Spain. They also wanted to avoid the tightly ordered hierarchical society that was evolving in Mexico. The cities and the farms in Florida prospered. One settler recorded, "I have planted with my own hands grapevines, pomegranates, orange trees and figs, wheat, barley, onions, garlic and many vegetables that grow in Spain." The colonists quickly took to the corn that was the staple of the Indian diet.

There were also slaves in St. Augustine from the beginning. Although his royal commission had authorized him to bring up to 500 African slaves to St. Augustine, De Avilés actually brought only about 50. In time, Spanish Florida had a black militia and included both African slaves and free Africans.

There was also intermarriage and more casual sexual encounters among Europeans, Native Americans, and Africans in Spanish Florida. In this outpost, the races blended, creating a new culture and new bloodlines. In addition, St. Augustine became a place where Europeans from other nations settled. Some settled of necessity after their ships were wrecked on the Florida coast. Others came to escape legal problems, military commitments, or families. Despite strict rules issued in Madrid, isolated places like St. Augustine reflected considerable diversity, including Jews escaping an increasingly intolerant Europe as well as French, Flemish, and German immigrants escaping religious persecution or simply wanting a new start in life.

After its founding in 1565 and up until 1705, St. Augustine was home to a large-scale effort to send Franciscan missionaries into the surrounding Native American territories. The Franciscans who traveled into the interior of Florida and Georgia to make converts also sought alliances with the Indians. Tribal leaders came to St. Augustine to trade and negotiate, and they accepted, however casually, Spanish rule. Eventually, about 80 mission centers were established from the Savannah River in Georgia to as far south as modern Daytona Beach. The Franciscans, however, also brought European diseases along with their preaching, and the American Indian population fell drastically. Nevertheless, for a century, Native Americans, missionaries, and soldiers traded religious and cultural ideas as well as the tools of commerce and war. They intermarried and substantially influenced each other and their offspring in Florida.

Despite occasional battles with the American Indians, raids by European navies, and hurricanes, life in Spanish Florida continued more or less uninterrupted well into the 1700s. While the English focused their efforts further north and the Spanish Empire centered on Mexico, Central, and South America, those who were in Florida were left alone. Except for a brief period of British rule between 1763 and 1784, Florida remained a Spanish colony until it was ceded to the United States in 1821, 256 years after the founding of St. Augustine.

Settling New Mexico: 1598

After Coronado's expedition to explore the North American Southwest returned to Mexico City in 1542, there was little further exploration of New Mexico for over half a century. Then in 1598, the Spanish viceroy in Mexico City decided it was time for another look at the lands of the north and appointed a new governor for what was called "New Mexico." The rumors that great wealth existed there had never died. More pragmatically, the Spanish were worried about the Protestant English. In 1579, Francis

Drake, an English privateer (a pirate working for the government), sailed up the coast of California, duplicating Cabrillo's route (and his failure to find San Francisco). Drake then turned west and duplicated the route of an earlier Spanish explorer, Ferdinand Magellan, sailing across the Pacific and on around the world before returning to London in 1580. To the authorities in Spain, this achievement was a real threat. Settling the interior of North America suddenly seemed imperative.

Don Juan de Oñate was appointed governor of New Mexico with instructions not to follow the harsh policies of Cortés or Pizarro. The King's appointment letter said, "You will endeavor to attract the natives with peace, friendship, and good treatment… and to induce them to hear and accept the holy gospel." A succession of Spanish monarchs never approved of the viciousness of the conquistadors, though they accepted the gold and silver that flowed back to Spain without asking too many questions about how it was acquired.

Oñate's expedition included 400 men, women, and children, among them a few Spanish soldiers, Franciscan friars, and Indians, along with supply wagons, cattle, sheep, and mules. Oñate's wife, Isabel Tolosa Cortés Montezuma, was herself a granddaughter of Cortés and a great-granddaughter of the Aztec emperor Montezuma. On April 30, 1598, the expedition stopped on the banks of the Rio Grande and claimed all of the lands and peoples to the north for Spain. Oñate named the place where he crossed the river El Paso del Norte the "pass to the north." Since Coronado's day, the Pueblo Indians had seen Spanish soldiers and missionaries come and go. The Spanish could be ruthless, but they also seemed to have little staying power. With the Oñate expedition, Spanish occupation of New Mexico would come closer to being permanent.

Oñate sought political allegiance from the Pueblos of southern New Mexico. In July 1598, he asked Pueblo chiefs to swear allegiance to Spain and convert to Christianity. Oñate chose to interpret their lack of hostility as agreement. He also built a capital, which he named San Gabriel. Something resembling a permanent settlement of 400 Europeans in the middle of thousands of Pueblo Indians took shape.

At first all was peaceful. Oñate divided New Mexico into administrative districts, each with a priest in each to try to convert the American Indians to Christianity. He allowed self-government to continue in each pueblo—he had little choice—but insisted that each one must have a political governor. He was more interested in exploring for the gold, silver, or pearls, which he was sure were just over the horizon, and did not try to force the Native Americans to labor for the Spanish.

The peace did not last, however. Zutucapan, the leader of the Acoma Pueblo, had avoided meeting Oñate because he did not want to cede any authority to the Spaniards. Late in 1598, he attacked a Spanish scouting party, and in 1599, Oñate struck back. After a fierce battle, the Spaniards, whose guns, swords, and horses gave them a huge advantage, burned Acoma to the ground. One thousand of its residents were killed, and the remaining 500 were taken as slaves. The male captives had one foot cut off. When the Jumano Indians also resisted Oñate, he hanged their chiefs and burned their village.

Oñate's cruelty and his failure to find riches led to his recall in 1609. The new royal governor Don Pedro de Peralta moved the capital further north to a new town that he created and named Santa Fe, in1610. There Peralta built the oldest public building still standing in the United States—the governor's mansion. The colony's attention turned from gold to farming. Churches were built at the center of each pueblo. The Spanish hoped these churches would become new centers of Indian life and faith, but tensions would continue that would eventually culminate some 50 years later in a surprising revolt.

2.3 | **Quick Review** How did Spanish exploration in North America change over time? What was different between the exploration that took place between 1513 and 1543 and the latter developments between 1565 and 1598? Identify and explain factors that most contributed to this evolution.

EXPLORATION AND ENCOUNTER IN NORTH AMERICA: THE FRENCH

2.4 Analyze early French exploration and claims in North America.

King Francis I of France (r. 1515–1547) did not want to leave the Americas to Spain or Portugal (which was quickly developing its own empire in Brazil). In 1524, some 30 years after Columbus made his journey, the French king commissioned an Italian sailor, Giovanni da Verrazano, to explore the Atlantic coast and find a sea route to Asia for France. Verrazano sailed from Florida to Newfoundland but concluded that an entire continent divided the Atlantic from the Pacific. After Verrazano, French interest in North America focused further north, on the St. Lawrence River Valley and what became Canada, especially after Jacques Cartier's visit of 1534 to that region, and after the destruction of Fort Caroline in 1565, as well as on islands in the Caribbean. Eventually, while the Spanish explored the Mississippi River Valley north from the Gulf of Mexico, the French would explore the same river coming south from their settlements near the Mississippi's headwaters and tributaries in what is today the Midwest.

First French Visit to the Atlantic Coast of the United States— Verrazano, 1524

Verrazano's ship *La Dauphine* left France in January 1524 and landed on what is now Cape Fear, North Carolina, 2 months later. He described the people he met there as, "of color russet, and not much unlike the Saracens; their hair black, thick, and not very long." He wondered if they might be Chinese.

On April 17, 1524, Verrazano became the first European to sail into New York Harbor, describing how the inhabitants of Manhattan "came towards us very cheerfully, making shouts of admiration, showing us where we might come to land most safely with our boat." He continued north, visiting Rhode Island's Narragansett Bay, Maine, and Newfoundland, and he mapped much of the Atlantic Coast of the future United States and Canada before returning to France.

Jacques Cartier Seeks a Sea Route to Asia, 1534

In 1534, France tried again to find a northern sea route to Asia. Jacques Cartier was authorized to make the effort for France. Cartier did not find the route—which did not exist except through then-frozen Arctic ice—but he explored Newfoundland and the gulf of the St. Lawrence River, laying the basis for future French claims to these lands. He also began a trade in furs that would have great significance for French and English relations with American Indians.

On a second voyage in 1535–1536, Cartier explored the St. Lawrence River far upstream (see Map 2-2), coming to the sites of Quebec and Montreal. More than a thousand friendly Indians came to the river to greet him. He traded European goods, including knives, for food, beginning a trading relationship that would transform the lives of native tribes and Europeans. But Cartier stayed too long, and when the winter closed in, he could not return to France because the river froze over. Cartier spent a terrible winter on the St. Lawrence, buried in deep snow and losing a quarter of his crew to disease and cold. Although Cartier's travels would be the basis for future French land claims, it would be another half-century before the French developed a serious interest in North America, after they discovered that there was no quick way around it to the Asian lands they really wanted to find.

2.4 **Quick Review** How did early French exploration differ from the Spanish? How was it similar?

EXPLORATION AND ENCOUNTER IN NORTH AMERICA: THE ENGLISH

2.5 Explain English explorers, privateers, and reasons for settlement.

Although Spanish conquistadors were the leading explorers of the Americas, an English-led expedition was among the first to follow Columbus. King Henry VII of England commissioned another Italian, Giovanni Caboto, or John Cabot, to sail across the Atlantic in 1497. Cabot made landfall in North America, most likely in Newfoundland, and may have traveled as far south as Maine. He did not meet any people, but erected a cross and banner to claim the lands for England. When he returned to London, he was given a rich reward.

In 1498, Cabot set out on a second voyage, but he and his companions disappeared—most likely their ships were sunk in a storm—and there is no clear evidence of further English discoveries or claims in the Americas until more than 50 years later when a very different England found new reasons to look more carefully across the Atlantic.

England's Reformation Shapes the Country

In the early years of the Protestant Reformation, few would have predicted that England would break with the Roman Catholic Church. When he became king in 1509, Henry VIII was a good Catholic. He even wrote a defense of traditional Catholic doctrine that led the pope to give him the title "Defender of the Faith." He had married Catherine of Aragon, daughter of the devoutly Catholic Ferdinand and Isabella of Spain. His closest advisor was Catholic Cardinal Thomas Wolsey. But Henry's marriage problems would eventually reshape the country and help it gain a powerful role in the Atlantic World.

By the late 1520s, Henry wanted to end his marriage with Catherine. Five of their six children had died. Only a daughter named Mary survived, and Henry wanted a male heir. He had also fallen in love with Anne Boleyn, a young woman at the court. Under pressure from the king, the English clergy had agreed to dissolve the marriage. But Pope Clement VII needed political support from Catherine's nephew, Charles V, King of Spain and Holy Roman Emperor, who opposed the divorce. The pope stalled and refused to approve the divorce.

A century, even a decade, earlier Henry would have had little room to maneuver. Now the Protestant Reformation gave him an opening. In 1534, Parliament passed legislation ending papal authority in England and declared Henry and his successors to be "the only Supreme Head in earth of the Church of England." Henry annulled his marriage to Catherine, married Anne, and celebrated the birth of a new daughter, Elizabeth, though he still longed for a son. He closed monasteries and sold off church land or used it to reward loyal followers. Henry did not embrace many Protestant teachings. Other than substituting his own authority for that of the pope, official Christianity in England remained closer to Catholicism than to the Protestantism of Luther or Calvin, a fact that would become especially significant in the next century.

When Henry died in 1547, England had three major religious groups. Some, known as **Anglicans**, were perhaps a majority and supported Henry's arrangement, including independence from the pope and preserving traditional Catholic religious forms. However, a growing Protestant minority, known as **Puritans**, wanted more radical religious change to "purify" the Church of England of Catholic practices, especially the leadership of bishops. In addition, many Roman Catholics could not agree to the break with Rome and remained loyal to the Catholic Church.

Henry's successor was his 9-year-old son Edward VI (r. 1547–1553) from the king's marriage to his third wife, Jane Seymour, after he tired of Anne and had her executed. In the end, Henry had six wives but only three children. The boy-king's regents sought to make the English church more Protestant in its doctrines and rituals. But when Edward died at age 15, his half-sister Mary I became queen and returned England—briefly—to Catholicism. However, Mary also died after a reign of only 5 years. In 1558, Elizabeth I (r. 1558–1603), daughter of Henry VIII and Anne Boleyn, succeeded her.

Anglicans
Within the Church of England, one group of Protestants who wanted to establish a church that was led by the English monarchy.

Puritans
Individuals who believed that reforms of the Church of England had not gone far enough in improving the church.

Queen Elizabeth ruled England from 1558 to 1603 during which time the country prospered internally and emerged as a major sea power in the world.

Elizabeth's reasons for embracing Protestantism were strong. If England were Catholic, then Henry's marriage to her mother would be illegal, and Elizabeth would be an illegitimate child and unable to assume the throne. If England were Protestant, she had every right to be queen of England. And Elizabeth meant to be queen. She did not want her subjects fighting with each other, however. In the Act of Uniformity of 1559, Parliament declared that she was "Supreme Governor" of the Church of England. Worship should follow the *Book of Common Prayer*, which preserved many Catholic rituals within a Protestant theology. Every person in England was required to attend church once a week or face a fine. Catholics who refused to break with Rome were persecuted. But as long as Protestants agreed to the Act of Uniformity and to attend church services that followed the *Book of Common Prayer*, Elizabeth's government left them free to disagree about their beliefs to their heart's content.

During Elizabeth's long reign, England became a major power in Europe and the world. Spain, under King Philip II, grandson of Ferdinand and Isabella, was at the center of a Catholic revival, and Philip's Spain and Elizabeth's England became bitter rivals. Queen Elizabeth subsidized Protestant rebels against Spain's rule of the Netherlands and even engaged in a correspondence with Ottoman Sultan Murad III about a possible joint Protestant-Muslim attack on Catholic Spain. King Philip, in return, plotted Elizabeth's overthrow and made plans to invade England to secure Spain's power and protect Catholic unity.

When Spain attacked England in July 1588, Spain's navy, known as the Spanish Armada, was defeated by the English navy and destroyed by storms. After 1588, England's navy dominated the Atlantic and eventually all of the world's oceans. English sailors grew more skilled, the country's shipbuilders became more sophisticated in their designs, and its navigators gained new understanding of winds and currents as well as their charts and instruments. For Elizabeth and many of her subjects, the defeat of the threatened Spanish Catholic invasion linked the Protestant religion and English patriotism indissolubly in their minds. A small nation, on the margins of Europe, was suddenly a major player in an emerging Atlantic world.

Elizabethan Explorers and Pirates

While Elizabeth I ruled England, English adventurers, with her support, set out to make a place for themselves in the new oceanic world. English and other European fishermen had fished off the North Atlantic coast of North America since the early 1500s. By the 1580s, however, warfare and piracy became the dominant role of the English who visited the Americas. Building settlements at that time was not a priority. If powerful Catholic Spain was exploiting the continents for gold and silver, England saw no reason not to relieve the Spanish ships of some of their treasure without going to the trouble of mining it themselves.

Francis Drake was perhaps the most famous pirate—or *privateer* as they were known when their exploits were commissioned by the government. Drake was licensed for piracy by Queen Elizabeth. Licensing individual captains to harass the Spanish treasure fleets was far cheaper than supporting a large royal navy, and the English government, at minimal risk, kept a fifth of whatever the pirates brought to England. Indeed, pirates may have supplied 10 percent of English imports in the 1590s. The decades of legalized piracy also helped expand the technical knowledge of English mariners. The role of this piracy was instrumental in laying a foundation for England's sea power.

✳ Explore Global Exploration on MyHistoryLab

HOW DID GLOBAL EXPLORATION CHANGE THE OLD AND NEW WORLD?

Beginning in the 1400s, explorers left Europe and headed west in search of faster trade routes to Asia to keep up with the growing European demand for luxury goods such as silk and spices. In the process, they encountered huge civilizations in the Americas: complex societies that often had high levels of economic and social interconnectedness. Over the next 2 centuries, Europeans attempted to conquer these Native American societies by force, set up colonies, and establish trade ties, connecting the Old World (Europe, Asia, and Africa) with the New World (the Americas). This Age of Global Exploration had a profound impact on world history and was especially destructive to societies in the Americas as vast numbers of people in New World succumbed to Old World diseases.

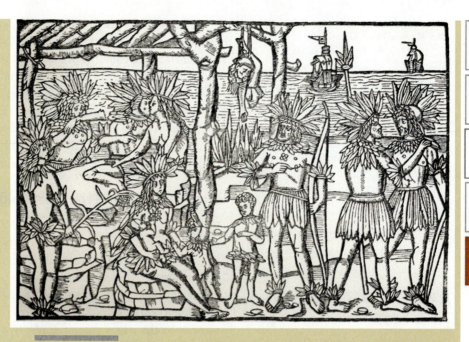

This illustration (c. 1500) of Italian origin is said to show the first European representation of people in the New World. Sadly it does not reflect much respect for the people who had so recently come to the attention of Europe.

POPULATIONS OF PRECONTACT NATIVE AMERICAN AND COLONIAL POWERS (C. 1500)

The Americas	Colonial Powers*

The Americas (60–70 million)	Colonial Powers (29.7 million)

Note: Each figure represents a million people.
*Colonial Powers: England, Spain, Portugal, France.

KEY QUESTIONS   Use **MyHistoryLab** *Explorer* to **answer** these **questions:**

Analysis ▶▶▶ *What global trade routes existed in the Old World prior to the Age of Global Exploration?*

Map the late medieval trade contacts between Europe, Asia, and North Africa.

Comparison ▶▶▶ *In what ways were societies in the Americas interrelated before the arrival of the Europeans?*

Map the economic interconnectedness of the New World.

Consequence ▶▶▶ *How did the new trans-Atlantic trade connect different parts of the world?*

Map the integration of the Old and New Worlds into a single trading network.

Francis Drake was an explorer as well as a privateer. During his voyage around the globe from 1577 to 1580—the first commander of such an expedition to survive—he confirmed the contours of the Americas for the English. He then continued across the Pacific and around Africa before returning to London. In 1585, he attacked and burned St. Augustine, Florida. In 1588, he helped defeat the Spanish Armada. His exploits brought considerable wealth to Queen Elizabeth's England while weakening Spanish control of the seas. By the time Drake died in1596, while again harassing the Spanish in Central America, English sailors were confident that they could travel anywhere without trouble, even if Spain still controlled the most valuable land in the Americas.

Walter Raleigh and the "Lost Colony" of Roanoke

In 1584, an ambitious young man, Walter Raleigh, was authorized by England to use his own funds to occupy lands in North America. Raleigh's role was to fund and authorize the missions. At the time, England and Raleigh himself were most interested in establishing a base from which privateers like Drake could easily operate and profit financially from these missions. The first mission in 1584 was a reconnaissance trip to identify potential sites. The small group discovered Roanoke Island and was received warmly by the Algonquian people, two of whom (Manteo and Wanchese) returned to England with the crew. In 1585, Raleigh sent 100 young men back to Roanoke on the Outer Banks of North Carolina along with the two Algonquian emissaries. It was the first English colony in what is now the United States. It was also short lived. When the men landed, one of their ships ran aground, and most of the food they had brought was ruined. The Roanoke Indians were not happy to feed the colonists whom they began to suspect of trying to dominate them, and a battle broke out in 1586 in which the Roanoke chief, Wingina, was killed. When Francis Drake arrived later that spring to rest his crews and refit his ships, he found the survivors in disarray. Instead of refitting, he agreed to take the survivors back to England when they decided to abandon the colony.

Raleigh was not discouraged, however. If a colony of men could not succeed, then perhaps one composed of families could. In 1587, he convinced English investors to create a new colony in a location on the Chesapeake Bay, which would have more navigable waters than the shallows around Roanoke. Colonists were promised 500 acres per family, a huge estate for the times, though one might question England's authority to give away land claimed by the Algonquians. Some 100 people left England to create this new colony, but events along the way landed them instead back at Roanoke, amid the Algonquians who had fought their predecessors. Nevertheless the colony was established, houses built, and the settlers began their new lives in this isolated place. Virginia Dare was born and baptized in this colony soon after the families arrived. She was the first English child known to be born in what is now the United States.

But the 1587, Roanoke colony also failed. Indeed, it came to be known as the "Lost Colony." The settlers had been left in what seemed like reasonably good shape with a promise that resupply ships would arrive the following spring. However, no ships were allowed to leave England in 1588 because of the threatened Spanish attack. The government commandeered every ship to oppose the mighty Spanish Armada. Nor did weather help the colony. Between 1587 and 1589, the worst drought in the area in 800 years struck. If the experience of later colonies is any guide, drought increased tensions with nearby American Indians who became much more reluctant to provide food when they faced their own shortages. When John White finally returned to Roanoke with the promised supplies in 1590,

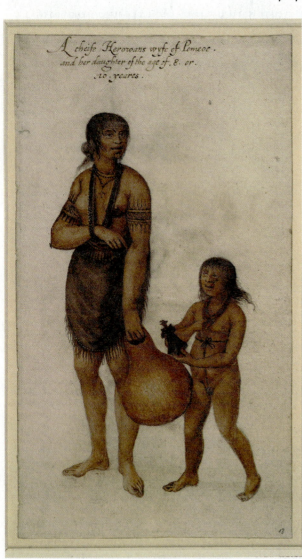

John White, himself an early English settler, drew this picture of a "woman and child of Pomelooc" in an effort to describe the Algonquians with whom the first English explorers came into contact.

he found the colony abandoned. Whether the colonists were massacred or simply melted into the surrounding Indian tribes is unknown.

> **2.5** **Quick Review** How did Francis Drake contribute to English wealth and power without establishing any colonies? Why were the English slower to establish colonies in the Americas than the Spanish or the French?

CONCLUSION

Through most of the 1500s, Cabrillo's, De Soto's, and Coronado's expeditions for Spain; Verrazano's and Cartier's voyages for France; and Raleigh's colonizing efforts for England were considered total failures. Fortunes had been spent, but few permanent settlements had been made. The explorers had found no gold and no quick route to China in the lands north of Mexico. Nevertheless, Spain, France, and England now had a much clearer picture of the geography of North America. Many of the native peoples of North America also had at least a vague knowledge of the militaristic Europeans whose presence would change everything for future generations. Half a century after Columbus had first landed, the Atlantic and Pacific coasts and most of the southern half of the United States had been the scene of many contacts between American Indians, Europeans, and often Africans. Even more than 100 years after Columbus, settlement was limited to a few Spanish posts in Florida and New Mexico. For the American Indians, Europeans were people who came quickly and left almost as quickly. While disease decimated some tribes, for most of the surviving native peoples of North America, daily life in the early 1550s, even in 1600, was barely different from what it had been a century before. They might have a few new trade goods or may have engaged in an occasional skirmish with Europeans, but that was about it. That situation would change quickly after 1600, however, as three great European powers, Spain, France, and England—and smaller ones including the Netherlands and Sweden— would establish permanent settlements and vie for control of North America.

> **CHAPTER REVIEW** How did European politics, economics, and religious issues lead to exploration and settlement in America? Of these three, which is the single most important category? Why?

COLUMBUS, THE COLUMBIAN EXCHANGE, AND EARLY CONQUESTS

2.1 Explain the reasons behind the voyages of Columbus, and describe early Spanish encounters with the peoples of the Caribbean, Mexico, and South America.

Review Questions

1. Contextualization

What do Columbus's words and actions on arriving in the New World tell us about his motives for making his voyages?

2. Crafting an Argument

Why did native populations decline so rapidly after 1492? Which cause for this was most important? Why?

3. Historical Interpretation

Who were the winners and losers in the shift toward an ocean-focused global trade system?

A DIVIDED EUROPE: THE IMPACT OF THE PROTESTANT REFORMATION

2.2 Explain how the Protestant Reformation and the development of the nation-state changed Europe and European ideas about how best to settle and govern America.

Review Question

4. Historical Interpretation

How did political and religious developments in 16th-century Europe shape the course of European settlement in the Americas?

EXPLORATION AND ENCOUNTER IN NORTH AMERICA: THE SPANISH

2.3 Analyze early Spanish exploration of America north of Mexico.

Review Questions

5. Contextualization

Why did the French try to colonize Florida? Why did the Spanish respond to these efforts as they did?

6. Historical Interpretation

How do you account for the failure to follow up on the De Soto, Coronado, and Cabrillo expeditions? Why did Spanish authorities remain uninterested in the future United States for so long?

7. Contextualization

How did the Pueblos respond to early Spanish efforts to find gold in their territory? What does their response tell us about their strategies for dealing with these newcomers?

EXPLORATION AND ENCOUNTER IN NORTH AMERICA: THE FRENCH

2.4 Analyze early French exploration and claims in North America.

Review Question

8. Comparison

Compare French lack of interest in a permanent settlement in the northern parts of the future United States and Canada in the 1500s with French and Spanish interest in settlement in Florida. How do you account for the differences?

EXPLORATION AND ENCOUNTER IN NORTH AMERICA: THE ENGLISH

2.5 Explain English explorers, privateers, and reasons for settlement.

Review Questions

9. Chronological Reasoning

How did events in the decades before Elizabeth I came to the throne shape her religious policies?

10. Contextualization

Why did contemporaries see most of the European expeditions in North America during the 1500s as failures?

Settlements Old and New

1607–1754

3 Settlements, Alliances, and Resistance

Trade in goods for furs from Native Americans and in colonial products, especially barrels of tobacco to Europe, was key to the success of European colonies in the 1600s, as illustrated by this encounter between an American Indian trapper and a French trader.

CHAPTER OBJECTIVE

Demonstrate an understanding of the motivations for and results of the European settlements in North America.

LEARNING OBJECTIVES

THE ENGLISH SETTLE IN NORTH AMERICA

3.1 Explain why the English began to settle in North America and how slavery was introduced in the English colonies.

ENGLAND'S WARS, ENGLAND'S COLONIES

3.2 Analyze the relationship between politics in England, internal colonial tensions, and life in the English colonies in North America during the 1600s.

FRANCE TAKES CONTROL OF THE HEART OF A CONTINENT

3.3 Explain France's growing role and power in North America and its impact on English and Spanish colonies.

DEVELOPMENTS IN SPANISH COLONIES NORTH OF MEXICO

3.4 Analyze the impact of Indian uprisings and the expansion of other European powers on Spain's colonies in New Mexico, Texas, and California.

For well over 100 years after Columbus, Europeans spent more time trying to get around or through North America to reach Asia than they spent paying attention to the lands that would become the United States or Canada. Spain's vast American empire was based in Mexico and Peru. The Spanish found Mexico, Central and South America, and the Caribbean more rewarding than they did North America, which lacked gold or silver and which they considered barren and icy.

For decades, most European contact with North America was limited to filling the enormous European demand for codfish. Fishermen from France, England, and the Basque regions of Spain spent summers off the coast of Canada and Maine. They set up temporary stations in Newfoundland, repaired their boats, and dried their fish. Few stayed the winter, and no permanent colonies were founded. The Native Americans found the fishermen intrusive. The fishermen resented that the Indians' plundered stores left behind over the winter. But most of the time, both sides simply avoided each other. Nevertheless, occasional contact was all it took to begin the spread of European diseases among the tribes of North America, well in advance of more sustained settlement.

By the late 1500s, however, some in England and France as well as Spain were developing new interests in North America. In 1585, Richard Hakluyt the elder wrote *Pamphlet for the Virginia Enterprise* in an effort to convince his countrymen that a settlement, or planting as he called it, was in their interests. He recognized that the native peoples might not welcome the English, but he said:

> We may, if we will proceed with extremity, conquer, fortify, and plant in soils most sweet, most pleasant, most strong, and most fertile, and in the end bring them all in subjection and to civility.

For Hakluyt, subjection and conversion of the Native Americans to Protestant Christianity meant a rich profit and a military base for England against Catholic Spain. Others agreed, including King James I, who succeeded Elizabeth I in 1603. With the settlement of Jamestown, Virginia, in 1607, the English came to America to stay. Only 1 year later, France established a permanent settlement at Quebec on the Saint Lawrence River. In 1610, Spanish authorities also moved to a new permanent capital for their vast New Mexico territory that they named Santa Fe. Spain may have been first, but England and France were not far behind in establishing North American colonies.

From the settlements of Jamestown and Quebec, England and France claimed huge tracts of lands that they would eventually come to dominate. The English expanded from tiny Jamestown to control most of the Atlantic coast north of Florida and west toward the Allegheny Mountains. From Quebec, the French built trade and military centers all along the Saint Lawrence River and down the Mississippi to New Orleans on the Gulf of Mexico, a vast region they called New France. After 1610, the Spanish expanded their settlements in New Mexico, though Florida was generally ignored.

In the 1500s, explorers had come and quickly departed from North America. In the 1600s, the Europeans began to stay. Initially some Indian tribes saw Europeans as welcome trading partners or military allies against other tribes. Especially in the later 1600s when settlements grew too quickly, disease spread too rapidly, or the Europeans became too demanding, Indian resistance stiffened. The story of the growth of European communities in North America and the responses by American Indian tribes—sometimes friendly trade and sometimes open warfare—is the heart of this chapter.

THE ENGLISH SETTLE IN NORTH AMERICA

3.1 Explain why the English began to settle in North America and how slavery was introduced in the English colonies.

When James I became king of England in 1603, he was anxious to make peace with Spain. He quickly ended the royal support for legalized piracy that Queen Elizabeth I had provided—though piracy itself flourished throughout the 1600s. But many in England wanted a larger role in the Americas. If they were not going to steal America's wealth from the Spanish on the seas, then they would need to find other ways to gain it. Investors seeking financial gain created the Virginia Company. They told those they sent to America "to try if they can find any mineral," and to seek "passage to the Other Sea," the longed-for shortcut to China. The investors also advised them to build settlements at some distance from the coast to avoid a Spanish attack and to gain as much knowledge and food from the Indians as possible "before that they perceive you mean to plant among them." Within about 30 years, England had settled or claimed large territories, and their claims continued to expand into the 1700s (see Map 3-1).

Colonizing Virginia: Jamestown

In 1607, 105 men from the Virginia Company arrived in North America. They named their new community Jamestown in honor of King James. The company appointed a council of six to govern the colony and left it to the council to elect its own president. But things in Jamestown did not go well.

Significant Dates	
1607	Jamestown, Virginia, founded by English
1608	Quebec founded by French
1610	Santa Fe founded as Spanish capital of New Mexico
1619	African slaves sold in Jamestown
1620	Plymouth, Massachusetts, founded by English Pilgrims
1624	Fort Orange (later Albany), New York, founded by the Dutch
1626	New Amsterdam (later New York City) founded by Dutch
1630	Boston, Massachusetts, founded by English Puritans
1634	Maryland founded by Lord Baltimore as a haven for English Catholics
1636	Rhode Island founded
1637	Pequot War in New England
1638	First African slaves brought to Boston, Massachusetts
1639	Fundamental Orders of Connecticut confirm government for Hartford-based colony (founded in 1637)
1642–1649	English Civil War
1649–1658	England governed as a Puritan Commonwealth
1660	Charles II begins to rule in England
1661	Maryland law defines slavery as lifelong and inheritable
1663	Carolina colony founded by England
1664	English capture New Netherlands colony, rename it New York
1675	King Philip's War in Massachusetts
1676	Bacon's Rebellion in Virginia
1680	Pueblo Indian Revolt in New Mexico
1681	Pennsylvania founded by William Penn as a haven for English Quakers
1682	LaSalle claims the Mississippi River Valley for France
1718	French establish New Orleans; Spanish found San Antonio, Texas

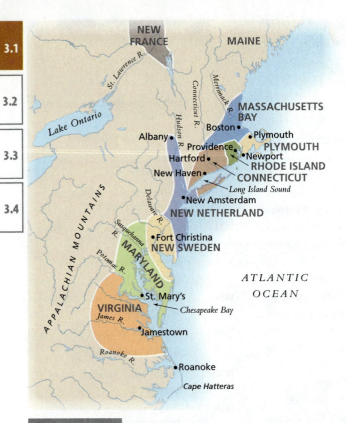

MAP 3-1 Spread of Settlement: Atlantic Coast European Colonies, 1607–1639. The earliest European colonies on the Atlantic coast north of Florida began as very small settlements close to the coast and then spread into the interior. New Sweden became the core of Delaware, while New Netherland, stretching along the Hudson River later became the core of both New York and New Jersey. Massachusetts Bay and Plymouth were separate colonies until merged with Massachusetts in 1686.

The unhealthy conditions at the site the colonists selected along the James River probably killed more of them than any other cause. Although they thought they had selected "a very fit place," they had in fact chosen land with a terrible water supply. The water from the James River was tidal. At high tide, it was salt water. At low tide, it was "full of slime and filth." The years 1607 and 1608 were drought years leading to a severe shortage of food. The winter of 1607–1608 was extremely cold. The Indians were suffering from the same drought and cold and were reluctant to trade food with the colonists. Waterborne disease and starvation weakened bodies, and few of the English escaped terrible bouts of sickness.

The members of the council constantly disagreed—they ended up executing one of the councilors as a Spanish spy—and the rest of the colonists fought each other bitterly. Although the colony's primary purpose was to enrich investors in London, those who were actually in Virginia found little reason to care whether the investors were enriched or not. England seemed far away. John Smith, the only member of the council not from the British nobility, complained, "Much they blamed us for not converting the Savages, when those [colonists] they sent us were little better if not worse." By 1608, only 38 of the 105 colonists were still alive.

The founders of Jamestown faced a different situation from what Columbus had encountered in 1492 when the Indians of Hispaniola gasped in awe at the ships, swords, and men with beards. By 1607, generations of Atlantic Coast Indians had substantial experience with Europeans. They had seen their ships, traded with them, and fought them. Some had even traveled to Europe and brought back reports of how these white adventurers lived. Europeans who were shipwrecked or from failed colonies—perhaps even from Roanoke—had melded into the Indian tribes and shared their knowledge with them. The Spanish at St. Augustine had tried to establish a northern outpost in the region. The Indians' opinion of Europeans was not favorable. For the Paspahegh tribe, on whose land Jamestown was built, the English were trespassing. And relationships between Jamestown and all of the local Indians, a confederation of Algonquian-speaking tribes of 13,000 to 15,000 people, were tense.

During its first weeks, the colony was attacked, and only after that did the settlers build a stockade. The English came to understand that the Paspahegh and some 30 other nearby tribes were under the rule of an overlord they called Powhatan whom the English described as functioning something like an emperor over the tribal chiefs. If the colonists wanted to make a lasting accommodation, it needed to be with him.

By his own account—his autobiography, *The True Travels, Adventures, and Observations of Captaine John Smith*, published in 1630—John Smith saved the colony. Smith was an experienced soldier who had fought in Austria against the Muslim Turks, had been captured and sold into slavery in Istanbul, escaped, and had made his way through Russia, Germany, and North Africa before coming home to England. He brought all of this experience to Virginia.

Early in his Virginia career, Smith had one of the most famous Indian encounters in American history. During the early months of the settlement, while Powhatan was trying to understand what these Englishmen wanted, Smith was exploring the countryside. He was taken prisoner by the Algonquians and brought before Powhatan. In Smith's telling, he was about to be executed—he was laid on the ground with his head on a rock, and men with clubs stood around him. Then Powhatan's daughter, Pocahontas, already known to Smith for her work as a negotiator with Jamestown, suddenly "got his head in her armes, and laid her owne upon his to save him from death." Powhatan granted Smith a reprieve. Most historians now believe that Powhatan scripted the whole event. After his rescue, Powhatan told Smith that "now they were friends" and gave him an Algonquian name. Far from being executed, Smith had been adopted. Perhaps Powhatan aimed to make Smith one of the many chiefs who reported to him.

Smith did not accept Powhatan's offer of a place within the Algonquian confederation though he did not formally reject it either. The English offered Powhatan an English crown that would symbolize his place in a world ruled by King James. Each side was jockeying for signs of submission from the other. In the early years, Powhatan could easily have destroyed Jamestown either by a direct attack or simply by withholding food. Instead, the Powhatan confederation fed the English and saw benefit in trading with them. The English brought valuable new goods. Powhatan meant to use the English to strengthen his position against other tribes. The English avoided war and starvation and survived only by making an alliance with Powhatan.

Smith's success in dealing with Powhatan was only part of his contribution to the colony. After he became governor in 1608, he instituted a policy that "he who does not work, does not eat." In a tiny colony, far from home, there could be no leisure class and no slackers. To survive, the colony needed the back-breaking labor of farming and stockade building. Smith set everyone to it. Jamestown would have gone the way of Roanoke or other failed ventures without his leadership.

But Smith returned to England in1609. As a result, he was not in Jamestown for the "starving time" of the winter of 1609–1610 when the colony was almost wiped out by starvation and disease. Realizing that the peaceful trade he hoped for was not materializing. Powhatan withdrew from contact with the Europeans. Consequently, the English could not rely on the Indians for food. The English attacked the Indians, burned their houses, plundered their sacred sites, and stole their valuables. But the English could not eat the valuables, and another party seeking food was found dead with their mouths stuffed with bread by the Indians.

Pocahontas gained fame first as the young woman who rescued Virginia's leader, John Smith, and later as the wife of tobacco planter, John Rolfe. She is shown here as she was seen in London, as Rebecca Rolfe, the first Native American to be seen by many in England.

In the spring of 1610, the surviving colonists decided to abandon Jamestown. They burned the town and sailed down the James River. However, before they reached the sea, they were met by an English fleet with 400 men led by the newly appointed governor, Lord de la Warr, and enough supplies to last a year. The colony was rebuilt where it had been.

While the colonists in Virginia had been starving, the Virginia Company in London had reorganized itself and sold stock to raise funds. It also enlisted clergy across England to preach on the importance of colonizing Virginia. The venture was no longer described as a way to acquire quick riches but as a kind of national mission. It was England's duty, the ministers said, to send missionaries and build a permanent Protestant base in the Americas that would convert Indians and serve England in future confrontations with Spain.

Jamestown survived. But for another decade, life remained precarious. Thousands of colonists arrived in Virginia, having fled England after being thrown off their land, but disease and limited food decimated their numbers. A new economic foundation for the colony's survival had to be found if Jamestown was to be of use. After a decade of investing in Jamestown, its backers in London were frustrated. No route to China had been found, and there were no precious metals in the colony. Farming kept the colonists alive but returned little to the investors, and there was conflict, not lucrative trade, with the Indians.

That something new turned out to be a product that Columbus had discovered—tobacco. Before 1492, no Europeans knew anything about tobacco, though the peoples of North and South America had used it for medicinal and religious purposes for hundreds of years. But Columbus took some tobacco leaves with him on his first return voyage. Within a few decades, smoking tobacco became popular in Europe. Spaniards smoked tobacco from Cuba. King James, who found smoking tobacco "loathsome to the eye, hateful to the nose, harmful to the brain, dangerous to the lungs," also saw in it a

This illustration was published in 1624 as part of John Smith's book about his time in Virginia showing, among other things, his battles with the American Indians, his rescue by Pocahontas, and his map of the colony.

way to make significant profits and created a royal monopoly. And Virginia, its settlers discovered, had the ideal climate and conditions for producing tobacco. The settlers might have preferred to find silver or gold, but tobacco quickly became valuable.

In 1622, led by Openchancanough, Powhatan's brother and the tribe's new leader, the Algonquians attacked and killed some 300 of the 1,200 English settlers. The Indians had lost patience with the continual encroachment of the English and the lack of trade or other benefits. Attacks continued for more than a decade. The conflict eventually bankrupted the Virginia Company, but in 1624, Virginia had been converted to a royal colony by the king, so efforts to settle the area continued.

The shift from trade with Indians to tobacco-based agriculture in the 1620s sealed the fate of the Indians who had been essential to the colony's early survival. Indian land became more valuable to the English than the Indians themselves, and disease was decimating Indian populations. The new emphasis on agriculture also meant that many from England would settle and farm the land. The shift also changed the lives of thousands of Africans who were brought to the Americas as slaves to produce the new crops. Tobacco was a key factor in reshaping who would be a part of this new English-speaking nation and the role they would play in the society that emerged.

The Massachusetts Colonies: Plymouth, Boston, and Beyond

During the first two decades of the 1600s, many in England were coming to see the country as overpopulated. Changes in agriculture were forcing people out of subsistence farming and into cities. England's economy was stagnating. What better outlet for excess population than the new colonies across the ocean? It was a great service, some argued, to ship the poor to do the agricultural work that was so badly needed across the sea.

King James especially wanted to see one group on its way across the ocean—the Protestant extremists who were forever agitating for more change within the Church of England (also known as the Anglican or Episcopal Church).

Protestants who wanted a more complete Reformation than the Church of England represented came to be known as Puritans. When Henry VIII and his successors had broken with the pope, they maintained a religious liturgy much like the Catholic Mass and a church governed by bishops. Queen Elizabeth I had sought religious peace by tolerating differences in viewpoints as long as people accepted her religious authority and agreed to use the form of worship prescribed in the *Book of Common Prayer*. But the Puritans wanted change—much more change. They believed that the office of bishop had no base in the Bible and that each individual congregation should be self-governing. They believed each individual was responsible for reading and understanding the Bible.

Those who opposed the Church of England's demands for religious uniformity also had major differences among themselves. Some believed it was their duty to stay within the Anglican Church and work for change. Others thought that change could come only from leaving the established church. The former tried to "purify" the Church of England and were known as Puritans. The latter group, called Separatists, thought that the church was hopelessly corrupt and that they needed to form their own separate religious communities. The Separatists were constantly in trouble with the authorities since everyone in England was expected to belong to the Anglican Church and attend its worship every Sunday. To separate oneself from the church, to worship in a place or form not authorized by the church, was treason. No wonder King James wanted to "harry them out of the land," and that so many of the Separatists wanted to leave.

Separatists, also known as **Pilgrims**, founded the second permanent English colony in North America at Plymouth, Massachusetts, in 1620. The origins of Plymouth colony lay in a small community of Separatists who left England for Holland in 1607 where they were welcomed along with other English religious dissenters.

But the Separatists still considered themselves English, and they worried about raising children in Holland who would become more Dutch than English. Eventually, they decided that English North America would be a happier place for them. In 1619, these Separatist Pilgrims secured a grant of land from the Virginia Company, got financial backing from investors, and hired a ship. After many delays, the *Mayflower* sailed from Plymouth, England, on September 6, 1620, with 102 passengers. Half the passengers were members of the congregation. The others were "strangers" along for adventure or profit. As William Bradford, who became Plymouth's historian, wrote of this congregation, "they knew they were pilgrims."

After a stormy 2-month voyage, they reached land far north of where they meant to go. Realizing that they were outside of the Virginia territory and that their new community was split between its religious members and others, they promised to "combine ourselves together into a civil body politic, for our better ordering and preservation." Future generations would see the **Mayflower Compact** as the beginning of government by the consent of the people. But historians have seen it as something more modest: an agreement among a diverse group of people to try to get along with each other through what they knew would be a hard winter in a strange land.

The Pilgrims' first landing in November 1620 was on the outer end of Cape Cod at what is now Provincetown, Massachusetts. By December, however, they had moved across Cape Cod Bay to a place they named Plymouth where a high hill offered protection, and a large level area leading down to the harbor was a good place to build a town. Plymouth was empty when the Pilgrims landed. As recently as 1616, 1,000 or more Indians had lived around Plymouth, but an epidemic had wiped them out. As had happened elsewhere in the Americas, disease traveled faster than people. Enough European fishermen and traders had been traveling along the coast to ensure a plentiful supply of microbes. The new community quickly built on the now empty land.

The Pilgrims had arrived too late to build the kind of shelter they needed for a New England winter. During the winter of 1620–1621, about half the community died from disease, cold, and malnutrition. Some families were wiped out altogether. They had no contact with Native Americans, but they knew they were being watched constantly.

Smoking tobacco quickly became a popular symbol of sophistication in Europe, making the production of tobacco in Virginia very profitable.

Pilgrims
A name given to the Separatists within the Church of England who settled Plymouth, Massachusetts.

Mayflower Compact
The 1620 agreement made among the Pilgrims and others (whom the Pilgrims called "Strangers") on board the ship that brought them to Plymouth.

This modern recreation of the Pilgrim Village at Plimoth Plantation (note old style spelling) has been built using extensive original records from 1627—seven years after the colony's founding when life had reached a bit of stability—on the site of the first Pilgrim colony in Plymouth, Massachusetts.

Then, in spring 1621, their luck changed. An Indian walked "very boldly" into the heart of the small Plymouth community. And when he arrived, to their utter amazement, he said, "Welcome, Englishmen!" The visitor was Samoset, a native of what is now Maine, where English fishermen had been landing for a century, hence his knowledge of the language. More important, he had been asked to visit them by Massasoit, the ruler of the Wampanoag Indians of the area. Massasoit was also familiar with English ships that had sailed along the coast and had sent exploring parties ashore. He was now ready to make contact.

Soon after Samoset's visit, Massasoit himself arrived with many warriors and a translator named Squanto who had been captured by previous English explorers and who had lived in London. He became a go-between for Massasoit with the Pilgrim community, even though neither side ever fully trusted him.

Squanto surprised the Pilgrims when he described parts of London and, more important, when he taught them how to find hibernating eels in nearby creeks. They had their best meal in months that evening. He also taught them to catch herring in the town brook and use them as fertilizer for planting corn. It proved to be the salvation of the colony. The Pilgrims concluded an agreement with Massasoit that led to 54 years of peace, an amazing development in the Americas.

In the fall of 1621, with peace concluded and the first successful harvest accomplished, Governor Bradford announced that it was time to "rejoice together" with the people who had helped, indeed allowed, them to survive. The first Thanksgiving (the Pilgrims never actually used that word) was a weeklong time of feasting on the fruits of the harvest and on turkeys, ducks, geese, deer, and stews. The Pilgrims were recreating something they knew well, a traditional English harvest festival. Most of those present at "the first Thanksgiving," however, were Wampanoags, including Massasoit himself who brought gifts of freshly killed deer to the festivities.

American Voices

Of Plymouth Plantation, by William Bradford, 1630–1651

William Bradford was one of the original Pilgrims. He wrote his classic book over a period of many years to inform an English audience—and English investors—of the state of the new colony or plantation.

Being thus arrived in a good harbor and brought safe to land, they fell upon their knees and blessed the God of heaven, who had brought them over the vast and furious ocean, and delivered them from all the perils and miseries thereof again to set their feet on the firm and stable earth....

Being thus passed the vast ocean and a sea of troubles before in their preparation (as may be remembered by that which went before), they had now no friends to welcome them, nor inns to entertain or refresh their weatherbeaten bodies, nor houses or much less towns to repair to, to seek for succor....

And for the season it was winter, and they that know the winters of that country know them to be sharp and violent and subject to cruel and fierce storms....Besides, what could they see but a hideous and desolate wilderness, full of wild beasts and wild men, and what multitudes there might be of them they knew not....

But that which was most sad and lamentable was that in two or three months' time half of their company died...being infected with the scurvy and other diseases, which this long voyage...had brought upon them; so there died sometimes two or three of a day in the aforesaid time, that of 100 and odd persons scarce fifty remained....

The spring now approaching, it pleased God the mortality began to cease amongst them, and the sick and lame recovered....Afterwards they...began to plant their corn, in which service Squanto stood them in great stead, showing them both... how to set it, and after how to dress and tend it...and where to get other provisions necessary for them, all which they found true by trial and experience....

They began now to gather in the small harvest they had, and to fit up their houses and dwellings against winter, being well recovered in health and strength, and had all things good plenty.

Source: William Bradford, *A History of Plymouth Plantation* (Boston: Massachusetts Historical Society, 1856)

Thinking Critically

1. **Documentary Analysis**

   What challenges did the first Plymouth settlers face?

2. **Historical Interpretation**

   What does Bradford's account tell us about the importance of Native American peoples to the initial survival of the settlement?

Another group of religious dissidents from England were not far behind Plymouth's Pilgrims. Puritan reformers who wanted to stay within the Church of England and change it were also having a hard time in the 1620s. King Charles I (r. 1625–1649) was extremely hostile to the **Puritans**. Advocating reform within the established church became more difficult and dangerous. The Puritans, however, were not without resources. A group of them controlled a corporation, the Massachusetts Bay Company, to explore and settle North America. It was similar to the Virginia Company except that Puritans led it. They planted their first colony in Salem, just north of present-day Boston in 1629, and soon wanted to expand. In late 1629, someone realized that wording in the charter would allow them to move the whole company—its charter and the control that went with it—out of England and into the colony that the Massachusetts Bay Company controlled. If successful, this move would create not only a self-governing Puritan company but also a company thousands of miles from the king and his bishops who were making things so difficult for Puritans in England.

John Winthrop, an ardent Puritan, was invited to be the governor of the new colony. In spring 1630, 14 ships left England for Massachusetts Bay with their new governor and their charter on board. By the end of the summer, more than 1,000 people and 200 cattle had landed in the Massachusetts colony. In the next decade, known as the Great Migration, some 20,000 people followed. The Puritan Massachusetts Bay Colony soon had more people than Plymouth and Jamestown combined.

The Massachusetts Puritans also had a clear sense of purpose. As Winthrop said: "Our immediate object is to seek out a new home under a due form of Government both civil and ecclesiasticall....we shall be as a Citty upon a hill. The eyes of all people are upon Us." The Puritan Commonwealth in New England could also be a new model for old England.

Puritans

A name given to those more extreme Protestants within the Church of England who wanted to stay in the church but "purify" it of what they saw as Roman Catholic ways.

The Charter of the Massachusetts Bay Company
The legal charter given to the London-based corporation that launched Massachusetts Bay colony.

Fundamental Orders of Connecticut
The 1639 charter that Massachusetts authorities allowed a new separate colony based in Hartford to adopt, which confirmed its independence from Massachusetts.

This 1922 statue of Anne Hutchinson at the Massachusetts State House commemorates a woman who caused considerable difficulties for the authorities who ruled in Boston during her own time.

The Pilgrims had written their Mayflower Compact as a simple basis for the colony's government. The Puritan migrants of 1630 meant to use the more detailed **Charter of the Massachusetts Bay Company** to organize a permanent self-governing colony in Massachusetts.

The first meeting of the Great and General Court—the colony's governing body—on New England soil took place in August 1630. What had started as a business venture in England was transformed into a government in Massachusetts. Annual elections chose the governor, deputy-governor, and members of the General Court (as the state legislature in Massachusetts is still called). Only church members in good standing could vote. This settlement was designed to be a model religious colony. When King Charles I realized what the Puritans had done, he sent a ship to recover the charter. Governor Winthrop called out the Puritan militia and mounted cannons at the entrance to Boston harbor. Those under royal command who had come for the charter decided that it would be wiser to sail back to England without it.

The Puritans valued literacy. If salvation depended on a personal encounter with the Christian faith, then Puritans needed to be able to read the Bible and have ministers and magistrates who were highly literate. In 1636, only 6 years after Boston was founded, the colony's legislature ordered the creation of a college that would soon be named Harvard for an early benefactor. They created Boston Latin School to prepare young men for college, and in 1647, the legislature required every township in the colony to provide for a school. Towns found ways to evade the law, but literacy was still high in Massachusetts.

The Puritans of Massachusetts Bay, however, had their differences with one another. Several splits occurred during the first decade of the colony. In 1637, Puritans on the Connecticut River found the government in Boston too restrictive and created their own independent colony of Connecticut based at Hartford. Two years later, with permission from the authorities in Boston, the Hartford colonists established a formal government for their colony known as the **Fundamental Orders of Connecticut**. The document offered more men the right to vote than did the rules then in force in Massachusetts Bay. Some have considered it as the first written constitution in the Americas, though others, looking at the Massachusetts charter and other such documents, dispute that claim. Other Puritans found the Boston government not strict enough and created a more theocratic colony at New Haven the following year.

More troublesome to the Puritans was Roger Williams, whose advocacy of freedom of conscience for every individual was almost unique in the 1600s. Williams was a supporter of the Puritan cause in England and arrived in Boston in 1631 only a year after the city's founding. But he quickly got into trouble with Boston's magistrates because he asserted that civil authority could not enforce religious laws, including a law against blasphemy. In 1635, he was convicted of "erroneous" opinions. In the winter of 1636, he walked from his old home in Salem, Massachusetts, to the top of Narragansett Bay (more than 65 miles) and soon established a new colony called Providence where he invited all those "distressed of conscience" to the first colony that would separate church and state and grant full liberty to people of any religious opinion, a direct slap at Puritan efforts at religious uniformity. Williams established close working relationships with both the Wampanoag and Narragansett tribes—and insisted on paying them for the land on which he established his colony, unlike the settlers of Boston or Plymouth. Under Williams' leadership Rhode Island became a haven for religious dissenters.

In addition, Anne Hutchinson caused a stir with her charismatic preaching and her belief that God's inspiration could be more immediate than most Puritans believed. While Puritans insisted that every man and woman should read and interpret the Bible, they expected the interpretation to follow certain paths. In addition, only men were supposed to preach. When Hutchinson said that she herself received direct revelations from God, she had moved beyond what the Puritans would tolerate and was banished from the colony. She and her followers made their way, first to Roger Williams's colony in Rhode Island, and then to Dutch New Amsterdam where she was killed in an Indian attack in 1643.

While the first generation of New England's founders argued about whose version of Protestant theology was correct, their American-born children and grandchildren sometimes wandered quite far from the theological interests of the founders. The first Massachusetts Puritans saw themselves as being on an "errand into the wilderness," as a 1670 sermon put it. Religious fervor and conversions were less common in the next generations.

In Massachusetts in the 1600s, only those who could convincingly demonstrate that they had a true religious conversion could be church members, and only church members could vote. Since one had to convince a congregation that he or she had truly been converted to become a church member, many, including the children of devout church members, could not qualify for either church membership or the right to vote. People who were excluded from these privileges did not make for happy colonial residents.

In 1662, Massachusetts clergy adopted the **Halfway Covenant**, which allowed adults who had been baptized as children, because their parents were church members, to have their own children baptized, even if they were not among the members of a congregation. The compromise was a significant one for a community in which church membership was central to all else. In time, that compromise also led to many Massachusetts churches allowing any who could demonstrate familiarity with Christian doctrine and led a good life to be church members—and therefore also voters.

Halfway Covenant
Plan adopted in 1662 by New England clergy that allowed adults who had been baptized because their parents were church members, but who had not yet experienced conversion, to have their own children baptized.

Maryland

After Virginia and the New England colonies, the next English colony to be established on the mainland of North America was Maryland. Earlier colonies had been founded by corporations or were royal colonies ruled by governors appointed by the king. Maryland represented something new, a proprietary colony. A **proprietary colony**—of which Maryland was the model—was essentially owned by one person and heirs who were, as the Maryland charter said, "true and absolute lords and proprietaries." The proprietor might allow others to own land and might take advice from local officials, but the whole colony was private property and, as such, could be passed from generation to generation within the proprietor's family. King Charles I established this model when he offered to give Maryland to George Calvert, the first Lord Baltimore.

Maryland was also different in another way. Lord Baltimore was a devout Catholic, and Catholics were persecuted in England. But King Charles was sympathetic despite popular opposition. Lord Baltimore, with the King's support, was determined to establish Maryland as a haven for English Catholics. After George Calvert died, his son, Cecil Calvert, the second Lord Baltimore, developed the colony. He realized that he had to recruit more people than a Catholic-only colony would attract. So, in 1649, Maryland granted freedom of worship to all Christians, including Protestants of any persuasion.

While the proprietors retained final authority in Maryland, they agreed in 1635 to call a representative assembly. After initially establishing a colony of large estates, they also decided, following Virginia's lead, to give every European settler 100 acres, another 100 for each additional adult member of the family, and 50 acres for each child. This **headright system**—as it came to be called—made moving to Maryland very popular. From the beginning, Marylanders also knew that, as in Virginia, tobacco would be the key to their economic success. With tobacco came the need for more workers. Thus, African slavery came early to Maryland. In 1661, Maryland was the first colony to formalize laws governing slavery. The laws included the stipulations that slaves inherited their status from their mother and that slavery for those born into it was for life.

proprietary colony
A colony created when the English monarch granted a huge tract of land to an individual as his private property.

headright system
A system of land distribution during the early colonial era that granted settlers a set amount of land for each "head" (or person) who settled in the colony.

Additional Colonies: Continued Settlement and Development

The first English colonies of Jamestown and Plymouth on the North American mainland were models for what came later. Plymouth and Boston learned from mistakes made at Jamestown. All of those who established later English colonies studied Jamestown, Plymouth, and Boston, borrowing what they liked and ignoring the rest. In addition, those colonies also studied the prosperous English colonies that were developing on the island of Bermuda and in the Caribbean. Those island colonies attracted their own settlers from England and brought far more slaves from Africa than did the mainland colonies. On the islands, slaves worked on the expanding sugar plantations. Table 3-1 shows all of the English colonies that were eventually established in North America and in the islands.

CONNECTICUT AND NEW HAMPSHIRE   After the creation of the colonies at Plymouth, Massachusetts Bay, Connecticut, and New Haven, the New England colonies continued

TABLE 3-1 England's American and Island Colonies

Colony	Founded	Official Religion	Crop	Government
Virginia	1607	Anglican	Tobacco	Corporation; Royal after 1625
Bermuda (island colony)	1612	Anglican	Mixed	Corporation
Plymouth	1620 Merged with Mass., 1685	Puritan	Farming	Corporation
St. Christopher (island colony)	1624	Anglican	Sugar	Royal
Barbados (island colony)	1627	Anglican	Sugar	Royal
Nevis (island colony)	1628	Anglican	Sugar	Royal
Massachusetts (included Maine, did not include Plymouth)	1630	Puritan	Farming, fishing	Corporation (based in Boston)
New Hampshire	Separate colony, 1630–1643; part of Mass., 1643–79; separate after 1679	Puritan	Farming	Corporation 1630–1679; Royal after 1679
Antigua (island colony)	1632	Anglican	Sugar	Royal
Montserrat (island colony)	1632	Anglican	Sugar	Royal
Maryland	1634	Founded as a haven for Roman Catholics with no established church; Anglican after 1692	Tobacco	Proprietary 1634–1690; Royal 1691–1715; Proprietary again after 1715
Rhode Island	1636	No established church, haven for dissenters, especially Baptists	Farming	Corporation
Connecticut (Hartford)	1636	Puritan	Farming	Corporation (from Massachusetts)
New Haven	1638; became part of Connecticut in 1665	Puritan	Farming	Corporation (from Massachusetts)
Jamaica (island colony)	1655 (captured from Spanish)	Anglican	Sugar	Royal
Carolina	1663; split into North and South Carolina, 1729	Anglican	Rice (south); tobacco (north)	Proprietary
New York	Settled by Dutch as New Netherlands colony, 1624–1626; became English and renamed New York, 1664	None	Farming, furs, trade	Proprietary, 1684; Royal after 1685
New Jersey	1664 (split from New York)	None	Farming	Proprietary
Pennsylvania	1681	None, established as a haven for Quakers	Farming	Proprietary
Delaware	1701 (split from Pennsylvania, but shared single governor until 1776)	None	Farming	Proprietary
Georgia	1732	None, haven for the poor rather than religious dissent	Farming	Proprietary; Royal after 1751

Source: Adapted from David Goldfield, et al., *The American Journey: A History of the United States*, 6th ed. (Upper Saddle River, NJ: Pearson Prentice Hall, 2011), p. 56.

to be reshaped. Connecticut was united with New Haven in 1662. Massachusetts Bay Colony merged with Plymouth in 1685. New Hampshire became a separate colony under a royal governor in 1691. (Vermont did not separate from New York until after the American Revolution, and Maine was part of Massachusetts until 1820.)

NEW YORK   New York was settled before Maryland, but not by the English. It became English only after the English Civil War (1642–1649). What is now New York was settled by the Netherlands, or Holland, a new Protestant country carved out of what had been Spanish possessions in the late 1500s. Sailing for the Dutch, Henry Hudson had explored much of the Atlantic coast in 1609. His voyage gave the Netherlands the basis for its claim to land in North America. The Dutch West India Company was set up in 1621, and it built a Dutch trading post at Fort Orange (now Albany, New York) in 1624. The economic base of the Dutch colony was the fur trade. The Iroquois were happy to trade with the Dutch. They benefited from fostering competition between Dutch and French traders to see who would offer the best price for furs and be the best military allies.

In 1626, the Dutch built a settlement and commercial center called New Amsterdam on Manhattan Island, which, according to legend, was purchased from local Indians for 60 Dutch guilders (calculated at approximately $24 by a historian in the 1840s, over $1,000 today but still exceedingly cheap). There is some debate about which tribe actually received any payment, though one was recorded in Holland. The payment, however, reflected a European understanding of land ownership. Most Native American tribes did not think in terms of someone actually owning land; to them, the land, air, and water were open to all.

Despite efforts by its long-time governor Peter Stuyvesant to enforce religious uniformity and ban Jews, New Amsterdam soon became a haven for religious dissenters including Jews, Catholics, Quakers, and Muslims. It was also home to Dutch, German, French, Swedish, Portuguese, and English settlers. The Dutch were active in the slave trade. New Amsterdam had the largest number of African slaves in North America in the 1600s. As a trading center, New Amsterdam also saw many Native Americans who came to the city to sell furs and buy European goods. Successive Dutch governors banned sexual contact between the Dutch residents and Indians, but the ban was not always honored.

While the heart of the Dutch colony remained on Manhattan Island, the Dutch authorities offered large tracts of land to wealthy Dutch citizens, known as **patroons**, to develop the lands along the Hudson River between New Amsterdam and Albany. Wealthy Dutch investors who promised to settle at least 50 people on their land were given huge tracts of land, which they controlled as private fiefdoms. Nevertheless New Netherlands never had more than 10,000 European and African residents.

patroons
Dutch settlers who were given vast tracts of land along the Hudson River between New Amsterdam and Albany in return for bringing at least 50 immigrants to work the land.

In 1664, King Charles II gave New Amsterdam to his younger brother, the Duke of York (who later became King James II). That the Dutch already had a settlement on the land did not bother either brother. Having been "given" the colony, the duke sent a fleet to New Amsterdam to take it. There was little resistance to the English take over; Governor Peter Stuyvesant was unpopular, and the English promised to respect Dutch property. The Dutch briefly recaptured the colony in 1673, but it returned to English rule permanently the following year. The heart of the Dutch oceanic empire was elsewhere. They were not going to fight the English over this remote outpost.

The Duke of York divided the colony, keeping New York for himself and giving New Jersey to two political allies. For the rest of the 1600s, New Jersey remained a colony of small farms of limited profit to its proprietors, although it attracted a diverse group of European settlers because its proprietors offered land at low prices and gave settlers significant religious and political freedom. But New York, with its great harbor and access to the interior via the Hudson River, quickly became one of the most valuable English colonies.

PENNSYLVANIA AND DELAWARE   The next English colony was Pennsylvania. Like Maryland, Pennsylvania was established as a proprietary colony and a haven for a persecuted religious group while being open to all. Pennsylvania's proprietor was William Penn, the son of Sir William Penn, an admiral in the Royal Navy with close connections to King Charles II. The younger William Penn inherited the right to collect a

This map of New Amsterdam just at the time the English first took control (note the English flag flying on the fort) shows the site of the fort at the tip of Manhattan and the British ships off shore.

substantial debt that the king owed to the Penn family. King Charles II repaid the debt in the form of land in North America. But while William Penn inherited both fortune and royal connections, unlike his admiral father, he was a member of a dissident religious community known as Quakers because they supposedly trembled—quaked—at the name of God. Quakers broke with much of the traditional theology and religious practice of the day. When they gathered for worship, Quakers sat in silence until someone was moved by the Spirit to speak. They did not have formal clergy and gave women equal standing with men in their community, known as the Society of Friends. In addition, they were absolute pacifists who would not serve in the military. Because of their refusal to serve in the military and attend the services of the Church of England, they were constantly in legal trouble. Penn himself was briefly jailed for following Quaker practices.

Penn received his land grant from King Charles II in 1681, and the next year he sailed to Pennsylvania and founded Philadelphia (the City of Brotherly Love). Penn recruited settlers widely, in Britain and on the European continent, especially in Germany. By 1700, 18,000 Europeans had arrived. In keeping with his Quaker beliefs, Penn insisted on peaceful trade with the Indians. Although he had been granted land from the king, Penn also paid the Indians for their land. During his lifetime, Pennsylvania was generally a peaceful place. Tribes from other colonies found a new home there.

Despite all of his commitment to peace with the Indians, Penn did not outlaw slavery in his colony. As early as 1684, 2 years after its founding, 150 African slaves arrived in Philadelphia. Slaves quickly came to have a key role as household servants, and by the early 1700s, slaves made up one-sixth of the city's population. In rural communities, slaves worked in iron furnaces, mines, tanneries, salt works, and on farms.

Penn tried to create a prosperous colony based on high ideals. But he was also an aristocrat who held absolute power. By the 1690s, many in the colony, including Quakers who appreciated their religious freedom, demanded more political freedom. In 1701, Penn reluctantly agreed to a Charter of Liberties that established an elected legislature, though the legislature and the Penn family would continue to argue until the beginnings of the American Revolution.

The 1701 charter also allowed the three most southern counties of Pennsylvania to create their own assembly, which became the core of the separate colony of Delaware. The first Europeans to settle in Delaware were from Sweden and Finland, creating the small New Sweden colony at Fort Christina—today's Wilmington, Delaware—in 1638.

The Dutch of New Amsterdam conquered the colony in 1655 before themselves being defeated by the English in 1664. The area was included in the land grant given to William Penn, but its separate history and geographical distance limited its relationship to the rest of Pennsylvania.

CAROLINA   South of Virginia, the land was contested between England and Spain, to say nothing of the Indian tribes who lived there. But England meant to claim the area. Soon after coming to the throne, Charles II rewarded eight of his supporters, and sought to secure England's land claims by creating a colony named Carolina (based on the Latin for *Charles*). The proprietors developed an elaborate system of government that prescribed a hierarchical society with themselves at the top followed by the local gentry, then poor white servants, with African slaves at the bottom. The city of Charles Town, later Charleston, became the colony's capital.

Carolina was a divided colony. In the north, most of the settlers were relatively poor white farmers from Virginia. Farther south, large-scale rice growing created a rich colony. Much of the colony's commercial success focused on the city—and harbor—at Charleston and on trade with the British Caribbean colonies, especially Barbados. Many of the early immigrants were from Barbados, both wealthy Europeans who became the elite of the mainland colony and African slaves who did the actual work of the rice farming. Following the model of Barbados in the Caribbean, which depended on plantations to grow sugarcane, the southern part of Carolina became one of the earliest plantation economies on the mainland of North America. The split between the north and south was formalized when King George II officially divided the colony into North and South Carolina in 1729.

GEORGIA   The last English colony that would later be part of the United States was Georgia, founded in 1733 for idealistic reasons. James Oglethorpe, a war hero in England, wanted to create a place where the poorest of England's poor, those in debtor's prisons because they could not repay what they owed, could find new lives. Oglethorpe also believed that England needed a strong frontier colony on the border with Spanish Florida. These settlers, people whose alternative might well be prison, would be inspired to be not only farmers but also soldiers within this frontier border. Given this focus, Oglethorpe excluded Catholics—who might be secretly loyal to Catholic Spain—and Africans, free or slave—since they might be tempted to run away. With Georgia, the 13 colonies that went on to unite in 1776 were in place.

PENNS TREATY with the INDIANS, made 1681 without an Oath, and never broken. The foundation of Religious and Civil LIBERTY, in the U.S. of AMERICA.

Although this painting was done long after the 1682 treaty shown here was concluded, it portrays Penn's commitment to negotiate with the tribes in Pennsylvania, including these negotiations to purchase the land on which Philadelphia was built.

Africans and Indentured Servants in England's Colonies

In 1619, a Dutch ship arrived at Jamestown. John Rolfe, anxious to expand the workforce for his tobacco farm, traded food supplies to the Dutch in return for 20 African slaves. Rolfe's 1619 purchase of other humans is usually given as the date for the beginning of slavery in what is now the United States. In fact, the Spanish had African slaves in Florida during the 1500s (see Chapter 2). A census of Virginia in 1620 that did not count Indians listed 32 Africans—17 women and 15 men—out of a total population of 982. Nevertheless, the exchange of American-grown foodstuffs for African people that took place in 1619 was significant. Although it would have been impossible to predict it then, slave labor would become the economic foundation of the colonies and of the new nation that emerged from them.

The slavery that existed in British North America in the early 1600s was profoundly different from what slavery had been in the early 1500s or from what it became in the colonies in the early 1700s. Many think of slavery as a static institution, but the nature of slavery changed often. For many Americans, the image of slavery is that of the large

This early picture of a Virginia tobacco plantation shows the role of African slave labor in doing the work of the plantation, the English elite in managing the work, and the overriding presence of Indians in the image of the colony.

indentured servants
An individual who contracted to serve for a period of 4 to 7 years in return for payment of passage to America.

plantations that existed in the South between 1800 and the 1860s. But understanding the development of slavery in the United States requires more careful observation. Slavery, though always terrible, meant different things at different times.

In the earliest years, slavery, though very difficult, was less harsh and hopeless than it became after about 1680. When John Rolfe purchased those 20 African slaves in 1619, it was not clear what their status would be. Slavery had not been codified either as a permanent life-long status or as something associated always with race.

The first generation of African slaves in Virginia often worked side by side not only with English and Irish servants—many of whom also had little choice about coming to America—but also with captured Indians. Race was always a factor, but racial lines were blurred. Servants and slaves lived together, created new families together, and resisted together when they felt ill-treated.

In the small farms of the Chesapeake, in the Middle Colonies, and in New England, slaves also worked side by side with those who owned the land and with **indentured servants** who were working for a specified number of years to pay off the cost of their travel to America. Some of these indentured servants came seeking a better life; others came as an alternative to prison in England. During a term of indenture, a servant was treated much like a slave. Indentured servants could be bought and sold and were often whipped. The difference between indentured servanthood and slavery, and it was significant, was that at the end of their term, ranging from 4 to 7 years, the servants were set free. Until the late 1640s the majority died before completing their term, and even after earning their freedom, most of the newly freed were not able to earn much, although a few prospered and joined the elite. Since an English indentured servant cost about half as much as an African slave, and since neither tended to live long, many Virginians initially preferred indentured servants. Servants and slaves often intermarried and saw themselves as a united group.

The Africans, like the European servants, dreamed of a day when they might be free to own their own land. That dream was not an impossible one in the early 1600s. For example, Anthony Johnson was sold as a slave in Jamestown in 1621. He worked on the farm of the Bennett family and became known for his "hard labor and…service." After more than a decade of labor on the Bennett property, he was allowed to farm independently while still a slave. He married a woman named Mary. Their children were baptized with the blessings of the authorities. Eventually, he gained his freedom and changed his name. When the Bennetts moved to eastern Virginia, the Johnsons moved with them. By 1651, Anthony Johnson owned a 250-acre farm with his own servants and at least one slave. His son John owned 550 acres, and another son owned 100 acres. The Johnson family, if not viewed as the equals of their white neighbors, were in many ways part of Virginia's landed gentry. During the 1600s, the Johnsons were not the only former slaves to achieve this status. No slaves in Virginia, Maryland, or the Carolinas, however, could hope to repeat this success in the 1700s or 1800s.

There was more to the experience of the Johnsons than the freedom they gained to own and work their own land. They were free to travel. They were members of Christian churches and participated in the financial and religious activities of the colony. The total number of Africans, slave and free, remained relatively small in Virginia before 1680. On the eastern shore where the Johnsons lived, there were some 40 free blacks out of a total black population of 300. While most Africans remained in slavery, 30 percent of the people of African descent in parts of Virginia were free in 1668. Race was not insignificant, but neither race as a marker of slavery nor slavery as an institution had been determined.

Slavery developed in the northern colonies as it did in those further south, coming to Massachusetts fairly soon after it came to Virginia. By the 1660s, Boston's elite lived in a slave-owning world. One-third of the slaves in Massachusetts lived in Boston. In the North, slavery was more urban than rural. In the cities, slaves worked as household servants, cooking, cleaning, sewing, tending gardens and stables, and running errands. They also worked on wagons and wharves. Northern slaves, like many southern slaves of the 1600s, were much more fully integrated into European-American society, had less contact with fellow Africans and African traditions, and had much more freedom than later generations of slaves.

3.1 **Quick Review** Compare the reasons for founding the different English colonies in North America during the 1600s. How might these different reasons lead to different developments in the colonies?

ENGLAND'S WARS, ENGLAND'S COLONIES

3.2 Analyze the relationship between politics in England, internal colonial tensions, and life in the English colonies in North America during the 1600s.

The tensions that led Pilgrims and Puritans to flee England erupted into a full-scale civil war in the 1640s in which King Charles I lost his head and a Puritan Commonwealth ruled the country for 11 years (1649–1660). The religious and political battles in England fueled settlement in North America. Puritans sought refuge in Massachusetts when they were feeling oppressed in England, supporters of the royal cause sought refuge in Virginia when the Puritans dominated at home, while Catholics moved to Maryland, and other dissidents found tolerant places like Rhode Island.

When the civil wars ended and a new king, Charles II, eldest son of Charles I, began to rule in England in 1660, he also rewarded supporters with grants of yet more colonial charters. All of England's tensions spilled over into its American colonies. More colonies were established, and many more English settlers arrived than might have been the case if their homeland had been at peace.

As England's American colonies were founded and began to grow, they were often violent places that reflected old and new tensions. In the 1670s, internal tensions burst into violence in the colonies. King Philip's War in Massachusetts was one of the most vicious wars ever fought in North America. In Virginia, backcountry farmers took up arms against the royal governor in 1679. The growth, the tensions, and the violence all helped create the political and cultural structures of the colonies of British North America in the 1700s.

Civil War and Revolution in England

When King James died in 1625, his son became King Charles I (r. 1625–1649). King Charles was known for his religious sincerity and lack of political skill. The king and his advisors pursued religious Anglican uniformity far more strictly than any of his predecessors had. The Puritan movement, however, grew despite royal opposition. By the late 1620s, Puritans were a majority in Parliament. As a result, in 1629, King Charles dismissed Parliament and did not convene it again for 11 years.

But in 1640, rebellion broke out in Scotland. To suppress it, Charles needed new taxes, and to get them, he had to call Parliament back into session. That move was his undoing. The Parliament that met in November 1640 was overwhelmingly Puritan and passed laws that favored the Puritans and limited royal authority.

By 1642, England was in a civil war. Parliament's army defeated the king, who was executed in 1649. General Oliver Cromwell ruled England as a Puritan Commonwealth from 1649 to 1658. By the time Cromwell died in 1658, many in England were tired of Puritan rule. In 1660, Parliament invited the son of Charles I to reign as King Charles II (r. 1660–1685). The Anglican Church again became the official state church, but the new king was more tolerant of religious differences than his father had been. Charles II also took an interest in expanding his North American colonies. Almost half of the colonies of the future United States—New York, New Jersey, Pennsylvania, North and South Carolina—date to his reign.

Rebellion in New England—King Philip's War, 1675–1676

The half-century of peace that the Pilgrims of Plymouth and the Wampanoag Indians experienced was unusual in North America. It seemed that the two cultures could live side by side in relative harmony. But while there was harmony in Plymouth between 1620 and 1675, there were also tensions, sometimes sharp ones.

Early in Plymouth's history, one incident showed just how violent the Pilgrims could be. When word came to Governor Bradford that their closest Indian ally, Massasoit, was desperately ill, Bradford sent Edward Winslow to treat the Wampanoag leader as a gesture of goodwill.

While he was recovering, Massasoit told Winslow that another tribe, the Massachusetts Indians, who lived north of Plymouth, were preparing to attack Plymouth. Whether the wily Massasoit was reporting the truth or using the Pilgrims to settle an old score is unclear, but Bradford took him seriously. Under the command of Miles Standish, Pilgrim soldiers killed two of the tribe's leaders. The Massachusetts Indians decided not to antagonize these violent Europeans and moved further north. Other tribes saw that, for good or ill, the alliance between Massasoit and the Pilgrims ran deep. But from Holland, the Pilgrim's spiritual guide Pastor John Robinson condemned "the killing of those poor Indians" warning, "where blood is once begun to be shed, it is seldom staunched of a long time after."

The Massachusetts Bay Puritans did not maintain peace for as long as the Plymouth settlers. Massachusetts Bay was larger, stronger, and less tolerant of outsiders than Plymouth. The Massachusetts Bay Puritans often traded with Indian tribes, especially the Pequots of the Connecticut River Valley. But when the captain of a trading vessel was killed in 1637, the Puritans responded harshly. Building an alliance with the Mohegans and Narragansetts, they attacked a Pequot fortress on the Mystic River, set the houses on fire, and attacked anyone who fled. In the short **Pequot War**, 400 Pequots were killed, and their village was annihilated. Surviving Pequots were sold into slavery. From the Mohegans' perspective, this conflict was an opportunity to expand their influence. From the perspective of the Narragansetts, it was horrifying. They were accustomed to Indian warfare that focused on the skill and bravery of a few, not the annihilation of the many. Europeans, they discovered, fought differently.

Pequot War
Conflict between English settlers and Pequot Indians over control of land and trade in eastern Connecticut.

Other tensions between the English settlers and Indian tribes were also evident. The English did not tend to intermarry or engage in sexual liaisons with Indians as frequently as the Spanish or the French. Many parts of New Spain and New France were conquered by unmarried men who quickly developed intimate relationships with native women and created a **mestizo** (mixed European and Indian blood) community. These relationships often helped to strengthen ties between cultures and reduce tensions. But New England was settled by English families, and their descendants tended to intermarry within the community. The English also had different views of appropriate sexual relationships. The Puritans were not as straight-laced as later generations came to picture them, but they seldom had sex outside their own community. The result was that mixed-race people who bridged cultures were rarer in English colonies than elsewhere in the Americas.

Additionally, the English, especially in New England, also wanted to convert the Indians to their religion. But most Indians resented and resisted missionaries, whether English, Spanish, or French. For all of his friendship with the Pilgrims, Massasoit distrusted Christianity. He saw the conversion of Indians on Cape Cod as a rejection of his role as their supreme chief.

What fostered the most tension, however, was the constant growth of the European community. The 40 miles between Plymouth and the heart of Massasoit's world provided a sufficient barrier for people who generally walked everywhere, but the European population was expanding. By the 1660s, English settlements were springing up in every direction and were beginning to dominate. European livestock ate Wampanoag corn. Land sales that had once seemed wise now seemed to confine a new generation of Wampanoags.

A new generation of Pilgrims and Wampanoags were coming to power—people who did not remember their early friendship. In 1657, Governor Bradford, who had led Plymouth for 37 years, died. At about the same time, Massasoit was succeeded, first by his son Alexander, and shortly after by his other son Metacom (who was known to the Pilgrims as King Philip).

Throughout the 1670s, rumors circulated that Metacom was preparing for war. He denied that he had anything but peaceful intentions, but he was also buying arms and ammunition. In January, 1675, a Christian Indian, John Sassamon, told Josiah Winslow, Bradford's successor as governor, that Metacom was indeed preparing for war. Winslow refused to believe Sassamon and sent him on his way. Soon thereafter, Sassamon's body was discovered. Metacom denied any role in his death and asked the authorities to allow the Wampanoags to settle what he saw as an internal matter. But instead, the Plymouth authorities hanged three of Metacom's associates.

The first skirmishes of what was known as **King Philip's War**—using Metacom's English name—took place within 2 weeks of the executions, in June 1675. People in outlying towns took refuge in fortresses. Abandoned homes were burned. When a father and son left the Swansea garrison and found Indians vandalizing their home, they fired on them. The Wampanoags did not want to draw the first blood, but once shots had been fired they fought furiously. Within days, at least 10 of the English were killed. When the Plymouth militia gave chase, Indians simply melted into the woods, crossed a river, and lived to fight another day—and fight they did. Early encounters between Europeans and natives of the Americas had pitted matchlocks (difficult-to-fire guns that were unusable in the rain) against Indian bows and arrows. However, in this war, both sides were armed with more modern flintlocks that they could use with deadly aim against the other.

As the war escalated, Europeans throughout New England lived in terror and died, whether in isolated settlements or larger towns. Colonial troops who did not understand Indian wars marched into ambushes and died by the scores. Indians died in even larger numbers, and the Wampanoag community was destroyed. Other tribes, even those that sought to remain neutral, were decimated. In western Massachusetts, after Indians burned the town of Springfield, colonists turned on friendly or neutral tribes, forcing them to join Metacom's side or die. Despite pleas from the missionary

mestizo
People of mixed bloodlines, usually the children of European fathers and Native American mothers and their descendants.

King Philip's War
Conflict in New England (1675–76) between Wampanoags, Narragansetts, and other Indian peoples against English settlers.

American Voices

Mary Rowlandson, The Sovereignty and Goodness of God, 1682

The journal of Mary Rowlandson describes an Indian attack on her town of Lancaster, Massachusetts, in 1676, the death of her daughter and many friends, and her subsequent experience as an Indian captive. Despite the terror and loss in her story, the Rowlandson journal also represents one of the first accounts of an American Indian war dance—just before her captors' successful attack on the town of Sudbury, Massachusetts. It also relates her relatively friendly conversations with Metacom (Philip) himself.

On the tenth of February, 1676, came the Indians with great numbers upon Lancaster. …Hearing the noise of some guns, we looked out; several Houses were burning….There were five persons taken in one house. The Father and the Mother and a sucking Child they knocked on the head; the other two they took and carried away alive….Some in our house were fighting for their lives, others wallowing in their blood, the House on fire over our heads….But out we must go, the fire increasing and coming along behind us roaring, and the Indians gaping before us with their Guns, Spears, and Hatchets to devour us…yet the Lord by his Almighty power preserved a number of us from death, for there were twenty-four of us taken alive and carried Captive.…

But now, the next morning, I must turn my back upon the Town, and travel with them into a vast and desolate Wilderness, I knew not whither. It is not my tongue or pen can express the sorrows of my heart and bitterness of my spirit that I had at this departure, but God was with me in a wonderful manner, carrying me along, and bearing up my spirit that it did not quite fail. One of the Indians carried my poor wounded Babe upon a horse;

it went moaning all along, "I shall die, I shall die." I went on foot after it with sorrow that cannot be expressed….This day in the afternoon, about an hour by Sun, we came to …An Indian Town called Wenimessett [today New Braintree, MA]…About two hours in the night, my sweet Babe like a lamb departed this life.…

During my abode in this place [after several moves], Philip spoke to me to make a shirt for his boy, which I did, for which he gave me a shilling…and with it I bought a piece of Horse flesh. Afterwards he asked me to make a Cap for his boy, for which he invited me to Dinner. I went, and he gave me a Pancake about as big as two fingers; it was made of parched wheat, beaten, and fried in Bear's grease, but I never tasted pleasanter meat in my life.

[Rowlandson was released by her captors in April as part of an unsuccessful peace initiative.]

Source: Mary Rowlandson, *The Sovereignty and Goodness of God, 1682*, in Nathaniel Philbrick and Thomas Philbrick, editors, *The Mayflower Papers: Selected Writings of Colonial New England* (New York; Penguin Books, 2007), pp. 166–211.

Thinking Critically

1. **Documentary Analysis**
   What connections can you make between this passage and the title of Rowlandson's work?

2. **Historical Interpretation**
   How would you explain the Indians' decision to take captives rather than simply killing all of the town's inhabitants? What uses might they have had for such captives?

John Eliot to protect the "Praying Indians"—converts to Christianity who were loyal to the Massachusetts authorities—they were taken to relocation centers in Boston Harbor where many died of exposure and malnutrition.

In one of the bloodiest battles of the war, known as the Great Swamp Fight of December 1675, a combined Massachusetts and Plymouth force attacked a fortress of the Narragansetts after tracking through swamps to get there. Even though the Narragansetts had remained neutral throughout the warfare, the English force destroyed the fort, killing perhaps 300 Narragansett warriors and burning alive another 300 women, children, and old people. Humanity seemed to have vanished from these descendants of those who sought to build a new Christian community.

Throughout the winter of 1675–1676, the outcome of the war was unclear. The European communities in New England risked being wiped out that winter. But in the summer of 1676, the Indians were running out of food. Some of the tribes that had been allied with Metacom drifted away or shifted their allegiance. The end came in August when Metacom and a few dedicated supporters were cornered in a swamp and killed.

In a grisly end to the war, King Philip's head was displayed on a pole in Plymouth for the next 20 years. Authorities in Plymouth and Boston expelled many of the Indians from New England. Over 1,000 Wampanoags and their allies, including Philip's wife and son, were sold into slavery in the Caribbean. John Eliot, the long-time pastor to Christian Indians wrote, "To sell souls for money seems a dangerous merchandise." But in the hatreds created by the war, these voices were not heard.

Of the 70,000 people of all races living in New England at the beginning of the war, some 5,000 were killed—1,000 of the English and at least 4,000 Native Americans. King Philip's War was one of annihilation; each side sought to destroy the other. In fact, the percentage of people killed in King Philip's War was larger than corresponding percentages for the American Revolution, the Civil War, or World War II. For the Wampanoags, the war ended the independent nation that Metacom and his father Massasoit had led (see Map 3-2).

Bacon's Rebellion in Virginia, 1676

As King Philip's War was being fought in New England, Virginia was also engulfed in violence. Like the war in Massachusetts, **Bacon's Rebellion** illustrated the instability of early colonial life and alliances that were constantly shifting. King Philip's War was a battle between Europeans and Indians. In Virginia, the conflict was more complex.

By 1660, Virginia had 40,000 colonists, including a small elite and many poor workers—Africans and Indians, some slave, some free, and current or former English

Bacon's Rebellion

A 1676 rebellion in Virginia, led by a recent immigrant from England, Nathaniel Bacon, in which a militia attacked not only Indian villages but also the royal governor before being defeated.

MAP 3-2 King Philip's War in New England in 1675–1676. As the map shows, King Philip's—or Metacom's—War involved all of New England in brutal conflict, not only in Plymouth where it began but throughout Rhode Island, Massachusetts, and the Connecticut River towns.

indentured servants. At this time, there were at least as many Indian as African slaves in Virginia. However, most of the Virginia tribes kept their distance from the white settlements, except for occasional trade.

Sir William Berkeley was the royal governor of Virginia from 1642 to the 1670s. He brought order to the colony, but it was an aristocratic order. He and an inner circle ran the government and retained most of the profits from the tobacco trade no matter who actually grew it. The corruption generated increasing tension among others as the social divide increased between rich whites and poor whites, between established landowners and newly arrived colonists (who could acquire land only along the western frontiers of the territory—closer to hostile tribes than colonists nearer the coast), and among Europeans, Africans, and Indians. Even if slaves and indentured servants did earn their freedom, land was increasingly difficult to acquire, and many were limited to becoming tenant farmers for wealthier land owners.

In 1675, resentment came to a head. The economy was in the doldrums. Neither the corn crop, which was essential for food, nor the tobacco crop, which was essential for money, was doing well. When Indians from the Doig tribe raided Thomas Mathew's plantation because Mathew supposedly had not paid for items obtained from the tribe, area colonists retaliated with an attack of their own. However, the colonists mistakenly attacked the Susquehanaug tribe instead of the Doigs. Violence was flaring.

At that point, Nathaniel Bacon, recently arrived in Virginia from a prosperous English family and already one of the largest landowners in the western part of the colony, organized a militia to attack the Indians. Bacon and his followers had heard news of King Philip's War where many tribes had united. They feared unity among Virginia's tribes and had no intention of discriminating between friendly and unfriendly Indians. Bacon and his militia began attacking Indians indiscriminately, seeing every Indian as an enemy. Governor Berkeley, however, believed that Virginia needed friendly tribes on its frontier to protect it from hostile tribes

THINKING HISTORICALLY

The Declaration of the People by Nathaniel Bacon, General, 1676

As the rebellion in Virginia continued, Governor Berkeley complained about trying to govern people who were poor, discontented, and armed. Bacon had the support of most of the people, white and black, who were poor, indebted, unhappy, and well armed. He issued a Declaration of the People, stating the many reasons—from high taxes, to elite control of the fur trade, to lack of support in his Indian wars—for the rebellion.

For having upon specious pretences of public works, raised unjust taxes upon the commonality for the advancement of private favourites and other sinister ends, but no visible effects in any measure adequate....

For having wronged his Majesty's prerogative and interest by assuming the monopoly of the beaver trade....

For having protected, favoured and emboldened the Indians against his Majesty's most loyal subjects, never contriving, requiring, or appointing any due or proper means of satisfaction for their many invasions, murders, and robberies committed upon us.

For having the second time attempted the same thereby calling down our forces from the defence of the frontiers, and

most weak exposed places, for the prevention of civil mischief and ruin amongst ourselves, whilst the barbarous enemy in all places did invade, murder, and spoil us, his Majesty's most faithful subjects.

Of these...we accuse Sir William Berkeley, as guilty.

Source: Selections from Louis B. Wright and Elaine W. Fowler, *Documents of Modern History: English Colonization of North America* (New York: St. Martin's Press), pp. 163–165.

Thinking Critically

1. **Historical Interpretation**
   What does the excerpt from Bacon's declaration tell us about the underlying causes of social tensions during the mid-1600s in Virginia?

2. **Contextualization**
   What role did Bacon and his followers believe the colonial government should play in Virginia? How might their views have differed from those of Berkeley and his supporters?

who lived further west. He refused to support Bacon's militia, and Bacon refused to have his militia disperse. Berkeley had Bacon arrested and then released him. Bacon marched his ragtag army of free Africans, slaves, and poor whites into Jamestown and set it on fire. In the face of the militia, Governor Berkeley fled, calling for help from England. The crown sent 1,000 English troops; it had no patience with rebels. Most rebels surrendered and were pardoned. In 1676, Bacon died at age 29 from dysentery. Twenty-three leaders of the short-lived rebellion were hanged. Virginia's poor had been crushed.

Bacon's Rebellion illustrates the complexity of American history. Berkeley was among the most overbearing aristocrats ever to govern a colony. During his more than 30 years as governor, he made evident his disrespect for the majority of people in his colony. Bacon's militia represented a racially diverse army of the dispossessed. But even as the rebels were demanding more equal treatment from Berkeley for themselves, they were also demanding the right to kill Indians indiscriminately and steal their land.

Bacon's Rebellion was a major turning point in the history of slavery in Virginia. Wealthy landowners now feared uprisings among current and former indentured servants, and they began to prefer slave labor, which they could more strongly control. Among the greatest losers in Virginia were the Native American tribes. While Bacon and his followers were defeated, the arrival of so many well-trained British troops reduced the power of the tribes to bargain. In 1677, the Indians of western Virginia ceded their remaining lands in the colony and moved west, continuing a process of "Indian removal" that would eventually span a continent.

3.2 **Quick Review** Identify two significant differences between the conflicts in New England and Virginia. How did the population and past events of each colony lead to the violence that occurred?

FRANCE TAKES CONTROL OF THE HEART OF A CONTINENT

3.3 Explain France's growing role and power in North America and its impact on English and Spanish colonies.

French explorers had been among the earliest Europeans to see much of the northern Atlantic coast of North America in the early 1500s. Little came of their discoveries, however, until a new European demand for beaver fur led French traders to set up trading outposts that became the permanent—if small—towns of Quebec and Montreal. During the long reign of King Louis XIV (r. 1643–1715), New France expanded from a tiny isolated community around Quebec to dominate the St. Lawrence River Valley. French communities were founded throughout the heartland of North America from Detroit and Chicago to New Orleans. By 1715, New France claimed far more of North America than either the English or Spanish (see Map 3-3).

Early French Settlement—Quebec, Montreal, and the Fur Trade

With the news that there seemed to be no way around North America, France, like England, lost interest in the land that Verrazano and Cartier had explored in the 1520s and 1530s. Later in the 1500s, however, a new trade emerged between Europeans and Native Americans to compete with the cod that had been the only North American resource of interest to most Europeans since before the days of Columbus. Beaver pelts were becoming popular for fur hats in Europe. Trade in beaver fur transformed the economies of both Europe and the tribes of North America as surely as the greed for gold and silver transformed South America. As tribes like the Montagnais and Hurons developed trading partnerships with the French, and the Iroquois with the English, trade and tribal warfare became more intense. Ancient rivalries among the Indians escalated as each tribe fought to control the supply of beaver furs that seemed in insatiable demand in Europe. While these tribes had long fought each other for honor, living space, and

MAP 3-3 France in the American Interior, 1670–1720. As this map shows, French exploration and claims to Montreal, the Saint Lawrence River Valley, the Great Lakes, and the Mississippi River all the way to the Gulf of Mexico gave it claim to the heart of North America but also completely encircled the English colonies on the Atlantic coast and challenged the Spanish for control of Texas.

captives, they now had European weapons, acquired through trades, that further fueled the warfare. For the first time, tribes seemed bent on annihilating their opponents. Even though the French and British fur traders preferred to make alliances with the Indians rather than enslave them, the results for many tribes were nevertheless disastrous.

The trade in beaver pelts also encouraged Europeans to make permanent settlements. Samuel de Champlain began exploring the St. Lawrence River in 1603 and founded the city of Quebec in 1608 as a representative of a private fur company—just 1 year after the English founded Jamestown. With only 28 men in his colony, Champlain knew that he needed alliances if Quebec was to succeed. So he joined the Montagnais and Hurons in a war against the Iroquois and solidified an alliance that would be the foundation of Quebec's trade. The Huron alliance also allowed Champlain to travel further west. He spent 1615–1616 exploring the Great Lakes.

After 1612, Champlain was also appointed as the king's viceroy for New France, uniting his commercial and governmental positions. As late as 1635, when Champlain died, Quebec had a population of only 300, but it was there to stay. Montreal was

This picture of Champlain and a group of Hurons attacking the Iroquois was published with Champlain's account of the battle. It is unlikely that Champlain was as heroic as the picture implies, or that there were any palm trees in what is now Canada.

settled in 1642 to expand trade. Jesuit missionaries arrived and lived among the Hurons learning their ways, and seeking to convert them to Catholic Christianity. New France, and the missions it sponsored, were as deeply Catholic as most of the English settlements were Protestant, fueling tensions between the French and English colonies that would last throughout their histories.

During the early 1600s, Quebec and Montreal were small French towns, thousands of miles from any other such town, but with their own European families, parishes, and culture. These isolated centers were surrounded by villages of French farmers who had decided to make a life in New France. New France came close to being wiped out in the late 1640s when the Iroquois Confederation overran Huron villages, torturing, killing, or taking prisoner everyone in sight. Jesuit missionaries died along with their Huron hosts. Once a nation of over 10,000 people, the Hurons disappeared as a recognizable group after 1648. The defeat of the Hurons was a huge blow to French missionaries and to the fur trade that was the economic anchor of New France.

The Iroquois also attacked French villages, and besieged Montreal itself. Two hundred French settlers were killed. Many more of the villagers left for France as quickly as they could. The future of New France was far from clear in 1650. Montreal and Quebec, however, remained militarily secure, and the Algonquians replaced the Hurons as the major French allies and the source of access to the fur trade.

Exploring and Claiming the Mississippi River Valley

In 1663, Louis XIV made New France into a royal province and sent 1,000 French soldiers to protect Quebec from Iroquois attack and establish it once and for all as the seat of what he expected to be a vast French empire. Plans were laid to make this expansion happen.

In 1672, Governor Louis de Frontenac sent Louis Joliet, who spoke a number of Indian languages, and Father Jacques Marquette, a Jesuit missionary, to find and explore a great waterway spoken of in Indian stories—the Mississippi (or *Mitchisipi*, "great water"), which he hoped might be the route to China. In June 1673, Marquette and Joliet paddled into the Mississippi, the first Europeans known to do so. Early in their trip, they were welcomed by the Illinois tribe and given a great feast. The encounter was the beginning of a long-term French-Indian alliance in the region.

Joliet and Marquette determined that the Mississippi flowed south into the Gulf of Mexico, not west to the Pacific and China as had been hoped. But they understood that they were in the midst of a land of great potential. They could develop a French colony that would allow a rich trade with the Indians and block the expansion of the English.

Fear of hostile tribes and of being captured by the Spanish led Joliet and Marquette to turn back before reaching the mouth of the Mississippi. On the return trip, they visited other Indian villages, including a Miami Indian village of *Checagou* or Chicago. Joliet returned to Quebec to report and draw maps of their travels. Marquette continued his missionary work until he died in 1675. What would, some two centuries later, become the Midwest of the United States was first described for Europeans and mapped by these two explorers. While the authorities in France wanted to strengthen the settlements in the St. Lawrence River Valley surrounding Montreal and Quebec before expanding further, Governor Frontenac had no patience with such caution. In young Robert de la Salle, he found a perfect ally for exploring the Mississippi Valley.

La Salle led a much larger expedition than that of Joliet and Marquette down the Illinois and Mississippi Rivers in 1679. La Salle's goals were to build an alliance with the Illinois and other tribes against the Iroquois and to establish a permanent French presence throughout the Mississippi Valley. In 1681–1682, he and his men traveled down the Mississippi to the Gulf of Mexico. In the name of King Louis XIV, he claimed "possession of this country of Louisiana," and of "the seas, harbors, ports, bays, adjacent straits, and all the nations, peoples, provinces, cities, towns, villages, mines, minerals, fisheries, streams, and rivers within it." It was a claim to more than one-third of North America.

Not content with reaching the mouth of the Mississippi, La Salle then continued as far west on the Gulf of Mexico as Texas. Eventually, he pushed his followers too hard, and some of them murdered him in 1687.

American Voices

Journal of the Voyage of Father Jacques Gravier, of the Society of Jesus [Jesuits], in 1700, from the Country of the Illinois to the Mouth of the Mississippi River

The Jesuit Relations *was a publication that gave regular reports on Jesuit missionary work and provided an extraordinary glimpse of the countryside and of the people who lived together along the Mississippi from modern-day Wisconsin to the Gulf of Mexico between the 1690s and the mid-1700s.*

I started in 1700, on the 8th of September, to come here.... I was accompanied by 5 Canoes manned by Frenchmen....We made only 4 leagues the 1st day, because one of our canoes was split by a snag hidden in the water, and we had to halt in order to repair it....I embarked in my Canoe to visit Monsieur Davion, a missionary priest, who was sick....In his mission, 3 different languages are spoken: the Iakou, with 30 Cabins; the Ounspik, with 10 or 12 Cabins, and the Toumika, who are in 7 hamlets, consisting in all of 50 or 60 small Cabins....

[Another] village is on the crest of a steep mountain, precipitous on all sides. There are 80 Cabins in it, and in the middle of the Village is a fine and very level open space, where from morning to night, young men exercise themselves. They run after a flat stone, which they throw in the air from one end of the square to the other, and try to Make it fall on two Cylinders, which they roll wherever they think the stone will fall. There is nothing fine about the temple except the Vestibule, which is embellished with the most pleasant and best executed grotesque figures that one can see....The Old man who keeps up the fire—the name of which, he told us, was *Louak ouloughé*—the "sacred fire."...

Since we have left the Natches, we have lived only on Indian corn with a few Squashes—For it is a long time since either wild oxen, Deer, or bears have been seen in this quarter; and if we have found a few bustards or wild geese, they have been so lean that they were as tasteless as wood. This has caused our Canoemen very often to sigh for the River of the Illinois, And the beauty of the country and of the landing-places; and for the numbers of wild oxen and Deer, and all Kinds of fat and excellent Game. The navigation of the Mississippi is very slow and tedious, and very difficult—especially in ascending it. It is also very troublesome on account of the gnats and other insects called Mosquitoes, midges, And black flies....At last, on the 17th of December, I reached fort Mississippi, after 68 Days of navigation in descending the river....The Commandant, Monsieur de Bienville, has there a small and very neat house.

Source: Reuben Gold Thwaites, editor, *Travels and Explorations of the Jesuit Missionaries in New France, 1610–1791*, Vol. LXV, *Lower Canada, Mississippi Valley, 1696–1702* (Cleveland: The Burrows Brothers, 1900), pp. 101–105, 127–129, 145–147, 159–161.

Thinking Critically

1. **Documentary Analysis**

   What kinds of communities did Father Gravier encounter on his journey?

2. **Historical Interpretation**

   What does Father Gravier's account suggest about the nature of French settlement along the Mississippi River in 1700?

Other French explorers and settlers followed in La Salle's wake. Working independently, French trappers and traders (known as *coureurs de bois* or "runners of the woods") established relationships with various Native American tribes and brought wealth back to New France. Some of them established a base called Fort Arkansas at the confluence of the Arkansas and Mississippi Rivers. French Jesuits built a mission at Chicago. In 1698, the Bishop of Quebec appointed missionary priests to a new mission at the Natchez Post on the Arkansas River. The French communities that dotted the Mississippi in the late 1600s and early 1700s were small. They included American Indians and French trappers, families, and missionaries. But they were there to stay.

Creating the French Gulf Coast—Biloxi, Mobile, and New Orleans

As a result of the reports from explorers and missionaries, Louis XIV decided to secure the French claim to the mouth of the Mississippi. Pierre d'Ibreville was commissioned in 1698 to scout the area.

D'Iberville landed on the east bank of the Mississippi River and built a fort near a Bilochi Indian settlement, which came to be called Biloxi. D'Iberville and his crew moved up the Mississippi River until they found a trail connecting the Mississippi to Lake Ponchartrain, and promised to return. To his surprise, d'Iberville also found a group of free blacks who were living with Indians and who did not take kindly to the arrival of Europeans.

Queen Anne's War of 1702–1713 (see Chapter 4) between England, France, and Spain made travel difficult and dangerous. With the coming of peace in 1713, d'Iberville's younger brother Jean-Baptiste de Bienville expanded the colony. When a veteran of LaSalle's trip down the Mississippi arrived in the area in 1713, d'Iberville gave the intrepid French explorer command of another French city on the Gulf coast, which they named La Mobile (now Mobile, Alabama).

In 1718, de Bienville built a colony that he called New Orleans on the land between the Mississippi and Lake Pontchartrain. New Orleans appeared on French maps, and stock was sold to develop it, well before any town existed. In March and April 1718, Bienville led some 50 men in tearing out cypress swamps and laying out a town on the crescent turn in the Mississippi River. After a hurricane destroyed the village in 1722, a new street grid was laid out—the French Quarter for which New Orleans is famous today.

The only contact the residents of New Orleans had with France was the occasional arrival of supply ships. Few volunteers moved to this isolated spot, even though French speculators, led by John Law, the most powerful banker in France, invested

A French visitor to New Orleans painted this view of Illinois Indians engaged in trade with the Europeans in 1735. Note that one of the tribe is most likely an escaped African slave.

heavily in the New Orleans venture and were desperate for the new colony to succeed. Most of the early immigrants from France were prostitutes and criminals who literally left France in chains. Many died in transit, but by 1721, New Orleans had 178 European residents who enjoyed the freedom their isolation gave them.

The French also introduced African slavery into the Mississippi Valley. While there had been slaves in Quebec, none of the early explorers coming south from Canada brought African slaves with them. But after 1700, slavery grew in French Louisiana. The first slave ships arrived in New Orleans in 1719. In 1721, ships brought 925 slaves from Haiti. A census in 1732 indicated that, of the 471 people living in the French towns in the Illinois River country, 168 were Africans.

Most slaves brought to New Orleans were from Senegal in West Africa. These Africans, if not Muslim themselves, were familiar with Islam and Muslim music that used chanting accompanied by stringed instruments. This music became part of the culture of New Orleans. The Senegalese also knew how to cultivate indigo, which thrived in Louisiana, and how to process it into dye. In addition, early slave ships brought sugar and rice, which the slaves also knew how to grow. Europe and Africa had been shaping each other's cultures for generations by the time New Orleans was founded, but the mix was especially deep in that city. With the French securely in control of both the headwaters and the mouth of the Mississippi River, France was in a strong position to be the dominant European power in North America, just as Spain was dominant further south.

> **3.3** **Quick Review** How did France's role in North America evolve from small settlements in Canada to become the "dominant European power"? Justify your answer.

DEVELOPMENTS IN SPANISH COLONIES NORTH OF MEXICO

3.4 Analyze the impact of Indian uprisings and the expansion of other European powers on Spain's colonies in New Mexico, Texas, and California.

Spain had established the first permanent settlements in the future United States— Florida in 1565 and New Mexico in 1598. Both remained isolated, but while St. Augustine, Florida, remained small, Spain claimed vast lands in New Mexico surrounding the new capital they built at Santa Fe in 1610. From Santa Fe, which was close to many of the Indian pueblos over which Spain claimed authority, the Spanish ruled with an iron hand, demanding more and more work from the Indians and trying to stamp out traditional Indian religious practices. For many years, the Spanish seemed to accomplish their goals, but eventually, to the surprise of the Spanish, the result was a large-scale rebellion. While the Spanish authorities reasserted their presence in New Mexico, they also worried about the territorial claims that England and France were making to other parts of North America. To counter those claims, the government of New Spain established small but permanent colonies across the Southwest from Texas to California (see Map 3-4).

The Pueblo Revolt—New Mexico, 1680

In August 1680, an uprising of the normally peaceful Pueblo Indians of northern New Mexico led by a charismatic leader, Popé, resulted in the greatest defeat of a European colony in the history of the Americas. In the **Pueblo Revolt**, nearly all of the Spanish who lived on isolated ranches and farms were killed. Survivors from the outlying communities poured into Santa Fe, which was then besieged. The Indians cut the city's water supply and burned outlying buildings. On August 21, Governor Antonio de Otermin decided to retreat to Mexico with the survivors.

During the retreat, one Indian told Otermin that the revolt happened because his people were "tired of the work they had to do for the Spaniards and the clergy [who] did not allow them to plant, to do other things for their own needs." Another old man

Pueblo Revolt
Rebellion in 1680 of Pueblo Indians in New Mexico against their Spanish overlords, sparked by Spanish suppression of native religious activity and excessive Spanish demands for Indian labor.

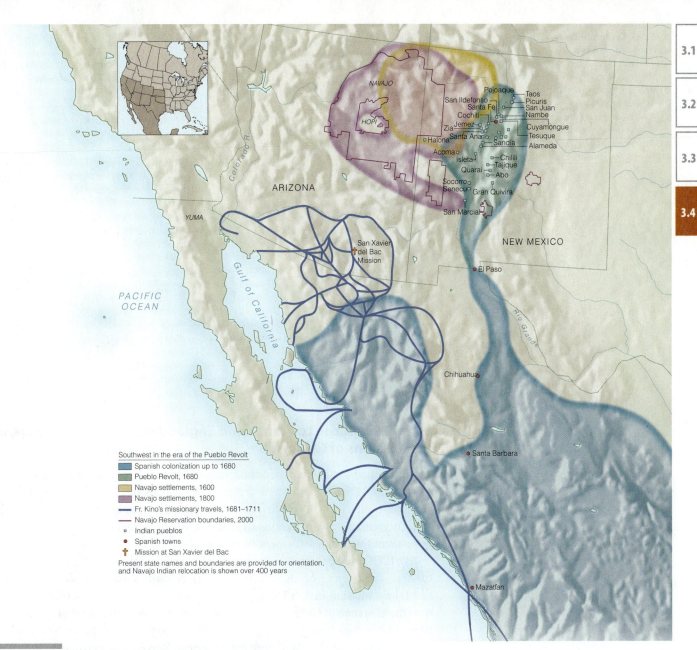

MAP 3-4 Changes in the Southwest. The heart of Spain's empire in the Americas always remained south of the future United States in Mexico and Peru. However, by the 1600s authorities based in Mexico had authorized the development of an important Spanish colony in territory they called New Mexico, among the Pueblo Indians in the area around Santa Fe and Taos. Spanish settlers also established a mission near the future Tucson, Arizona, though it would be after 1700 before there was Spanish settlement in Texas or California.

told the governor that it was because the Spaniards had tried to take away "the ways of their ancestors, the faith by which they have lived and thrived." Both of these grievances—the harsh workloads and religious repression—were crucial in fueling the revolt, as was hope that life might return to a happier day before the Spanish arrived.

After the success of the revolt, Indian leaders lived in the governor's mansion in Santa Fe. Churches were leveled, statues destroyed. Pueblo life returned more or less to what it had been before 1598. The distant and defeated Spanish were mocked.

The Spanish eventually regained control of New Mexico, but it took 12 years. Nowhere else in the Americas, not even among the powerful Aztecs and Incas, was a revolt so successful or long lasting. In 1690, the Spanish viceroy in Mexico City appointed a new governor for New Mexico, Don Diego de Vargas, who had an ability to compromise that many of his predecessors had lacked. Vargas left El Paso with his army in 1692. He offered each pueblo a full pardon in exchange for their reconversion to Christianity, but he did not try to stamp out tribal religion. The Indians could retain both faiths and agreed to his terms.

3.1

3.2

3.3

3.4

MAP 3-5 California Missions. Once they had founded San Diego in 1769, the Spanish authorities in Mexico commissioned a Franciscan priest, Father Junipero Serra, to create a string of missions along the Pacific Coast of what they called Alta (or upper) California. Serra and his successors created these missions as far north as San Francisco, the farthest northern reach of Spanish settlement into the Americas.

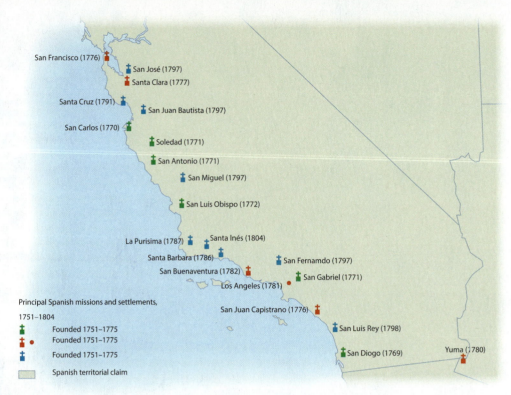

San Francisco (1776)

San José (1797)

Santa Clara (1777)

Santa Cruz (1791)

San Juan Bautista (1797)

San Carlos (1770)

Soledad (1771)

San Antonio (1771)

San Miguel (1797)

San Luis Obispo (1772)

La Purisima (1787)   Santa Inés (1804)

Santa Barbara (1786)

San Fernamdo (1797)

San Buenaventura (1782)

San Gabriel (1771)

Los Angeles (1781)

San Juan Capistrano (1776)

San Luis Rey (1798)

San Diogo (1769)

Yuma (1780)

Principal Spanish missions and settlements, 1751–1804

Founded 1751–1775

Founded 1751–1775

Founded 1751–1775

Spanish territorial claim

Spain's Response to France and England—San Antonio, Texas, and the Missions of California

Word that La Salle had claimed the coast of Texas for France frightened authorities in New Spain. When the French founded New Orleans in 1718, the Spanish decided to act. They built a new city of their own, San Antonio, to assert their claims to Texas. San Antonio remained a small and isolated outpost of a great empire, but it was the first permanent European settlement in present-day Texas.

By 1769, the Spanish were also worried about English explorations and Russian fur-trading activities on the Pacific coast. In response, the Spanish established a fort and then a mission in San Diego, the first permanent European settlement in what is now the U.S. state of California. From there, Spanish Franciscan missionaries created a string of missions from San Diego to San Francisco to convert the Indians and develop the economy of California. Before the American Revolution, permanent Spanish communities could be found on the Atlantic Coast in Florida, in Texas and New Mexico, and on the Pacific Coast in California (see Map 3-5). It would be many more years before any of these were much more than small dusty outposts. Nevertheless, they were the foundation for the much more extensive settlement that would follow.

3.4   **Quick Review** Why was Spain so concerned about English and French colonization?

CONCLUSION

The nations of Europe showed little interest in establishing settlements north of Mexico until the early 1600s. The coast of what is now the United States served as little more than a way station for cod fishermen throughout all of the 1500s. After Richard Hackluyt published his *Pamphlet for the Virginia Enterprise* in 1585, some English investors began to take a second look and see the merit of establishing colonies in North America not only to trade with the Indians but also to Christianize them and enlist them as an ally against England's rival Spain. The first successful English colony was established at Jamestown, Virginia, in 1607. The colony would not have lasted without the leadership of the English adventurer John Smith or the assistance of

Powhatan, an Algonquian chief, who saw an advantage in establishing trade with the English and using them as allies against other Indian tribes.

Unlike Jamestown, which had been established as a commercial enterprise by the Virginia Company, the colonies in the areas of present-day New England were established as refuges for England's persecuted and restive religious nonconformists, including the Puritans and Pilgrims, who founded colonies in Plymouth and Boston in Massachusetts. Soon, dissenters from these colonies founded their own new English colonies in Connecticut and Rhode Island.

The New England colonies coexisted for some time with nearby Indian groups. However, unlike the French and Spanish colonists, very little intermarriage took place, which might have increased the degree of animosity that soon developed as the New England colonies grew in size and encroached on Indian lands. This hostility ultimately led to King Philip's War in the 1670s, in which the English colonists destroyed Indian settlements, ending the era of coexistence that some in the first generation had enjoyed. While King Philip's War was being fought in New England, a different kind of violence engulfed the Virginia colony. White immigrants, mostly poor people, living at a distance from the coast, made alliances with Africans, slave and free, in attacks on the nearby Native American tribes. These allied groups also attacked the royal government based on the Atlantic coast, which sought peaceful relationship with the Indian tribes as a way of preserving the colony. The revolt was soon defeated, but it resulted in the expulsion of most tribes from Virginia as well as a decision by the authorities to limit the immigration of poor whites and rely more on African slave labor in the colony.

After the establishment of Virginia and the New England colonies, other English colonies became established in quick succession. Maryland became a haven for Catholics, who were also being persecuted in England. Carolina began to expand production of rice and tobacco. New York was acquired from the Dutch, and New Jersey split off of New York. Pennsylvania was established initially for the Quakers, and Delaware eventually split from that colony. Finally, Georgia was founded, thus establishing England's 13 colonies on the mainland of North America.

All of the English colonies permitted slavery of Africans and American Indians, and slaves were found in all of the English colonies on the North American mainland and in even greater numbers on the English-controlled islands of the Caribbean. However, during most of the 1600s, slaves worked and lived alongside—and even rebelled with—white indentured servants and members of the white lower classes. Some slaves were even able to farm their own land, and in some cases earn their freedom—something that would be much more difficult to achieve after 1700.

Meanwhile, as England monitored its colonies, France and Spain had claimed control over much of the rest of North America. New France claimed not only vast areas surrounding Quebec but also a huge slice of the interior along the entire length of the Mississippi River down to New Orleans. New Spain expanded into the Southwest of the future United States from Texas to California. New France and New Spain exploited their territories and related to Indians in far different ways. French explorers along with Jesuit missionaries created small settlements and expanded the fur trade throughout their vast territory. Spain also created settlements in their region and sent priests to live with many of the tribes. In one case, however, Spanish efforts to subjugate the Indians of New Mexico led to the Pueblo Revolt of 1680. In spite of revolts, wars, and tensions, however, by the end of the 1600s, settlements established by England, France, and Spain dotted the land that would one day be the United States. Individual colonies might prosper or fail, but the territory that most Europeans had ignored for a hundred years after Columbus was slowly becoming a permanent home to generations of European immigrants and the African peoples they brought with them.

CHAPTER REVIEW How did the English, French, and Spanish interaction with American Indians and Africans differ? Identify two reasons for this difference in relations, and explain your choices.

THE ENGLISH SETTLE IN NORTH AMERICA

3.1 Explain why the English began to settle in North America and how slavery was introduced in the English colonies.

Review Questions

1. **Chronological Reasoning**
   How and why did the relationship between the Jamestown colonists and the local Indians change during the settlement's first two decades?

2. **Contextualization**
   What kind of society did the Puritans of Massachusetts hope to establish? In this context, why did North America seem like a good place to settle?

3. **Historical Interpretation**
   What was the nature of slavery in British North America before the 1680s?

ENGLAND'S WARS, ENGLAND'S COLONIES

3.2 Analyze the relationship between politics in England, internal colonial tensions, and life in the English colonies in North America during the 1600s.

Review Questions

4. **Historical Interpretation**
   How did civil war in England shape the development of British North America?

5. **Comparison**
   Compare and contrast Maryland, New York, and Pennsylvania in the 1600s. How would you explain the differences you note?

6. **Crafting an Argument**
   Why did friendly relations collapse between Indians and colonists in New England during the 1600s?

FRANCE TAKES CONTROL OF THE HEART OF A CONTINENT

3.3 Explain France's growing role and power in North America and its impact on English and Spanish colonies.

Review Questions

7. **Historical Interpretation**
   How did the fur trade reshape relations between the Indian peoples who participated in it?

8. **Comparison**
   Compare and contrast Anglo-Indian and Franco-Indian relations. How would you explain the differences you note?

DEVELOPMENTS IN SPANISH COLONIES NORTH OF MEXICO

3.4 Analyze the impact of Indian uprisings and the expansion of other European powers on Spain's colonies in New Mexico, Texas, and California.

Review Question

9. **Crafting an Argument**
   What role did religion play in the Pueblo Revolt?

Creating the Culture of British North America

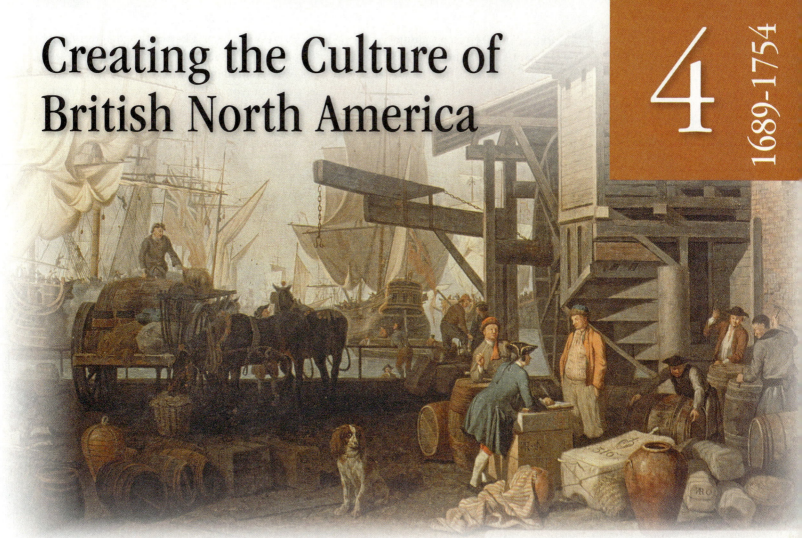

Raw materials, most of which were produced with slave labor from Britain's colonies in North America and the Caribbean, were bringing great wealth to the nation as illustrated in this picture of sailing ships from North America unloading at London's Old Custom House dock.

I n 1733 a young apprentice, John Peter Zenger, was hired to start a new newspaper in New York, the *New York Weekly Journal*. Newspapers, though long popular in England, were still fairly new in British North America. The first regularly published colonial newspaper, *The Boston News-Letter,* began publication in 1704, but it was subsidized by the British government. Later newspapers, including James Franklin's *New England Courant* that began publication in 1722, were more independent. The *Journal*'s New York backers were part of a political faction in the colony that opposed Royal Governor William Cosby. Zenger quickly began printing stories about official corruption and government actions he considered to be dictatorial. Within a year, he was indicted for printing seditious libel. British law at the time made it a crime to print attacks on public officials that challenged their authority—whether the articles were false or true—and Zenger had clearly printed attacks on Governor Cosby. But Zenger and his backers fought back, defending themselves in court.

In a well-publicized trial that lasted into 1735, Zenger's attorney argued for rights of speech and the press that far exceeded what then existed in Britain. He asked the jury, "Shall the press be silenced that evil governors may have their way?" The trial, the attorney said, was not about Zenger but "every free man that lives under a British government on the main of America." The jury acquitted Zenger in spite of the law.

4

1689-1754

CHAPTER OBJECTIVE

Demonstrate an understanding of how local and global developments shaped the lives and thoughts of those residing in British North America from the Glorious Revolution to the beginnings of the American Revolution.

LEARNING OBJECTIVES

ENGLAND'S GLORIOUS REVOLUTION AND "THE RIGHTS OF ENGLISHMEN," 1689

Analyze the impact of England's Glorious Revolution on the thinking and political organization of British colonists in North America.
4.1

THE PLANTATION WORLD: FROM A SOCIETY WITH SLAVES TO A SLAVE SOCIETY

Explain why and how slavery developed as it did in the late 1600s and early 1700s.
4.2

STABILITY AND INSTABILITY IN THE AMERICAN AND BRITISH WORLDS

Analyze the changes in the ideas and daily lives of the people in British North America in the 1700s as a result of events within and beyond the colonies.
4.3

The *New England Courant*, one of the early colonial newspapers, was published from 1722 to 1726, but both its publisher James Franklin and his younger brother Benjamin continued to publish newspapers in the 1720s and 1730s.

Glorious Revolution

Bloodless revolt that occurred in England in 1688 when parliamentary leaders invited William of Orange, a Protestant, and his wife Mary, the daughter of King James II, to assume the English throne in place of James II.

Zenger's acquittal has been celebrated ever since as a key victory for freedom of speech and freedom of the press. In part it *was* a victory. Zenger was free to keep up his critique, and other publishers were emboldened by the result. On the other hand, the laws against seditious libel were not repealed, and every editor of Zenger's day knew that there was a danger of arrest and trial before a jury that might not be as sympathetic as the one Zenger faced. Nevertheless, by the 1730s, there were more than 20 newspapers being printed in the North American colonies, and the majority included not only critiques of royal governors and colonial governments but also republished articles from the English press demanding freedom and calling attention to what they called "the rights of Englishmen." These newspapers also published news from other colonies and began to create a stronger sense of unity among Americans—a name that residents of the British colonies were starting to call themselves.

The defense of freedoms that Zenger and his attorneys considered basic to their rights as residents of the British colonies clearly reflects the views of a growing number of English inhabitants of North America at the time. The great divisions over religious and political authority, which had created turmoil and uprisings in England and in the colonies, were receding into the dim past. In spite of numerous new tensions, many who lived in America between 1690 and 1760 were feeling a strong sense of pride in being British—enjoying the prosperity that the British Empire was creating and appreciating an elected Parliament that was playing a dominant role in asserting individual liberties. However that pride in British institutions and British rights slowly changed as some colonists began to shift their loyalties. Over time, many came to distrust the British government as protector of their rights and began to talk of a way to separate from that government and protect their own rights as colonists. Understanding that shift is key to understanding the decades before the American Revolution.

ENGLAND'S GLORIOUS REVOLUTION AND "THE RIGHTS OF ENGLISHMEN," 1689

4.1 Analyze the impact of England's Glorious Revolution on the thinking and political organization of British colonists in North America.

The 25 years between 1675 and 1700 were times of turmoil in England and its North American colonies. A little more than a decade after King Philip's War and Bacon's Rebellion convulsed the colonies, the English Parliament came to distrust King James II who they believed was centralizing too much authority and who they suspected of privately supporting Catholicism. They ousted him in 1689 in what was known as the **Glorious Revolution**. For many in England and its colonies, it was an exciting time, an assertion of "the rights of Englishmen" and the authority of elected assemblies to control their destiny. Initially, news of the overthrow of James II brought rebellions in many of the colonies. Royal governors were arrested, and popular assemblies demanded new authority, just as Parliament had done in London. Soon enough, a new English government asserted its authority in colonial matters. In the process, a new sense of rights had been created on both sides of the Atlantic Ocean.

Parliament's Decision to "Elect" a New King and Queen

King James II (r. 1685–1688), who came to the English throne at the death of his brother Charles II, was a Catholic, even though he was officially the head of the Protestant Church of England. As he expanded religious freedoms for Catholics and appointed some to high office, his moves aroused serious opposition in Britain's Protestant majority, many of whom associated Protestantism with British independence and Catholicism with foreign domination, especially by the Spanish and French.

James also wanted to assert royal authority, especially in England's increasingly independent colonies. He appointed a single royal governor, Sir Edmund Andros, over a newly designated Dominion of New England, which comprised Plymouth, Massachusetts, New Hampshire, Connecticut, Rhode Island, as well as New York and New Jersey. He also abolished most of the local autonomy that the colonies had enjoyed.

The colonists resented the unwanted merger of their colonies as well as the new king and governor who were enforcing it, but they could do little about it. However, in England, Parliament turned against James II. Rather than risk losing his head like his father, James fled the country. Parliament invited James's Protestant daughter, Mary, and her husband Prince William of Orange, rulers of the Netherlands, to come to England as joint sovereigns. This move by Parliament was a dramatic change that would have far-reaching effects. The concept of the **divine right of kings**, by which the sovereign—good or bad—inherited the throne from the previous sovereign and ruled with unquestioned authority, was already in decline. But now, Parliament had decided not only to limit royal authority but also to take some control over the choice of a king or queen themselves.

To justify the ouster of one king and the virtual election of new monarchs, English people had to rethink how they understood themselves and their system of government. Kings and queens retained power after 1689, but their supremacy was now bound by law. After 1689, it was clear that Parliament, as representative of the people, was a deciding force in England.

John Locke—Defending the Right to Revolution

The most famous English philosopher at the time of the Glorious Revolution, John Locke, justified the revolution by insisting that all government rested on the **natural rights** of the governed. This concept was a novel idea in 1689, but Locke, who was living in exile in Holland because of his opposition to James's rule, wrote that humans were born free in a state of nature and only agreed to a social compact when it suited their purposes. If the people no longer agreed, then monarchs had no right to continue to rule. The basic "rights of all Englishmen" to accept or reject their government came to be the dominant political ideology of the English nation—as it then existed on both sides of the Atlantic.

In his *Second Treatise on Government*, Locke described civil society as a social contract made by free people to live together, but one in which everyone retained "his natural freedom, without being subjected to the will or authority of any other man." Neither kings nor Parliament were supreme. The people were. Locke insisted, "There remains still in the people a supreme power to remove or alter the legislative [power] when they find the legislative act contrary to the trust reposed in them." Locke's revolutionary ideas helped justify the Glorious Revolution of 1689. A hundred years later, his ideas would be cited often in North America.

North American Responses

In England's American colonies, news of the Glorious Revolution brought rejoicing. In New England, the colonists arrested Governor Andros and sent him back to England, though he later returned as Governor of Virginia. The new monarchs, William and Mary, allowed the New England colonies to return to their former separate existences. However, when the king and queen reestablished the governments of Massachusetts and Connecticut, they included a clause in the royal charters granting "liberty of conscience" to all Protestants—but not Catholics. Baptists, Anglicans, and others were now free to build their own churches and worship as they wished. Some Puritans protested against this "tolerance for error," as they called allowing other churches to conduct their own services, but the rules stuck in spite of their protests.

Significant Dates

1662	Halfway Covenant in Massachusetts
1689	The Glorious Revolution, James II replaced by William and Mary
1692	Salem witch trials
1701–1713	Queen Anne's War
1704	Mohawk Indians destroy Deerfield, Massachusetts
	Esther Williams taken hostage
	First regular colonial newspaper begins publication in Boston
1707	Act of Union between England and Scotland
1715–1716	Yamasee War in South Carolina
1721	First smallpox inoculations advocated by Cotton Mather and administered in Boston
1730s	Jonathan Edwards leads religious revivals
1732	Georgia established
	Benjamin Franklin begins publication of *Poor Richard's Almanack*
1734	Beginning of First Great Awakening
1735	John Peter Zenger acquitted in trial for libel
1739	Stono slave rebellion in South Carolina
1739	War of Jenkins' Ear between England and Spain in the Caribbean
1741	Slave conspiracy in New York City
1744–1748	King George's War between Britain and France
1754	Albany Plan of Union advocates unifying the colonies for war with France

divine right of kings
A belief that the king—or queen—was selected by God through birth in the royal family and that it was irreligious to question either a monarch's fitness to serve or a monarch's decisions. During the 1600s, England overthrew two monarchs, and afterwards, few still held such a belief.

natural rights
Political philosophy that maintains that individuals have an inherent right, found in nature and preceding any government or written law, to life and liberty.

Other Protestants were free to build churches—at their own expense—and worship freely, but everyone paid taxes to support the Congregationalists, and Catholic worship was not allowed in New England.

In New York, news of the change in England brought a general uprising. Those on the bottom of the social order—merchants, dockworkers, and traders—seized power under the leadership of a German immigrant, Jacob Leisler. Leisler held power for 2 years, but when he was slow in ceding power to the new royal governor appointed by William and Mary, he was arrested and executed for treason. However, those loyal to Leisler remained a faction in New York politics for a generation to come.

In Maryland, there was also an uprising. The Catholic proprietor was driven from office and lost ownership of the colony. Maryland became a royal colony with a governor appointed by the king and queen, and the Anglican Church of England became the colony's official church. After the Glorious Revolution, Maryland, a colony that had been chartered in 1632 to protect Catholics, excluded Catholics from public office.

In the Americas, the Glorious Revolution produced winners and losers. After 1689, independent corporations like the Virginia Company and the Massachusetts Company, as well as colonial proprietors like Lord Baltimore or William Penn, faced a decline in power. Catholics in England and Maryland lost hard-won political rights as the new monarchs asserted England's status as a Protestant nation. All Protestants gained rights, and Protestant men who had been excluded from the voting lists because they belonged to a dissenting religious group could now vote. Elected legislatures (elected by landowning white males) competed with royal governors to make the laws governing each colony. In all the colonies, changing one's social and economic status was becoming more difficult. An English colonial elite, supported by English military authority, now dominated colonial life. The British communities became larger, more secure, and wealthier.

> **4.1** **Quick Review** 1. How do the colonists' reactions to the Glorious Revolution reflect their sense of connection to ideas and events in England?
> 2. Based on what you read, for whom in the British colonies did the Glorious Revolution have a positive effect? A negative effect?

THE PLANTATION WORLD: FROM A SOCIETY WITH SLAVES TO A SLAVE SOCIETY

4.2 Explain why and how slavery developed as it did in the late 1600s and early 1700s.

Amid all the talk of "the rights of Englishmen," one group of North American residents lost rights after the 1680s—African slaves. All of the British colonies had slaves in the late 1600s, but the institution of slavery changed most dramatically in the southern colonies—Maryland, Virginia, and soon also the Carolinas. Bacon's Rebellion brought great changes to Virginia and its neighbor Maryland after 1676. Once the planter elite had defeated Bacon's ragtag militia, they quickly consolidated their power. They did not want another rebellion like the one they had just lived through in which poor whites allied with Africans, slave and free. Having decided that slaves would make better and more dependable workers than indentured servants, this planter elite wrote new slave codes that more clearly made slavery an inherited and permanent status. They also imported many more African slaves and reduced the numbers of English indentured servants allowed into these colonies. Historian Ira Berlin described this shift: "A society with slaves gave way to a slave society." It was a significant change—from a society in which slavery existed to a society in which the institution of slavery dominated all aspects of society—particularly for those who were enslaved. Although this shift began in Virginia and Maryland, its effects would eventually extend to other southern colonies.

Seeking Stability by Creating a Slave Society

As the institution of slavery came to be more rigidly defined, it also came to be linked more closely to race. Africans were seen as slaves. Europeans—even the poorest Europeans—were seen as free. More and more Indians were simply excluded from the colonies. Those Africans who had already achieved their freedom, and those few who did so during the 1700s, lived in a dangerous world. While Anthony Johnson had moved from slavery to freedom and prosperity in the Virginia of the mid-1600s (see Chapter 3), his children and grandchildren fled from Virginia in the late 1600s to avoid the risks of slavery, some of them living with the Nanticoke Indians in a small community of African, European, and American Indian origin.

Children of mixed race were marginalized or simply declared to be African slaves. Any child born to a black woman was automatically considered to be African even if, as was often the case, the father was a European slave owner. But mixed-race children born to white mothers were more problematic to marginalize or cast into slavery, so stringent efforts were made to prohibit sexual liaisons between white women and males of other races.

While there were slaves in all of England's North American colonies, as slavery became institutionalized, the numbers of African slaves in the southern colonies rose dramatically. In the 1680s, approximately 2,000 Africans were shipped to Virginia. Between 1700 and 1710, approximately 8,000 arrived. In 1668, white indentured servants outnumbered African slaves by five to one, and there were about equal numbers of Indian and African slaves. By 1700, nearly all tobacco and rice workers in Virginia and the Carolinas were African slaves (see Map 4-1).

The Atlantic Slave Trade, the Middle Passage, and the Nature of Colonial Slavery

North American slavery was always a relatively small part of the Atlantic slave trade. The sugar plantations of the Caribbean, Brazil, and New Spain needed many more slaves—and slaves there died much more quickly—so there was a constant flow of slaves to islands controlled by the English, French, Dutch, Danish, and Spanish and to the South American mainland. Some 10–15 million Africans were forced across the Atlantic between 1500 and 1900, but only a fraction came to the mainland British colonies (see Map 4-2).

As economic developments in all of North and South America came to depend more and more on slavery, the hunt for slaves went deeper and deeper into the African continent, leading to slave coffles—as they were known—in which newly captured people were marched hundreds of miles to the coast for transport across the Atlantic in numbers never before seen.

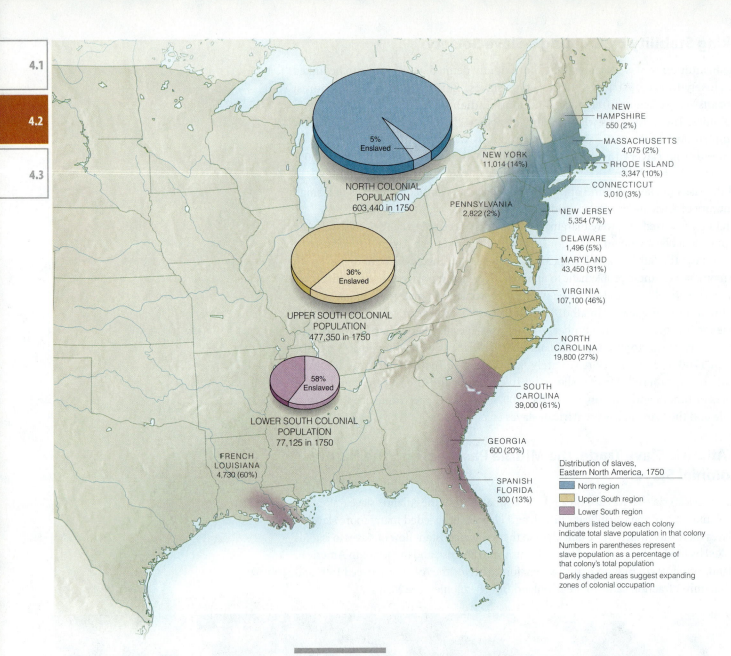

NORTH COLONIAL
POPULATION
603,440 in 1750

5%
Enslaved

UPPER SOUTH COLONIAL
POPULATION
477,350 in 1750

36%
Enslaved

LOWER SOUTH COLONIAL
POPULATION
77,125 in 1750

58%
Enslaved

FRENCH
LOUISIANA
4,730 (60%)

NEW
HAMPSHIRE
550 (2%)

MASSACHUSETTS
4,075 (2%)

RHODE ISLAND
3,347 (10%)

CONNECTICUT
3,010 (3%)

NEW JERSEY
5,354 (7%)

DELAWARE
1,496 (5%)

MARYLAND
43,450 (31%)

VIRGINIA
107,100 (46%)

NORTH
CAROLINA
19,800 (27%)

SOUTH
CAROLINA
39,000 (61%)

GEORGIA
600 (20%)

SPANISH
FLORIDA
300 (13%)

NEW YORK
11,014 (14%)

PENNSYLVANIA
2,822 (2%)

Distribution of slaves,
Eastern North America, 1750

- North region
- Upper South region
- Lower South region

Numbers listed below each colony
indicate total slave population in that colony

Numbers in parentheses represent
slave population as a percentage of
that colony's total population

Darkly shaded areas suggest expanding
zones of colonial occupation

MAP 4-1 Enslaved People in British North America in 1750. Between 1700 and 1750 there were grow-ing numbers of slaves in all 13 of the mainland British colonies in North America but hardly in equal num-bers. By 1750 the percentage of slaves in most of New England was 2–3% of the population, while in Rhode Island and New York—the northern colonies with the most slaves—they represented 10–14%. But there was a much higher proportion of slaves in the southern colonies ranging from 27% of the population of North Carolina to 61% of the population of South Carolina.

New states in West Africa—Asante, Dahomey, and Oyo—emerged along the African coast, fueled by the transfer of slaves from the interior of Africa to the coast for sale and shipment to the Americas. Some African states such as Benin refused to engage in the slave trade. But those that did grew rich as the slave trade grew rapidly. What had been a limited, if brutal, business now seemed to have no limit. For most West Africans, the huge growth of the African slave trade was a disaster. In addition to the warfare and fear among Africans that the slave trade inspired, the continent lost millions of people, which sapped its strength.

Once slaves arrived on the African coast, they were kept naked in cramped quar-ters in what were called slave factories. They were fed only bread and water. Those found to be fit were "marked on the breast, with a red-hot iron, imprinting the mark

Middle Passage

The horrendous voyage in which slaves were taken from West Africa to slave colonies in the Americas during which as many as a quarter died.

of the French, English, or Dutch companies, that so each nation may distinguish their own." Sorted and branded, the slaves were held for sale to ship captains who would take them across the Atlantic.

The **Middle Passage**—the transit of slaves from Africa to the Americas—was a horrifying experience. One slave ship captain said that slaves were packed "like books upon a shelf…so close that the shelf would not easily contain one more" up to 400 on a ship. Men were chained shoulder to shoulder. Women were generally not chained but packed just as tightly for a voyage that took 7 weeks in a filthy ship's hold that stank of human waste. The rate of disease was high: 25 percent of slaves died on the voyage. Slaves were force fed to reduce the loss of valuable cargo to starvation. One slave trader noted the tendency of slaves "to revolt aboard ships." Slaves would, he said, "watch all opportunities to deliver themselves, by assaulting a ship's crew, and murdering them all." Slaving was a dangerous and dirty but profitable business.

The first generation of slaves in North America, those arriving in the early 1600s, came from the coast of West Africa. They were familiar, at least in a general way, with each other and with European culture and languages since Europeans had been trading along the coast for more than 100 years. Those who arrived later often had been captured much further inland. They knew little about European ways or about each other.

The first generation of slaves were allowed some dignity, but by the late 1600s, every effort was made to rob slaves of their self-respect. Slaves were inspected like animals by those who bought and sold them. Masters used names as part of an effort to break the slaves' spirits. New slaves were named Jack or Sukey or Jumper or Hercules. Slave marriages were not recognized by law, and a master could sell husband away from wife or children from parents.

Olaudah Equiano was born around 1745. According to his autobiography, he was captured when he was 11 years old, shipped to America, and put to work first as a domestic servant in Virginia and then aboard a ship. He had much better luck than most slaves, eventually purchasing his freedom and writing a description of his experiences that became an early tract for the budding antislavery movement. He reported what it meant to be taken onboard a slave ship on the coast of Africa:

> I was soon put down under the decks, and there I received such a salutation in my nostrils as I had never experienced in my life: so that, with the loathsomeness of the stench, and crying together, I became so sick and low that I was not able to eat, nor had I the least desire to taste anything. I now wished for the last friend, death, to relieve me; but soon, to my grief, two of the white men offered me eatables; and, on my refusing to eat, one of them held me fast by the hands, and laid me across I think the windlass, and tied my feet, while the other flogged me severely.

Millions of other Africans suffered the same experiences but never achieved the freedom that Equiano did.

Most Africans, especially those imported into the southern colonies after the 1680s, faced a lifetime of slavery on a tobacco, cotton, or rice plantation. Their difficult lives were not long ones. Until the mid-1700s, one-quarter of newly arrived slaves died within a year. Young children often worked in the fields alongside adults, and the labor for women and men was backbreaking from sunup to sundown. The law gave plantation owners a free hand in how they treated their slaves. Slaves were whipped, branded, tortured, and executed for the smallest infractions to warn

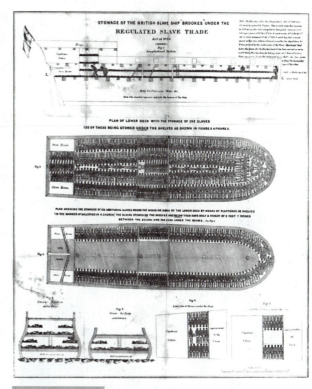

This sketch of the inside of a slave ship and the chart showing British rules for the slave trade, shows how tightly slaves were packed for the horrendous Middle Passage from Africa to the Americas. Not surprisingly a quarter of the slaves often died on the voyage, and survivors never forgot the trauma.

According to his popular autobiography, Olaudah Equiano was captured in Nigeria in 1756 when he was 11 years old, sold into slavery, and unlike the vast majority of slaves of his generation, eventually was able to purchase his freedom and rise to prosperity. *The Interesting Narrative of the Life of Olaudah Equiano*, which he wrote, was published in 1789 and became an important antislavery tract that provided a firsthand account of the experience of slavery.

ATLANTIC
OCEAN

NORTH AMERICA

4% Chesapeake

15%
11%
16%
38%
16%

Origin of Africans, 1700–1800
- Senegambia
- Windward Coast
- Gold Coast
- Bight of Benin
- Bight of Biafra
- West Central Africa
- Mozambique

23%
18%
40%
7% 9%
3%   Carolinas

Over 5,800,000
Africans arrived
in the Americas
(1700–1800)

The Atlantic Slave Trade during the 18th Century

9%
25%
25%
1%
3% 18% 19%

Africans reaching the New World, 1700–1800
- British North America (522,400)
- British Caribbean (1,439,500)
- Spanish Americas (1,114,460)
- French Americas (1,044,800)
- Dutch Americas (208,960)
- Danish Americas (46,450)
- Portuguese Brazil (1,427,900)

SOUTH AMERICA

PACIFIC
OCEAN

**MAP 4-2 Origin and Destinations of Enslaved
Africans, 1700–1800.** This map shows not only
the places of origin in Africa for most of the slaves
transported across the Atlantic between 1700 and
1800 but also their destinations in the Americas.
While perhaps half a million humans were sold
into slavery in British North America, almost three
times as many people were sold into the British
Caribbean colonies and an equal number to
Portuguese Brazil.

others of what resistance would mean. Total and unquestionable authority became the
order of the day for male owners, making them absolute monarchs over their slaves.
By the early 1700s, a small group of plantation owners controlled nearly all aspects of
life in the southern colonies. It was a society in which slaves were given no respect, a
few wealthy white males had unlimited power, and the institution of slavery defined
the social order.

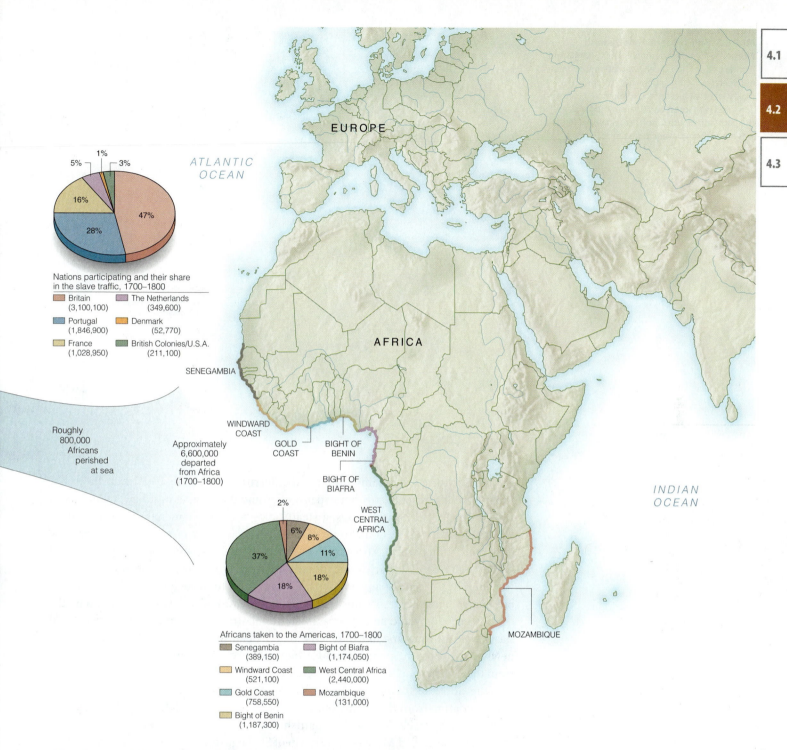

Nations participating and their share in the slave traffic, 1700–1800

- Britain (3,100,100)
- Portugal (1,846,900)
- France (1,028,950)
- The Netherlands (349,600)
- Denmark (52,770)
- British Colonies/U.S.A. (211,100)

Roughly 800,000 Africans perished at sea

Approximately 6,600,000 departed from Africa (1700–1800)

Africans taken to the Americas, 1700–1800

- Senegambia (389,150)
- Windward Coast (521,100)
- Gold Coast (758,550)
- Bight of Benin (1,187,300)
- Bight of Biafra (1,174,050)
- West Central Africa (2,440,000)
- Mozambique (131,000)

The Fear of Slave Revolts: South Carolina and New York

In the early 1700s, British landowners, especially in the southern colonies, imported more and more slaves from Africa. The production of tobacco, rice, and indigo was growing quickly. Charleston, South Carolina, became the largest slave trading center in mainland North America. But slaves did not accept their fate easily. They longed for and sometimes fought for their freedom. As more white colonists came to depend on slave labor for their growing prosperity, they also lived in constant fear of slave revolts, uprisings that were far from uncommon in all of the colonies. Two examples reflect the volatile conditions throughout the colonies.

THE STONO SLAVE REBELLION OF 1739 England and Spain were often at war, making the border between Spanish Florida and British South Carolina and Georgia a tense boundary (see Map 4-3). In 1693, Spain offered freedom to all fugitives from

MAP 4-3 British Georgia and Spanish Florida. While the border between Georgia and Florida was considered an international boundary between the British and Spanish colonies, the reality was that most of the unguarded territory was filled with forest and swamp, and for slaves the path from South Carolina to Spanish Florida was a path from slavery to freedom.

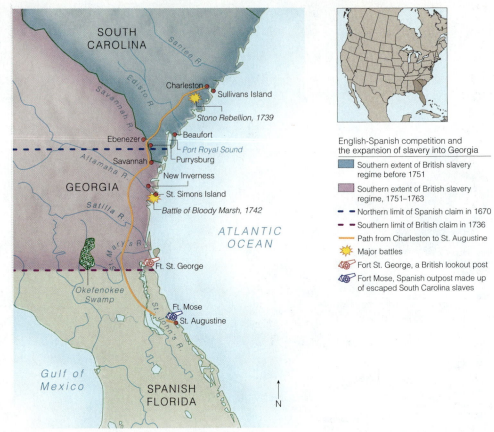

English-Spanish competition and the expansion of slavery into Georgia

- (blue) Southern extent of British slavery regime before 1751
- (purple) Southern extent of British slavery regime, 1751–1763
- – – Northern limit of Spanish claim in 1670
- – – Southern limit of British claim in 1736
- —— Path from Charleston to St. Augustine
- ✹ Major battles
- Fort St. George, a British lookout post
- Fort Mose, Spanish outpost made up of escaped South Carolina slaves

British territories who came into Spanish territory and converted to Catholicism. Many Carolina slaves heard about Spain's offer, and the number of runaways increased.

Throughout the early 1700s, a steady stream of slaves managed to make their way to Florida and freedom. Some of these runaways were already Catholic because they came from parts of Africa, such as the Kingdom of Kongo, long since converted by Portuguese missionaries. For others, converting to Catholicism was a route to freedom. At first, the Spanish authorities were slow to make good on their promise, but they soon realized the value of their policy. The runaway slaves were a drain on the Carolina economy and an embarrassment to the British. In addition, the newly freed slaves were a strong first line of defense on the Spanish side of the border. After all, as newly free people in Spanish Florida, they had special reason to defend the territory from the British, who wanted to perpetuate their slavery.

One of these former Carolina slaves, Francisco Menendez, won a special commendation from the Spanish in 1728 for his heroism in defending St. Augustine from English attack. When the Spanish authorities decided to create a separate settlement they called Mose—to the north of St. Augustine—as a buffer against further attacks, the Spanish governor placed Menendez in charge. Mose was more a fort than a town, but it was home to approximately 100 Africans who defended Florida and organized attacks on the British in South Carolina.

A large effort by Carolina slaves to gain freedom in Spanish Florida in 1739 came to be called the **Stono Rebellion**, the largest slave uprising in the colonies before the American Revolution. It terrified slave masters throughout the British colonies. The rebellion began when some 60 slaves from the South Carolina rice plantations, led by a slave named Cato, walked off their plantations, armed themselves, burned buildings of the slave owners, and killed whites who got in their way as they sought freedom in Spanish Florida. Fearful slave owners sent the South Carolina militia to stop them. In a battle at Stono, South Carolina, 50 miles from what was then the Florida border, many of the rebels and their white pursuers were killed. Other slaves were captured and returned to slavery. But some made it to freedom in Florida and

Stono Rebellion
Uprising in 1739 of South Carolina slaves against whites; inspired in part by Spanish officials' promise of freedom for American slaves who escaped to Florida.

joined the free black community there. In response, the white planter government of South Carolina temporarily restricted the importation of more African slaves and permanently curtailed the rights of slaves to assemble with one another.

After the Stono Rebellion was crushed, individual slaves continued to escape south across the border. Menendez, the former slave, had further adventures. Traveling to Spain, he was captured by the British and threatened with execution, but he eventually escaped and, by 1752, was again back leading the militia in Florida. By 1763, Mose had a population of 3,000, mostly escaped slaves. When Spain ceded Florida to Britain in that year, they moved the Mose Africans to Cuba, where they were given land, tools, a subsidy, and ironically, a slave for each leader in the community.

TENSIONS IN NEW YORK CITY, 1741 In the 1700s, slavery was not limited to the southern colonies. New York City and Providence, Rhode Island, had some of the largest concentrations of slaves in North America at that time. New York's African-American community included approximately 2,000 out of the city's 10,000 residents. Slave labor in New York might not have been as backbreaking as on a Virginia tobacco or Carolina rice plantation, but it was slavery nonetheless. Slaves did the worst jobs, got no pay, and had limited freedom. They could also be sold south at any time. Nevertheless, unlike rural slaves, urban slaves had a chance to meet other slaves, either at their work or in those taverns that welcomed them. Some of these opportunities frightened whites, leading them to react to what they assumed was pending rebellion.

In the early months of 1741, fires swept New York, destroying businesses and homes including the governor's house. Governor George Clarke became convinced that "The Negros are rising." Whether or not slaves had anything to do with it, the 1741 fires were real. New Yorkers were suffering through a harsh winter. News of South Carolina's Stono Slave Rebellion was in circulation, and memories of other slave revolts were fresh. There had been a slave revolt in the Caribbean in the 1730s. In 1712, New York slaves had killed nine whites and wounded six more. Fear spread easily.

A zealous prosecutor became convinced that there was a conspiracy to kill the city's whites, so he brought charges against targeted suspects, pitted accused against accused, and elicited confessions. Thirty Africans, most of them slaves, and four whites were executed, either hanged or burned at the stake. Eighty-four other suspects were transported to slavery in Jamaica. The degree to which New Yorkers experienced an actual revolt as opposed to being caught up in a fear-induced mass hysteria will never be known, but the trials illustrate the way those who enslaved others also feared the reality that they had created.

4.2 **Quick Review** What is the difference between a "society with slaves" and a "slave society," and how did part of North America become the latter?

STABILITY AND INSTABILITY IN THE AMERICAN AND BRITISH WORLDS

4.3 Analyze the changes in the ideas and daily lives of the people in British North America in the 1700s as a result of events within and beyond the colonies.

In 1706–1707, the English and Scottish Parliaments passed the **Act of Union**, formally uniting England and Scotland to create Great Britain. Although the two countries had been ruled by a single monarch since James I came to the throne in 1603, they were separate nations with separate Parliaments, and the American colonies were English colonies. After 1707, England and Scotland were one country, and the English colonies became British North America. The act extended the political stability of the Glorious Revolution. By 1707, third and fourth generations of people living in the American colonies had never seen Britain, even though they were of English and

Act of Union
The 1707 vote by the Scottish and English Parliaments to become one nation of Great Britain.

As their dress and the picture's background illustrate, Charles and Anne Byrd Carter of Virginia were among the colonial elite when these pictures were painted in the 1730s.

occasionally Scottish descent. They were being joined by other Europeans, especially immigrants from Ireland and Germany along with increasing numbers of unwilling and unfree Africans.

The British economy on both sides of the Atlantic was changing, and people were prospering. Although many people were still poor, the desperate starving time in Virginia and similar early struggles elsewhere were far behind. In British cities on both sides of the Atlantic and on the great plantations developing in the southern colonies, a growing social and economic elite lived comfortable lives, largely made possible by the slave trade and the backbreaking work of African slaves. The wealthiest colonial residents were those who lived on the tobacco, rice, and indigo plantations of Virginia and the Carolinas, including people like Charles and Anne Byrd Carter, whose families owned thousands of acres as well as many slaves and produced some of the goods most in demand in Great Britain and Britain's other colonies around the world.

Nevertheless, colonial life was still full of uncertainty. The hysteria that led to the Salem witch trials in the 1690s reflected these deep-seated fears that were just under the surface of much of colonial society. Rural women were often isolated, and even urban women were confined to domestic worlds, which could be boring and lonely. Fears and uncertainties were often shaped by information about events that took place in another colony. The ever-present danger of Indian raids continued to threaten British colonies, just as raids by settlers were a constant danger for tribes living near the colonies. The wealthy elite, whose wealth depended on slaves, feared slave revolts. In addition, wars in Europe often led to battles in North America.

By the early 1700s, England was the world's dominant sea power, bringing great financial benefits to those who controlled the trade in goods and people across the Atlantic and bringing prosperity to those who lived in port cities on both sides of the ocean. As trade and prosperity grew, the quest for commercial success began to replace religious devotion as the prime focus of many people's lives.

The Salem Witch Trials of 1692

Underlying tensions in colonial life surfaced in Massachusetts during the harsh, unrelenting winter of 1691–1692. The residents of Salem and the surrounding Massachusetts communities also lived in fear because New England was under siege from Indians allied with French Canada. In midwinter, Indians killed 50 residents of York, Maine, and took another hundred hostage. Residents of other Maine communities fled in terror and were living in or near Salem. Exiles from Maine may have been especially traumatized, but all of the residents feared further attacks. Moreover, other tensions were brewing in the port city of Salem. Many poorer residents resented their neighbors who formed a more prosperous commercial elite. In addition, women in Salem, like in all English colonies, lived, often unwillingly, within strict submissive gender roles; women who were unusually assertive, especially women who lived alone or were of non-English backgrounds, were not trusted.

As these tensions simmered, Salem fell into a kind of mass hysteria late that winter. Two young girls in the home of Reverend Samuel Parris of Salem Village—his daughter Betty and her cousin Abigail—began to suffer fits. They seemed to be "bitten and pinched by invisible agents." The town doctor wondered if their disease might be a result of witchcraft. In March, the girls accused Tituba, the family's Indian slave, of bewitching them. Thus began the **Salem witch trials**, one of the best-known episodes of mass hysteria in the English colonies.

Soon other young women came forward with tales similar to those of Betty and Abigail. As a result, formal charges were brought, and court proceedings began. In time, some of those accused, including Tituba, "confessed" to being witches. Witnesses turned against one another, and convictions for witchcraft became common.

Between February 1692 and May 1693, legal action was taken against 144 people—106 women and 38 men. Six men and 14 women, including Tituba, were executed. That so many people in Salem believed their illnesses and troubles were the work of witches was not strange in the 1600s. Most people in Europe believed that there were witches—people who had made a compact with the devil and could appear as ghosts and make other people and animals sick. Hundreds of supposed witches were executed in England in that century, and many other accusations of witchcraft had surfaced in New England, although never on the scale of what happened in Salem. In Salem, the whole community became involved as the accusations spread quickly from one household to another. Virtually all of the accusers were young women under age 25, and most of the victims were also women—though often older.

The hysteria ended almost as quickly as it had begun. By the fall of 1692, Massachusetts authorities—clergy and political leaders—were starting to have doubts about the trials and executions. Most people in the colony probably still believed in witchcraft, but they were increasingly uneasy about what was happening in Salem. By spring 1693, it was all over. One of the judges, Samuel Sewall, publicly apologized for his role and asked God's pardon. Reverend Parris was forced to leave Salem, and the Massachusetts authorities voted compensation for victims and families. The Salem witch trials were one of the last times that people were executed for explicitly religious reasons in North America.

Women's Lives

By the middle of the 1700s, the white culture of British North America was generally divided between the public and private realms. Because women were generally relegated to the private realm, many of them lived cut off from society.

Urban women had much more opportunity for social contact with other women and men than those living in more isolated regions. In Williamsburg, Virginia, two women—Anne Shields and Jane Vobe—both ran their own taverns. Mary Channing ran a large store in Boston, and Lydia Hyde had her own shop in Philadelphia. While these women may have been the exception, city women did have many opportunities to interact.

However, more than 90 percent of the British residents of North America lived on farms, sometimes very isolated farms, and the lives of rural women could be frighteningly lonely. In more settled communities, especially in southern New England, women could often find limited contact with other women in ways that allowed them to build some friendships, such as gathering to trade soap, candles, cheese, and butter or attending church. Growing commercial prosperity also meant that some women were able to purchase imported goods including tea, china, and—for a few—even silk.

An illustration from the book *Full and Plain Evidence Concerning Witches and Apparitions*, published in London in 1681, represented beliefs on both sides of the Atlantic about the powers of those who made a pact with the devil.

Salem witch trials
The 1692–1693 hysteria in Salem, Massachusetts, during which women and men were accused of being witches who had made a pact with the devil, some of whom were executed for the crime.

As the American population expanded, finding land often required moving to more isolated rural areas, which could make contact and community life more difficult, especially for women. While male farmers also lived very isolated lives, they traveled to town to sell goods and buy necessities more often than women. These trips provided men far more opportunity to meet neighbors and participate in the social and political discussions. In contrast, women were limited not only by assumptions that they should stick to household matters and leave political discussion and trade to their husbands but also by the physical demands of pregnancy, birth, nursing, and child rearing as well as by the daily chores of a farm—taking care of the animals, cultivating the vegetables, preserving food, preparing meals, spinning wool, weaving cloth, and making clothes.

Women's work also included playing the role of physician or pharmacist because most farm families did not have access to more formal medical care. Women had to be familiar with medical information and herbal medicines. Manuals such as *Aristotle's Complete Masterpiece: Displaying the Secrets of Nature in the Generation of Man* provided many women with detailed information on sexual matters, childbirth, and child rearing. In addition, the opportunities women had to share medical and child-rearing information, provide medical care, and support each other through medical emergencies and childbirth were extremely important to women's community life. Midwives and healers had special status, but any nearby farm wife might be summoned to attend a birth, and a woman in labor might well have 6–10 female attendants. The times surrounding a birth were an important social occasion as women had time to sew, tell stories, and catch up with each other.

At the bottom of the social hierarchy were enslaved women. For women living in slavery, the usual gender distinctions of white society had less meaning. On farms and plantations, male and female slaves all worked long hours in the fields. In urban areas, where there might be greater gender distinctions in specific forms of work, enslaved women were still afforded little of the protections that were expected—if not always enforced—for white women.

There were, of course, exceptions to the general isolation that women living outside of cities experienced. Eliza Lucas (1722–1793) was born to a wealthy English sugar-growing family on the island of Antigua in 1722. She was educated in London and then joined her family in South Carolina in 1738. She quickly became a popular member of Charleston's elite. However, in 1739, war between England and Spain required her father to return to Antigua. She was left in charge of three Carolina plantations at the age of 16. In 1744, Eliza married Charles Pinckney. He also traveled a great deal and left her in charge of the plantations. Like male plantation owners, Eliza Pinckney supervised a large labor force of slaves whose labor was the basis of her wealth and leisure. Her position gave her time and opportunity to develop her agricultural ideas and cultivate her intellect, which she did throughout her life. She experimented with new crops and crop rotations. She also helped develop cultivation of the indigo plant, which was used to create a blue dye that was popular in England and which soon rivaled rice as a source of wealth in South Carolina.

The Growth of Cities: Philadelphia, New York, Boston, Charleston

In 1700, British North America had a population of approximately 250,000, including both Europeans and Africans, but not Indians. Boston was the largest city in the colonies with 8,000 inhabitants, followed by New York City with 6,000. Philadelphia and Charleston were both under 3,000, but Philadelphia was growing fast. By contrast, the capital of New Spain, Mexico City, had 100,000 residents, and London had over 500,000 in 1700. With growing trade and prosperity, the British North American population would dramatically increase (see Table 4-1).

TABLE 4-1 Estimated Populations of the Four Largest Cities in British North America between 1700 And 1775

City	1700	1720	1750	1775
Boston	8,000	12,000	16,000	17,500
Philadelphia	2,000	10,000	15,000	31,000
New York	6,000	7,000	14,000	21,500
Charleston	2,000	3,500	6,500	11,000

By the 1770s, on the eve of the American Revolution, Philadelphia would have 30,000 residents, followed by New York with 25,000, Boston with 16,000, and Charleston with 12,000. The total colonial population would be 2.5 million, including 500,000 slaves of African origin.

Many colonists responded to the growing trade and prosperity with pride in being part of the British Empire. In the 1690s, Virginia moved its capital from Jamestown to Williamsburg, complete with a new capitol building that reflected this pride. The structure had two wings—one for the elected legislature, the House of Burgesses, and one for the royally appointed council—just as the Parliament that sat in London had places for the elected House of Commons and the hereditary House of Lords. The governor's elegant Williamsburg residence reflected the status of the crown's representative in the colony.

Although most people still lived on farms or in small towns, the port cities were becoming significant centers of trade and culture for the whole British Empire. Between 1701 and 1754, the cities of British North America moved from being rude outposts to cities that looked and felt very much like similar cities in Britain. They were important to the British Empire's commercial and maritime success, and residents were proud of their connection to the mother country.

In the early 1700s, New York City, Philadelphia, Boston, and Charleston all emerged as significant trading centers for the British world. The ocean-based commerce of these cities was based on their good harbors, Britain's growing dominance of the world's oceans, and industries that included Britain's naval building, the tea trade, and the slave trade. Ships based in North America carried food—cornmeal, pork, and beef—and naval stores—tar, pitch, turpentine, and lumber—to the great sugar plantations of the British West Indies. These prosperous plantations on Barbados, Jamaica, and other British-controlled islands were far richer than anything on the mainland of North America. They also had many more slaves than any plantation on the mainland. But they depended on outsiders, often colonists living on the vast mainland of North America, to supply their food and building supplies. The ships returned to North American ports with slaves, sugar, rum, molasses, cotton, and fruit from the Caribbean; manufactured goods from Great Britain; and letters of credit that expanded the cash in circulation in the colonies and in London.

Cities also became safer places to live after Boston clergyman Cotton Mather championed the first vaccinations against smallpox in 1721. While smallpox had been a major cause of death among Indians who had never developed immunity to the disease, many Europeans also died of it. Mather, a Puritan theologian and pastor, was also an acute scientific observer. He had read about a Turkish doctor who had produced light cases of smallpox by deliberately infecting healthy people with the disease, which produced immunity in them against more lethal strains.

When the smallpox epidemic of 1721 hit Boston, Mather advocated using that doctor's inoculation approach, and a physician, Zabdiel Boylston, tried it. Mather collected the statistics. Of some 300 people inoculated, only five or six died compared with 900 deaths among the 5,000 who were not inoculated. The statistics were compelling. Smallpox inoculations spread throughout the colonial world though it was another 30 years before smallpox inoculations were common in England.

American Voices

Benjamin Franklin, *The Way to Wealth*, 1757

Benjamin Franklin (1706–1790) was born in modest circumstances in Boston, Massachusetts, in 1706. At age 12, after 2 years of schooling, Franklin became an apprentice—an indentured servant—to his older brother, James, a printer in Boston. In 1723, at the age of 17—and 4 years before his indenture expired—Benjamin took advantage of a loophole in the contract and left Boston for Philadelphia. By 1729, at the age of 23 he was sole owner of a printing business having bought out a partner. While he made money printing government documents and publications for private businesses, Franklin also produced Poor Richard's Almanack *that predicted the weather for the coming year and shared friendly advice. By 1748, when he was 42 years old, Franklin, with his flourishing printing business, was one of the richest people in the northern colonies and decided that it was time to retire from work, live the life of a gentleman, and devote himself to public service. Public service had always been important to Franklin, and it was a measure of the status he sought. He had already helped launch the Library Company of Philadelphia. Soon after he retired, Franklin engaged in his famous experiment with a kite to prove that lighting was, indeed, electricity. In 1755 he helped found the College of Philadelphia that would become the University of Pennsylvania. In 1757, Franklin wrote a preface to the last edition of his almanac he had published for 30 years. He used a fictional Father Abraham to quote all of the best passages that he had written over the years. This preface was subsequently published as* The Way to Wealth, *one of Franklin's most enduring works, which reflected a growing emphasis on financial success. The advice from Poor Richard shed light on a changing colonial culture, one in which religious orthodoxy and national loyalties mattered less and individual commercial success mattered much more.*

I stopped my horse lately where a great number of people were collected at a vendue [sale] of merchant goods. The hour of sale not being come, they were conversing on the badness of the times, and one of the company called to a plain, clean old man with white locks: "Pray, Father Abraham, what think you of the times? Won't these heavy taxes quite ruin the country? How shall we be ever able to pay them? What would you advise us to?…

"Friends," says he, "and neighbors, the taxes are indeed very heavy, and if those laid on by the government were the only ones we had to pay, we might more easily discharge them; but we have many others, and much more grievous to some of us. We are taxed twice as much by our idleness, three times as much by our pride, and four times as much by our folly; and from these taxes the commissioners cannot ease or deliver us by allowing an abatement. However, let us hearken to good advice, and something may be done for us; 'God helps them that help themselves,' as Poor Richard says in his almanac of 1733.…

"'If time be of all things the most precious, wasting time must be,' as Poor Richard says, 'the greatest prodigality'; since as he elsewhere tells us, 'Lost time is never found again'; …and 'Early to bed and early to rise, makes a man healthy, wealthy, and wise'.… Diligence is the mother of good luck,' as Poor Richard says…and 'By diligence and patience the mouse ate in two the cable'; and 'Little strokes fell great oaks,' as Poor Richard says in his almanac—the year I cannot just now remember…

"And now to conclude, 'Experience keeps a dear school, but fools will learn in no other, and scarce in that'; for it is true, 'We may give advice, but we cannot give conduct,' as Poor Richard says…"

Thus the old gentleman ended his harangue. The people heard it and approved the doctrine, and immediately practiced the contrary, just as if it had been a common sermon.

Source: Benjamin Franklin, *The Works of Benjamin Franklin*, with Notes and a Life of the Author by Jared Sparks. (London: Benjamin Franklin Stevens, 1882)

Thinking Critically

1. **Documentary Analysis**
   What values did Franklin endorse?

2. **Historical Interpretation**
   What groups in colonial society would have been most likely to see Franklin's values as their own? Why?

---

mercantilism
Economic system whereby the government intervenes in the economy for the purpose of increasing national wealth.

capitalism
Economic system best described by Adam Smith in 1776 in which trade is seen as the source of wealth rather than as exchange of goods themselves; as a result, wealth can continually expand as trade expands.

Commercial Attitudes, Commercial Success—Mercantilism and the New Trading Economy

The economy of Europe and Europe's American colonies changed drastically between 1689 and 1754. Since at least the time of Queen Elizabeth, the western world's economy, and certainly the economy of Britain and Britain's possessions, had been organized around an economic system known as **mercantilism**. But as trade developed in the colonies, the seeds of what would later be described in 1776 as **capitalism** were already taking hold. Advocates of mercantilism believed that economic transactions should be directed to increase the nation's wealth without regard for other participants in those transactions, that the world's wealth was finite, and that for any nation to grow in wealth some other nation needed to be the loser. Using this mercantile approach, the British Empire closely guarded the colonies so that their wealth went exclusively to Britain and not to other European countries. Economists of the time believed that it was critical that the colonies be used only to produce raw materials that would enrich the European nation that claimed them and that colonies also consume manufactured products from their mother country. Any trade outside of this closed loop, they claimed, ran the risk of diluting the nation's wealth. As the later idea of capitalism emerged, advocates for that concept saw the economic world very differently. Economists who favored capitalism believed there was no limit to the world's wealth because it was trade, not the goods that were being traded, that was the ultimate key to wealth. Thus, trade between individuals and between nations allowed continuing growth for all parties.

The prime example of mercantilism in the Americas were the British Navigation Acts of 1650 and 1660. The 1660 Navigation Act proclaimed that, "from thenceforward, no goods or commodities whatsoever shall be imported into or exported out of any lands, islands, plantations, or territories to his Majesty belonging or in his possession…but in such ships or vessels as do truly and without fraud belong only to the people of England or Ireland, dominion of Wales or town of Berwick upon Tweed." In other words, anything shipped *to* North America or to other British colonies had to be transported in English ships, and everything shipped *from* the colonies had to be transported in English ships bound for England. The goal was clear: the colonies would produce raw goods—as the act stipulated, "sugars, tobacco, cotton wool, indigoes, ginger, fustic, or other dyeing wood"—and ship them only to England. England would produce manufactured goods, and the colonies would be limited to buying goods only from England. The arrangement was a closed economic system, and it was designed to ensure that wealth from the colonies flowed only to London, not back to the colonies and certainly not to any other country. Clearly, Britain had no interest in cultivating wealth within the colonies themselves.

The problem with mercantilism was that it focused too much on *control* of things and too little on the *trade* of things. The efforts on the part of Spain to maintain its wealth by controlling the world's supply of silver and gold are illustrative of that problem as was the effort of British pirates to steal the same gold. Many European wars of the era were fought over issues related to mercantilism as each European power sought to control the greatest amount of what they saw as the world's limited wealth. As the Navigation Acts made clear, for much of the 1700s, even as Britain itself was beginning to focus on developing an economy based on trade, its government attempted to use mercantile principles to control that trade with the American colonies.

The **Triangle Trade** that developed in response to British mercantile policies involved the shipment of slaves from Africa to the West Indies and North America in exchange for rum (see Map 4-4). Sugar and rum (made from sugar) were also shipped to Britain, and goods manufactured in Britain were shipped to Africa, the West Indies, and to the mainland of North America. But there was also significant trade directly between North America and Britain. Raw materials, including fur, grain, tobacco, rice, and indigo—the last three all produced by slave labor—were shipped directly to Britain in return for manufactured products that by law—though not always in reality—could be produced only in Great Britain.

For British colonists living in North America, the trade problems were more real life than theoretical. They hated mercantilism and the Navigation Acts, not because they opposed slavery or the introduction of slave labor into the colonies or because they thought capitalism was a better economic theory, but because the British policies were keeping them from getting rich. Molasses could be bought more cheaply from French colonies than from British. Slaves could sometimes be bought more cheaply

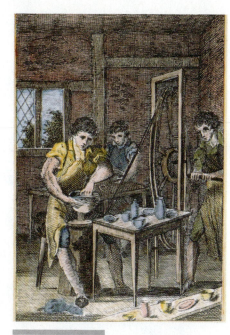

As colonial life became more settled in British North America between the 1680s and the 1750s, economic patterns became more established. In the early 1700s a British study reported the kinds of trades practiced in the colonies, including this illustration of a male master and apprentice working in a shop.

Triangle Trade
A pattern of trade that developed in the 1700s in which slaves from Africa were sent to the West Indies and mainland North America while goods and other resources were shipped between the West Indies and North America and Britain.

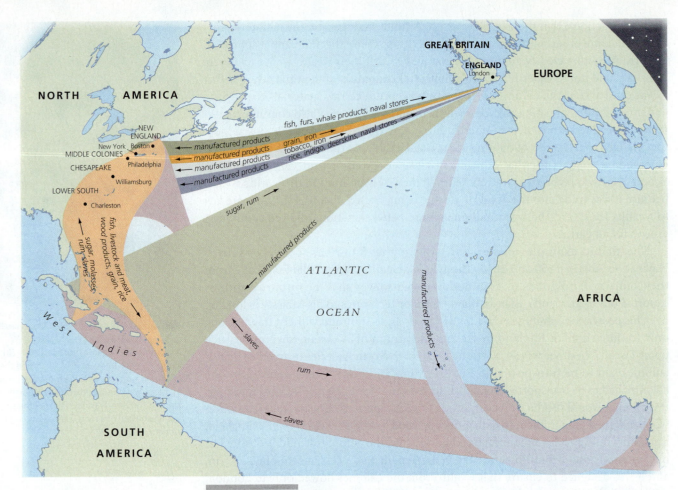

MAP 4-4 The Triangle Trade. As this map shows, the so-called triangular trade was not a perfect triangle. But for the British colonies the most significant trade focused on England from which manufactured products were shipped to the Americas and to Africa. In return, African slaves were shipped to the Caribbean and to North America, Caribbean rum was shipped to Africa and to England, and raw materials—including fish, fur, grain, rice, indigo, and tobacco—were shipped directly from North America to England which, according to mercantile laws, was the only place where raw materials could be turned into finished manufactured goods.

from Dutch traders than from English. Similarly, goods produced in the colonies—tobacco, rice, foodstuffs and ships' stores—could often fetch higher prices elsewhere in the world than in Britain. Trading with a wider world, especially the rich colonies of the Caribbean, made more sense and produced greater profit than limiting trade to England alone.

Circumventing the Navigation Acts, either through finding legal loopholes or simply sailing off in a different direction than British laws allowed, became a major enterprise and source of wealth throughout all of the British colonies. The involvement of the colonies in worldwide trade—even when that trade was illegal—foreshadowed not only American independence but also a shift in economic systems from the closed world of mercantilism to a more open and elastic world in which trade and commerce, rather than simply ownership of things, was the key to wealth.

Trade was also increasing the exchange of information. Cotton Mather learned about smallpox inoculations from Turkish physicians through contacts in London. New York's traders interacted with merchants in Jamaica and Barbados as well as Africa and England. Jews whose forbearers had been exiled from Spain mingled on the streets of New York and Philadelphia with Africans captured from Kongo and servants fleeing poverty in London. News of attacks by Indians allied with France or Spain sparked uncertainty, even hysteria, among colonists. Slaves from the Carolinas heard about offers from Spanish Florida and escaped to freedom. And as the next section in this chapter relates, the most influential preacher of the Great Awakening, George Whitefield, traveled back and forth across the Atlantic 13 times, preaching transformative sermons to huge crowds in England and America. These kinds of exchanges gave many people new knowledge of a wider world. Although the world of British North America could be limited and most people did not travel very far, colonial society was very much an international society—a context that shaped the life of every British North American resident in the mid-1700s.

At the same time, trade, travel, and communication among the colonies grew, even though London tried to tighten its control and its separate connections with each of the 13 mainland British colonies. People along the Atlantic Coast, from New England to the Carolinas, began to take greater notice of one another, exchanging ideas and seeing new reasons to defend their common interests. By the 1750s, colonists were identifying some of those common interests even as they jealously guarded their own colony's independence. The years between 1707 and 1754 were years of relative stability in British North America, but they were also years in which the availability of information, attitudes and opinions about the value of British political power in colonial life changed dramatically.

Changing Social Systems

As the economic systems gradually shifted, starting in the 1730s, social systems in British North America also began to change, reflecting those economic trends. Although society in North America was not as highly stratified as in Britain itself, the strong sense of social class had been growing since the late 1600s. Among the many social gradations in British North America, those at the top believed that there were really only two social classes in the early to mid-1700s. A small class of gentlemen and ladies, who did not have to work for a living, were on top. Gentlemen and ladies might engage in public service, and the gentlemen might sit in legislative assemblies or engage in certain professions, but they did so as a sign of their social status and not because they needed the money. Below that elite group, separated by a great gulf, were those who had to work for a living—farmers and tradespeople known as "mechanics" and, below them, the servants and slaves. However prosperous the mechanics and farmers might become, they were still stigmatized. They were expected to know their place and maintain proper deference to society's elite. At the very bottom were those in varying degrees of unfreedom—slaves, indentured servants, or simply desperately poor people. Members of this group were disregarded in terms of having any say or influence. People in these classes typically acknowledged duty to those above them and deference to those below. The notion of society as a hierarchy was commonplace.

By the 1720s, however, some of the mechanics and farmers were beginning to recognize a new social class: the "middling sorts." These prosperous working people earned their success through hard work and frugality, both of which the elite scorned. Over generations, this group would evolve into what we now call the middle class. The middling social class, including printers, most physicians, small farmers, and those who sailed on ships, differentiated themselves from working people in the less prosperous trades and the servants and slaves. A new perspective was taking shape. People began to question the notion of a society that expected deference to those of higher status. The assumption that one stayed in the class to which one was born was quickly disappearing. Benjamin Franklin, though much more successful than most, was far from the only resident of colonial America to move from one class to another. Of course, social movement was not the only in an upward direction. As class roles weakened, some also moved downward or moved outside of the class system altogether, such as the most famous outlaw of the mid-1700s, Thomas Bell.

THINKING HISTORICALLY

Thomas Bell, A Very Different American Life

If one depended on colonial newspapers rather than on the work of subsequent historians, then the best-known American of the first half of the 1700s was not Benjamin Franklin or Jonathan Edwards (see next section on religion) but Thomas Bell. The February 10, 1743, issue of Benjamin Franklin's newspaper the *Pennsylvania Gazette* describes Bell's renown:

> He has it seems made it his business for several years to travel from Colony to Colony, personating different People, forging Bills of Credit, &c. and frequently pretending Distress, imposed grossly on the charitable and compassionate.

This "famous American traveler" was known for his thefts, swindles, and escapes in Massachusetts, New York, New Jersey, Virginia, Maryland, the Carolinas, and island colonies including Barbados and Jamaica.

Bell was about the same age as Benjamin Franklin or Jonathan Edwards. Born in Boston in 1713, he attended Harvard College but was expelled because he "stole a cake of chocolate…has been guilty of the most notorious, complicated lying." He quickly left town. In 1738, he was arrested in Williamsburg, Virginia, and again in New York City, "for falsely, unlawfully, unjustly, knowingly, fraudulently, and deceitfully, composing, writing, and inventing a false, fictitious, Counterfeit, and invented Letter."

A year after his arrests in Williamsburg and New York, Bell sparked a riot between Jewish and Christian communities in Barbados when, pretending to be the son of the governor of Massachusetts, he got himself invited to a Jewish wedding. During the celebration, he was caught pilfering the family's goods. Bell denied the obvious theft and appealed to the Christian community to defend him, setting off a Christian attack on Jews.

Two years later, in the summer of 1741, Bell stopped at a tavern in Princeton, New Jersey. When he was mistaken for the Reverend John Rowland, a Presbyterian minister, Bell sensed an opportunity and offered to preach at the Presbyterian Church. Just before Sunday services, he rifled the goods in his host's home, stole his horse, and departed. When the real Rowland returned to New Jersey, the famous minister was arrested for the theft, and it took a considerable time before the Supreme Court of New Jersey cleared up the matter of the mistaken identities.

After several more daring escapades, Bell met his end in Kingston, Jamaica, where in 1771 he was hung for piracy. Bell's story and mark in history has faded with time, but it represents a part of the story of America's people that has continued throughout American history, including outlaws in the West and gangsters in the 1900s.

Thinking Critically

1. **Contextualization**

   How would you explain Bell's fame during his own lifetime? Why might his successful acts of impersonation have captured the imagination of the colonial public?

2. **Historical Interpretation**

   What role did newspapers play in creating Bell's fame? What does his story tell us about the role of newspapers in colonial popular culture?

A Changing Religious Landscape—From the Halfway Covenant to the First Great Awakening

With the first settlement in British North America, there was a sense that somehow this new land was a divinely planned opportunity to begin the world again and make it right. In 1702, Cotton Mather, perhaps the best known minister in Boston at the time, published a highly romanticized religious history of New England that confirmed this sense. The book reflected a theme that would be repeated throughout American history, the belief that the country had a special divine mission to fulfill. Mather praised God that Europe had made contact with the Americas after the Protestant Reformation so British North America was being built by Protestants and not by Roman Catholics. At the same time, some Catholics saw their mission from the opposite side of the Reformation divide. Giovanni Botero wrote in 1595 that it was only divine providence that led the kings of France and England to reject overtures from Columbus so that his initial "discovery" could be made while sailing for Catholic Spain.

Not all Europeans accepted their mission as a special part of divine providence, however. Roger Williams, who led Rhode Island as a haven for religious tolerance, insisted that God did not choose special elect nations—not England and not New England. A group of settlers in northern New England reminded one missionary who spoke of their divine mission, "Sir,…our main end is to catch fish." Nevertheless, by the early 1700s, the notion that America was part of a divine drama of salvation was widespread.

By the early 1700s, however, the sense of being on a divine mission had declined among many colonists. The grandchildren and great-grandchildren of the original Puritan settlers were living increasingly comfortable lives in the commercially prosperous British Empire. Religious fervor and religious conversions were less and less common, and many were much more tolerant of the growing religious diversity in all of the colonies. This growth of religious toleration in the 1700s—something not imagined in the 1600s—prompted more Europeans to come to the British colonies in search of religious freedom that they could not find in their homelands.

Increasingly, more of those who already lived in the colonies began to consider alternatives to the religious dogmas of their parents and communities. The growth of new philosophical ideas in Europe led many intellectuals, and eventually more and more people in general, to look more to science and human reason than to faith in trying to understand their world. They called the time in which they were living the **Age of Enlightenment**. Some in this period rejected all religious teachings, while others simply placed less emphasis on matters of faith and more on reason. In the colonies as in Europe, some people began to take religion with a large grain of salt, being convinced by Enlightenment philosophies that most religious matters were mere superstitions that were, at best, unprovable by the scientific tools of the new age. Some simply turned their attentions to other matters.

Describing his travels in Pennsylvania between 1750 and 1754, the German Protestant minister Gottlieb Mittelberger described a scene not at all to his liking:

> We find there Lutherans, Reformed, Catholics, Quakers, Mennonists or Anabaptists, Herrnhuters or Moravian Brethren, Pietists, Seventh-Day Baptists, Dunkers, Presbyterians, Newborn, Freemasons, Separatists, Freethinkers, Jews, Mohammedans, Pagans, Negroes, and Indians….Many pray neither in the morning or in the evening, neither before nor after meals. No devotional book, not to speak of a Bible, will be found with such people.

Mittelberger may have been happy to leave Pennsylvania and return to his ministry in Germany. However, while many ministers expressed similar worries about a religious decline in the colonies in the early 1700s, especially New England, other preachers sought ways to release religious energy. Prompting some of these religious stirrings were the sermons of Solomon Stoddard, who served as the minister of the Congregational church in Northampton, Massachusetts, and who had been one of the authors of the Halfway Covenant. By the 1720s, Stoddard's sermons were leading to a resurgence of religion not only in Northampton but also in much of western Massachusetts and Connecticut.

Stoddard's grandson and successor, Jonathan Edwards (1703–1758), became famous for leading even larger religious revivals. Edward's sermons in western Massachusetts, like those of John Wesley in England, led many to report that their "hearts were strangely warmed" and that they were experiencing a new sense of divine presence. The **First Great Awakening**, a series of religious revivals that swept all of the North American colonies in the late 1730s had begun. Word of the awakening spread quickly across the colonies as well as Great Britain and the rest of Europe.

Edwards prided himself on preaching in a low voice and seeking to convert people solely by the power of the logic of his words. He rejected any anti-intellectual religion as "heat without light." Although the revivals led by Edwards and others of his day resulted in a significant emotional release for many, they were nothing like the revivals of later times. If there was music, it was not central, and sermons were

The Age of Enlightenment
Major intellectual movement occurring in Europe beginning in the 1600s that led many to look more to scientific advances and the role of human reason in understanding the world than to religion.

First Great Awakening
A significant religious revival in colonial America begun by the preaching of Solomon Stoddard and Jonathan Edwards in the 1720s and 1730s and expanded by the many tours of the English evangelical minister George Whitefield that began in the 1730s.

While a Massachusetts pastor, Jonathan Edwards was one of the first preachers to stir some of the religious fervor of the First Great Awakening. George Whitefield, an English preacher shown here, was its most prominent leader. Whitefield crossed the Atlantic 13 times beginning in 1739 and was probably heard by more Americans than any other individual before the Revolution.

designed to be long rational arguments for the importance of changing one's life that depended less on the preacher's charisma than any ability to persuade. But by the 1730s, these logical sermons were creating their own dramatic results. Many in Edwards's congregation were undergoing deeply emotional conversion experiences while listening to his sermons, taking religion seriously in a way that they never had before. In a short period of time, 300 conversions were reported, increasing church membership considerably.

For Jonathan Edwards, the purpose of revival preaching was to convince individuals of their sinfulness and move them through an emotional catharsis of conversion to a new life and a new relationship to God. In perhaps his best known sermon, Edwards said, "The God that holds you over the pit of hell, much as one holds a spider, or some loathsome insect, over the fire, abhors you, and is dreadfully provoked; his wrath towards you burns like fire…yet it is nothing but his hand that holds you from falling into the fire every moment." Edwards was urgently pleading with his hearers to rethink the direction of their lives.

Later in the 1730s, George Whitefield (1714–1770) became the most powerful preacher of the Great Awakening. Whitefield lived in Britain but preached to huge audiences in both Britain and North America. His first trip to North America began in Georgia in 1738. In 1739 and 1740, he crossed the Atlantic again, making a preaching tour that started in Georgia, moved through the middle colonies (including Philadelphia, where his preaching deeply impressed Benjamin Franklin who became a lifelong friend if not a convert), and progressed to Boston where huge audiences attended a series of sermons, including one on Boston Common that drew a crowd of 30,000 listeners. Whitefield also visited Northampton and preached at Edwards's church to great acclaim.

Whitefield had high regard for Edwards and Presbyterian ministers like Gilbert Tennent. He had a much lower opinion of the majority of preachers and said that, "the reason why congregations have been so dead, is because dead men preach to them." Timothy Cutler, an Episcopal priest in Boston, responded by describing Whitefield's sermons as "his beastly brayings."

Cutler was not the only minister to resist the emotionalism of Whitefield and Edwards. The leaders at Harvard and Yale did not like the revivalists whom they saw as emotional and divisive. Churches were split. The Presbyterian Church was split into New Light (pro-Awakening) and Old Light (anti-Awakening) bodies. Many Congregational churches were split, and towns that had supported one church for much of the past century now supported two, or three, or even four. In contrast, the Baptists, who generally sided with the Awakening, grew dramatically.

The Great Awakening changed American society. Many who had previously shown little interest in religion became converted. Many who thought of themselves as deeply religious now saw their faith in more emotional and ethical terms. The revivals of the Great Awakening cut across many of the traditional divides of class and race, even gender. While more women than men responded to the religious energy, some of the rules segregating classes and races seem to have been suspended for these revivals. Africans—slave and free—and American Indians were also converted and became enthusiastic members of religious bodies. Samson Occom, a Mohegan Indian from Connecticut, was a convert in the Awakening who went on to be a revival leader, preaching to white and Native American audiences.

The Awakening transformed American higher education, which at that time was closely connected to the churches. Harvard resisted the movement while Yale, first split by it, eventually moved into the Awakening camp. Prorevival ministers founded Dartmouth—initially meant to serve American Indians—and Princeton to support the revival cause and help prepare a new generation of revival-oriented ministers.

American Voices

Jonathan Edwards, *A Treatise Concerning Religious Affections*

In his book, *A Treatise Concerning Religious Affections, published in 1746 after the Great Awakening had run its course, Edwards asked a fundamental question about any religious experience, "How does one judge if it is real or not?" He answered that the key was found in the way a person lived. Edwards believed that a person who did not live out what religious truths he or she claimed to believe surely signaled that his or her religious experience was not sincere.*

What is the nature of true religion?...Gracious and holy affections have their exercise and fruit in Christian practice. I mean, they have that influence and power upon him who is the subject of 'em, that they cause that a practice, which is universally conformed to, and directed by Christian rules, should be the practice and business of his life....Slothfulness in the service of God, in his professed servants, is as damning, as open rebellion....Christ nowhere says, ye shall know the tree by its leaves or flowers, or ye shall know men by their talk, or ye shall know them by the good story they tell of their experiences, or ye shall know them by the manner and air of their speaking, and emphasis and pathos of expression, or by their speaking feelingly, or by making a very great show by abundance of talk, or by many tear and affectionate

expressions, or by the affections ye feel in your heart towards them: but by their fruits you shall know them...."Let your light so shine before men, that others seeing your good works, may glorify your Father which is in heaven" (Matt. 5:16)....Hypocrites may much more easily be brought to talk like saints, than to act like saints....There may be several good evidences that a tree is a fig tree; but the highest and most proper evidence of it, is that it actually bears figs....[W]e should get into the way of appearing lively in religion, more by being lively in the service of God and our generation, than by the liveliness and forwardness of our tongues.

Source: Jonathan Edwards, *A Treatise Concerning Religious Affections* (Boston: S. Kneeland and T. Green, 1746, reprinted and edited by John E. Smith, New Haven: Yale University Press, 1959).

Thinking Critically

1. **Documentary Analysis**
   How did Edwards define "true religion"?
2. **Historical Interpretation**
   What does this passage tell us about Edwards's views on the state of contemporary colonial religious practice?

Ongoing Wars in Europe and British North America

Between 1689 and 1815, England and France were engaged in more or less continual war with each other for control of global empires. Spain was often allied with France in these wars. For those living in North America, each war involved not only international struggles but also local battles, especially with Indian tribes that were in their own shifting alliances with European powers. From Europe's perspective, the American Revolution itself could be seen as just one battle in that ongoing war. But long before the Revolution, colonial life in Britain's colonies, as well as in colonies claimed by France and Spain, was shaped by these wars.

France still claimed the St. Lawrence River Valley and the Mississippi Valley—an area spanning from what is now Minnesota to New Orleans. In 1724, Cadwallader Colden, a surveyor, reminded the governor of New York that, "the French plainly shew their intention of enclosing the British Settlements and cutting us off from all Commerce with the numerous Nations of Indians." Despite the larger population of the British colonies, many colonists shared his fear that Britain's colonies were encircled by French ones. They also worried because Spain controlled Florida, many Caribbean islands, and the rich lands of Central and South America, giving Spain great power and wealth in its confrontations with Britain on both sides of the Atlantic. In addition, Indian tribes, many allied with the French, were often the dominant power in territory from western New York through Pennsylvania and into the western portions of the Carolinas and Georgia (see Map 4-5).

It was not always clear who was winning and who was losing in the ongoing struggles, but war was a fact of daily life for much of the colonial era, sometimes devastatingly close to home and sometimes more generally reflected in concerns about who would control the future of North America. When William and Mary came to

MAP 4-5 French, English, and Spanish Claims, 1608. Although it did not have the European population of the British colonies, New France, which was settled along the St. Lawrence River to the north and the Mississippi River to the west, was much larger than the British colonies. The large areas of land claimed by France along with the area of Florida claimed by Spain prevented British colonies from growing further and created hostile tensions.

the throne in England in 1689, King Louis XIV of France objected to their elevation by Parliament. Louis, a Catholic, had already fought William, a Protestant, in Holland, and now he did so again in what the British colonists called King William's War. It lasted from 1689 to 1697. The war's outcome was inconclusive, but the battles had devastating consequences for towns in the northern British colonies as Indian tribes who were allied with France attacked English settlements. It was as part of these battles that York, Maine, was attacked, sending residents fleeing to Salem, Massachusetts, perhaps helping to provoke the Salem witch hysteria. European settlement of Maine was delayed for a generation.

Soon after that war ended, another war began in Europe, the War of the Spanish Succession, over rival claimants to the Spanish throne, one of whom was strongly backed by France, which sought to tighten its alliance with Spain. The other claimant was supported by Britain, in part, because Britain greatly feared a strong French-Spanish alliance. The war lasted from 1701 to 1713. The British colonists in North America called this war Queen Anne's War for the British monarch who ruled during this time. During this conflict, major battles took place between Spanish and British forces in Florida and the Carolinas. In the same period, battles continued to erupt between French and British forces in Canada and New England, with various Indian tribes allied on all sides. In one attack, Indians who had allied with the French devastated the town of Deerfield, Massachusetts.

As Britain, France, and Spain fought their wars in the 1600s, the five nations of the Iroquois were firmly allied with the English against the French and France's Indian allies. In 1689, a leader of the Mohawks—one of the five Iroquois nations—said of his people that, "as they are one hand and soul with the English, they will take up the ax with pleasure against the French." By the beginning of Queen Anne's War, however, some Iroquois were beginning to believe that their alliance with the English meant that the Iroquois did all the fighting but received little in return. In 1701, Iroquois leaders signed a separate treaty of peace with the French that gave them new trading rights, especially at French-owned Detroit.

For the next several decades, most of the Iroquois tried to keep clear of the continuing British-French tensions. Some Mohawks had different ideas, however. Despite their long alliance with the English, a group of Mohawks settled near Montreal in French Canada and converted to Catholicism. Among these settlements were also settlements of refugees from non-Iroquois tribes who had been defeated in King Philip's War (1675–1676). These refugees harbored an intense dislike of the English, especially the English in Massachusetts. They and their Canadian-based Iroquois allies nurtured a desire to show their support for France and seek revenge on Massachusetts for the loss of Indian lives in King Philip's War.

In February 1704, Canadian-based Mohawks destroyed the town of Deerfield, Massachusetts, and a frontier outpost near the New York border. Fifty colonists were killed, and perhaps 70 more were taken captive. By the end of the day, the town was a burning ruin. Deerfield's Congregational minister, Reverend John Williams, as well as his wife and remaining children, were taken hostage after one of the children was killed in the attack. His wife died on the forced march to Canada where the captives were taken. Eventually, Massachusetts officials ransomed Williams and most of the captives. The minister wrote an account of the attack and his captivity that became a best seller at the time.

To the utter surprise of Rev. Williams and the Massachusetts officials, however, some of the Deerfield captives preferred to stay in Canada with the Mohawks. Among them was Eunice Williams, the minister's daughter. She married a Mohawk, changed her name to A'ongote Gannenstenhawi, converted to Catholicism, and was the mother of three children raised in the Mohawk community. She lived a long life among her adopted community and died there in 1785 at the age of 95.

Even when there were periods of relative peace among the European powers, Indian tribes fought their own battles with the colonists. As white settlement expanded in the Carolinas, the Tuscarora tribe began to resist. In 1711, the Tuscaroras captured a leader of Swiss and German immigrants, Christoph von Graffenried, and the Carolina surveyor-general, John Lawson. Graffenried was freed, but the Tuscarora executed Lawson. In response, the South Carolina authorities declared war on the Tuscarora and enlisted another tribe, the Yamasee, as their allies. Within 2 years, most Tuscarora villages were burned, and a thousand of its tribe were killed. The remaining Tuscaroras moved west to avoid white settlement and, seeking further protection, affiliated with the Iroquois in 1722, enlarging the Iroquois League to six nations rather than five.

After the war, the Yamasee expected to be rewarded by the Carolina authorities for supporting their efforts. When no rewards were forthcoming, and when whites continued taking Yamasee as slaves, the Yamasee, in alliance with the Creeks, attacked Carolina plantations, killing settlers and traders in one of the bloodiest wars in colonial history. For a time, it was unclear whether the Carolina colony would survive, but officials sought an alliance with the powerful Cherokees, who had become dependent on trade with the British for the clothes and rifles. The Cherokees quickly defeated the Yamasees. Those Creeks and Yamasees who survived fled to Spanish Florida, leaving virtually no Yamasee or Creeks in the Carolinas. The British community also suffered significant loss of life in the Yamasee Wars, but it was clear they were the victors.

In 1739, after 25 years of peace between the major European powers that held claims in North America, Britain and Spain again went to war—the so-called War of Jenkins' Ear—when Spain claimed a right to search British ships in the Caribbean for contraband goods and Britain objected. (The odd nickname for the war referred to a British ship's captain, Robert Jenkins, whose ear was cut off by a Spanish boarding party.) The British defeated Spain in this war, which confirmed the dominance of British sea power in the Atlantic and Caribbean and made colonial trade with Britain and Britain's Caribbean colonies much easier.

Before the war of 1739 with Spain had ended, Britain and France were fighting again in the War of the Austrian Succession (referred to as King George's War in North America). Much of New York and New England was engulfed in that war. The result, again, was modest victories and land transfers, but with considerable loss of life to British and French colonists and to their Indian allies.

By 1754, another war erupted, known in Europe as the Seven Years' War and in British North America as the French and Indian War. Unlike the previous wars, the British would be decisively victorious at the end of the French and Indian War in 1763 (see Chapter 5). However, the consequences of expanding the British Empire in North America would be significant.

The many wars between 1689 and 1763 (see Table 4-2) disrupted life in North America. Colonial militias were called up. Colonial shipping was attacked. Settlements of colonists and Indians were damaged or ruined. Indian alliances shifted. Various tribes were either decimated or fled their homelands. Many colonists and Indians died, and for many of those who survived, life was far from secure.

The Unifying Effects of the Wars on British Colonies

During the many wars that took place in the 1700s, many English colonists developed a deep sense of patriotism to the British cause, often linked to an equally strong dislike of all things French and of the Indian nations allied with France. At the same

TABLE 4-2 Wars in British North America Between 1689 and 1763

Dates	Who Fought	Name of War in North America	Name of War in Britain	Impact/Outcome
1689–1697	English and British colonies allied with Iroquois against France, New France, and Indian allies	King William's War	War of the League of Augsburg or War of the Grand Alliance	Considerable devastation, especially in Maine; no border changes as a result
1702–1713	Same as King William's War, with Spain joining as an ally of France	Queen Anne's War	War of Spanish Succession	Primarily fought in Europe, but also in New England (against French Canada) and the Carolinas (against Spanish Florida); France and Spain determine to create Gulf colonies—New Orleans and San Antonio.
1739–1742	Britain against Spain; France remained neutral	War of Jenkins' Ear		Fought mostly in the Caribbean, though Georgia-based forces attacked Saint Augustine in Spanish Florida.
1744–1748	Britain against France	King George's War	War of Austrian Succession	French forces attacked and destroyed communities in New York; significant loss of life in New York and New England.
1754–1763	Britain against France and Spain with important Indian allies	French and Indian War	Seven Years' War	Largest war; Britain wins control of all of French Canada.

time, they came to realize that the British army was sometimes far away when it was most needed and that they needed to develop their own militias to protect themselves. The British monarchs were distracted by these wars and were inclined to neglect the colonies in the intervening years. As a result, colonial governments grew stronger and more independent through the early decades of the 1700s.

For most of his life, Benjamin Franklin was a loyal subject of the British Empire. In 1754, Franklin wrote that his greatest desire was for the people of Great Britain and the people of Britain's American colonies to "learn to consider themselves, not as belonging to different Communities with different Interests, but to one Community with one Interest." In 1754 many colonists agreed with Franklin.

By the early 1750s, it was clear to many who were living in British North America that the tension between England and France, which was playing out on both sides of the Atlantic, would soon lead to another war. In the early summer of 1754, several of the North American colonial governments appointed commissioners to meet in Albany, New York, to negotiate stronger mutual defense treaties with the Six Nations of the Iroquois and to discuss the common defense of the British colonies. Benjamin Franklin, who was chosen as one of Pennsylvania's four commissioners, wanted far more. He arrived in Albany with a plan for "one general government [that] may be formed in America, including all the said colonies." The particulars of the **Albany Plan of Union**, as it came to be known, included a provision that each colony would retain its own government, but that the new united colonies would be led by a council of representatives from the 13 colonies and a single "president general" appointed by the Crown. The unified government would have authority to raise soldiers, build forts, and regulate trade with the Indians. It would help the 13 colonies realize Franklin's

Albany Plan of Union
Plan put forward in 1754 by Massachusetts governor William Shirley, Benjamin Franklin, and other colonial leaders, calling for an intercolonial union to manage defense and Indian affairs.

Even as late as 1774, Benjamin Franklin, shown here with members of Parliament, considered himself a loyal British subject, trying his best to reduce tensions between the colonies and the authorities in London.

dream of being "one community with one interest" in relation to each other as well as to Great Britain. Franklin could not understand why the colonists couldn't borrow an idea from the Six Nations of the Iroquois with whom they were negotiating. As Franklin said, if the Iroquois "should be capable of forming a Scheme for such an Union" he could not understand why "a like Union should be impracticable for ten or a Dozen English Colonies."

In fact, Franklin's proposed plan, though supported by the commissioners who met in June and July of 1754, was defeated resoundingly by the colonies. Every colonial legislature rejected the plan, fearing it meant giving up too much control to other colonies and especially to the Crown, who would appoint the leader. At the same time, officials in London rejected the plan because they saw it giving too much power to the colonies. They preferred to have each colony accountable separately to London. Nevertheless, quite a few colonial leaders met each other for the first time at the Albany gathering, and the possibility of union had been mentioned and considered.

Tensions continued to grow between Britain and France and between Britain's Iroquois allies and the tribes allied with the French forces. As the British colonies saw the world moving toward a war between Great Britain and France—a war they knew would be fought in large part on the border between British North America and New France—colonial legislatures sought to raise taxes to provide for their defense. This need was especially urgent in Pennsylvania where Indians, allied with France, had defeated several western settlements and were within a day's distance of Philadelphia itself.

Even in this desperate situation, however, the Penn family, which still controlled the colony, refused to allow their own lands to be taxed. Although William Penn had founded the colony as a refuge for persecuted Quakers, his son Thomas saw it mostly as a source of income. By 1757, the Pennsylvania legislature decided to send a delegation to England to negotiate directly with Thomas Penn to get him to pay his fair share of the funds to protect his colony or, if that failed, to request the English government to give them a royal governor rather than one appointed by the Penn family. The obvious representative for Pennsylvania to send was Benjamin Franklin. The 51-year-old Franklin sailed for England that summer and, except for brief trips home, lived there until 1775. He did not get the funds from Penn but enjoyed London and, for many years, remained a very loyal British subject, even attending the coronation of King George III in 1760. However, beginning in the early 1760s, the pressure of war as well as issues of politics, trade, and taxes began to drive Britain and the colonists apart.

Quick Review How did European nations and the colonies' interaction with them affect life in British North America?

CONCLUSION

The Glorious Revolution of 1689 changed the balance of power in England's government. Although kings and queens were much more than figureheads, Parliament assumed greater control over the nation and its overseas territories. In 1707 England united with Scotland to become Great Britain and, with its colonies in North America and elsewhere around the world, became a true empire. The wars Britain conducted on the European mainland over the course of the 1700s with its old enemies France and Spain would lead to parallel conflicts between the North American colonies of these empires, conflicts that also involved Native American tribes allied with each one of them. Great Britain also exerted its economic control over the British colonies by enforcing mercantilism, a closed economic system that allowed for trade only between the colonies and the mother country. This system was designed to ensure the colonies supplied Great Britain with raw materials; in return, the colonies did not manufacture their own goods or buy them on a world market but, rather, purchased manufactured goods only from Great Britain. Nevertheless, Britain's American colonies grew and prospered with thriving port cities and an emerging colonial elite who sometimes became quite good at evading the British government's regulations.

The social and economic life of the American colonists also changed after the 1680s. In response to the revolt of slaves, indentured servants, and poor white farmers in Bacon's Rebellion, a trend among the wealthy elite to use more slaves and fewer indentured servants led to deeper divisions along racial lines in Virginia. The southern colonies, where the greatest growth of the slave population was taking place, enacted laws that created a slave society in which African slaves could expect a lifetime of servitude. The slave trade of the notorious Middle Passage brought increased numbers of slaves to support a growing slave-plantation economy.

In addition, underlying tensions connected to Indian attacks were growing. This tension, along with long-standing tensions about the role of women in society and beliefs across European cultures about the active role of witches in society, led to the Salem witch trials that involved an entire community in hysterical accusations, legal actions, and 20 executions.

Women's roles were largely relegated to the private realm—raising children and working in the home. Rural women often led lonely lives with few opportunities to connect with other women. Helping other women through childbirth was an important way rural women connected. Urban women had more options to socialize, particularly in the trade of household necessities such as preserved foods, soap, and candles. Some women joined their husbands as part of the privileged social and economic elite of the colonies.

From the first settlement in British North America onward, colonists maintained a sense that somehow their new land was a divinely planned opportunity to begin the world again and make it right. Cotton Mather, a well-known minister in Boston, confirmed this sense in his writings. By the early 1700s, however, the sense of being on a divine mission had declined among many colonists, and tolerance for religious diversity was growing. Those in Europe and in the colonies who began to look more to science and human reason than to faith in trying to understand their world, called this time the Age of Enlightenment. Some in this period rejected all religious teachings while others simply emphasized reason over faith. Many ministers worried about a religious decline in the colonies, and some sought ways to release religious energy, spawning the First Great Awakening. Yet other colonists came to a growing regard for other forms of self-improvement and interest, like those championed by Benjamin Franklin in his *Poor Richard's Almanack*. Increasingly, in spite of philosophical differences, colonists came to regard themselves more and more as Americans and less and less as simply British subjects living on a different side of the Atlantic Ocean.

CHAPTER REVIEW How did events throughout the 1700s transition the North American colonies from separate entities into a colonies with more common pursuits?

ENGLAND'S GLORIOUS REVOLUTION AND "THE RIGHTS OF ENGLISHMEN," 1689

4.1 Analyze the impact of England's Glorious Revolution on the thinking and political organization of British colonists in North America.

Review Questions

1. Comparison

Compare and contrast British ideas of kingship before and after the Glorious Revolution. What was the most important change brought about by the events of 1688 and 1689?

2. Historical Interpretation

What impact did the Glorious Revolution have on the political landscape of British North America?

THE PLANTATION WORLD: FROM A SOCIETY WITH SLAVES TO A SLAVE SOCIETY

4.2 Explain why and how slavery developed as it did in the late 1600s and early 1700s.

Review Questions

3. Chronological Reasoning

How and why did the relationship between slavery and race in British North America change between 1650 and 1750?

4. Contextualization

Describe the sequence of events that took the typical African slave from his or her homeland to the Americas. What physical and psychological hardships did slaves experience during this journey?

STABILITY AND INSTABILITY IN THE AMERICAN AND BRITISH WORLDS

4.3 Analyze the changes in the ideas and daily lives of the people in British North America in the 1700s as a result of events within and beyond the colonies.

Review Questions

5. Synthesis

What generalizations can you make about the lives of women in British North America during the 1700s? What are the limits of those generalizations?

6. Historical Interpretation

What role did cities play in the growing colonial economy of the 1700s?

7. Contextualization

What were the goals of the leaders of the First Great Awakening? How did they try to achieve them?

8. Historical Interpretation

How did wars between Europe's powers disrupt life in colonial America?

9. Contextualization

From the point of view of the British government, how did the American colonies fit into Britain's imperial trading economy?

A New Birth of Freedom— Creating the United States of America

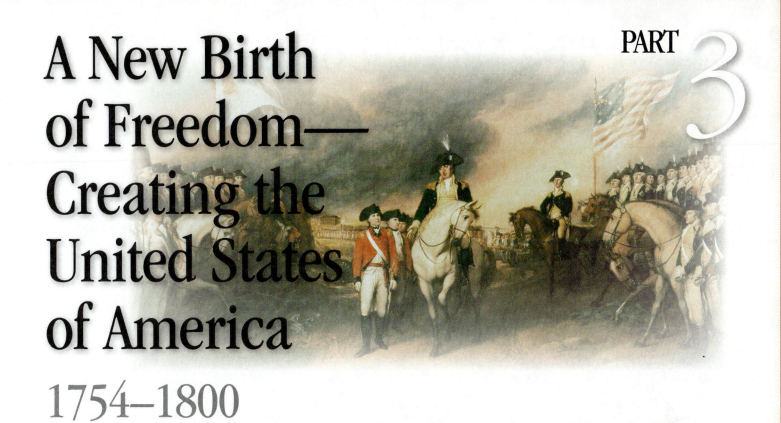

1754–1800

5 The Making of a Revolution

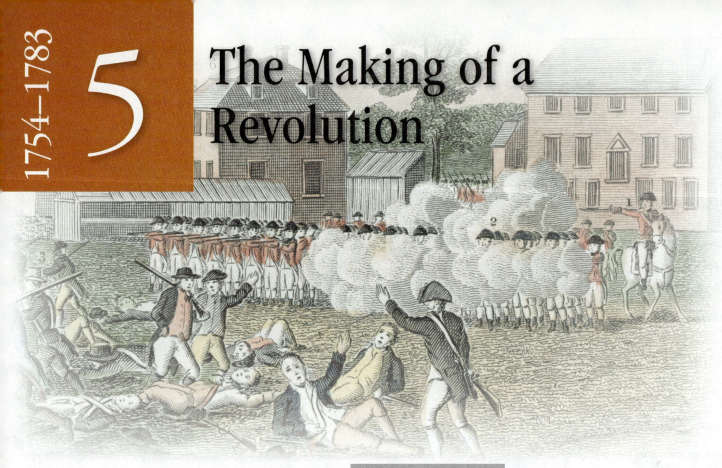

Far more than anyone else, George Washington dominated the era leading up to and through the American Revolution. It is important to remember that for much of this time, he was—as pictured here—an officer in the British army.

CHAPTER OBJECTIVE

Demonstrate an understanding of how Britain's victory over France in the war of 1754–1763 exacerbated the grievances of many colonists and led to renewed conflict culminating in the American Revolution and the Declaration of Independence.

LEARNING OBJECTIVES

PRELUDES TO REVOLUTION

5.1 Explain Britain's victory over France in the French and Indian War and what conflicts followed this victory.

THE REVOLUTION WAS IN THE MINDS OF THE PEOPLE

5.2 Explain why, in the 15 years before the Revolutionary War began, support for the patriot cause spread so quickly among many different groups of North Americans who opposed Britain for different reasons.

THE WAR FOR INDEPENDENCE

5.3 Explain how political and military strategy, support for the patriot cause, and American alliances with France and Spain led to an American victory in the war for independence.

On May 28, 1754, George Washington, then a 22-year-old gentleman farmer recently promoted to lieutenant colonel in the Virginia militia, and Tanaghrisson, an Iroquois chief, led a force of Virginia militia and Indians to attack French soldiers in what is now western Pennsylvania. The French troops had been sent from Fort Duquesne—modern Pittsburgh—to look for Washington's force. Fort Duquesne was part of a string of French forts built along the Ohio and Mississippi Rivers to maintain New France's claims in the region. The French perspective was that the English were trespassing on their territory. Washington, however, was asserting the British claim to the Ohio River Valley.

The English-Iroquois force surprised the French with a dawn attack. It had been raining and the French had failed to post sentries. Ten of the French were killed and 22 taken prisoner. The shots fired that May morning in what came to be called Jumonville Glen, after the French commander who was killed there, were among the first in a war that would have effects worldwide.

Although Washington defeated the French in that first attack, he knew that a much larger French force actually controlled the Ohio River Valley. He retreated from Jumonville Glen and built a small armed camp that he named Fort Necessity. In July, 50 French soldiers and 300 of their Indian allies forced Washington to surrender. The French allowed the English to return to Virginia but only after Washington signed a document admitting that he had attacked and killed—or assassinated, depending on how one translated the French—French troops in the May skirmish while Britain and France were officially at peace. That skirmish in Western Pennsylvania helped provoke a world war in the 1750s, and that war then influenced the residents of British North America, including George Washington, to fight for and win their independence in the 1770s.

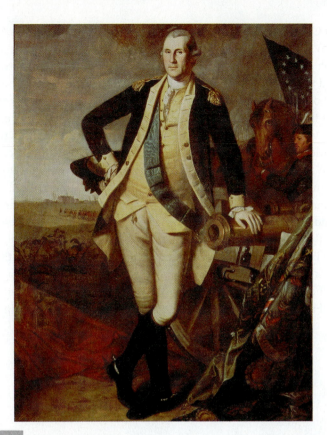

Far more than anyone else, George Washington dominated the era leading up to and through the American Revolution. It is important to remember that for much of this time, he was an officer in the British army before becoming—as shown here—a leader of the American forces.

Significant Dates

5.1

5.2

5.3

1754–1763	French and Indian War
1763–1766	Pontiac's Rebellion
	Paxton Boys attack Pennsylvania Indians
1765	Stamp Act crisis
Mid-1760s	Regulator movement in North and South Carolina
1770	Boston Massacre
1772	Slavery declared illegal in England
1773	Boston Tea Party
1774	Closing of the Port of Boston, Quebec Act, and other Intolerable Acts
	First Continental Congress meets in Philadelphia
1775	First battles of the Revolution at Lexington and Concord
	Second Continental Congress convenes at Philadelphia
	Battle of Bunker Hill
	British governor of Virginia, Lord Dunmore, declares freedom for slaves that join the British cause
1776	Thomas Paine's *Common Sense*
	British evacuate Boston but take New York City
	Congress adopts the Declaration of Independence
	Washington's troops capture Trenton, New Jersey
1777	Congress adopts the Articles of Confederation to govern the new United States
	American victory at Saratoga, New York
1778	France and United States agree to an alliance
1779	Washington's troops attack British-allied Iroquois villages
	Spain enters war against Britain
1780	British victories in the South
	British take Charleston, South Carolina
1781	American victory at Cowpens, South Carolina
	Lord Cornwallis surrenders to George Washington and allied French forces
1783	Treaty of Paris

PRELUDES TO REVOLUTION

5.1 Explain Britain's victory over France in the French and Indian War and what conflicts followed this victory.

In North America, the world war that started near Pittsburgh was known as the **French and Indian War**. Because of its outcome, French Canadians came to call it the War of Conquest. In most of Europe, it was called the Seven Years' War. Whatever the war was called, it was fought over more of the planet than any previous war. The voyages of Columbus and subsequent maritime trade and migrations had created a vast interactive world, and in 1756, that world exploded.

The French and Indian War, 1754–1763

In North America, the formal declaration of war in 1756—two years after Washington's skirmish with the French—surprised no one. The English and their Iroquois allies were in constant tension with the French and their Ottawa, Delaware, and Shawnee allies. Both sides hated each other and were ready for war.

During that time, Britain and France were also sliding toward war in Europe, Asia, Africa, and the Caribbean. In January 1756, England and the German kingdom of Prussia agreed to defend each other's territory. In response, Austria signed a treaty with France. War among these countries was declared in May 1756, and the French navy defeated a British fleet in the Mediterranean the next month. Counting on his English allies to provide support, King Frederick the Great of Prussia then attacked Austria and Russia. Sweden and Saxony joined the French alliance against Prussia.

The war quickly spread to Asia. The British East India Company and the French Compagnie des Indes each controlled parts of the Indian subcontinent, either directly or through alliances with local rulers. Suraj ud Dowlah, the ruler of Bengal, who was allied with France, used the situation to attack and capture British Calcutta. A British force

French and Indian War
Known in Europe as the Seven Years' War and in French Canada as the War of Conquest, this war was fought in North America between 1754 and 1763 and ended with the defeat of the French.

under Robert Clive retook the city and the French post at Chandernagor. British control of Bengal, won in that war, laid the foundation for Britain's 200-year rule in India.

The British also attacked the main African slave-trading island of Goree off the coast of Senegal and took control of it from the French, hurting the French economy but having no impact on the slave trade on the island. Goree had been the port for transshipment of slaves since the Portuguese founded it in the 1500s and was valuable no matter which government controlled the island because many nations purchased slaves there.

While battles took place in North America, Europe, India, and Africa, much of the Seven Years' War was fought in the Caribbean. British warships based in Jamaica captured the French islands of Grenada, the Grenadines, St. Vincent, Dominica, and Tobago as well as Martinique and Guadeloupe with their rich sugar plantations. At the war's end in 1763, Martinique and Guadeloupe were returned to France in exchange for concessions in North America, but the British kept the remaining islands. After Spain entered the war on the side of France in 1761, the British captured Havana, Cuba, and Manila in the Philippines, all of which were returned to Spain in 1763 in exchange for Spanish Florida.

The war changed the landscape of North America (see Map 5-1 and Map 5-2). In 1758, after a French force defeated the English at Fort Ticonderoga in New York, a

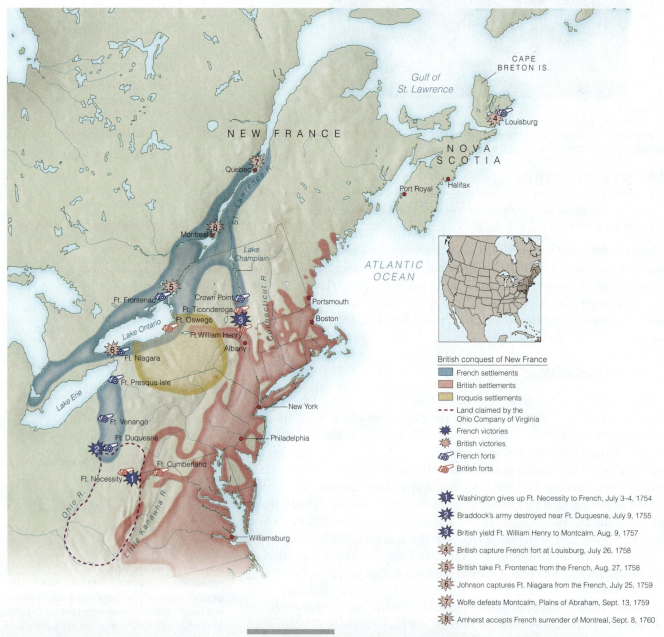

British conquest of New France
- French settlements
- British settlements
- Iroquois settlements
- – – – Land claimed by the Ohio Company of Virginia
- French victories
- British victories
- French forts
- British forts

1. Washington gives up Ft. Necessity to French, July 3–4, 1754
2. Braddock's army destroyed near Ft. Duquesne, July 9, 1755
3. British yield Ft. William Henry to Montcalm, Aug. 9, 1757
4. British capture French fort at Louisburg, July 26, 1758
5. British take Ft. Frontenac from the French, Aug. 27, 1758
6. Johnson captures Ft. Niagara from the French, July 25, 1759
7. Wolfe defeats Montcalm, Plains of Abraham, Sept. 13, 1759
8. Amherst accepts French surrender of Montreal, Sept. 8, 1760

MAP 5-1 North America Before and During the French and Indian War, 1754-1763.

British dominance in eastern North America
- Acquired by Britain from France
- Acquired by Britain from Spain
- Prior British colonies, as of 1763
- Reserved to Indians under British rule
- Spanish Louisiana

Points of violence, 1763–1766
- British forts seized during Pontiac's Rebellion in 1763
- Towns demonstrating against the Stamp Act in 1765

Distribution of British troops
- British posts 100–250 soldiers
- British posts 250–600 soldiers
- British posts over 600 soldiers

MAP 5-2 North America After the French and Indian War, 1763. Maps 5-1 and 5-2 show the extraordinary changes brought about by the French and Indian War of 1754–1763. The first map shows the relatively limited range of control exercised by both the British and the French colonies in North America when the war began, as well as significant battles between the powers. The second map shows the huge expanse of territory claimed by the British at the war's end in 1763 including the 13 colonies along the Atlantic coast, the large Indian reserve of land promised to the tribes that had supported the British, the former French colonies in Canada and the former Spanish colonies of East and West Florida that were also in British hands.

British force—with George Washington as one of its officers—took Fort Duquesne, renaming it Fort Pitt (today's Pittsburgh) in honor of William Pitt, who had led Britain as prime minister during the war. That same year, Teedyuscung, leader of the Delaware tribe, decided that his French allies could not be trusted and sought an alliance with the English and the Iroquois. Although Teedyuscung and the Delaware did not get the Pennsylvania lands they sought, they and the Iroquois received a British promise that after the war there would be no white settlement west of the Alleghenies—a promise the British attempted to keep until the American Revolution.

In the most significant North American battle, a British army under General James Wolfe defeated a French army led by the Marquis de Montcalm and captured Quebec, the capital of French Canada, in September 1759. The British victory ended French control of all of Canada.

By the early 1760s, both Britain and France were exhausted from the fighting. Although Britain had won major victories, its new king, George III (r. 1760–1820) wanted peace, and in 1763, the two countries signed the Treaty of Paris to end the war. (Both this treaty and the later treaty ending the American Revolution in 1783 were known as the Treaty of Paris.)

The world war had many outcomes. All of the governments that fought the war emerged deeply in debt. In Europe, little land changed hands, but in other parts of the world, the changes were dramatic. Britain made concessions to bring hostilities to an end, but was still the biggest winner. Its dominance of India was secure, and the British presence on the coast of Africa and in the Caribbean was enhanced. In addition, Spain ceded Florida to England. Most significantly, the war eliminated France as a North American power although France did regain its control of the rich sugar-producing islands of Guadeloupe and Martinique in the Caribbean. France ceded Canada and the land east of the Mississippi River to the British. To compensate its Spanish allies for their support, France also ceded its claim to the lands west of the Mississippi River, along with New Orleans, to Spain. The French threat to New England and New York ended. Britain now controlled most of North America east of the Mississippi River.

Pontiac and Indian Responses

Pontiac's Rebellion
Indian uprising (1763–1766) led by Pontiac of the Ottawas and Neolin of the Delawares.

For American Indians living between the Mississippi River and the Atlantic, the end of the French and Indian War was an unmitigated disaster. As a British official had said, "to preserve the balance between us and the French is the great ruling principle of the modern Indian politics." For the tribes further south—including the Cherokee and Creeks—the Spanish presence in Florida had allowed them to play a three-way balancing act between Britain, France, and Spain. But with the French and Spanish out of eastern North America for the time being, the potential for bargaining virtually disappeared.

Even for the Iroquois, the cost was high. Although they were allied with the British, Iroquois power had partly come from Britain's need for Iroquois allies in its competition with the French. After 1763, the French were gone. At the war's beginning, the Iroquois Chief Hendrick, or Theyanoguin, had told the representatives of the British colonies who met at Albany, New York:

> Brethren—The Governor of Virginia and the Governor of Canada, are both quarrelling….The Governor of Virginia and Pennsylvania have made paths thro' our Country…they should have first asked our consent.

SOI-EN-GA-RAH-TA,
OR
KING HENDRICK.

Hendrick, a chief of the Mohawk tribe—one of the nations of the Iroquois—was a close ally of the British until killed in battle in 1755.

Without the presence of the French in Canada, the British governors of Virginia and Pennsylvania had little reason to ask the Iroquois for consent to anything. The British general Lord Jeffrey Amherst, seeking to save money for his government and seeing no reason now to placate the Indians, refused to provide the gifts of ammunition and gunpowder that various tribes had come to see as a kind of rent for the use of their lands. The Indians considered the move to be both an insult and a fundamental threat since the tribes' survival depended on the gunpowder to hunt deer.

For the Indians who had sided with the French, the outlook was even worse. Neolin, a Delaware, living on the Ohio River, preached resistance to the "dogs clothed in red" as he called the British. His visionary message, calling on the Indians to return to the "original state that they were in before the white people found out their country," sparked a wide-ranging Indian movement to return to former Indian ways.

Pontiac, an Ottawa chief, was inspired and heeded Neolin's call, sparking what came to be known as **Pontiac's Rebellion**. In the spring of 1763, only months after the Treaty of Paris was signed, Pontiac

THINKING HISTORICALLY

Pontiac's Vision

Seeking support for an uprising, Pontiac described a vision similar to Neolin's in which the Master of Life or the Great Spirit told him to return to living by "the bow and arrow" with no need of "gun or powder" and to cleanse his people and their land of the ways of the whites. Pontiac said:

> This land where ye dwell I have made for you and not for others. Whence comes it that ye permit the Whites upon your lands? Can ye not live without them? I know that those whom ye call the children of your Great Father supply your needs, but if ye were not evil, as ye are, ye could surely do without them. Ye could live as ye did live before knowing them—before those whom ye call your brothers had come upon your lands.

Thinking Critically

1. **Documentary Analysis**
   Who did Pontiac blame for the occupation of Indian lands by whites, the English colonists or his own people?

2. **Historical Interpretation**
   In what ways does Pontiac's vision represent a call for cultural and spiritual reform? What connections might Pontiac have seen between such reforms and successful resistance to white encroachment?

convened a meeting of Ottawa, Chippewa, Pottawatomi, and Wyandot people near Detroit. Pontiac told his listeners of his vision in which he had been promised that, if they would cleanse themselves of the ways of the whites, they would see their lands and old powers restored. He insisted, "It is important for us, my brothers, that we exterminate from our lands this nation which seeks only to destroy us."

Pontiac and his followers attacked British forts across the region. The British held Detroit and Fort Pitt, but many other forts surrendered to the Indians: Fort Miamis, near Fort Wayne, Indiana; Fort Ouiatenon, near Lafayette, Indiana; Fort Michilimackinac on the Great Lakes; and most of the old French posts in Indiana and Ohio. Most of the Ohio country was again in Indian hands. The British were caught off guard but fought back.

The English commander, Jeffrey Amherst, ordered his troops to put "every Indian in your Power to Death." His troops won several battles. Amherst also encouraged the distribution of smallpox-infected blankets to Indians, a move that rapidly spread the disease. In October, Pontiac received a letter from the French telling him that the French were not going to come to his aid. On receiving this news, Pontiac initiated a peace process. He met with the British authorities in Oswego, New York, in July 1766 and signed a treaty of peace. Three years later, he was murdered, probably by other Indians who resented both the deaths his rebellion had caused and his relatively quick surrender that meant the deaths were in vain.

The Proclamation Line of 1763

Soon after the long French and Indian War, the new British monarch King George III and his first minister George Grenville tried to ensure peace in North America. They meant to honor the commitments they had made in 1758 to the Delaware and Iroquois tribes and protect them from white settlement. Already embroiled in Pontiac's conflict, which largely involved formerly French territories, they did not want other rebellions, and they were wary that land-hungry settlers would quickly begin to expand into Indian-dominated areas. In October 1763, the king issued a proclamation that there should be no British settlement west of the crest of the Appalachian Mountains and that Indian rights to western lands would be protected forever. The proclamation also directed any colonists who had already settled in these lands "forthwith to remove themselves from such Settlements." For many of the tribes who lived on the

The Proclamation Line
Royal proclamation of 1763 designed to protect Indian tribes by setting a boundary at the peaks of the Appalachian Mountains beyond which no western white settlement was to take place.

western slopes of the mountains and beyond, the **Proclamation Line** fulfilled what they believed they had been promised.

The Grenville administration took other steps to keep peace with the Indians. They replaced Amherst with the more conciliatory General Thomas Gage, who immediately resumed negotiations and gift giving with the tribes. The Grenville administration also strengthened the authority of the superintendents of Indian affairs, who had sought accommodations with the tribes since the 1750s.

The Proclamation Line slowed white settlement into western Pennsylvania, Ohio, and what would become Kentucky. But it also infuriated the British colonists—both land-hungry farmers and rich speculators—and did far too little to protect the Indians. Grenville and Parliament were too far away, and despite the British military outposts, their efforts to enforce the line were ineffectual, which had fateful consequences in the next decade.

The Paxton Boys and Rural White Responses

In the town of Paxton, in Pennsylvania's Lancaster County, a group of farmers decided that the way to end warfare between whites and Indians on the frontier was to get rid of all Indians, whether they were allied with the British or the French. Calling themselves the Paxton Boys or the Hickory Boys, these frontier vigilantes said:

> We have long been convinced from sufficient evidence that the Indians that lived as independent commonwealths among us or near our borders were our most dangerous enemies.

In December 1763, the Paxton Boys attacked a Delaware village, killed six people, and burned the town. Then they killed 14 Indian survivors who were in protective custody in the town of Lancaster. They began a march to Philadelphia to find other Indians, especially Delawares, who had taken refuge there. Before the mob got to Philadelphia, Benjamin Franklin and a delegation of the colony's leading citizens negotiated an end to the rebellion, but the hatred of Indians would haunt the inhabitants of North America for a long time to come. After 1763, many white residents of British North America began to lump all American Indians together as an enemy race, even though their parents and grandparents had viewed different tribes quite separately, depending on a tribe's relationship to the British cause. Like many earlier wars, the fighting in the French and Indian War was between the British and the Iroquois allies on one side and the French and the Ojibwa, Ottawa, Shawnee, Wyandot, and other tribes allied with them. Soon after the war, the lines came to be seen as much more racial, with all whites allied against virtually all Indians. This change in attitudes had far-reaching consequences for the residents of North America.

Threats of New Taxes

Relations between the British colonists and the American Indians were not the only concern of British authorities after 1763. Victory in the war had virtually drained the kingdom's treasury. Britain's national debt was double what it had been when the war began. In 1764, George Grenville and the majority in Parliament asked Britain's North American colonists to pay what the authorities in London thought was a fair share of the war's cost. Their argument was that the war had protected colonists far more than it had anyone living in Britain. What seemed just and equitable in London, however, was seen quite differently in the colonies. These differences on who should bear the cost of the war would soon have significant consequences.

5.1 **Quick Review** What expectations and concerns did Indians come to have regarding the British in the aftermath of the war of 1756–1763? What expectations and concerns were colonists beginning to have regarding Native Americans? Regarding the British government? How were the various expectations and concerns in conflict?

"THE REVOLUTION WAS IN THE MINDS OF THE PEOPLE"

5.2 Explain why, in the 15 years before the Revolutionary War began, support for the patriot cause spread so quickly among many different groups of North Americans who opposed Britain for different reasons.

Long after the Revolution was over, former president John Adams wrote to another former president, Thomas Jefferson, describing the Revolutionary War that began in 1775 as "only an effect and consequence." According to Adams, "The Revolution was in the minds of the people, and this was effected from 1760 to 1775, in the course of fifteen years before a drop of blood was shed at Lexington." He was right. For many British North Americans, a revolutionary change did indeed take place in their minds between 1760 and 1775, and it took place for many different reasons.

While people like Adams and Jefferson and many of their peers moved from being loyal British subjects to revolutionary advocates of independence in those years, others did not. People such as Thomas Hutchinson of Massachusetts, William Franklin (Benjamin's son), and perhaps a fifth of the white colonists remained **Loyalists**— Americans who wanted to maintain loyal ties to Great Britain and who opposed the American Revolution. For reasons of their own, a majority of African slaves were probably also Loyalists. The Loyalists lived through the same momentous changes as those who embraced the revolutionary cause, but they came to different conclusions. Still other colonists remained neutral throughout the struggle, focusing on personal matters or simply not caring who ultimately governed them.

Loyalists
The name given to those in the colonies— perhaps one-fifth to one-third of the total population—who supported the British and opposed American independence.

In addition, people in the colonies came to their own differing conclusions at varying times. Sailors and shop owners in Boston, New York, and Philadelphia as well as backwoods farmers in western Pennsylvania, Virginia, and the Carolinas were sometimes much more ready for revolution, much sooner, than their better-known leaders.

For African slaves, the growing spirit of revolution held both potential and danger. Some slaves and free blacks saw in the revolutionary rhetoric the possibility of their own freedom. In contrast, other African-Americans saw the British government as a potential protector and even liberator against slave owners who embraced the patriot cause. Potential for freedom was not a guarantee in any scenario, however.

The Iroquois, Cherokee, and other Indian tribes knew that frontier whites had little use for the king's ban on white settlement and, if freed from British authority, would stream west. As the possibility of expanded settlement fueled revolutionary fervor among frontier whites, it also fed fears among Indians, most of whom sided with the British after 1776.

In effect, during the 15 fateful years that John Adams described above, many different groups of people with wide-ranging hopes and fears considered the possibility of an American Revolution and arrived at different conclusions. Each of these groups fought their own revolutions, sometimes in alliance with each other, sometimes acting at cross-purposes. Far from being clear, the goals and tactics of the revolutionaries were an ever-changing patchwork as different groups fought for their own purposes and made shifting alliances.

Transition from the "Rights of Man" to Revolt

Many residents of the British colonies had grown up reading John Locke's defense of Britain's Glorious Revolution of 1689. Long before tensions between the colonies and the government in London reached a crisis, colonists believed, as Locke said, that the people always retained "a supreme power to remove or alter the legislative" authority when they wanted to. Throughout the 1770s, Locke's ideas guided some of the Revolution's most articulate advocates such as Thomas Jefferson, John Adams, and Benjamin Franklin as well as backwoods rebels like Ethan Allen, a man of modest

republicanism
A complex, changing body of ideas, values, and assumptions that held that self-government by the citizens of a country, or their representatives, provided a more reliable foundation for good society and individual freedom than rule by kings or any other distant elite.

education who was the leader of Vermont's Green Mountain Boys. Using Locke's arguments in their speeches and lawsuits, they taunted royal governors, and ultimately, they used Locke's ideas to justify armed resistance.

Revolutionary leaders also read and cited French philosophers—Voltaire, Rousseau, and Montesquieu—and authors from ancient Greece and Rome, all of whom advocated a commitment to liberty and the need to overthrow unjust authorities. Leaders of the patriot cause became convinced that England represented the evils of empire while the colonists represented the virtues of **republicanism**, which supported a broad distribution of power to people, enabling them to determine how and by whom they would be governed.

Leaders on both sides of the Atlantic, those who argued for independence and those who argued to maintain the ties between Britain and the American colonies, all read the same literature. Nearly all of them believed that George III ruled only by the consent of Parliament, not from any sort of divine right. For a hundred years before the American Revolution, British subjects in the old and new worlds constituted a community of people who valued "the rights of Englishmen" and distrusted efforts to undermine those rights. When, in 1776, Thomas Jefferson wrote that the colonies had a right to independence because it was a self-evident truth that "all men are created equal; that they are endowed by their creator with certain unalienable rights," he was reflecting a way of thinking that was familiar in America and Britain.

Those who shared common ideas about rights, liberty, and freedom extended beyond just residents of Britain and North America. The world that was at war in the 1750s and 1760s became a world involved in revolution in the 1770s and 1780s and beyond. Although the government of the King Louis XVI of France would play an essential role in the American victory, Louis XVI himself would lose his throne and his head to a French revolution within the next decade. The French and American Revolutions led to further revolutionary efforts across much of Europe as people in Germany, Poland, Scandinavia, and Italy attempted their own revolutions. Future president James Madison wrote in 1792 that "America has set the example and France has followed it, of charters of power granted by liberty."

Madison did not, however, mention another revolution that was much closer to the United States than those in Europe. In 1791, slaves in the French colony of Saint Domingue (modern Haiti) rebelled. Saint Domingue was one of the richest and most oppressive slave systems in the world, where some 500,000 African slaves grew sugar and coffee that made the 40,000 French owners very rich. A free black, Toussaint L'Overture—who quoted the same philosophers as North American revolutionaries— led the rebels in Haiti to win a series of victories. L'Overture himself was captured and died in France, but a new free Republic of Haiti was proclaimed in 1804. The rebellion was the most successful slave revolt in history and another in a long line of revolutions against distant authorities.

In addition, not long after the American Revolution, between 1810 and 1826, most of Latin America expelled its Spanish and Portuguese colonial masters. Simón Bolívar led revolutionary movements in his native Venezuela and helped establish the Republics of Columbia, Ecuador, Peru, and Bolivia. His 1812 *Manifesto of Cartagena* expressed the same philosophical ideas as those of his counterparts in North America and Europe. The American Revolution, then, was part of a worldwide revolution against distant authorities and old ideas, and it was based on a new philosophical understanding of "the rights of man" and the way the world should be organized.

The Accompanying Revolution in Religion

In 1740, a Presbyterian minister, Gilbert Tennent, one of the leaders of the Great Awakening (see Chapter 4), preached a sermon on "The Danger of an Unconverted Ministry" in churches throughout New Jersey and Pennsylvania. Tennent's sermon, with its plea to test the personal faith of ministers, was a direct challenge to the leaders of the major Protestant denominations—Presbyterian, Congregational, and Episcopal. As a result of the Great Awakening, church members claimed permission—indeed, the responsibility—to judge their ministers. It was not a great leap for citizens to claim the same permission, and responsibility, for judging those in civil authority.

One visiting revivalist asserted that Patrick Henry, rector of the Episcopal church in Hanover, Virginia (and uncle to the patriot leader Patrick Henry), was a "stranger to true religion." Reverend Henry, in return, demanded that Virginia's governor stop these "strolling preachers" who were, in his view, "a set of incendiaries, enemies not only to the Established Church, but also common disturbers of the peace." In a way, Henry was right. The Great Awakening disturbed the peace, split churches, and undermined all authorities.

Seaport Radicalism—From the Stamp Act to the Boston Massacre and Boston Tea Party

The Boston Tea Party of 1773 was probably the most famous act of resistance in America before the Revolution, but it was far from the first. Between 1747 and 1774, dockworkers, sailors, and townspeople drove the leading British officials—customs officials, navy officers, and even governors—away from the docks and out of Boston five times. Similar acts of rebellion took place from New York to the Carolinas.

Impressment had been British navy policy for centuries and, since the 1690s, had been a source of riots in colonial ports. When a warship was short of sailors, which happened often due to high rates of death and desertion, the captain had the authority to impress (or kidnap) likely sailors from merchant ships or ports and sign them up for naval service. Commercial sailors were paid higher wages than those in the navy and often had better working conditions, so impressments were, as one senior British naval officer noted, a source of "Hatred for the King's Service . . . [and] a Spirit of Rebellion," for many who lived along the waterfront.

Impressment
The British policy of forcibly enlisting sailors into the British navy against their will. It had long been a source of resentment toward the British government in port towns.

In November 1747, British Commodore Charles Knowles sent sailors in search of new recruits while his ship was in Boston Harbor. They impressed 46 men into service. A rebellious crowd responded, taking some of Knowles's officers hostage and chasing the royal governor out of town. A successful brewer, Samuel Adams, defended the rioters as an "Assembly of People drawn together upon no other Design than to defend themselves and repel the Assaults of a Press-Gang." He insisted that they "had a natural right" to do so. Perhaps his cousin, John Adams, should have considered an earlier date than 1760 for the start of revolutionary thinking in the colonies.

British actions in the 1760s and 1770s escalated tensions in North American cities. The British government desperately needed to pay off the debt from the French and Indian War and attempted to do so, in part, by imposing new taxes. With each attempt—the Sugar and Currency Acts of 1764, the Stamp Act of 1765, the Townshend duties of 1767, and the Tea Act of 1773—colonial resistance grew. In a spiraling series of encounters, Parliament sought to raise funds, backed off in the face of colonial resistance, and then enacted new "get tough" policies that also backfired (see Table 5-1). The impact of the persistent but failed efforts to raise taxes fueled colonial resistance and the sense that resistance was effective. The taxes seemed fair only to those in Britain who were in power. The colonists saw each tax as a new attack on their liberty and each British effort at compromise as a sign of weakness.

The Sugar Act of 1764, the first tax, and the Currency Act of 1764 provoked limited but spirited resistance. The tax on sugar included rum and molasses, both made from sugar. The Currency Act prohibited colonies from issuing their own paper money as legal tender for either public debts, including paying taxes, or private debts, including paying merchants for goods made in Britain. In response, merchants and artisans in New York and Boston joined in a nonimportation movement in 1764 that was the beginning of a growing refusal to buy or use anything manufactured in Britain.

TABLE 5-1 Parliamentary Acts that Fueled Colonial Resistance

Name of Act	Description
The Sugar Act of 1764	Increased duties and strengthened collection of customs on rum and molasses, which particularly affected merchants and importers
The Currency Act of 1764	Prohibited the colonies from issuing their own paper money as legal tender for public or private debts to Britain
The Stamp Act of 1765	Taxed all legal and commercial documents, creating an immediate hardship for business leaders and building resentment in many ports where people depended on those businesses for jobs
The Declaratory Act of 1766	Repealed the Stamp Act but said Parliament could legislate for the colonies in "all cases Whatsoever"
The Revenue Act of 1766	Restricted trade in sugar, which helped British and Caribbean merchants at the expense of North American merchants
The second Revenue Act of 1767 (also known as the Townshend duties after Charles Townshend, chancellor of the Exchequer)	Placed new duties on paper, lead, paint, glass, and tea. All but the tax on tea were repealed in 1770—the same day as the Boston Massacre.
The Tea Act of 1773	Allowed the British East India Company to ship tea to the colonies without having to pay normally required duties, making it cheaper than most smuggled tea. The Townshend tea tax would still apply once it reached the colonies. The Act supported the East India Company, almost bankrupt because so many customers were purchasing cheaper, smuggled tea from elsewhere.
The "Intolerable Acts" of 1774	Parliament's response to the tea riots; they closed the port of Boston, expanded the royal governor's authority, shifted control of the Ohio River country to the British governor in Quebec (the Quebec Act), and allowed British troops to use any uninhabited building as a barracks, without the owner's authorization (the Quartering Act).

Sons of Liberty

Secret organizations in the colonies formed to oppose the Stamp Act. From 1765 until independence, members spoke, wrote, and took direct action against British measures especially the Stamp Tax and the tax on tea.

A year later, resistance to the Stamp Act of 1765 was stronger, and it united colonists of many social classes. The act required legal and commercial documents, including magazines, newspapers, and playing cards to be printed on special paper showing an official stamp. Payment for the stamped paper had to be in British currency. In the spring of 1765, Patrick Henry asked Virginia's legislature, the House of Burgesses, to pass resolutions that came to be known as the Virginia Resolves opposing the tax. Middling and upper-class New Yorkers—including lawyers and merchants who would have had to pay the highest taxes if the law was enforced—began writing articles against the tax in the city's many newspapers, which circulated widely. Some also formed a new secret organization, the **Sons of Liberty**, which sent delegates to all the colonies to create a kind of underground resistance to the tax—a tax they described as a sign of British tyranny. Nine colonies sent delegates to a gathering known as the Stamp Act Congress in New York City in October 1765. There they issued a Declaration of Rights and Grievances, which said that Parliament had no right to tax the colonies, and they petitioned for a repeal of the Stamp and Sugar Acts.

More important than the petition was the fact that leaders of the growing resistance movement met together and began to sense their unity. As one of the organizers of the congress said, "There ought to be no New England men, no New Yorker, etc. known on the Continent, but all of us Americans." This appeal to unity was a new sentiment in colonies that had, up until now, jealously guarded their independence from each other. Britain's parliamentary action had provoked this increasing unity.

While colonial leaders met and wrote petitions, some of the strongest resistance to the stamp tax developed in the working-class taverns where laborers and sailors gathered. Poor people had little reason to actually pay the tax because they did not use many legal documents or paper products that would require the stamped paper, but the tax was a symbol of British arrogance and threatened to slow the colonial economy, which could put sailors and laboring people out of work. To the poor, the haughty British authorities were becoming intolerable.

When Lieutenant Governor Cadwallader Colden placed the embossing stamps in Fort George—at the tip of Manhattan—until the new tax went into effect on November 1, 1765, public protests mounted into what came to be known as the New York Stamp Act Riot. New York merchants and groups like the Sons of Liberty agreed not to import any British goods while the Stamp Act was in force. In taverns across the city, angry citizens shared their discontent with the British. On the evening of November 1, a crowd paraded around the city with torches as well as effigies of the lieutenant governor and the devil. They dared the British troops to fire on them and burned Colden's coach. Next, the crowd broke into the home of Major James of the Royal Artillery, drank his considerable supply of liquor, and burned the house. Calling themselves the Sons of Neptune to distinguish themselves from the more middle class Sons of Liberty, the crowd resisted efforts to end the violence. Months later, when news reached New York in May 1766 that the Stamp Act had been repealed, celebrating crowds fired guns, broke windows, and erected a "liberty pole" to taunt British authorities.

Similar riots by the "lower sorts" took place in other colonial cities. In Boston, a mob ransacked the governor's home, and in Annapolis, Maryland, a crowd burned the stamp distributor's warehouse and forced him to flee the colony. In Wilmington, North Carolina, a mocking, angry crowd paraded the stamp collector through the streets. And in Charleston, South Carolina, a crowd of workers and seamen burned effigies of the stamp distributor.

In response to the unrest, British authorities under the new prime minister, the Marquess of Rockingham, decided to repeal the Stamp and Sugar taxes but also to show force. In 1766, while repealing the taxes, Parliament also voted the Declatory Act, which claimed its right to tax and regulate the colonies "in all cases Whatsoever." In addition, Parliament passed the Revenue Act of 1766, restricting trade in sugar, which helped British and Caribbean merchants at the expense of colonial merchants.

A year later, Charles Townshend, chancellor of the Exchequer (treasurer) in a new British government, imposed new taxes on lead, paint, paper, and tea, known as the second Revenue Act of 1767 (also known as the Townshend duties of 1767). The new British government was desperate to find a way to pay off the war debt but also wanted to assert Parliament's authority over the colonies. In particular, Parliament wanted to curtail smuggling by some of the most prosperous colonial merchants and to control the mobs that kept rioting in Boston and New York. In September 1768, the warships of the Royal Navy arrived in Boston, and British troops marched through town in a show of the government's authority. According to Paul Revere, the troops "Formed and Marched with insolent Parade, Drums beating, Fifes playing, and Colours flying, up King Street." The presence of so many troops created a sense of siege in Boston.

A year and a half later, British soldiers were still stationed in Boston, creating constant tensions with residents who resented their presence. One source of the tension was the fact that off-duty soldiers were allowed to work on their own part-time, increasing competition with colonists for jobs by accepting lower wages. On the evening of March 5, 1770, an angry crowd began to throw snowballs at British soldiers. They taunted the lone British sentry at the State House, Private Hugh White. As the crowd around White grew, more people joined in the taunting or watched from the sidelines. John Adams called the crowd "a motley rabble," but they had strong support in a city tired of the presence of so many soldiers.

British Captain Thomas Preston sent more soldiers to support White while the crowd grew to 300 or 400. Preston asked the crowd to disperse, assuring them that the soldiers would not fire since he himself was standing directly in front of them. However, someone threw something that knocked one of the soldiers down, and some of the soldiers started firing, even though no one heard Preston give any orders. Three men were killed—including a seaman, Crispus Attucks, a former slave who was part African and part American Indian and who would be celebrated as the first man and first black

The BOSTONIAN'S Paying the EXCISE-MAN, or TARRING & FEATHERING.
Plate I.

This picture, titled "The Bostonians Paying the Excise-Man," shows many forms of resistance to British taxes that developed, including the mob actions that sometimes coated an offending tax collector with tar and feathers or forced him to drink boiling tea. In the background, a Liberty Tree—symbol of freedom—sports a hangman's noose, and colonists dump tea off a ship.

Boston Massacre

After months of increasing friction between townspeople and the British troops stationed in the city, on March 5, 1770, British troops fired on American civilians in Boston who were throwing projectiles at them, killing five and stirring even greater hatred toward the British army.

person to die in the Revolution. Two more later died of their wounds. The **Boston Massacre**, as colonists called it, fueled anger at the British authorities. To avoid further confrontation, the Royal Governor pulled the troops out of Boston. His action also left most of the town in the hands of an increasingly anti-British population.

Some of the British troops involved were accused of murder. John Adams defended them in a subsequent trial (in which they were found not guilty). Later, Adams said that his defense of the soldiers, though highly unpopular, was, "one of the most gallant, generous, manly and disinterested Actions of my whole Life." Nevertheless, Adams also said that there was "no Reason why the Town should not call the Action of that Night a Massacre." Paul Revere described the event as a deliberate military attack on a peaceful crowd. Sam Adams created a "committee of correspondence" to encourage resistance in other colonies. With such rhetoric, many Bostonians would likely never again be loyal British subjects.

In 1773, Britain decided to maintain the tax on tea, but repeal the other Townshend duties. The Tea Act of 1773 not only asserted Parliament's authority to levy whatever taxes it wished but also attempted to protect the almost-bankrupt British East India Company, which was struggling because customers were purchasing cheaper, smuggled tea elsewhere. Under the act, the East India Company could ship large quantities of tea to the colonies without paying required duties, making the tea cheaper for the colonists, even with the Townshend tea tax. The plan was to encourage colonists to buy the taxed British East India Company tea instead of smuggled teas.

Given the tension and anger in Boston, the city's response could easily have been predicted. City residents had no intention of paying that tax, even on discounted tea. In New York, Philadelphia, and Charleston, patriotic groups, often led by the Sons of Liberty, convinced merchants not to allow the tea to land from the British ships. "No taxation without representation," became the rallying cry from colonists who were fed up with having no say in matters that affected them.

In November 1773, a shipment of British tea arrived in Boston on the ship *Dartmouth*. Even before it arrived, crowds had forced the tea merchants to barricade themselves in their warehouse. Once the *Dartmouth* appeared, a crowd forced the ship to move to Griffin's Wharf where dockworkers, sailors, and merchants, not the British authorities, controlled the dock. The customs commissioners fled rather than risk getting tarred and feathered, an increasingly popular punishment by patriotic crowds for those who supported royal authority. Governor Thomas Hutchinson would not let the *Dartmouth* sail back to England, and the crowd would not let the tea be unloaded. The stand-off lasted into December.

In this print, designed to fuel hostility toward the British more than provide an accurate record, Paul Revere showed the British soldiers—more organized than they actually were—firing on a helpless crowd.

On December 16, angry citizens met at the Old South Meeting House. When the governor would not back down, Samuel Adams said, "This meeting can do nothing more to save the country." The crowd's response—probably well rehearsed—was a series of faked Indian war whoops, a shout of "Boston harbor a tea-pot tonight," and a call to gather at Griffin's Wharf. As thousands watched from the shore, men, slightly disguised as Mohawks, boarded the *Dartmouth* and dumped the tea into Boston Harbor.

The Boston Tea Party galvanized anti-British sentiment in other colonies, and the city was seen as the incubator of revolutionary activity long before the next shots were fired. In response to the incident, the British closed the port of Boston to all shipping, creating a financial crisis that led to further anger and unrest among not only dockworkers but also the merchant elites who depended on the port for their wealth.

Daughters of Liberty

Organized as a women's response to the Sons of Liberty, the Daughters opposed British measures, avoided British taxed tea, spun their own yarn, and wove their own cloth to avoid purchasing British goods.

Women, too, became increasingly involved in leading their own protests. In response to the Stamp Act crisis of 1765, small groups of women who were determined to boycott British goods in protest began calling themselves the **Daughters of Liberty**. New England women organized spinning bees to make their own cloth so they could avoid buying English textiles. Among the elite and working people, wearing homespun clothing became a symbol of loyalty to the patriot cause. Their efforts continued to strengthen and spread, especially with the strong support they got from newspapers. In 1774, 51 women in Edenton, North Carolina, promised not to consume English goods, including tea, and other women organized similar boycotts elsewhere. When war broke out after 1775 and many goods became scarce, women protested when colonial merchants hoarded goods or demanded higher prices. In 1777, women in Poughkeepsie, New York, broke into the house of a merchant they thought was hoarding goods. As the war continued, women led food riots throughout the colonies.

Revolts in the Back Country

Rural people on the frontier from New York to the Carolinas were also taking matters into their own hands, but for different reasons. Back-country Virginians had rebelled in various ways against royal authority since Bacon's Rebellion in 1676, and in all of the colonies, major splits reflected gaps between coastal areas that had more access to, and more representation in, colonial governments than rural inland settlements.

In the mid-1760s, feeling ignored and cheated by what they saw as distant and corrupt coastal authorities, farmers in the western regions of North and South Carolina created what they called the Regulator movement. In South Carolina, Regulators attacked when gangs of outlaws stole from isolated farms. The governor eventually agreed to create circuit courts in the back country, which diminished the violence. In North Carolina, the movement protested corrupt practices of sheriffs and court officials who forced settlers to pay illegally high taxes and legal fees. Regulators rallied settlers, who refused to pay the taxes, closed the courts, and attacked officials. The governor sent in state militia from the coastal areas, and in their largest encounter with the Regulators, 29 people were killed and 150 wounded.

A British publication ridiculed American women's efforts to boycott tea, but the hostility shown in the cartoon reflects the degree to which women's protests were effective.

Throughout the colonies, however, the most contentious issue for inland communities was relationships with Indian tribes. Inland people complained that those on the coast used inland settlers as a buffer from the Indians. In Pennsylvania, there were also ethnic splits between the regions. Pennsylvania's mostly English Quaker elite had settled around Philadelphia. As pacifists, they tried to maintain peaceful relations with the Indians. But between the Quakers and the Indians was a zone inhabited by Scots-Irish and Germans who did not share the pacifism of the Quakers and who found themselves much closer to potential Indian hostility.

The rapid growth of the white population exacerbated the conflicts between frontier whites and Indians. The ever-increasing pressure for more land, a lot more land, could be satisfied only by white movement into areas that belonged to Indian tribes. As whites encroached, attacks by Indians increased. Settlers wanted, and expected, the British to protect them. But after 1763, King George's Proclamation Line halted further movement west—at least legally. The British-imposed barrier caused intense anger on the frontier.

British agents sought to not only relieve the pressure among land-hungry white settlers but also honor the king's commitment to the Indians. A 1768 treaty allowed white settlement in present-day West Virginia and Kentucky. A similar treaty opened parts of western Pennsylvania and New York to white settlement. But colonists wanted much more land than these treaties gave them and were prepared to fight to get it— whether with Indian tribes or with the king's representatives.

Violence extended all along the lines of settlement. A German immigrant, Frederick Stump, was arrested for murdering 10 Indians in western Pennsylvania in 1768 and then freed from jail by a white mob. In Virginia, vigilantes who called themselves the Augusta Boys killed Cherokees.

General Thomas Gage, the senior British commander in North America, found the situation intolerable. He complained to London that, "all the people of the frontiers

First Continental Congress
Meeting of delegates from most of the colonies and held in Philadelphia in 1774 in response to the British efforts to tax the colonies.

Somerset Decision
A 1772 ruling by Britain's Lord Chief Justice in the case of James Somerset that set him free and essentially declared slavery illegal in England, though not in British colonies.

Phillis Wheatley lived an unusual life for an African slave. Before she was given her freedom, she was given considerable opportunity to learn and to write by the Wheatley family that claimed her. Her poems reflected the yearning for freedom that all colonists felt, but specifically the hopes of enslaved Africans among them.

from Pennsylvania to Virginia inclusive, openly avow, that they never find a man guilty of murder, for killing an Indian." In response to the frontier resistance, Parliament passed the Quebec Act of 1774, assigning all lands north and west of the Ohio River to the British-controlled Province of Quebec. That action effectively took Indian policy out of the hands of frontier agitators or royal governors along the coast. The Quebec Act also recognized the legal rights of the Catholic Church, which deeply offended the overwhelmingly Protestant Americans. Colonists saw the Quebec Act as one of what they called the Intolerable Acts, a series of laws that included the act that closed the port of Boston until the price of the tea and the tax on it was paid, a revision of the colonial charter of Massachusetts, and a Quartering Act that allowed governors to place troops in any uninhabited building. Patriots insisted that because Parliament was enacting these laws with no representation from colonists, Britain was violating the rights of English subjects in North America. Parliament's actions, including closing the port of Boston and challenging frontier farmers, were unintentionally provoking a common sense of grievance among people who had previously been quite separate in their complaints.

Growing Unity in the Colonies—The First Continental Congress

While people began to organize and challenge British authorities from Virginia to Massachusetts, leaders of the rebellion in Massachusetts asked the other colonies to join it in united action against what they saw as British tyranny. All of them except Georgia—which was fighting Creek Indians and wanted Britain's support—sent delegates to Philadelphia in September 1774 to what became known as the **First Continental Congress**.

Most of the delegates who came to Philadelphia agreed that Parliament had no right to tax the colonies without their consent. The delegates also sought unified opposition to the British treatment of Boston. However, few were ready for a break with Britain. The Virginians wanted to continue to export tobacco, and South Carolina depended on the export of rice and indigo. Finding common ground was not easy. But the delegates did gain experience working together, even when they argued—which they did a lot.

There was little talk of war or independence at the 1774 gathering. But before they adjourned on October 26, the delegates declared that their rights were based on the laws of nature, the British constitution, and the colonial charters, and were not to be trifled with. They also agreed to a ban on British imports to take effect in December 1774, a ban on exports that would take effect in September 1775 (after the tobacco and rice crops were safely on their way to Britain), and—for symbolic reasons—an immediate ban on the consumption of tea from the East India Company. They agreed to meet again in May 1775 if relations with Britain did not improve.

Talk of Freedom for Slaves

For African slaves in British North America, the most revolutionary moment of the 1700s took place in London in July 1772. An American slave named James Somerset had been taken from Virginia to England as a personal servant by his master Charles Stewart. In London, Somerset became friends with free blacks and white abolitionists. In October 1771, he ran away. He was caught and put on a ship bound for Jamaica. But Somerset's white friends petitioned for a writ of habeas corpus, requiring that Somerset be brought before a judge to determine whether he was imprisoned lawfully. They insisted that he was held against his will—which, like all slaves, he certainly was. Eventually, the Lord Chief Justice ruled that since Parliament had never legalized slavery in England itself, as opposed to the English colonies, Somerset had to be freed because "the state of slavery is of such a nature, that it is incapable of being introduced on any reason, moral or political; but only by positive law." This decision basically ended slavery in England itself.

The **Somerset decision** caused a considerable stir in the colonies and in Britain. In September 1773, the *Virginia Gazette* noted that, as news of the decision spread, running away to England was "a notion now too prevalent among the Negroes, greatly

American Voices

Phillis Wheatley, Poem to the Earl of Dartmouth, 1773

Phillis Wheatley was born in West Africa in 1753. She was captured at age seven or eight and brought to Boston as a slave where she was purchased by John and Susanna Wheatley, who provided her with a good education. The young Phillis was moved by English poets, Christianity, and the talk of democracy that she heard in upper-class Boston in the 1760s and 1770s— which, she believed, applied to slaves as well as free people. In response, she wrote poems about religion, slavery, and freedom, including this one titled, "To The Right Honorable William, Earl of Dartmouth, His Majesty's Principal Secretary of State for North America, &c." She was allowed to travel to London to see some of her poems published in 1773 and was later freed on the eve of the American Revolution. She died in 1784.

No more, America, in mournful strain
Of wrongs, and grievance unredress'd complain,
No longer shalt thou dread the iron chain,
Which wanton Tyranny with lawless hand
Had made, and with it meant t'enslave the land.

Should you, my lord, while you peruse my song,
Wonder from whence my love of Freedom sprung,
Whence flow these wishes for the common good,

By feeling hearts alone best understood,
I, young in life, by seeming cruel fate

Was snatch'd from Afric's fancy'd happy seat:
What pangs excruciating must molest,
What sorrows labour in my parent's breast?
Steel'd was that soul and by no misery mov'd
That from a father seiz'd his babe belov'd;
Such, such my case. And can I then but pray
Others may never feel tyrannic sway?

Source: Phillis Wheatley, "To The Right Honorable William, Earl of Dartmouth, His Majesty's Principal Secretary of State for North America, &c," in Herb Boyd, editor, *Autobiography of a People* (New York: Anchor Books, 2001, pp. 29–30.)

Thinking Critically

1. **Documentary Analysis**
   How did Wheatley connect her personal experiences to the revolutionary cause?

2. **Historical Interpretation**
   What light does this poem shed on Wheatley's hopes for the coming revolution? How might her vision of revolution have differed from that of her white Bostonian neighbors?

to the vexation and prejudice of their masters." Benjamin Franklin, who was living in London, had once owned slaves, but now, like many others, he was turning against the institution, calling it "this pestilential detestable traffic in the bodies and souls of men." In Massachusetts, after successfully defending a slave in a trial to obtain his freedom in the Nantucket Court of Common Pleas, John Adams said, "I never knew a jury by a verdict to determine a negro to be a slave. They always found him free."

Legal challenges were not the main ways in which slaves sought freedom before and during the American Revolution, however. Slaves heard about the protests of the Stamp Act and saw how effective mob action was. Some 107 slaves ran away from a plantation near Charleston to join other runaways who were creating their own communities in hard-to-penetrate swamps.

Whites on both sides of the Atlantic noted the absurdity of colonists protesting their own perceived enslavement by Parliament while, as one wrote, those same colonists enslaved "thousands of tens of thousands of their fellow creatures!" The most consistent voice for abolition in the 1760s and 1770s came from the Quakers, who made it mandatory for members of their denomination to free their slaves or allow them to purchase their freedom. Others such as Virginia's Arthur Lee—from a great slaveholding family in the colony—wrote that "freedom is unquestionably the birth-right of all mankind, of Africans as well as Europeans." In the 1700s, the slave trade was still a profitable institution. While some whites wrote anti-slavery letters and pamphlets, 7,000 slaves were imported into Charleston in 1765. The debate around slavery was as heated as the debate around British rule, and no one living through these years could fail to notice the contradiction of fighting for liberty and enforcing slavery.

5.2 **Quick Review** Did Americans' revolutionary ideas contradict their attitudes towards Indians and slaves? To answer this question, consider the time and context in which the American Revolution took place.

THE WAR FOR INDEPENDENCE

5.3 Explain how political and military strategy, support for the patriot cause, and American alliances with France and Spain led to an American victory in the war for independence.

As talk of rebellion spread in 1774, not long after the Boston Tea Party, John Adams overheard rural farmers discussing the events in Boston. One insisted, "If parliament can take away Mr. Hancock's wharf and Mr. Rowe's wharf, they can take away your barn and my house." Adams realized that if isolated farmers were agreeing with a mob in Boston, revolution was possible. Indeed, battles would soon break out in Lexington and in Concord, starting the American Revolution. At the same time, word was quickly spreading among Africans regarding the disputes about slavery. They were poised to take action to support either the colonists or the British—whichever side would benefit them the most. Beginning in 1775, what had been occasional mob actions turned into outright warfare as increasingly well-disciplined colonial militia fought against the British army. While some colonial leaders met in Congress and declared independence in 1776, other colonists, later aided by French forces, fought a long and bitter series of battles that won the actual independence that had been declared.

From Lexington and Concord to Bunker Hill—Revolt Becomes War

General Thomas Gage also understood the growing rebellion. When Parliament passed the Intolerable Acts, Gage was charged with moving British troops back into Boston and allowing no trade until Massachusetts submitted to the crown (see Map 5-3). Gage recommended to London that efforts be made to conciliate the colonists. But the leaders in Parliament were in no mood for conciliation, and Gage received orders to restore order at all costs. As he moved his troops, Gage kept a close eye on the Massachusetts rebels who kept an equally close eye on him. Paul Revere, who had helped lead the Boston Tea Party, now led an informal group of unemployed artisans who noted every troop movement in Boston.

THE BATTLES OF LEXINGTON AND CONCORD, APRIL 1775   In the inland towns of Concord and Worcester, the colonial militia was collecting arms, and Gage knew it. Hoping for secrecy, he ordered troops to prepare to march to Concord to seize the arms. The colonists had been expecting such a move. Paul Revere was to report any troop movements by hanging lanterns in the steeple of the North Church—one lantern if the troops moved inland and "two if by sea," meaning by boats across the Back Bay. When the British troops started to move, Revere had two lanterns hung in the steeple (the British took the water route). Then he and William Dawes began their famous rides through the night to alert the colonial militia. Revere himself was arrested by British troops, but Dawes woke Sam Adams and John Hancock, who made it to Concord to organize the militia.

When the British reached Lexington Town Green at little after 4:30 a.m. on April 19, 1775, they were met by colonial militia. Shots were fired, killing eight militiamen and wounding 10 others. Only one British soldier was wounded in this first battle of the Revolution.

There was no further gunfire until the British entered the town of Concord where they found few arms. As they left to march the 16 miles back to Boston, militiamen hidden behind trees, buildings, rocks, and fences attacked their easy targets. At the end of the day, the British had 273 casualties, the militia 95. What had been unrest was now a war.

Word of the battles of Lexington and Concord spread quickly. Many shared Thomas Jefferson's belief that "the last hopes of reconciliation" had now ended. People who were not sure about independence felt they had to make decisions. Some, perhaps as many as a third of all white colonists, remained loyal to the crown, though in New England they did so quietly. But many began to commit to what they saw as a patriotic cause, some even taking matters into their own hands. Ethan Allen, who, since

MAP 5-3 British Courts and Troops Stationed in the Colonies as the Revolution Began. As unrest grew in the colonies, British authorities made every effort to assert control. They stationed more troops in all of the colonies, especially in restive Boston, and established a series of courts—Vice-Admiralty Courts—in Charleston, Philadelphia, Boston, and Halifax, Nova Scotia. Stationing more troops and clamping down on smuggling did nothing to end colonial resistance and, as word spread of the battles of Lexington and Concord after April 19, 1775, colonial resistance only grew.

1770 had led his Green Mountain Boys in challenging royal authority in Vermont, and Benedict Arnold of Connecticut, then on the rebels' side, organized their own militia and captured Fort Ticonderoga on Lake Champlain on May 10, 1775. The cannons from the fort would play a large role in the coming struggle.

FROM THE BATTLE OF BUNKER HILL TO THE FORMATION OF THE COLONIAL ARMY In the weeks after the battles at Lexington and Concord, the Massachusetts militia, fortified with recruits from Connecticut, began to dig in on the hills surrounding British-occupied Boston—Dorchester Heights to the south, Bunker Hill, and Breed's Hill to the north. Colonel William Prescott of the Massachusetts militia was put in charge of fortifying the northern hills.

General Gage again felt that he had to act. On June 17, Gage ordered an attack on Breed's Hill. It was a British victory, but at a high cost—226 British dead and 828 wounded compared with 140 militia killed and 271 wounded. As one Englishman remarked, "If we have eight more such victories, there will be nobody left to bring the news."

The battle, which later became known as the Battle of Bunker Hill, even though it had taken place on Breed's Hill, had been between ill-organized militia and regular units of the British army. After that battle, however, the American forces became better organized and gained support from all 13 colonies.

African-Americans in the Armies of Both Sides

The outbreak of war opened a new avenue to freedom for American slaves. While some, like Wheatley, embraced revolution for liberty and freedom, others heeded different words. Jeremiah, a free black in Charleston, heard the rumor that the British intended to "come to help the poor negroes." He did not wait for that help but began to organize one of several slave uprisings in the Carolinas in 1775 and 1776. Jeremiah's plans for an insurrection were discovered, and he was hanged and burned at the stake in August 1775 by prorevolutionary authorities in South Carolina.

There was a good reason for the rumors among the slaves. In 1775, Lord Dunmore, the royal governor of Virginia, under attack from the rebels, fled Williamsburg. In November of that year, from his refuge on a British warship, he announced:

> I do hereby further declare all indented servants, Negroes, or others...free, that are able and willing to bear arms, they joining His Majesty's Troops as soon as may be.

The proclamation terrified whites. With it, the slaves' perspective of the revolutionary struggle was transformed into a struggle about who would "give them their liberty." And in South Carolina, where there were 80,000 slaves—60 percent of the population—such liberty would be a radical revolution indeed.

Many slaves responded to the invitation. Between 800 and 1,000 slaves joined the British army. Dunmore organized them into what he called the Ethiopian Regiment, whose members wore a sash reading "Liberty to Slaves." In one engagement, an American colonel, Joseph Hutchings, was captured by two of his own former slaves. When the British landed on Staten Island in 1776, New York and New Jersey slaves joined them. When they Royal Navy sailed up rivers in Pennsylvania and Maryland, more slaves joined them, and when the British attacked Charleston, still more joined.

Runaway slaves built forts, tended the wounded, carried supplies, and fought alongside white soldiers. British generals understood that in recruiting slaves they were also disrupting the economies of the rebellious colonies. Although disease took a terrible toll among black soldiers and their families, and though many were captured and reenslaved, the loyalty of slaves to the British cause eventually brought freedom to some of them. Approximately 300 former slaves sailed with Dunmore when he left Virginia in 1776, and by the end of the war, British forces had relocated some 3,000 more in Canada or in colonies in West Africa.

The American army was much slower to enlist free blacks or slaves than the British. African-Americans, however, did serve among the colonial troops at Lexington and Concord in 1775, including Lemuel Haynes, who became one of the leading ministers in Massachusetts after the war.

Washington was reluctant to arm black soldiers, fearing not only the reaction of white troops but also the possibility that arms given to black soldiers might eventually support a slave revolt. Nevertheless, by the winter of 1777–1778, when things looked grim for the Revolution, Washington finally embraced black volunteers. Shortly after, in February 1778, Rhode Island offered freedom to "every able bodied Negro, Mulatto, or Indian Man slave in this state...to serve during the continuance of the present war with Great Britain." Perhaps one in four male slaves in the state eventually enlisted in what was known as Rhode Island's Black Regiment. Those who survived the war were given their freedom in 1783.

Moving Toward Independence

When the delegates to the **Second Continental Congress** gathered as promised in Philadelphia on May 10, 1775, the Battles of Lexington and Concord had changed everything. They knew that they had to manage a war and attempted to create the Continental Army. The obvious choice to command it was George Washington, a respected member of Congress and veteran of the French and Indian War.

Washington took command of the colonial militia, such as it was, in Cambridge, Massachusetts, on July 2, 1775, shortly after the Battle of Bunker Hill. American resistance would be more coordinated than it had been during the early skirmishes. Washington commanded between 9,000 and 14,000 troops—he was never sure—while Gage led about 5,000 in Boston. Despite the difference in numbers, the Royal Navy controlled the water, and Gage's troops were highly disciplined soldiers. Washington's troops were a ragtag army, capable of effective guerrilla fighting and great courage, but hard to discipline, easily bored, and ready to return to their homes if fighting dragged on.

After selecting Washington and beginning to find the money—mostly in foreign loans—to support an army, the Second Continental Congress turned to another pressing question: What did they want from the war? John Dickinson of Pennsylvania wanted reconciliation with Britain if Parliament would respect the rights of the colonists. John Adams and most of the Virginia delegates wanted independence. Others were not sure. It took a year for the debate to be resolved, and before then, other matters intervened.

THOMAS PAINE'S *COMMON SENSE* While the Congress debated independence, a new arrival from England, Thomas Paine, published a pamphlet, *Common Sense*, in January 1776. Soon, over 100,000 copies were in circulation. Paine asked, "Why is it that we hesitate?…For God's sake, let us come to a final separation.…The birthday of a new world is at hand." Paine made two basic points: that monarchy was always a bad way for people to be governed and that the time was right to declare independence. With his passionate words and exquisite timing, Paine shaped public opinion. *Common Sense* appeared on the same day George III declared the North American colonies to be in a state of rebellion. The two events could not have contrasted more clearly. John Adams was no admirer of Paine or his pamphlet, which he saw as simple minded and needlessly antagonistic, though he agreed with its conclusion. Nevertheless, Adams said that he expected *Common Sense* to become the "common faith" of the new nation.

Declaring Independence, 1776

On June 7, 1776, after months of debate in the Congress, Richard Henry Lee, a delegate from Virginia, offered a motion:

> Resolved…that these United Colonies are, and of a right ought to be, free and independent states, that they are absolved from all allegiance to the British Crown, and that all political connection between them and the state of Great Britain is, and ought to be, totally dissolved.

John Adams immediately seconded the motion.

In the debate that followed, delegates led by John Dickinson opposed the resolution. Most of the delegates had likely come to this Congress with the hope of reconciliation, not with any plan for permanent separation. But the fighting with British troops and the influence of publications like *Common Sense* had changed many minds. Congress eventually agreed to delay a vote on independence until July 1 but to also appoint what became known as the Committee of Five—Thomas Jefferson, Benjamin Franklin, John Adams, Roger Sherman, and Robert Livingston—to draft a declaration in case Congress did vote for independence.

Jefferson, known for his skill with words, was chosen to write the first draft. Adams and Franklin, and ultimately the full Congress, made adjustments, which frustrated and hurt the sensitive Jefferson. The most important changes included removing

Recently arrived from England, Thomas Paine took up the patriot cause with a fervor that many more established colonists lacked. In his easy-to-read pamphlet, *Common Sense*, he attacked not only the British treatment of the colonies but also the very idea of monarchy. His words were significant in fanning the flames of the independence movement.

Second Continental Congress
An assemblage of delegates from all the colonies that convened in May 1775 that eventually declared independence, adopted the Articles of Confederation, and conducted the Revolutionary War.

Jefferson's passionate attack on the slave trade, which was hypocritical in light of the fact that Jefferson owned many slaves and made no move to free them. In addition, far too many of the others in the Congress had investments in the trade to accept Jefferson's language anywhere in the document. However, no one suggested removing Jefferson's assertion that the king "has endeavored to bring on the inhabitants of our frontiers, the merciless Indian savages," even when they all knew that it was whites on the frontiers who were invading Indian territory, and the king's government was trying to keep the two apart. Those in Congress saw the frontier whites as essential supporters of the patriot cause and were in no mood to antagonize them.

The waiting period before the vote paid off. By July 1776, no one was willing to go on record as being opposed to independence. On July 2, a unanimous Congress voted for independence, and on July 4, they adopted a declaration of independence that began with these powerful words:

> When, in the course of human events, it becomes necessary for one people to dissolve the political bands which have connected them with another, and to assume among the powers of the earth, the separate and equal station to which the laws of nature and of nature's God entitle them, a decent respect to the opinions of mankind requires that they should declare the causes which impel them to the separation.
>
> We hold these truths to be self-evident, that all men are created equal; that they are endowed by their Creator with certain unalienable rights; that among these are life, liberty, and the pursuit of happiness.

The philosophical ideas that John Locke had used to defend England's change in monarchs were now, a hundred years later, used to announce to the world that monarchy itself was being abolished in England's former colonies. In Philadelphia, people celebrated with "bonfires and ringing bells, with other great demonstrations of joy."

When word of the Declaration of Independence reached New York City, a mob of soldiers and residents celebrated by pulling down the statue of King George III that stood on lower Broadway. The metal was eventually melted down to make bullets for the revolutionary cause.

A crowd in New York tore down the statue of George III, Washington built up morale in the army by reading the Declaration to his troops, and the celebrations continued up and down the coast.

THE ARTICLES OF CONFEDERATION   A year later, the Congress adopted a governing document for the new and fragile country they had created. In 1777, the **Articles of Confederation** created a national, though weak, government for what was now called the United States of America. Although 11 of the colonies ratified the Articles within a year, the last, Maryland, did not do so until 1781. Nevertheless, with the Articles of Confederation, states banded together in a formal—and ultimately successful—alliance to prosecute the war and govern the nation in the peace they hoped would follow. With the Declaration of Independence, the 13 different colonies declared themselves to be 13 independent states that agreed to work together for certain limited common purposes. Although they were committed to cooperate, especially in fighting for independence, the representatives were distrustful of centralized government. Under the Articles of Confederation, there would be no national executive or court system in the new nation. In addition, Congress could raise money through taxes only if every state agreed. Nevertheless, this government—really, an alliance of independent states more than anything that looked like a modern nation—was able to coordinate its fight and win the Revolution. Whether such a government could build a nation, however, remained to be seen.

5.1

5.2

Articles of Confederation
Written document setting up the loose confederation of states that made up the first national government of the United States from 1781 to 1788.

5.3

George Washington and His Victorious Patchwork Army

The American Revolution was a long and bloody war between two strikingly different armies. On one side were Washington's patchwork Continental Army and various rebel militias—later supported by troops from France and Spain. In the course of the long war, some 200,000 of the 350,000 men who could have served participated in some military activity, but the turnover was such that no more than 25,000 served at any one time. Fighting against them was a corps of extremely well-trained British troops, supported by organized units of Loyalist colonists (as many as 8,000 at the start of the war and increasing as the war continued) and hired soldiers from Germany. Ultimately, many factors led to the success of the ragtag rebels and their allies in their battles with the British troops (see Map 5-4) and perhaps more important their ability to survive in spite of the British effort to eliminate them as a fighting force.

Most of the revolutionary Minute Men who fought at Lexington and Concord (called Minute Men because they had pledged to be ready to fight on a minute's notice) were farmers who owned their own weapons and knew how to shoot. In some of the early battles, the popular image of the "citizen soldier" may have been true as farmers and townspeople took up arms to defend their communities. But as the war continued, and as Washington and his officers created the kind of discipline necessary for an effective army, more and more of the early volunteers faded away, replaced by recently indentured servants, impoverished transients, or those who traded a jail cell for a uniform. A colonial officer called the troops, "a wretched motley Crew," but Washington was an effective leader who never seemed to lose control when others started to panic, and he was deeply committed to the cause.

Despite being ill-trained, ill-fed, ill-clothed, and restless, these troops continued to fight, even after seeing the "horrors of battle…in all their hideousness," as one soldier remembered. Surprisingly, these often forgotten men are who won the independence that others celebrated.

A few women also took a direct role in the war. Armies in the 1700s usually included women known as camp followers. Some were the wives of soldiers, who could not or would not leave their husbands. Others were single women seeking adventure or simply survival in army life and army rations. Camp followers carried water to the battlefield, fed and supported the troops, nursed the wounded, and occasionally fought in battles. Mary Ludwig Hays, known as Molly Pitcher (for the water she carried),

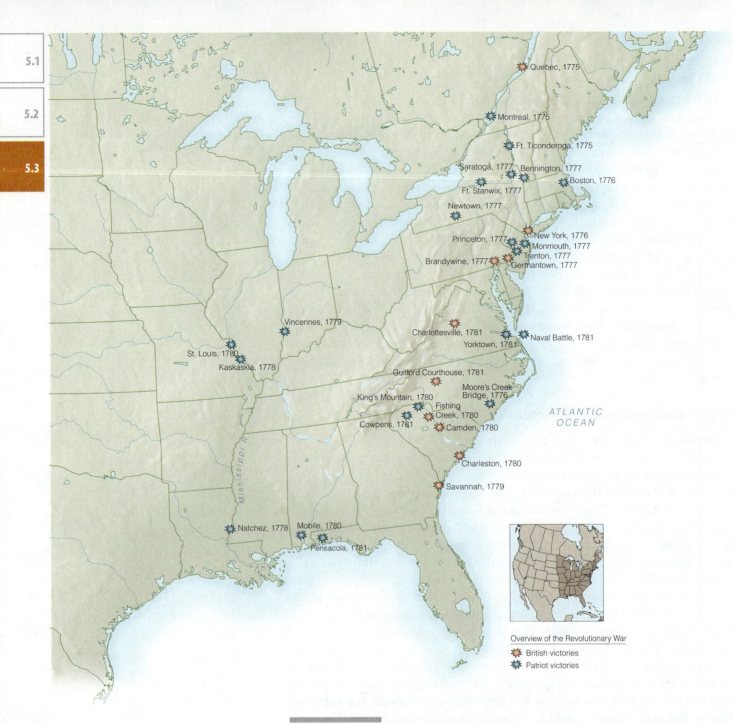

Quebec, 1775

Montreal, 1775

Ft. Ticonderoga, 1775

Saratoga, 1777   Bennington, 1777

Ft. Stanwix, 1777   Boston, 1776

Newtown, 1777

Princeton, 1777   New York, 1776
                               Monmouth, 1777
                               Trenton, 1777
Brandywine, 1777   Germantown, 1777

Vincennes, 1779   Charlottesville, 1781
                                          Naval Battle, 1781
St. Louis, 1780   Yorktown, 1781

Kaskaskia, 1778

                   Guilford Courthouse, 1781

                                   Moore's Creek
King's Mountain, 1780   Bridge, 1776

          Fishing
          Creek, 1780
Cowpens, 1781   Camden, 1780

                                          ATLANTIC
                                           OCEAN

                   Charleston, 1780

                   Savannah, 1779

Natchez, 1778   Mobile, 1780

          Pensacola, 1781

MISSISSIPPI R.

Overview of the Revolutionary War

✴ British victories

✴ Patriot victories

MAP 5-4 Major Battles of the American Revolution. The Revolutionary War was fought all across British North America, not only in almost all of the 13 colonies along the Atlantic coast but well into British Canada and in the Mississippi River Valley.

also supposedly loaded her husband's cannon after he was wounded at the Battle of Monmouth in 1778. Deborah Sampson disguised herself as a man, joined the army, and fought for years until a doctor discovered her identity after she was wounded.

Washington understood that though his army could fight, it could not withstand a direct battle with British regulars. He told Congress that he needed to fight a defensive war and avoid any general action. For much of the war, his goal was not a decisive victory, but avoiding a decisive loss. The longer Washington was able to keep his army together and out of too many battles, the better the chance that the British would tire of the war. He knew how well-trained the British army was—having served in it—but he also expected that training and discipline had narrowed their conception of war and would give him the edge as long as his troops could use nontraditional tactics and avoid capture or defeat.

American Voices

Joseph Plumb Martin, *Narrative of a Revolutionary Soldier*, 1775–1783

Joseph Plumb Marin was a private in the American army through eight years of war. He saw few direct battles but many small skirmishes. Martin knew that his primary task was to survive and avoid capture. His humorous journal, written when he was 70 years old, makes clear that his greatest enemies were neglect and hunger.

I, the redoubtable hero of this Narrative, first made my appearance in this crooked, fretful world, upon the twenty-first day of November, in the year 1760....I remember the stir in the country occasioned by the stamp act, but I was so young that I did not understand the meaning of it; I likewise remember the disturbances that followed the repeal of the stamp act, until the destruction of the tea at Boston and elsewhere; I was then thirteen or fourteen years old, and began to understand something of the works going on. . . . Time passed smoothly on with me till the year 1774 arrived, the smell of war began to be pretty strong, but I was determined to have no hand in it, happen when it might; I felt myself to be a real coward. What—venture my carcass where bullets fly! That will never do for me....I was ploughing in the field about half a mile from home, about the twenty-first day of April [1775], when all of a sudden the bells fell to ringing, what the cause was we could not conjecture....During the winter of 1775–6, by hearing the conversation and disputes of the good old farmer politicians of the times, I collected pretty correct ideas of the contest between this country and the mother country, (as it was then called)....I felt more anxious than ever, if possible, to be called a defender of my country.

1777—Next morning, we joined the grand army near Philadelphia, and the heavy baggage being sent back to the rear of the army, we were obliged to put us up huts by laying up poles and covering them with leaves; a capital shelter from winter storms....About this time the whole British army left the city, came out and encamped, or rather lay, on Chestnut-hill in our immediate neighborhood; we hourly expected an attack from them; we had a commanding position and were very sensible of it. We were kept constantly on the alert, and wished nothing more than to have them engage us, for we were sure of giving them a drubbing, being in excellent fighting trim, as we were starved and as cross and ill-natured as curs. The British, however, thought better of the matter, and after several days maneuvering on the hill, very civilly walked off into Philadelphia again. Starvation seemed to be entailed upon the army and every animal connected with it....

1780—Here was the army starved and naked, and there their country sitting still and expecting the army to do notable things while fainting from sheer starvation.

Source: Joseph Plumb Martin, *A Narrative of the Adventures, Dangers, and Sufferings of a Revolutionary Soldier* (originally published 1830 republished New York: Signet Classics, 2010.)

Thinking Critically

1. Documentary Analysis

How did Martin characterize his own journey toward support of the revolutionary cause?

2. Historical Interpretation

What does this passage suggest about the differences between the American and British armies?

THE BRITISH EVACUATE BOSTON   After the Battle of Bunker Hill, the British controlled Boston but were hemmed in there. Through the winter of 1775–1776, Washington commissioned a promising soldier, Henry Knox, a young Boston bookseller, as a colonel in the Continental Army and sent him and his men to move the guns captured at Fort Ticonderoga on sleds over snow-covered mountains to Boston. On the night of March 1, 1776, Washington's troops assembled the guns on Dorchester Heights and then bombarded the city until March 17 when the British finally evacuated Boston.

THE WAR IN THE NORTH—MANHATTAN, TRENTON, AND VALLEY FORGE   The victory in Boston was one of the few outright victories Washington would achieve. Washington's goal, however, was to engage in more indirect strategies that would wear down the British while preserving his own limited troops.

Just as the American Congress was declaring independence in Philadelphia in 1776, Sir William Howe, who had replaced Gage as the British commander, landed his army on Staten Island, across from Manhattan. Howe had some 32,000 troops, including 8,000 German mercenaries—essentially soldiers for hire—known as Hessians (since many were from the German province of Hesse). During the war, some 30,000 Hessians fought for the British, approximately a quarter of all of their soldiers. Hessian troops were recruited, often by force, from among the poorest Germans, and German princes would rent them out as units, especially to the British. Many Hessians soldiers had little interest in the British cause, but had little choice except to fight for it. Washington had his own morale problems, but his soldiers were somewhat more willing to fight.

As the two sides watched each other, Washington's troops dug fortifications to defend Brooklyn and Manhattan. In late August, Howe's larger and better-trained force attacked Brooklyn. Rather than risk battle and capture at this point, Washington abandoned Brooklyn and brought all 9,500 of his troops across the East River to Manhattan on the night of August 30. When Howe attacked Manhattan in September, Washington again retreated. Throughout the early fall, Washington continued a retreat, and the British advanced through New Jersey. As they settled down for the winter, the British held most of New Jersey, while Washington's army was across the Delaware River in Pennsylvania.

Then, on Christmas night of 1776, Washington and 2,400 troops made a daring raid across the Delaware River and captured Trenton, New Jersey. They also captured many Hessian soldiers, some of whom quickly joined the rebel side. In January, they would go on to successfully attack a British force in Princeton. By the winter of 1776–1777, Washington controlled southern New Jersey while the British held northern New Jersey and New York City, which they would control throughout the war.

In May 1777, British General John Burgoyne assembled a large army in Canada. His plan was to proceed down the Hudson River and smash the "unnatural Rebellion" in New York and New England. Initially, the plan went well. Burgoyne had some 8,300 men, including 3,000 German troops. He led his army across Lake Champlain, overran the Americans at Fort Ticonderoga, and continued south into New York's Hudson River Valley, an exhausting effort that involved moving a large army with heavy supplies through dense forests. As he moved through the area, Burgoyne's sometimes pompous pronouncements to colonists and the German troops' inability to communicate with them bred additional colonial resentment and motivated fresh volunteers for the American cause.

In September 1777, near Saratoga, New York, Burgoyne's army encountered American troops under the command of an experienced general, Horatio Gates, and Benedict Arnold (still on the American side, but soon to be caught negotiating a plan with the British to defect). The British were surprised that their bayonet charge could not break the American lines. Both armies suffered heavy losses, but neither won a decisive victory. Burgoyne's army was now cut off from its winter quarters and, shortly after, was forced to negotiate. Some 5,800 British troops were captured and held as prisoners until the end of the war. The Battle of Saratoga, was a turning point for the colonial cause. It eliminated a significant British force, and it proved to the world—especially those in France and Spain who were watching the war closely—that the Americans could stand up to Britain's toughest troops. As a result, American diplomats including Benjamin Franklin were able to negotiate an agreement with the French and later the Spanish to recognize the united colonies and provide military assistance.

The British wanted not only to split the colonies and, especially, to capture Washington and his army, but also to catch the members of the Continental Congress by overtaking Philadelphia where the Congress met. In September 1777, British troops captured Philadelphia, but the members of Congress escaped before the British arrived. Washington was able to block supplies into the city, and the following spring, the British abandoned Philadelphia, which remained in colonial hands for the rest of the war, though there were continued riots between patriots and Loyalists in the city.

Before the British left Philadelphia, however, the American forces had to survive perhaps their most difficult winter. Washington selected Valley Forge, Pennsylvania, 18 miles northwest from Philadelphia as a place to keep an eye on the British in the city. His army was exhausted, cold, and hungry, and they got colder and hungrier as the winter continued. For weeks, there was little to eat. In time, however, Washington was able to appoint commissary officers who found food and clothing for the soldiers. A Prussian officer volunteering in the American cause, Baron von Steuben, began training the troops in close order drills. Von Steuben possessed expertise in military training and hoped to make a name, and a home, for himself in a free America. In addition, a French officer, the Marquis de Lafayette, was recruited to lead forces that harassed the British. By the time the British sailed out of Philadelphia, the American troops were better fed and clothed, better trained, and ready for new battles—preparation they would need in the next years.

In 1778, General Sir Henry Clinton replaced Howe, and a new British strategy took shape. Clinton ordered the Royal Navy to harass the colonists up and down the Atlantic coast and encouraged Britain's Indian allies to attack frontier settlements. In addition, he sent the main British land force south to overrun the Carolinas and Georgia. If he could detach those three colonies, Clinton thought, the Revolution might crumble. After 1778, the major battles of the war would be in the colonies' western and southern regions.

THE IMPORTANCE OF FRANCE AND SPAIN   The Revolution was won by the rebels for many reasons, including the key fact that France and Spain were willing to help. The two countries had their own reasons for wanting to embarrass the British and reduce Britain's power on the world stage. In particular, both France and Spain wanted greater access to trade with North America, which was highly restricted as long as the British controlled the colonies. By the 1770s, the French still resented the British victory in the Seven Years' War and wanted to ensure that France, not Britain, was the dominant power in Europe. As early as 1775, France sent agents to America to see what might be gained from assisting in the rebellion. Similarly, Spain started to supply the colonists with food and gunpowder from Spanish-held New Orleans and Cuba.

While they were willing to support the rebellion, neither France nor Spain wanted to engage in war with Britain unless the colonists were serious. In arguing for a declaration of independence in 1776, Adams told the Congress: "Foreign powers cannot be expected to acknowledge us, till we have acknowledged ourselves and taken our station among them as a sovereign power, an independent nation." He had two specific foreign powers in mind.

In 1776, Benjamin Franklin led an American delegation in Paris to seek further help. Franklin with his simple fur cap and plain spectacles, yet sophisticated manner, charmed the French. However, Franklin needed more than charm to win real help. With the Americans' declared independence and victory over Britain's troops at Saratoga, French leaders started to take him more seriously. His diplomatic efforts secured important supplies and, in February 1778, a full French alliance with the United States of America, the first diplomatic recognition of the new nation. A few months later, France formally declared war on Great Britain. For the rest of the war, Washington could count on the French army and navy to fight the British.

In 1779, Spain also declared war on Britain. Spanish forces moved up the Mississippi River from New Orleans and along the Gulf Coast and took the British forts at Baton Rouge, Natchez, Mobile, and Pensacola. Spanish attacks in the Mississippi River Valley diverted British troops from the Atlantic coast, helping the American effort.

Once France and Spain went to war with Britain, the American Revolution became a world war. The French and British navies fought in the English Channel, Spain attacked British-held Gibraltar in the Mediterranean, and all of them fought battles in the Caribbean. Most important for the American cause, the French fleet supported Washington's troops throughout the latter part of the war while Spanish funds and smuggling efforts provided badly needed supplies.

THE IROQUOIS AND THE BRITISH   The Iroquois were divided about how to respond to the rebellion, and at the beginning of the war most sought to remain neutral. However, many saw Britain as the key to their independence, and as the war continued, neutrality faded. Beginning in the summer of 1777, Mohawks under the leadership of Thayendanegea, also known as Joseph Brant, attacked white communities across New York and Pennsylvania. The attacks on farms threatened a crucial colonial food supply. In response, in the summer of 1779 Washington sent perhaps a third of his army to attack the Iroquois and "lay waste all the settlements around…that the country may not be merely overrun but destroyed." From Washington's perspective, the Iroquois had to be stopped. For the Iroquois, Washington's fierce response was proof that the American leadership would always be an implacable enemy. Both sides adopted brutal scorched-earth tactics that left long-lasting hatreds.

BRITISH LOYALISTS   Colonists who remained loyal to Britain formed their own militia, and in the Carolinas, an army of over a thousand Loyalists challenged rebel forces. Other Loyalists joined British regiments. American rebels had nothing but contempt for them. In the New York-New Jersey area, Catherine and Phillip Van Cortland, one of the area's leading families, remained loyal to Britain. When Washington gained control of their part of New Jersey, he ordered that the Van Cortland house be used as an army hospital. With her husband away, Catherine and her children were told to leave. She described their February 1777 departure:

> Our youngest children could not pass a far yard where they were milking cows without wishing for some. My little Willing was almost in agonies, springing in my Arms and calling for milk. I therefore rode up and requested the good man to let me have some from one of his pails.…the man stopped, asked who we were, and…swore bitterly he would not give a drop to any Tory Bitch. I offered him money, my children screamed; and, as I could not prevail, I drove on.

In some cities including Newark, New Jersey, in 1777 and Philadelphia in 1780, the wives of missing Loyalists were exiled by the American forces. Some Loyalist families were able to blend back into their old homes after the war, but many left for Canada or England and never returned.

Sarah Franklin Bache, unlike her half-brother William, was a staunch defender of the patriot cause. She led an effort to raise funds for the troops in the Continental Army and later led an effort in which Philadelphia women made 2,200 shirts for the soldiers.

WOMEN'S SUPPORT FOR WASHINGTON'S ARMY   In 1780, at a particularly bad time for the Continental troops, Esther De Berdt Reed (wife of the governor of Pennsylvania) and Sarah Franklin Bache (Benjamin Franklin's daughter) asked patriot women to give up all luxuries and contribute to a fund for the Continental Army. Eventually, the women raised $300,000, a huge sum at the time.

The women's goal was to give $2 in hard currency to every soldier. Washington refused the offer and asked the women instead to buy cloth and sew shirts for the soldiers. The women agreed and produced thousands of shirts for the ill-clad troops. The experience also led to the creation of the Ladies Association, the first intercolonial organization of women in America and a model for future national organizations of women.

Women throughout the colonies found additional ways to support the cause. In Fishing Creek, South Carolina, young girls went from farm to farm, asking, "Is the owner out with the fighting men?" If the answer was yes, then they harvested the land. In five or six weeks, they had completed the harvest for the whole county, saving patriot farmers from economic ruin and providing food stores for the revolutionary cause. Stories of similar efforts abounded.

THE WAR IN THE SOUTH—FROM CHARLESTON TO YORKTOWN   After capturing Savannah, Georgia, in December 1778, the British attacked Charleston, South Carolina, in 1780, and on May 12, 1780, that city surrendered. The loss was significant. If the British took control of Georgia and the Carolinas, it would be hard to continue the resistance in the name of the united colonies and the strategy seemed to be working.

As the battle for control of the south continued, Washington named one of his generals, Nathaniel Greene, to lead a southern campaign. Greene divided the American forces, taking command of half and assigning others—a contingent of Maryland and Virginia militias—to Daniel Morgan, an experienced officer from Virginia. The British commander, Lord Cornwallis also divided his army between himself and Lieutenant Colonel Banastre Tarleton, who had a reputation for exceptional cruelty.

While the two armies maneuvered, smaller independent units fought their own battles. Not every resident of South Carolina supported independence, and local Loyalists fought against colonial units. Throughout 1780 and 1781, the South Carolina backcountry was filled with ugly and often personal conflicts. Unlike other colonies, the civilian death toll was high in South Carolina as a result.

Morgan made a stand against the British forces in a South Carolina pasture known as Cowpens in January 1781. In one of the last full-scale battles of the war, the American troops defeated Tarleton's army and captured some 800 British soldiers—a crucial American victory. Although the British still held Charleston and small units loyal to the British harassed the revolutionaries, after Cowpens, the Americans were in control of the South Carolina countryside.

Cornwallis saw little chance of further success in the Carolinas and marched into Virginia in May 1781. He decided to fortify Yorktown on the York River where he thought he could count on being resupplied by water. As Cornwallis's troops dug in at Yorktown, Washington was in the north planning another attack on New York City. Greene's army was far to the south. At the prodding of the French, Washington moved quickly to take advantage of the situation. In September, the French navy blockaded the York River and cut Cornwallis off from resupply. Then, supported by French troops under the Count de Rochambeau, Washington marched his own army from New York 450 miles south at surprising speed. On September 28, Washington's 16,000 troops attacked Yorktown. The siege continued for the next 2 weeks, but after failing at an attempted escape, Cornwallis surrendered on October 17, 1781.

Pleading illness, Cornwallis actually failed to show up for the surrender ceremony, which was handled by junior British officers. But everyone knew how significant the event was. Without the army that Cornwallis led, British efforts to defeat the Continental Army were at a standstill.

✳ Explore the American Revolution on MyHistoryLab

The idealized prominence of General George Washington as a war leader is shown as he meets with other generals and officers of the American colonies in a large state room.

HOW DID THE AMERICAN REVOLUTION UNFOLD?

Between 1775, when fighting broke out near Boston, and the 1783 Treaty of Paris, the British and rebellious American colonists fought the Revolutionary War. This war, however, was in reality a civil war, as some colonists remained loyal to the British Empire while their neighbors rebelled against imperial power. Even though George Washington's Continental Army was outmatched in military manpower and lost more major battles than it won, the superior decision making of its leaders combined with patriotic support throughout the colonies led to a victory for the Americans, and the Thirteen Colonies emerged as the independent United States of America.

HIGHEST LEVEL OF TROOP STRENGTH

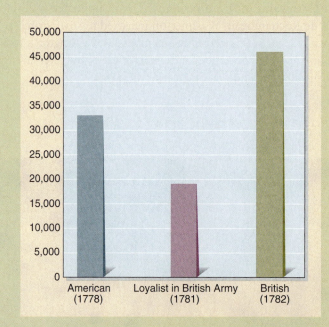

Source: Longman American History Atlas, 1998

KEY QUESTIONS

Use **MyHistoryLab** *Explorer* to **answer** these **questions:**

Comparison ▶▶▶ *Where did the Americans have military successes?*

Map the losses and victories of the two sides in the Revolutionary War.

Analysis ▶▶▶ *Which regions were Loyalist and Patriot strongholds?*

Consider the roles of these two groups in the unfolding of the war.

Response ▶▶▶ *What position did the major cities play in the conflict?*

Understand the importance of urban areas for the two sides.

THE TREATY OF PARIS The surrender of Cornwallis at Yorktown did not end the war, but it virtually guaranteed that it would eventually end favorably for the Americans. British troops still controlled New York City, Charleston, Savannah, and parts of the countryside, but many in Parliament were tired of the war, and public opinion in Britain had turned against continued hostilities. In June, 1780, Congress had sent John Jay to join Benjamin Franklin and John Adams in Paris to negotiate peace. After news of the Yorktown surrender arrived, the British delegates agreed to a draft treaty that began, "His Britannic Majesty acknowledges the said United States . . . to be free Sovereign and independent States." The two sides continued to negotiate boundaries, fishing rights, and legal claims, and Britain concluded separate treaties with France and Spain. The final treaty was signed in Paris on September 3, 1783. The Revolutionary War was over, and a new nation had been born.

 Quick Review Did the French and Indian War lead directly to the coming of the American Revolution? What other factors might have prevented or caused the outbreak of war in 1775? Make a list of some of the different groups that came to the conclusion that life would be better for them if the colonies were independent from Great Britain. Why did they want independence? Could any independent nation satisfy such diverse goals?

CONCLUSION

Many factors led to the beginning of the American Revolution. As American colonists sought to evade British taxes, John Locke's ideas about the "Rights of Man" influenced some men—and women—and provided a moral justification for disobeying the crown. The First Great Awakening led many to challenge religious and civil authority.

While ideas fueled the conflicts, the aftermath of the French and Indian War led to some of the most decisive events leading up to the colonies' break with Britain. While the colonists benefitted from the British takeover of New France, many rebelled against Parliament's efforts to get colonists to help pay the cost of this war through increased taxation without representation in Britain's Parliament. Many colonists, too, would not honor George III's Proclamation Line of 1763, which prevented them from appropriating Indian land. Slaves in the American colonies welcomed news that courts in England were moving toward outlawing slavery there; however, plantation owners, who depended on slavery and the slave trade, now had another reason for supporting an open break with the mother country. As resistances to British policies and taxes grew, Parliament responded with new taxes and sent more troops, which only inflamed colonists' passions and further united them against British rule.

At the first and second Continental Congresses, representatives of the colonies debated the best course of action. In 1775, violence escalated. The combination of unwanted British armed forces in North America as well as unwanted taxes and oppressive laws culminated in armed resistance by the colonists. By mid-1775, Americans had formed their own army under George Washington. The protracted war that followed engulfed the colonies, involving not only white men but also white women, slaves, and the Indians, along with armies and aid from France and Spain. Finally, after years of avoiding capture by the British army and some successful victories by the patriot forces, new alliances with France and Spain helped the colonists' army, commanded by George Washington, win the surrender of the largest British army in North America. With the surrender of the British forces at Yorktown in 1781, and the Treaty of Paris in 1783, the independence of the United States became a reality.

CHAPTER REVIEW Which factors do you think were most important in leading to the colonists' victory against the British Empire?

Chapter 5   Chapter Review

PRELUDES TO REVOLUTION

5.1 Explain Britain's victory over France in the French and Indian War and what conflicts followed this victory.

Review Questions

1. Crafting an Argument
   Is it valid to describe the Seven Years' War as a "world war"? Why or why not?

2. Comparison
   Compare and contrast the position of the European powers in North America before and after the Seven Years' War. What were the most important changes?

3. Historical Interpretation
   How did British victory in the Seven Years' War alter the relationship between Indian peoples and British colonists?

"THE REVOLUTION WAS IN THE MINDS OF THE PEOPLE"

5.2 Explain why, in the 15 years before the Revolutionary War began, support for the patriot cause spread so quickly among many different groups of North Americans who opposed Britain for different reasons.

Review Questions

4. Contextualization
   Explain what John Adams meant when he said that the Revolution "was in the minds of the people, and this was effected from 1760 to 1775, in the course of fifteen years before a drop of blood was shed at Lexington."

5. Historical Interpretation
   What were the political consequences of the "revolution in religion" during the mid-1700s?

6. Historical Interpretation
   What might explain the fact that seaport cities were important centers of revolutionary activity?

7. Crafting an Argument
   Why, in some ways, is the term *American Revolutions* more appropriate than *American Revolution*?

THE WAR FOR INDEPENDENCE

5.3 Explain how political and military strategy, support for the patriot cause, and American alliances with France and Spain led to an American victory in the war for independence.

Review Questions

8. Chronological Reasoning
   How and why did colonial resentment of British policies move from protest and demonstration to war and the Declaration of Independence between 1774 and 1776?

9. Contextualization
   What do the Articles of Confederation indicate about the political ideals and hopes and fears of the delegates to the Second Continental Congress?

10. Crafting an Argument
    What factors do you think are most important in explaining the American victory in the Revolutionary War?

Creating a Nation

Having won independence, the new United States faced many crises. In an effort to resolve some of the tensions, some of the nation's leaders proposed a new form of government and met in Philadelphia over the long hot summer of 1787 to produce a new Constitution.

In 1787, a Philadelphia physician, Benjamin Rush, wrote, "The American war is over, but this is far from the case with the American Revolution. On the contrary, nothing but the first act of the great drama is closed." For the generation that had lived through the 1760s and 1770s, opportunities abounded to help shape the new nation they had created. When Congress adopted the official seal of the new nation (found today on the back of every dollar bill), they included the Latin phrase *Novus Ordo Seclorum*, "a new order of the ages." Thomas Paine wrote, "We have it in our power to begin the world over again." Many in the new United States of America thought they could do just that.

The revolutionary leaders—Washington, Adams, Jefferson—have become cardboard characters. Their words have been invoked too often, their deeds too sanitized. But if today's citizens are to make sense of the Revolution and the creation of a new nation, they need to see those leaders as real. In addition, people today need to realize that many other actors were also asserting their place in—or, in the case of American Indians and Loyalists, on the margins of—the new nation. Those known as the "founding fathers" were far from the only actors. Women who had lived through the Revolution were far less willing to leave political or domestic decisions to men than their mothers and grandmothers had been. Poor farmers often felt

CHAPTER OBJECTIVE

Demonstrate an understanding of how the Revolution affected diverse groups of people and how independence ultimately led to the adoption of a new form of government.

LEARNING OBJECTIVES

THE STATE OF THE NATION AT WAR'S END

Explain how the outcome of the American Revolution affected different groups in the new United States. **6.1**

CREATING A GOVERNMENT: WRITING THE U.S. CONSTITUTION

Explain the needs, pressures, and compromises that led to writing and adopting the Constitution. **6.2**

democracy
A form of government in which power is vested in the people and exercised by them directly or indirectly through a system of representation.

that their grievances had not been addressed by independence, and they continued to complain. Even among those who led the Revolution itself, there were great differences of opinion, especially regarding the best ways to govern the new nation and to maintain the liberty for which had fought. What that new order would look like depended on not only where one stood in 1783 but also where one had stood before and during the Revolution. Exploring the efforts that helped create a stable and strong nation out of 13 British colonies requires, first, understanding what the end of the Revolution meant for different groups of people who found themselves in different circumstances.

THE STATE OF THE NATION AT WAR'S END

6.1 Explain how the outcome of the American Revolution affected different groups in the new United States.

For people of all classes, races, and political persuasions in British North America, the Revolution brought extensive change. Great inequality remained, but few people were willing to defend it as they had in the colonial era. Despite Abigail Adams's plea to her husband John that the Continental Congress should "remember the ladies" or Jefferson's assertions about the evils of slavery in his original drafts of the Declaration of Independence, sexism, slavery, and many forms of inequality survived the Revolution intact. Nevertheless, something had changed. No form of inequality survived the separation from Great Britain untouched. Forces had been unleashed, intended or not, that would undermine oppression. Thomas Paine, ever the optimistic recorder of events, wrote, "We see with other eyes; we hear with other ears, and think with other thoughts, than those we formerly used." And he explained that freedom, to him, meant "perfect equality.…The floor of Freedom is as level as water." Not all of his contemporaries wanted "perfect equality," but passive acceptance of inequality or hierarchy was much less common after the Revolution.

For the Revolutionary Army Officers: The Newburgh Conspiracy

The American experiment in creating an independent nation that would be a **democracy**, governed by the will of the majority—or at least the white male majority—almost died before it was born. During the long months between the victory at Yorktown in late 1781 and the treaty that ended the war in March 1783, the army that had won the war came close to a military takeover of the government—a *coup d'état* and a military dictatorship. Once the army had won its final battle, the Continental Congress asked the soldiers to wait. And the army, especially the officers, did not wait patiently in the year and a half that followed.

By the spring of 1783, the soldiers and officers had many reasons for complaint. The northern army was in barracks in Newburgh, New York. They were bored. By December 1782, they had not been paid for months. Pensions that the Congress had promised looked like they might never be paid. General Alexander McDougall and Colonels John Brooks and Matthias Ogden took a petition from Newburgh to the Congress in Philadelphia that said, "We have borne all that men can bear—our property is expended—our private resources are at an end, and our friends are wearied out and disgusted with our incessant applications." Borrowing money from friends to survive did not sit well with these officers. They warned that "any further experiments on their [the army's] patience may have fatal effects."

The petition arrived in Philadelphia at a crucial moment. The new nation was governed by the Articles of Confederation that had been adopted during the Revolution. Under the Articles, which did ensure a democratic government, led by a Congress of representatives elected by the voters of the 13 states, the national government could not levy taxes or raise funds without the unanimous approval of all the states. In late 1782, some of the states had rejected a proposal to tax imports. Alexander Hamilton wrote, "Without certain revenues, a government can have no power." The government that received the petition from the officers was in just that situation.

Those in the Congress who supported the idea of a more powerful central government used the army's petition to demand that the Congress be given the power to tax so it could raise its own funds and not have to depend on the generosity of state legislatures. These Federalists, who in the next decade formed the nucleus of the Federalist Party, led by Alexander Hamilton, made it clear to the army's representatives that they needed to support the move to give the Congress the power to tax if they were ever going to get paid. The other main faction in Congress, however—leaders who later became the Republican-Democrat Party that emerged in the 1790s—feared maintaining a standing army and opposed a larger government fueled by national taxes. They wanted to maintain the national government just as it was—as a weak alliance of individually strong states.

Deadlock followed. It was a dangerous moment. The threat by the army's officers to use force was real. They had been promised payment. Congress had now linked the payments to other agendas and postponed action. While most of those in the army were angry, there were also significant differences among them. A group of young officers were ready for action. They thought that George Washington was far too moderate. Their hero was Horatio Gates, who had led the victory at Saratoga and who disliked Washington. Some around Gates, perhaps in consultation with some Federalists in Congress, began planning for a military takeover of the new Republic. In March 1783, Major John Armstrong, Jr., published the first of what were called the "Newburgh Addresses," anonymously belittling the "milk and water style" and "meek language" of the previous petitions to Congress and calling for a meeting of the officers to discuss the situation.

General Washington was horrified. Military action would undermine everything for which he and the officers had fought. But Washington was a crafty politician. He simply asked the officers to postpone their meeting by a few days, invited Gates to preside, and requested a full report, implying that he would not be there. The officers who wanted action thought they had won and that they could meet with Washington's blessing.

But when Gates called the meeting to order, Washington entered the room and requested permission to speak. Though he was furious, Gates knew he could not refuse Washington in front of the other officers. Washington then attacked the anonymous "Newburgh Addresses" as "unmilitary" and "subversive of all order and discipline." He reminded the officers, "I have been…the constant companion and witness of your distresses." Would the army, he asked, contemplate attacking the Congress? "My God!" he said, "What can this writer have in view," by recommending such measures?

The speech worked. The officers cheered Washington. All threat of military action against the weak civil government was over. Congress voted to give a lump sum payment to all the officers who had been promised a pension and passed a tax on imports to pay off the national debt, including the debt to the army.

The so-called Newburgh Conspiracy was defeated. In November, the last British troops left New York City, and the American officers and their troops marched into the city and began its transition to civilian leadership. Instead of seizing power, the Continental Army began to disband, with payment as promised. Washington made a triumphal entry into the city and, on December 4, 1783, gave an emotional farewell to his officers. He then returned to civilian life at his home in Mount Vernon, Virginia. By January 1784, the army had shrunk to some 600 soldiers, ensuring a transition to civilian rule.

For Poor White Farmers: Shays's Rebellion

Like the officers of the Continental Army, the poor of colonial society—now the poor of the new nation—were also unhappy, in some cases violently unhappy. Some had served as enlisted soldiers in the Revolutionary army and had their own complaints about salaries. Beginning in 1784, the influx of imported goods that came with the war's end created an economic depression that hit hardest those who were already

Having led the American army through the hard years of the Revolutionary War and ensured a transition to civilian government, George Washington said farewell to many of the officers who had served with him. He retired to Mount Vernon in December 1783.

Shays's Rebellion

An armed movement of debt-ridden farmers in western Massachusetts in the winter of 1786–1787 who objected to the state's effort to tax them to pay off the Revolutionary War debt.

poor. The most famous response to this unhappiness in the first years of the new Republic took place in Massachusetts and came to be known as **Shays's Rebellion**, named for one of its leaders, Daniel Shays. Those who participated in the rebellion called themselves Regulators—not to be confused with those in the Carolinas who had taken the law into their own hands before the Revolution, but simply people who wanted to regulate the power of the new state governments.

In 1786, farmers in western Massachusetts began petitioning the state legislature for relief from economic hardships brought on by a significant increase in their taxes as the legislature tried to pay off Revolutionary War debts and by the postwar economic depression that reduced the value of farm products. For farmers who were used to being self-sufficient, the reduction in their income and demands for taxes to be paid in cash were too much to accept. They were being threatened with foreclosure and their way of life was being destroyed because they could not raise the money demanded of them. They had to do something.

When faced with the petitions of the farmers, the Massachusetts legislature, dominated by commercial leaders from the eastern part of the state, blamed the farmers for their own plight. In response, the farmers decided on direct action. They simply stopped the courts from issuing foreclosure rulings. On August 29, 1786, 1,500 farmers armed with clubs and muskets shut down the court in Northampton as it attempted to hear cases. They also stopped courts in four other towns.

The governor and legislature reacted by passing a Riot Act that prohibited 12 or more armed persons from gathering and authorized county sheriffs to kill those who disobeyed the law. They also suspended the writ of habeas corpus and authorized the governor to arrest and hold without bail "any person or persons whatsoever."

Shays's Rebellion, an uprising of poor farmers who were in danger of losing their land because of increased taxes, symbolized the discontent that many Americans felt during the economic downturn after the Revolution, but it also struck fear into many other Americans who believed the nation was on the edge of anarchy and needed a much stronger central government to deal with matters.

But the farmers, many of whom had fought as soldiers in the Revolution, were prepared to fight a second time for their rights as free citizens. From their perspective, the Massachusetts legislature was acting like the former royal governor. Shays and several thousand of his fellow citizens now took up arms, fearing for "our lives and families which will be taken from us if we don't defend them."

By January 1787, the Regulators had decided to overthrow the government of Massachusetts. Shays himself planned to attack the federal arsenal in Springfield and then march to Boston to "destroy the nest of devils, who by their influence, make the Court enact what they please, burn it and lay the town of Boston in ashes." He came close to succeeding.

By late January, thousands of well-armed farmers surrounded the federal arsenal in Springfield, which was defended by 1,000 state militia under the command of Major General William Shepard. Unfortunately for the rebellion, different groups thought the assault was set for different days, and so on January 25, as a smaller group than expected marched on the arsenal, Shepard's troops fired over their heads but then directly into their ranks. Four or five were killed, and the rest retreated. They did not immediately give up their idea of overthrowing the state government, but no other attack came as close to doing so.

As 1787 wore on, the rebellion slowly ended. The Regulators had few friends in the government of Massachusetts or the surrounding states and were not able to establish a political base. In 1788, the economy began to recover, which made life more tolerable for farmers. Some of the rebels left Massachusetts for more remote places. Shays himself settled in Vermont. But the rebels had terrified the nation's elite and hastened the movement toward a stronger national government.

Fears of the rebellion in Massachusetts inspired other revolutionary leaders to act. When he first heard news of Shays's Rebellion, Washington told Henry Lee of Virginia that the rebellion was "proof of what our trans-Atlantic foe has predicted…that mankind when left to themselves are unfit for their own Government." But, despite their worries, men like Washington and Lee were determined not to let such a proof stand. The convention that met in Philadelphia in the summer of 1787 was a direct result.

For White Settlers Moving West

The new nation was huge compared to the territorial size of the European powers. The Treaty of Paris recognized the eastern border of the United States as running along the Atlantic coast from Maine to Georgia. Since Britain had returned Florida to Spain at the end of the Revolutionary War, the new nation was cut off from the Gulf of Mexico, and Spain was not always a friendly southern neighbor. The Treaty of Paris also made the eastern shore of the Mississippi River the nation's western boundary. The British proclamation line that had protected Indian tribes in the Ohio region and caused so much tension was not mentioned in the treaty. Control of the Mississippi River itself—the right to travel on it—would remain contested, especially since the river ended at the city of New Orleans, which Spain zealously guarded (see Map 6-1).

Within this vast territory, the 13 states hugged the Atlantic coast. American Indians dominated the interior, but without even the modest protection from white settlers that Britain had provided. More whites were crossing the mountains and claiming western lands despite the lack of government approval and the dangers of Indian attack. Royal charters gave many of the states' claims to lands far into the interior. But soon after the Revolution ended, the Continental Congress began resolving conflicting land claims and creating new states and territories west of the original 13 states.

One of the first issues to be resolved was over the conflicting claims of New York and New Hampshire to the land on the eastern side of Lake Champlain. Many of the whites who had settled the region wanted independence from both. Local heroes, such as Ethan Allen and his Green Mountain Boys, had fought for the American cause in the region and wanted to control their home. As a result, Vermont became the first new state in 1791 (see Map 6-2).

One of the most significant accomplishments of the Congress that operated under the Articles of Confederation was the creation of the Northwest Territory out of lands claimed by Pennsylvania, New York, Connecticut, and Massachusetts. Between 1784 and 1787, Congress set up territorial governments for what would become Ohio, Indiana, Illinois, Michigan, and Wisconsin. It took years of difficult negotiations before the original states gave up their conflicting claims to the interior lands, but ordinances passed between 1784 and 1787 created a new structure for the future Midwest. In 1785, Congress ordered that the lands be surveyed, set off into a grid pattern with most sections to be sold, while some were reserved for future government needs and specifically for the support of schools. The grid system established in 1785 was used in future territories, creating clear and well-organized boundaries for farms and towns, but encouraging widely dispersed settlements

MAP 6-1 The American-Spanish Border, 1783–1795. In the Treaty of Paris, Great Britain not only recognized American independence but returned control of Florida to Spain, creating the southern border for the United States; though, as the map shows, the border was far from clear. West of the United States was the vast Louisiana Territory, for the time being also under Spanish control.

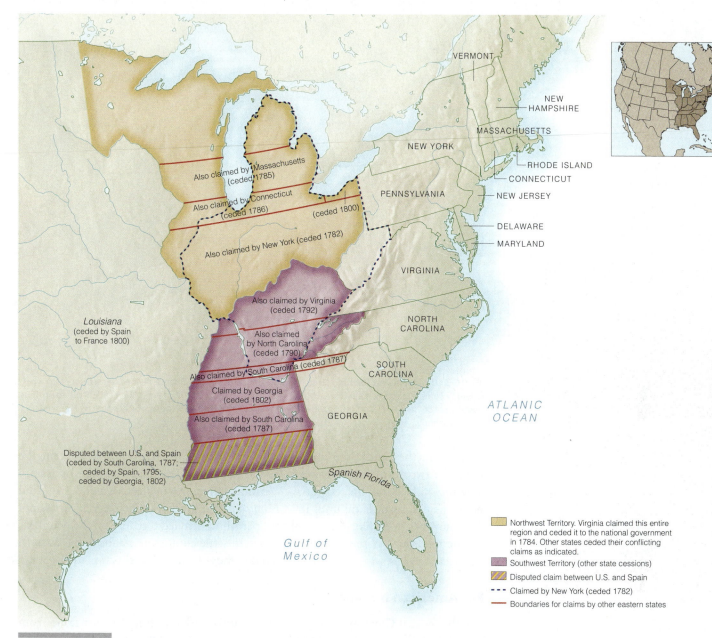

VERMONT

NEW
HAMPSHIRE

MASSACHUSETTS

NEW YORK

RHODE ISLAND

CONNECTICUT

NEW JERSEY

PENNSYLVANIA

DELAWARE

MARYLAND

VIRGINIA

NORTH
CAROLINA

SOUTH
CAROLINA

GEORGIA

Louisiana
(ceded by Spain
to France 1800)

Also claimed by Massachusetts
(ceded 1785)

Also claimed by Connecticut
(ceded 1786)

(ceded 1800)

Also claimed by New York (ceded 1782)

Also claimed by Virginia
(ceded 1792)

Also claimed
by North Carolina
(ceded 1790)

Also claimed by South Carolina (ceded 1787)

Claimed by Georgia
(ceded 1802)

Also claimed by South Carolina
(ceded 1787)

Disputed between U.S. and Spain
(ceded by South Carolina, 1787;
ceded by Spain, 1795;
ceded by Georgia, 1802)

Spanish Florida

*ATLANTIC
OCEAN*

*Gulf of
Mexico*

- Northwest Territory. Virginia claimed this entire region and ceded it to the national government in 1784. Other states ceded their conflicting claims as indicated.
- Southwest Territory (other state cessions)
- Disputed claim between U.S. and Spain
- - - Claimed by New York (ceded 1782)
- Boundaries for claims by other eastern states

MAP 6-2 State Claims to Western Lands. The huge tract of land that the King's Proclamation Line had reserved for Indian tribes before the Revolution became part of the United States in 1783. Different original states claimed this land and one of the first duties of Congress was to sort out those conflicting claims. After 1783 no one in government spoke for the rights of the Native Americans whose land much of the territory had been.

rather than compact communities (see Map 6-3). **The Northwest Ordinance of 1787** banned slavery in these territories as well as mandating religious freedom and the development of public schools. The act also declared that "the utmost good faith shall always be observed towards the Indians; their lands and property shall never be taken from them without their consent," though little was done to enforce this provision.

Further south, white settlement was, if anything, proceeding faster. An accomplished soldier, hunter, and trapper, Daniel Boone first explored the trans-Appalachian territory that would be known as Kentucky in 1767 when it was still off limits to whites. As the Revolution was starting in 1775 and the British ability to stop settlement was ebbing, Boone blazed the "Wilderness Trail" through the Cumberland Gap in the Appalachians and established a settlement he called Boonesborough. During and after the war, many more settlers followed the Wilderness Trail. Virginia gave up its long-standing claims to the region, and the federal government, recognizing that there were already slaves in the territory, admitted Kentucky to the union as a slave state in 1792 and Tennessee in 1796.

The Northwest Ordinance of 1787
Legislation passed by Congress under the Articles of Confederation that provided for public schools, the sale of government land, and prohibited slavery in the Northwest Territories.

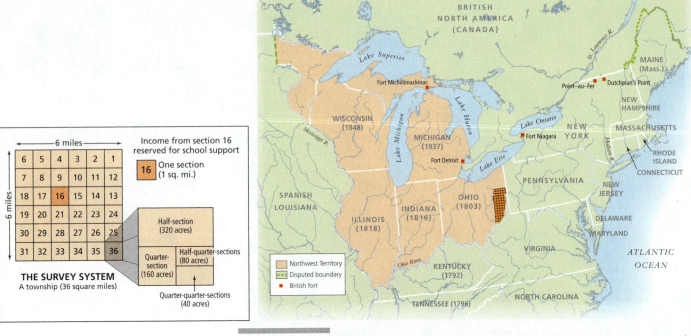

THE SURVEY SYSTEM
A township (36 square miles)

MAP 6-3 The Northwest Territory Grid System. The Northwest Ordinance divided the territory into what would become five states. It also created a survey system in which the land would be divided into townships made up of 36 "sections," 35 of which would be available to settlers and one of which would be reserved to support schools.

Even further south, the land west of Georgia that would eventually become the northern two-thirds of Alabama and Mississippi was organized as the Mississippi Territory in 1798, but the territorial government there was ineffective, and Georgia did not give up its own claims until 1802. (The southern third of Alabama and Mississippi was known as West Florida, part of the Spanish-controlled territory on the country's southern border.) While the Congress tried to settle conflicting claims to the western lands, the Indians, who had the oldest claim to the land, had no inclination to give it up.

For American Indians

For the federal Congress, the greatest threat to the new United States came from American Indians. For most of the tribes who lived between the Atlantic coast and the Mississippi River, the end of the American Revolution was one more disaster among many. Despite the loyalty of the Iroquois to the British during the Revolution, the king's government agreed to the Treaty of Paris in 1783, which ceded all the lands between the Atlantic coast and the Mississippi and south of the Great Lakes and Canada to the new United States, without consulting with their old allies. The Proclamation Line limiting white settlement was gone. Among the many Indian tribes, even among the Iroquois, there were differing responses to the British failure to honor their loyalty. Many Indian leaders saw no reason to honor a treaty in which they had played no part and continued to act as if much of New York and Pennsylvania and all lands west of the Ohio River belonged to them.

Under the leadership of Joseph Brant, the Mohawks, who had fought so hard for the British between 1776 and 1781, petitioned the British authorities in Quebec for land on the British side of the new border and were granted a large tract in Canada. But they, like other tribes, did not let an international boundary limit their range of hunting or living. New York and Pennsylvania petitioned the Congress for help with the Indian tribes on their western frontiers, and the New York legislature considered expelling all the tribes of the Six Nations because of their alliance with the British during the war (see Map 6-4).

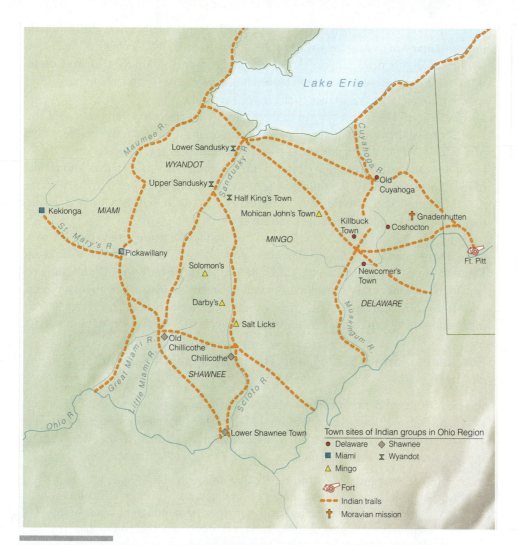

Town sites of Indian groups in Ohio Region
- ● Delaware   ◆ Shawnee
- ■ Miami   ✕ Wyandot
- ▲ Mingo

Fort

Indian trails

✝ Moravian mission

MAP 6-4 Ohio in the 1780s. The land that would later become the state of Ohio was a battlefield in the 1780s. While Great Britain included the land as part of the newly independent United States in 1783, in reality Native American tribes were the dominant force in the region and they often received aid from their Canadian-based British allies.

Through the Treaty of Paris, the British also promised to withdraw from all forts south of the Great Lakes. As a result, a power vacuum was looming in the region, though the British were slow to honor their commitment to leave their western forts. Rather than depend on state militia, Congress in 1783 began to create the U.S. Army to occupy Fort Niagara near today's Buffalo, New York, and Fort Pitt, today's Pittsburgh. Although Congress could create an army, its difficulty in raising funds meant that the Secretary of War, former General Henry Knox, had to beg for money to keep the army paid, fed, and supplied, which strengthened the hand of Indian leaders committed to resisting white expansion. And many meant to resist.

The Iroquois were far from the only Indians who began to resist American expansion violently. These tribes had never formally agreed to peace with the new nation, and they attacked both the army and the settlers. The small battles—individual attacks, kidnappings, and destruction of property—continued as they had during the Revolution. The U.S. Army was far too small, ill-trained, and ill-supplied to be much of a deterrent. Given how weak the army was, the Indians held the upper hand in the Northwest Territory and Kentucky.

A temporary peace along the New York border was secured in October 1784 by the **Treaty of Fort Stanwix** between some of the Iroquois and the U.S. government. But many, including Sagoyewatha (Red Jacket) of the Seneca and Joseph Brant opposed the treaty, and it did not hold. In fact, the Indians of the Northwest Territory would remain virtually at war with the United States from 1785 until 1795.

Treaty of Fort Stanwix
A 1784 treaty between one faction of the Iroquois and the U.S. government that sought to end the violent battles over land in New York, Pennsylvania, and the Ohio River Valley to the west.

Chapter 6 Creating a Nation   **157**

Joseph Brant, or Thayendanegea, was a leader among the Mohawks, who convinced many in the Iroquois federation to support the British cause during the Revolution and oppose American expansion after the war, as he negotiated for Native American rights. He was one of the very few people of any race to meet with both George Washington and King George III.

After the Treaty of Fort Stanwix was signed, Brant sailed for London where he met with many high-ranking British officials and had an audience with King George III. He sought financial support for his people as compensation for their role on the British side in the Revolution, and he—and his British hosts—also seem to have developed a plan for Indian resistance to the new American nation.

In 1785 and 1786, Brant began to create an Indian confederation that could successfully resist the United States. The confederation included not only representatives of the Iroquois but also many other tribes who had been traditional enemies of the Iroquois as well as Cherokees from much further south and smaller tribes who resided in the Ohio River Valley. It would be one of the most unified and effective adversaries that the United States would face. The Indians demanded that the Congress ensure that white settlement ended at the Ohio River.

While the Indians and Congress negotiated fitfully, the frontier remained a violent place. In the late 1780s, 1,500 white settlers and at least as many Indians in Ohio and Kentucky were killed (see Map 6-5). The United States had no intention of ceding as much land to the Indians as they demanded, but under the Articles of Confederation, it was difficult to organize an army to enforce the government's claims. The need to create a government strong enough to counter the Indians led many to support the Constitution in 1787.

For Slaves, Former Slaves, and Those Who Claimed Ownership of Them

In 1791, Benjamin Banneker, a free African-American whose parents had been slaves, wrote to Thomas Jefferson, then Washington's secretary of state, reminding him that in 1776 Jefferson had written, "that all men are created equal, and that they are endowed by their creator with certain inalienable rights." Banneker continued:

> [B]ut sir, how pitiable is it to reflect that although you were so fully convinced of the benevolence of the Father of mankind…you should…counteract his mercies, in detaining by fraud and violence so numerous a part of my brethren, under groaning captivity and cruel oppression, that you should…be found guilty of that most criminal act, which you professedly detested in others, with respect to yourselves.

Banneker would not let Jefferson forget the contradiction at the heart of the new American enterprise and Jefferson's own life.

As Banneker's letter indicates, many slaves and former slaves understood that the words *freedom* and *liberty* also ought to count for them. By the end of the Revolution, many whites agreed. Back in 1775, Thomas Paine asked how Americans could complain about British tyranny "while they hold so many hundreds of thousands in slavery?"

The issue of freedom and liberty seemed to be gaining ground for some slaves after 1776. News traveled slowly, but word spread that in 1794, in the midst of the French Revolution, the French National Convention had abolished slavery, and then that slaves in France's most lucrative Caribbean colony had won independence for what became the black-led Republic of Haiti.

When Cornwallis surrendered at Yorktown in 1781, he had between 4,000 and 5,000 former slaves with his army. Many more were in other British-held areas, especially New York City. As the war ended, the British returned some slaves to old masters, gave others to new masters in the Caribbean, or simply abandoned them. But many former slaves also sailed with the British when they left the colonies, some settling as free people in Canada, England, or West Africa. A former slave named Boston King wrote that, "The English had compassion upon us in the day of distress. Soon after, ships were fitted out, and furnished with every necessary for conveying us to Nova Scotia." Life was not easy for African-Americans in Nova Scotia, but they were free.

By the time George Washington was inaugurated president in 1789, slavery had been abolished in Massachusetts, New Hampshire, and Vermont and was dying—though slowly—throughout the north. Northern slaves worked as household help and

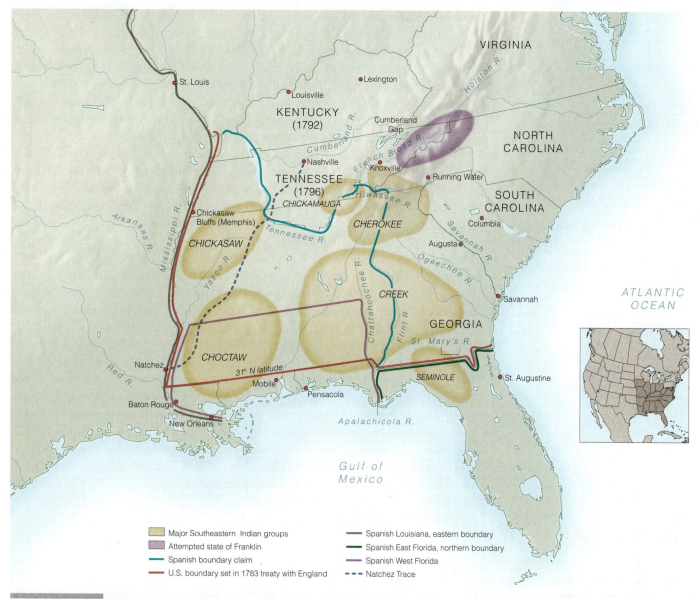

MAP 6-5 Tribal Land Claims 1783–1788. Especially in the southwest of the new United States, strong Native American tribes clamed large areas and did not much care whether the U.S. or Spain claimed the territory since they did not want settlers from either country.

labored in factories and farms. New York had the most slaves in the north, concentrated in Manhattan but also working on the great estates of the Hudson Valley. New Jersey and Rhode Island were next in number. In the north, however, more money was made on the slave trade than on slave labor. The Northwest Ordinance prohibited slavery in the Ohio region. Many thought slavery would also die out in Delaware, Maryland, and Virginia. Only in the Carolinas, Georgia, and the new western areas of Kentucky and Tennessee was slavery still strong.

Despite the regional differences, by 1789, 1 in 10 African-Americans was a free person. Some had won their freedom through the army. Some had won through state action. Some had been set free by individual slave owners. But in 1789, one could not assume that to be black was to be a slave. That truth was a significant change from 1776 when free blacks were a definite exception in every one of the 13 colonies.

After Massachusetts, New Hampshire, and Vermont abolished slavery, other northern states with more slaves moved exceedingly slowly toward gradual emancipation (Table 6-1). The Pennsylvania law of 1780 declared slavery "disgraceful to any people," but then set up a system in which the first slaves would not be freed until 1808 and the last would not be emancipated until 1847. New York's abolition law of 1799 and New Jersey's of 1804, as well as similar laws in Connecticut and Rhode Island, were equally slow in their operations. Although every northern state had started the process of ending slavery before 1800, it was almost 1850 before slavery disappeared in the north.

Free blacks sometimes found work in the same households where they had been slaves. Black men worked on merchant ships, whaling vessels, or even in the navy. (The racially diverse crew of the whaling ship *Pequod* in Herman Melville's 1851 novel *Moby Dick* was not unusual.) In Philadelphia, New York, Providence, and Boston, many blacks worked on the docks. Throughout the northern states more and more free blacks referred to themselves as Africans or, as the Free African Society of Philadelphia said, "free Africans and their descendants."

In the region encompassing Delaware, Maryland, Virginia, and North Carolina, slavery did not die out, but slave life changed after the Revolution. Some masters heeded the revolutionary language of freedom. James Madison freed one slave named Billy because he came to fear that Billy's love of freedom meant he was no longer "a fit companion for fellow slaves." George Washington wrote often of his wish that slavery could be gradually abolished and left instructions in his will that all his slaves should be free after he and Martha died. Other planters in the region also freed slaves. Slaves who had run away during the war managed to establish new identities and maintain their freedom, especially in cities like Baltimore, Richmond, and the new District of Columbia. By 1810, almost a quarter of the African-Americans in Maryland, a third in the District of Columbia, and six or seven percent in Virginia and North Carolina were free. A thriving community of free people of African descent emerged. As a sign of their growing confidence, in 1792, Thomas Brown, a black Revolutionary War veteran in Baltimore, ran, although unsuccessfully, for the Maryland legislature, promising to "represent so many hundreds of poor Blacks."

TABLE 6-1 The Free Black Population in the Early United States

State	Free black population in 1790	Total black population in 1790	Percentage of free blacks in total black population	Free black population in 1810	Total black population in 1810	Percentage of free blacks in total black population
New Hampshire	630	788	80%	970	970	100%
Vermont	255	271	94%	750	750	100%
Massachusetts	6,001	6,001	100%	7,706	7,706	100%
Connecticut	2,808	5,572	50%	6,453	6,763	95%
Rhode Island	3,407	4,355	78%	3,609	3,717	97%
New York	4,654	25,978	18%	25,333	40,350	63%
New Jersey	2,762	14,185	19%	7,843	18,694	42%
Pennsylvania	6,537	10,324	63%	22,492	23,287	97%
Delaware	3,899	12,786	30%	13,136	17,313	76%
Maryland	8,043	111,079	7%	33,927	145,429	23%
Virginia	12,866	305,493	4%	30,570	423,088	7%
North Carolina	4,975	105,547	5%	10,266	179,090	6%
Kentucky	114	12,544	1%	1,713	82,274	2%
Tennessee	361	3,778	10%	1,317	45,845	3%
District of Columbia	—	—	—	2,549	7,944	32%
South Carolina	1,801	108,895	2%	4,544	200,919	2%
Georgia	398	29,662	1%	1,801	107,019	2%

American Voices

Prince Hall, "From Slavery to Equality," 1797

Born a slave, Prince Hall was freed before the Revolution, and after the war he played a leading role in abolishing slavery in Massachusetts. Hall helped create the African Lodge of the Masons in Boston and delivered the following speech to that group. He makes it clear that although African-Americans in his city are free, they are far from equal; still, he urges his audience to take heart at the promise of freedom seen in the revolution in Haiti.

Now, my brethren, nothing is stable; all things are changeable. Let us seek those things which are sure and steadfast, and let us pray God that, while we remain here, he would give us the grace of patience and strength to bear up under all our troubles, which, at this day, God knows, we have our share of. Patience, I say; for were we not possessed of a great measure of it, we could not bear up under the daily insults we meet with in the streets of Boston, much more on public days of recreation. How, at such times, are we shamefully abused, and that to such a degree that we may truly be said to carry our lives in our hands, and the arrows of death are flying about our heads. Helpless women have their clothes torn from their backs....I was told by a gentleman who saw this filthy behavior in the Common that, in all places he had been in, he never saw so cruel behavior in all his life; and that a slave in the West Indies on Sundays or holidays enjoys himself and friends without molestation....

My brethren, let us not be cast down under these and many other abuses we at present are laboring under, for the darkest hour is just before the break of day. My brethren, let us remember what a dark day it was with our African brethren, six years ago, in the French West Indies. Nothing but the snap of the whip was heard, from morning to evening. Hanging, breaking on the wheel, burning and all manner of tortures were inflicted upon those unhappy people. But, blessed be God, the scene is changed. They now confess that God hath no respect of person and, therefore, receive them as their friends and treat them as brothers. Thus doth Ethiopia stretch forth her hand from slavery, to freedom and equality.

Source: Prince Hall, "Thus Doth Ethiopia Stretch Forth Her Hand from Slavery, to Freedom and Equality," (1797) in Manning Marable and Leith Mullings, editors, *Let Nobody Turn Us Around: Voices of Resistance, Reform, and Renewal* (Lanham, MD: Rowman & Littlefield, 2000), pp. 16–18.

Thinking Critically

1. Documentary Analysis

What light does Hall's speech shed on race relations in Boston in the late 1700s?

2. Historical Interpretation

What connection did Hall make between the revolts that would produce an independent Haiti and the situation confronting African-Americans? How might his analysis of events in the French West Indies have differed from that of many white observers?

In this region, slaves and free blacks worked in an economy that was more diverse than before the war. By 1790, slaves in Virginia and Maryland, for example, were increasingly engaged in growing wheat, a crop that required horses that needed tending, plows, and fertilizer. They also worked in flour mills and the ironworks, blacksmith shops, and other enterprises that were springing up in the region. Some slaves were "rented out" and moved from job to job, giving them a chance to learn more skills, travel short distances, make a little money, and gain a taste of freedom.

Other slaves from the region were far less fortunate. In the years after the Revolution, with the plantations of Virginia and Maryland stabilized in size, slave owners needed fewer slaves. So they increased their wealth by developing a new internal market in humans. They encouraged slaves to have more children and then, as those children reached adolescence, sold them, as they sold other agricultural products, for transport to places that needed more and more slave labor. Slaves were taken to join the white settlers who established the new states of Kentucky and Tennessee. Other slaves were transported to South Carolina and Georgia.

Further south, in South Carolina and Georgia, life for slaves was very different. Some of the fiercest fighting of the Revolution had disrupted almost every aspect of life in South Carolina and Georgia, and slaves had more opportunities to run away. With the coming of peace, however, the planter elite in these states was determined to reestablish a way of life that depended on slavery. Slaves represented between 40 and

60 percent of the population in South Carolina and Georgia. Slave labor had produced great fortunes for the plantation owners before the war, and it would produce new fortunes for them after the war ended.

Whereas many planters in Delaware, Maryland, Virginia, and North Carolina felt the need to consider the rhetoric of freedom and perhaps modify the tyranny of slavery, planters in South Carolina and Georgia made it clear that they believed such language did not apply to slaves. As a result, the few free blacks in the southernmost states, often people who had black, white, and Indian heritage, were kept as far away from the slave community as possible so the slaves would not hear the contagious language of freedom.

In the 20 years after 1790, the number of slaves doubled in South Carolina from 100,000 to 200,000, and in Georgia it more than tripled from 30,000 to over 100,000. The rapid growth of the slave population in South Carolina and Georgia at the end of the 1700s also led to a new kind of community life in the slave quarters of these large plantations. Unlike those who owned a lone slave or a single slave family, which could be closely supervised, the largest plantations in South Carolina and Georgia had hundreds of slaves in the 1790s. Slave labor created great wealth, and the owners of these plantations were the economic elite of their states, but they were often away, preferring the social life of Charleston or Savannah. Slaves, though driven by overseers, were able to develop their own community lives and norms within the slave quarters, which had not been possible on the smaller farms and plantations of an earlier era. Having their own vegetable gardens sometimes gave slaves limited economic freedom. Religious gatherings provided communal support.

For Women: The Rise of Republican Motherhood

In April 1776, Abigail Adams wrote to her husband John while the future president was attending the Congress that would issue the Declaration of Independence in Philadelphia and she was managing the family and farm in Quincy, Massachusetts, from which he was so often absent. She told him to "remember the ladies." And she warned, "Do not put such unlimited power into the hands of husbands....If particular care and attention is not paid to the ladies we are determined to foment a rebellion, and will not hold ourselves bound by any laws in which we have no voice or representation." Abigail was quite serious in her demand. Her husband, however, treated his wife's plea as a kind of joke. John Adams wrote back to his wife saying, "Our struggle has loosened the bonds of government everywhere; that children and apprentices were disobedient," but, he said, Abigail's letter "was the first intimation that another tribe, more numerous and powerful than all the rest, were grown discontented." We do not know how she responded to having her husband lump her plea for a voice in government with the discontent of children and apprentices. Abigail and John had a close marriage, but while she was serious about wanting the American Revolution to recognize more rights for women, he was equally determined to ignore her plea.

Women, of course, fell into all of the different groups that men did. American Indian women, most of whom like the men had supported the British, often paid a high price for their loyalty to Britain. Mary (Molly) Brant, the sister of Joseph Brant, convinced many Iroquois to support an Iroquois-British alliance during the war. When the war ended, she found a new home in Canada, reminding the British authorities that they were not providing the support they had promised her people.

Slave women also sided with the British more often than with the American Revolutionaries. With British armies operating in the southern colonies, and the British welcoming slaves to their side, women as well as men fled to freedom with the British. Of the 23 slaves who ran away from Thomas Jefferson's plantations during the Revolution, 13 were female. More than 40 percent of all of the former slaves who left with the British at the end of the war were women.

Some white women—rich and poor—also supported the British cause and paid dearly for it. With the coming of the war, many Loyalist wives stayed behind to mind their homes when their husbands joined the British army or fled to Canada. These women faced hostile neighbors and local governments, and many lost their homes.

For white women who supported the Revolution, life was also hard, but the outcome was usually better. The Revolutionary War shaped the lives of most women who had supported it. For some, it changed virtually every aspect of life. After the war, Deborah Sampson, who had pretended to be a man and fought in the war, married and lived in Sharon, Massachusetts, but she was also entertained by President Washington, was granted a revolutionary soldier's pension by Congress, and became something of a national hero. Other women did not easily return to their old ways, limited to the private sphere of their families. With many men away for months or years, women took on household duties that were, by long tradition, men's exclusive sphere. Mary Bartlett, whose husband represented New Hampshire in Congress, reflected a changed attitude experienced by many. In her first letters in 1776, she wrote about "Your farming business," but by 1778, it had become "our farming business." The difference of one word that made it clear she now included herself in the ownership of their farm was an important change.

Many women who had coped with years of isolation during the war found that the political independence of the United States brought personal independence, too. More women postponed marriage, demanded divorces from unhappy marriages, and sought higher education as well as new—if limited—political involvement in the new republic.

For many Americans, women and men, the book, *A Vindication of the Rights of Woman*, written in 1792 by British writer Mary Wollstonecraft, gave words to ideas that had been taking shape since the Revolution. In her appeal for equality, Wollstonecraft called for equal education, and coeducation, for girls and boys. In America, Judith Sargent Murray expanded Wollstonecraft's arguments and insisted that women are indeed "in every respect equal to men."

Important as they were, the ideas about total equality developed by Wollstonecraft and Murray did not become the dominant ideology of the new nation. Instead, something much more moderate, known as **Republican Motherhood**, came to dominate public discussions of women's place in the new United States. As the ideology of Republican Motherhood was developed in pulpits and magazines after the Revolution, women would have an important role, but a limited one—not full citizenship but also no return to a merely passive role in the domestic sphere that had been prescribed before 1776. Republican Motherhood was a kind of middle position. Its advocates suggested that women would advise their husbands and raise their sons to be active citizens and their daughters to be part of another generation of republican mothers who shaped the nation from home. But to play this role, its advocates insisted that women also needed an education, perhaps a different education from men, but a better one than that given to their mothers and grandmothers.

In 1778, Abigail Adams wrote, "I regret...how fashionable it has been to ridicule Female learning." After the war, she and many others planned to do something about it. Private academies, which had educated white male leaders for a century, began to open their doors to women, or more often, separate private academies for women were founded like the Young Ladies' Academy of Philadelphia that Benjamin Rush opened in 1787. Rush, whose views reflected his belief in the ideology of Republican Motherhood, believed that the "attention of our young ladies should be directed as soon as they are prepared for it to the reading of history, travels, poetry, and moral essays...to the present state of society in America." When Priscilla Mason graduated from Rush's Young Ladies' Academy in 1794, however, she condemned the arbitrary limitations that "have denied us the means of knowledge, and then reproached us for the want of it." She continued, "The Church, the Bar, and the Senate are shut against us.

Having lived through the Revolution in Massachusetts and become a leader in the Universalist churches, Judith Sargent Murray also came to be one of the strongest voices demanding absolute equality for women in the new nation.

Republican Motherhood
The belief that women should have more rights and a better education so that they might support husbands and raise sons who would actively participate in the political affairs of society.

American Voices

Judith Sargent Murray, *On the Equality of the Sexes*, 1792

Judith Sargent Murray was born into a merchant family in Massachusetts in 1751 and lived through the Revolution as a young woman. She was a leader of the Universalist movement in religion, which believed that all people were saved, a belief that led them to emphasize equality, including equality of the sexes. She argued that differences between the sexes were due to educational opportunities rather than inherent qualities, and she wanted an education that would make women the equals of their brothers, husbands, and sons. She argued that the way society constructed women's roles perpetuated the stereotype of women as overly emotional and not thoughtful. With an equal education, she insisted, women could at least equal men. Her most famous book, On the Equality of the Sexes, was published in 1792.

Is it upon mature consideration we adopt the idea, that nature is thus partial in her distributions? Is it indeed a fact, that she hath yielded to one half of the human species so unquestionable a mental superiority?…May we not trace its source in the difference of education…the one is taught to aspire, and the other is early confined and limited. As their years increase, the sister must be wholly domesticated, while the brother is led by the hand through all the flowery paths of science. Grant that their minds are by nature equal, yet who shall wonder at the *apparent* superiority, if indeed custom becomes *second nature*…. At length arrived at womanhood, the uncultivated fair one feels a void, which the employments allotted her are by no means capable of filling.…She experiences a mortifying consciousness of inferiority, which embitters every enjoyment.…Now, was she permitted the same instructors as her brother, (with an eye however to their particular departments) for the employment of a rational mind an ample field would be opened.…A mind, thus filled, would

have little room for the trifles with which our sex are, with too much justice, accused of amusing themselves, and they would thus be rendered fit companions for those, who should one day wear them as their crown.…

Should it still be vociferated, "Your domestic employments are sufficient"—I would calmly ask, is it reasonable, that a candidate for immortality, for the joys of heaven, an intelligent being, who is to spend an eternity in contemplating the works of Deity, should at present be so degraded, as to be allowed no other ideas, than those which are suggested by the mechanism of a pudding, or the sewing the seams of a garment? Pity that all such censurers of female improvement do not go one step further, and deny their future existence; to be consistent they surely ought.

Yes, ye lordly, ye haughty sex, our souls are by nature *equal* to yours; the same breath of God animates, enlivens, and invigorates us; and that we are not fallen lower than yourselves.

Source: Judith Sargent Murray, "On the Equality of the Sexes," first published in the *Massachusetts Magazine*, April 1790, reprinted in Eve Kornfeld, *Creating an American Culture, 1775–1800: A Brief History with Documents* (Boston: Bedford St. Martin's, 2001), pp. 127–132.

Thinking Critically

1. **Documentary Analysis**
   What differences did Murray note between the education of boys and girls? What consequences did she attach to those differences?

2. **Historical Interpretation**
   What vision of republican womanhood did Murray support? How did her vision differ from that embodied in the emerging ideology of Republican Motherhood?

Who shut them? Man, despotic man." An education that produced such a speaker, may have been more than Rush envisioned when he proposed the school.

Women also took a more direct role in politics when they could. New Jersey's 1776 Constitution gave women the right to vote, but the provision was repealed in 1807. The Bill of Rights that was added to the federal Constitution in 1791 gave all citizens—women as well as men—the right to "petition the government for a redress of grievances," and women regularly petitioned Congress and state legislatures. After the Revolution, women also gained significant new rights to control their own property, which they had not had before the war. It would be a long time before law and culture would support the equality that Abigail Adams or Judith Sargent Murray advocated. But attitudes had begun to change.

Within the ideology of Republican Motherhood, however, two double standards emerged. First, middle- and upper-class white women were expected to be the guardians of sexual morality. Men might stray, but, as a Philadelphia newspaper editorialized, "Ladies, much depends on you, towards a reformation in the morals of our sex." And if men did stray, it was expected they would do so only with lower-class or poor white women or with blacks, slave or free. Second, servants and working women were

Although it is often forgotten, New Jersey's 1776 state constitution gave that state's women the right to vote, a right they exercised enthusiastically until the provision was repealed in 1807.

not included in either the rules or the opportunities for education and influence that the ideal of Republican Motherhood gave to supposedly all women, but in reality the increasingly well-educated and active women of higher social and economic status.

 Quick Review Did the Revolutionary War have a truly revolutionary effect on Britain's former colonies? Address the changes, or lack thereof, among at least two groups in your answer.

CREATING A GOVERNMENT: WRITING THE U.S. CONSTITUTION

 Explain the needs, pressures, and compromises that led to writing and adopting the Constitution.

The years immediately after the Revolution were not easy ones in the new United States of America. Many Americans were unhappy with the situation in which they found themselves. Farmers were angry about taxes. Frontier whites and Indians fought for control of the land. Many women were agitating for their own rights. Some of the most famous revolutionary leaders, including Washington, Franklin, and Hamilton, were determined to end the growing chaos and reshape the new nation they had helped to create.

The Crisis of the 1780s: The Failure of the Articles of Confederation

The problems that the nation faced in the 1780s had many sources. The Articles of Confederation that governed the nation were essentially a treaty among 13 independent nations. All 13 states needed to agree to levy any taxes, and 9 states had to agree to pass a law. Real sovereignty—in this case, the ability to make the most important decisions about how Americans should govern themselves and pay for their government—rested with the state governments.

For present-day citizens, who live in a world in which a national government rules almost every spot on the planet, such a loose federation may seem surprising. But for the revolutionary generation, the arrangement was not strange at all. The separate colonies had experienced over a century of independent relationships with London. Until the 1760s, the links between each colony and Britain were much stronger than the ties between the various colonies. When Americans looked to Europe, they saw that small independent states and cities were the rule in what is now Germany and Italy. In that context, viewing Massachusetts, New York, and Virginia as independent states that were linked only in a loose confederation did not seem odd.

Nevertheless, leading citizens were concluding that the American confederation was not working. They believed that it was too weak, the state legislatures too strong, and that this imbalance was causing serious problems. Unlike their European models, the American confederation had acted as a united front to achieve independence, and that effort had a ripple effect on subsequent actions. Under the treaty that ended the Revolution, the United States—all of the states together—had promised to pay debts that it had incurred during the war—pensions for soldiers as well as the repayment of loans to U.S. citizens and foreign creditors. But Congress had no money and could not seem to raise any, given the requirement that all 13 states agree to any tax. The credit rating of the new nation was dropping quickly, and the lack of faith in the government's ability to pay its debts was strangling the national economy. If the government could not pay off the loans negotiated during the Revolution, many European creditors thought, why loan any more money to either the American government or American commercial enterprises?

The financial crisis had additional impacts. Indian tribes along the frontier were growing stronger, and the new nation risked losing control of its western lands because it could not afford a strong army to protect them. In 1785, a Shawnee leader, Piteasewa, told commissioners sent by the Congress, "We are aware of your design to divide our Councils, but we are unanimous." Although the tribes were never actually unanimous, in the 1780s they were still more than a match for the U.S. Army or the various state militias.

Moreover, many state legislatures not only failed to raise taxes or pay their state debts but also often simply gave in when mobs of farmers like those in Massachusetts took control of the court houses and stopped trials of those who had failed to pay debts or taxes. Charles Lee, one of Virginia's leading citizens, complained to George Washington in 1788 of the legislature's willingness to grant too much tax relief: "the public debts and even private debts will in my opinion be extinguished by acts of the several Legislatures."

In September 1786, five states sent delegates to a convention in Maryland—known as the **Annapolis Convention**—to try to deal with yet another weakness of the Articles of Confederation—economic rivalry between the states that had led to a battle over navigation rights on the Potomac River between Maryland and Virginia and to a violent boundary dispute between New York and what would become Vermont. The convention never had a quorum and did no business, but it did give some leaders a chance to talk about the nation's problems. As a result, Alexander Hamilton wrote to the Congress asking that the states appoint delegates to meet in Philadelphia in May 1787 "to devise such further provisions as should appear to them necessary to render the constitution of the federal government adequate to the exigencies of the union."

In February 1787, 5 months after receiving Hamilton's letter, the Congress agreed to call a convention, but with limitations. They voted to ask the states to send delegates to Philadelphia "for the sole and express purpose of revising the Articles of Confederation, and reporting to Congress and the several legislatures such alterations and provisions therein as shall when agreed to in Congress and confirmed by the States, render the federal Constitution adequate to the exigencies of Government and the preservation of the Union." On the surface, this call was hardly a mandate for wholesale change. But it launched the Constitutional Convention of 1787, and the Convention would far exceed its authority. Some, including Madison and Hamilton, planned it that way from the beginning. The result would be a radically different form of government than the one under which the United States had won its freedom.

Annapolis Convention
Conference of state delegates that issued a call in September 1786 for a convention to consider changes to the Articles of Confederation.

The Constitutional Convention of 1787

The 55 white men who gathered in what later came to be known as Independence Hall in Philadelphia in spring of 1787 for the **Constitutional Convention** had instructions from Congress merely to propose amendments to the Articles of Confederation. The group represented the elite of the new nation. They had been appointed by 12 states; Rhode Island's legislature distrusted any effort to strengthen the central government and refused to send anyone to Philadelphia. Most were fairly young. Twenty-nine had college degrees at a time when that achievement was rare. Only eight had signed the Declaration of Independence in 1776. Except for George Washington and Benjamin Franklin, some of the most prominent leaders of the Revolution were absent. Virginia's Patrick Henry and Massachusetts's John Hancock and Sam Adams refused to attend because they, too, worried that the convention would undermine the rights of individual states. Jefferson was away as U.S. ambassador to France. John Adams was ambassador to Britain. Women and the rebels of western Massachusetts who had marched with Daniel Shays, slaves and free blacks, and American Indians were not represented. But in that summer gathering in 1787, the delegates produced a frame of government that has served the United States well for more than 200 years.

DECISIONS ON THE STRUCTURE OF A UNIFIED GOVERNMENT Coming to agreement at the Constitutional Convention involved long arguments and difficult compromises. The final result that the convention produced in September 1787 disappointed many. Surprisingly, all the delegates, even those who left in anger, kept to a pledge to keep their deliberations secret. All of the delegates wanted to be sure they had the time and freedom to talk through the difficult issues of the day without undue pressure from outside groups. No one outside the convention, including members of Congress that were still meeting in New York, had a clue what the distinguished group in Philadelphia would recommend.

Constitutional Convention
Convention that met in Philadelphia in 1787 and drafted the Constitution of the United States.

In the spring of 1787, delegates from 12 of the 13 states gathered in Independence Hall—now a national historic site—to write a new plan of government. After a summer of hard negotiations, they proposed what became the Constitution of the United States.

Although he held no special office at the Constitutional Convention—serving simply as one of several delegates from Virginia—James Madison planned carefully and did his best to guide the convention's deliberations. His notes on the meeting provide the best record of what happened that summer.

Virginia Plan

The first proposal put forward at the Constitutional convention, which included two houses of Congress, both elected by proportional representation, and a national executive and judiciary.

separation of powers

A core aspect of the Constitution by which different parts of the new national government would have their authority always limited by other parts.

federalism

A system of government in which power is clearly divided between state governments and the national—or federal—government.

proportional representation

A way of selecting representatives in Congress based on the total population of a state, as opposed to having each state receive equal votes in Congress.

New Jersey Plan

A proposal of the New Jersey delegation to the Constitutional Convention by which both houses of Congress would be elected by states, with equal size delegations for every state.

Connecticut Plan—or the Great Compromise

Plan proposed for creating a national bicameral legislature in which all states would be equally represented in the Senate and proportionally represented in the House.

A relatively young delegate from Virginia, James Madison (1751–1836), who had served in the Virginia legislature during the Revolution and had authored the Virginia Statute of Religious Freedom, was the key architect of the Constitution that emerged, although he never held a special office at the convention. In preparation for the convention, Madison privately arranged for the Virginia and Pennsylvania delegates to arrive in Philadelphia a week before the convention opened. He used that week to craft a plan that could be presented as soon as the convention got underway.

On May 29, the first day of business at the convention, Virginia's Governor Edmund Randolph, following Madison's plan, presented what came to be known as the **Virginia Plan**—the first outline of a new constitution. In Randolph's plan, a new Congress with two houses, whose members would be elected based on proportional representation reflecting the population of the various states, would replace the current Congress. The new government would represent the people, not necessarily 13 equal states. If more people lived in certain states, especially Virginia and Massachusetts, then those states would have more votes in the Congress. The Congress would have the power to levy taxes, regulate interstate commerce, and veto state laws. Randolph also proposed creating a "national executive" and judiciary, or a set of federal courts.

The next day, May 30, the delegates endorsed a resolution from Pennsylvania's Gouverneur Morris that "a national government ought to be established consisting of a supreme legislative, executive, and judiciary." The basic outline of a strong new national government—one that included the **separation of powers** between the Congress, the executive branch, and the courts—had emerged quickly. The new system that Madison, Randolph, and Morris were proposing was also known as **federalism**, a system of government in which both the central national government and the individual state governments had real power, but in separate spheres of influence. But there would be many days of meetings in a hot and stuffy Independence Hall before the details would be resolved and the Constitution itself would be completed.

From the opening day, there was a battle between those, generally from larger states, who wanted the new Congress to have **proportional representation**—that is, representatives elected directly by the voters of districts based on the size of a state's population—and those, generally from smaller states, who wanted Congress to be made up of representatives of the states themselves, so that each state would have an equal number of votes. The Virginia Plan called for proportional representation, but a subsequent plan put forward by New Jersey's William Paterson—not surprisingly known as the **New Jersey Plan**—called for a Congress in which both houses would be made up of delegates elected by state legislatures with an equal number from each state. While the delegates from the largest states, especially James Madison and Edmund Randolph, insisted that proportional representation was essential to a strong and democratic national government, Paterson, along with delegates from Delaware and surprisingly some from New York and Massachusetts, insisted that members of Congress should represent only state governments and that each state should be treated equally.

A compromise, first proposed by Connecticut's Roger Sherman—and sometimes called the **Connecticut Plan**—was to split the difference and create a House of Representatives with members elected by districts based on population and a Senate made up of two senators from each state no matter what its population, elected by the state legislature. But adopting this **Great Compromise**, which was the key to the future Constitution, did not come easily.

Other issues were even more difficult to resolve. The convention came to a standstill over the office of president. Everyone assumed that the convention's presiding officer, George Washington, would be the first president in the new government, but few could agree on the details of the office or on how to select his successors. Some wanted an executive of several individuals in a cabinet of equals, while others insisted on a single leader. Most wanted to ensure that only the "wisest and best" citizens voted for the president, and almost none trusted the people to elect the president by a direct popular vote. But how to select the president—by the Congress, by state legislatures, or by some other formula—seemed impossible to resolve until Madison proposed the **Electoral College**. He suggested that each state select presidential electors according to the number of its senators and representatives in Congress by whatever method it preferred, and that these electors would then select the president. If a majority of the electors did not agree on any one candidate, the choice would fall to the House of Representatives—but with each state delegation in Congress having only one vote. This proposal seemed like a compromise that could work. The convention also decided on a 4-year term for the president, with no limit on the number of terms that could be served.

There were many arguments about how much power to give the president. Delegates remembered that they had just fought a war against the tyranny of George III's government. On the other hand, after a decade of chaos, they wanted a strong executive who could make tough decisions and have the authority to make them stick. The delegates compromised and agreed that the president could veto legislation, but that a two-thirds vote of each chamber of the Congress could override a veto. Those wanting a strong executive won, though it would fall to Washington and subsequent presidents to flesh out the job.

The delegates spent almost no time on the judiciary. They created a Supreme Court and lower courts but left the details to subsequent generations. While they considered an arrangement whereby the judges of the Supreme Court and the president together might declare both federal and state laws unconstitutional they dropped the idea. Only later, after John Marshall became chief justice in 1800, did the Supreme Court take on its role as arbiter of the constitutionality of laws.

The Effects of Slavery on a Unified Government

While the convention spent much of its time debating issues that divided large states from small ones, Madison understood that the real divide was between northern and southern states, or more specifically, between states where slavery was growing rapidly and those where it was dying out. Later, he remembered that "the institution of slavery and its implications formed the line of discrimination" on many issues. The existence of slavery in the United States embarrassed most of the framers of the Constitution. They were careful not to use the words "slave" or "slavery" even once in the final document. But they were equally careful to protect the institution and appease slaveholders.

Madison, like his fellow Virginians, Jefferson and Washington, embodied all the contradictions of slavery. Madison owned slaves, yet despised slavery. He told the convention that the "distinction of color" represented the basis for "the most oppressive domination ever exercised by man over man." Nevertheless, he later assured the Virginia convention that ratified the Constitution that the Constitution offered slavery "better security than any that now exists." He was right in his assurance.

Although many of the delegates, including some who were slaveholders, understood that slavery was incompatible with "life, liberty, and the pursuit of happiness," they were willing to live with the contradiction. The framers of the Constitution were also willing to live with slavery because of their belief that a key to securing life, liberty, and the pursuit of happiness was ensuring the inviolable right of private property. Slaves were seen, first, as the private property of their owners and only second as human beings, if as humans at all. For many at the convention, all private property, including property consisting of other humans, was sacrosanct. Without the security of property, they did not think any of their other rights were

Electoral College
A system in which each state selects presidential electors according to the number of its senators and representatives in Congress by whatever method it prefers, and these electors then select the president.

secure. They were willing to sacrifice their moral qualms about slavery to protect their rights to their own property.

The first time slavery intruded into the convention was when the delegates argued about representation in Congress. If representation was to be by population, then *who* would be counted as *people*? Defenders of slavery wanted slaves to be counted in equal numbers with free citizens in assigning seats in the House of Representatives to states. Delegates from states where slavery was shrinking or gone wanted to count only free citizens. Pennsylvania's James Wilson offered a compromise resolution, quickly seconded by South Carolina's Charles Pinckney (who owned more slaves than almost any other delegate), which said that representation in Congress would be apportioned:

> In proportion to the whole number of white and other free Citizens and inhabitants of every age sex and condition including those bound to servitude for a term of years and three-fifths of all other persons not comprehended in the foregoing description, except Indians not paying taxes, in each state.

Everyone knew that "all other persons" meant slaves. After further debates, the final document kept the **three-fifths clause**.

Some delegates objected. Pennsylvania's Gouverneur Morris condemned the three-fifths clause as creating a situation in which

> the inhabitant of Georgia and South Carolina who goes to the Coast of Africa, and in defiance of the most sacred laws of humanity tears away his fellow creatures from their dearest connection and damns them to the most cruel bondages, shall have more votes in a government instituted for the protection of the rights of mankind, than the citizen of Pennsylvania or New Jersey who views with laudable horror so nefarious a practice.

But in the end, the "nefarious practice" won.

Moreover, the three-fifths clause was far from the only concession to slaveholders. When a committee was appointed to start drafting a document, Charles Cotesworth Pinckney warned them, "If the Committee should fail to insert some security to the Southern states against an emancipation of slaves, and taxes on exports, I will be bound by duty to my state to vote against the report." He need not have worried. The first draft of the Constitution included a clause that said Congress could neither tax nor prohibit "the migration or importation of such persons as the several States shall think proper to admit." "Such Persons" referred to slaves, and the insistence that Congress could not tax or prohibit their "migration or importation" meant that the new government could not use its power in interstate commerce to limit the slave trade. However, the wording of the final draft did allow Congress to change the policy after 1808, and when that year arrived, Congress did end the slave trade and stop the importation of slaves from Africa. Nevertheless, between 1787 and 1808, over 200,000 Africans were forcibly taken from Africa and sold into slavery in the American South. In that one short 21-year period, half as many slaves were brought to the United States as the 400,000 Africans who had been brought to America over the previous 177 years between 1610 and 1787.

The final compromise about slavery came quickly. The draft of the Constitution prepared by the Committee of Detail had said that each state had an obligation to "deliver up" any person charged with a serious crime in another state. Delegates from South Carolina and Georgia asked the convention to add a clause that required "fugitive slaves and servants to be delivered up like criminals." Delegates from Pennsylvania and Connecticut objected. However, when it came time to vote, the convention embraced the request without a single dissent. It was the end of August. The delegates were tired and anxious to end their work. And the issue of slavery was just not as important to northerners as it was to southerners. As a result, the final version of the Constitution contained a clause (Article IV, Section 2) that

three-fifths clause

Another compromise from the Constitutional Convention by which slaves—though the term was never used—would be counted as three-fifths of a person for purposes of establishing a state's representation under the proportional representation plan.

required states to extradite criminals from one state to another and a separate clause that stated:

> No Person held to Service or Labour in one State, under the Laws thereof, escaping into another, shall, in Consequence of any Law or Regulation therein, be discharged from such Service or Labour, but shall be delivered up on Claim of the Party to whom such Service or Labour may be due.

Once again, the word *slavery* did not appear, but the meaning of "Person held to Service or Labour" was slaves.

The fugitive slave clause gave slaveholders a new and powerful tool. As the 1800s wore on, it led to increasing strife because many northerners resented it, and southerners became angry at northern slowness in complying with one of the planks of the Constitution that united them.

The delegates who met in Philadelphia in 1787 compromised on many issues—slavery most of all—but one area where they did not compromise, despite the pleas of several delegates, would bedevil them for some time. On September 10, only a week before their final vote, George Mason of Virginia said he wished "the plan had been prefaced with a Bill of Rights," a guarantee of freedom of speech, press, religion, trial by jury, and so on, that would "give great quiet to the people." Mason had been the author of the Virginia Declaration of Rights, and he anticipated that the lack of a formal guarantee of rights in the final document would create strong opposition. But not a single state delegation approved Mason's proposal, though several states now had their own bills of rights. Some delegates argued that such guarantees were unnecessary, but more of them were hot, tired, and ready to be done with their work. It was too late to add something new, but the failure to include a Bill of Rights in the original document almost derailed the whole plan for a new federal government.

Forty-one of the original 55 delegates gathered for the final vote. Edmund Randolph who had introduced the Virginia Plan to the convention would not sign the final document. The Constitution gave far more power to the federal government than he ever imagined it would. George Mason worried about the lack of a Bill of Rights. Elbridge Gerry of Massachusetts objected to the Constitution because, first, the three-fifths clause gave too much power to slaveholding states and, second, the power to raise armies was a dangerous step toward a military establishment. The remaining 38 were ready to sign the document that began with these words:

> We the people of the United States, in order to form a more perfect union, establish justice, insure domestic tranquility, provide for the common defense, promote the general welfare, and secure the blessings of liberty to ourselves and our posterity, do ordain and establish this Constitution for the United States of America.

Many perhaps agreed with Benjamin Franklin, who said that there were "several parts of this Constitution which I do not at present approve," but "the older I grow the more apt I am to doubt my own judgment and pay more respect to the judgment of others." And, he added a realistic note, "I doubt too whether any other Convention we can obtain may be able to make a better Constitution."

Debating and Adopting the Constitution

As mandated by the call to the Constitutional Convention, once the 38 delegates had signed the draft Constitution, it was sent to the Congress that was meeting in New York. Ten of the delegates from the Philadelphia convention were also members of that Congress, and they transported the document. The delegates meeting in Philadelphia had far exceeded their instructions to propose amendments to the Articles of Confederation, but those members of the Congress who had not participated in drafting the new document were in no mood for a fight. They simply sent the proposed Constitution to the states for their consideration, even though they understood that it replaced rather than amended the Articles of Confederation and were aware that the Constitution itself stated the conditions for its national launch: ratification by only 9 of the 13 states. However, the members of Congress did require that the battles about whether to adopt this radical new experiment in government would be fought on a state-by-state basis in conventions of specially elected delegates who would choose to ratify, or not ratify, the Constitution. This approach would increase the power of the voters in each state to decide instead of representatives in the political bodies of the legislatures. In the fall of 1787, the outcome was by no means clear.

To ensure that the document they had worked so hard to create actually became the fundamental law of the United States, delegates from the Constitutional Convention quickly went to work. James Madison, one of the chief architects of the new Constitution, set out to persuade the state conventions to adopt it. In the fall of 1787, he, along with Alexander Hamilton and John Jay—three leaders who did not normally get along with one another—wrote 85 newspaper articles to support the Constitution, later published as *The Federalist Papers*. In these articles, the three argued passionately that the new nation needed a strong national government and described the problems that they believed the Constitution addressed.

The Constitution's advocates, who called themselves **Federalists**, entered the state conventions with important advantages. They had a specific document and specific arguments on how theirs was a clear plan for improving the government. The new Constitution addressed the fears of many who would vote for delegates to the conventions and sit in them. For those afraid of another Shays's Rebellion, for those wanting a strong U.S. Army to protect them from Indians along the Allegheny frontier, and for those worried about the nation's credit rating, the Constitution provided reassurances not found in the Articles of Confederation.

In contrast, for those known as **Antifederalists**, people who worried that a strong national government would trample on the rights of sovereign states and the liberties of individual (white, male) citizens, the Constitution offered little to calm their fears. The Constitution, which lacked a Bill of Rights and shifted significant powers from the states to the federal government, provoked attacks by many who had fought hardest against British authority in the Revolution. Like many Antifederalists, Virginia's Richard Henry Lee feared that a new "consolidated government" had been created and would be dominated by a "coalition of monarchy men, military men, aristocrats, and drones." Ratification would not be easy.

The Pennsylvania legislature, which met upstairs in the same building as the one the Constitutional Convention had met in, ordered the election of delegates even before Congress officially sent the Constitution to the states. Although backcountry farmers in Pennsylvania resisted strong government in any form, the majority of delegates to the Pennsylvania convention wanted to ratify the document and, if possible, be the first state to do so, possibly securing the seat of the national government in Pennsylvania. But while Pennsylvanians debated, a convention in Delaware unanimously adopted the Constitution after only 5 days of discussion, beating Pennsylvania as the first state to ratify. Delegates to New Jersey's convention who liked the idea that taxes on imports arriving through New York Harbor would now be paid to the federal government instead of to the state of New York also ratified quickly. They were joined by Georgia, which wanted immediate protection from Indian raids, and by Connecticut, which had a strong Federalist party. Decisions among other states got more difficult.

Federalists
Supporters of the Constitution; those who favored its ratification.

Antifederalists
Opponents of the Constitution; those who argued against its ratification.

American Voices

James Madison, The Federalist Papers, 1787, and Patrick Henry's response, 1788

James Madison, Alexander Hamilton, and John Jay published their Federalist Papers as individual pieces in newspapers in the fall and winter of 1787–1788. Hamilton wrote 51 of them; Madison, 29; Jay only 5. Madison's were among the most articulate arguments for a strong federal government, including his argument in Federalist No. 10 that a national government would reduce the danger of a political faction trampling on the liberties of others. These articles were later collected as a book, The Federalist Papers, and remain one of the most often cited descriptions of the meaning of the new Constitution. But not everyone was convinced by the arguments put forward by the Constitution's defenders in the Federalist Papers and in the various state conventions. There was opposition to adopting the Constitution in almost every state. In Virginia, Patrick Henry, one of the Constitution's staunchest opponents, gave a stirring speech against the proposed new form of government. Where Madison placed his faith in a strong federal government, Henry trusted state governments as more accountable to the people and therefore more likely to protect their liberty.

James Madison, *Federalist No. 10*, November 22, 1787

Among the numerous advantages promised by a well constructed Union, none deserves to be more accurately developed than its tendency to break and control the violence of faction....

A zeal for different opinions concerning religion, concerning government, and many other points, as well of speculation as of practice; an attachment to different leaders ambitiously contending for pre-eminence and power; or to persons of other descriptions whose fortunes have been interesting to the human passions, have, in turn, divided mankind into parties, inflamed them with mutual animosity, and rendered them much more disposed to vex and oppress each other than to co-operate for their common good. So strong is this propensity of mankind to fall into mutual animosities, that where no substantial occasion presents itself, the most frivolous and fanciful distinctions have been sufficient to kindle their unfriendly passions....But the most common and durable source of factions has been the various and unequal distribution of property. Those who hold and those who are without property have ever formed distinct interests in society. Those who are creditors, and those who are debtors, fall under a like discrimination. A landed interest, a manufacturing interest, a mercantile interest, a moneyed interest, with many lesser interests, grow up of necessity in civilized nations, and divide them into different classes....

A rage for paper money, for an abolition of debts, for an equal division of property, or for any other improper or wicked project, will be less apt to pervade the whole body of the Union than a particular member of it; in the same proportion as such a malady is more likely to taint a particular county or district, than an entire State.

In the extent and proper structure of the Union, therefore, we behold a republican remedy for the diseases most incident to republican government. And according to the degree of pleasure and pride we feel in being republicans, ought to be our zeal in cherishing the spirit and supporting the character of Federalists.

Patrick Henry, "Speech against the Federal Constitution," June 5, 1788

Patrick Henry, a firebrand during the Revolution, spoke to the Virginia Convention called in 1788 to consider ratifying the Constitution. Although Madison tried hard to persuade him to support the document, Henry was adamant in his opposition.

Here is a resolution as radical as that which separated us from Great Britain....The rights of conscience, trial by jury, liberty of the press, all your immunities and franchises, all pretensions to human rights and privileges are rendered insecure, if not lost, by this change, so loudly talked of by some, and inconsiderately by others. Is this tame relinquishment of rights worthy of freemen? Is it worthy of that manly fortitude that ought to characterize republicans?...

Guard with jealous attention the public liberty. Suspect everyone who approaches that jewel. Unfortunately, nothing will preserve it but downright force. Whenever you give up that force, you are inevitably ruined....We are come hither to preserve the poor commonwealth of Virginia, if it can be possibly done: something must be done to preserve your liberty and mine.

The Confederation, this same despised government, merits, in my opinion, the highest encomium: it carried us through a long and dangerous war; it rendered us victorious in that conflict with a powerful nation; it has secured us a territory greater than any European monarch possesses; and shall a government which has been thus strong and vigorous, be accused of imbecility, and abandoned for want of energy?...

I am not well versed in history, but I will submit to your recollection, whether liberty has been destroyed most often by the licentiousness of the people, or by the tyranny of rulers. I imagine, sir, you will find the balance on the side of tyranny....

Before you abandon the present system, I hope you will consider not only its defects, most maturely, but likewise those of that which you are to substitute for it. May you be fully apprized of the dangers of the latter, not by fatal experience, but by some abler advocate than I!

Thinking Critically

1. **Documentary Analysis**

   According to Madison, what led to the emergence of political factions? Why did he think a strong federal government would limit the impact of factions?

2. **Historical Interpretation**

   Compare and contrast Madison's and Henry's views on the new Constitution. What do they tell you about how each man saw the challenges and dangers facing the new nation?

THINKING HISTORICALLY

James Madison vs. Patrick Henry

Madison said he wanted a strong national government because, while a political faction might capture a particular state, there was far less chance of such a group capturing the national government. Thus, he saw a strong national government as the best means of protecting liberty. In opposing adoption of the Constitution, Patrick Henry had the opposite fear, that a strong national government would not only be distant from the people, but would lead inevitably to a loss of "the rights of conscience, trial by jury, liberty of the press, all your immunities and franchises," which were best protected by state and local governments.

Thinking Critically

1. Contextualization

Looking back over the story of the American Revolution and this chapter what sorts of liberties do you think Madison and Henry were worried about? Whose liberty was more—or less—important to them?

2. Crafting an Argument

How did the proposed Constitution—without the Bill of Rights—protect or threaten liberties? Two hundred years later, whose fears do you think were more justified, Madison's or Henry's? Why?

In Massachusetts, the outcome was far from certain. Although reaction to the rebellion of western Massachusetts farmers had helped launch the Constitution, these farmers themselves sent delegates to Boston who did not trust "these lawyers, and men of learning, and moneyed men, that talk so finely, and gloss over matters so smoothly, to make us poor little people swallow down the pill," as an Antifederalist delegate said. Two of the state's most respected revolutionaries—Governor John Hancock, whose name was at the top of the Declaration of Independence, and Sam Adams of Boston Tea Party fame—believed that the Constitution sought to solve problems that were not serious and that the states, not the national government, were best situated to protect individual liberty. In the end, the Massachusetts convention adopted the Constitution by a close vote of 187 to 168 but only on the condition, as Adams insisted, that it be immediately amended to further protect the people's liberties and the rights of state governments. The Constitutional Convention's failure to add a Bill of Rights to the Constitution was already creating problems.

The next states to consider the document faced even more difficulties. The ratifying convention in New Hampshire adjourned without taking action. In addition, just as they had refused to attend the Constitutional Convention, the Rhode Island legislature refused even to call a convention. (They did, however, submit the question to town meetings in the state, and the voters rejected it, 2,708 to 237.) Maryland's convention approved the document, but also called for 28 amendments to limit the power of the federal government. South Carolina approved the Constitution despite delegates' fears about "the interests of the Northern states" and the federal government's potential to limit that state's "peculiar species of property" (slaves). Because of these fears, South Carolina's convention voted for an amendment that would guarantee that states "retain every power not expressly relinquished by them."

Virginia, the largest state in the Union, was divided. Madison and Washington were strong advocates for the Constitution. But others were not enthusiastic. George Mason worried about the lack of a Bill of Rights. Patrick Henry, perhaps the most respected Virginian after Washington, adamantly opposed the Constitution. His loyalty was to the sovereign state of Virginia. He was willing to be part of a loose federation of states, but only one that ensured that real authority rested with a government

"*When opposite Bowling Green, the president and members of Congress were discovered standing upon the fort, and the Ship instantly brought to and fired a salute of thirteen guns, followed by three cheers, which were returned by the Congressional dignitaries.*" *Page 325*

As it became clear that the Constitution would be ratified and that the country would have a new and stronger government, crowds celebrated. In spite of the strong opposition to the Constitution, once it became law, most Americans supported it, though many also insisted that a Bill of Rights be added as quickly as possible.

close enough to its citizens to ensure their rights. In the end, Virginia ratified the Constitution in June 1788, partly because its opponents were split among themselves. Virginia's convention also demanded a Bill of Rights as soon as possible. With the vote in Virginia and a positive vote in a reconvened convention in New Hampshire earlier that same month, the Constitution was ratified, having reached its quota of nine states to support it.

Although enough states had supported ratification to launch the Constitution, no national government could thrive without New York. New York was already emerging as the financial center of the new nation, and the state sat in a strategic location between New England and the rest of the country. The New York convention debate was long and bitter. Alexander Hamilton led the charge for the Constitution, but Antifederalists were strong in New York. Given what was happening in other states, it would have been hard for New York to reject the Constitution, especially when many New Yorkers still hoped that the federal capital would remain in New York City. In the summer of 1788, the New York convention considered 55 possible amendments, a call for a second convention to revise the Constitution after its adoption, and a conditional vote that would ratify the document only *if* it were amended. In the end, however, by a slim margin (30–27), New York ratified the Constitution in July 1788, the 11th state to do so.

The last states to ratify the Constitution, North Carolina and Rhode Island, made their choice only after the new government was already functioning. By the time they acted, there was no practical way for any state to remain outside of the new United States or its government. Refusing to ratify would have made a state a foreign government amid the formal United States. It remained for Americans to translate the document into an actual government and work out their complex relationships across divisions of class, race, gender, and degrees of freedom and nonfreedom as well as the extraordinary distances in geography and belief that separated them.

6.2 **Quick Review** What failures of the Articles of Confederation did the Constitution address?

CONCLUSION

With the end of the Revolution and the recognition of American independence, the government of the new United States now faced the same problem that had faced the British royal government in the past: how to pay for a war and how to govern a restive populace enjoying both the benefits and disappointments of their liberty. Officers in the Continental Army threatened to rebel when payment for their services was not forthcoming. Poor farmers, some of whom had served in the army during the Revolution and had never been paid, suffered because an influx of expensive imported goods that came with the war's end created an economic depression. Many began petitioning state legislatures for relief and resorted to rebellion when that approach failed. From New York and Pennsylvania to the Carolinas and Georgia, various Native American tribes challenged the new United States as white settlers streamed over the Allegheny Mountains into territory that the British government had kept off limits before the Revolution. At the same time, Congress began to resolve states' claims to lands far into the interior, creating new states and territories for white settlers.

The issues of freedom and liberty that had rallied a new nation also took hold with slaves, and they and some white allies increasingly began to call for changes. Northern states, where slavery was less essential to the economy, slowly began to phase out slavery, but southern states, whose economic base depended on slave labor, were adamantly against emancipation and imported record numbers of new slaves. In addition, women in all levels of society began to expect more equal treatment and broader opportunities, particularly the right to education. Women's expectations were translated in the male-dominated society to an ideology of Republican Motherhood in which women were expected to be better educated than their mothers and grandmothers but only so they could support the political development of their husbands and sons.

Many believed that at the core of many of the new nation's problems was the fact that the governing document for the United States, the Articles of Confederation, was too weak a foundation on which to base a central government, in part, because it lacked the means to support itself through any kind of taxation. The Constitutional Convention that met over the summer of 1787 had been tasked by Congress to revise the Articles of Confederation. Instead, the representatives debated and designed a completely new Constitution, a very different document laying out a new form of government with three branches of government: an executive branch, including the president and cabinet; a legislative branch, consisting of two houses of Congress; and a judicial branch, including a Supreme Court. A key purpose of this design was to balance power, preventing one person or group from dominating the government while at the same time giving the national government the authority to act.

In many ways, the U.S. Constitution reflected the needs and aspirations of its creators—white men who were the elite of their society. Although the Constitution's language never used the terms *slave* or *slavery*, the ideas and points within it upheld the institution, a benefit to many of the Constitution's creators.

When the Constitution was presented to Congress for approval, Congress mandated that each state should call a special convention of delegates specifically elected to ratify, or not ratify, the document. As laid out in the body of the Constitution itself, a total of nine states would be needed to launch this new form of government. Throughout the states, debate was heated. Federalists and Antifederalists (supporters and opponents of the Constitution) took strong and contentious stands. Eventually, all states ratified the document, some by very narrow margins. No state wanted to be left behind on its own. However, no state found the document to be completely acceptable, and demands were strong to amend it immediately, particularly, by adding a Bill of Rights to protect all citizens. But by 1788, even before those changes were enacted and even before the last two states had ratified the Constitution, a new form of government for the United States was ready to be launched.

CHAPTER REVIEW Does the Constitution created in Philadelphia in 1787 embody or contradict the goals of the Revolution? Why?

Chapter 6   Chapter Review

THE STATE OF THE NATION AT WAR'S END

| 6.1 | Explain how the outcome of the American Revolution affected different groups in the new United States. |

Review Questions

1. **Historical Interpretation**

   What light do the Newburgh conspiracy and Shays's Rebellion shed on the economic challenges facing the new nation at the conclusion of the Revolutionary War? What do they suggest about the connection between economic problems and political divisions during the period?

2. **Comparison**

   Compare and contrast the situation of African-Americans, both enslaved and free, in the northern states, the middle states, and the southern states in the decades following the American Revolution. What might explain the differences you note?

3. **Contextualization**

   How did revolutionary ideology shape ideas about gender roles in the late 1700s and early 1800s?

CREATING A GOVERNMENT: WRITING THE U.S. CONSTITUTION

| 6.2 | Explain the needs, pressures, and compromises that led to writing and adopting the Constitution. |

Review Questions

4. **Historical Interpretation**

   What role did economic issues play in prompting calls for the creation of a stronger central government?

5. **Crafting an Argument**

   Is it fair to describe the Constitution, as ratified in 1788, as a proslavery document? Why or why not?

6. **Contextualization**

   Why did Antifederalists view the Constitution as a threat to liberty? How did the experience of British colonial rule shape their views?

Practicing Democracy

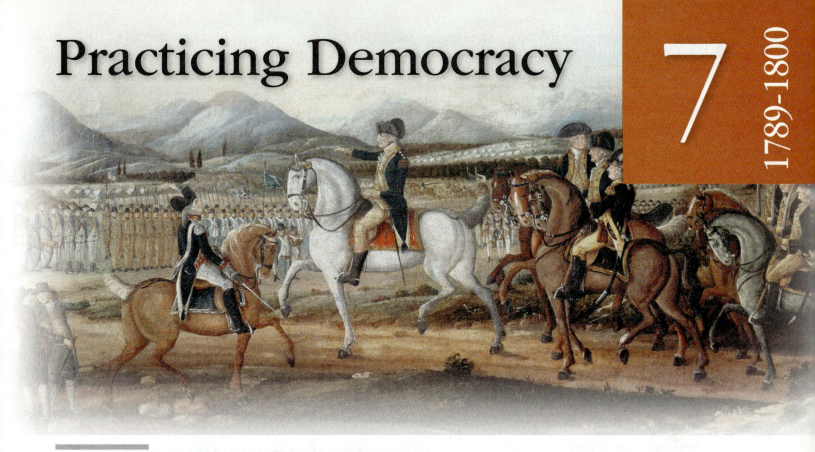

President George Washington reviews troops at Fort Cumberland on the Potomac before leading them to suppress the Whiskey Rebellion. Frederick Kemmelmeyer, "General George Washington Reviewing the Western Army at Fort Cumberland the 18th of October 1794," after 1794. Oil on paper backed with linen, 18 1/8 x 23 1/8. Courtesy of Winterthur Museum.

When New Hampshire and Virginia voted to ratify the Constitution in June 1788, it became the law of the land. But putting that new law into effect was not easy. The old Congress as well as local and state officials in the 13 states needed to conduct elections. Those elected to the new positions, as members of the U.S. House of Representatives and Senate and as the new president, would breathe life into the words of the Constitution and set precedents based on their interpretation of its meaning—or their preferences—that would last for generations. Different Americans, however, interpreted the Constitution differently. Americans discovered that they wanted the country to develop in diverse ways and began long-term arguments with one another about policy.

Soon after the new Congress was elected, it created and enacted the Bill of Rights, 10 amendments that many thought should have been part of the original document. With this addition, more Americans felt comfortable that they had created a government that would protect their rights and maintain their freedom. Once elected as president, George Washington quickly set out to define this important American role. He appointed the first members of the Supreme Court and other judges and created a presidential cabinet to carry out the work of his administration. One cabinet member, Secretary of the Treasury Alexander Hamilton, laid the foundation for the nation's economic system. Washington himself asserted federal authority and expanded the U.S. Army to win Indian Wars on the nation's frontier. Washington's vice president, John Adams, and his secretary of state, Thomas Jefferson, who would later become the next two presidents, worked together in this early government, but eventually became bitter rivals whose arguments represented different directions for the country.

CHAPTER OBJECTIVE

Demonstrate an understanding of how the federal government worked under the new Constitution.

LEARNING OBJECTIVES

CONVENING A CONGRESS, INAUGURATING A PRESIDENT, ADOPTING A BILL OF RIGHTS

Analyze the first federal elections and the adoption of the Bill of Rights.

7.1

CREATING AN ECONOMY: ALEXANDER HAMILTON AND THE U.S. ECONOMIC SYSTEM

Analyze the enduring argument begun by Hamilton's economic vision for the United States and the alternative vision of Jefferson and Madison.

7.2

SETTING THE PACE: THE WASHINGTON ADMINISTRATION

Explain the precedents set by George Washington's presidential administration.

7.3

THE BIRTH OF POLITICAL PARTIES: ADAMS AND JEFFERSON

Explain the growing split between the Federalist and Democratic-Republican Parties, including how the French Revolution and the personal differences between Hamilton, Adams, and Jefferson affected American politics.

7.4

Significant Dates

1789	New House and Senate elected
	George Washington elected and inaugurated as first U.S. president
	French Revolution begins
1790	Federal government assumes state Revolutionary War debts
	Washington, D.C., selected permanent U.S. capital (the government actually moved there in 1800)
	Judith Sargent Murray's "On the Equality of the Sexes" published
1791	Bill of Rights ratified
	First Bank of the United States chartered
	Ohio Indian tribes defeat U.S. Army in Northwest Territory
	Hamilton's *Report on Manufactures*
1793	Washington reelected president
	Citizen Genêt arrives as ambassador to the United States
1793–1794	Whiskey Rebellion
1794	Western Indian Confederacy is defeated at Battle of Fallen Timbers
	Jay's Treaty negotiated between the United States and Britain (ratified by the Senate in 1795 and effective in 1796)
1795	Treaty of Greenville ends Indian Wars on Ohio frontier
	Pinckney's Treaty with Spain
1796	John Adams elected president
1797	Beginning of the Quasi-War with France
1798	XYZ Affair
	Congress passes Alien and Sedition Acts
	Kentucky and Virginia Resolutions declare Alien and Sedition Acts unconstitutional
1799	George Washington dies
1800	Adams concludes peace with France and signs Judiciary Act
	Jefferson defeats Adams for president

The policies that were set and institutions that were created during the first years of the new government lasted for decades, but the philosophical differences about the role of government in the nation's life that emerged have persisted to the present.

CONVENING A CONGRESS, INAUGURATING A PRESIDENT, ADOPTING A BILL OF RIGHTS

7.1 Analyze the first federal elections and the adoption of the Bill of Rights.

In one of its last acts under the Articles of Confederation, the outgoing Congress set the dates for elections for the House of Representatives, the Senate, and presidential electors to occur in early 1789. The Constitution left it to each state legislature to decide how to manage these elections. No one had conducted elections like these before, and it took time to work out the process.

Elections for members of the House were held in January and February of 1789. As permitted in the Constitution, different states had different rules for who could vote. Some House races were hotly contested, including the one in Virginia's fifth district that pitted two future U.S. presidents, James Madison and James Monroe, against each other. Madison won and played a crucial role in the first Congress. State legislatures then elected the members of the U.S. Senate, as they would do until 1913. Presidential electors were chosen by different methods depending on the state, and they cast their ballots for the first president.

Congress and President Washington: Setting to Work

By early spring, the new Congress began to assemble in the nation's temporary capital, New York City (the location that many of its residents hoped would become permanent). Congress was supposed to convene on March 4, but it was not until April that either house of Congress could muster a quorum—a majority of the total members, which was required to do business. Much business awaited. The Constitution required each house to set up its own rules of operation. The Senate had to confirm the election of the president. The Constitution also gave the new government the power to set and collect taxes. The need for a tax law was urgent: each day that Congress delayed, thousands of dollars went uncollected.

On April 14, Charles Thomson, the secretary of Congress, arrived at Mount Vernon to officially inform George Washington of what he already knew: he had been unanimously elected president of the United States by the 69 presidential electors who also elected John Adams as vice president though by a smaller vote. Washington quickly traveled to New York where he and Adams were formally inaugurated on April 30, 1789. He then set to work creating the executive branch of the federal government.

The 58-year-old George Washington had no precedents to guide him. An independent republic with an elected citizen at its head was an unprecedented development for the world of 1789. Some, led by Alexander Hamilton who loved British models, recommended that Washington establish a court similar to that of King George III. Others, including Vice President John Adams, recommended a more egalitarian approach. Washington steered a middle course, insisting on formal state dinners and fairly formal relationships with those who came to call on him, but avoiding a throne or robes of office. He was called simply "Mr. President" instead of "your Highness." Although he was the only president never to live in the White House, he did help to design it, although African slaves did most of the work building it. While in office, he maintained a formal presidential residence in New York City and in Philadelphia when the capital moved there in 1790.

The Bill of Rights

On May 4, 1789, only a month after the House of Representatives had begun its work, James Madison told the House that he would soon fulfill his promise and propose amendments to the Constitution. On June 8, he offered amendments that included line-by-line changes in the Constitution. Proposing amendments was easy. Getting them passed was not. Some of Madison's strongest partners in getting the Constitution adopted were neutral or hostile to amending it. President Washington, at Madison's request, made a brief reference to amendments in his inaugural address. Later, Washington said of the proposed amendments "Some of them, in my opinion, are importantly necessary, others, though of themselves (in my conception) not very essential, are necessary to quiet the fears of some respectable characters and well-meaning men." It was hardly a ringing endorsement. On the other hand, some Federalists in Congress thought it was far too early to amend the Constitution, especially when other issues, like balancing the budget, were pressing.

During the ratification process, however, Madison had promised to add a **Bill of Rights** to the Constitution, guaranteeing citizens important rights under a federal government. Without a promise for those added rights, key states would not have ratified the Constitution. While he was determined to fulfill his promise, Madison also knew that Antifederalists sought more far-reaching changes, and he wanted to act faster than those opponents. Representative Theodorick Bland, a close ally of Patrick Henry, proposed a second convention to consider "the defects of this Constitution." If Congress did not act to quiet this movement, the whole constitutional structure could unravel.

Madison quickly abandoned his original proposal for new clauses to be included throughout the body of the Constitution and decided instead to propose amendments to be added at the end of the document. The House initially passed 17 amendments, but the Senate changed them, and on September 25, Congress sent 12 amendments to the states for ratification. It was fast work for a body that had not existed 6 months earlier. An amendment setting the size of the House was not ratified; neither was an amendment limiting Congressional pay (it was ratified finally in 1992). The other 10 amendments became the Bill of Rights, added to the Constitution in 1791 after three-fourths of the state legislatures approved them. The first of these amendments said:

> Congress shall make no law respecting an establishment of religion, or prohibiting the free exercise thereof; or abridging the freedom of speech, or the press, or the right of the people peaceably to assemble, and to petition the Government for a redress of grievances.

Other of the amendments included "the right of the people to keep and bear Arms," freedom from being required to house soldiers in private homes (a major grievance against the British before the Revolution), the right to be "secure in their persons, houses, papers, and effects, against unreasonable searches and seizures," the right to trial by jury, the right to a speedy trial, and limits on excessive bail.

Finally, the Tenth Amendment—perhaps most important to many Antifederalists, especially those who worried about federal intervention in the institution of slavery—limited the powers of the national government:

> The powers not delegated to the United States by the Constitution, nor prohibited by it to the States, are reserved to the States respectively, or to the people.

Bill of Rights
The first 10 amendments to the Constitution passed by Congress in 1789 and ratified by the states in 1791.

The Methodist Church on John Street in New York City is the oldest Methodist Church in the United States. Since Methodist and Baptist churches never received public support in any of the former colonies, they were among the strongest supporters of the prohibition on any Congressional action to create a state church for the United States that was included in the Bill of Rights.

The Constitution had replaced a weak national government with a strong one, but the amendments meant that the new government would operate within clear limits.

7.1 **Quick Review** Why was the Bill of Rights added to the Constitution?

CREATING AN ECONOMY: ALEXANDER HAMILTON AND THE U.S. ECONOMIC SYSTEM

7.2 Analyze the enduring argument begun by Hamilton's economic vision for the United States and the alternative vision of Jefferson and Madison.

President Washington faced difficult problems, many of them economic. The inability of the federal government under the Articles of Confederation to collect taxes meant that federal debts were not being paid and that the financial status of the United States was in serious trouble. The government could not afford an army sufficient to protect the frontier. Tensions with Britain were made worse because Britain had not withdrawn its troops from western forts as promised in the Treaty of Paris and because London merchants who were owed large sums from Americans were angry. Although the Continental Congress had adopted the dollar as the national currency in 1785, there was no official currency; Congress, state governments, and private banks had printed a variety of paper notes, all of which could be easily counterfeited, and the ease with which they were put into circulation led to inflation. In the new United States, as during much of the colonial era, people bought and sold with an amazing variety of paper notes and coins from around the world, especially Spanish gold and silver. Solving the financial crisis and regulating the currency was essential for national prosperity.

In the summer of 1789, Congress adopted a five percent customs tax on all imports into the United States, creating a solid financial footing for the new government. It also set up a system of federal courts and approved the establishment of four senior positions within the executive branch: secretaries of state, war, and the treasury, and an attorney general. These four officials became the first presidential cabinet.

Washington quickly appointed Thomas Jefferson, then U.S. Ambassador to Paris, as his secretary of state; General Henry Knox, his deputy in command throughout the Revolution, as secretary of war; and his friend, the former governor of Virginia, Edmund Randolph, as attorney general. But given the nation's financial problems, the most important and powerful position would be secretary of the treasury, and to that office, Washington appointed New Yorker Alexander Hamilton. A brilliant and ruthless political infighter, Hamilton could handle the economic crisis better than anyone else, even if Washington also knew from bitter experience that he could never completely trust Hamilton, who had served as Washington's chief aide during the Revolution and had sometimes gone behind his commander's back or quarreled directly with him.

The Secretary of the Treasury's Key Role

On his first full day on the job, Secretary Hamilton negotiated a $50,000 loan from the Bank of New York to keep the new government solvent. He also set about creating a Customs Service to collect the five percent import tax that Congress had already passed, and he organized what would become the U.S. Coast Guard to be sure that imports were not smuggled into the country without being taxed. Hamilton had once said, "I hate procrastination in business," and he was not about to make a slow start on the new job. Ten days after his appointment, the House of Representatives asked him for a report on the public credit of the United States—the most pressing national issue in virtually everyone's view—and gave him until January to prepare it.

Debt and Taxes

Hamilton's *Report Relative to a Provision for the Support of Public Credit* was the foundation of the economic development of the new nation. Hamilton had read widely in philosophy and economics, as if preparing for the moment when he would be asked to design a new economic system. As he looked at the crushing debt that the nation faced from the Revolution—$54 million in federal debt and $25 million more in state debts—he knew that radical action was required. Few people, including foreign and domestic investors and foreign governments, trusted the new country's ability to pay its bills. As a result, neither the state and federal governments nor private businesses could borrow money. The government could not finance desperately needed activities, including the creation of an army. Private businesses could not restart commerce, which had been mostly frozen since the Revolution. Revolutionary War veterans who had been paid in government promissory notes had sold them for as little as 15 cents on the dollar rather than trust a government that seemed untrustworthy to pay what it had promised. In this crisis, Hamilton saw only one solution. The federal government, he believed, needed to assume all of the Revolutionary War debt—state and federal—and promise to pay it all off, dollar for dollar, while establishing a tax policy that would show wary observers that the government would meet its obligations. "Credit is the entire thing," Hamilton argued.

Not everyone in Congress agreed. To Hamilton's surprise, his close ally in the fight over adopting the Constitution, James Madison, led the opposition to debt assumption in the House, and more quietly, Secretary of State Jefferson led similar opposition within the administration. States like Virginia and North Carolina that had paid off most of their own war debts were unhappy with the idea that they would pay taxes to cover the debts of what they considered less responsible states like Massachusetts and South Carolina. Veterans who had sold their government promissory notes at highly depreciated rates during the 1780s to eat and live were appalled that the civilian speculators to whom they had sold them would get rich on the 100 percent payment of the debt. And for those who shared Jefferson's view of a democratic nation of small farmers, Hamilton's plan created a national government that was too big, would raise too much in taxes, sustain a standing army, and shift power from farmers to urban and commercial interests. They would have none of it.

In the spring of 1790, the House, led by Madison, rejected Hamilton's proposals each of four times he submitted it. Ever the wily politician, Hamilton sought a compromise and Secretary of State Jefferson made it happen. Many years later, Jefferson told the story of how he hosted a dinner at his home in New York at which he, Madison, and Hamilton struck a deal by which each one got something that he considered important. Hamilton wanted New York City, his home and the nation's commercial center, to be the permanent U.S. capital. But others—especially Jefferson and Madison—wanted to locate the capital further south. They disliked the difficult travel to New York, and they also disliked urban life. They feared that a northern capital would fuel northern antislavery tendencies in Congress. Not incidentally, Madison, like George Washington, owned land on the Potomac River that would become more valuable if the capital were nearby. If Hamilton would agree to support Jefferson and Madison on the location of the capital, then the two Virginians would support Hamilton's economic plan.

In July, Congress made the compromise official. Philadelphia, not New York, was designated as the new temporary capital and the law also stipulated that a 10-square-mile site on the Potomac River between Maryland and Virginia should become the nation's permanent capital. They gave President Washington a free hand to select the specific site and plan the new center of government. Congress also passed Hamilton's financial plan, including the assumption of state debts by the federal government. Henceforth, the new nation would have a government on a solid financial footing with a guaranteed credit rating, just as Hamilton wanted.

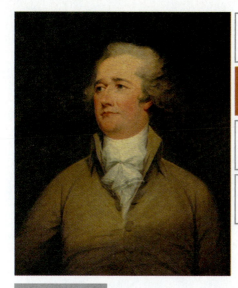

This painting of Alexander Hamilton (ca. 1804) was done by the artist John Trumbull after Hamilton had left office. Hamilton's fiscal program was controversial from the beginning but it launched the nation's economy in a commercial direction and also created political division that continued for decades in the United States.

The compromise solved the immediate issues, but the split on economic policy would lead to the creation of two hostile political parties—which came to be known as the Federalists and the Democratic-Republicans (known at first as Antifederalists)—that would dominate the nation's politics for the next decade. In the first years of the new government, those who supported the Constitution called themselves Federalists (wanting a strong federal government), and those opposed to the adoption of the Constitution and then Hamilton's interpretation of it were happy to be known simply as Antifederalists. But as the battle over Hamilton's plans intensified, those in the government and the newspapers who supported Madison's and Jefferson's opposition began to call themselves Democratic-Republicans, claiming that they, not those following Hamilton, were the true defenders of the republic. Most everyone, including Hamilton, Jefferson, Madison, and especially Washington, abhorred the idea of opposing political parties, but such parties were beginning to form before Washington finished his first term in office, though no one yet called them that.

To a degree, the political divisions reflected a sectional split. Supporting Hamilton were bankers in New York and Philadelphia as well as merchants, especially those engaged in seagoing trade based in Boston or other ports. Those tending to support the Democratic-Republican cause included southern plantation owners, who always worried that the new government would move against slavery and who saw little value in banks and commercial development; farmers, ranging from supporters of Daniel Shays in Massachusetts to farmers in the backwoods of Kentucky; and small-town merchants who were less dependent on international credit. Supporters of each side also had their own newspaper. John Fenno had launched the *Gazette of the United States* in 1789 to support the Federalist cause. Two years later, Madison and Jefferson convinced Philip Freneau to launch the staunchly Antifederalist *National Gazette*. To support that paper, Jefferson, to his later embarrassment, also put Freneau on the federal payroll as an official of the State Department. The lines between two groups were growing stronger.

The First Bank of the United States

Once he had resolved the debt issue, Hamilton's next move widened the divide between those who, like him, wanted an activist government and a robust commercial economy and those who preferred Jefferson's vision of an agrarian nation made up of small independent farmers with a very modest national government. In December 1790, Hamilton submitted another report to Congress that called for creating a **Bank of the United States**, modeled on the Bank of England. Hamilton's fondness for British models was one reason many Americans never trusted him. But Hamilton did not want to be part of Britain. He wanted to use Britain's economic model to build a nation that would become as powerful as Britain. Achieving that vision meant creating a federal bank that would manage the economy and fund a strong government, as Britain's bank did for that country. As with the debt, not everyone agreed.

The Bank of England was a joint public-private venture. Most of its shareholders were private investors, but it played a key role in guaranteeing and repaying Britain's public debt, and its paper bank notes were accepted as official currency in Britain. Hamilton did not trust Congress or the states to issue paper currency. He feared—all too realistically, given what had happened during the Revolution—that Congress and the states would solve financial problems by printing more currency and, thus, quickly debase its value and re-create the inflation that the nation faced in the 1790s. But Hamilton was confident that no investors would risk their funds by allowing more currency to circulate than they could afford to redeem. He was anxious to have those Americans who had funds to invest become strongly attached to the new government. Currency from a semiprivate bank could be trusted because the bank would have to redeem its paper currency in gold or silver. Hamilton believed the United States could have a stable currency that everyone trusted if the Bank of the United States were chartered.

Bank of the United States
The first federal bank, chartered in 1781, issued currency for the country and stabilized the economy.

The 1799 building that was designed for the First Bank of the United States in Philadelphia reflected the solid structure and grand hopes that Hamilton had for his bank.

A central bank could also make loans, thus expanding the amount of credit available. With resources backed by both private investors and government guarantees, the bank could ease the credit squeeze and stimulate commerce and trade. Businesses could get loans. Investment in new enterprises could begin. Much of the bank's financing would also be promissory notes from the government itself—notes that Hamilton had just guaranteed would maintain their full value.

For southern plantation owners like Jefferson and Madison, the bank plan was much worse than the plan to assume all debt for the Revolutionary War. The bank plan would centralize power in the big northern cities—Philadelphia, New York, and Boston—where the nation's largest banks were. Jefferson did not like cities. He preferred small rural communities, which he believed were far more democratic places. He said, "I think our governments will remain virtuous for many centuries as long as they are chiefly agricultural." And, he continued, when people "get piled upon one another in large cities, as in Europe, they will become corrupt as in Europe." In addition, Jefferson, like most Democratic-Republicans of his day, did not like banks. The battle over the Bank of the United States was a key battle in a war between those who wanted an urban commercial nation and those who wanted a nation based on independent farmers. It would not be the last such battle.

Jefferson feared that banks would keep the poor in poverty and enrich those who were already wealthy through ill-gotten gains based on speculation rather than hard work. For most farmers, who were always in debt given their need to buy seed and fertilizer before they could plant and harvest a crop, banks were the distant institutions that hounded them to repay loans. For Jefferson and Madison, and even for John Adams, the thought that the government they had worked so hard to create was now about to create a bank was galling. Although Hamilton and Madison had both helped write and defend the Constitution, they now parted company forever over their interpretation of it.

Despite the opposition of some of the nation's most eloquent leaders, the bank bill sailed through Congress. Almost all northern representatives voted for it, and almost all southern ones against it. The sectional lines, and the lines between the Federalist and Democratic-Republican factions (they were not yet political parties) were clearly emerging.

Once the bill passed both houses of Congress, Washington had to decide whether to sign it. For Madison, who had been operating as Washington's key spokesperson in Congress, the bank was an unconstitutional extension of federal power, and he argued privately and persuasively that Washington should veto the bill. Washington then turned to his cabinet for advice. Attorney General Randolph and Secretary of State Jefferson both urged a veto. The Tenth Amendment was clear, they said, that anything not mentioned in the Constitution was left to the states, and the Constitution certainly did not authorize a federal bank. For Secretary of the Treasury Hamilton, however, the bank was essential, and the Constitution, he said, gave Congress the authority to do everything "necessary and proper" for the smooth functioning of the nation. He warned Washington that if the national government did not invoke the "necessary and proper clause," then Americans would become "a people *governed* without *government*." Washington signed the bill in February 1791, and the United States now had a bank and deeper political divisions than previously imagined.

After the bank bill, Hamilton proposed a federal mint to create uniform coins for use throughout the country. For almost 20 years after the Revolution, people had used foreign coins. Hamilton wanted U.S. coins based on the U.S. dollar, not the British pound. It was not a controversial proposal, and the federal mint was soon established. With the mint in place, Hamilton resigned as Secretary of the Treasury in 1795, and Washington appointed Oliver Wolcott in his place. Though he remained a close presidential advisor until the end of Washington's term, Hamilton preferred to make money as a private citizen.

Hamilton's Commercial Nation vs. Jefferson's Agrarian Vision

Hamilton's last major report to Congress was his *Report on Manufactures*. Unlike the earlier reports, this one was not a plea for immediate legislation, but rather a blueprint for the future of the nation as Hamilton saw it. Where Jefferson wanted an agrarian nation that exported raw materials, Hamilton wanted a more complete economy within the United States. He, too, saw farming as the backbone of the economy, but he also wanted to support factories that would create finished goods from the products of the fields, forests, and mines for both domestic consumption and export. In addition, he wanted the nation to make everything its military might need, from uniforms to gunpowder and warships.

Hamilton was a harsh critic of slavery, but although he did not mention slavery in his *Report on Manufactures,* the document was suffused with what 70 years later a new Republican Party would call "free labor." Hamilton's vision promoted open immigration. Immigrants from Europe would work in the emerging factories, Hamilton said, and a plentiful supply of new workers would keep wages low and factories profitable for their owners. He had no fear of child labor either, noting, "in general, women and children are rendered more useful, and the latter more early useful, by manufacturing establishments than they would otherwise be."

Hamilton wanted a federal government that would shape the nation's economy rather than leave economic development to individuals. He believed that higher tariffs should protect new industries and that government incentives should help launch those ventures when private investment was not sufficient. He saw strong patent protection as essential to invention. Moreover, he wanted to build a network of roads and canals to help commerce flow.

These ideas frightened Jefferson and Madison. At one point, Jefferson told Washington that he thought his treasury secretary was expanding the "general welfare" clause of the Constitution to give Congress the authority to regulate every aspect of the nation's economy. Jefferson would continue to worry, especially as Washington sided with his treasury secretary more often than not.

Although Hamilton was a brilliant if sometimes unscrupulous leader, not all of his ideas were his alone. He was regularly looking to Europe, especially Britain, for ideas, and there were many economic ideas ready for export. Hamilton greatly admired the British industrialists who were creating mechanized production on a scale never seen before. He was also influenced by the Scottish philosopher Adam Smith whose book, *Wealth of Nations,* was published in 1776.

In the economic world that Smith described, wealth was generated, not by the simple ownership of things—land or gold or products—but, rather, by the free trade of goods and services and by competition to expand trade. As people competed to make a profit on their transactions, they increased the circulation of money, lowered the cost of goods, and created general prosperity—the wealth of nations and of individuals. Competition, Smith said, was the key to wealth. Thus he wrote, "It is not from the benevolence of the butcher, the brewer, or the baker that we expect our dinner, but from their regard to their self-interest." As that self-interest is satisfied through competition, there is more meat, beer, and bread at lower cost available for everyone while the butcher, brewer, and baker live well. For Smith, who called Britain "a nation of shopkeepers," it was the shopkeepers and manufacturers and traders, not the hoarders of gold and silver, who made wealth.

THINKING HISTORICALLY

Hamilton vs. Jefferson

In his 1791 *Report on Manufactures*, Alexander Hamilton defended "the expediency of encouraging manufacturers in the United States." Contrasting farming with manufacturing, he noted:

> labour employed in Agriculture is in a great measure periodical and occasional, depending on seasons, liable to various and long intermissions; while that occupied in many manufactures is constant and regular, extending through the year, embracing in some instances night as well as day.

Hamilton knew that not everyone agreed with him. Some believed that it was wrong to use the government "to accelerate the growth of manufactures." Critics, he knew, liked a world in which, "the less independent condition of an artisan can be exchanged for the more independent condition of a farmer."

Hamilton's critics, led by Thomas Jefferson and James Madison, feared an activist government and thought his plans were an anti-democratic effort to strengthen the power of the financial elite and their political allies. Where Hamilton wanted the federal government to foster manufacturing and commerce, Jefferson and his supporters wanted a passive federal government that stayed out of people's way. While still secretary of state, Jefferson wrote, "Hamilton's financial system…had two objects; 1st, as a puzzle to exclude popular understanding and inquiry, 2nd, as a machine for the corruption of the legislature." Jefferson believed that independent farmers were far more likely to maintain a strong democratic government than paid employees, who, in giving up their economic freedom, would soon also give up their political freedom. He saw Hamilton's plan as a way to confuse the true agents of democracy. This debate from the 1790s is still alive today.

Thinking Critically

1. **Contextualization**

   What regions of the country in the 1790s best reflected Jefferson's view of America? What regions reflected Hamilton's view?

2. **Historical Interpretation**

   What groups in American society stood to gain the most if Hamilton's vision was enacted? Which groups would gain from Jefferson's vision?

Smith's book was a direct attack on the earlier ideas of mercantilism that saw wealth as a matter of getting and hoarding wealth. In the new world of a capitalist system or a market economy where commerce and trade were most significant, Great Britain, with its growing factories and its Royal Navy controlling the oceans, was destined to great wealth. As Smith was trying to describe the economic system in Great Britain, Hamilton was trying with surprising success, in spite of the opposition, to duplicate the system in the United States.

> **7.2** **Quick Review** How did Hamilton's ideas for the young United States differ from those of Jefferson? How might different groups of Americans line up as supporters of one or the other?

SETTING THE PACE: THE WASHINGTON ADMINISTRATION

7.3 Explain the precedents set by George Washington's presidential administration.

While President Washington tended to leave economic policy to his secretary of the treasury, he was far from a passive bystander during his 8 years in office. Although economic issues were the top priority, Washington also faced many others. Having spent most of his adult life in public service, Washington knew how fragile the new republic was. The votes to adopt the new Constitution had been close in several states, and powerful leaders, including Patrick Henry in Virginia and John Hancock in Massachusetts, would have been happy to return to a system in which the states were supreme and the national government only a weak federation. Many rural Americans, including the poor white farmers who made up most of the citizens, distrusted all governments and felt they got little benefit from them while the tax on imports raised the cost of necessities. An obscure Massachusetts farmer, William Manning, who had fought at the battle of Concord, now wrote a pamphlet, *The Key of Liberty,* in which he argued that "friends to liberty and free government" needed to be watchful of the "few" who were dominating the new administration and needed to be prevented from destroying "free government" and "tyrannizing over" the people. While farmers like Manning complained, Britain was alert, maneuvering in military and diplomatic actions along the borders of the fledgling republic, prepared to reopen hostilities and, indeed, retake the newly independent nation.

Washington was especially worried that the new nation would lose the land west of the 13 original states. Although Britain had ceded all its claims to land east of the Mississippi River to the United States, Indians who lived in that huge territory had not agreed, and when Washington took office, the tribes were considerably stronger than the U.S. Army. In addition, the British had not removed all of their forces from forts in that area, even though they had agreed to at the end of the Revolution. The British saw the Indians as a useful instrument to help them reignite a war that would end American independence and return the country to the empire.

Many western whites were so fed up with the lack of protection by the federal government that there was talk of forming a separate western nation. Between 1785 and 1788, John Sevier led settlers in the western counties of North Carolina—now the state of Tennessee—to form a state they called Franklin, or sometimes, the Republic of Franklin. They were desperate for support in their battles with local Cherokee and Chickasaw. When their petition to become a state failed, they virtually governed themselves as an independent nation. Sensing an opportunity, Spanish authorities offered financial support to the settlers if they would affiliate with Spain rather than the United States, but North Carolina authorities successfully reasserted authority in the region. When he became president in 1789, Washington wanted to be sure there were no similar interests in independence or foreign alliances in the western lands claimed by the United States.

As one of his first moves after taking office, Washington set out on a series of grand tours of the United States. He meant to see and be seen with the citizens of the country. People loved seeing in person this war hero, now president, and the tours were an important effort to solidify the country behind the president and the constitution. A lifelong soldier, Washington also played a major role in the wars between the United States government and the Native American tribes that dominated the Ohio region when he came to office. In spite of a series of defeats for the U.S. Army, Washington kept pressing his case and eventually defeated the tribes that had long inhabited the Ohio River Valley. When Hamilton's efforts to raise taxes created an armed uprising of farmers along the Pennsylvania frontier—the so-called Whiskey Rebellion—Washington himself took charge of the army that put down the rebellion but also treated the rebels far more leniently than some like Alexander Hamilton wanted. Finally, in his second term in office, Washington turned most of his attention to foreign policy, specifically the growing tension between revolutionary France and the United States, which continued even after he left office.

The President Tours the Nation

To use his personal prestige to consolidate public support for the new government, Washington went on tours of the nation, not an easy task at a time when roads were poor and horses and carriages were the only means of transport once one left the waterways.

American Voices

Moses Seixas and George Washington, 1790 Letters

In 1790, as part of one of his national tours, Washington visited Newport, Rhode Island, and its Touro Synagogue, the oldest synagogue in the United States. Moses Seixas, speaking for the congregation, wrote to Washington, thanking him for the visit. Washington responded with a statement of his commitment to religious freedom. In a nation that was still sorting out the meaning of democracy, and at a time before the First Amendment was added to the Constitution, Washington's letter was an important statement of American freedom.

Letter from Moses Seixas

Permit the children of the stock of Abraham to approach you with the most cordial affection and esteem for your person and merits—and to join with our fellow citizens in welcoming you to Newport….Deprived as we heretofore have been of the invaluable rights of free Citizens, we now with a deep sense of gratitude to the Almighty disposer of all events behold a Government, erected by the Majesty of the People—a Government, which to bigotry gives no sanction, to persecution no assistance—but generously affording to all Liberty of conscience, and immunities of Citizenship: deeming every one, of whatever Nation, tongue, or language equal parts of the great governmental Machine….

Letter from G. Washington to the Hebrew Congregation in Newport Rhode Island

While I receive, with much satisfaction, your Address replete with expressions of affection and esteem; I rejoice in the opportunity of assuring you, that I shall always retain a grateful remembrance of the cordial welcome I experienced in my visit to Newport….The Citizens of the United States of America have a right to applaud themselves for having given to mankind examples of an enlarged and liberal policy: a policy worthy of imitation. All possess alike liberty of conscience and immunities of citizenship. It is now no more that toleration is spoken of, as if it was by the indulgence of one class of people, that another enjoyed the exercise of their inherent natural rights. For happily the Government of the United States, which gives to bigotry no sanction, to persecution no assistance, requires only that they who live under its protection should demean themselves as good citizens, in giving it on all occasions their effectual support.

Source: George Washington Papers, 1741–1799, Library of Congress, Letterbook 39.

Thinking Critically

1. **Documentary Analysis**
   What claims do Seixas and Washington make about religious toleration in the United States of the 1790s?

2. **Historical Interpretation**
   Washington wrote his letter before the First Amendment was added to the Constitution. What does he mean by "more than toleration" and "natural rights" to "free religious expression"?

Nevertheless, between 1789 and 1791, he rode by carriage and horseback from New York through much of New England and across the South. The trip allowed him to address important issues such as religious freedom, hear from citizens, and personalize a distant national government. Welcoming the nation's greatest hero and leader was the social event of the season for these small-town residents, and for many it consolidated the sense of belonging to one nation. Privately, Washington sometimes complained about the accommodations, but he was convinced that his speeches and meetings had done much to build good will and support for the nation and his administration.

Indian Wars: Building the U.S. Army

Washington was deeply concerned about how to handle the frontier Indian tribes. He blamed much of the problem on the "turbulence and disorderly conduct" of settlers who would not wait for permission or protection to enter the new territories but then who complained bitterly when Indians attacked them. Still, he needed to act with caution because he wanted these new settlers to be loyal citizens despite his frustration with them. On a personal level, he himself, like many members of Congress, had speculated in western lands and stood to make money if the land could actually be opened to white settlement. But given the poverty of the federal government—including only 600 soldiers in the army when Washington became president—the president hardly commanded a force that could make much of a difference in the vast western territory.

The chief representative of the U.S. government on the western frontier, Arthur St. Clair, was both the appointed governor of what were then the Northwest Territories of the United States—lands Indians claimed—and a major general in the army. Congress had ordered him to end all Indian titles to the lands between the Ohio and Mississippi Rivers. But St. Clair lacked the resources to do his job. His strategy, as he wrote to Washington, was to divide and conquer—to seek many treaties with individual tribes rather than one overall treaty with all the tribes. But this strategy did not go well. In 1789, just before Washington's inauguration, St. Clair negotiated several treaties with one group of Indian leaders at Fort Harmar, but most other leaders and most tribes rejected these treaties, making them virtually useless.

In 1790, Washington asked Congress to expand the army so it could force the tribes of the Ohio region to "sue for peace before a blow is struck at them." Congress agreed to expand the army to 1,000 men and added 1,500 state militia from Kentucky, Virginia, and Pennsylvania. This increased force, however, was still not strong enough to win the victories the president thought essential.

In September 1790, 1,450 troops under General Josiah Harmar marched into the territory of the Miami and Shawnee to destroy villages and crops as a show of force that might stop the attacks on frontier settlements. In October, Harmar's army was attacked by Shawnees, Miamis, and Pottawattamies, and 500 of the Americans were killed before the rest retreated. After this defeat, attacks on white settlements continued, and attempts at negotiating peace failed. Although some Indians, led by a Seneca named Cornplanter, sought to make a separate peace for their tribes, most others rejected the government's proposed treaties.

In 1791, President Washington ordered a new attack. General St. Clair himself led 2,000 troops in a direct assault on the Miamis on the Wabash River in what is now Indiana. On November 4, 1791, 1,500 Indians from several tribes led by Mishikinakwa—or Little Turtle—of the Miami and Blue Jacket of the Shawnee killed over 500 troops and most of the expedition's female camp followers. Washington was shocked that St. Clair had allowed his army "to be cut to pieces, hacked, butchered, tomahawked," and relieved St. Clair of his command. As 1792 began, most of the area the United States called its Northwest Territory was in Indian hands.

The battles between the U.S. military and a confederation of tribes that were fought between 1785 and 1795 were sometimes referred to as the Northwest Indian War, or Little Turtle's War, in recognition of the central role of the Miami leader, Little Turtle, in the early defeats of the U.S. forces.

Throughout 1792, the Washington administration and many of the Indians tried to negotiate. In June 1792, Joseph Brant, the Mohawk leader who had earlier traveled to London to meet with King George III, went to Philadelphia and met with President Washington, becoming one of the few people to meet with both national leaders. The meeting with Washington was cordial but did not lead to any final agreements, and Brant continued to strengthen his ties with Britain. Brant and most of the Iroquois, Shawnee, and Miami leaders were determined to allow no white settlement west of the Ohio River and demanded that the United States abandon its forts in that territory. But white settlers continued to move across the Ohio River. They and their government wanted more land. Some of the negotiations were good faith efforts. Some were a sham. All failed.

While some in Congress and the press argued for peace and an end to the waste of money and lives in western military campaigns, Washington called for a full-scale war on the Indians. Secretary of War Knox began to create a truly professional army of 5,000 men. In late 1793, he launched a third military campaign in the Northwest Territory.

In place of the disgraced St. Clair, Washington appointed Anthony Wayne (known as "Mad" Anthony Wayne) as major general of the U.S. Army. Wayne trained his army, and during the winter of 1793–1794, they built a new base, Fort Recovery, on the site of St. Clair's defeat. In August 1794, Wayne's army defeated a large Indian force led by the Shawnee Blue Jacket at the Battle of Fallen Timbers, near present-day Toledo, Ohio. After fierce fighting among twisted tree limbs and trunks, the Indians broke ranks and retreated. British forces at the nearby Fort Miami did not support their Indian allies, and Wayne decided not to attack the British fort (see Map 7-1).

A year later, the **Treaty of Greenville** ended major hostilities between Indians and whites in the future states of Ohio and Indiana. The treaty established Indian reserves

Treaty of Greenville
A treaty agreed to in 1795 in which Native Americans in the Northwest Territory were forced to cede most of the present states of Ohio, Indiana, Illinois, Michigan, and Wisconsin to the United States.

MAP 7-1 Indian Removals and Resistance, 1790–1814. Between the end of the Revolution in 1783 and the Treaty of Greenville in 1795, there was almost constant warfare between Native American tribes and the U.S. Army in the Northwest Territory and further battles well into the 1800s elsewhere in what was then the West of the country.

After a series of Native American victories, the U.S. Army's victory at the Battle of Fallen Timbers in 1794 brought organized resistance to an end. A year later, in 1795, defeated tribal leaders agreed to the Treaty of Greenville, ceding most of the land of the Northwest to white settlement. This picture shows Little Turtle talking with General Anthony Wayne.

while ceding most of the remaining lands to white settlers. For the tribes of the Northwest, the Battle of Fallen Timbers and the Treaty of Greenville were the end of their control of the territory. The defeated Indian leader Little Turtle was blunt, telling General Anthony Wayne, "You have pointed out to us the boundary line between the Indians and the United States, but I now take the liberty to inform you, that the line cuts off from the Indians a large portion of the country, which has been enjoyed by my forefathers from time immemorial, without molestation or dispute." But after Fallen Timbers there was little that the tribal leaders could do. Many Indians moved to British Canada or further west into the Louisiana Territory, still formally controlled by Spain. Although groups of Indians and settlers continued minor skirmishes for another 20 years, 1795 was the end of the Indian Wars in the Ohio region. Efforts to survey settlements and create local governments came quickly.

Washington's goals for the Northwest Territory and for dealing with the Indians were mostly accomplished. White settlers got the lands they wanted, the British lost their most powerful ally in the region, and the power and prestige of the U.S. Army were enhanced. Settlement continued long after Washington left office, and Ohio was admitted as a state in 1803. Indiana followed in 1816, Illinois in 1818, but Michigan and Wisconsin much later in 1837 and 1848, respectively.

Whiskey Tax, Whiskey Rebellion

When a compromise by Hamilton, Jefferson, and Madison led Congress to pass Hamilton's economic plan in 1782, it solved one set of problems but created new ones. Paying off the debt required more income for the federal government than the customs tax alone could raise. After considering several options, Hamilton hit on the idea of taxing whiskey. If there were to be new taxes, a tax on whiskey seemed less undesirable than most options. Even Hamilton's long-time opponent James Madison supported it as a way to increase "sobriety and thereby prevent disease and untimely deaths." Like the "sin taxes" of later generations, the tax on whiskey seemed an easy call. However, what seemed easy in New York and Philadelphia was seen by farmers in western Pennsylvania as a direct attack on their livelihood.

Western Pennsylvania and neighboring parts of Appalachia had been settled long before the Revolution, primarily by Scots-Irish Presbyterians who were willing to fight Indians for land and who wanted to maintain their culture, including their love for whiskey. Turning corn, their staple crop, into whiskey was also the best way to get the crop to market. A farmer could distill corn into whiskey at home and then transport a keg, or several kegs, on a horse or mule over the mountains and sell the liquid corn at $16 a keg in East Coast markets, making a considerable profit. It was much easier and more profitable than trying to transport raw corn over the mountains, and between 1783 and 1795 when Spain closed the port of New Orleans to American goods, transporting any products down the Ohio and Mississippi Rivers was not an option.

Hamilton's tax, however, ate up the profit. Since the tax was applied uniformly to all producers, small producers of whiskey ended up paying a higher percentage of their income than did those producing larger amounts. Moreover, the tax singled out these whiskey-making farmers and not others such as land speculators (of which Washington was one). Western farmers complained that the tax discriminated against them, and it did. They were already angry. Most frontier farmers had opposed adopting the Constitution when it was being debated in 1787 and 1788. Now only a few years later, the first administration elected under that document wanted to destroy their best hope of economic prosperity. They rebelled.

The **Whiskey Rebellion** began with modest protests. The Pennsylvania, North Carolina, Maryland, Virginia, and Georgia legislatures passed resolutions opposing the tax. When these actions were not heeded by the administration, protests escalated quickly. Tax collectors were shot at, tarred and feathered, or beaten and threatened with scalping. In a mass meeting in Pittsburgh, rebels agreed to fight for the repeal of the tax and to treat tax collectors with the "contempt they deserve." In 1793 and 1794, no federal taxes were collected in Kentucky or Pennsylvania's western counties. A convention of more than 200 farmers at Parkinson's Ferry debated armed resistance to the national government. In 1794, a federal marshal, David Lennox, and John Neville, a friend of Washington's from the Revolution, were attacked by armed men when they tried to collect the tax. Neville's house was burned, and he and his family barely escaped. On August 1, 6,000 rebels met outside of Pittsburgh and, modeling their behavior on revolutionaries in France, created a Committee of Public Safety, erected a guillotine, and made plans to attack the government garrison at Pittsburgh to gain weapons.

Hamilton advised Washington to "exert the full force of the Law against Offenders." But Washington worried about losing the westerners' allegiance to the United States. Throughout 1792 and 1793, he sought to negotiate with the whiskey makers. Washington's overtures were seen as weakness by some of the Whiskey Rebels. Farmers who paid the tax were attacked and their stills destroyed.

Whiskey Rebellion
Armed uprising in 1794 by farmers in western Pennsylvania who attempted to prevent the collection of the excise tax on whiskey.

Western farmers who opposed the whiskey tax turned to increasingly violent means of resistance, including tarring and feathering U.S. tax agents as others had done to British tax agents before the Revolution.

By the summer of 1794, as the riots spread and after the attack on Neville, Washington had had enough. He saw the attacks on federal officials and the refusal to pay the taxes as part of a plot to overthrow the Constitution. He decided to act.

Given the size of the insurgency, Washington called for 12,000 troops to be drawn from the militias of New Jersey, Maryland, and Virginia. The president himself took command of the force and, with Hamilton at his side, marched across Pennsylvania. While Hamilton promised that every rebel they caught would be "skewered, shot, or hanged on the first tree," Washington remained "grave, distant, and austere."

In the end, the sheer size of Washington's army frightened the rebels and ended the rebellion. Most of the rebel farmers either accepted Washington's offer of amnesty if they would swear loyalty to the United States or melted away into the woods and hollows. The army arrested 150 rebel leaders, but only two were convicted of treason, and Washington pardoned both of them. But the back of the rebellion had been broken. Federal authority—loved by some, hated by others—was supreme.

The French Revolution Comes to America

News and ideas moved slowly in the 1700s. People had to wait weeks to hear about developments in another state and months to hear about foreign events. Yet to a surprising degree, Americans in the 1790s were well informed about and influenced by developments in Europe, most of all by the French Revolution about which most Americans had strong opinions.

If much of Washington's first term was taken up with economic matters and Indian wars, his second term (1793–1797) was dominated by the French Revolution (Table 7-1). Indeed, if revolution had not erupted in France, Washington might have served only one term and retired as he wanted to do.

TABLE 7-1 Interplay of the French Revolution and the United States, 1789–1801

Developments in the United States	Developments in France
April 1789—George Washington is inaugurated as the first U.S. president; Washington appoints Alexander Hamilton (generally pro-British) Secretary of the Treasury and Thomas Jefferson (generally pro-French) Secretary of State.	July 1789—A Paris mob storms the Bastille Prison and sets prisoners free (keys to the Bastille are eventually given to George Washington).
September 1789—Congress approves the Bill of Rights, including freedom of religion and the press and guaranteed due process. (Ratified December, 1791)	August 1789—The French National Assembly issues the Declaration of the Rights of Man and Citizen—"Men are born and remain free and equal"—and affirms freedom of thought, religion, petition, and due process.
	September 1791—A New French Constitution creates a constitutional monarchy.
November 1792—George Washington is elected to a second term as president after agreeing to be a candidate primarily because of concerns with the French Revolution.	April 1792—The National Assembly declares war on Austria, beginning 23 years of war in Europe; French monarchy is overthrown.
April 1793—Citizen Genêt arrives as French ambassador.	January 1793—Louis XVI is executed in Paris.
1793–1794—Democratic-Republican Societies spring up around United States in support of French Revolution and Jefferson-Madison policies at home; during the Whiskey Rebellion, farmers create a "Committee of Public Safety," modeled on France, and set up a guillotine.	June 1793–June 1794—Reign of Terror, under a "Committee of Public Safety," over 40,000 people are executed; the terror ends with the execution of Maximilian Robespierre.
1797—John Quincy Adams reports a French plot to create a breakaway republic in southwest United States, President Adams fears a French-Jeffersonian plot to create a Directory in the United States.	1795–1799—France is governed by a five-member Directory.
1798–1800—XYZ Affair; United States fights undeclared naval war with France.	1799—Napoleon Bonaparte stages a coup d'état and rules France until 1814.
1801—Thomas Jefferson is elected president, reducing tensions with France.	
1803—Jefferson purchases Louisiana Territory from France.	

By 1792, Washington believed that he had stabilized the country and would have been happy to retire. However, both Hamilton and Jefferson, by then bitter enemies, told Washington that the country still needed him, in part because each saw Washington as a buffer against the other's policies. Most of their followers agreed. The most powerful argument for a second term, however, was Washington's realization that revolutionary France would soon be at war with Austria and Britain, and that war would make American diplomacy much more difficult. He could not walk away from what he saw as a coming foreign policy crisis even as he insisted "at my age, the love of retirement grows every day more & more powerful." His personal popularity exceeded any disagreement with his policies, and he was reelected unanimously.

When word of the European war reached Philadelphia in the spring of 1792, the Washington administration issued a formal Proclamation of Neutrality. Where Washington had seemed to favor Hamilton in economic matters, he favored Jefferson—and Jefferson's successor Edmund Randolph—on foreign policy. When France's revolutionary government asked for America to pay off debt from the Revolutionary War earlier than negotiated, Washington agreed. When the French announced plans to send a new ambassador, just after the execution of King Louis XVI in January 1793, Washington agreed to receive him. Washington was determined to maintain neutrality. He would not let Hamilton's pro-British views draw him into a war, much as he disliked some of the news from France.

However, the new French ambassador, Edmond-Charles Genêt—Citizen Genêt as he was called, using the title that every person in France adopted if they wanted to keep their head—was as undiplomatic as a diplomat could be. He landed in Charleston, South Carolina, and immediately began commissioning American vessels to attack British shipping in direct violation of Washington's neutrality policies. He also purchased munitions for France and enlisted volunteers to attack Spanish Florida. Then he went to Philadelphia to meet the president.

Washington had long mastered the art of showing icy displeasure. Having heard about Genêt's actions in Charleston, he met Genêt with great formality, standing under a picture of Louis XVI, America's ally during its Revolution, whom Genêt's government had just executed. In the nation's capital of Philadelphia, Genêt continued to raise arms for privateers to attack the British and recruit soldiers from Kentucky to attack Florida. Washington then demanded that the French government recall Genêt, which it did early in 1794. (Fearing execution if he returned to France, Genêt then asked for asylum and settled in New York as a private citizen.) But in Genêt's brief tenure as ambassador, the **Citizen Genêt Affair**, as it came to be called, did lasting harm, inspiring hostility toward France among President Washington, Vice President John Adams, and other officials, while arousing more enthusiasm for the French Revolution among some Americans.

While Washington found it easy to dismiss Citizen Genêt, he could not as easily dismiss Americans' support for the French Revolution. In the first years of the revolution in France, most Americans strongly supported developments in the country's oldest ally. When French citizens stormed the Bastille prison in July 1789, Lafayette, who had fought with Washington during the Revolution, sent the keys to the former prison to the president. Conservative Federalists joined with staunch Antifederalists in celebrating the emergence of a new constitutional state in Europe.

Some Federalists soon began to have doubts about the French Revolution, however. For those who worried that deference and hierarchy were disappearing all too fast in the United States, news of riots and killings in France were terrifying. For the emerging republican movement, however, the news from France was most encouraging. Thomas Jefferson never stopped believing that the revolution was a grand moment in history, even if he was uncomfortable with what he viewed as its excesses. Once Britain joined the war against revolutionary France, many Americans sided with France despite official neutrality.

Citizen Genêt Affair
The efforts of Edmond-Charles Genêt, French ambassador to the U.S. (1793–1794), to stir up military support for France and the French Revolution among Americans, leading to long-term anti-French sentiment.

Democratic-Republican Societies supporting the French Revolution sprang up across the United States. The first society was established in Philadelphia, but before long there were dozens, from Maine to South Carolina and from coastal cities to backcountry hamlets. These grassroots societies were more radical than anything even Jefferson was comfortable with. Some of those who joined the Democratic-Republican Societies were farmers who were angry with the federal government and ready for some revolutionary activity of their own. But the largest societies were in East Coast cities, where anti-British sentiment still ran deep. There, small-time merchants and manufacturers, mechanics, and other citizens were angry at the arrogance of an older, Federalist aristocracy and anxious to make their own place in the new nation. Members of these societies had great hopes for the ideals—if not all the tactics and the bloodshed—of the French Revolution and wanted to defend it. Not accidentally, most of the members of these societies also disliked Hamilton's economic policies as well as the expanding power of the federal government and supported the Jeffersonian opposition in elections, even if the Democratic-Republican leaders in Congress kept their distance from them.

Regardless of differences, the president was generally considered above politics, so dissenters usually avoided direct criticisms of Washington himself. Even so, the Democratic-Republican Societies became bastions of hostility to many of his policies and closest allies. If the birth of the two-party system can be traced to the split between Hamilton and Jefferson over economic issues, then the deep divides over the revolution in France solidified the organization of the Federalists and the Democratic-Republican Societies and inspired the creation of the Democratic-Republican Party in the United States (see Table 7-2). The Federalists were pro-British and wanted a strong federal government and army as well as economic policies that supported commercial development. The Democratic-Republicans were pro-French and wanted a small federal government, more independence for the states and individuals, less commercial development, and more focus on independent farmers. Ironically, given all the republican talk of liberty and equality, the groups associated with Jefferson were also much more sympathetic to slavery. Many among the Democratic-Republicans saw states' rights as a vehicle for protecting slavery. By contrast, the Federalists tended to see slavery as morally wrong and harmful to the nation's commercial development.

Washington, who hated the very idea of permanent factions or parties, tried hard to stay "above the fray" and unite the factions. For a time he succeeded, which explains part of the reason he was unanimously reelected in 1792, but by the end of

TABLE 7-2 Characteristics of the Emerging Political Parties or Factions

Topic	Federalists	Antifederalists or Democratic-Republicans
Leaders	Alexander Hamilton and John Adams (personal enemies)	Thomas Jefferson and James Madison (personal friends)
Foreign policy	Generally pro-British; want to model United States on British institutions	Strongly pro-French; generally supportive of the French Revolution
Influence of federal government	Strong federal government with strong army	Weak federal government; strong states' rights
Economic policy	Commercial nation; favor building roads and canals and support the Bank of the United States	Agrarian nation; oppose federal spending for roads and canals and oppose Bank of the United States
Regional base	Strongest in New England	Strongest in the southern states
On slavery	Mildly against slavery	Favor protecting states' rights as a vehicle to protect slavery
Alien and Sedition Acts (see "The Birth of Political Parties" later in this chapter)	Sponsor and enforce Alien and Sedition Acts	Sponsor Kentucky and Virginia Resolutions declaring Alien and Sedition Acts "nullified"

his second term in office in 1797 more people were coming to see him as another Federalist leader. If he had run for a third term—something he had no intention of doing—the election would certainly not have been unanimous, though it is difficult to imagine a person of his enormous popularity being defeated.

U.S. anger at Britain was not fueled only by memories of 1776. In the 1790s, British soldiers still held Fort Detroit and Fort Niagara (near present-day Buffalo) in violation of the Treaty of Paris. In the summer of 1793, fearing that American neutrality was a cover for selling American grain to all sides in the European war, the British government issued Orders in Council (orders from the King through his Privy Council—the equivalent of Executive Orders in the United States) that banned all American commercial links with France or the French Caribbean islands. By 1794, the Royal Navy had taken 400 merchant sailors prisoner. Farmers could not sell their wheat, and dockworkers had no jobs. There were growing calls for war with Britain, which might help France, rid the frontier of the British, and end the restrictions on shipping. Washington, however, was determined to avoid war. He sent Chief Justice John Jay, who had been foreign secretary under the Articles of Confederation, to London to resolve the problems. For a short moment, Jay's appointment as U.S. representative to London quieted the calls for war.

But the treaty Jay negotiated with Britain late in 1794 accomplished little of what Washington wanted. Britain did agree to pay compensation for its attacks on shipping since 1793, but not to end the ban on neutral shipping to France or to pay compensation for earlier American losses. While Britain also promised again to remove its troops from the Mississippi Valley, it had been ignoring its own promises to do so for a decade, and there was little reason to assume that it would now change policy. The most Jay could say of the treaty he had negotiated was "It breaks the ice." Washington was bitterly disappointed that Jay had not accomplished more but sent **Jay's Treaty** to the Senate for ratification anyway. The Senate vote in 1795 showed the growing divisions in the country. All 20 Senators identified with the Federalists in the Senate voted for the treaty, and all 10 associated with the Democratic-Republicans voted against it. The public attacks against Washington, which had been muted up to this point—in part because of his personal popularity and in part because many believed the president should be above attack—now became much louder.

In the final year of the Washington administration, one significant diplomatic victory helped to balance out the previous controversies. While Jay had been in London, Washington had sent Thomas Pinckney to Madrid. Where Jay had failed, **Pinckney's Treaty** succeeded beyond expectations. Worrying that Britain and the United States might settle their differences at Spain's expense, the Spanish agreed to a treaty that pushed the northern border of Florida farther south and westward to the Mississippi and, far more important, opened the Mississippi River and the port of New Orleans to U.S. commerce. Access to New Orleans was very important. During the colonial era Spain had allowed travel on the Mississippi River but, fearing the rising power of the new United States, had closed the port to all American citizens after the Revolution. With Pinckney's Treaty, western farmers could again ship goods down the Mississippi through New Orleans to world markets instead of having to struggle across the Appalachians. In addition, for all the uproar over Jay's Treaty, the British actually honored it, removing their soldiers from Niagara and Detroit. Washington believed he could now retire in confidence that the nation was secure.

Jay's Treaty
A treaty with Britain, negotiated in 1794, in which the United States made major concessions to avert a war over the British seizure of American ships.

Pinckney's Treaty
A treaty with Spain that set the border between the United States and Spanish Florida.

7.3 **Quick Review** How did the Washington Administration try to strengthen the nation's security between 1789 and 1796?

THE BIRTH OF POLITICAL PARTIES: ADAMS AND JEFFERSON

7.4 Explain the growing split between the Federalist and Democratic-Republican parties, including how the French Revolution and the personal differences among Hamilton, Adams, and Jefferson affected American politics.

The framers of the Constitution feared the idea of political parties and the idea of people voting for specific candidates in a national election for president. Because of these fears, they designed the election of the president to be a complex process in which each state would have the number of presidential electors equal to its representation in Congress. These electors would form the Electoral College. State legislatures could select these electors any way they wished. The plan did not entail candidates being nominated for the presidency. Each elector would get two votes, technically one for president and one for vice president, but electors would not differentiate the offices on their ballots. Instead, each elector would vote for whomever he wished as long as his two candidates were from different states. Whoever got the most votes from all the electors would be president. The runner up would be vice president. If no one got a majority of the electoral votes, then the election would be resolved in the House of Representatives where each state delegation would have one vote in selecting among the top three vote getters in the electoral college. No one knew how this complex system would work, but the avoidance of nominations or indeed the identification of actual candidates before the selection of presidential electors was an attempt to prevent the influence of specific factions. Since there had been a national consensus that George Washington should be the first president and since he was reelected unanimously, only Washington's retirement tested the system. The first two tests, in 1796 and 1800, did not go well.

John Adams's Difficult Presidency

The election in 1796 that made John Adams president was an odd one. By 1796, Adams, though never a close friend or political ally of Hamilton, had come to represent the Federalists, those who supported the Washington administration's foreign policy and most of Hamilton's economic policies. Most Federalists also supported Thomas Pinckney of South Carolina for vice president and a few, including Hamilton, tried to maneuver Pinckney into the presidency.

Thomas Jefferson was the logical candidate of the Democratic-Republicans, that large group—though not yet an organized political party—who sympathized with the French Revolution and thought Hamilton had shifted too much power to the federal government and to the urban economic elites of New York and Philadelphia. Although Aaron Burr of New York was not an official running mate, many Democratic-Republicans supported him as their vice presidential candidate. Advocates of these views had formed Democratic-Republican Societies in all parts of the country, organized their own newspapers, sympathized with the Whiskey Rebels, and adopted the French tricolor of red, white, and blue as their political colors. They were ready to become a political force in presidential politics.

Adams and Jefferson remained at home throughout 1796—actually *wanting* to be president after Washington was considered unseemly—but many others campaigned for them. A Democratic-Republican paper in Philadelphia called Adams "His Rotundity" (he was heavy) and said that he was the "champion of kings, ranks, and titles." Federalist papers said that Jefferson was an atheist, a friend of the radical French Revolutionaries, and a danger to democracy. There were also battles within the factions. After Adams learned of Hamilton's efforts to make Pinckney president instead of him, he called Hamilton "as great a hypocrite as any in the U.S."

George Washington also entered the campaign, though without formally endorsing a candidate. In September 1796, Washington gave what he called his farewell address 6 months before he left office. Later generations saw the speech as the grand nonpartisan benediction of the nation's founder. Contemporaries understood it differently. In the address, Washington said he wanted to warn his country "against the baneful effects of the spirit of party generally." A political party would "distract the public councils and enfeeble the public administration. It agitates the community with ill-founded jealousies and false alarms." He also warned "that foreign influence is one of the most baneful foes of republican government."

In 1796, most people took the speech to mean "vote for Adams not Jefferson." In Washington's mind, the Democratic-Republican Societies embodied "the spirit of party generally," and he had seen how they could foment "riot and insurrection" when he had led the army against the Whiskey Rebels. He also feared that Jefferson's pro-French views represented the "insidious wiles of foreign influence." Although he would never say so directly, Washington wanted his vice president to be his successor. He got his wish.

Of the 139 electoral votes cast in the 1796 election, Adams received 71, all from New England, New York, and New Jersey, while Jefferson received 68, all from Pennsylvania and the southern states. So Adams and Jefferson, these two long-time political rivals, became president and vice president, respectively.

The anger of the 1796 campaign cooled quickly. The pro-Jefferson newspaper, the *Aurora*, declared that Adams was a man "possessing great integrity." One of Jefferson's strongest supporters in Congress, William Branch Giles of Virginia, said, "The old man will make a good President, too." Jefferson and Adams exchanged cordial letters, and Adams invited the vice president to sit in the Cabinet—which Washington had never done for him—but Jefferson declined. The two dined with Washington just after Adams's inauguration, and in his inaugural address, Adams insisted that it was his "inflexible determination" to maintain peace with all nations, including France, words that surely reassured Jefferson and his followers.

But the split between the Federalists and the Democratic-Republicans went too deep for soothing words to heal. Differences came to a head in Congress in January 1798 when Matthew Lyon, a Democratic-Republican from Vermont, ridiculed the ceremonial greeting for President Adams and insulted Federalist Roger Griswold of Connecticut. Griswold then insulted Lyon who spat in Griswold's face. Griswold attacked Lyon with his cane, and Lyon grabbed a pair of fireplace tongs to fight back on the floor of the House of Representatives. The two were pulled apart, but the incident symbolized the hatred between the two parties and the depths to which public discourse had sunk.

Nothing, however, represented the split between the two factions as much as their attitudes toward the French Revolution. Barely a week after his inauguration, Adams received troubling news that the French Directory, the five-member council then ruling revolutionary France, had refused to receive Adams's choice as U.S. ambassador to France. Adams had actually chosen Charles Cotesworth Pinckney (brother of the Federalist candidate for vice president) to improve the U.S.-French relationship, but the French did not see it that way. The Directory also launched an undeclared war on U.S. shipping. In the following months, the French captured 300 American merchant ships. From his son, John Quincy Adams, who was serving as U.S. Ambassador to Prussia, Adams also heard of a French plan to stir up revolt and secession in the western U.S. territories. The Federalist press called for war against France while the Democratic-Republicans claimed it was a false crisis made up by the pro-British Federalists.

Adams, who was more nonpartisan than his Federalist backers had hoped, sought a middle ground. He sent Elbridge Gerry of Massachusetts and John Marshall of Virginia to join Pinckney in Paris and try to reopen negotiations. But he also asked Congress to establish a navy and provide funds to prepare for war if it came. The response to the new president's actions broke along partisan lines, with Federalists supporting Adams and Democratic-Republicans opposing him. But Adams won authorization for a new Department of the Navy and funds to build and support three medium-sized warships called frigates.

In this popular drawing that was widely circulated, Roger Griswold, a Connecticut Federalist, attacked Matthew Lyon, a Vermont Republican, who fought back with fire tongs. Few images so starkly described the state of partisan politics in the new nation.

 This cartoon reflects the anti-French sentiment of many Americans, showing France as having five heads (for the five-member Directory that ruled at one point), the bloody guillotine in the background, and the demand for a bribe from the upright American delegates. Note also the Africans representative of French-owned Haiti.

However, Adams's peace overtures to the French did not go well. When his new delegation arrived in Paris, the French foreign minister Charles Maurice de Talleyrand arranged for agents, whom Adams identified only as "X, Y, and Z," to inform the Americans that negotiations could proceed only if Talleyrand was paid a bribe of $250,000 and the French government received a loan of $10 to $12 million as well as an apology for what the French considered Adams's belligerent tone. Pinckney's famous response was "No, no, not a sixpence." In fact, the commissioners were prepared to pay a bribe, not an unusual part of diplomacy at the time, but the amount demanded was far too high.

When word of the so-called **"XYZ Affair"** reached Congress and the American public in March 1798, Adams's popularity soared, and many called for a war against France to avenge U.S. honor. Federalists in Congress voted to increase the size of the U.S. Army and shift its focus from the western frontier to a presumed threat of French invasion on the Atlantic coast. Given British naval supremacy, a French invasion was improbable. Even if the British did not like the United States, they certainly did not want their archenemy France to control any territory in North America. Adams, unlike most Federalists, feared a large standing U.S. Army, especially after Hamilton won appointment as a major general within it. Adams preferred to strengthen the Navy to protect U.S. interests.

In 1798 and 1799, though there was no formal declaration of war, the United States engaged in what became known as the **Quasi-War** with France or, as Adams preferred to call it, the "Half-War." Treaties with France dating back to the American Revolution were repealed, and the United States began a trade embargo against France. The United States also supported the independence of Haiti, something it had not done during the Washington administration. Congress created the Marine Corps along with the Navy and armed merchant ships so they could attack French ships near the U.S. coast or in the Caribbean. Even if France had the most powerful army in Europe, Talleyrand did not really want war with the United States, and he began to make peace overtures. U.S. neutrality, if not friendship, would be important, Talleyrand thought, if France were to launch a planned invasion of England.

The war hysteria also led Congress to pass the **Alien and Sedition Acts**, actually three separate acts, that irreparably hurt Adams's reputation even though he did not directly request any of them. Federalists had become increasingly fearful of pro-French agitation. Massachusetts Congressman Harrison Gray Otis asked, "Do we not know that the French nation have organized bands of aliens as well as their own citizens, in other countries?" Many Federalists wondered, could it not happen here?

XYZ Affair

Diplomatic incident in 1798 in which Americans were outraged by the demand of the French for a bribe as a condition for negotiating with American diplomats.

Quasi-War

An undeclared war—1797 to 1800—between the United States and France.

Alien and Sedition Acts

A series of three acts passed by Congress in 1798 that made it harder for new immigrants to vote and made it a crime to criticize the president or Congress.

To make sure that French efforts, aided by Jeffersonian Democratic-Republicans, could not undermine the government and its Federalist leaders, Congress passed the Naturalization Act and the Alien Friends Act in June 1798, which were referred to as the Alien Acts. These laws lengthened the time to qualify for citizenship from 5 to 14 years—to ensure that recent pro-French immigrants could not vote—and allowed the government to deport anyone deemed dangerous to the United States. While no one was actually deported under the acts, many French citizens left the United States on their own rather than wait and see what might happen.

A month later, on July 14, 1798, Congress passed the Sedition Act by a slim majority, and Adams signed the law. The Sedition Act targeted primarily newspaper editors like Benjamin Franklin Bache, editor of the Democratic-Republican *Aurora*, making any "false, scandalous, and malicious" speech against the government, particularly Congress or the president, a crime. Unlike the Alien Acts, the Sedition Act was vigorously enforced. Democratic-Republican Congressman Matthew Lyon—who earlier had the wrestling match with Griswold—was convicted under the law for continuing to criticize the Adams administration and spent 4 months in a Vermont jail. (His constituents made it clear what they thought of the act when they overwhelmingly reelected Lyon to Congress once he was released from jail.) All told, 17 people were tried under the act, including a drunk in New Jersey who had "cast aspersions on the President's posterior" and was fined the then enormous sum of $150. But newspapers were not silenced, and the attack on free speech undermined support for the Federalists.

The Democratic-Republicans attacked the Alien and Sedition Acts. Vice President Jefferson initially counseled "patience with what he saw as "the reign of the witches" in the Adams administration, but soon came to view the Alien and Sedition laws as a fundamental threat to democracy. In the fall of 1798, he drafted resolutions, and his friends and supporters in the Kentucky legislature adopted his words, that asserted a state's right to declare federal law "void and of no force" within the state's jurisdiction. Virginia's legislature adopted similar resolutions drafted by James Madison. Both legislatures invited other states to join them, but none did. Nevertheless, the **Kentucky and Virginia Resolutions** drew a sharp line between the two political factions. On the Democratic-Republican side, Madison, like Jefferson, saw the resolutions as an appropriate protest within the framework of the Constitution he had helped write, and both men saw them as the basic right of state legislatures to nullify federal law. But the Federalists saw both resolutions as a fundamental attack on the basic authority of the federal government and, indeed, on the Constitution itself.

Kentucky and Virginia Resolutions
Resolutions written by Thomas Jefferson and James Madison that criticized the Alien and Sedition Acts and asserted the rights of states to declare federal law null and void within a state.

While Adams never repudiated the Alien and Sedition Acts, he did end the war fever. Through emissaries, Adams received a signal that France did not want war, and after British Admiral Horatio Nelson destroyed the French fleet in the Battle of the Nile in October 1798, any remote possibility of a French invasion of the United States disappeared. Adams had become convinced that Hamilton was trying to stir up a war for his own political ambitions. The president called him "a man devoid of every moral principle." In February 1799, Adams told the Senate that he himself was committed "to embrace every plausible appearance of probability of preserving or restoring tranquility," and he also asked them to approve a new ambassador to France to replace Pinckney. Many Federalists were enraged that Adams would try yet again for peace, and he had to endure a shouting match with Hamilton—now a private citizen but an influential one. He also had to fire his own Secretary of State Timothy Pickering, who was ready for war, and replace him with a close political ally, John Marshall (who would later become chief justice of the Supreme Court). But the Senate approved William Vans Murray as the new ambassador, and the new mission worked. It took all of 1799 and 1800 to negotiate, during which time the government of France changed from the Directory to the dictatorship of Napoleon Bonaparte, but peace came. The Convention of Mortefontaine ended the Quasi-War and protected U.S. shipping. Adams disbanded part of the army in May 1800 over the opposition

American Voices

The Kentucky Resolutions of 1798

When Congress passed the Alien and Sedition Acts in 1798, a firestorm of protest broke out. Leaders of the Democratic-Republican Party saw the new laws as a direct attack on freedom of speech, a bedrock of democracy. They also opposed the legislation because they feared it would foster war with France and expand the army, navy, and federal power in general. In response they sought to undermine the laws. Jefferson secretly drafted the resolutions below, which were adopted by the Kentucky legislature in November 1798, while Madison drafted similar resolutions for Virginia. These Kentucky and Virginia Resolutions not only attacked the Alien and Sedition Acts but also declared that, since the federal government was a compact of the states, any state could declare any federal law unconstitutional within the bounds of that state. This claim would have far-reaching implications in the decades leading up to the Civil War. Although most historians see the Alien and Sedition Acts as a dangerous attack on free speech, they also see the resolutions as an equally dangerous effort to undermine national unity.

1. *Resolved*, That the several states composing the United States of America are not united on the principle of unlimited submission to their general government; but that, by compact, under the style and title of a Constitution for the United States, and of amendments thereto, they constituted a general government for special purposes, delegated to that government certain definite powers, reserving, each state to itself, the residuary mass of right to their own self-government; and that whensoever the general government assumes undelegated powers, its acts are unauthoritive, void, and of no force; that to this compact each state acceded as a state, and is an integral party; that this government, created by this compact, was not made the exclusive or final judge of the extent of the powers delegated to itself, since that would have made its discretion, and not the Constitution, the measure of its powers; but that, as in all other cases of compact among powers having no common judge, each party has an equal right to judge for itself, as well of infractions as of the mode and measure of redress.

2. *Resolved*... therefore, also, the same act of Congress, passed on the 14th day of July, 1798, and entitled "An Act in Addition to the Act entitled 'An Act for the Punishment of certain Crimes against the United States;'" [the Sedition Act]...(and all other their acts which assume to create, define, or punish crimes other than those so enumerated in the Constitution,) are altogether void, and of no force; and that the power to create, define, and punish, such other crimes is reserved, and of right appertains, solely and exclusively, to the respective states, each within its own territory.

Source: Library of Congress http://lccn.loc.gov/09021366

Thinking Critically

1. **Documentary Analysis**
   What argument did Jefferson make in favor of a state's right to nullify federal legislation?

2. **Historical Interpretation**
   In what ways did Jefferson's position constitute a threat to national unity?

of his own party. He also pardoned John Fries who had led a nonviolent rebellion against federal war taxes in Pennsylvania in 1799 and had been sentenced to death for treason. These actions cost Adams dearly, particularly among his own Federalists. But he considered the choice for peace against war his crowning achievement and ordered that his gravestone read "Here lies John Adams, who took upon himself the responsibility for peace with France in the year 1800."

The Election of 1800

The political differences between the two leading candidates for president in 1800, President John Adams and Vice President Thomas Jefferson, could not have been clearer. But the methods for actually selecting the next president and vice president in 1800 could not have been more convoluted. None of the problems with the Electoral College that were seen in 1796 had been resolved. At that time, political parties had been informal alliances of like-minded individuals. By 1800, however, the Federalists and Democratic-Republicans were much better organized. They had come to represent two distinct philosophies and sets of personal allegiances. Nevertheless, Americans still distrusted formal political parties. Within the parties, advocates of different positions schemed to defeat not only the other party but also rivals within their own party. In December 1799, just as the maneuvering for the 1800 election was starting, news came that George Washington had died at his home in Mount Vernon, Virginia. People of all political factions mourned the loss of a unifying leader but also knew that the next election would be more divisive than ever.

Despite the fact that most of the Constitution's authors did not want nominations of presidential candidates to occur before the selection of presidential electors, in 1800, each party's Congressional delegations nominated the candidates in semisecret caucuses. When the Democratic-Republican caucus met on May 11, 1800, it was clear that Jefferson would be their nominee for president. Several candidates were considered for vice president, but the Democratic-Republicans wanted someone who would help them win New York, which they saw as the key to the White House. The man to deliver New York's votes was Aaron Burr. Few politicians, including Jefferson, trusted or respected Burr, but Jefferson did not intend to lose the presidency twice. In an ill-fated decision, the caucus and party leaders pledged that every elector would vote for both Jefferson and Burr. Everyone simply assumed that somehow Jefferson would receive the most votes and become president with Burr, the runner up, becoming vice president, but that assumption proved to be a serious mistake.

Federalist maneuvering was equally complicated. There was general agreement that failure to support Adams would fatally split the party. But the caucus also chose Charles Cotesworth Pinckney of South Carolina, the brother of their 1796 vice presidential nominee, to be vice president, in part because he was known to be loyal to Hamilton and in part because his refusal to give a bribe to France in the XYZ Affair had made him a hero. Behind the scenes, Hamilton hoped, as he had in 1796, that he could somehow engineer Pinckney's election as president. Once again, Adams found out about Hamilton's plans and was furious.

Because the Constitution gave each state the right to choose its presidential electors any way it wished, the actual voting for those electors was spread out over most of the year. In an early but crucial test, Burr was able to ensure New York's electoral votes for the Jefferson-Burr ticket. Pennsylvania's Democratic-Republican governor also promised to deliver its electoral votes for the Jefferson-Burr ticket or, if that failed, to simply prevent a vote to choose electors from taking place in that state so Adams could not receive any votes there.

As other states continued to select their presidential electors in the summer and fall of 1800, the contest remained fierce. A Federalist newspaper said a vote for the Democratic-Republicans was a vote "for the tempestuous sea of anarchy and misrule; for arming the poor against the rich; for fraternizing with the foes of God and man" while a Democratic-Republican paper asked people to choose between, "Peace or war, happiness or misery, opulence or ruin!" The Sedition Act made direct attacks on President Adams dangerous, but the press was far from neutral, and anger at that act added fuel to the Democratic-Republican fire.

Slaves could not vote, and slavery had not been a major issue in the previous presidential campaigns, but it was in 1800. Gabriel Prosser and Jack Bowler were slaves on a Virginia plantation not far from the state capital in Richmond. Throughout the summer, they were planning a slave uprising. Prosser promised death to all whites except "Quakers, Methodists, and French people," that is, whites known to support abolition. Over 1,000 slaves were involved, forging swords from sickles, making their own bullets, and designing a flag that read "Death or Liberty." The uprising was set for Saturday, August 30, when they planned to meet at the Prosser plantation, kill the white owners, and march on Richmond. However, a terrible storm on August 30 scattered the slave army, and Governor James Monroe discovered the plan and called out the state militia. The leaders of the uprising were quickly tried and executed, but the prospect of a slave uprising terrified the southern states.

Campaign banners were popular in the 1800 campaign, including this streamer that says, "T. Jefferson, President of the United States of America; John Adams—no more."

The issue of slavery also complicated the presidential campaign. Both political parties were divided internally over it. Adams hated slavery, but Pinckney, his running mate, was one of the largest slave owners in South Carolina. Both Jefferson and Burr owned slaves, Jefferson many of them. But Jefferson had also written in opposition to slavery. He needed northern Democratic-Republican votes in Pennsylvania and New York where abolitionism was gaining ground. Governor Monroe and Jefferson feared that too many slave executions would spark an abolitionist upheaval and cost them votes. On the other hand, leniency could cost them votes in the fearful southern states where Adams and Pinckney suddenly looked like the forces of stability.

Some slaves saw the ironies of the situation. Most of those arrested, including Prosser, simply remained silent, knowing that nothing they said would save them. One, however, calmly told the judges:

> I have nothing more to offer than what General Washington would have had to offer, had he been taken by the British officers and put to trial by them. I have ventured my life in endeavouring to obtain the liberty of my countrymen, and am a willing sacrifice to their cause; and I beg, as a favour, that I may be immediately led to execution. I know that you have predetermined to shed my blood, why then all this mockery of a trial?

The tension between American freedom and American slavery, which was at the heart of the republic, surfaced in the 1800 contest.

Jefferson's religious beliefs also became a major election topic. Yale's president, Timothy Dwight, gave a speech asking whether the country was going to elect "men who set truth at nought…who doubt the being and providence of God." Everyone knew who Dwight was talking about, given Jefferson's liberal religious views. Many clergy and laypeople claimed that Jefferson had renounced the basic beliefs of Christianity. In fact, Jefferson was a deist who believed that God tended to leave the universe on its own. Adams himself, who tended to agree with Jefferson in religious matters, though he was more discreet and more often seen in established churches, privately expressed "indignation at the charge of irreligion," but did not say anything publically during the heat of the campaign.

The Hamilton-Adams feud could not be kept so quiet. In the summer of 1800, Hamilton wrote *A Letter from Alexander Hamilton, Concerning the Public Conduct and Character of John Adams, Esq., President of the United States.* Hamilton seems to have meant the 54-page document for the private use of a few electors, whom he was attempting to switch from Adams to Pinckney, but a delighted Democratic-Republican press found the document, and it became public. In words that could, ironically, have been prosecuted under the Sedition Act, Hamilton attacked Adams for his "great intrinsic defects of character," including "his disgusting egotism," "eccentric tendencies," "bitter animosity," and "ungovernable temper." The split among the Federalists was complete. Noah Webster, a tough Federalist from Connecticut and author of the first American dictionary, wrote to Hamilton that, if Jefferson was elected as a result of this Federalist split, "the fault will lie at your door and…your conduct on this occasion will be discerned little short of insanity.

In 1800, the candidates campaigned openly, unlike 1796. The ever-diffident Adams, surprisingly, seemed to enjoy campaigning, giving speeches in key states. Jefferson considered similar campaign stops but was dissuaded by Virginia's Governor Monroe. Instead, he engaged in a nonstop correspondence with supporters and in less public forms of campaigning, offering financial and editorial advice to friendly newspaper editors.

Given the advantages that the Democratic-Republicans held, ranging from the unpopularity of the Alien and Sedition Acts to the split among the Federalists, the election was surprisingly close. Adams swept New England and most of the northern states while Jefferson held strong in New York and Pennsylvania and most of the southern states. The three-fifths clause, which counted slaves in the population though they were not allowed to vote, gave the southern states an advantage in the electoral college that ultimately tipped the election for Jefferson. The last state to vote was South Carolina, and when the Jefferson-Burr ticket carried every electoral vote in that state, the new Washington, D.C., Democratic-Republican paper *The National Intelligencer* ran a headline on December 12, "Splendid Intelligence…Mr. Jefferson may…be considered as our future President." But it was not to be so simple (see Map 7-2).

Because the Democratic-Republicans had been so well organized, Jefferson and Burr each received 73 electoral votes, putting them well ahead of Adams and Pinckney. But because Jefferson and Burr had *each* received 73 votes, the House of Representatives would now have to decide between two candidates who had tied in the election. In addition, though the Democratic-Republicans had also won a majority in the new Congress, the old Congress, with a Federalist majority, would decide the election. Many Democratic-Republicans, including Jefferson, thought that Burr had engineered this outcome to make himself president. Many Federalists suddenly gave Burr a second look. As far as anyone knows, Burr did not negotiate with the Federalists. But he also did not give way to Jefferson. The country was stuck.

When Congress heard the tally of electoral votes, the outcome was 73 for Jefferson, 73 for Burr, 65 for Adams, 64 for Pinckney, and one for John Jay. The House then began to vote between the top two. But it remained deadlocked. Finally, Hamilton, who had fought for so long with Thomas Jefferson on almost every major government policy, convinced his fellow Federalists that Burr, whom he knew all too well from New York politics, was a dangerous man of too much ambition and too little morality. On February 17, Thomas Jefferson was elected president by a vote

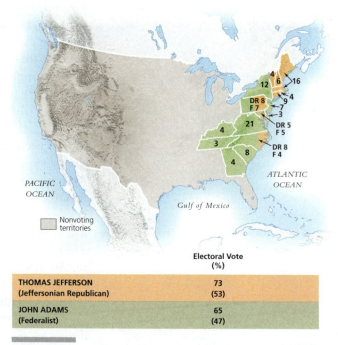

	Electoral Vote (%)
THOMAS JEFFERSON (Jeffersonian Republican)	73 (53)
JOHN ADAMS (Federalist)	65 (47)

MAP 7-2 The 1800 Presidential Election. The 1800 electoral contest between incumbent John Adams and Thomas Jefferson reflected regional differences—Adams carried all of New England and Jefferson most of the South, but middle states, especially New York, decided the outcome.

of 10 state delegations to four, with two not voting. Burr became vice president. It had been a long year and a long election cycle, and it would never be repeated in quite the same form.

> **7.4**   **Quick Review**   Why did factions and political parties arise in the 1790s?

CONCLUSION

George Washington was elected unanimously as the first president of the United States in 1789. This unity, largely the result of his popularity as the general who had defeated the British, would be short lived as factions began to form around personalities and around very different ideas of what the government of the new nation should look like. Alexander Hamilton, Washington's secretary of treasury, was an especially forceful advocate of a strong and activist central government. Those who agreed with this position came to be known as the Federalists. Hamilton had been charged with making the government financially solvent. He quickly convinced Congress to pass import taxes to pay off the Revolutionary War debts, to build up the national government, and especially to fund the U.S. Army. In addition, Hamilton persuaded Congress to launch the Bank of the United States as well as establish a currency system and a mint. He believed that making possible financial credit for both government and business would ensure the strength of the new republic.

In opposition to Hamilton, Thomas Jefferson, Washington's first secretary of state, envisioned an idealized agrarian republic with a weak central government. He believed that the strongest powers should remain with the states and in the hands of the people. Jefferson distrusted banks, a standing army, and centralized authority.

As promised to many who ratified the Constitution, James Madison authored amendments to the Constitution that became the Bill of Rights. These amendments spelled out limits on the federal government. They guaranteed that the nation could not establish a state religion, limit free speech or a free press, or prohibit people from keeping firearms. They also promised protection from illegal search and seizure. Perhaps most important to those who initially opposed the Constitution, the Bill of Rights limited the power of the federal government itself to only those things that were specifically mentioned in the Constitution and reserved all else to the states and the people.

Washington's tenure as president during two terms in office was filled with conflict. He took the role of mediator and negotiator as often as possible, including efforts to balance Hamilton and Jefferson, but mediating was a messy business. In the Northwest Territory, he tried to control disorderly settlers whose support he also needed. After illegally moving into territory in the Ohio River Valley and Kentucky, those settlers expected support from state and national governments when Indians defended their lands. As president, Washington sought a more powerful army to manage the conflict. In spite of initial Native American victories, before Washington left office, all of the tribes of the region then known as the Northwest had been defeated and millions of acres opened for white settlements. In response to a new federal tax on whiskey, a rebellion—the Whiskey Rebellion—broke out among settlers in western Pennsylvania who had no intention of paying the tax. With a massive show of force, the Washington administration brought the rebellion to an end, but once the rule of federal law had been secured, Washington pardoned individual rebels. The French Revolution began just as Washington was taking office, but it was during his second term (1793–1797) that it dominated the administration's interest. Washington was determined to maintain neutrality as revolutionary France went to war with Great Britain and as large numbers of Americans came to support each side in the war.

After serving as president for two terms, Washington retired. In a close race, his vice president John Adams defeated former secretary of state Thomas Jefferson, and under the rules then in force, Adams became president and Jefferson vice president. Four years later, the two again ran against each other, but this time, after a hard fought and exceedingly complicated election process, Thomas Jefferson became the third president of the United States.

By the time Jefferson was inaugurated, the factions that Washington abhorred had begun to harden into two political parties. The Federalists who supported a strong central government, a national bank, and the development of commercial enterprise were represented in the presidential contests by John Adams, but Alexander Hamilton, who privately feuded constantly with Adams, drove the party's ideas. On the other side, the Antifederalists, or Democratic-Republicans, led by Jefferson, were the party of those supporting states' rights, a weak federal government, and agrarian—often slaveholding—interests. Once Jefferson defeated Adams, the Federalists would never elect another president, but the philosophical divide between the two parties would dominate American politics for decades.

 CHAPTER REVIEW How well did the early American government under the Constitution uphold its spirit and ideals? How did issues not addressed within the document lead to controversy later on?

Chapter 7 Chapter Review

CONVENING A CONGRESS, INAUGURATING A PRESIDENT, ADOPTING A BILL OF RIGHTS

7.1 Analyze the first federal elections and the adoption of the Bill of Rights.

Review Questions

1. **Contextualization**
   What were the most important priorities for the new Congress? Why?

2. **Chronological Reasoning**
   What concerns raised by the Antifederalists during the debate over ratification were addressed by the first 10 amendments to the Constitution?

CREATING AN ECONOMY: ALEXANDER HAMILTON AND THE U.S. ECONOMIC SYSTEM

7.2 Analyze the enduring argument begun by Hamilton's economic vision for the United States and the alternative vision of Jefferson and Madison.

Review Questions

3. **Constructing an Argument**
   Why was the resolution of the federal government's fiscal problems so critical to the success of the new nation?

4. **Historical Interpretation**
   What larger political and regional divisions were reflected in the debates over debt assumption and the First Bank of the United States?

5. **Comparison**
   Compare and contrast Hamilton's and Jefferson's visions of the future development of the United States. Why did Jefferson believe that small, independent farmers were the foundation of American society and government? Why did Hamilton disagree?

SETTING THE PACE: THE WASHINGTON ADMINISTRATION

7.3 Explain the precedents set by George Washington's presidential administration.

Review Questions

6. **Historical Interpretation**
   Why did events in the western regions of the country occupy so much of Washington's time and attention? Why did he think events in the region were so important to the country's future?

7. **Crafting Arguments**
   In your opinion, why did diplomatic efforts fail to resolve the conflict in the Northwest Territory between Indian peoples and white settlers? What evidence can you provide to support your argument?

8. **Contextualization**
   Why did so many Americans identify with the revolutionary cause in France? How did public reaction to the French Revolution contribute to the increasingly partisan nature of American politics in the 1790s?

THE BIRTH OF POLITICAL PARTIES: ADAMS AND JEFFERSON

7.4 Explain the growing split between the Federalist and Democratic-Republican Parties, including how the French Revolution and the personal differences among Hamilton, Adams, and Jefferson affected American politics.

Review Questions

9. **Crafting Arguments**
   Should the election of 1796 be considered a contest between two political parties? Why or why not?

10. **Contextualization**
    What light do the Alien and Sedition Acts shed on the nature of American politics at the end of the 1700s? How might a supporter of the acts have defended them?

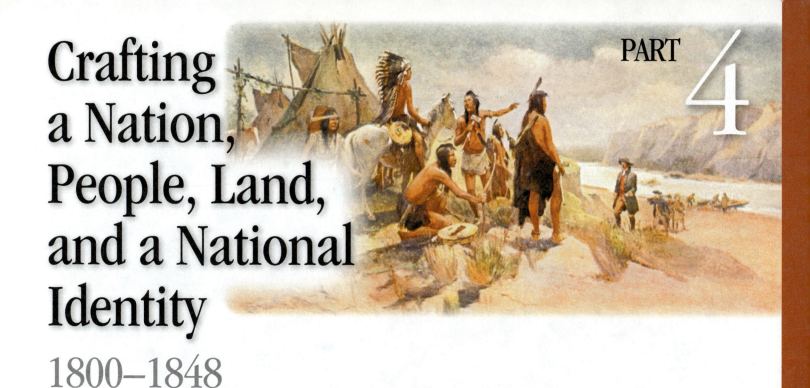

Crafting a Nation, People, Land, and a National Identity

1800–1848

PART 4

8 Creating a New People, Expanding the Country

CHAPTER OBJECTIVE

Demonstrate an understanding of how the post-Revolutionary generation created a new culture for the country while also expanding the land area of the United States.

LEARNING OBJECTIVES

JEFFERSON AND THE REPUBLICAN IDEAL

8.1 Explain how Jefferson's republicanism shaped and reflected the nation's democratic culture.

THE IDEAL OF RELIGIOUS FREEDOM

8.2 Explain how Americans applied new individualist ideals in their religion and how the expansion of faith-based organizations supported, yet also challenged, Jeffersonian republicanism.

BEYOND THE MISSISSIPPI: THE LOUISIANA PURCHASE AND THE EXPEDITION OF LEWIS

8.3 Explain what effects the Louisiana Purchase and the westward expansion had on how Americans saw themselves.

THE WAR OF 1812

8.4 Analyze the causes and impact of the War of 1812.

EXPANDING AMERICAN TERRITORY AND INFLUENCE

8.5 Analyze how the United States acquired new territory and increased influence abroad.

The Conestoga wagon pulled by a team of oxen—as shown here—or horses and pulling white settlers west became a symbol of the changing United States after 1800 as explorers and then settlers moved ever further toward the west, displacing the original inhabitants and building new communities.

On Inauguration Day, March 4, 1801, Thomas Jefferson had breakfast at his boardinghouse in Washington, D.C., and then walked up New Jersey Avenue to the unfinished Capitol building to take the oath of office as the nation's third president. He was sworn in by one of his political archenemies, the Federalist Chief Justice John Marshall. In his inaugural address, Jefferson acknowledged the bitterness of the 1800 presidential campaign but continued:

> But every difference of opinion is not a difference of principle. We have called by different names brethren of the same principle. We are all Republicans, we are all Federalists. If there be any among us who would wish to dissolve this Union or to change its republican form, let them stand undisturbed as monuments of the safety with which error of opinion may be tolerated where reason is left free to combat it.

Federalist ideas, which were at the core of the Constitution and the first two presidential administrations, were increasingly out of touch with the democratic tone of the new century. As the new president made clear, more trust and less fear as well as dynamic exchanges and significant freedom were to characterize Jeffersonian democracy and his emerging Democratic-Republican Party.

Republican ideals and an explosion of interest in religion defined the politics and culture of Jeffersonian America. This chapter will examine these ideals and explore their effect on the growth of religious bodies as well as on the expansion and consolidation of American territory and power through the Louisiana Purchase, the War of 1812, and policies such as the Monroe Doctrine.

JEFFERSON AND THE REPUBLICAN IDEAL

8.1 Explain how Jefferson's republicanism shaped and reflected the nation's democratic culture.

From the moment he took office, Jefferson set a new tone for the federal government. His inaugural address emphasized conciliation and national unity while his actions involved dramatic changes. Jefferson wanted to preside over a country in which social equality (among white male citizens) and individual freedom were the order of the day. The social hierarchies that had characterized the colonial era and the first years of the republic were, he thought, long out of date. He wanted a limited government that fostered the kind of freedom that was his ideal. Most of his countrymen, it seems, agreed.

Jefferson quickly sold the horses and coaches that John Adams had used. In place of formal state dinners, he held smaller dinner parties. What some called a "pell-mell" seating arrangement marked these gatherings at the White House. There was no assigned seating and no respect for the rank of the dignitaries who attended. The president simply sat down with whomever he found interesting and expected the other guests to do the same. A British diplomat described the new president as a host "with a most perfect disregard to ceremony both in his dress and manner" and vowed never to attend another White House dinner.

These changes in tone were not trivial. They represented what was quickly becoming the dominant ideology of the United States quite different from that of the Federalists: a commitment to a Democratic-Republican government but also **republicanism** in personal styles and political beliefs (see Table 9-1). Americans valued equality not only in terms of representation in government but also in terms of how Americans treated others—at state dinners in the White House, at town meetings, and in taverns and family homes. They also valued a notion of freedom in which a nation of independent farmers could make their own decisions, independent of one another if they preferred. American republicanism was a new way for citizens to relate to each other, emphasizing equality and independence far more than the class separation, deference, and dependence that had marked British North America and Great Britain itself.

TABLE 8-1 Comparison of the First Political Parties: Federalists and Democratic-Republicans

Federalists	Democratic-Republicans
Originally organized by supporters of the Constitution	Began as an informal protest movement led by Jefferson and Madison in response to Hamilton's economic plans
Although George Washington insisted he stood above party and hated the idea of political parties, he was usually considered to be a Federalist. The Federalists supported John Adams for president in the elections of 1796 and 1800.	By the 1796 and 1800 elections, Democratic-Republicans formed a well-defined caucus within the Congress, though hardly a modern political party. Between 1800 and 1820s, it was the nation's majority party—the Democratic-Republican Party—sometimes called the Jeffersonian Republican or simply the Republican Party.
The party wanted a strong national government, favored Hamilton's economic reforms, and generally supported stronger U.S. ties with Great Britain.	The party sought a smaller federal government, wanted less federal involvement in economic matters, and generally favored France over Great Britain.
After the 1800 election, the Federalists never again dominated the national government but remained strong in New England for another 20 years. They nominated their last presidential candidate in 1816.	By the 1820s, it was the only remaining political party before splitting into the Democrats and the Whigs.

Significant Dates

1800	Thomas Jefferson elected president
1803	Louisiana Purchase
	U.S. Supreme Court's *Marbury* v. *Madison* decision
	Ohio admitted to the Union
1804–1806	Lewis and Clark Expedition
1807	*Chesapeake-Leopard* affair
	Congress passes Embargo Act
1808	James Madison elected president
1812–1815	War of 1812
1812	American defeat at Detroit
1813	American victories on Great Lakes and Battle of the Thames
	Death of Tecumseh
1814	Jackson victory over Creeks at Battle of Horseshoe Bend
	The British burn Washington, D.C.
	Treaty of Ghent signed (ratified 1815)
1815	U.S. victory at Battle of New Orleans
1816	James Monroe elected president
1817	Rush-Bagot Treaty demilitarized the Great Lakes between the United States and Canada
1818	Anglo-American Convention set the border between the United States and Canada and included an agreement for temporary joint ownership of the Oregon Territory
1819	Adams-Onís Treaty—Spain cedes Florida to the United States
1822	Plans for slave revolt in Charleston led by Denmark Vesey
1823	Monroe Doctrine

republicanism
A complex, changing body of ideas, values, and assumptions that developed in the United States in the late 1790s and early 1800s around Thomas Jefferson and James Madison's political organizing and their campaigns for the presidency.

There are many ironies in Jefferson's success. Jefferson, whose lack of religious orthodoxy was an issue in his campaigns, led the country during one of the great revivals of religion. Jefferson, the sophisticated aristocrat in his personal life, presided over White House events with a sense of informality that many officials found insulting. Jefferson, a slaveholder who had great misgivings about slavery, led the country during the time when slavery became stronger and more entrenched as well as a source of bitter divisiveness. And Jefferson, the believer in an agrarian vision of the United States, presided over a growing commercial economy that saw an expansion of U.S. territory as well as the rise of cities, banks, and corporations, which would have pleased his old rival Alexander Hamilton much more than it ever impressed Thomas Jefferson. The apparent disconnect between Jefferson the political leader and Jefferson the person generated much criticism but, those ironies also reflected the dramatic changes afloat in the nation.

Jefferson the Political Leader

Jefferson's changes in the government went far beyond symbolism. He shrank the federal bureaucracy while doubling the landmass of the United States. Jefferson thought the bureaucracy he had inherited from John Adams was "too complicated, too expensive" and vowed to cut it, though that government was hardly a large one. The largest federal office, the War Department, included the secretary of war, one accountant, 14 clerks, and two messengers. The secretary of state had one chief clerk, six other clerks, and a messenger. The attorney general did not even have a clerk. Still, Jefferson thought it was too big and cut it. In addition, having always feared the impact of a standing army, he cut the size of the army in the west and the size of the navy that patrolled the Atlantic Ocean. He founded the military academy at West Point only because he wanted to replace Federalist officers with a thoroughly professional (and Republican) officer corps. Jefferson's secretary of the treasury persuaded him to keep Hamilton's Bank of the United States, but Jefferson was never enthusiastic about the bank, and a Republican Congress refused to renew its charter in 1811, after he had left office.

tariff
A tax on imports into any nation.

While he kept the **tariff**—the tax on imported goods—Jefferson abolished all internal taxes. Most Americans dealt with the federal government only through the post office during the Jefferson, Madison, and Monroe administrations. Washington, D.C., had fewer than 10,000 residents, most of whom lived in boardinghouses. A British diplomat described it as a capital city "like no other in the world" where one could get stuck in the mud on Pennsylvania Avenue, and a carriage had to avoid tree stumps and grazing cows, but there was "excellent snipe [a type of game bird] shooting…close under the wall of the Capitol." Jefferson liked it that way. He wanted a small federal government. For Jefferson, the states, not the federal government, were supposed to have the "principal care of our persons, our property, and our reputation."

One of Jefferson's early efforts to shrink the federal government sparked one of the most significant Supreme Court decisions in U.S. history. The new Jeffersonian majority in Congress repealed the Judiciary Act of 1801, which had expanded the number of federal judges and which John Adams had signed just before leaving office. Following Jefferson's views, Congress wanted fewer federal judges, and it especially disliked the Federalist judges that Adams had appointed in his last days in office, which some called **"midnight judges"** because of the hour at which the outgoing president appointed them. Congressional leaders and President Jefferson virtually dared the Supreme Court, particularly, Chief Justice Marshall, a Federalist whom Adams had appointed, to declare Congress's actions unconstitutional. They promised that if the Court did so, Congress would reduce the Court's authority. But Marshall was a wily judge. He waited for the right case to make his decision. One of the many last-minute court appointments that Adams had made was to name William Marbury a justice of the peace for the District of Columbia. But Adams left office before Marbury's commission was delivered, and President Jefferson and his secretary of state, James Madison, refused to

midnight judges
The name the Jeffersonian Democratic-Republicans gave to those judges appointed by the outgoing Federalist president John Adams.

deliver it. Marbury sued, and in 1803, the Supreme Court, led by John Marshall, issued its decision in the case of **Marbury v. Madison**.

Marbury v. *Madison* was a complex decision with far-reaching consequences. Marshall began by saying that Jefferson had, indeed, been irresponsible in failing to deliver the commission, for even a president "cannot at his discretion sport away the vested rights of others." However, Marshall also said, the Court could do nothing because the clause in the Judiciary Act of 1789 giving the federal courts the right to issue writs requiring governmental action was unconstitutional because the Constitution did not give the judiciary such authority. The result of the ruling was three-fold. First, Marbury did not get his job. Second, while the Court slapped Jefferson's wrist, it also gave him the legal victory in the case because he was not forced to appoint Marbury, and his party's overturning of the Judiciary Act of 1801 stood. Since Jefferson had won, there was nothing in the Court decision for him to challenge. But third, Marshall also made a point of saying that the Court had the authority to declare an act of Congress unconstitutional. It was the first time the Court asserted this power of **judicial review**. The Court would not use this power to determine the constitutionality of an act of Congress again until 1857, long after Marshall was gone, but Marshall had dramatically expanded the authority of the federal courts while also ensuring that they would not be challenged by Jefferson or the Republican Congress.

Rural America and the Agrarian Ideal

In 1801, the occupations, opinions, and manners of most American voters were compatible with Jefferson's agrarian ideal of a nation of independent farmers, and they provided a solid foundation on which to build political consensus. The population of the United States when Jefferson took office was just over 5.3 million, almost 900,000 of whom were African slaves. Ninety percent of whites lived on farms.

However, far from being permanently attached to their isolated rural communities, many moved often, seeking more and better land in Ohio, Kentucky, and Tennessee. Older farms were sold and resold regularly. A French observer, the Duc de La Rochefoucauld-Liancourt, visited the United States just before Jefferson's inauguration. He wondered whether American farmers had any of the French peasant's attachment to a particular piece of land, but when he asked the Americans, they said that such attachments represented a lack of pluck. So he wrote, "It is a country in flux…that which is true today as regards its population, its establishments, its prices, its commerce will not be true six months from now."

For many in the Republic, all forms of authority, in government and in manners, were suspect. Republican virtue was to be found in equality, at least among white men. While voting restrictions related to race and gender continued, and even grew in the early 1800s, virtually all property qualifications for voting disappeared, and many people now wanted to vote. As a result, the number of voters, which had previously included around 20 percent of the white male population, expanded in most states to 70 and 80 percent. Compared to any earlier era, the white male electorate was large. It was also opinionated and individualistic.

European visitors were fascinated and appalled by the manners and morals of Americans. An Englishman, Charles William Janson, who lived in the United States from 1793 to 1806, called Americans "the only remaining republicans in the civilized world," but he also found them "in every respect uncongenial to English habits, and to the tone of an Englishman's constitution." Everyone in the United States, Janson said, from the poorest and least educated to the most elite, "consider themselves on an equal footing with the best educated people in the country."

The United States of the early 1800s was also a violent place. Political arguments were often settled with fists. Urban riots were not unusual when crowds poured out of a tavern, theater, or factory. Observers worried that the country was losing its cohesion. Fighting was as common in rural communities. Daniel Drake, who grew up

Marbury v. Madison
Supreme Court decision of 1803 that created the precedent of judicial review by ruling part of the Judiciary Act of 1789 as unconstitutional.

judicial review
A power implied in the Constitution that gives federal courts the right to review and determine the constitutionality of acts passed by Congress and state legislatures.

During Jefferson's time in office, the nation's capital in Washington, D.C., was little more than a sleepy village along the shores of the Potomac River. Jefferson liked it that way, as a symbol of a weak federal government.

in Kentucky and became one of the leading citizens of Cincinnati, described his childhood home in the early 1800s as a place where men fought with "no holds barred" using hands, feet, and teeth and "scratching, pulling hair, choking, gouging out each other's eyes, and biting off each other's noses."

Men of higher social standing often settled minor grudges with a duel. Jefferson's Vice President Aaron Burr, who never forgave his longtime political rival former Treasury Secretary Alexander Hamilton for his role in the final outcome of the 1800 election, later challenged him to a duel in response to unkind comments Hamilton made. Hamilton agreed as a point of honor, and Burr killed him in the resulting fight in 1804. Long before he became president in 1829, Andrew Jackson was shot in a duel over a bet on a horserace in Tennessee in 1806. He carried that bullet in his chest for the rest of his life; his opponent was killed in the encounter.

One cause of the violence was the high level of alcohol consumption. Most Americans with access to alcohol—which did not include slaves—enjoyed a drink during the colonial era. But in the early 1800s, drinking doubled from an average of 2.5 gallons per person per year in 1790, to five gallons in 1820. One doctor complained that 40 of the 100 physicians in New York City were drunks. Charles Janson reported his "horror" at "boys, whose dress indicated wealthy parents, intoxicated, shouting and swearing in the public streets." Another observer estimated that some workers were consuming a quart of hard liquor every day.

The violence, lack of manners, and "shouting and swearing" were not limited to duels among the elite or fist fights on the frontier. Interracial violence between white Americans and Indians continued long after the Indian Wars in the east had ended. Individual Indians were easy marks for attack. Similarly, slaves could do little to protect themselves against the violence that was always a part of the slave system. The beating, rape, even killing of slaves was seldom considered a matter of concern for anyone but those on the plantation.

Family life, too, was not exempt from violence. When a New Yorker, Stephen Arnold, was tried for the murder of his adopted daughter, many saw it as government intrusion into a family matter. But while violence toward wives and children may have increased, it was also resisted as it had not been earlier. Divorce rates increased as women refused to stay in violent or unhappy marriages or remain legally connected to a man who had left them long before.

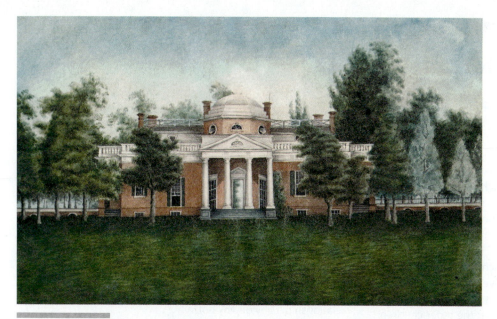

Jefferson built a grand home, Monticello, for himself and his family, near Charlottesville, Virginia. Slave laborers expanded the house according to Jefferson's plans and attended to his personal needs.

Jefferson the Individual

While Americans debated the many meanings of freedom and unfreedom in the democratic experiment of which they were a part, they also debated the personal life of their president and whether he was himself a good example of the ideals he espoused.

While Jefferson insisted on a simplified social scene at the White House, his life at his grand house in Monticello was anything but. At Monticello, he entertained lavishly and served the finest food and wine, while continually expanding the house and the library. Slaves did all of the hard work and took care of the president's every need. The defender of republican equality in social relations lived an aristocratic private life.

The president's private life became national news soon after he took office. On September 1, 1802, the *Richmond Recorder*, edited by James Callendar, a former Jefferson ally-turned-enemy, carried a story that began, "It is well known that the man, whom it delighteth the people to honor, keeps, and for many years has kept, as his concubine, one of his slaves. Her name is SALLY." Thus did rumors of Thomas Jefferson's longtime relationship with his slave, Sally Hemings, become national news. Not everyone believed the story, and Jefferson remained silent, but his opponents used the story of his life with Sally Hemings and the birth of their children to smear the president. The Federalists made a major issue of the relationship when Jefferson ran for reelection in 1804. He still won easily, but the rumors persisted long after he died and Hemings's children were free. With the advent of DNA testing in the late 1990s, it has been established as highly likely that the children of Sally Hemings, four of whom survived into adulthood and were set free, were also the children of Thomas Jefferson. Although not without debate, this conclusion is the consensus of most historians who have studied Jefferson's life.

8.1 **Quick Review** Jefferson called his election the "Revolution of 1800." Considering the changes in the government during his administration, do you agree with him? Why or why not?

THINKING HISTORICALLY

Thomas Jefferson and Sally Hemings

As a young man, Jefferson married Martha Wayles Skelton, like himself a wealthy young Virginian. Martha Jefferson died at Monticello in 1782, and Jefferson never remarried. In 1787, a 16-year-old slave, Sally Hemings, who was the half-sister of Jefferson's wife Martha by her slave-owning father, became a servant in Jefferson's Paris home while he was ambassador to France. When Jefferson returned to the United States in 1789, Hemings could have stayed in France and been free by French law, but she returned with him. While much is not known about their relationship, Jefferson seems to have promised Hemings that he would free the children of their union. Hemings and many of her family lived at Monticello near the older children from Jefferson's marriage. Sally Hemings's last child was born there in 1808, and Hemings stayed at Jefferson's home until he died in 1826, when she went to live with her own free children.

In her book, *The Hemingses of Monticello: An American Family* (New York: W. W. Norton, 2008), historian Annette Gordon-Reed traces not only the story of Sally Hemings, but the story of the intertwined generations of the Jefferson and Hemings families. The story raises many questions for historians, including questions about the relevance of Jefferson's personal relationship with Sally Hemings in terms of judgments about his political career and as president.

Thinking Critically

1. **Contextualization**

   Was it possible for a slave woman and a powerful older free man who claimed ownership of her to form a truly consensual relationship? Why or why not?

2. **Historical Interpretation**

   What bearings might Jefferson's relationship with Sally Hemings have on his complex attitudes about the institution of slavery? What does an understanding of Jefferson's family with Sally Hemings and her family tell us about the nature of American slavery and society in the early 1800s?

THE IDEAL OF RELIGIOUS FREEDOM

8.2 Explain how Americans applied new individualist ideals in their religion and how the expansion of faith-based organizations supported, yet also challenged, Jeffersonian republicanism.

On his first New Year's Day in the White House, Thomas Jefferson wrote to the members of a committee of the Danbury, Connecticut, Baptist Association:

> Believing with you that religion is a matter which lies solely between man and his God, that he owes account to none other for his faith or his worship, that the legislative powers of government reach actions only, and not opinions, I contemplate with sovereign reverence that act of the whole American people which declared that their legislature should "make no law respecting an establishment of religion, or prohibiting the free exercise thereof," thus building a wall of separation between Church and State.

wall of separation between church and state

A phrase coined by Thomas Jefferson to make clear his belief that the First Amendment to the Constitution guaranteed that governments should not interfere with the work of churches, and churches should not interfere with, or expect support from, government.

With the wide distribution of that letter, the "**wall of separation between church and state**" became part of the American lexicon. Some have pointed out that the "wall of separation" is merely a phrase coined by one president and not part of the Constitution or law of the land. They are right. But in 1802, Jefferson was expressing another aspect of the republican ideal. More and more Americans believed that two of the most important arenas of American life—politics and religion—should stay as far away from each other as possible. People who wanted to be treated equally with everyone else, no matter what their wealth or family; who wanted to be free to curse, drink, and fight without the law's intrusion; and who wanted to be left alone on their own farms also wanted to be able to pursue their religious beliefs as they chose.

A decade before Jefferson wrote to the Connecticut Baptists, President George Washington had written to the Sephardic Jewish congregation in Newport, Rhode Island, expressing similar views (see Chapter 7). Like the letter that Washington wrote, Jefferson's letter was written to a specific audience, but unlike Washington, Jefferson sought a change in government policy—specifically *state* government policy in New England.

In 1802, when he wrote the letter, Connecticut was one of four states that still had an official, state-supported church, a so-called "**religious establishment.**" Connecticut required all of its citizens, including its Baptists and nonbelievers, to pay taxes to support the state's Congregational churches, as did New Hampshire and Massachusetts. Maryland required support for the Episcopal Church. When it was adopted in 1791, the First Amendment to the U.S. Constitution, indeed all of the Bill of Rights amendments, applied only to the federal government. States could do as they pleased in church-state matters. Only after the Civil War was the reach of the Bill of Rights broadened. Long before the Revolution, all of the states had stopped requiring church attendance or prosecuting people for heresy, but the clergy in the four states of Connecticut, New Hampshire, Massachusetts, and Maryland were still civil servants supported by the state government. Some of the governed, including Connecticut's Baptists and Maryland's Catholics, resented paying a tax that benefited other religious bodies but not their own. So in the 1802 letter, Jefferson was telling these Connecticut Baptists just what they wanted to hear. Not surprisingly, some of the Congregational leaders in Connecticut did not agree.

The Separation of Church and State at the State Level

Jefferson, along with James Madison, had convinced the Virginia legislature to end public financial support for the Episcopal Church in that state in 1786, 5 years before Madison helped shepherd the First Amendment through Congress. That victory had not been an easy one.

The fiercest battle over state support for specific churches, however, was fought in Connecticut. Timothy Dwight, who became president of Yale in 1795, was a firm Federalist who hated Jefferson's republicanism and who could not imagine good government or moral citizens without a state church. One of Dwight's students at Yale, Lyman Beecher, organized the Connecticut Society for the Suppression of Vice and the Promotion of Good Morals and published *The Connecticut Evangelical Magazine and Religious Intelligencer* in an effort to maintain the special status of the Congregationalist churches. But he lost. In 1817, Oliver Wolcott, who opposed a state-supported church in Connecticut, defeated a Federalist for governor, and Connecticut would end its state support for all religious bodies. Beecher was heartbroken. Years later, however, he changed his mind:

> The injury done to the cause of Christ, as we then supposed, was irreparable. For several days I suffered what no tongue can tell for the best thing that ever happened to the State of Connecticut….By voluntary efforts, societies, missions, and revivals, they [clergy] exert a deeper influence than ever they could by queues, and shoe-buckles, and cocked hats, and gold-headed canes.

Religion in Connecticut, as Beecher noted, actually survived and flourished without state support and, not long afterward, Massachusetts, the last holdout, followed the same path to separate church and state.

New Religious Expressions

Direct government support for churches disappeared in the early 1800s, but the importance of religious freedom did not. The ideals of individual freedom in all areas of life generated an amazing growth in religious organizations and ideas in the same era.

Church attendance in America dropped during and after the Revolution. Many of the elite, like Jefferson, were **deists** who saw God as, at most, a distant force in human affairs; many working people ignored religious matters altogether. During Jefferson's presidency, however, Americans participated in an outpouring of evangelical

religious establishment
The name given to a state-church or to the creation of an "established church" that might play a role in, and expect support and loyalty from, all citizens.

deist
One who has a religious orientation that rejects divine revelation and holds that the workings of nature alone reveal God's design for the universe.

Second Great Awakening
A series of religious revivals in the first half of the 1800s characterized by great emotionalism in large public meetings.

Christianity—the beginning of the **Second Great Awakening**. This religious revival paralleled and, indeed, exceeded the Great Awakening of the 1740s that had transformed American Christianity. Although major developments of the Second Great Awakening occurred largely in the 1820s and 1830s, the movement began in the late 1790s and the early 1800s.

Cane Ridge and the Revivals of the Early 1800s

In 1796, a Presbyterian minister named James McGready moved from the Carolinas to Kentucky. Most of those who had moved across the Appalachian Mountains into Kentucky had left their religion at home, if they ever had any at all. McGready described "Rogue's Harbor" in Logan County, Kentucky, as a place of horse thieves, murderers, robbers, counterfeiters, and runaways. They were the same people whom Daniel Drake had described as fighting with "no holds barred." McGready set out to make them good church-going Christians. He was surprisingly successful. In 1799, he and other preachers held a church service at the Gaspar River Meeting House. John McGee, one of the others involved, remembered, "I left the pulpit and went through the audience shouting and exhorting with all possible ecstasy and energy, and the floor was soon covered with the slain." (Revivalist preachers often called those who experienced emotional conversion "the slain" because they were seen as having died to their old, sinful lives.)

The revival of 1799 led to more religious gatherings, and they grew so big that they needed to be held at outdoor campgrounds. In one of the largest religious gatherings before the Civil War, perhaps 20,000 people—10 percent of the state's population—gathered at Cane Ridge in Bourbon County, Kentucky, for a 5-day camp meeting in August 1801 that was led by Presbyterian and Methodist ministers. Preaching continued from dawn to midnight with little time for meals or rest. James Finley, who was himself converted to Christianity at the Cane Ridge Camp Meeting and went on to a long career as a frontier revivalist, described the days:

> I counted seven ministers all preaching at once, some on stumps, others in wagons, and one…was standing on a tree trunk which had, in falling, lodged against another. Some of the people were singing, others praying, some crying.

Barton W. Stone, the pastor of the Cane Ridge Presbyterian Church that hosted the gathering, remembered, "Many things transpired there, which were so much like miracles, that if they were not, they had the same effect as miracles on infidels and unbelievers."

Methodists, Baptists, and Other Protestants

Although Cane Ridge was a joint Presbyterian-Methodist endeavor, it was the Methodists and Baptists who grew the most from the revival movement. Indeed, the revivals that began in the early 1800s made these two denominations the largest Protestant groups in the country during that time.

Methodism had come to America through John Wesley (1703–1791), who founded the Methodist movement in England along with his brother, Charles, the hymn writer (1707–1788). John Wesley had also preached in Georgia. But it was the first American Methodist Bishop, Francis Asbury (1745–1816), who established American Methodism. Asbury created a new form of Protestant ministry, the Methodist circuit riders, who moved from community to community preaching with great fervor and organizing churches at every stop.

This popular illustration of an early camp meeting gives some sense of what went on at a camp meeting, though especially in the west, the crowds who attended were larger and more diverse than indicated here.

John Wesley believed that it was in the power of every person to decide whether they wanted to experience salvation. His emphasis on the need for free individuals to make their own decisions appealed in freedom-loving Jeffersonian America. In addition, Wesley's experience of having his "heart strangely warmed" allowed a level of emotionalism in Methodism that was lacking in other denominations.

Baptists had been in North America for almost as long as the Puritans. They were the largest religious body in Rhode Island, where they founded Brown University. The Baptists of the Second Great Awakening, however, were a different breed from their earlier, New England Baptist counterparts. Their religious events were more emotional, and they were more individualistic and determined to assert local authority.

Where Methodism was tightly organized from bishops to preachers to congregations, Baptist organization was highly decentralized, with each congregation retaining total control. While Methodists were largely united until the coming of the Civil War, Baptists tended to splinter into rival groups—Regular Baptists, Anti-Mission Baptists, Freewill Baptists, Church of God Baptists, Seventh-Day Baptists, Six-Principle Baptists, Hard Shell Baptists. The model Methodist minister was the circuit rider; the typical Baptist minister was a farmer-preacher who grew up in a particular congregation and was selected to lead it while he continued to support himself by his own labor. Despite their differences, however, both the Methodist and the Baptist ministers were highly effective in changing the religious outlook of the country after 1800.

Faith in the Slave Quarters and Free Black Churches

White communities were not the only ones experiencing a revival of religion in the early 1800s. At revivals like Cane Ridge, blacks and whites, whether slaves or free people, mixed with surprising freedom. Revivals in some parts of the South, especially in the early 1800s, were seen as a kind of holiday, and many of the rules of daily life, including racial segregation, were suspended.

Many plantation owners organized religious services for slaves that focused on the virtues of submission and obedience. But slaves passed along memories of another form of worship—congregations that met, often at night in secluded places. The scholar and activist W.E.B. Dubois (1868–1963) described the meetings of these clandestine congregations as occasions to speak of "the longing and disappointment and resentment of a stolen people" and about their deep passion for liberty.

Litt Young, a slave on a plantation near Vicksburg, Mississippi, remembered that the mistress of the plantation

> built a nice church with glass windows and a brass cupola for the blacks. A yellow man [a light-skinned African-American] preached to us. She had him preach how we was to obey our master and missy if we want to go to heaven, but when she wasn't there, he come out with straight preachin' from the Bible.

Clara Young recalled her favorite preacher was a man named Matthew Ewing who, even though he could not read or write, "sure knowed his Bible." For these slaves, effective preaching involved knowing the Bible, either by memory or from the rare—and illegal—ability to read it, and an ability to preach with passion about freedom in the next life and quite possibly in this life. Worship included singing, dancing, and a cathartic emotional release and renewal.

Any unsupervised meeting of slaves frightened whites. Denmark Vesey, a free black Sunday school teacher who saw himself as a latter-day Moses, ready to lead his people to freedom, led a slave revolt in South Carolina in 1822. In 1831, Nat Turner would lead the largest slave revolt before the Civil War. When Turner told the authorities that he knew he "was ordained for some great purpose in the hands of the Almighty," and that "the great day of judgment was at hand," he confirmed what they had been fearing about slave religion.

The longing for freedom usually took less violent paths, however. Slavery depended on hopelessness, and religion gave slaves hope that could lead to resistance. The songs of the slave quarter are often songs of freedom. Thus slaves sang:

> Steal away, steal away, steal away to Jesus!
> Steal away, steal away home, I ain't got long to stay here!

Sometimes these lyrics meant stealing away to the religious meeting, but they could also mean stealing away from slavery to flee North.

At the same time, northern free blacks began to form their own religious organizations. Richard Allen was born a slave in Delaware. He converted to Methodism and was able to purchase his freedom and begin preaching. Although Allen preached to white and black congregations, he "soon saw a large field open in seeking and instructing my African brethren, who had been a long forgotten people and few of them attended public worship."

Because white churches were not always welcoming, Allen became convinced that a racially integrated congregation was impossible. In response, he organized the Bethel Church in Philadelphia in 1794. Thus was born the African Methodist Episcopal Church, which by 1820 had 4,000 members in Philadelphia and 2,000 more in Baltimore. Other black Methodists founded the African Methodist Episcopal Zion Church in New York. African-American Baptists also created their own congregations. Fears of religiously inspired slave rebellions, especially after Denmark Vesey's rebellion of 1822, led southern governments to block the growth of independent black churches, but in the North, free black churches thrived as their members exercised leadership, developed their own ideas, and worshipped among themselves.

American Catholic and Jewish Communities

In the early years of the Republic, there were few Roman Catholics or Jews in the areas of the original 13 colonies. During the late 1700s and early 1800s, the largest number of Catholics in North America lived in New Orleans, which had become part of the United States only in 1803, and in Texas, New Mexico, and California, which were still part of Mexico until the 1840s. Nearly all white immigrants to the British colonies had been at least nominally Protestant, except for Catholics who had been granted safe haven in Maryland. Religious freedom in the Jeffersonian era was tremendously important to those who were in the smallest minorities. The freedom to form their own religious organizations, free of government control and often free of full authority by their own senior leaders, was important to Catholics and Jews in Jeffersonian America.

In 1790, John Carroll was appointed the first Catholic bishop in America. He was based in Maryland, where Catholics, having lost their right to govern the colony, had again gained religious freedom after the Revolution (see Chapter 7). Carroll was later promoted to Archbishop of Baltimore when the Vatican appointed bishops for Boston, New York, and Bardstown, Kentucky. Carroll worked hard to build Catholic strength and to fit into the democratic spirit of America. He established the first American Catholic college at Georgetown, Maryland (later part of the District of Columbia), and a Catholic seminary at Baltimore. In many places, Catholic laypeople created their own churches, appointed themselves trustees, and when possible hired their own priests. Vatican responses to the radical secularism of the French Revolution led to pressure on Carroll to curtail this trend among the American laity and, instead, agree to the hierarchical appointment of priests, but throughout the early 1800s, American Catholicism had remarkably strong lay leadership.

At the time of the Revolution, most of the few American Jews lived in East Coast cities such as Newport, Philadelphia, and New York City. Between then and 1820, new congregations and synagogues were formed in Richmond, New Orleans, Cincinnati, and Baltimore. Jewish religious communities, like those of Catholics and Protestants, took on republican sentiments. In New York City, Congregation Shearith Israel adopted the words "Whereas in free states all power originates and is derived from the people" as the beginning words to their new congregational constitution.

8.2 **Quick Review** How does this trend toward religious freedom epitomize the republican values of the Jefferson administration?

BEYOND THE MISSISSIPPI: THE LOUISIANA PURCHASE AND THE EXPEDITION OF LEWIS AND CLARK

8.3 Explain what effects the Louisiana Purchase and the westward expansion had on how Americans saw themselves.

Jefferson was a political philosopher committed to a small federal government and religious freedom, but he was also a pragmatic politician. One of the practical issues that he faced in leading a country of independent farmers was that those farmers living in western regions were not happy.

Geography shaped American politics at the beginning of Jefferson's term in office. Before the advent of railroads, farmers west of the Alleghenies found it very difficult to ship their goods over the mountains to the Atlantic coast or transport them down the Mississippi through New Orleans. These difficulties had helped fuel the Whiskey Rebellion and the short-lived effort to make Kentucky the independent nation of Franklin during Washington's administration (see Chapter 7), and Jefferson worried that frustrated frontier farmers might still seek to form an independent country, as some of them advocated to do. He also worried about European influence still among them and knew that having many unhappy citizens was not good for the future of a sitting president. He was determined to do something about it.

French explorers were the first Europeans to reach and settle the banks of the Mississippi River, and most European influences in the region were still French, reflected in French place names from Detroit to Saint Louis to New Orleans. However, at the close of the French and Indian War in 1763, France ceded to Spain the area west of the Mississippi and the city of New Orleans. Throughout the Washington and Adams administrations and into Jefferson's, in spite of the provisions of the Pinckney Treaty, Spain periodically restricted non-Spanish vessels from sailing on the Mississippi and collected customs duties on all goods moving through New Orleans. That practice was detrimental because more than half of all the goods shipped out of the United States were shipped down the Mississippi River and through the port of New Orleans, not Atlantic ports. By 1800, Spain had become weaker, prompting Jefferson to write that Spanish control of the river and New Orleans "would hardly be felt by us."

However, Napoleon Bonaparte, who now ruled France, negotiated a secret treaty with Spain to return New Orleans and the entire Louisiana Territory to France. When word of the treaty reached the United States in 1802, it provoked a crisis. Jefferson believed that for France, then the strongest nation in Europe, to control American commerce was intolerable. The president told the American ambassador in Paris,

"There is on the globe one single spot, the possessor of which is our natural and habitual enemy." That spot was New Orleans.

The Louisiana Purchase

The solution for more secure commerce, Jefferson thought, was to buy the city of New Orleans from France. Once the port was under American control, Jefferson was confident that he would have solved a long-term problem for his western constituents and won an important political victory. Jefferson dispatched two of his most trusted associates, James Monroe and Robert Livingston, to Paris to offer $6 million for the city. If they could not reach an accommodation with the French, Monroe was to proceed to London and try to make an alliance against France with Great Britain.

While Jefferson worried about control of New Orleans, Napoleon had worries of his own. Although he was victorious on the European continent, Napoleon needed money. In addition, French efforts to put down the slave uprising in Haiti had gone terribly. Militant slave resistance and yellow fever had killed 24,000 French soldiers, and Haitian independence seemed inevitable. New Orleans and the Mississippi Valley, which supplied Haiti with food and raw materials, would become much less important to France if France no longer controlled the Haitian sugar and coffee plantations. So when the Americans offered $6 million for one city, Napoleon's government offered to sell the whole middle third of the present-day United States for $15 million.

Jefferson was thrilled with Napoleon's offer. He worried, however, that a strict reading of the Constitution did not authorize the federal government to make such a huge purchase of land; it certainly did not mention that authority in the powers granted to the national government. Nevertheless, the practical political benefits of the **Louisiana Purchase** overcame his constitutional doubts. Some Federalists in Congress opposed the purchase, fearing—correctly—that the influence of New England—the last Federalist region of the country—would be diminished in a vastly larger nation. But most Americans, even most Federalists, were enthusiastic. Congress acted quickly, and the treaty confirming the transfer of 828,000 square miles from nominal French control to the United States was easily ratified. The United States had solved the problem of New Orleans and secured control of both sides of the Mississippi River from the Great Lakes to the Gulf of Mexico, while almost doubling the nation's land area. How to incorporate this land into the United States, whether as states or territories, would be left for future administrations to determine.

The City of New Orleans

New Orleans was unusual for an American city when it became part of the United States in 1803. Many of its inhabitants spoke French or Spanish, but they now lived in a country where business was conducted in English. It was a Catholic city that was now part of an overwhelmingly Protestant country. Its citizens were a cosmopolitan mix with attitudes toward many things—including race and sexuality—that were different from those of most Americans.

Slavery in Spanish and French colonies varied widely. Some of the harshest slavery in the world was in the sugar plantations of French Haiti and in Spanish Cuba. But slaves in cities like Havana and pre-1803 New Orleans could maintain stable families, enjoy their own holidays, and earn money to buy goods for themselves and, sometimes, even their freedom. In New Orleans, slaves and free blacks could gather at Congo Square on Sundays to dance, play drums, and sing in their own languages under the watchful eye of whites but with a freedom of action unimaginable elsewhere in the United States. The music that they brought from Africa and developed in New Orleans was the foundation of American jazz music.

There was also considerable racial mixing in New Orleans. Mixed-race people faced discrimination, but many black women nonetheless became long-term partners to white men. Indeed, such unions were an avenue of upward mobility for some black

Louisiana Purchase
The 1803 U.S. purchase of the vast land holdings that France claimed along the west side of the Mississippi River beginning in New Orleans and extending through the heart of North America to the Canadian border.

women, not only in New Orleans but also in many of the Spanish and French colonies in ways that were not true in British colonies or in the United States. That African women could maintain their own gardens, buy and sell goods, and be involved in intimate relationships with white men led to complex family negotiations. A libre (as free blacks were called) woman, Carlota d'Erneville, purchased her freedom in 1773 and the freedom of her son Carlos in 1775. She later became rich enough to own her own tavern and houses that she rented to others.

The New Orleans that Jefferson purchased in 1803 had a population of 8,000 with their own churches, dance halls, theater, newspapers, and police force. One-third of all people of African origin in the city were free compared with less than two percent in nearby Kentucky or Tennessee and under 10 percent in the United States as a whole.

Many of the French-speaking women and men of New Orleans, black or white, slave or free, tended to refer to any citizens of the United States as "Kaintucks" or Kentuckians—no matter where in the United States they came from. Kaintucks were the tough backwoods farmers and slaves who crewed flatboats. These large floating rafts, often 15 feet wide by 50- to 80-feet long, carried up to 100 tons of grain. For the Americans who came down the Mississippi on a flatboat, New Orleans was a city of pleasure that lured many to stay and create a new American population. Although the racial and cultural diversity of New Orleans frightened some Americans, its essential geographic location made it the prize of the Louisiana Purchase.

The Lewis and Clark Expedition

Jefferson wanted to assert American dominance in North America. In 1803, before he even knew the outcome of the Monroe-Livingston negotiations for New Orleans that he had authorized, he asked Congress to support a "scientific expedition" to study the people, lands, and animal and plant species of the North American continent across the Louisiana territory and on to the Pacific Ocean. While he wanted the scientific information, Jefferson was even more interested in a full report on Spanish and French military power in the region. The expedition was to be led by his private secretary, Meriwether Lewis, and an army officer, William Clark. Before Lewis and Clark could depart, word came of the Louisiana Purchase. Suddenly, the United States owned much of the land the expedition was authorized to explore. The news changed nothing; the order still stood: learn as much as possible about the new American lands and the places beyond them, and make treaties with as many of the original inhabitants as possible. It was a daunting assignment that would become one of American history's most celebrated exploits.

Lewis and Clark and their **Corps of Discovery**—the team of soldiers, civilian woodsmen, boatmen, interpreters, and Clark's slave York—prepared for the trip during the winter of 1803–04 in St. Louis on the west bank of the Mississippi River. The site was a Spanish/French trading post of about a thousand people, which was a gateway to the territory the United States had just acquired. French explorers were familiar with much of the land over which the expedition would travel, as was a British trader, Alexander Mackenzie, who had been the first European to cross North America in 1792–93. Of course, the Indians living along the route knew their homelands well. Still, for Americans, this vast area was unknown land. On May 14, 1804, the Corps of Discovery left Camp River Dubois in Hartford, Illinois, to travel up the Missouri River into the heart of the Louisiana Territory. By the end of October, they reached an area close to the current U.S.-Canadian border in North Dakota. There, near a Mandan Indian village on the Missouri River, they made camp for the winter. The Mandans lived in earth lodges in settled villages. They had traded with the French for over a hundred years, had been decimated by European smallpox, and knew European ways, but the arrival of the Lewis and Clark expedition was their first contact with Americans. The Americans traded goods and celebrated feasts, including New Year's Day, with the Mandans, drinking, dancing, and playing the fiddle to the surprise of their hosts.

8.1
8.2
8.3
8.4
8.5

In 1803 President Thomas Jefferson sent James Monroe and Robert R. Livingstone to Paris to negotiate the American purchase of the city of New Orleans. In their meeting with the French foreign minister Charles Maurice de Talleyrand, shown in this contemporary engraving, the French offered, and the Americans accepted, the transfer of the entire Louisiana Territory to the United States.

Corps of Discovery
The name given to the expedition led by Lewis and Clark in 1804–1806 that explored the Louisiana Purchase and the Oregon lands extending to the West Coast.

Critical to the success of the corps were French trapper Toussaint Charbonneau and his Shoshone partner Sacagawea, who joined the expedition with their newborn child. Whether Sacagawea was the slave or the wife of Charbonneau is unclear, but she became an essential guide and an American legend. Sacagawea began as a cook and laundress for the corps while she carried her baby on her back but quickly used her knowledge of the countryside to find food and translate with some of the tribes they met. At the end of their journey, Lewis and Clark paid Charbonneau $500 for his services, but later they wondered whether they should have paid Sacagawea, too. According to unverified Shoshone tradition, Sacagawea lived to an old age, dying at the Wind River Indian Reservation in 1884.

As they tried to cross the Rocky Mountains in September of 1805, the corps moved beyond the rather inexact western boundary of the Louisiana Purchase into Oregon Country that was claimed by Britain, Russia, and Spain, but not the United States. As instructed by Jefferson, they kept going, and almost starved. They had assumed that the Rocky Mountains were like the Appalachians. They crossed through a valley expecting to see downward slopes, but instead, Clarke noted in his journal, they faced higher mountains "in every direction as far as I could see." At Weippe Prairie in what is now Idaho, they stumbled into a party of Nez Perce Indians, by far the largest tribe in that part of the western Rockies, who brought them to a "large spacious lodge" and fed them. An Indian leader known as Twisted Hair drew a map of the river system leading to the Columbia River and the Pacific coast and taught the Americans how to make dugout canoes out of pine. The food saved the explorers lives, and the canoes saved the trip.

On November 24, 1805, the Corps of Discovery left their horses with Twisted Hair and, following the route he mapped for them, reached the Pacific Ocean. They built Fort Clatsop near present-day Astoria, Oregon, and wintered there until March 23, 1806, when they began the long, arduous journey home, reaching Saint Louis on September 23, 1806 (see Map 8-1). Word spread quickly to the nation and to Jefferson at the White House that the party, whom many had given up for lost, had made it back.

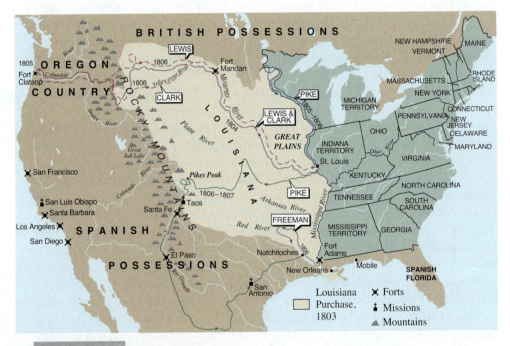

MAP 8-1 Exploring The New Territory. This map shows the size of the Louisiana Purchase in comparison with the original land of the United States and the route of the Lewis and Clark expedition through and beyond Louisiana.

While Lewis and Clark were exploring the northern parts of the Louisiana Purchase and the Oregon coast, Jefferson launched other expeditions. Zebulon Pike led an expedition that departed from St. Louis in the fall of 1805 to explore the Mississippi and Arkansas Rivers and much of the present-day state of Colorado. In 1806, Jefferson appointed a third expedition led by Thomas Freeman, an astronomer and surveyor, to track the Red River Valley in the southern portion of the new territory. The reports from these expeditions opened the way for other adventurers and traders, some of whom, like New York's John Jacob Astor, made a fortune in the fur trade. The result for the Mandans, Nez Perce, and other tribes was far too often disease, war, and the loss of lands and a way of life.

8.3 **Quick Review** What key aspects of the Louisiana Purchase were of particular importance to the United States, and how would they change life for different groups of Americans?

8.1

8.2

8.3

8.4

8.5

American Voices

William Clark and Red Bear—Two Views of the Lewis and Clark Experience

The rescue of the Lewis and Clark expedition by the Nez Perce in September 1805 was critical to the success of the expedition. But the explanation for why the Nez Perce were so friendly depends on who was describing the event. For William Clark, it was an appropriate response to his gifts and skill as a negotiator. For the Nez Perce, it was a response to a much earlier Nez Perce tradition.

From the Journals of Lewis and Clark	Red Bear
September 20—I Set out early and…decended the mountain to a leavel pine Countrey proceeded on through a butifull Countrey for three miles to a Small Plain in which I found maney Indian lodges, at the distance of 1 mile from the lodges I met 3 boys, when they Saw me ran and hid themselves searched…found gave them Small pieces of ribin & Sent them forward to the village a man Came out to meet me with great Caution and Conducted me [us] to a large Spacious Lodge which he told me (by Signs) was the Lodge of his great Chief…great numbers of women gathered around me with much apparent Signs of fear, and apr. pleased they (those people) gave us a Small piece of Buffalow meat, Some dried Salmon beries & roots in different States, Some round and much like an onion which they call (Pas she co) quamash the Bread or Cake is called Pas-she-co Sweet, of this they make bread & Supe they also gave us the bread made of this root all of which we eate hartily, I gave them a fiew Small articles as preasents, and proceeded on with a Chief to his Village 2 miles in the Same Plain, where we were treated kindly in their way and continued with them all night. Those two Villages consist of about 30 double lodges, but fiew men a number of women & children; They call themselves *Cho pun-nish* or *Pierced Noses*; their dialect appears very different from the (flat heads) Tushapaws (I have seen).	[From an oral history recorded in 1926 with Red Bear's grandson] Chief Red Bear first learned of white people through a girl of his band living on Tamonmo [the Salmon River]. When small she was stolen by the Blacklegs in the buffalo country, who sold her to some tribe farther toward the sunrise. In time she was bought by white people, probably in Canada, where she was well treated. It is a long story; how in time, carrying her little baby, she ran away and after several moons reached the friendly Selish, who cared for her and brought her in a dying condition to her own people at White Bird. Her baby had died on the way. She was called Watkuweis [Returned from a Faraway Country]. She told of the white people, how good they had been to her, and how well she liked them. When the first two white men, Lewis and Clark with their followers, came Watkuweis said to her people, "These are the people who helped me! Do them no hurt!" This was why the strange people had been received in friendship. There had been a prophecy about Red Bear and a new people, which was thus fulfilled in 1805. He met the strangers. They first have a smoke. If no smoke, then they must fight. Red Bear made presents of dressed buckskins, and they gave him beads and a few other articles. They afterwards found the white man's gifts to be cheap.

Source: Frederick E. Hoxie and Jay T. Nelson, editors, *Lewis & Clark and the Indian Country: The Native American Perspective* (Urbana: University of Illinois Press, 2007), pp. 136–141.

Thinking Critically

1. Documentary Analysis
How did Clark explain the friendly reception they received from the Nez Perce? What was Red Bear's explanation for the same reception?

2. Historical Interpretation
What light do these documents shed on the assumptions white Americans often brought to their interactions with American Indians and Indians brought to white Americans?

THE WAR OF 1812

Analyze the causes and impact of the War of 1812.

Jefferson expanded the United States, but he had been able to do little about the British and French navies that threatened the country as a result of conflicts between the two European powers. The actions Jefferson took to protect the United States on the seas actually hurt the country economically. What had begun as an irritating concern to Jefferson escalated into the War of 1812 during the presidency of his successor James Madison.

That conflict, which continued from 1812 to 1815, deserves more attention than it often receives from historians. The war resolved issues that had limited U.S. development for decades, and its conclusion launched a new period of growth for the country. It was the last war ever fought between the United States and Great Britain. The two nations had been in conflict almost nonstop since 1775, but the end of this war brought real peace. It was also the last war in which Indian tribes were allied with one nation or against another. After the war, no tribe was ever again able to make an alliance with a foreign nation, and the U.S. government treated the tribes less and less as sovereign nations and more as an "internal matter."

Renewed Tension Between the United States and Great Britain

The tensions that led the United States and Great Britain to go to war in 1812 had existed since the battles of Lexington and Concord in 1775. Despite treaties, the two nations were never fully at peace, and each made alliances with Indian tribes to make trouble for the other.

For the British, troubles in North America were a sideshow to a world war with France that had begun in 1689 and continued, with brief pauses, until 1815. English colonists fought on the British side until the French and Indian War ended in 1763. In 1778, France had come to the aid—decisive aid—of the American colonists in the Revolution. With the coming of the French Revolution in 1789 and the rise of Napoleon in 1799, the war between Britain and France took on a deeper ideological tone. While earlier wars had primarily been territorial disputes, after their Revolution, the French saw themselves as the agents of democracy against a despotic coalition led by Britain. Especially after the rise of Napoleon, the British saw themselves as defenders of the free world against Napoleonic tyranny. In the United States, the greatest divide between the emerging political parties was the Federalist tilt toward Britain and the Democratic-Republican tilt toward France. By early 1806, Napoleon's armies controlled most of the European continent while the British Royal Navy controlled the oceans. For the United States, British control of the seas was a much larger threat than worries about who controlled the European continent.

With Britain and France each casting itself as the defender of freedom while fighting for national preservation, the war was intense. To survive, Britain depended on its navy to protect the island nation from invasion and to dominate the oceans. But the Royal Navy was always short of sailors, and one of the reasons for the shortage was the tendency of British sailors to desert and join the crew of a U.S. merchant vessel where the working conditions were better and the pay up to five times higher. The British regularly stopped U.S. merchant vessels and occasionally warships on the high seas, in violation of international law, to search for their own sailors and, all too often, also to force any able-bodied seaman, British or American, into service.

This policy of seizing sailors, or impressment, was seen as vital to Britain, but it was a direct threat to American freedom and to the economic survival of the United States. Impressments had long infuriated Americans and, in fact, had helped spark the Revolution in 1776 (see Chapter 5). Between 1803 and 1812, 3,000–6,000 American citizens were pressed into service on British warships against their will, many of whom never returned. The practice was an assault on individual liberties that challenged everything the American Revolution stood for. A major crisis erupted in June 1807 when the Royal Navy's HMS *Leopard* opened fire on the USS *Chesapeake* after its commander refused to let British officers board the ship to look for deserters. Three American sailors were killed in the fighting, and the British then took four sailors off the *Chesapeake* who were either deserters from their navy or Americans resisting impressments. President Jefferson wrote, "This country has never been in such a state of excitement since the battle of Lexington."

Jefferson and Congress, however, knew that the United States was too weak for a fight, in part, because of the cutbacks Jefferson had authorized in the navy and army that Adams had previously built up. Congress initially passed a Non-Importation Act, hoping that boycotting British goods would be an effective strategy, but it failed to have an effect. Consequently, Jefferson urged the **Embargo Act**, which Congress passed in December 1807, preventing U.S. trade with any foreign ports to keep ships and sailors "out of harm's way." The president was confident that the major impact would be on Britain, which he thought could not survive without American food-stuffs, and that the American people would be willing to suffer short-term loss to gain peace. He was wrong on both counts. British warehouses were full, the country was having a good harvest, other nations were willing to sell food, and they could wait out the Americans. Most Americans were anxious to maintain the income that commerce provided. New England shipping was devastated, and farmers in all of the states lost money as cotton, grain, and tobacco piled up and could not be shipped. Smugglers became active, by land, across the border between New England and Canada, and by sea, eluding the small U.S. Navy that tried to enforce the embargo. The Massachusetts and Connecticut legislatures, following the precedent of Jefferson's own earlier Kentucky and Virginia Resolutions, declared the embargo illegal in their states, thus setting up talk of secession or civil war.

As a compromise that was meant to appease New England merchants, Congress replaced the embargo with the **Non-Intercourse Act** in 1809, just days before Jefferson left office. The new act authorized trade with everyone except Britain and France. (France had plundered U.S. ships for supplies during their war with Britain.)

During Madison's first term as president, tension continued to grow between the United States and Great Britain. In 1810, a further modification of the Non-Intercourse Act, known as Macon's Bill No. 2, created new tensions, especially between the United States and Britain. British impressments of U.S. sailors continued unabated while each new act continued to hurt commercial ties between the two countries.

Renewed Tension Between Whites and Indians

While tensions mounted between the United States and Great Britain, warfare between the United States and Indian tribes broke out in the Ohio country. After the U.S. Army's victory at the Battle of Fallen Timbers and the subsequent Treaty of Greeneville in 1795, the Old Northwest had been at peace. But a new generation of Indians was much less willing to live with what they saw as an unfair treaty. A new tribal alliance led by a charismatic religious figure named Tenskwatawa, or the Prophet, and his half-brother, the military leader Tecumseh, frightened white settlers and seriously challenged the small U.S. Army. Many correctly deduced that Tecumseh and Tenskwatawa were aided by the British.

After their losses from the Treaty of Greenville in 1795, many Shawnees came to believe that their sorry state was due to their having displeased Waashaa Monetoo, the Good Spirit, who, their traditions said, had recreated the world after its destruction by a flood. In the early 1800s, a spiritual leader, Tenskwatawa, told the tribes that their dependence on white culture was the source of the Good Spirit's unhappiness. After 200 years of coexistence, tribes like the Shawnees had become dependent on European muskets, wore cotton clothing, cooked in European cookware, and even lived in European-style houses. Tenskwatawa promised that, if his people would renounce

Embargo Act
An act passed by Congress in 1807 prohibiting American ships from leaving for any foreign port.

Non-Intercourse Act
An act, passed by Congress in 1809, designed to modify the Embargo Act by limiting it to trade with Britain and France so as to extend U.S. commerce in the rest of the world.

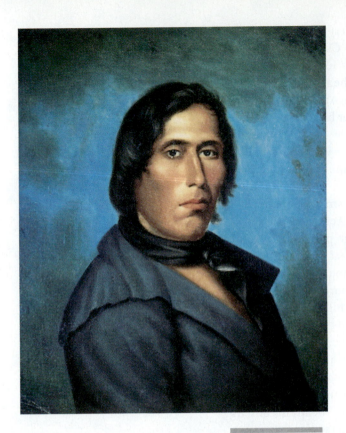

Two Shawnee leaders and half-brothers—Tecumseh, who led a diverse Indian military alliance, and Tenskwatawa, known as The Prophet—proposed a revival of Native American religion in opposition to white expansion.

European ways and goods, they could renew their culture and drive whites out of their country. He created a new settlement at what is now West Lafayette, Indiana, called Prophetstown, where Shawnees and other tribes gathered for spiritual renewal.

While Tenskwatawa preached, Tecumseh prepared for war. Tenskwatawa was a religiously inspired leader, Tecumseh an inspired military tactician. White colonists had killed their father Pukeshinwau at the beginning of the American Revolution. The brothers had seen whites make and break treaty after treaty. Tecumseh traveled throughout the Ohio territory and sought help from British authorities in Canada who, he remembered, had sought to exclude whites from the Ohio region before the American Revolution. Tecumseh traveled as far south as Tennessee and Alabama to recruit Cherokees, Choctaws, and Creeks. In a meeting with Choctaw and Chickasaw leaders in the spring of 1811, Tecumseh (speaking in the Shawnee language) said:

> The whites are already a match for us all united, and too strong for any one tribe alone to resist; so that unless we support one another with our collective and united forces; unless every tribe unanimously combines to give check to the ambition and avarice of the whites, they will soon conquer us apart and disunited and we will be driven away from our native country and scattered as autumnal leaves before the wind.

Tecumseh was willing to negotiate with the United States, but his goal was an all-Indian alliance to drive all whites from the land south of Canada and from between the Alleghenies and the Mississippi.

Whites on the frontier were frightened. In September 1807, Thomas Kirker, the acting governor of the new state of Ohio, met with Tecumseh, and the two agreed to peace. But in November 1811, while Tecumseh was away seeking Cherokee allies, William Henry Harrison, governor of the Indiana Territory, attacked Prophetstown with 1,000 U.S. troops. Harrison's troops burned the village to the ground, though

American Voices

Tecumseh, Speech to the Governor of Indiana, 1810

Before William Henry Harrison, Governor of Indiana Territory, led the U.S. Army to attack the Shawnee encampment at Prophetstown, Tecumseh met with Harrison in hopes of establishing a peace agreement. For all of his distrust, Tecumseh was willing to negotiate, and the two met in August 1810. Tecumseh spoke little or no English, but the 1810 meeting included interpreters. The U.S. government interpreters were careful to transcribe the speech as accurately as possible, and the copies they sent to Washington became the most accurate account on record of Tecumseh's words.

Brother, I wish you to listen to me well. I wish to reply to you more explicitly as I think you do not clearly understand what I before said to you. I shall explain it again….

You ought to know that after we agreed to bury the Tomahawk at Greenville we then found their new fathers in the Americans who told us they would treat us well, not like the British who gave us but a small piece of pork every day. I want now to remind you of the promises of the white people. You recollect that the time the Delawares lived near the white people (Americans) and satisfied with the promises of friendship and remained in security, yet one of their towns was surprised and the men, women, and children murdered.

The same promises were given to the Shawnees, flags were given to them and were told by the Americans that they were now children of the Americans. These flags will be as security for you; if the white people intend to do you harm hold up your flags and no harm will be done you. This was at length practiced and the consequence was that the person bearing the flag was murdered with others in their village. How my Brother after this conduct can you blame me for placing little confidence in the promises of our fathers the Americans?

Brother. Since the peace was made you have kill'd some of the Shawnee, Winnebagoes, Delawares, and Miamies and you have taken our lands from us, and I do not see how we can remain at peace with you if you continue to do so.

Source: In spite of the government's care, there are differing accounts of the speech. See for example Camilla Townsend, *American Indian History: A Documentary Reader* (Malden, MA: Wiley-Blackwell, 2009), pp. 96–99.

Thinking Critically

1. Documentary Analysis

How did Tecumseh characterize past interactions between whites and Indians?

2. Crafting an Argument

In your opinion, why was it so difficult for whites and Indians to live side by side in peace? What ideas does this document provide on this question?

---

the Prophet and most residents escaped. A year later, when the United States went to war with Great Britain, Tecumseh, strengthened by support from the British who had never stopped stirring up Indian opposition to the United States, led his tribal confederation in an all-out war on the Americans. With the United States and Britain formally at war, the Shawnee alliance with Britain was a major threat to the Americans.

War and Its Consequences

As hostilities grew between the United States and Great Britain and its Indian allies, some in Congress, known as the **War Hawks**, saw a war with Britain as just what the country needed. Republicans, led by Henry Clay of Kentucky and Felix Grundy of Tennessee, argued that war was key to territorial expansion. They were confident that if the United States went to war with Britain, those French inhabitants who remained in Canada after France ceded the territory to Britain would revolt, allowing the United States to seize Canada. The war hawks also wanted to attack the small Spanish colonies in Florida and claim that territory for the United States. With Britain and Spain out of the picture, the country could then settle things once and for all on the Indian frontier. Republican leader Elbridge Gerry of Massachusetts, eager to stop British disruptions to American trade in the Atlantic, told President Madison, "By war, we should be purified, as by fire."

Federalists, however, saw war as just one more step in a process by which the Democratic-Republicans had moved the country into an unnecessary, and commercially foolish, hostility with Britain. When Madison asked Congress for a declaration

War Hawks

Members of Congress, mostly from the South and West, who aggressively pushed for a war against Britain after their election in 1810.

of war in June 1812, it passed by the smallest margin of any U.S. declaration of war—79–49 in the House and 19–13 in the Senate. The nation was far from unanimous in its commitment to war, and the war did not go well.

Madison was confident that the war would be quick and cost little in terms of money or American lives. He was terribly wrong. The attack on Canada was a disaster. Jefferson and Madison, with their commitment to a small government and modest taxes, had kept the army weak while many in Congress who voted for war had also voted against every military appropriation in the time leading up to the war. Far fewer of the people in Canada, English or French, wanted to become part of the United States than the Americans expected. In addition, the British army was strong and had been cultivating Indian alliances.

In July 1812, Detroit fell to British soldiers and Indians led by Tecumseh, and an American attack on British forts on the Niagara River failed. Far from taking Canada, the opening battles of the war had left the Northwest more open to attack by the British and Tecumseh's tribal alliance. Tecumseh is still remembered as a hero in Canada for his role in defending that country. Battles along the frontier were brutal. The Kentucky militia scalped British soldiers, and Indians scalped American settlers. Both sides complained of atrocities.

At first, the Royal Navy enforced a much tighter blockade on the Atlantic coast than Jefferson's embargo had ever accomplished, wrecking the U.S. economy. British landing parties attacked coastal towns at will. However, an American naval victory on Lake Erie by ships under the command of Oliver Hazard Perry gave the country a new hero. Shortly after, Tecumseh was killed in October 1813 when the U.S. Army won a significant victory over combined British and Indian forces at the Battle of the Thames in southern Canada. The combined victories brought some safety to the New York, Pennsylvania, and Ohio frontier, but all thought of conquering Canada disappeared.

By 1814, the war turned further against the United States. Napoleon's abdication in April 1814 freed the British for a full-scale fight. In August, British troops raided Washington and burned the Capitol and the White House. First Lady Dolly Madison collected state papers and the famous Gilbert Stuart painting of George

In August 1814, only a short time after 1800 when they had begun serving as the center of the American government, British troops burned both the Capitol building and the White House. The deserted husks of both buildings stood until the war ended and they could be rebuilt.

Washington and fled just ahead of the British. However, on September 13, the British bombardment of Fort McHenry in Baltimore harbor failed to dislodge the American garrison. When Francis Scott Key, who was temporarily being held in British custody, saw that the American flag had not been struck in defeat, he was inspired to write "The Star-Spangled Banner." That same month, American forces also stopped a British invasion of New York. But stopping invasions was hardly winning the war.

On the Indian front, however, American forces were achieving some important victories. Like the French and Indian War and the American Revolution, the War of 1812 was a disaster for Indians living east of the Mississippi. Tecumseh's death at the Battle of the Thames ended the fragile coalition he had built and opened all of Ohio and Indiana Territory to rapid white settlement. In the south, at the Battle of Horseshoe Bend in March 1814, Andrew Jackson defeated a Creek and Cherokee alliance, killing close to 1,000 Indian fighters and 2,000 more in subsequent battles, 15 percent of the tribes' total population. "My people are no more!" the Creek leader Red Eagle, or William Weatherford, said. In the Treaty of Fort Jackson, the Creeks were forced to give up almost 25 million acres in Georgia and Alabama, half of their total land.

While both sides were winning and losing battles, an American peace delegation of Henry Clay, Albert Gallatin, and John Quincy Adams, son of the former president, met with their British counterparts in Ghent, Belgium, to negotiate what would become the **Treaty of Ghent**. Despite its strong position in the war, Britain, having ended its hostilities with France, was fearing that peace would not last, and it wanted to end its battles with the United States to conserve resources. Initially, the British asked for significant concessions, including a large protected zone for their Indian allies, but the American delegation stalled through much of 1814. Late in the year, fearing the situation with France, the British agreed to a treaty that essentially returned all borders and issues to their status quo before the war began. It was a wise move for them. Napoleon, living in exile on the island of Elba off the Italian coast since his defeat in 1814, returned to power briefly in 1815. He again ruled France until his final defeat by British and German troops at the Battle of Waterloo in June 1815. If the British had lost at Waterloo, and the battle was a close call, it might have been because their best troops were in North America.

Even as the Ghent negotiations were taking place, Federalists in New England were taking actions against the war. Many New Englanders saw little value in the territorial expansion of the country and were convinced that new lands would only mean new Democratic-Republican representatives in Congress. Even more, the war had devastated the New England economy, which was dependent on international shipping. In protest, New England governors ordered their state militias to serve only within the borders of their own states. In December 1814, Federalist delegates from across New England convened the **Hartford Convention** in Hartford, Connecticut, to demand peace and consider New England's secession from the Union if peace did not come quickly. While a majority of the delegates ultimately opposed secession, the convention insisted on the right of nullification, the right of state governments to impede Congressional actions within their own boundaries, and proposed amendments to the Constitution to protect New England's power. Delegates to the convention expected the Madison administration to give in to their demands, but when news arrived of Jackson's victory in New Orleans and then the peace treaty, the convention did more to discredit the Federalist Party than support their cause. Nevertheless, it signaled the level of hostility to what many came to call "Mr. Madison's War."

The war's final dramatic Battle of New Orleans was fought after the peace treaty was already signed but before news of it had reached Jackson or the opposing British army. The British planned to attack New Orleans so they could win control of the Mississippi River and cut U.S. trade on it. Major General Sir Edward Pakenham and his 8,000 troops were battle-hardened from years of fighting the French, but in New Orleans, they faced Jackson's 4,700 American troops, a collection of regular militia, Tennessee and Kentucky volunteers, and pirates and smugglers under the command

Treaty of Ghent
A treaty signed in December 1814 between the United States and Britain that ended the War of 1812.

Hartford Convention
A meeting of Federalist delegates from the New England states to protest the continuation of the War of 1812.

of the infamous Jean Lafitte. On January 8, 1815, Pakenham's troops marched straight into a line of fire organized by Jackson's army. When, after hours of fighting, the British called for a truce, almost 700 British soldiers had been killed and 1,400 wounded. Of the Americans, 8 were killed and 13 wounded. It was one of the great victories of the war, and it made Jackson a hero and would help make him president. And, though it came after the peace treaty, it helped convince the British that they should, indeed, honor the terms of the treaty, which they might not have done if they had taken New Orleans (see Map 8-2).

Far more Americans, Indians, and British soldiers and sailors died in the War of 1812 than anyone expected when the war began. Indian tribes from the Shawnees to the Creeks would never have significant power again. The United States was virtually bankrupt as a result of the war. Secretary of the Treasury George W. Campbell reported that the government needed to borrow $50 million in the fall of 1814 and resigned when he could not raise it, and the government, for the only time in history, defaulted on its debts.

Nevertheless, news of the Treaty of Ghent and of Jackson's victory in New Orleans was met with national celebrations. Henry Clay asked, "What is our present situation?" and answered his own question: "Respectability and character abroad—security and confidence at home." Daniel Webster, who as a representative from Massachusetts had opposed the war, now said:

> The peace brought about an entirely new and a most interesting state of things: it opened us to other prospects and suggested other duties. We ourselves were changed, and the whole world was changed.

It was an odd mood for a nation that had lost more battles than it won, come close to bankruptcy, and still had its new capital city laying in ashes. But Webster captured the national mood better than the statistics. The end of Britain's long war with France also brought an end to Britain's war with the United States, which had continued in various forms of conflict for 40 years.

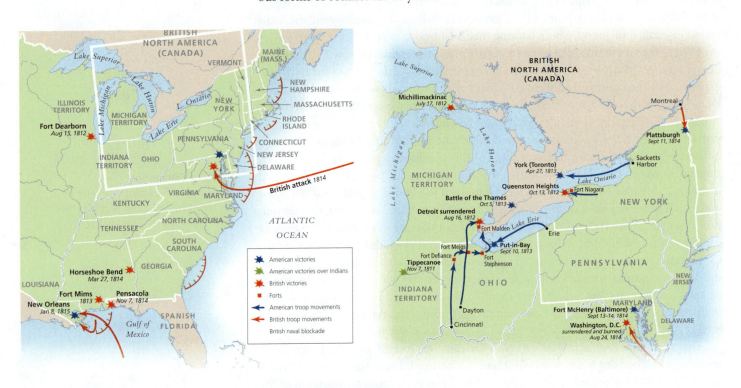

MAP 8-2 Fighting the War of 1812. Few parts of the United States were exempt from the fighting of the War of 1812. The British navy maintained a highly effective blockade of the nation's ports, bringing commerce to a stall and making it easy to attack and burn the capital in 1814. The American navy was more successful in battles on the Great Lakes while armies fought all along the Mississippi River from Tippecanoe in Indiana Territory to the final battle in New Orleans at the war's end.

Almost immediately after the war ended, Britain and the United States negotiated a commercial treaty that gave the United States trading rights with Britain and much of Britain's empire. Two years later, in 1817, the Rush-Bagot Treaty guaranteed the disarmament of the Great Lakes, and the year after that another treaty, the Anglo-American Convention, resolved much of the border between the United States and Canada. These treaties were the beginning of long-lasting peace on the northern border of the United States. Indeed, after 1815, both Europe and America settled into a long period of relative peace and mutual prosperity.

In spite of all the complaints about the war, the years during which the region's ports were closed were a time when some residents began manufacturing enterprises that in the years ahead would fuel rapid industrialization of the region. The United States was considerably more self-sufficient at war's end than it had ever been before. Still, trade with Europe after the war's end not only resumed but also quickly exceeded all previous levels. In addition, with peace came further territorial expansion and an extraordinary economic and commercial transition that fundamentally changed the nation. Perhaps most important of all, as Webster and Clay both claimed, the overall effect of the war left the United States a much more confident and proud nation than it had been up to that time. Men like Webster and Clay who were prophets of that confidence and pride, would be national leaders for the next several decades of the nation's life.

8.4 **Quick Review** Why did the War of 1812 and the events leading up to it split the nation? Based on events in the early 1800s, did Madison make the right decision?

EXPANDING AMERICAN TERRITORY AND INFLUENCE

8.5 Analyze how the United States acquired new territory and increased influence abroad.

In spite of wars and tensions, territorial expansion continued under Jefferson's handpicked successors, presidents James Madison (1809–1817) and James Monroe (1817–1825) as it had under Jefferson. During this 24 year period, three men who were political allies from the same political party and the same state governed the nation, seeking many of the same goals. Rapid growth fundamentally changed the country. In 1799, Daniel Boone, who had created the first white settlements in Kentucky during the Revolution, moved with his family yet again, this time across the Mississippi River into Spanish-controlled Missouri. Other American settlers from Kentucky followed, seeking ever more land. They assumed that their rights as American citizens went with them and that, eventually, American sovereignty would follow. The Louisiana Purchase in 1803 confirmed Boone's assumptions.

Other Americans followed Boone's pattern in Florida, Texas, New Mexico, and California. Americans ventured far beyond the borders of the United States and expected, often demanded, that the American government continue to protect them and eventually annex new lands to the Union. Many in the government agreed with the settlers, and successive governments, anxious to expand or consolidate regional control, approved.

During the War of 1812, the military victories of William Henry Harrison over the Shawnees in the Old Northwest finalized the opening of Ohio and the future states of Indiana and Illinois to white settlement. At the same time, Andrew Jackson's defeat of the Creeks and Cherokees in the Old Southwest opened up huge new tracts of land in what would become the states of Mississippi and Alabama. With the lands ceded by Britain in 1783 and the vast Louisiana Purchase now firmly under American control, the most obvious pieces of real estate left for further U.S. annexation after the War of 1812 were the territories known as West and East Florida, still controlled by Spain, and the Oregon Territory that several European powers claimed.

Florida and Oregon

West Florida was more or less the southern third of what would eventually be Mississippi and Alabama, while East Florida was what is today the state of Florida. To the United States, foreign control of those lands represented multiple threats. It gave Spain control of most access to the Gulf of Mexico, which was a threat to U.S. shipping. Slaves and others seeking to escape U.S. jurisdiction could easily escape south along a long, unguarded border and melt into the vast, unruly lands of Florida. Seminole Indians, already refugees from the growing white population north of Florida, often welcomed escaped slaves and created new communities that were united in their dislike of the Americans. Americans just north of the Florida border were hungry for more land. Many ignored international boundaries and crossed into Florida to farm and build settlements. These settlers in turn demanded U.S. protection from the Seminoles and Creeks, who had been displaced by the Treaty of Fort Jackson and were determined to defend their new land in Florida.

In 1817, Andrew Jackson, a military hero after his victories in 1814 and 1815, told President James Monroe and Secretary of State John Quincy Adams that he could seize Florida in 60 days. The president and Adams did not want a war with Spain but, in language that was deliberately vague, called on Jackson to attack the Seminoles who were harassing white settlers and gave him "full powers to conduct the war in the manner he may judge best." Given how Jackson had conducted the war against the Creeks, Monroe and Adams knew what their orders meant.

Jackson's army marched into Florida. They could not find many Seminoles, who were adept at disappearing into swamps and marshes, but they burned their villages and crops. They also seized Spanish forts and arrested a Scots trader named Alexander Arbuthnot and another British subject, Robert Armbrister, charged them with assisting the Seminoles, and after a quick trial executed both. When his troops did find Seminole and Creek leaders, Jackson simply executed them, including Hillis Hadjo, a Creek spiritual prophet who had been part of Tecumseh's movement.

The execution of Indians did not cause an uproar in the United States or Europe, but an American general executing British subjects in Spanish territory caused an international incident. Monroe and Adams, however, were skillful diplomats. They managed both to distance themselves from Jackson and use what Adams called "the Jackson Magic"—his immense popularity after his victories in the War of 1812—to bring pressure on Spain.

In fact, Spain did not care much about Florida but did have serious concerns about the independence movements in the Spanish colonies in Mexico and South America. The Spanish authorities wanted assurance that the United States would not aid or recognize these revolutions. Spain was also deeply worried about its control of the land from Texas to California. It was more than willing to trade Florida for assurances about Texas and the revolutions further south. Monroe briefly considered making a bid for Texas, but he decided that it was more trouble than it was worth and agreed to the treaty.

Instead of pursuing a claim to Texas, Monroe and Adams decided to ask Spain for its support in the areas that Lewis and Clark had explored. Spain, Great Britain, and Russia all claimed the same territory along the Pacific coast known as Oregon. By the late 1700s, explorers from New Spain were making claims as far north as Alaska. At the same time, Russian fur traders and explorers had established permanent Russian settlements, complete with Orthodox churches, in Alaska and almost as far south as San Francisco. British sea captains, notably James Cook in the 1770s, had explored the Oregon coast. British explorers coming overland from Canada made land claims, among them the Hudson's Bay Company trading post at the mouth of the Columbia River, which represented the largest European settlement in the region. An earlier U.S. claim, based on Lewis and Clark's explorations in 1805, was weak by comparison, and there were no U.S. settlements in Oregon. Of course, the native peoples of the region had little use for any of the claims, though they traded with all the claimants. Nevertheless, despite its weak claim, the United States had an interest in Oregon. While some in Congress thought Oregon was far too distant and barren to be of interest, Adams—prompted by the merchant and fur trader John Jacob Astor—saw the value of an American presence at the mouth of the Columbia River, not only for access to the fur trade there but as a way to enter the Pacific trade with Asia.

In the 1819 **Adams-Onís Treaty** with Spain, Spain not only ceded Florida to the United States but also agreed to transfer Spanish rights to the Oregon Territory to the United States. It was a significant accomplishment. The United States paid $5 million in Spanish debts, and the deal was done. All of Florida was now a U.S. territory. While the United States was negotiating with Spain, it was also negotiating with Great Britain about Oregon. In 1818, Adams negotiated the Anglo-American Convention in which Britain and the United States agreed to joint control of the Pacific Northwest for 10 years and to resolve other issues in the future. The two treaties with Spain and Britain gave the United States as strong a claim to Oregon as either Britain or Russia, a claim it would not forget. Just before he ended his tenure as Secretary of State, Adams agreed to an 1824 treaty with Russia that set the border of Alaska much farther north, leaving it to the United States and Britain to resolve questions about Oregon, which they finally did; only in 1846 (see Map 8-3).

Adams-Onís Treaty

An 1819 treaty between the United States and Spain that led to American acquisition of Florida and American rights in the Oregon Territory in return for a $5 million payment to Spain.

MAP 8-3 Expanding Borders, 1817–1823. During his term as secretary of state, John Quincy Adams negotiated a series of treaties that established the border between Maine and the Louisiana Territory and British Canada as well as created a joint U.S.-British ownership of Oregon, and also acquired Florida from Spain.

Monroe Doctrine
A declaration by President James Monroe in 1823 that the Western Hemisphere was to be closed off to further European colonization and that the United States would not allow European interference in the internal affairs of independent nations anywhere in the Americas.

The Monroe Doctrine

Having taken Florida and asserted a claim to Oregon, the United States agreed—for the time being—to stay out of Spain's way in Texas and California. Nevertheless, the Monroe administration took further steps to consolidate U.S. power in the Americas. In 1822, despite earlier promises to Spain, the United States officially recognized the new independent states of Chile, Colombia, Mexico, and Peru. If Latin America was, in fact, going to be independent of Spain, then the United States meant to be both the region's benefactor and prime trade partner.

Then, going a big step further in a speech to Congress in December 1823, President Monroe declared that, henceforth, the United States would not allow European intervention or the acquisition of any new territory by a European power in North and South America. Coming less than a decade after the United States had almost lost its independence in the War of 1812, it was a bold announcement. A complex set of international developments led Monroe and Secretary of State John Quincy Adams to formulate this stance, which became known as the **Monroe Doctrine**.

On the Pacific coast, Russian Tsar Alexander I was pressing Russian claims not only to Alaska but also to much of the Oregon Territory in the Pacific Northwest. In 1821, Alexander issued an imperial edict that claimed much of the Pacific coast and gave the Russian-American Company the right to trade there. The Russians threatened to confiscate American ships that traveled too far north, even though more American than Russian sailors were actually taking the sea lions and whales and trading with the Alaskan natives. Nevertheless, for the United States, Russian actions represented a dangerous European intrusion.

Halfway across the world, Greek patriots, borrowing language from the American Revolution, declared independence from the Ottoman Empire, and liberal constitutionalists briefly took power in Spain. The Greek and Spanish revolts were tricky for Monroe and Adams. Many Americans were sympathetic with the Greeks, but the administration also wanted good relationships with the Ottomans. In addition, American sentiment was on the side of a revolution in Spain. These situations in

Russian claims to Alaska dated back to the 1700s, but by the 1820s, the Russians were building up colonies, including their largest one in Sitka, Alaska. These outposts, complete with Russian Orthodox churches, fostered trade with indigenous Alaskans and provided fresh supplies for ships taking fish and sea lions off the coast.

Europe, though not the center of American concern, still had to be responded to carefully, given the strength of public opinion. Much more pressing, however, was the revolutionary activity in the Americas. Taking the wrong side in the revolutions of Latin America could hurt the United States politically and economically for a long time to come while little could be gained from interfering in Europe.

At the tense moment when the United States was considering ways to respond to Russian pressure and to revolutions around the world, British Foreign Secretary George Canning proposed a joint British-American declaration in which both nations would oppose European intervention in the Americas, including efforts to restore Spain's control, and that neither Great Britain nor the United States would have any territorial interests in the Americas. Canning's proposal was a problem for Monroe and Adams. They did not want Spain to reassert power in the Americas, and Britain's influence would be helpful in preventing it. But both the president and his secretary of state had their eyes on eventual U.S. takeover of parts of the Spanish Empire, from Texas to California and perhaps Cuba. Canning's hands-off agreement would jeopardize long-term American interests.

In the end, Monroe and Adams concluded that they would leave it to the Europeans to deal with Greece and Spain and essentially declared noninvolvement in the "internal affairs of Europe." On the other hand, they used President Monroe's December 2, 1823, message to Congress to say that any nation of the Americas that had assumed "free and independent conditions" would "henceforth not be considered as subjects of colonization by any European power." Many Europeans were amazed at what they saw as the arrogance of the new and still relatively weak United States. It was not clear that the country could enforce the new policy. But the Monroe Doctrine, which began as a simple diplomatic maneuver, became a bedrock of U.S. foreign policy. The independence not only of the United States but of all of the independent Americas from European control was, it seemed, the country's business. The new policy had no impact on Britain's long-standing control of Canada or Russia's dominance of Alaska or, indeed, on those colonies that Spain still claimed in Latin America. But it did announce that the United States would oppose any *new* colonies anywhere in the Americas. With the Monroe Doctrine, the U.S. government was again reflecting Jeffersonian pragmatism. It might be a small country of farmers, but the United States was claiming vast new influence in all of North and South America. It was a diplomatic expansion that was being matched by an era of economic expansion, growth that was unimagined when Thomas Jefferson took the oath of office in 1801.

> **8.5** **Quick Review** How did the outcome of the War of 1812 allow the U.S. government to pursue its expansionist goals and issue the Monroe Doctrine?

CONCLUSION

When Thomas Jefferson became president of the United States in 1801, much of the country's population, cities, seaports, agriculture, industry, indeed, much of its economy, was contained within the original 13 states. Within the next 20 years, under his leadership and that of handpicked successors James Madison and James Monroe, the country's territorial claims would extend to the Pacific Ocean. Much of this growth originated in Jefferson's republican beliefs and his agrarian ideal of a nation of independent farmers rather than a nation run by any elites.

Significant political and social developments also occurred during the first two decades of the 1800s. With the U.S. Supreme Court's *Marbury v. Madison* decision in 1803, the Court essentially gave itself the authority to decide the constitutionality of any law passed by Congress. Religion played an increasing role in society, even as the last states ended their support for specific churches. Many Protestant groups made significant new gains among both white and black adherents with revivals in what came to be known as the Second Great Awakening.

The Louisiana Purchase opened up trade along the Mississippi River and through New Orleans. Lewis and Clark led an expedition to explore the huge expanse of new U.S. territory, even venturing beyond its scope to reach the Pacific Ocean. Their explorations, aided greatly by various Indian tribes, revealed tremendous potential for future American growth.

Tensions leading up to the War of 1812 began during Jefferson's term and came to a head under the administration of Madison. Ultimately, the inconclusive war resolved issues that had limited U.S. development for decades, and launched a new period of growth for the country. It was the last war ever fought between the United States and Great Britain. It was also the last war in which Indian tribes were allied with another nation against the United States, and afterward, the United States dealt with Native Americans as an "internal matter" rather than a focus of foreign policy.

Although the cost was high in terms of lives lost, money spent, and economies devastated, the end of the war left the United States more confident, proud, and self-sufficient than ever before. With peace came further territorial expansion, especially a series of treaties between 1817 and 1823 that established the border with Canada, gave the nation joint ownership of the Oregon Territory with Great Britain, and gave the country control of Florida. The end of the war also launched an extraordinary economic and commercial transition that fundamentally changed the nation and transformed the lives of Americans. The bold new confidence of the United States, reflected in the Monroe Doctrine declaring that there could be no new European claims on any lands in North or South America, surprised the world.

CHAPTER REVIEW — What are the most significant differences between the United States in 1800 and the United States in 1823? Why are these differences more important than others?

Chapter 8   Chapter Review

JEFFERSON AND THE REPUBLICAN IDEAL

8.1   Explain how Jefferson's republicanism shaped and reflected the nation's democratic culture.

Review Questions

1. **Contextualization**
   What did Americans in the early 1800s mean by the terms *equality* and *independence*? What role did these terms play in shaping their social and political ideals?

2. **Crafting Arguments**
   Defend or refute the following statement: Thomas Jefferson, in both his policy choices and personal life, embodied the spirit of republicanism in the early 1800s. What evidence can you present to support your position? What evidence might support a different argument?

3. **Comparison**
   How did the political culture of the United States in the early decades of the 1800s differ from the political culture of the late 1700s? How would you explain the differences you note?

THE IDEAL OF RELIGIOUS FREEDOM

8.2   Explain how Americans applied new individualist ideals in their religion and how the expansion of faith-based organizations supported, yet also challenged, Jeffersonian republicanism.

Review Questions

4. **Comparison**
   Compare and contrast the views of Thomas Jefferson and Lyman Beecher on the relationship between church and state. What conflicting values were at the heart of their disagreement?

5. **Historical Interpretation**
   When some historians have described the United States as being built on faith in "dynamic democracy" and "evangelical religion," what did they mean? Is this description an accurate interpretation of U.S. history in the years from 1800 to 1820?

6. **Crafting Arguments**
   Why did African-Americans, both slave and free, develop their own segregated religious institutions and gatherings over the course of the early 1800s? What needs might such churches and gatherings have met that white churches did not?

BEYOND THE MISSISSIPPI: THE LOUISIANA PURCHASE AND THE EXPEDITION OF LEWIS AND CLARK

8.3   Explain what effects the Louisiana Purchase and the westward expansion had on how Americans saw themselves.

Review Questions

7. **Chronological Reasoning**
   How did events in Europe and Haiti create the opportunity for the United States to acquire the Louisiana Territory?

8. **Comparison**
   Compare and contrast race relations in New Orleans and the rest of the United States during the early 1800s.

THE WAR OF 1812

8.4   Analyze the causes and impact of the War of 1812.

Review Questions

9. **Chronological Reasoning**
   Trace the growing tensions between the United States and Britain between 1783 and 1812. What events were most crucial in propelling the two nations toward war?

10. **Historical Interpretation**
    How would you explain the sectional divide over the War of 1812? Why did the war find the most support in the southern and western states and territories and the least support in New England?

11. **Synthesis**
    What were the long-term consequences of the war? Is it fair to describe the War of 1812 as an inconclusive war? Why or why not?

EXPANDING AMERICAN TERRITORY AND INFLUENCE

8.5   Analyze how the United States acquired new territory and increased influence abroad.

Review Questions

12. **Crafting Arguments**
    Evaluate the role of individual American settlers in shaping American foreign policy in the early 1800s. How did the desire of Americans to move beyond the boundaries of the United States create both opportunities and challenges for the federal government?

13. **Historical Interpretation**
    In what ways did the articulation of the Monroe Doctrine represent a turning point in American history? What light does the doctrine shed on the vision of America's future shared by the doctrine's supporters?

9 New Industries, New Politics

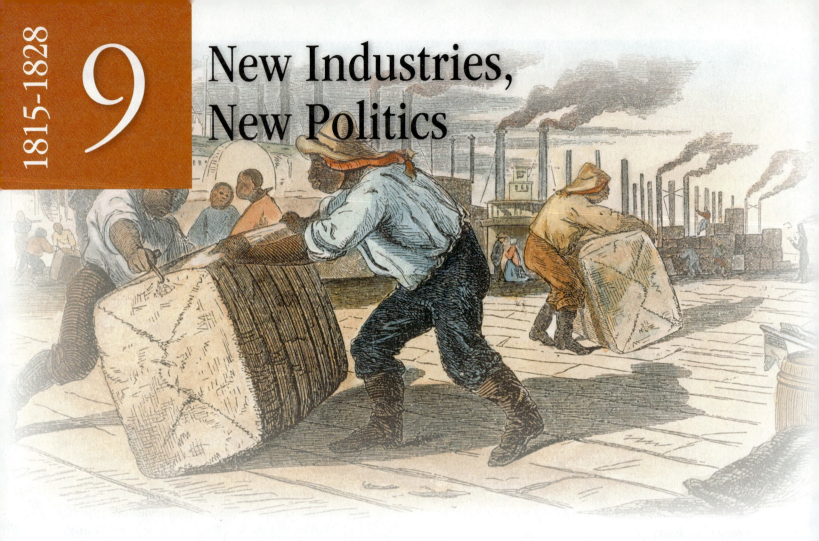

CHAPTER OBJECTIVE

Demonstrate an understanding of the changes in the U.S. economy brought about by the rapid expansion of cotton production, other commercial and financial developments, and the impact of these changes on U.S. political life.

LEARNING OBJECTIVES

CREATING THE COTTON ECONOMY

9.1 Explain the role of cotton in transforming the land and the lives of diverse people in the United States.

COMMERCE, TECHNOLOGY, AND TRANSPORTATION

9.2 Analyze the technological and financial changes that led to the emergence of a new market economy in the United States.

FROM THE ERA OF GOOD FEELINGS TO THE POLITICS OF DIVISION

9.3 Explain the political developments in the United States during the 1820s, including the shift of power toward the South and West that resulted from the changing economic situation.

This picture of large bales of cotton being loaded onto steamships by slave labor reflects much of the economic development of the nation in the decades after the end of the War of 1812.

The end of the War of 1812, Andrew Jackson's victory at New Orleans, the American takeover of Florida, and the Monroe Doctrine were all far from primary concerns of many Americans in the years after 1815. Something much closer to home—cotton—was transforming their lives. The rapid growth of cotton production changed the lives of more Americans, whether or not they were directly involved in cotton production, than any other development between 1800 and the Civil War. Cotton transformed the nation's physical, commercial, and political landscape.

Henry Bibb, a former slave, described what cotton meant to him and his fellow slaves on a Louisiana cotton plantation that had only recently been developed:

> The object of blowing the horn for them two hours before day, was, that they should get their bit to eat, before they went to the field, that they need not stop to eat but once during the day....I have often heard the sound of the slave driver's lash on the backs, of slaves, and their heart-rending shrieks....I have known the slaves to be so much fatigued from labor that they could scarcely get to their lodging places from the fields at night.

Slaves working on the new cotton plantations of the ever expanding cotton-growing regions of the nation knew little respite from the fatiguing labor. They had to clear the land before they could plant, and once planted, the cotton plants needed almost constant care. The harvest was intensive, and much work was required afterward to prepare the harvest for market. Because of the value of the cotton crop and increasing demands for it, there was constant pressure to work harder and no end to the punishment for those who did not produce as expected.

While Bibb and thousands of other slaves cultivated the cotton, young women working in the mills, or textile factories, of Lowell, Massachusetts, turned it into cloth to be sold around the world. An anonymous worker described her life in a mill:

> Since I was between seven and eight years old, I have been employed almost without intermission in a factory, which is almost 18 years....I do not wonder at your surprise that the operatives were worked in the summer season, from five in the morning till seven in the evening....The time we are required to labor is altogether too long. It is more than our constitutions can bear. If any one doubts it, let them come into our mills of a summer's day, at four or five o'clock, in the afternoon, and see the drooping, weary persons moving about, as though their legs were hardly able to support their bodies.

North or South, for slaves in fields and workers in factories, cotton was wearying work. For some, cotton brought extraordinary wealth as "King Cotton" came to dominate the U.S. economy, but for others, drudgery permeated life. In one way or another, the rise and dominance of the cotton industry affected almost all Americans.

The transformation of the U.S. economy immediately after the War of 1812 involved many changes that made cotton dominant, including new inventions like cotton gins and steamboats, new institutions like corporations, and a different kind of bank—all of which worked together to expand the national economy. These changing economic and social structures also affected the political scene. The new cotton-based economy made slaves much more valuable and slave owners more anxious to defend slavery. At the same time, many northerners, including northerners in cotton industries, became more hostile to slaveholding, which led to deep national divisions.

CREATING THE COTTON ECONOMY

9.1 Explain the role of cotton in transforming the land and the lives of diverse people in the United States.

Cotton's dominant role in the economy came about quickly. In 1800, a few southern plantations grew enough cotton to make cloth for their own use and ship a few bags to England, but the dominant plantation cash crops were rice, indigo, tobacco, and in southern Louisiana, sugar. But after the War of 1812, cotton quickly outstripped every other American export and remained a major American industry until the 1930s.

Demand and Technology

Two developments in the late 1790s set the stage for the rapid expansion of cotton production in the United States. First, during this period, many Europeans came to prefer cotton clothing to the wool or linen that had clothed them for generations. Cotton was cooler and more comfortable than wool, and it was getting cheaper. Most of Europe's cotton came from India via Great Britain's East India Company, but India could not produce enough cotton to meet Europe's growing demand.

The second development was a set of technological changes that launched the worldwide expansion of cotton. In England in 1733, John Kay invented a "flying shuttle" that made weaving cloth much faster and allowed a single weaver to handle a loom that previously required many weavers. In 1764, James Hargreaves invented the spinning jenny, which could run multiple spindles, each spinning cotton into thread. By 1800, a single jenny could be seen operating up to 120 spindles at once. In 1769, Richard Arkwright patented a "water frame" that used waterpower to drive the spinning process, a major step toward mass production, while James Watt's coal-powered

1794	Eli Whitney patents the cotton gin
1812	Francis Cabot Lowell returns from England after memorizing plans for Manchester's mills
1813	Boston Manufacturing Company chartered to build mills in United States
1815	The end of the War of 1812 launches era of economic prosperity
1816	Beginning of "Alabama Fever"—development of Alabama and Mississippi cotton plantations
1817	New York legislature authorizes construction of Erie Canal
1819	Financial panic
	Dartmouth College v. Woodward and *McCulloch v. Maryland* Supreme Court cases
1820	Missouri Compromise
1823	Lowell, Massachusetts, laid out as a new mill town
1824	John Quincy Adams elected president after disputed election
1825	Erie Canal completed
1828	Tariff of Abominations
	Andrew Jackson elected president

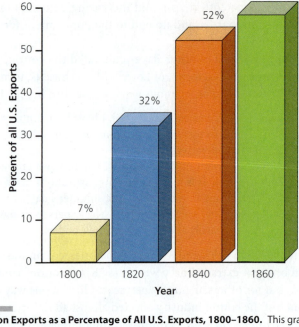

FIGURE 9-1 Cotton Exports as a Percentage of All U.S. Exports, 1800–1860. This graph illustrates the growing significance of cotton in the U.S. economy during the early 1800s. While all exports from the country were growing, cotton was quickly outstripping everything else, increasing from a tiny fraction in 1800 to one-third of all exports in the 1820 and to more than half by 1840.

A simple machine, the cotton gin dramatically speeded the cleaning of green-seed cotton, making cotton production inexpensive and enormously profitable.

cotton gin
Originally designed by Eli Whitney in 1793–94, the cotton gin (*gin* is short for *engine*) allowed the inexpensive processing of cotton.

steam engine, designed in 1763, added steam power to the English mills, expanding their size long before it provided the energy for railroads and ships.

Although developed in England, much of this technology was soon brought to the United States through transfers, legal or otherwise. British authorities knew that their new means of production were key to their industrial and political might. They provided patents for their inventors and kept their production process secret. However, in 1789, an Englishman, Samuel Slater, having been sworn to secrecy and apprenticed in Arkwright's textile business, sailed to New York to bring the industry to the United States. Slater ignored Arkwright's patents and recreated Arkwright's mechanical spinning in mills in Rhode Island. More technological transfers followed.

Despite the worldwide demand for cotton and England's growing industrial capacity for turning raw cotton into cloth, American farmers and plantation owners were skeptical that they could make money on it. Green-seed, or upland, cotton was the only kind that would grow in the American South, except for a few places on the coast or coastal islands where a more profitable variety of long-stem cotton grew. But each ball of cotton produced on a green-seed cotton plant contained many of those green seeds. They had to be removed by hand before the cotton could be spun into threads. A slave, working hard all day, could clean about 1 pound of cotton, hardly enough to make a meaningful profit. Many people sought a mechanical way to clean cotton. Eli Whitney, a recent Yale graduate who had gone south to work as a tutor, lived on the Greene family plantation at Mulberry Grove in Georgia where he became interested in devising a machine to clean cotton. He gained fame, if not fortune, for his patent on the **cotton gin** (*gin* was short for *engine*).

While serving as a tutor and tinkering with how to clean cotton, Whitney decided to try pulling the picked cotton through a screen that would allow the seeds to fall out and the clean cotton fibers to be baled for shipment. When the first model failed because the wooden teeth were too brittle, Catherine Greene, the matron of the plantation, suggested wire (from her bird cage) and a brush to keep the seeds from clogging the works. The cotton gin that Whitney patented in 1794 could clean 50 pounds of cotton a day. Others quickly improved on Whitney's model, and manufacturing cotton gins became a big business from Natchez, Mississippi, to Bridgewater, Massachusetts.

Whitney did not make his fortune from this invention; too many other people were improving it too quickly. However, he did become rich developing the idea of interchangeable parts and manufacturing rifles with such parts for the U.S. government. Interchangeable parts made everything from rifles to farm implements easier to repair since a replacement part could be counted on to work in the original gun or machine.

The cotton gin transformed the nation. The United States now had an export crop that could make it prosperous. The cotton market and the technology that made it possible led to the rapid development of new lands, especially the great plantations of Alabama, Mississippi, and Louisiana. In turn, the New England factory system that began in Rhode Island expanded to the great mill center of Lowell, Massachusetts, in 1823 and then to factories and factory towns all over the region. As the cotton market continued to grow, coastal and transatlantic shipping also expanded as more and more southern cotton was brought to the mills of New England and to the even larger mills of Manchester and Birmingham in England itself. This rather plain and simple product was a driving force for economics and technology in the period, and it seemed to have no limits.

The Land of Cotton

While some of the nation's first export cotton, the long-stem variety, was grown along the Atlantic coast and especially on the Sea Islands off the coast of the Carolinas and Georgia, the greatest cotton production involved the green-seed variety on the plantations of the so-called **black belt** (named for its rich black soil), stretching from Georgia to Louisiana. The quality of the soil made it perfect for growing cotton.

Within this black-belt area, only Georgia was one of the 13 original states. The northern parts of Alabama and Mississippi were part of the land Britain ceded to the United States at the end of the Revolution. The Louisiana Purchase added Louisiana. Andrew Jackson's defeat of the Creeks during the War of 1812 and the "Creek Cession" that he negotiated in 1816 opened much new land to white settlement, while the 1819 U.S. treaty with Spain placed the Gulf Coast of Mississippi and Alabama under U.S. control. White settlers—often single men, sometimes families—from Georgia, Tennessee, the Carolinas, and Europe, especially many Scots-Irish, poured in and brought black slaves with them. A land rush that was known as "Alabama Fever" began in 1816 just as the War of 1812 ended. Alabama was admitted as a state in 1819 with a non-Indian population of 128,000, five times what it had been in 1810. Louisiana and Mississippi were admitted in 1812 and 1817, respectively (see Map 9-1).

The federal government played a central role in the development of these lands. The first European settlers were illegal white squatters moving onto farms recently abandoned by Indians, but after the coming of peace in 1815, the federal government quickly began official surveys and legal sales of the land. Before the War of 1812, the largest sales of federal lands in 1 year had been 350,000 acres. In 1815, a million acres of newly acquired lands were sold at $2 per acre, and in 1818, 2.5 million acres were sold as the government acquired land from the Creeks and then from Spain and quickly made it available for sale. These sales helped the federal budget, and white settlement surged. The government spent some of the revenue from land sales on maintaining the army that protected the new lands. It also aided settlement by building a road from Columbia, South Carolina, to Columbus, Georgia, and then farther into the black-belt region (see Map 9-2).

The new land was fertile. Planters who had grown 300 pounds of cotton per acre in South Carolina could grow 800 to 1,000 pounds an acre in the black belt. In 1801, nine percent of the world's cotton came from the United States while 60 percent came from India. By 1820, the United States was exporting more cotton than India. By 1850, the American South was producing more than two-thirds of the world's cotton. The new technology, the new land, and the institution of slavery created great wealth for some; a poor, hard-earned living for others; and backbreaking, torturous misery for slaves.

black belt
The cotton-growing region that was developed in the early 1800s, stretching from Georgia through Alabama, Mississippi, and Louisiana, named for its rich black soil.

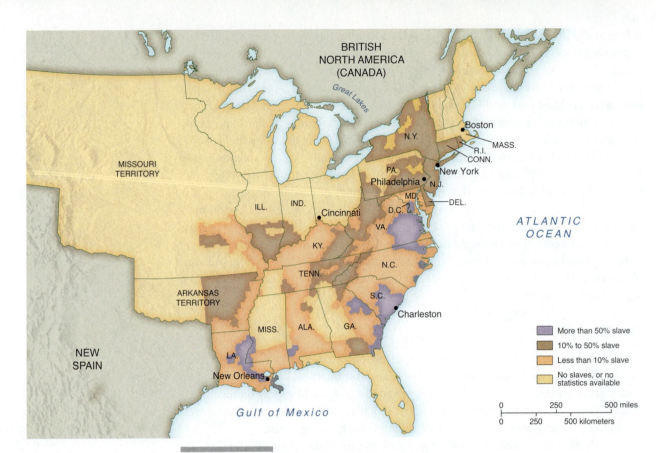

MAP 9-1 The Growth of Slavery in the Black Belt. As the black-belt area of cotton production expanded, slave labor became they key to its success and the number of slaves grew dramatically.

The People Who Worked the Land—Cotton and the Transformation of Slavery

The white settlers who were able to buy large parcels of land in the rich new territory of what was known as the Old Southwest did not do most of the hard work of actually planting, hoeing, and picking the cotton that would be grown there. Other Americans did that work: African slaves, whose lives were also transformed by the explosive growth of cotton production and whose value to their white owners increased even more than the value of the new land on which they labored.

Between 1800 and 1860, more than 1 million black Americans were forced to move from the homes they knew—and often from their families, too—to new homes in the interior cotton-growing lands of Georgia, Alabama, Mississippi, and Louisiana and later Arkansas and Texas. While slavery slowly disappeared in the North after 1800 and the slave population of Maryland, Virginia, and the Carolinas stabilized or declined, slavery exploded in the new land. In the 60 years before the Civil War, more slaves made the journey from coastal states to inland plantations than had made the terrible Middle Passage from Africa to North America in the previous 200 years.

In some ways similar to the passage from Africa to North America, the journey from a settled community in Virginia, Maryland, or the Carolinas to the new interior plantations was a terrible ordeal. As more slaves were sold into the interior or sold from place to place within it, slaves on the coast lived in terror of being sold and losing all connections to family and birthplace. Slave owners used the threat of sale, or the sale of a perceived troublemaker, to maintain discipline in the slave quarter. Slaves often pleaded with masters not to be sold. Sometimes the pleas were successful but often not. Jeff Randolph, the executor of Thomas Jefferson's estate, was considered especially humane because he refused to sell the former president's slaves to a buyer from Georgia but sold them instead, at less profit, to other Virginians. The sale of a

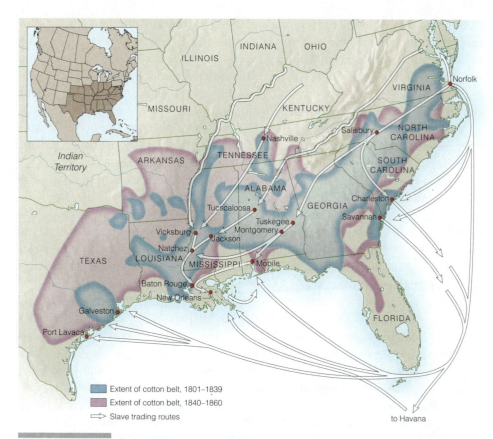

Extent of cotton belt, 1801–1839
Extent of cotton belt, 1840–1860
Slave trading routes

to Havana

MAP 9-2 The Expanding Cotton Belt. The areas of greatest cotton production in the United States grew dramatically between 1801 and 1860.

spouse broke up one slave marriage in five, and one-third of all slave children were sold away from their parents. Men were sold more often than women; planters wanted male muscle, and slave owners in older regions were happy to keep women so that they could bear more children who could, in turn, also be sold. Slaves between ages 14 and 35 were sold much more often than the very young or the aging. A literate slave, Arena Screven, learned that he was to be sold from Georgia to New Orleans and wrote to his wife "with much regret" that he hoped "if we shall not meet in this world I hope to meet in heaven." Laura Clark, a slave, remembered her mother asking another slave, who had been sold in the same group as she to "take care of my baby child... and if I never sees her no more raise her for God." Such heartbreak led many slaves to despair, to run away, or to rebel.

Once sold, either to a plantation owner who had come east for additional slaves or more often to a slave trader whose job was brokering other humans, slaves were organized in groups called slave coffles to walk west. Coffles of 20 to 50 slaves, sometimes more, trudging west became a normal sight of southern life. Walking 15 to 20 miles a day, it could take the slaves 2 months to go from Virginia to the Mississippi Valley, often longer when rain flooded streams and turned roads to mud. In later years, more slaves were transported by ship to New Orleans, which became the largest slave-trading center in the United States by the 1820s.

When they could, slaves rebelled. Slave trading was a dangerous business, and stories of slaves murdering slave traders were well known. In 1841, slaves being shipped from Norfolk, Virginia, to New Orleans on the *Creole* forced the captain to deliver them to the Bahamas, a British colony, where they found freedom because Britain had abolished slavery in 1833. More often, slaves simply ran away when they could, though many went home to family where they were recaptured and sold again.

Once slaves arrived at their destination, they often faced difficult and unfamiliar work. Work in cotton fields was backbreaking for men, women, and children. While tobacco and rice required more skill, cotton required long hours and hard work.

Cotton was planted in the early spring and required constant attention and weeding throughout the growing season. On most plantations, there was a strict gender divide: men plowed, and women and children hoed. Harvest began as early as August and lasted through September and October. Slaves worked the longest hours—from sunrise to sunset, and if there was a moon, much longer—to get the whole crop in before storms could hurt it. Prickly cotton pods cut their hands, and slaves who did not produce their quota were beaten at day's end. Finally, with the full crop in, there was a brief respite. But the winter was the time for the women to work the cotton gin and pack the cotton for market while men cleared more land and repaired buildings.

Contrary to many images of the old South, most cotton was grown on relatively small farms. Many of those who first settled and began growing cotton on the new rich lands owned relatively small plots of land and one or a few slaves. These white owners worked in the fields with the slaves or, if the farm was larger, served as their overseers. Less than one percent of the population owned the great plantations for which the South became known. In the largest plantations owned by the most wealthy planters, slaves worked in large gangs with certain slaves appointed as "drivers" to get the work done and poor whites employed as overseers to manage the whole labor force. It was on the large plantations, with constant pressure on the overseers to ensure profits, that slaves faced some of the worst conditions.

Slaves established new communities within the slave quarters. Young slaves met new partners, children were born, and the rhythms of community life were reestablished, but always under threat of dissolution. New leaders emerged within the slave community, often preachers and deacons selected by other slaves. Although legally banned from learning to read or write, slaves sometime secretly did both and taught others to do so. As memories of Africa or the African-American communities on the east coast faded in later generations, a new culture was created in the slave communities, drawing on older traditions and adapting to new contexts. Often with the permission of their owners, slaves grew their own food, made cloth for better clothing than their owners gave them, and even earned cash by selling surplus food and clothing to the free people in surrounding communities or to their own masters. While owners saw slaves exclusively as a source of muscle and work, many slaves and ex-slaves made it clear through their stories that for them family, community, faith, and the

As this picture illustrates, slaves spent long hours in the fields surrounded by the cotton they were expected to cultivate and pick with no reward for their backbreaking labor.

American Voices

Charles Ball, *Fifty Years in Chains; or, The Life of an American Slave*, 1810–1860

Charles Ball was born a slave on a tobacco plantation in Maryland. He remembered his grandfather telling of being captured into slavery in Africa. After establishing his own family in Maryland, Ball was sold to a slave trader who in turn sold him to a cotton and rice plantation in Georgia. He never saw his home or family again. Half a century later, he escaped, hid on a ship bound for Philadelphia, and lived out his days in freedom. His autobiography, *Fifty Years in Chains*, was a popular publication among abolitionists—those who supported the end of slavery.

My master kept a store at a small village on the bank of the Patuxent River….Whilst I was eating in the kitchen, I observed him talking earnestly, but low, to a stranger near the kitchen door. I soon after went out, and hitched my oxen to the cart, and was about to drive off, when several men came round about me, and amongst them the stranger whom I had seen speaking with my master. This man came up to me, and, seizing me by the collar, shook me violently, saying I was his property, and must go with him to Georgia. At the sound of these words, the thoughts of my wife and children rushed across my mind, and my heart beat away within me. I saw and knew that my case was hopeless, and that resistance was vain, as there were near twenty persons present, all of whom were ready to assist the man by whom I was kidnapped. I felt incapable of weeping or speaking, and in my despair I laughed loudly. My purchaser ordered me to cross my hands behind, which were quickly bound with a strong cord; and he then told me that we must set out that very day for the South. I asked if I could not be allowed to go see my wife and children, or if this could not be

permitted, if they might have leave to come to see me; but was told that I would be able to get another wife in Georgia.

My new master, whose name I did not hear, took me that same day across the Patuxent, where I joined fifty-one other slaves…. A strong iron collar was closely fitted by means of a padlock round each of our necks. A chain of iron, about a hundred feet in length, was passed through the hasp of each padlock, except at the two ends, where the hasps of the padlock passed through a link of the chain….

Our master ordered a pot of mush to be made for our supper; after dispatching which all lay down on the naked floor to sleep in our handcuffs and chains. The women, my fellow-slaves, lay on one side of the room; and the men who were chained with me, occupied the other. I slept but little this night, which I passed in thinking of my wife and little children whom I could not hope ever to see again. I also thought of my grandfather, and of the long nights I had passed with him, listening to his narratives of the scenes through which he had passed in Africa.

Source: Charles Ball, *Fifty Years in Chains; or, The Life of An American Slave* (New York: H. Dayton, 1860), pp. 28–31, 240–241, 280.

Thinking Critically

1. **Documentary Analysis**
   What aspects of his sale were most traumatizing for Ball? Why?
2. **Historical Interpretation**
   What light does Ball's story shed on major trends in slavery and slave ownership in the first half of the 1800s?

hope for freedom were the highest priority. Studies of the advertisements for runaway slaves also made it clear that slaves never stopped running away no matter how far they might have to run. Similarly, small- and large-scale slave revolts never stopped.

Cotton in the North—Factories and the People Who Worked in Them

The technology that made cotton the core of the Industrial Revolution in the United States developed in England and North America during the 1700s. Just before the War of 1812, American Francis Cabot Lowell, who had spent 2 years working in and observing the British mills in Manchester, brought the technology he learned there to the United States. When he left Britain, customs agents searched his baggage to be sure he was not bringing with him drawings or plans from the British mills, which were a closely guarded national secret. But Lowell had simply been memorizing the plans. Like Slater, an Englishman who had transferred British secrets about mechanic spinning to Rhode Island mills in 1789, Lowell was ready to build a British-style mill in Massachusetts. Lowell also brought with him a second, equally important idea—the multishareholder corporation that could raise more money than any one individual could provide and could offer less risk to investors.

In 1813, Lowell incorporated a new business with Patrick T. Jackson and Nathan Appleton: the Boston Manufacturing Company. Lowell and his mechanic, Paul Moody, recreated a British-style power loom in Massachusetts. With these steps, they established what would be the heart of American manufacturing for the next century: the multiowner corporation that produced cotton fabric in a large factory.

The partners built their first factory, or mill, at Waltham, Massachusetts, on the Charles River. After Lowell's death in 1817, they then created a new city in 1823: Lowell, Massachusetts, that housed an even larger complex, using the 30-foot drop of the Merrimack River to power mills that could turn cotton into cloth for a domestic and international market at an astounding rate. Similar large operations sprang up on New Hampshire rivers in Manchester, Dover, and Nashua and on other Massachusetts rivers in Chicopee, Holyoke, and Lawrence. Where Samuel Slater's mills in Rhode Island had been rather small, family affairs, the factories and towns that Lowell and his colleagues built transformed the industry and the lives of the people involved in it. With the creation of Lowell as a new industrial city, the American Industrial Revolution was born.

The Boston Associates needed workers for their giant looms and mills. They turned first to young women from the farms where most New Englanders still lived. More men than women had been heading west for decades, and New England had a surplus of young women. Farm life was hard, young women were kept in subservient positions, and the independence and the potential to earn their own money appealed to many young women. To avoid the squalid conditions of the English factories, Lowell and his colleagues built clean, company boarding houses for their female employees, complete with chaperones and opportunities for religious and educational activities. For the most part, they hired only single young women whose living conditions (and virtue) they could control (see Map 9-3).

The young women who worked in Lowell's mills in the early 1800s were known as "factory girls." Lowell was a show town, and its owners published the *Lowell Offering* to tell the world about the success of the venture and the good life the women who worked there enjoyed. The *Lowell Offering* attracted new investors to the business and new young recruits to work in the mills. But life at Lowell and the other mill towns was less rosy than the *Lowell Offering* reported. Conditions may have been better than in the "dark satanic mills" of Britain, but the work was hard, the hours long, and the conditions harsh.

This idealized print of women working at their machines gives little hint of the noise, danger, and drudgery of 14-hour work days where a moment's lack of attention could lead to a disaster.

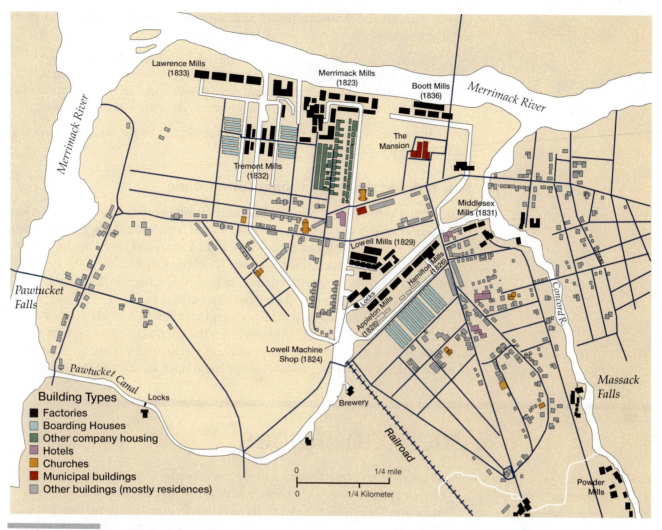

Building Types

- ■ Factories
- ■ Boarding Houses
- ■ Other company housing
- ■ Hotels
- ■ Churches
- ■ Municipal buildings
- ■ Other buildings (mostly residences)

0   1/4 mile

0   1/4 Kilometer

MAP 9-3 Lowell, Massachusetts in 1832. The water-powered mills of the new company town of Lowell, Massachusetts, had to be very close to the rivers that surrounded the town, but the company also built boarding houses for the workers in close proximity to the mills making the trip to work and the supervision of the workers quite easy.

A New Hampshire newspaper, the *Dover Gazette,* friendly to the factory girls, reported on an 1834 strike by the young women, one of the first strikes in America:

> In consequence of the notice...[that] their wages would be reduced, to enable their employers to meet the *"unusual pressure of the times,"* the girls, to the number of between 600 and 700, assembled in the Court-House on Saturday afternoon, to devise ways and means to enable themselves to meet the *"pressure of the times"* anticipated from this threatened reduction.

The first strikes did not last long and did not win concessions. The company had too much power and the women too little. Still, news of the unrest tarnished the image of Lowell as a benevolent community run in the interests of its workers. A second strike 2 years later—described by one of the participants in the following American Voices feature—also failed.

By the 1840s, conditions had become much tougher in Lowell. The mill owners' benevolence had worn off. The option of quitting and returning home, which had provided a way to escape the mill life during the 1830s, was disappearing because of an agricultural depression in New England. Young women stayed in Lowell, not necessarily because they wanted to, but because they had few other choices. Period publications like *The Voice of Industry* published their letters and articles, which described the challenges they faced and what hopes they had. One woman, known only as Ada, shared these challenges and hopes in biblical terms that her peers would appreciate:

> "Do unto others, as ye would that they should do to you," is a great precept, given to us by our great Teacher....What but the neglect of this great principle, has brought into the world all this confusion, this disorder, this isolated state of interest, between man and man; all this monopoly and competition in business?

As the Industrial Revolution expanded, Ada would not be the last one to ask that question.

New York and the International Cotton Trade

As significant as the mills of New England were in cotton production, most American cotton was shipped in its raw state to Manchester and Leeds in England. The permanent peace that had been established between the United States and Great Britain after the end of the War of 1812 made this trade easy. New York City became the center of the shipment of cotton across the Atlantic and, in the process, became the nation's largest city and commercial center, a position it has retained ever since.

New York City enjoyed several advantages that allowed it to play such a dominant role in the nation's cotton economy, even though no cotton was grown within hundreds of miles of the city and few cotton mills were nearby. First, New York had an extraordinary deep-water harbor. Ships could dock directly in Manhattan and

American Voices

Harriet H. Robinson worked in the cotton mills at Lowell from 1835 to 1848. She was 10 when she began and left at age 23 to be married. She published her story half a century later. The book, Loom and Spindle: Or Life Among the Early Mill Girls, remains a classic story of what life was like for the first generation of young women, most fresh from the farms, to take these jobs.

The working-hours of all the girls extended from five o'clock in the morning until seven in the evening, with one-half hour for breakfast and for dinner....

One of the first strikes of cotton-factory operatives that ever took place in this country was that in Lowell, in October, 1836. When it was announced that the wages were to be cut down, great indignation was felt, and it was decided to strike, *en mass.* This was done. The mills were shut down, and the girls went in procession...and listened to "incendiary" speeches from early labor reformers.

One of the girls stood on a pump, and gave vent to the feelings of her companions in a neat speech, declaring that it was their duty to resist all attempts at cutting down the wages. This was the first time a woman had spoken in public in Lowell, and the event caused surprise and consternation among her audience....

My own recollection of this first strike (or "turn out" as it was called) is very vivid. I worked in a lower room, where I had heard the proposed strike fully, if not vehemently, discussed; I had been an ardent listener to what was said against this attempt at "oppression" on the part of the corporation, and naturally I took sides with the strikers. When the day came on which the girls were to turn out, those in the upper rooms started first, and so many of them left that our mill was at once shut down. Then, when the girls in my room stood irresolute, uncertain what to do, asking each other, "Would you?" or "shall we turn out?" and not one of them having the courage to lead off, I, who began to think they would not go out, after all their talk, became impatient, and started on ahead, saying, with childish bravado, "I don't care what you do, I am going to turn out, whether anyone else does or not;" and I marched out, and was followed by the others.

As I looked back at the long line that followed me, I was more proud than I have ever been since at any success I may have achieved, and more proud than I shall ever be again until my own beloved State gives to its women citizens the right of suffrage.

Source: Harriet H. Robinson, *Loom and Spindle: Or Life Among the Early Mill Girls* (Boston: T.Y. Crowell, 1898.), pp. 31, 83–85.

Thinking Critically

1. Documentary Analysis
How did Robinson explain the factors that led to her decision to join the strike at her mill?

2. Contextualization
How did work in a textile factory change Robinson's outlook? What connections can you make between her strike experience and her commitment to the suffrage movement?

Brooklyn without needing to anchor offshore and unload goods to smaller boats. The port was also easily accessible by coastal vessels from southern ports. As the production of cotton expanded after 1815, most of the South's cotton was shipped north to New York and then reshipped either across the Atlantic to English ports or up Long Island Sound to Boston for the New England mills. Second, New York already had the infrastructure necessary to accommodate this level of shipping, including miles of docks and a community of merchants. Third, New York, an established port already, had experienced workers, including dockworkers and longshoremen (who handled cargo), to handle the hundreds of ships that did business there. The already large numbers of workers grew rapidly as New York (not counting Brooklyn, which was a separate city until 1898) grew six times its size between the American Revolution and 1820. In 1820, it mushroomed again from 125,000 residents, and to over 500,000 in 1850.

New York businesses sent agents (called "factors") to Charleston, South Carolina; Savannah, Georgia; Mobile, Alabama; and New Orleans to buy cotton for shipment to New York. In turn, the cotton was transferred from coastal ships to larger transatlantic ships that sailed to ports in England, racing each other to make the trip in the shortest amount of time.

On the return trip from England, these ships brought cash from the sale of cotton and all sorts of British and European goods—iron and steel tools from Sheffield, England, wine from France, and manufactured goods that the United States needed and that could often be bought in New York for less than it cost to make them elsewhere in America. While American manufacturers disliked this reality, merchants from across the country flocked to New York to stock up on cheap goods, enhancing the city's commerce.

In 1818, shipping across the Atlantic was improved when a Quaker businessman, Jeremiah Thompson, founded the Black Ball Line and established a fixed schedule of weekly departures of fast ships from New York to Liverpool, England. The Black Ball Line announced that it had "undertaken to establish a line of vessels between NEW YORK and LIVERPOOL, to sail from each place on a certain day in every month through the year," and printed the schedule. Until that time, commercial vessels waited to fill their holds with cargo, however long that took, before sailing. Now with the fixed schedule, passengers and goods could be sure of leaving on time, and factories in England could be sure of a steady flow of cotton to keep their mills operating.

The new ships were called packet ships because the line had a contract with the federal government to carry packets of U.S. mail. These packet ships became a regular feature of world commerce and New York's waterfront. Any packet ship captain who made the trip to Liverpool in under 22 days or the return trip to New York (which took longer because of less favorable winds) in under 35 days would be rewarded with a new coat and a dress for his wife, courtesy of Thompson. Competition with the Black Ball Line soon developed, and the passenger cabins became elegant as different lines competed for business. Shipwrights along New York's East River changed the construction of new ships so they could make the voyage even more quickly than the original schedule. But most important, the Black Ball Line's ships and its many competitors that emerged in the 1820s and 1830s ensured a steady supply of cotton for English mills and steady profits to U.S. cotton growers.

New York was also the place in the United States to raise money. From the time Alexander Hamilton established the first Bank of the United States in New York City in 1791, some New Yorkers grew rich financing commercial activities that were far away from the city itself. Many farmers had long needed to borrow money for seed and fertilizer to plant a crop. After industrialists like Francis Cabot Lowell began creating giant new corporations to build the factories for producing the cotton cloth that launched the industrial revolution, they too needed ways to borrow much larger amounts of money as well as longer periods of time to make profits and pay off the loans. Without such financing, the Industrial Revolution would never have happened. Financial brokers had agreed to work together in New York in 1792, and the New

York Stock Exchange was founded in 1817, to support this large-scale commerce by allowing investors to pool funds and create new industries as well as commercial enterprises that were larger than any one person, even a rich one, could fund alone.

New York was also home to many banks, investment houses, and insurance companies that helped finance the cotton industry. Nautilus Insurance Company wrote over 300 life insurance policies on slaves, which protected the investments of plantation owners even if those policies did nothing for the slaves themselves. The investment house that became Brown Brothers, Harriman loaned millions of dollars to southern growers to finance the planting and shipping of cotton as well as the buying of slaves. At one point, the company owned three plantations and 346 slaves in Louisiana when owners defaulted on their loans. In general, however, New York financiers made their profits in trade and commerce and kept their distance from the institution of slavery and the risks of cotton growing. Jeremiah Thompson of the Black Ball Line made his fortune transporting slave-grown cotton, though as a Quaker, he opposed slavery itself.

The extraordinary growth of cotton production in the South, the shipment of cotton within and beyond the United States, and the seemingly insatiable European demand for cotton cloth resulted in a rapid growth of the industry. In 1800, Great Britain imported 56 million pounds of raw cotton, 16 percent from the United States and most of the rest from India. After an economic downturn that disrupted the entire industry and more, production once again began to pick up, and by 1830, Britain imported 264 million pounds of cotton, 77 percent from the United States, and by 1840, 592 million pounds, 81 percent from the United States. Once again, the demand seemed endless, but many were now a bit wiser.

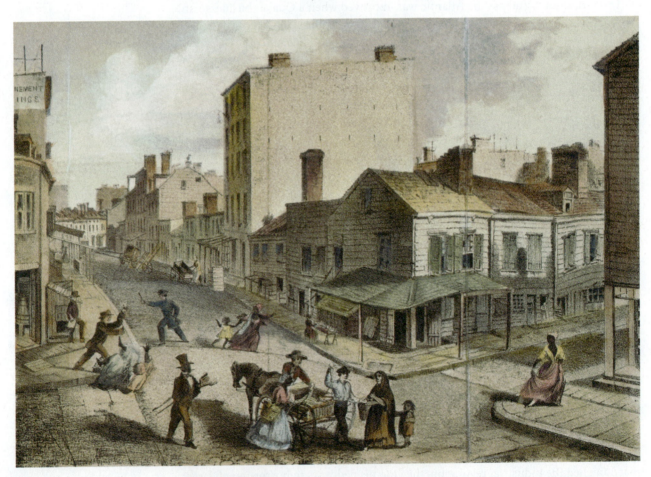

With the development of the trans-Atlantic cotton trade and the opening of the Erie Canal, New York City grew rapidly in its commercial success. However, especially in hard times, the city was also plagued with areas of squalid poverty. Many New Yorkers lived in the most difficult conditions, especially in the notorious crime-filled Five Points neighborhood of Lower Manhattan.

The Panic of 1819

The boom in the industry was not, as it turned out, a continual progression. As more Americans invested in land or slaves to grow cotton or in the commercial activities that flowed from cotton, the optimism led them to become financially overextend. Suddenly in 1819, the growth came to a sudden if temporary halt. After 4 years of peace, Europe was growing more food, and a good harvest in 1818 meant less need for imported American grain. In addition, more raw cotton was being delivered to Liverpool than the mills could process, and new mills took time to build. The value of cotton fell from 32.5 cents a pound in October 1818 to 24 cents a pound in December. By early 1819, it was only 14 cents a pound. At that price, it was not profitable to grow cotton, to invest in land to plant more cotton, or to ship cotton either to New York or to Europe.

Unfortunately, the Bank of the United States decided to protect itself by limiting credit and calling in loans. State banks followed suit, and investors and farmers could not pay their debts. Small businesses failed, farms were foreclosed, and people across the country lost their jobs. The great migration west came to a halt, at least for the time being, and the business cycle slowed dangerously. At the time, no one knew when or indeed if, prosperity would return. A national economy was a new thing in the United States, and it was not well understood. In earlier eras, what happened to New England shipping had little impact further south, and a crisis in southern tobacco never had much impact further north. By 1819, however, the nation's economy was interconnected as never before and, as a result, a widespread depression affected all Americans. The boom-and-bust cycle of this young industrial economy was also new, and people were shocked. Eventually, the economy and the country recovered, but it took years and much hardship. In the middle of that first national depression, however, Americans worried about the future. The price of cotton and the value of the cotton industry eventually rebounded and grew beyond anything imagined before the panic, but those successes would be at least partly tempered by what had happened.

9.1 Quick Review Why did cotton come to be known as King Cotton in the early 1800s?

COMMERCE, TECHNOLOGY, AND TRANSPORTATION

9.2 Analyze the technological and financial changes that led to the emergence of a new market economy in the United States.

While cotton was the prime factor in the growth of the U.S. economy after 1815, it was not the only one. North American wheat and corn had been feeding Britain and continental Europe long before North American cotton began to clothe them. Trees from North American forests provided wood for ships and buildings on both sides of the Atlantic. North American furs remained in demand as they had been before the American Revolution. And as more Americans moved further into the interior, improvements in internal transportation became essential for the country's commercial development.

The Erie Canal

The Hudson River offered easy north-south connections between New Yorkers in Manhattan and Brooklyn and farmers along the river valley up to Albany and beyond, but the heartland of New York State, far to the west of the Hudson, was isolated. The Mohawk River had never been navigable, and rural roads were in terrible shape. The treaties with the Iroquois after the American Revolution opened up tens of thousands of acres, many of them rich lands that white farmers could settle, but these farmers faced terrible isolation and difficulty in selling their crops. Beginning in the 1790s, many New Yorkers wanted a way to ease transport across the state, but no easy approach seemed possible. Indeed, Americans throughout the rest of the growing country had similar needs—and a similar lack of know-how.

After Congress refused to fund a canal linking rural upstate New York with the Hudson Valley, former New York City Mayor DeWitt Clinton ran for governor in 1816 with a promise to build a canal using state funds. The canal that Clinton proposed avoided the hard-to-navigate Mohawk River and Lake Ontario (using the lake would have lowered construction costs but risked diverting trade to Canada). Instead, he proposed a canal that would follow an old Mohawk Indian trading route (the governor knew his New York history) and run from the Hudson Valley directly to Buffalo on Lake Erie. Such a canal would give farmers along its route a link to markets and would connect all of New York state to the growing Ohio region and eventually to the Mississippi River. It would make New York City the commercial capital of the nation.

The plan called for an unimaginable engineering feat. Thomas Jefferson called it "madness." The canal needed a series of locks to raise and lower water to accommodate changes in elevation of 565 feet. The United States had few engineers, and no one really knew how to build such locks. The longest canal in the country at that time was only 26 miles, less than one-tenth of the projected plan. None of those problems discouraged Clinton or the canal's backers. When the anti-Clinton faction, led by Martin Van Buren, realized how much enthusiasm there was for the canal, they ended their opposition, and the project quickly moved through the state legislature.

At dawn on July 4, 1817, a gala ground-breaking celebration was held at Rome, New York, when the symbolic first shovel of dirt was dug to build the **Erie Canal**, a manmade waterway that would extend 363 miles between Albany and Buffalo and contain a total of 83 locks. Clinton was a wily politician. He made sure that many different

Erie Canal
Completed in 1825, the canal linked the Hudson River with the Great Lakes and gave farmers all along its route new ways to be part of a global economic system of trade.

The Erie Canal crossed rural New York State, connecting villages all along the way. Travelers needed to keep their heads down when traveling under bridges and wait as locks raised and lowered boats, but the canal boats provided transport at a speed unimagined before it was built.

contractors got a piece of the action digging the canal. He built political support by ensuring that up to three-quarters of the 9,000 men who did the actual digging were Dutch or English farmers and laborers from New York State and future Clinton voters. As soon as the section near Rome was completed, Clinton used the revenue it generated to cover the interest on the $7 million in bonds that had been floated to pay for the canal, reducing the cost to taxpayers.

Clinton found contractors willing to experiment with new approaches to construction. In one section, near the town of Lockport, locks needed to be constructed to raise and lower the boats over changing elevations. Contractors used gunpowder to blast out the rock, and horses hauled away the debris. By 1825, the canal, four-feet deep and 40-feet wide, was completed. Governor Clinton traveled from Buffalo across the state on the canal and then down the Hudson to mark the official opening by pouring water from Lake Erie into New York Harbor.

Many admired the engineering of the canal and many more enjoyed its economic impact. Goods and exports that had cost $100 a ton to ship from Lake Erie to New York City before the canal now shipped for $9, or even $3, a ton. Farmers in distant upstate New York and in Ohio could get their wheat to international markets through New York Harbor. Formerly isolated farm families could now send letters and even visit friends and relatives. They could also import goods that had earlier been unimaginable luxuries because they had been too heavy or perishable to transport. A newspaper in Batavia, New York, celebrated the arrival of "Oysters! Beautiful Oysters," from Long Island to a town where fresh seafood had never been available. Farmers and small town residents now could not only eat sea food but also buy a clock for their wall, a mattress for their bed, or curtains for their home at a fraction of the price these goods had cost before the canal opened. By the 1830s, the Erie Canal carried more than twice the freight of the Mississippi River, and Rochester, Syracuse, and Buffalo boomed. Where cotton had made New York City the nation's commercial center, foodstuffs and other products from upstate New York and even western Pennsylvania and Ohio now cemented the city's role as the place where the nation's trade, commerce, and finance met. Other shorter canals were built in many other parts of the country, but none had the commercial impact of the Erie Canal.

Steamboats, Roads, Travel, and News

Erie Canal boats were pulled by horses walking along the bank. The packet ships that crossed the Atlantic were powered by sail as ships had been for thousands of years. But the invention of the steamboat revolutionized water transportation. In 1807, Robert Fulton built the first commercially successful steamboat, the *Clermont*, which significantly cut the travel time from New York to Albany. Within 2 decades, New York Harbor and adjacent areas had become a hive of steamboat activity for both commerce and passengers, and many steamboat lines competed for the trade, none more successfully than the line Cornelius Vanderbilt owned.

Steamboats also transformed trade on the Mississippi River. In the early 1800s, farmers floated down the river on large riverboats with their goods and then sold the boats for lumber when they reached their destination and walked or rode horses home. Steamboats, however, could travel up the river against the current. In 1817, a steamer went from New Orleans to Louisville, Kentucky, in 25 days, an unheard-of speed. In less than a decade, the travel time had been cut to 8 days as faster boats competed for the Mississippi River business and became a colorful part of America in the 1800s (see Map 9-4).

In certain areas, water transport was the fastest and easiest way to travel through and around the United States, but roads were also important. In 1802, Congress authorized the use of funds from the sale of government lands in Ohio to build a gravel road to the interior of the country. Beginning in 1811, at Cumberland, Maryland, the National Road was built across the Appalachian Mountains. When it reached its original terminus at Wheeling, Virginia (after the Civil War, West Virginia), in 1818, it

MAP 9-4 Canals and Road in the United States. Although the Erie Canal was without question the most important canal in the nation, a huge network of canals, dirt and gravel roads, and later, railroads connecting to rivers and ocean ports, connected inland areas to world markets.

not only had crossed the mountains but also had linked the Potomac River with the Ohio River, which flowed into the Mississippi, and from there to the Gulf of Mexico. Later, slowly, the National Road was extended across Ohio, Indiana, and Illinois, connecting to the Mississippi River itself. While many, notably Jefferson's Secretary of the Treasury Albert Gallatin, argued for more federally financed construction, Presidents Jefferson, Madison, and Monroe—all three advocates of a small federal government—doubted whether the national government could finance such undertakings without an amendment to the Constitution. Those three were also Virginians, and Virginia, with a long coastline, benefited more from coastal shipping than from canals or roads. On occasion, they put their doubts aside and signed bills providing federal funding for specific projects, but none of those who lived in the White House between 1801 and 1825 were enthusiastic about federal support for a transportation infrastructure for the nation.

In addition, states built their own roads, like the Lancaster Turnpike across Pennsylvania, but travel by road was slow and expensive throughout the 1820s and 1830s. A stagecoach could travel 6–8 miles an hour on a good road—11 on the best road between New York and Philadelphia. Wagons could haul goods as far as the next river or canal. Tollbooths collected fees to pay for the roads, but on a poor road in the wilderness, it was easy to detour around the tollbooth. Until railroads arrived in the 1840s, proximity to a canal, river, or the Atlantic and Gulf coasts was essential for the productive commerce in goods and services. People who lived near land or water routes for transport were able to get their goods to market, receive newspapers, and stay connected to an increasingly national economy and culture. Those who lived farther away from such transportation lived isolated lives—all the more isolated as others became more connected.

With increased speed in travel, news also moved more quickly (see Table 9-1). Packet ships from Liverpool brought European news, and as the ships cut trans-Atlantic travel time from 50 days in 1816 to 42 days in the 1820s, that news traveled faster. Within the United States, by 1817, a man on a horse could bring news from New York to Philadelphia or Boston in 2 days. A steamboat traveling through Long Island Sound could also bring the news to coastal cities in Connecticut and to Boston in about the same amount of time. For southern coastal cities, the travel time was slower, and for inland towns, much slower. Newspapers sprang up across the country, and the federal government developed an extensive post office system (since the Constitution clearly sanctioned the post office and post roads) that helped Americans connect for personal and business matters. The packet ships, stagecoaches, and canal boats also depended on contracts with the federal post office to make their routes profitable. Commercial leaders and traders on the New York Stock Exchange were anxious to have the latest news, especially about crops, but also about European and American demand for goods. They supported the post office and newspapers as essential for the growing, unified market economy.

While steamships like Robert Fulton's *Clermont* made for easy and fast travel up the Hudson River and along other rivers around the nation they were limited to water transport, while stage coaches, which were much slower, were essential for travel over the country's poorly constructed roads until replaced on many routes by railroads..

TABLE 9-1 Changes in Travel Times Within the United States as a Result of the Revolution in Transportation

Route	1800	1830	1860
New York to Philadelphia	2 days	1 day	Less than 1 day
New York to South Carolina	More than 1 week	5 days	2 days
New York to Illinois	6 weeks	3 weeks	2 days
New York to New Orleans	4 weeks	2 weeks	6 days
New York to Florida	2 to 3 weeks	1 to 2 weeks	3 days
New York to Ohio	2 to 3 weeks	1 week	2 days

Banks, Corporations, and Finance

In the early years of the Republic many Americans harbored deep distrust of large business enterprises. The family farm was the business model with which most people were familiar, and other businesses were expected to be small, individual or family ventures. People might join together to finance a voyage or a project, but these efforts were short-term partnerships. At the time of the American Revolution, there were only seven American corporations, each chartered by colonial legislatures. State legislatures chartered 40 more corporations in the 1780s and some 300 in the 1790s, but gaining a corporate charter remained difficult. In general, such charters were given only to colleges or other nonprofit agencies to serve the public good. Commerce was considered as being for individual gain and therefore not something worthy of a state charter.

Some of the first corporations were banks. Congress had chartered the nation's first bank, the Bank of North America, at Hamilton's urging in 1781. By 1815, the United States had 200 state-chartered banks. Banks offered two essential services. First, they printed paper currency—bank notes—that were backed by the bank's gold and silver deposits (known as specie), making commercial transactions much easier than hauling actual gold and silver around. Second, banks also made loans and collected interest, making funds available to people who wanted to develop a new enterprise and making the banks themselves profitable investments. Soon, banks also began to issue bank notes not only on the species they held but also on the loans in their portfolio. This development made banking more risky but expanded the amount of money in circulation and the credit available, essential elements in the growth of a commercial republic.

As commerce developed, however, larger commercial and industrial ventures, like the mills at Lowell, were too large and risky to be financed solely by individuals, even if those individuals could secure large bank loans. A new idea, that of a corporation as a free-standing commercial venture with multiple stockholders, took hold slowly. Two key elements in a corporation—limited liability for individual stockholders and the corporation's freedom from having its charter withdrawn or altered by the government—were new in the United States. Individually owned businesses came and went, but corporations with their many stockholders and secure charters eventually became a permanent and important feature of American economic life after 1815.

The Reality of the New Market Economy

In 1819, Washington Irving, already a well-known author, published *Rip Van Winkle*. The story has entertained generations of readers, but it captured the changes in the United States in the first decades of independence. In the story, Rip, a lazy fellow living in New York's Catskill Mountains, takes a nap in the woods on a fine fall day. He awakes 20 years later and finds everything has changed in his home village.

The picture on the sign over the inn was of someone named "General Washington" instead of King George III, but even more surprising, the whole town was different:

> The very village was altered; it was larger and more populous. There were rows of houses which he had never seen before, and those which had been his familiar haunts had disappeared....The very character of the people seemed changed. There was a busy, bustling, disputatious tone about it, instead of the accustomed phlegm and drowsy tranquility.

Rip had been a passive subject of King George III. When he awoke, he was a citizen in an independent country that took politics, voting, and political parties very seriously. When he was asked whether he "was Federal or Democrat," Rip was equally at a loss. But Irving was saying something more about the decades after the Revolution—that "the very character of the people seemed changed." Where once rural America had moved to a relaxed, slow pace, the whole country was now a more unified commercial enterprise in which a "busy, bustling, disputatious tone" was the norm because people needed to work and work fast.

There were many real-life Rip Van Winkles who, while not necessarily having the benefit of a 20-year nap, still came to live in an adult world utterly different from that of their youth. Ichabod Washburn was born in the small town of Kingston, Massachusetts, in 1798. His widowed mother supported the family with a loom in her home. When his mother could not feed her whole family, Washburn was "put out" to work as a harness maker and told that a boy should not ask too many questions about the world around him. Later, he found work in one of the factories that were springing up around New England and then founded his own business. Washburn & Moen Wire Manufactory became the largest wire maker in the country, sending its products all over the world and making Washburn a rich man. Not all Americans became as rich as Washburn, but many people in many parts of the land moved from isolated family businesses to work in large nationally and internationally connected industries. They went from a slow-paced world of barter to a cash economy based on trade, and they moved from rural isolation to participate in the exchange of information within a much larger world.

The growing economy and the revolution in transportation only increased demand for the nation's raw materials such as lumber, which new machinery made easy to cut into standard-sized boards for shipment and use in building houses and ships.

Before the American Revolution, most farmers lived in a barter economy in which most goods and services were simply traded. In that economy, life moved at a slow and predictable pace, and little money was transacted. By the 1820s, the barter economy had disappeared in all but the most remote areas. Farmers sold their goods on the world market and used the cash they received to purchase not only necessities but also, often, luxuries that their pre-Revolutionary forbearers never imagined.

To many Americans—not just to national leaders—distances seemed shorter, money more important, and politics more omnipresent after 1815 than one would have thought possible even a few years before. Visitors to remote farm settlements in Illinois in the 1820s found that cloth coats and calico dresses purchased from a trader or a store were replacing homespun and buckskin. Once one family made the shift, everyone in the village felt pressure to earn enough money to keep up. As people worked harder and longer, public clocks—with an added hand that noted minutes, not just the passage of the hours—became more prominent. Chauncey Jerome's Connecticut clock company made a fortune manufacturing and shipping clocks to every part of the nation. As one 1840 traveler reported, "In every dell of Arkansas, and in cabins where there was not a chair to sit on, there was sure to be a Connecticut clock." Rip Van Winkle was not the only one waking up in a different time and in a money-conscious country.

> **9.2** **Quick Review** How did new trading routes progressively improve the U.S. economy and, in doing so, change the United States?

FROM THE ERA OF GOOD FEELINGS TO THE POLITICS OF DIVISION

> **9.3** Explain the political developments in the United States during the 1820s, including the shift of power toward the South and West that resulted from the changing economic situation.

James Monroe's two terms as president from 1817 to 1825 were known as the **Era of Good Feelings** because of the lack of rancor in his virtually unanimous election and reelection during a time when the opposing Federalist Party had almost disappeared. The period was quite a change from the days when John Adams and Thomas Jefferson contested the presidency and Federalists and Democratic-Republicans fought in the press and on the floor of Congress. But even during the Era of Good Feelings, all was not calm on the political front. The Supreme Court was rapidly expanding its reach and the reach of the federal government into new aspects of the country. In addition, political tensions over the cotton economy, territorial expansion, and slavery exploded with surprising force in the 1820s. The good feelings were not destined to last.

The Supreme Court Defines Its Place

John Marshall served as chief justice of the U.S. Supreme Court from 1801 to 1835. Throughout his long tenure on the Court, Marshall was usually able to convince a majority of the justices to go along with his views no matter what their prior political beliefs were. He used his position to define the role of the court as arbiter of the Constitution, and he expanded the role and power of the federal government in many aspects of national life.

Early in his tenure, Marshall's 1803 *Marbury v. Madison* decision claimed a role for the Supreme Court in reviewing the constitutionality of acts of Congress. Marshall never again invoked that right, but in a series of subsequent decisions, he created the same right for the court in relationship to state legislatures and state courts. Two 1819 decisions from the Marshall court were especially important in expanding the role of the Supreme Court and the federal government.

Era of Good Feelings
The period from 1817 to 1823 in which the decline of the Federalists enabled the Democratic-Republicans to govern in a spirit of seemingly nonpartisan harmony.

In an appeal to the Supreme Court in the case of *Dartmouth College v. Woodward* (1819), the old Federalist Marshall reviewed a decision by lower courts that began when the Democratic-Republican-dominated New Hampshire legislature revised the original charter of Dartmouth College, converting the school from a private to a state college. The Supreme Court ruled that state charters, including charters from colonial legislatures like Dartmouth's, were contracts and that contracts, once agreed to, were inviolable; thus, the legislature's actions were unconstitutional. The case was important not only because it asserted the right of the Supreme Court to review the actions of state legislatures, not just Congress, but also because it asserted the inviolability of contracts. As a result, it became an important bedrock of the American economic system. After the Dartmouth College decision, the nation's growing businesses and industries were able to be certain that their contracts, once agreed to, could not be overturned by legislative action.

The other important 1819 decision was *McCulloch v. Maryland*. Congress had chartered the Second Bank of the United States at the end of the War of 1812 to stabilize the nation's finances. But the bank was not popular with many people, especially farmers and others who saw it as an instrument of the commercial elite. In response to the general opposition to the bank and to charges of irregularities in the bank's Maryland branch, the state of Maryland imposed a tax on the bank as a way to drive it out of business, or at least out of Maryland. In response, the bank brought suit in the federal courts and the case worked its way up to the Supreme Court. In the decision, written by Marshall, the court took Alexander Hamilton's view that the "necessary and proper" clause of the Constitution meant that Congress had the right to charter a bank if it thought it was in the national interest, despite the Tenth Amendment's mandate that states should retain any power that was not specifically delegated to the national government in the Constitution. Marshall went further, saying that "the power to tax involves the power to destroy" while the "power to create" that Congress had invoked in the case of the bank, "implies a power to preserve." The issue Marshall referred to was not obscure. With *McCulloch v. Maryland,* the Supreme Court declared that states could not interfere with the workings of the federal government.

The Marshall Court continued to expand federal authority in subsequent cases. In *Gibbons v. Ogden* (1824), the court ruled that the state of New York did not have a right to give Ogden, a partner of Robert Fulton, a monopoly to ferry service in New York harbor since the harbor connected New York and New Jersey and thus involved interstate commerce, which only Congress could control. Later, in *Worcester v. Georgia* (1832), the court ruled that the state of Georgia could not regulate private dealings by U.S. citizens within the territory controlled by the Cherokee tribe since tribes had their own sovereign rights, subject only to the authority of the federal government. In these and other decisions, the court affirmed what came to be known as a "loose construction" of the Constitution, which as Marshall explained, enabled the Constitution "to be adapted to the various crises of human affairs" to preserve its relevance through time. Not everyone agreed with Marshall's perspective, and when he died in 1835, a Democratic-Republican paper did not mourn "the political doctrines" of a justice who sought "to strengthen government at the expense of the people." Nevertheless, many felt that both the Constitution and the rights of people were stronger for his efforts.

The Politics of Cotton and the Missouri Compromise of 1820

Although Missouri was too far north to be a cotton-growing state, its population also grew as a result of America's westward movement, and by 1819 Missouri applied to Congress to be admitted as a new state. A bill to authorize a state constitutional convention was introduced in Congress with little fanfare early in 1819. However, Congressman James Tallmadge, Jr., of New York introduced an amendment to the

Missouri statehood bill to prohibit the introduction of new slaves into the state and gradually free those who were already there. Tallmadge's amendment created a huge crisis in which southern representatives and senators attacked it and its author.

In language that prefigured the heated debates of the next four decades, Georgia Representative Thomas W. Cobb told Tallmadge, "You have kindled a fire which all the waters of the ocean cannot put out, which seas of blood can only extinguish." Tallmadge responded in kind: "If a dissolution of the Union must take place, let it be so! If civil war, which gentlemen so much threaten, must come, I can only say, let it come." Threats of disunion were as old as the Constitutional Convention of 1787, but this language was harsher than Congress had heard in a long time. The reasons were clear.

When the Constitution was adopted, many from both the South and the North believed that slavery was dying; even its defenders tended to describe the institution as a sad though necessary evil. When George Washington and others of his generation freed their slaves, the economic impact was limited since slaves were not of great value. But that period was before cotton transformed the economics of slavery. A slave in the prime of life who might be sold for $400 or $500 in 1814 could be sold for $800–$1,100 in 1819, and though the price of slaves, as of land, decreased with the panic of 1819, values in both cases recovered and then kept rising. Slaves had become valuable, whether as workers or as "products" to be sold. If Virginia and Carolina planters could not use all the slaves they owned, instead of freeing them, they could now sell them to cotton growers in Georgia, Mississippi, and Alabama at a substantial profit. Missouri had few slaves, but by 1820, slave owners were not about to allow an attack on the institution of slavery. Although much of the debate about Missouri was spoken in the language of popular will and the sovereign right of (white) people there to decide their own policies, it took place as economic and racial realities were changing quickly.

In the North, hostility to slavery was growing. Many northerners, including many whose pre-Revolutionary parents and grandparents had owned slaves, now hated the whole idea of human slavery and disliked a constitutional system that protected it. Even before 1820, some people were starting to call themselves abolitionists—those committed to completely ending slavery. Many other northerners had more strategic objections to the constitutional protection of slavery. The three-fifths clause in the Constitution gave the slaveholding South 17 more seats in the House of Representatives and, thus, 17 more electoral votes in presidential elections than an allocation of representatives based on only free people would have done. As a result, four of the five U.S. presidents who had served by 1820 had come from Virginia. The nation was becoming divided between a commercial North and an agricultural South, and although neither region was purely for or against slavery, the fact that slavery gave the South a political edge came across to many northerners as being unfair.

The debates about Missouri, despite all the anger voiced by Tallmadge and Cobb, were not as vitriolic as future debates would be. There were not yet many radical abolitionists in the North, and so far, few in the South were saying that slavery was a positive good. But already in 1819, neither side would back down, and Congress adjourned without doing anything about Missouri.

Before Congress reassembled in 1820, President Monroe and Henry Clay of Kentucky, the speaker of the House of Representatives, designed a compromise to resolve the issue. While the North had a solid and growing majority in the House, the Senate was evenly divided between slave and free states. Since each state had two senators no matter what its population, 11 free states and 11 slave states meant a Senate that was split 22-22 on the issue of slavery. In addition, while Congress had debated what to do about Missouri, the region known as the District of Maine, within the Commonwealth of Massachusetts, was also petitioning for statehood with the blessing of the Massachusetts legislature. The compromise proposed that if Maine and Missouri were admitted at the same time, and if Missouri was allowed to be a slave state, then the balance in the Senate would be maintained. However, this proposed compromise would also restrict the spread of slavery: while Missouri would be admitted as a slave state, all other states north of the 36° 30´ north parallel, that is, the southern border of Missouri, would be admitted as free states. Although most northerners in the House and Senate voted against it, some supported the compromise, as did almost all of those from the South, and the **Missouri Compromise** passed Congress, allowing Missouri and Maine to be admitted to the Union. The crisis had been averted. The success would be the first of many such compromises for which Henry Clay would become known as the "great compromiser" over the next 3 decades. However, the need for this compromise signaled more clearly than ever before that slavery had become a divisive issue that would not go away (see Map 9-5).

The Contested Election of 1824

As President Monroe came to the end of his second term, the political good will that had marked his tenure disappeared. Although no constitutional limitation had yet been set on presidential terms, Washington had set a precedent for stepping down after two terms, which others had followed. In 1824, as the nation sought a new president,

Missouri Compromise
A compromise in Congress in 1820 that admitted Missouri to the Union as a slave state and Maine as a free state as well as prohibited slavery in the rest of the Louisiana Purchase territory above 36°30´ north latitude.

MAP 9-5 The Missouri Compromise Line. This map shows the way the nation was divided in an equal number of free and slave states by the Missouri Compromise.

The Missouri Compromise

When he heard about the Missouri Compromise, the aging Thomas Jefferson, who had been infuriated by the Tallmadge amendment because it interfered with the rights of states, wrote to John Holmes, a Massachusetts congressman:

> I had for a long time ceased to read the newspapers or pay any attention to public affairs, confident they were in good hands, and content to be a passenger in our bark to the shore from which I am not distant. But this momentous question, like a fire bell in the night, awakened and filled me with terror. I considered it at once as the knell of the Union. It is hushed indeed for the moment. But this is a reprieve only, not a final sentence. A geographical line, coinciding with a marked principle, moral and political, once conceived and held up to the angry passions of men, will never be obliterated; and every new irritation will mark it deeper and deeper.

While Clay was being hailed as a national hero for crafting the compromise, Jefferson, perhaps, had a better sense of what lay ahead. The former president and slaveholder who also wrote passionately against slavery knew that, in the long term, no issue would so greatly divide the nation's citizens, and as he grew old, he saw the division become increasingly intense.

Thinking Critically

1. Contextualization

How would you characterize pro- and antislavery forces in 1820? What might explain the widespread belief that the issue of slavery had been resolved with the passage of the Missouri Compromise?

2. Historical Interpretation

In hindsight, it is clear that Jefferson was correct and the Missouri Compromise was only a "reprieve." What evidence was available in 1820 to support Jefferson's point of view? What trends had already begun to emerge that would lead the intensification of the conflict over slavery in the decades to come?

the United States experienced one of the most contested and confusing presidential elections in its history. For citizens of a nation that had elected James Monroe almost unanimously in 1816 and 1820, the ill will of 1824 was a surprise.

In one sense, the election of 1824 proceeded just as the writers of the Constitution—who hated the idea of political parties—envisioned: a contest in which members of the House, with each state's delegation having one vote, would decide on a president from among several of the nation's leading citizens who had been identified by the votes of the Electoral College. With the demise of the Federalists, the Democratic-Republican Party was the only party in the nation. It had been as that party's candidate that Monroe had been elected by an almost unanimous vote since the Federalists did not nominate a candidate in 1820 or anytime after that.

By 1824, however, the usual process in which a party caucus within Congress would select a presidential nominee had broken down, and three members of Monroe's cabinet along with the speaker of the House of Representatives all sought the presidency. A fifth candidate from the same Democratic-Republican Party, Senator Andrew Jackson, the national war hero from Tennessee, also joined the race. In this type of contest, personal animosity and political intrigue were inevitable.

At first, many thought Secretary of the Treasury William H. Crawford of Georgia was the obvious choice. Crawford had stepped out of the way to support Monroe's election, and he and many of his supporters thought it was now his turn. The congressional caucus that traditionally nominated presidential candidates, in fact, did choose Crawford. However, in what was clearly a warning of trouble to come, less than a fourth of the members of Congress showed up to vote in the caucus. Others, in Congress and outside of it, would find other candidates and other ways to support them.

Secretary of State John Quincy Adams of Massachusetts had a good claim to consideration. Many considered the office of secretary of state as the natural stepping stone to the presidency. Monroe had been Madison's secretary of state as Madison had been

Jefferson's, and Jefferson had been Washington's. In addition, Adams had served the nation well. He had acquired Florida for the United States, arranged treaties that opened vast new lands to settlement, and handled South American revolutions and potential European interference skillfully. As a former ambassador, senator, son of a former president, and favorite of the antislavery North, Adams had much going for him.

Secretary of War John C. Calhoun from South Carolina was another candidate. Calhoun had not yet become the fierce advocate of states' rights that he was later. In 1824, he was a strong nationalist. He advocated for a strong army and for using army engineers to conduct a national survey that would lead to federally supported roads, bridges, and canals connecting all parts of the nation. He also supported the Bank of the United States. Calhoun initially backed Adams, but when he became convinced after the Missouri crisis that southern and border state electors would never support a New Englander, his own ambition was fired up and he campaigned actively.

Henry Clay of Kentucky, also a contender, was speaker of the House of Representatives and an ardent nationalist. Like Calhoun, he supported an expansive federal government that controlled the currency through a strong national bank and that built roads and bridges as well as supported commerce. From his political base in Kentucky, Clay hoped to be the first president from west of the Alleghenies. He was also shrewd enough to guess that with so many candidates in the race, the House of Representatives, which he controlled, might make the final decision.

Finally, there was Andrew Jackson of Tennessee. At first, Jackson seemed an unlikely candidate for president. Unlike any president after Washington, Jackson had never served in the cabinet or represented the nation abroad. Instead, he was the hero of the Battle of New Orleans. He had served for 1 year in the Senate and in other government posts, but his primary public role was as a military leader, and in the 1820s, the military was not always a popular institution. His wife, Rachel Jackson, strongly opposed his seeking the presidency. In 1822, however, the Tennessee legislature formally nominated Jackson as a candidate for president, primarily as a way to block the then frontrunner Crawford. At that point, Jackson probably supported Adams, in part, because Adams had supported Jackson's actions in Florida, while Crawford and Clay had not.

No one, including Jackson, counted on how popular he would be with the electorate. When a tavern keeper in Pennsylvania wrote, asking whether Jackson would indeed seek the presidency, the canny general, knowing that his response would be published, replied that it was his "undeviating rule neither to seek or decline public invitations to office." His response seemed the height of statesmanship to a country that had seen Monroe's almost unanimous election in the Era of Good Feelings replaced by a divisive contest for the presidency.

The Constitution allows each state to decide how to choose presidential electors. By 1824, most states allowed voters to select electors pledged to a specific candidate, thus greatly democratizing the presidential selection process. That electorate had changed since the Constitution was adopted in 1789. Since 1808 when New Jersey retracted its decision to give women the right to vote, only men voted. Property restrictions on voting, still common when Washington was elected, were long gone in most states, so nearly all white men could now vote, and in some northern states, so could free black men. In New York City, free blacks sometimes held the balance of power among various factions. Excluded from voting were women of all races, most blacks including all slaves, and Indians. Nevertheless, this broad male electorate valued widespread popularity as more important in selecting a president than the voice of a few members of the social and economic elite. By 1824, the (white male) popular will was coalescing behind Jackson far more than anyone expected.

In a nation increasingly divided by sectional issues, a nationally respected war hero had great appeal. In addition, a fierce opponent of banks like Jackson was popular with many people who were convinced—at least partially rightly—that the Bank of the United States had brought on the panic of 1819. In places like Mississippi and Alabama where some people were growing rich on farmlands that Jackson had wrested from their Indian owners, he was a local hero. Particularly in a country where an elite's economic decisions had hurt many farmers and workers, a candidate who had been born in a log cabin and grown up poor, though he had become wealthy as an adult, had deep appeal. Popular appeal had not been a major factor in the elections of Madison and Monroe, but it was *the* factor in 1824.

In the 1824 election, Jackson won the popular vote. Calhoun, who had withdrawn from the campaign after deciding that Jackson was too popular to beat, was easily elected as vice president since the Twelfth Amendment, ratified in 1804 in the aftermath of the Jefferson-Burr fiasco, mandated that presidential electors cast separate ballots for presidential and vice presidential candidates. In addition to Pennsylvania, Jackson easily carried the black-belt states of Georgia, Alabama, Mississippi, and Louisiana as well as most of the rest of the South, a region benefitting from its population of nonvoting slaves, which strengthened its electoral votes as a result of the three-fifths clause to the Constitution. Jackson defeated Adams in New Jersey, Crawford in North Carolina, and Clay in Indiana and Illinois. Adams carried New England, some of the mid-Atlantic region, and the Northwest. However, although Jackson won the most popular votes, no one had the 131 electoral votes needed for a majority:

Jackson	99 electoral votes
Adams	84 electoral votes
Crawford	41 electoral votes
Clay	37 electoral votes

Clay's prediction was right; the election had been tossed into the House of Representatives. Not since 1800 had the House of Representatives been called on to decide the outcome of a presidential contest.

Ironically, however, since the Constitution required the House to choose from among the top three candidates, Clay himself had been eliminated. Moreover, although his supporters had kept it hidden, Crawford had had a stroke and could not possibly assume the presidency. So the election came down to Jackson and Adams, and Adams was determined to fight for the office, despite ranking second in the popular and electoral votes. The Constitution mandated a process, and Adams wanted to follow it. Many of Adams's followers, and the supporters of other candidates, saw Jackson as a would-be American Napoleon who would undermine American democracy. No one held that concern more strongly than Henry Clay—who was master of the House and determined that Jackson should not be president. When the House met on February 9, 1825, Adams was elected president by a vote of 13 states, with seven states for Jackson and four for Crawford.

On the evening of the vote, outgoing President Monroe held a party at the White House. Jackson approached Adams, and they greeted each other with considerable formality. Observers thought Jackson was "genial and gracious," while Adams was "stiff, rigid, cold as a statue." The two would not often meet again, but the interaction that night imprinted an image on the public that would follow them, to Jackson's benefit, for the next 4 years and beyond.

Whether Adams had made any secret agreement with Clay will never be known. But 5 days after the vote, Adams appointed Clay to be his secretary of state and thus his successor if the previous pattern held true. Jackson denounced both men for making a "corrupt bargain," resigned from the Senate, and returned to his home in Nashville to begin what was essentially a 4-year campaign against Adams, Clay, and their administration, as well as a campaign for his own election to the office that he and his followers believed he had won in 1824. Adams and Clay had underestimated the popular feeling for Jackson. The animosity of the campaign and Jackson's rancor would make the next 4 years difficult for an administration led by two of the nation's most gifted political and diplomatic leaders.

The Adams-Clay Agenda

In his inaugural address in March 1825, Adams acknowledged that he came to the presidency, "less possessed of your confidence in advance than any of my predecessors." Nevertheless, it was his goal to unify the nation and improve all parts of the country. He was the last president to believe that the "baneful weed of party strife" might be avoided, and he struggled—unsuccessfully—to avoid the creation of political parties and permanent national divisions.

Adams proposed a list of national improvements to be implemented by the federal government. Support for federally funded improvements such as roads, canals, and so on would be a hallmark of the Adams administration. An emerging political faction that supported national development and strong federal actions to deal with national problems agreed with the direction that the Adams administration was taking. Jackson and another emerging faction would strongly oppose this sort of activist federal government, advocating instead for states' rights.

Improvement, both personal and political, was a popular ambition in the 1820s. Adams worried about becoming a better person, and he swam naked in the Potomac every day to improve his body. But he also wanted to improve the country, and he saw the money freed from paying off the Revolutionary War debt and the income from sales of federal lands as the perfect opportunity for investing in the country. The General Survey, conducted by army engineers when John C. Calhoun was secretary of war, was the blueprint. Adams, with an eye to southern voters, proposed a second National Road to link Washington, D.C., to New Orleans. He proposed, and Congress approved, building the Chesapeake and Ohio Canal that would connect with the original National Road and link the Potomac with the Ohio and Mississippi Rivers. Postmaster General John McLean built post offices in rural areas and subsidized the stagecoach industry to carry the mail and connect the nation's far-flung people to one another. Adams also proposed a new national university to be based in Washington and a national observatory—a "lighthouse of the skies." All of these activities were designed to knit the nation together, advancing knowledge and making it easier to transport goods. In addition, the intent was to unite the nation in a single political entity and a market economy, especially after the divisions sparked by the debates around the Missouri Compromise (see Map 9-4 on page 256).

Secretary of State Clay was involved in all these efforts and, in fact, during the presidential campaign, had described a program of internal improvements and protective tariffs that came to be known as the "**American System**." In Clay's mind, the American System would reduce poverty by linking all Americans (all *white* Americans; Clay considered neither his own 50 slaves nor others' slaves to be Americans) in a prosperous commercial community. The system was American because it made the federal government an agent of economic development. Clay believed that the roads and canals, as well as the support of interstate commerce that he and Adams wanted to foster on a federal level, would make a stronger and more united America, commercially, geographically, and socially. Ultimately, Clay wanted transportation and commerce to bridge traditional sectional divides and create a thriving commercial nation that was united by common national investments. Moreover, the system was potentially a way to protect the country by building an infrastructure that could serve military needs, allowing troops to move quickly from one part of the country to another when necessary. Finally, the American System would protect infant American industries through a strong tariff that would allow them to develop and thus reduce American dependence on cheaper foreign imports.

In one of his last acts as speaker in 1824, Clay led an effort to increase the average tariff from 20 percent to 35 percent. The new higher tariff made him a hero to New England mill owners and their workers whose jobs it protected. It was also popular in commercial centers like Cincinnati, Ohio, and Clay's hometown of Lexington, Kentucky, where new industries needed protection. But the improvements and tariffs

American System

The program of government subsidies to improve roads and canals and to foster economic growth and protect domestic manufacturers from foreign competition.

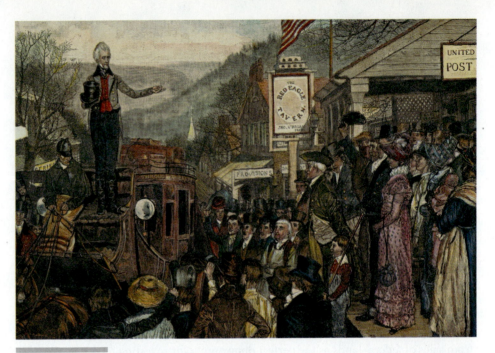

This stylized picture of Andrew Jackson speaking to a crowd begins to suggest the enormous popularity that the former war hero had as he connected with diverse audiences of voters in a way no leader since George Washington had done.

of the American System were not popular in other parts of the country. A high tariff raised the cost of everything southern cotton planters had to buy but did nothing to raise the price of their cotton in the market. They saw the tariff and the president's antislavery opinions as a sign of a federal government that was working against their economic interests, and many in the South hardened their opposition to Adams, Clay, and the American System.

As the 1828 presidential campaign built steam, Adams and Clay continued their pitch for the costs and benefits of the American System. Jackson, however, had a more focused agenda: to replace Adams, the minority president, with the man who had rightfully won in 1824. Ironically, although Adams ardently wanted to avoid the "baneful weed of party strife," it was during his term that new American political parties were born.

The Jackson Victory of 1828 and the Rebirth of Political Parties

From the day he left Washington, D.C., in 1825, Jackson was running to become president in 1828. He believed that he and his supporters had been cheated, and he meant to be vindicated. Nevertheless, it took time for the campaign to take shape. It is easier to understand the birth of political parties in retrospect than it was at the time. Many Americans were glad to see the old Federalist Party gone; at the same time, they hated to see the Democratic-Republicans splinter. At first, the two factions in Congress were described simply as "Adams men" and "Jackson men." After the midterm Congressional elections of 1826, the "Jackson men" controlled Congress. The "Adams men" then started to call themselves National Republicans, that is, Democratic-Republicans who supported the national administration led by President Adams. This group, led primarily by Henry Clay, would become the core of the new **Whig Party**, the party that advocated for a strong national government role in the economy, internal improvements such as roads and canals, and social reform movements in general. The "Jackson men" continued to call themselves Democratic-Republicans, emphasizing that they were the rightful winners of the last election and represented the democratic will of the people, which had been thwarted by Adams and Clay in the 1824

Whig Party
Political party that began to take shape in support of the Adams-Clay American system and was first known as the National Republicans, but became the Whig Party in the 1830s in opposition to the Jacksonian Democrats.

election. Soon, the Jacksonians dropped the "Republicans" in their name and were simply known as Democrats, forerunners of the **Democratic Party** that throughout the 1800s argued for the rights of the "common man" to be left alone by centralized government and economic interests.

Neither party was fully organized in the 1828 election and though each had newspapers that were strongly on their side, other hallmarks of national political parties like national nominating conventions came later. Nevertheless, from 1828 on, most Americans expected presidential elections to be hotly contested by two or more candidates representing their respective political parties and running on specific promises. The era of electing a few wise men to select the best president was over forever.

The prime architect of Jackson's campaign and his political agenda, besides Jackson himself who delegated little, was Senator Martin Van Buren of New York. Van Buren was a strict constructionist of the Constitution who believed that the American System advocated by Adams and Clay violated the Constitution because it involved the federal government in many matters not specifically assigned to it by the Constitution. Although a New Yorker, Van Buren was closely allied with many in the South who liked Van Buren's commitment to a small federal government because they feared that if the federal government could involve itself in shaping the nation's economy, it could also interfere with slavery, a threat that terrified the slaveholding class.

The campaign of 1828 was as nasty as any in American history. Newspapers took on a larger role than ever before endorsing candidates and spreading slander about the opposition. The National Republicans reminded voters of Jackson's temper and his many brawls and duels, which they said were unpresidential, as well as the times he may have exceeded his authority in attacking Indians or executing British subjects. In addition, they attacked his marriage to Rachel Jackson. More than 30 years earlier, the Jacksons had been married before Rachel's divorce from her first husband was final, so she was thus guilty of bigamy. The attack on their marriage infuriated Jackson and deeply hurt Rachel. When she died shortly after the election, Jackson never forgave his adversaries.

The campaign organized by Jackson and Van Buren was equally nasty. They reminded voters of the supposed "corrupt bargain" that had put Adams in the White House and claimed—with no proof—that Adams, as ambassador to Russia, had procured young American women for the Czar's pleasure. They portrayed Adams as cold and elitist and attacked his Unitarian beliefs as un-Christian compared with Jackson's devout Presbyterian faith. For the Democrats, the campaign was not about the American System but a choice "Between J.Q. Adams, who can write, and Andy Jackson who can fight." The fighter won easily.

The popular vote nearly tripled between 1824 and 1828, and 57.5 percent of all eligible voters actually voted. All but two states, Delaware and South Carolina, chose presidential electors by popular vote for slates pledged to one candidate or another in 1828. Campaigning had risen to new heights, and more voters believed that their votes counted. Political parties organized a new get-out-the-vote effort, which for the first time, included election materials such as buttons, mugs, posters, and slogans. In the end, Jackson won 647,286 votes—56 percent of the popular vote—and 178 electoral votes, and Adams won 508,064 popular votes and 83 electoral votes. (Four years earlier the popular vote had been 153,554 votes for Jackson to 108,740 votes for Adams.) There was no need for the House of Representatives to be involved. A new style of electioneering had emerged.

9.1

9.2

9.3

Democratic Party
Political party that favored states' rights and a limited role for the federal government, especially in economic affairs.

9.3 | **Quick Review** How did the nation evolve from the Era of Good Feelings to the partisanship of the mid to late 1820s? What were the most important factors in this transition?

CONCLUSION

Washington Irving's story, *Rip Van Winkle*, published in 1819, tells the story of a man who awakens after a 20-year nap to find that everything in his village has completely changed. The story captures the transformation of the physical, commercial, and political landscapes of the United States and the corresponding changes in the lives of Americans during the first decades of independence—largely caused by the rapid growth of cotton production and technological innovation. Although it would have seemed unimaginable even a few years earlier, after 1815 distances seemed shorter, money and material goods more important, and politics omnipresent to many Americans, not just national leaders. Production of cotton and all the accompanying commerce it generated changed the lives of nearly all of the country's residents and focused the attention of many Americans on productivity and hoped-for prosperity. Slavery expanded from the Atlantic coast as thousands of enslaved people were forced to move into the interior of the country where the black belt, stretching from Georgia through Alabama, Mississippi, and Louisiana, became the center of cotton production based on the back-breaking labor of slaves. At the same time, many white Americans, especially young women, who had been used to the rhythms of farm life, went to work in highly regimented mills, spinning cotton into cloth. Other Americans transported cotton between states and across the Atlantic Ocean at speeds their forbearers could not have imagined. The new prominence of public clocks with a hand that noted minutes in addition to the passage of hours reflected this shift. The demand for cotton and the labor-intensive process of its cultivation led to the explosion of slavery in the South, the growth of the textile industry in the North, and a revolution in industry and transportation.

New York City emerged as a transportation hub connecting the United States to the international cotton trade. The Erie Canal also secured New York's place as a commercial center as it made transport between interior locations and coastal ports more efficient. Steamboats, canal boats, transatlantic packet ships, and stagecoaches traveled the routes in ever-faster circuits. Banks, some of the first and most important corporations in the young nation, played an essential role in the market economy. Corporate shareholders, a dramatically new development, deepened the stability of businesses and extended their ability to operate. However, the cotton market slumped in 1819, which caused an economic downturn and financial panic among Americans. Although the economy would eventually recover and thrive, the experience reflected a new and not fully understood national economy.

During Monroe's administration, the Supreme Court, led by Chief Justice John Marshall, decided a series of cases that expanded the power of the federal government and limited that of the states, claiming a role for the Supreme Court in reviewing the constitutionality of acts of state legislatures, which would become important in the years to come. Despite general calm during the Era of Good Feelings of Monroe's two-term administration, political tensions over the cotton economy, territorial expansion, and slavery exploded with surprising force in the 1820s. When Missouri applied to become a state in 1819, the divisions over slavery intensified, and although the Missouri Compromise was meant to resolve the differences, many agreed with the aging Thomas Jefferson that it was "a reprieve only." The Era of Good Feelings gave way to divisive contests for the presidency in 1824—a victory for John Quincy Adams—and in 1828—a victory for Andrew Jackson—and the rebirth of political parties. Jackson's political agenda reflected his concerns for the economic and political interests of a broad spectrum of white America that was growing in influence in the government, and he represented the symbolic voice of a new generation.

CHAPTER REVIEW How did the economic changes fostered by the growth of cotton production and the new national market economy in the United States affect national politics and governmental decisions? Why were economic and political trends so closely connected?

Chapter 9 Chapter Review

CREATING THE COTTON ECONOMY

9.1 Explain the role of cotton in transforming the land and the lives of many diverse people of the United States.

Review Questions

1. **Chronological Reasoning**
   How did events and developments in the 1790s set the stage for the rapid expansion of cotton production in the United States in the early 1800s? What role did events taking place outside of the United States play in this process?

2. **Historical Interpretation**
   How did the expansion of cotton production shape the development of slavery in the United States? In what ways did it make life harder for enslaved African-Americans?

3. **Historical Interpretation**
   How did the expansion of cotton production shape the development of the commercial economy in the United States? What new opportunities and challenges did it create for northern workers?

COMMERCE, TECHNOLOGY, AND TRANSPORTATION

9.2 Analyze the technological and financial changes that led to the emergence of a new market economy in the United States.

Review Questions

4. **Historical Interpretation**
   How did the transportation revolution create new connections between Americans and alter old ones? How did it facilitate the movement and exchange of people, products, and ideas?

5. **Crafting Arguments**
   Defend or refute the following statement. "The emergence of the market economy in the early 1800s would not have been possible without significant government involvement." What evidence can you provide to support your position?

6. **Comparison**
   What were the most important social, political, and economic differences between the United States in 1800 and the United States in 1820? How would you explain the changes you note?

FROM THE ERA OF GOOD FEELINGS TO THE POLITICS OF DIVISION

9.3 Explain the political developments in the United States during the 1820s, including the shift of power toward the South and West that resulted from the changing economic situation.

Review Questions

7. **Comparison**
   Why was the sectional divide over slavery deeper in 1820 than it had been in 1790?

8. **Historical Interpretation**
   How did Andrew Jackson's unexpected popular success in the election of 1824 foreshadow broader changes in the nature of American politics? To whom did Jackson appeal? Why?

9. **Historical Interpretation**
   How did the economic policies of the Adams administration contribute to the emergence of new political parties? How was the growing sectional divide reflected in the new parties?

10 Democracy in the Age of Andrew Jackson

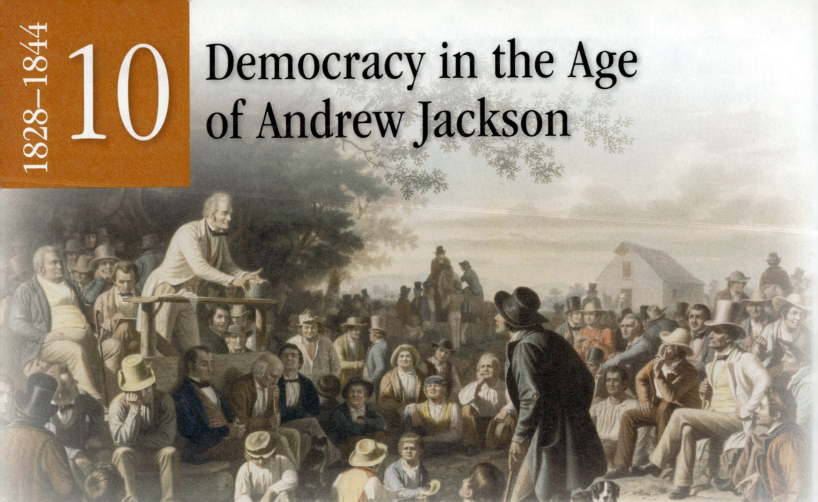

Politics dominated the thinking of many Americans in the Age of Jackson. This painting titled *Stump Speaking* captures the scene as a large group of white men gathered to hear a political speaker.

CHAPTER OBJECTIVE

Demonstrate an understanding of the changing definitions of democracy in the Age of Jackson and what Jacksonian Democracy meant for different groups of Americans.

LEARNING OBJECTIVES

JACKSONIAN DEMOCRACY, JACKSONIAN GOVERNMENT

10.1 Analyze Jackson's advocacy for Indian Removal, his opposition to the Bank of the United States, his support for a tariff, and the impact of these policies on other Americans.

DEMOCRATIZED RELIGION: THE SECOND GREAT AWAKENING

10.2 Analyze the diversity of American religious experience and how the freedom of the era gave rise to diverse religious expressions.

DEMOCRATIZED EDUCATION: THE BIRTH OF THE COMMON SCHOOL

10.3 Explain the development of public education as a result of, and in response to, the cultural currents of the 1820s and 1830s.

A ndrew Jackson's inauguration as president in March 1829 was a somber affair for Jackson himself, who was still mourning his wife Rachel's death the previous December. He did not make the traditional call on the outgoing president, blaming John Quincy Adams for attacks that he believed hastened Rachel's death, and he did not attend his own inaugural ball. For his supporters, however, Jackson's inauguration was a raucous celebration of democracy. When Jackson arrived at the White House, a festive crowd overran the place, stood on the furniture, broke china, and had to be lured outside with bowls of spiked punch. A Washington observer, Margaret Bayard Smith complained about what she saw as the rabble that inundated the White House, describing their behavior as "scrambling, fighting, romping." Supreme Court Justice Joseph Story called it "the reign of King Mob." But order was restored, and Jackson's agenda began to emerge.

Jackson cared about a few big issues, and these shaped his agenda as president. He did not worry much about how the issues were connected. During both of his campaigns for the presidency in 1824 and 1828, he had promised to acquire land for white settlement by forcing Indian tribes to move west of the Mississippi River. He also promised to undermine the Bank of the United States and the power of northern economic elites.

This illustration of the crowd at the White House after Jackson's inauguration captures the mood of the day, even though the artist was not present and created it based on stories told by others.

Significant Dates

<table>
<tr><td>1826</td><td>Charles B. Finney leads religious revivals in western New York</td></tr>
<tr><td>1828</td><td>Tariff of Abominations; Jackson defeats Adams for president</td></tr>
<tr><td>1829</td><td>Andrew Jackson inaugurated president</td></tr>
<tr><td>1830</td><td>Congress passes Indian Removal Act
Nullification Crisis begins
Joseph Smith founds the Church of Jesus Christ of the Latter-Day Saints</td></tr>
<tr><td>1832</td><td>Jackson vetoes recharter of Second Bank of the United States
South Carolina legislature nullifies federal tariffs
Black Hawk's War in Illinois</td></tr>
<tr><td>1833</td><td>Congress passes compromise tariff
Nullification debate ends</td></tr>
<tr><td>1835</td><td>Treaty of New Echota
Catharine Beecher publishes Essay on the Education of Female Teachers</td></tr>
<tr><td>1836</td><td>First McGuffey Reader published
Second Creek War in Alabama</td></tr>
<tr><td>1837</td><td>Horace Mann elected Secretary of the Massachusetts Board of Education</td></tr>
<tr><td>1838</td><td>Ralph Waldo Emerson "Divinity School Address"</td></tr>
<tr><td>1838–1839</td><td>Trail of Tears</td></tr>
</table>

10.1

10.2

10.3

He was opposed to Henry Clay's American System and wanted to keep taxes low and the role of the federal government modest. That said, Jackson understood power and was committed to expanding the power of the presidency itself. As he proceeded with his agenda, he was often challenged, and his response was to fight back with all the resources he could find.

The era during which Jackson led the country was known as the Age of Jackson. Jackson was the symbolic voice of a new generation and a specific class of American people. The first president born west of the Alleghenies, he was not connected to the Founding Fathers as all of his predecessors had been. He spoke for the economic and political interests of a broad spectrum of white America that was growing in influence in the government. Although it was not his doing, Jackson also presided over a nation in which the churches and the schools expanded and changed significantly.

JACKSONIAN DEMOCRACY, JACKSONIAN GOVERNMENT

10.1 Analyze Jackson's advocacy for Indian Removal, his opposition to the Bank of the United States, his support for a tariff, and the impact of these policies on other Americans.

Jackson knew what he wanted to accomplish as president. Before implementing any other policies, he planned a clean sweep of senior federal office holders, some of whom had served under several presidents. Jefferson's successors—Madison, Monroe, and John Quincy Adams—had made few changes below the level of the Cabinet itself, partly because they were all from the same political party and partly because they did not see it as the president's role to make wholesale personnel changes. In a significant change of practice, Jackson replaced many officials, and in the process, created the suspicion that there had been corruption without evidence for it. Jackson believed in what came to be called the "**spoils system**," which was a patronage system in which a victorious political party rewards a candidate's supporters with government jobs. Jackson used the term "rotation in office," but his supporters believed "to the victor belongs the spoils." Suddenly with Jackson in office, experienced officials, including 25 customs collectors and 423 postmasters, were fired from what had been a small, stable federal bureaucracy. Services deteriorated, and the quality of some federal services like the postal service did not recover until civil service reform took hold in the 1880s.

spoils system
A way of selecting people for government jobs based on the idea that "to the victor belongs the spoils."

Martin Van Buren, architect of Jackson's 1828 campaign for president, became secretary of state. But Jackson's other cabinet officers were less talented, and Jackson often ignored them. Instead, he surrounded himself with informal advisors who came to be known as his "Kitchen Cabinet," longtime friends and advisors who worked closely with the president, particularly to accomplish removing Indians from wanted lands, revoking the charter for the Second Bank of the United States, and preserving the authority of the federal union against radical supporters of states' rights.

Jackson's Presidential Agenda

Jackson had several interlocking, but not entirely consistent, priorities. He distrusted government at all levels but had unbounded trust in his own ability to govern. He meant not only to be an activist president—John Quincy Adams and other presidents had also followed strong agendas—but also to make the presidency the center of the American government. He would not defer to Congress in ways that all of his predecessors had done. He vetoed more congressional bills than all of his predecessors combined and made it clear that Congress would have to reckon with him. As he had announced before the election, he was determined to force the Indians who lived in northern Georgia, Alabama, and Mississippi to move west to clear the land for white settlement. Although he supported a modified tariff, he meant to scale back the size of the federal government. He hated the Bank of the United States and was determined to destroy it. He saw its charter as an inappropriate use of federal authority and was convinced, probably rightly, that the bank had contributed to Adams's campaign. And perhaps most of all, Jackson was determined to preserve the Union at a time when southern leaders were insisting that each state had the right of **nullification**, the right to declare that specific federal legislation was null and void within its borders. Jackson was a slaveholder and a defender of slavery, but if slaveholders threatened national unity, they would have to deal with him.

In his two terms as president, Jackson realized most of his goals, despite fierce opposition. He established permanent precedents for presidential authority. He was a hero to some and an evil genius to others. For most historians, he remains one of the most complex American leaders, expanding the roles of poor and working-class whites in the political process and of the presidency in American life, while reducing the rights of Indians, slaves, federal employees, bankers, and indeed anyone who disagreed with him.

The Indian Removal Act, the Trail of Tears, and the Settlement of Oklahoma

For some white Americans, "Indian Removal"—Jackson's policy of forcing the Cherokee Nation and other tribes to move to reservations in distant Oklahoma, or Indian Territory as it was called, was a great achievement. For the tribes caught in Jackson's web, the policy led to war within the tribes, terrible losses, resistance, resignation, and reinvention. Their white supporters, though passionate, were ineffective against Jackson.

Known as the **Five Civilized Tribes**, the Cherokees, Chickasaws, Choctaws, Creeks, and Seminoles had for generations lived in the region known as the Old Southwest—Georgia, Alabama, Mississippi—as well as in Arkansas, and Florida. These tribes had traded and fought with Spanish, French, and English settlers and had sold or ceded much of their land, but based on treaties with the U.S. government, they still owned huge tracts of land in the heart of the cotton-growing South.

Far more than the Indians of the Northwest or the West, the Five Civilized Tribes had adopted many white ways and customs, intermarried with whites, and created a unique culture based on farming and trade. Of the five tribes, the Cherokee Nation had the most sophisticated political, economic, and cultural institutions. Stretching over northwest Georgia, Alabama, Tennessee, and North Carolina,

nullification
A constitutional doctrine holding that a state has a legal right to declare a national law null and void within its borders.

Five Civilized Tribes
The Cherokees, Chickasaws, Choctaws, Creeks, and Seminoles, who had established treaty agreements with the United States in the late 1700s or early 1800s, lived in peace with their neighbors and adopted more of the ways of the whites than most Native Americans.

the Cherokees expected to be treated as a sovereign country. The Cherokees, who had supported the British during the Revolution, had signed a treaty with the new United States government in 1785 and never again waged war against the United States. They supported Jackson in his battle with the Creeks and lived at peace with their neighbors, but that did them little good once Jackson determined his course of action.

After making peace with the United States in the 1780s, the Cherokees took well to the European-style of communication and farming. In 1821, a Cherokee warrior, Sequoyah, intrigued by what he called the "markings" of written English, invented an 86-character alphabet that represented the syllables of spoken Cherokee. The new alphabet caught on quickly, not only in handwritten form but also in typeface for printing. The *Cherokee Phoenix*, published in both English and Cherokee, became an important means of communication. Sequoyah, who never learned English, created a similar alphabet for the Choctaw language. His achievement to invent a written language while being illiterate in all languages had never before been done. In addition, the Cherokees set up a large and effective trading network with other tribes and the white community. In 1827, they adopted a written constitution for the Cherokee Republic.

Beginning in the 1790s, Christian missionaries came to live among the Cherokees. The Cherokees welcomed them, though most never became Christians. Using Sequoyah's alphabet, the missionaries translated the Bible into Cherokee and later became some of the most heroic defenders of Cherokee rights.

Cherokees also cultivated cotton as their white neighbors did, and some owned African slaves. An 1825 census counted 13,563 Cherokees, 220 whites (some of whom were married to Cherokees), and 1,277 African slaves in the Cherokee Republic. Of all the American Indian tribes, the Cherokees were the model of assimilation that presidents from Washington to Jefferson claimed to want. But white settlers and President Jackson decided to ignore the assimilation. They wanted the land.

Georgia took the lead in seizing Indian land. In 1824, Governor George Troup announced that he was ending treaty rights for the Cherokee and Creek tribes. When President John Quincy Adams opposed him, citing the tribes' treaties with the U.S. government, Troup and his successor, John Forsyth, campaigned for Jackson in 1828. In December 1828, the Georgia legislature declared that, starting in June 1830, Georgia state laws would extend to all parts of the Cherokee Republic despite federal treaty agreements to the contrary. White Georgians then began moving onto Cherokee lands, and Jackson withdrew U.S. troops that had been protecting the Cherokees.

It was in this context that Jackson addressed Congress, advocating an **Indian Removal Act** to "protect" the Cherokees from Georgia laws. The president gave the tribes what seemed like a choice: "voluntarily" move west to new lands where their independence would be honored or choose to stay where they were. But if they chose to stay, they would be subject to the laws of Georgia, laws that said Indians could not vote, own property, testify against a white person in court, or obtain credit. It was not much of a choice, as Jackson himself said in private.

The land that the government offered the tribes was completely unfamiliar to the tribes of the Old Southwest. Most people thought of it as simply a desert where farming would be impossible. Indian Territory, which eventually became the state of Oklahoma, was a portion of the Louisiana Purchase just north of Texas. The land was not empty, though the government tended to treat it that way. Some of the plains tribes—the Wichitas, Kiowas, Kiowa Apaches, and especially Osages—had lived there for generations. Some tribes from the Ohio-Illinois area—Shawnees, Delawares (Lenapes), Miamis, Kickapoos, Sacs, and Fox—had been relocated to that territory after defeats by the U.S. Army. In addition, there were a few white settlers and some slaves and former slaves seeking refuge in the region. Nevertheless, under Jackson's plan, the government was now offering the territory to the Cherokees and others of the Five Civilized Tribes (see Map 10-1).

While Cherokee, Creek, Chickasaw, Choctaw, and Seminole leaders had long feared just such a move and had been protesting against it, many whites now rallied to their side. In Congress and the national press, Indian Removal became a major fight.

Sequoyah was intrigued with the way reading seemed to give whites power. He created an alphabet for the Cherokee language and, later, a similar one for the Choctaw language.

Indian Removal Act
Legislation passed by Congress in 1830 which provided funds for removing and resettling eastern Indians in the West. It granted the president the authority to use force if necessary and resulted in the involuntary transfer of thousands of Native Americans to new homes in Oklahoma.

MAP 10-1 Indian Removal. While Indian Removal began with the forced relocation of the Sac and Fox tribes from Illinois and Iowa, by far the largest relocation of tribes took place when the five Indian nations who were living in large territories in Georgia, Alabama, Florida, and Mississippi were forced far to the west to the newly created Indian Territory.

Catharine Beecher, a reformer associated with many causes, organized women across the Northwest to defend Indian rights and flooded Congress with petitions. Missionaries campaigned against the bill so vigorously that Georgia sentenced two of them to prison at hard labor for refusing to abandon the Indians.

In the Senate, Theodore Frelinghuysen of New Jersey, long a supporter of Protestant missionaries and reform efforts, led the opposition to the Indian Removal Bill. Frelinghuysen insisted that the government was bound by its treaties and that, if need be, should use the U.S. Army to force Georgia to retract its claims to the Indian lands. Henry Clay, who had not previously spoken in favor of Indian rights, joined the antiremoval forces. In the end, the removal bill passed the Senate 28 to 19, but passed the House by only a 102–98 vote. Among those voting no was Congressman Davy Crockett of Tennessee, who called the bill "oppression with a vengeance." But Jackson signed the law May 28, 1830, making half a century of treaties void. The tribes would have to move. While all of the tribes resisted, negotiated, and ultimately had to surrender, the Cherokees went to U.S. courts to assert their claims to their lands. Initially,

American Voices

Perspectives on Indian Removal, 1818–1829

Americans responded differently to President Andrew Jackson's plan to remove American Indians from the Old Southwest to reservations west of the Mississippi. Most whites in Georgia and many elsewhere applauded. In the north, many opposed Indian Removal, and Catharine Beecher organized a petition campaign in which women petitioned Congress to stop what they saw as an immoral process. Not surprisingly, most Cherokees, like the other tribes involved, also opposed removal. Writing a decade before Jackson's speech, Cherokee women demanded that the tribal elders not cede land to the United States. The following three documents represent three different American voices.

Andrew Jackson, Message to Congress, December 8, 1829	Statements of Residents of Steubenville Ohio, February 15, 1830	Cherokee Women's Petition, June 30, 1818
The condition and ulterior destiny of the Indian tribes within the limits of some of our States have become objects of much interest and importance. It has long been the policy of Government to introduce among them the arts of civilization, in the hope of gradually reclaiming them from a wandering life. This policy has, however, been coupled with another wholly incompatible with its success. Professing a desire to civilize and settle them, we have at the same time lost no opportunity to purchase their lands and thrust them farther into the wilderness. By this means they have not only been kept in a wandering state, but been led to look upon us as unjust and indifferent to their fate. . . Our ancestors found them the uncontrolled possessors of these vast regions. By persuasion and force they have been made to retire from river to river and from mountain to mountain, until some of the tribes have become extinct and others have left but remnants to preserve for awhile their once terrible names.… Humanity and national honor demand that every effort should be made to avert so great a calamity.… As a means of effecting this end I suggest for your consideration the propriety of setting apart an ample district west of the Mississippi, and without the limits of any State or Territory now formed, to be guaranteed to the Indian tribes as long as they shall occupy it, each tribe having a distinct control over the portion designated for its use. There they may be secured in the enjoyment of governments of their own choice, subject to no other control from the United States than such as may be necessary to preserve peace on the frontier and between the several tribes.…	THAT your memorialists are deeply impressed with the belief that the present crisis in the affairs of the Indian nations, calls loudly on *all* who can feel for the woes of humanity.…It is readily acknowledged, that the wise and venerated founders of our country's free institutions, have committed the powers of government to those whom nature and reason declare the best fitted to exercise them; and your memorialists would sincerely deprecate any presumptuous interference on the part of their own sex, with the ordinary political affairs of the country, as wholly unbecoming the character of American Females.… yet all admit that *there are times* when duty and affection call on us to *advise* and *persuade*, as well as to cheer or to console. And if we approach the public representatives of our husbands and brothers, only in the humble character of suppliants in the cause of mercy and humanity, may we not hope that even the small voice of *female* sympathy will be heard?… In despite of the *undoubted natural right*, which the Indians have, to the land of their forefathers, and in the face of solemn treaties, pledging the faith of the nation for their secure possession of those lands, it is intended, we are told, to force them from their native soil, and to compel them to seek new homes in a distant and dreary wilderness. To you then, as the constitutional protectors of the Indians within our territory and as the peculiar guardians of our national character, and our country's welfare, we solemnly and earnestly appeal to save this remnant of a much injured people from annihilation, to shield our country from the curses denounced on the cruel and ungrateful, and to shelter the American character from lasting dishonor.	We have called a meeting among ourselves to consult on the different points now before the council, relating to our national affairs. We have heard with painful feelings that the bounds of the land we now possess are to be drawn into very narrow limits. The land was given to us by the Great Spirit above as our common right, to raise our children upon, & to make support for our rising generations. We therefore humbly petition our beloved children, the head men & warriors, to hold out to the last in support of our common right, as the Cherokee nation have been the first settlers of this land; we therefore claim the right to the soil. We well remember that our country was formerly very extensive, but by repeated sales it has become circumscribed to the very narrow limits we have at present. Our Father the President advised us to become farmers, to manufacture our own clothes, & to have our children instructed. To this advice we have attended in everything as far as we were able. Now the thought of being compelled to remove [to] the other side of the Mississippi is dreadful to us, because it appears to us that we, by this removal, shall be brought to a savage state again, for we have, by the endeavor of our Father the President, become too much enlightened to throw aside the privileges of a civilized life. We therefore unanimously join in our meeting to hold our country in common as hitherto. Some of our children have become Christians. We have missionary schools among us. We have h[e]ard the gospel in our nation. We have become civilized & enlightened, & are in hopes that in a few years our nation will be prepared for instruction in other branches of sciences & arts, which are both useful & necessary in civilized society.…

Sources: Andrew Jackson, Annual Message to Congress, December 8, 1829, Messages and Papers of the Presidents, ed. J. D. Richardson, National Archives and Records Administration, (1896), II, 456–459 (Dec. 8, 1829); Ladies of Steubenville, Ohio, Petition Against Indian removal (February 15, 1830), Ellen Skinner, Women and the National Experience: Sources in Women's History, third edition (Boston: Prentice-Hall, 1996), pp.42–143; "Petition of Nancy Ward and Other Cherokee Women to the United States Congress, 19\818," in Karen L. Kilcup, editor, Native American Women's Writings, 1800–1924: An Anthology (Malden, MA: Blackwell, 2000), pp. 29–30.

(continued)

Thinking Critically

1. Documentary Analysis

How did Jackson attempt to argue that Indian Removal was in the Indians' best interest? How might opponents of Indian Removal have responded to his position?

2. Contextualization

How might the fact that two petitions in opposition to Indian Removal were written by women have affected their reception? How might it have helped the authors' cause? How might it have hurt?

3. Contextualization

The Cherokee women say that they hope that, soon, their people "will be prepared for instruction in other branches of sciences & arts, which are both useful & necessary in civilized society." What does this statement mean? What do you think is the strongest reason they give for asking not to be moved west?

they won. In *Cherokee Nation v. Georgia* (1831) and *Worcester v. Georgia* (1832), the U.S. Supreme Court, under Chief Justice John Marshall, ruled that the Cherokees were a "domestic dependent nation" and could not be forced by the state of Georgia to give up land that treaty rights agreed to by the United States government had given them. Jackson simply ignored the court. Jackson is supposed to have said, "John Marshall has made his decision, now let him enforce it." No one actually heard Jackson say that, but Jackson controlled the army and he was not about to enforce the court's decision. No other president before or after ignored the Supreme Court in that way.

The Indian Removal Act and the implementation that followed was a disaster for the Five Civilized Tribes. The government had seized their homes and offered in return land that was thousands of miles away and completely foreign to them. Moreover the tribes were divided about how to respond. While most of the country was focused on the Cherokees, Jackson sent Secretary of War John Eaton to negotiate with the Choctaws. By excluding those he considered troublemakers and bribing others, Eaton got a small group of Choctaw leaders to agree for the tribe to leave its homes in Mississippi, but most in the tribe considered those who negotiated the removal treaty to be nonrepresentative and refused to abide by it. The federal troops enforced it anyway.

The French observer Alexis de Tocqueville, who became famous for his analysis of American life in the Jacksonian era, described the day the Choctaws crossed the Mississippi River on their way west:

> At the end of 1831, I stood on the left bank of the Mississippi....It was then the depths of winter and the cold was exceptionally severe...the snow had frozen hard on the ground; the river was drifting with huge ice-floes. The Indians had brought their families with them and hauled along the wounded, the sick, newborn babies, and old men on the verge of death. They had neither tents nor wagons....I saw them embark to cross the wide river and that solemn spectacle will never be erased from my memory. Not a sob or complaint could be heard...they stood silent. Their afflictions were of long standing and they considered them beyond remedy. Already the Indians had all embarked upon the boat which was to carry them; their dogs still remained upon the bank. When these animals finally saw they were being left behind forever, they raised all together a terrible howl and plunged into the icy Mississippi to swim after their masters.

Within the decade most members of the Cherokee, Chickasaw, Creek tribes had made the same crossing. Only the Seminoles avoided their fate.

Alabama and Mississippi followed Georgia's lead and voted to end tribal rights for the Creeks. In March 1832, the Creeks surrendered all land east of the Mississippi, and most of them moved to Oklahoma. Those that took advantage of a promise that they could stay in the East as private citizens soon lost their lands. Some of the remaining Creeks began violent resistance to state and federal authorities, but the so-called Second Creek War of 1836–37 ended quickly when Jackson's secretary of war ordered federal troops to expel all Creeks from lands east of the Mississippi. The Creeks who were deported after the Second Creek War suffered higher mortality rates than the Cherokees; perhaps half lived to see Oklahoma.

Among the Cherokees, a civil conflict broke out about how to respond to the demand that they move to Oklahoma. Principal Chief John Ross and most of the Cherokees were determined to fight for their lands. A minority, some of whom were among the rising middle class and slave holders within the tribe, decided that a compromise was better than forced expulsion. John Ridge and Elias Boudinot, publisher of the *Cherokee Phoenix*, signed the Treaty of New Echota in December 1835, trading land in Georgia for new land in Oklahoma and $5 million. The U.S. Senate barely ratified the treaty after Daniel Webster and Henry Clay pointed out how fraudulent it was since the majority of the Cherokees opposed it.

After Ridge and Boudinot and their followers departed for Oklahoma, or Indian Territory as it was called, the U.S. Army put most of the remaining members of the tribe in detention camps. A few were able to flee into the wilderness and remained in their homelands but without their land. Others fought, but in the end, Chief Ross and General Winfield Scott negotiated a settlement to avoid further bloodshed. Even though Jackson had left office by then, his successor, Martin Van Buren was determined to enforce his predecessor's policy. From the detention camps, soldiers forced 12,000 Cherokee men, women, and children to march west in the fall and winter of 1838–39. It was an especially cold winter and a terrible time to make a march of over a thousand miles into the unknown. The Cherokees never had enough food, blankets, or warm clothing, and as they moved in large groups, disease and exposure took a terrible toll. On what became known as the **Trail of Tears**, perhaps a quarter to a third of the marchers, including Ross's wife, died before they reached Oklahoma.

Seeing what was happening to other tribes, the Chickasaws moved west quickly on their own. The Seminoles of Florida Territory had no intention of moving, however. Although a minority of Seminoles agreed to move, most stayed in Florida, disappearing into the swamps and hiding places they knew well. When soldiers tried to force them to move, the Seminoles annihilated them. The Second Seminole War was not resolved until 1842. Fewer Seminoles than members of any other tribe ever moved to Oklahoma.

Trail of Tears
The forced march in 1838 of the Cherokee Indians from their homelands in Georgia to the Indian Territory in the West; thousands of Cherokees died along the way.

Cherokee men, women, and children, and their U.S. Army guards, rode or walked on the long march from their ancestral homes across a thousand miles to new territory in Oklahoma.

Chapter 10 Democracy in the Age of Andrew Jackson **279**

In the meantime, the Sac and Fox tribes, which had already been exiled to the Indian Territory as a result of earlier removals from the Old Northwest, were not too happy about life there. In April 1832, a chief named Black Hawk led 1,000–2,000 Sac and Fox people back east across the Mississippi, closer to their old homelands. The Sac and Fox Indians were moving mostly to escape from hostile Sioux groups on the Great Plains and Iowa Territory. The Illinois governor took the tribes' move into Illinois as an attack, called out the militia, and asked for federal troops. In Black Hawk's War, federal and state troops on the east side of the Mississippi and Sioux warriors on the west virtually annihilated the Fox and Sac tribes, to the delight of whites who were happy to see these tribes completely out of their way.

In fact, Jackson had meant to use the removal law for Georgia to force all Indians east of the Mississippi out of their lands. When the forced exile finally reached its goal by the end of the 1830s, only the Iroquois in New York, a few Cherokees in North Carolina, and scattered small communities remained legally east of the Mississippi, although others like the Seminoles simply melted into the woods and could not be found by the government. All in all, 46,000 Indians were forcibly removed during the Jackson administration, and subsequent administrations removed as many more.

The Cherokees and other tribes tend to disappear from the history books after the Trail of Tears. But the Cherokees, Choctaws, and Creeks were resilient people. Forced onto an inhospitable and alien land, they sought to reestablish their communities and culture. To a surprising degree, they succeeded. As the last Cherokees arrived in Indian Territory in 1839, the tribe adopted a new Constitution and established Tahlequah as their capital. In 1844, they began publishing the *Cherokee Advocate* in both English and Cherokee. They also set up a school system with elementary schools as well as higher education institutes and seminaries to prepare teachers—European and Cherokee—for their schools. In the U.S. Civil War, parts of the tribe favored each side, and the divided tribe fought internally. But again they rebuilt after the war. Today, there are some 200,000 to 300,000 Cherokees, of whom 70,000 live within the Cherokee Nation in northeast Oklahoma and the rest are scattered around the country, making them the largest federally recognized tribe today.

Jacksonian Economics—The War on the Bank of the United States

The Second Bank of the United States
A national bank chartered by Congress in 1816 with extensive regulatory powers over currency and credit.

In his campaign for president, Jackson pledged to do something about the Bank of the United States, which he and many others blamed for the Panic of 1819 and saw as an elitist threat to a democracy. **The Second Bank of the United States** was patterned on the first Bank of the United States that had been a cornerstone of Alexander Hamilton's economic plans for the new nation (see Chapter 7). The first bank had been chartered in 1791 for a period of 20 years. In 1811, the Jeffersonian Republicans refused to extend its charter and it closed. Henceforth, it seemed, state banks would issue currency in the form of banknotes backed by gold or silver, federal funds would be deposited in state banks, and the federal government, like everyone else, would borrow money from these banks when needed. Then came the War of 1812.

As the War of 1812 threatened to bankrupt the country, some of the nation's richest men, led by John Jacob Astor, met with Treasury Secretary Albert Gallatin and offered to loan the nation the funds it needed if the Bank of the United States were rechartered. They believed that only a national bank could build long-term prosperity and ensure that their loan would be repaid. As a result, a charter for a Second Bank of the United States passed Congress in 1816. The Madison, Monroe, and John Quincy Adams administrations were strong advocates for a unified national market economy that could foster prosperity and stability, and they had used the bank to support that economy. Jackson wanted prosperity, but he disagreed about the government's role in the nation's economy.

The Second Bank of the United States was never without enemies. The Constitution never mentioned a bank, and strict constructionists—who thought the government should limit its role to things specifically included in the Constitution—always opposed it. The bank was also seen by many as a way to expand the power of the commercial elite based in New York and Philadelphia and, thus, was seen as an enemy by farmers whether they lived on small out-of-the-way farms in the still very rural country or on the bourgeoning plantations of the cotton-growing South. In the opinion of many farmers, whether small or large scale, Jackson was the defender of their interests against threatening commercial elites. Particularly since the Supreme Court's ruling on *McCulloch* v. *Maryland* that Congress had the right to charter a bank if it thought it was in the national interest, popular support for the Bank had weakened (see Chapter 9). Many farmers did not believe "the national interest" that Congress saw was in their interests.

During his first months in office, Jackson did not say a lot about the bank, but in December 1829, he told Congress: "Both the constitutionality and the expediency of the law creating this bank are well questioned....[I]t has failed in the great end of establishing a uniform and sound currency." In spite of Jackson's challenge, the bank's charter ensured that it could continue for 7 more years, but Jackson had fired a warning shot. Before long, he would do much more.

Many of Jackson's strongest supporters disagreed with him about the bank. The country was prospering, credit was solid, and the soundness of the currency, despite Jackson's words, seemed secure. The federal bank's policies of calling in loans may have helped start the Panic of 1819, but Nicholas Biddle, the bank's president, had done as much as anyone in the country to end the hard times after the Panic of 1819. Nevertheless Jackson was a populist, intending to represent the common people politically. And although the nation's elite supported the bank, many citizens did not like any banks. In a meeting at the White House he told Biddle, "I do not dislike your bank any more than all banks," but the federal bank was the only one Jackson could do something about. His attack on the bank was as emotional as it was calculated.

For the next few years, Biddle led the bank in continued efforts to stabilize the currency, help state banks through difficult times, and expand the nation's credit, something that both northern mill owners and western land promoters liked. The bank also concentrated wealth and power within the economy in the hands of a commercial elite and strengthened the nation's unified market economy based on currency and trade. That uneven concentration of wealth and power was something Jackson would not forgive.

In 1832, Jackson launched his campaign for reelection. For the first time, something resembling modern political parties played a role. Under Jackson's leadership, the Democratic-Republicans had become simply the Democrats. They easily nominated Jackson for a second term and his handpicked running mate, Secretary of State Martin Van Buren, for vice president. The opposition to Jackson, sometimes known as the National Republicans because they had supported a strong national government, now became known simply as the Whig Party. They nominated Henry Clay for president and John Sergeant of Pennsylvania as vice president. Unlike the Jacksonian Democrats, the Whig Party was committed to Alexander Hamilton's vision of a federal government that took an active role in shaping the economy, so they strongly supported the Second Bank of the United States. The Whig nominee, Henry Clay, urged Biddle to secure the bank's future as well as that of the pro-bank Whig Party. If Biddle were to request an extension of the bank's charter, even though the original charter would not expire for 4 years, Clay would promise to make the bank an issue in the campaign. Either Biddle would win the recharter fight immediately, or he would provide Clay a weapon with which to attack Jackson. Biddle, who was astute at counting votes in Congress, took Clay's advice and applied for a new charter. The charter bill passed both houses of Congress easily. But Jackson vetoed it. He told Martin Van Buren, who was now his running mate, "The bank, Mr. Van Buren, is trying to kill me, but I will kill it."

By the time Jackson became president, political cartoons were becoming popular, including this one that shows Jackson using his order to withdraw government funds to topple the pillars of the bank as Nicholas Biddle, the bank's "devil president," and investors run.

In November 1832, Jackson defeated Clay 219 electoral votes to 49. Congress refused to override the president's veto.

Biddle still tried to rally support in Congress. He made arguments, offered congressmen loans, and ensured that the bank's lead attorney was elected to Congress from Philadelphia. When Massachusetts Senator Daniel Webster complained that his annual retainer from the bank had not been "refreshed as usual," Biddle promised quick action. Biddle also loosened credit across the country, ensuring short-term prosperity but provoking an eventual reckoning. He was desperate to save his bank.

Jackson then made his move. He ordered his treasury secretary to remove federal deposits from the bank and place them in 23 state banks that he selected—banks that were quickly called Jackson's "pet" banks by his opponents. The move was meant to destroy the Second Bank of the United States. But the law said that federal funds could be withdrawn only if there was clear evidence that the deposits were not secure. Even Jackson's handpicked auditors could find no such evidence. When Treasury Secretary McLane refused the president's order to move the funds, Jackson promoted him to secretary of state. When another treasury secretary also refused, Jackson fired him.

Finally, Jackson's third treasury secretary, Roger B. Taney, who also had doubts about the legality of removing federal funds, hit on a compromise. He would not actually remove federal deposits from the bank, but he would do something just as effective to undermine the bank. Going forward, Taney regularly paid the government's bills with funds from the accounts that the government had in the Bank of the United States, but he stopped depositing new federal revenue in the bank. Instead, the government's income went to the state banks. It was a mortal blow. The federal government's accounts slowly shrunk to zero and the Second Bank of the United States was dead, though it took a few years to die.

Led by Clay, the Senate censured the president, saying he had "assumed upon himself authority and power not conferred by the Constitution and laws." But the censure did not hurt Jackson or save the bank. Biddle's politically motivated loans and payments sapped support for the bank. The Second Bank of the United States became a wholly private bank and soon went bankrupt. The combination of inflation caused by Biddle's too-easy credit and the loss of a national bank that could stabilize the currency caused financial distress. By 1837—just after Jackson left office—the nation experienced another financial panic, and there was no national entity to help stabilize the economy. Nevertheless, efforts to revive the bank failed. For decades, all of the paper currency in circulation would be issued by state banks, some of less than solid credit. Only in 1863, during the Civil War, did the U.S. government again issue paper money, and not until the creation of the Federal Reserve Bank in 1913 did the nation again have a central bank to regulate the economy.

The Tariff, the Union, and the Nullification Crisis

The battle over the tariff began as a modest disagreement over federal tax policy. Before it ended, that battle was the greatest constitutional crisis the nation faced between the adoption of the Constitution in 1789 and the Civil War in 1861. To a degree, it was a personal battle between two proud and stubborn men, Andrew Jackson and John C. Calhoun. In another sense it was a battle about the fundamental nature of the U.S. government.

ANDREW JACKSON VS. JOHN C. CALHOUN   John C. Calhoun of South Carolina had been elected vice president when John Quincy Adams won the presidency in 1824, and he was reelected to that office in 1828 to serve with Jackson. Because separate ballots were cast for presidential and vice presidential candidates after the passage of the Twelfth Amendment in 1804 and before the rise of party nominating conventions in 1832, no one thought it strange that two leaders as hostile to each other as Adams and Jackson would have the same vice president. As a congressman and as secretary of war under President James Monroe, Calhoun had been a nationalist who favored internal improvements as much as Henry Clay or John Quincy Adams. He sought a strong national government and had supported the Bank of the United States. Although his views differed from Jackson's on some issues, everyone expected Calhoun and Jackson, as proslavery southerners, to have a close partnership. It was not to be.

One of the first wedges between them was purely social. Jackson's Secretary of War John Eaton had married the recently widowed Margaret O'Neale Timberlake, but rumors swirled that she was a widow only because her first husband, a naval officer, had committed suicide when he learned of her long adulterous relationship with Eaton. Jackson, who had been deeply hurt by attacks on his own marriage, defended the Eatons. Others in Washington, led by Mrs. Calhoun, snubbed Peggy Eaton. When Emily Donelson, Jackson's official White House hostess, joined with Mrs. Calhoun, Jackson temporarily banished her from the White House. He never forgave the Calhouns.

Another reason for the growing split between Jackson and Calhoun centered on the fact that Calhoun's political beliefs were changing. By 1828, Calhoun, who had previously advocated for a strong federal role in the life of the nation—far stronger than anything Jackson ever advocated—was becoming the nation's strongest defender of states' rights against federal authority. This new stance may have reflected an honest change of heart, but it also served a political purpose. Regardless, it guaranteed a clash with Jackson since no matter how much Jackson might have favored states' rights in the past, he would not tolerate any challenge to his authority as president.

Many of the leaders in South Carolina, Calhoun's home state, were becoming very fearful of the federal government, and South Carolina was developing the strongest antifederal stance in the Union. The South Carolina Radicals, as they were called, dominated state government. They advocated the right of states to declare any federal law null and void or even to secede from the Union. The reason was clear: South Carolinians feared for the future of slavery more than people in any other state. Most residents of South Carolina—54 percent—were enslaved people of African descent. In some rice-growing regions of the state, that figure was closer to 90 percent. A wealthy but deeply fearful white elite governed these slaves and depended on their labor to generate continuing wealth. In 1827, a pamphlet called *The Crisis; or, Essays on the Usurpations of the Federal Government* argued that federal tariffs, internal improvements, and other federal activities were all means to enable the national government, if it chose, to abolish slavery. As word spread that Parliament was about to abolish slavery throughout the British Empire in the 1830s, the fear grew that Congress might try to do the same. Calhoun had to decide whether he was with his state's planter elite or against them. He might have dreamed about becoming president someday, but in the meantime, he would have to win elections in South Carolina. He made his choice.

NULLIFICATION AND THE FUTURE OF THE REPUBLIC In 1828, Calhoun wrote a pamphlet arguing that a state could declare a tariff or any other federal law null and void. Calhoun claimed that since state-by-state conventions had ratified the Constitution, state conventions, not the Supreme Court, had the authority to decide what was constitutional. In his view, once a state convention declared a federal law void, other states would have to weigh in, and only a new amendment to the Constitution could force the law on the dissenting state. Calhoun did not advocate secession as many of the South Carolina Radicals did. Instead, he hoped nullification in response to a tariff or to restrictions on slavery would make secession unnecessary. He was thus more moderate than many South Carolinians, but that moderation would not continue to be the case.

The tariff, not the issue of slavery, brought the issue of nullification to the fore. The tariff, or tax on imported goods, had been the major source of financial support since the Washington administration, and it had been an issue in the 1828 election in which Jackson defeated Adams. As Jackson's supporters prepared for that election, Jackson's chief advisor Martin Van Buren realized that, even though he and Jackson opposed a high tariff—in part, because they thought the federal government needed less money and, in part, because the tax raised the cost of foreign-made consumer products in the United States—the Adams-Clay tariff was popular in many parts of the country because it protected local industries from foreign competition and because many people liked the internal improvements like roads and canals that the tariff helped finance. Adams and Clay might want to fight the 1828 election on the issue of tariffs, but Van Buren did not. When the Adams administration suggested a new tariff, Van Buren and his congressional allies decided to reshape it rather than oppose it. They knew they could not win New England in the next election, so they did not hesitate to modify the proposed tariff by reducing the protection for the cotton produced by New England mill owners, thus allowing foreign-made cotton to be sold more cheaply than might otherwise have been the case. They also raised tariffs to protect export of products like molasses, hemp, iron, and wool, which were produced in the mid-Atlantic states, especially in Pennsylvania, to woo voters there by protecting their industries and jobs from foreign competition. The result was a tariff that raised the price of products that many Americans bought from foreign sources and that angered the cotton mill owners who originally wanted the tariff but now saw the protection of their industry disappear. The new tariff also infuriated rural interests, especially southern plantation owners, who saw the cost of everything they needed go up while no protection was provided to the price of the goods they produced and sold on the international market. The 1828 tariff came to be known as the **Tariff of Abominations** because it was so uneven and obviously unfair in the industries and regions it protected, but it passed Congress and set the stage for a confusing presidential campaign and the crisis that followed.

Planters in South Carolina saw the tariff as a terrible hardship and an unfair use of federal power. To a degree, they were right. A tax on imports raised the cost of virtually everything the planters needed. Planters claimed that 40 out of every 100 bales of cotton they produced went to pay the tariff. This claim was an exaggeration, but the tariff may have raised the cost of living in South Carolina by 20 percent. In addition, planters worried that a tariff on imported goods might cause other nations to purchase less cotton either in retaliation or because, with Americans buying less from abroad, other nations might not have had the funds to purchase American grown cotton. With their state's economy hurting, public opinion in South Carolina supported nullification of the tariff.

The issue of states' rights versus the rights of the federal government was argued on the floor of the U.S. Senate in January 1830. It was a debate that would be remembered for generations. South Carolina Senator Robert Y. Hayne, a protégé of Calhoun's, claimed that the federal government was making the North the winner and the South the loser and that the pro-Northern policy "has invaded the State of South Carolina, is making war upon her citizens, and endeavoring to overthrow her principles and institutions." Everyone understood that Hayne was talking about the tariff but also the issue of slavery. He was determined to defend the right of South Carolina to nullify federal law and, if still dissatisfied, to secede from the Union if Congress ever made a move against slavery. Massachusetts Senator Daniel Webster's "Second Reply to Hayne" staked out a different position. Webster pleaded for a strong federal union that no state should be allowed to undermine. His closing line, "Liberty and Union, now and forever, one and inseparable" became part of American lore. Hayne congratulated Webster on winning the war of words, though Hayne never changed his mind.

Tariff of Abominations
A revised federal tariff (or tax on imports) that lowered the tax on cotton products but raised it on many of the products made in the mid-Atlantic states.

At first, people wondered how the president would respond to the debate. Jackson had campaigned for reducing the federal role in people's lives, but he did not like to be crossed. He was not elected to see the government over which he presided pushed aside. As a military man, he would not countenance mutiny. As a politician, he despised Calhoun's self-serving strategic maneuvering. To the surprise of some, Jackson, the president elected with virtually no support from New England, embraced Webster's speech in spite of the fact that it was given by the senator from Massachusetts. Four months after the Hayne-Webster debate, political leaders were asked to make toasts at a banquet. Looking directly at his vice president, Jackson, offered a simple toast, "Our Union: *It must be preserved.*" Calhoun responded, "The Union. Next to our liberty, the most dear. May we always remember that it can only be preserved by respecting the rights of the states...." It marked the final break between the two men.

Nevertheless, as strongly as Jackson believed in asserting federal authority, he was still prepared to compromise about the tariff itself. The actual rate charged in the tariff mattered far less to Jackson than the principle that no state had a right to nullify federal law. A compromise seemed possible when Congress convened in 1831. Former President John Quincy Adams had been elected to the House of Representatives from Massachusetts (the only former president in history to return to Congress), and the congressional leaders asked him to write a new tariff to replace the Tariff of Abominations. Adams took the job seriously. He reduced the duty on goods not produced in the United States and therefore not in need of protection, but retained tariffs to protect growing U.S. industries, especially iron and cotton textiles. He also reduced the tariff on cheap woolens—which slaves wore—from 45 percent to 5 percent, a significant concession to the slave states.

Most of the South found Adams's tariff reasonable. Besides, much of the cotton-growing South was prospering, despite the tariff, because of other Jacksonian policies, especially from the new land that Indian Removal had made available for growing cotton. Other states were in no mood to press the nullification issue.

But South Carolina was different. Much of the state's farmland had been exhausted by decades of overuse, and its dependency on slave labor made its leaders more fearful of federal intervention in the institution of slavery than those of any other state. Led by Calhoun, the state's leaders believed that they had to win the right to nullify the tariff to establish the larger principal that states could nullify any law. For them, the Adams tariff was not enough. In November 1832, a South Carolina state convention declared that both the tariffs of 1828 and 1832 were unconstitutional and that "it shall not be lawful…to enforce payment of duties imposed by the said acts within the limits of this state" after February 1833. They also said that the state would secede if the federal government tried to force it to back down. The South Carolina legislature elected Robert Hayne, who had debated with Webster, as the governor to lead the state through these difficult times and elected Calhoun to replace Hayne in the Senate. Calhoun would essentially be South Carolina's ambassador to the federal government for the next 2 decades. Calhoun resigned as vice president in December 1832, a little more than 2 months before his term ended, and returned to the Senate as a member, a very belligerent member. The stage was set for a major confrontation.

In November 1832, the South Carolina legislature also raised a state militia of 25,000 volunteers. Jackson responded with a proclamation, stating that the state's vote was "in direct violation of their duty as citizens of the United States." According to Jackson, they had no right to nullify federal law and certainly not to raise their own army and,

In January 1830 as tensions were building over the right claimed by South Carolina to nullify federal law, Massachusetts Senator Daniel Webster—shown here—defended the priority of the federal government and the cause of the national union.

he said, "Disunion by armed force is treason." He told a South Carolina congressman, "I will hang the first man of them I can get my hands on to the first tree I can find." He backed his words with action, reinforcing federal garrisons and sending armed revenue ships to Charleston Harbor. He also shifted the collection of customs duties in Charleston to warships offshore. When Governor Hayne told Senator Thomas Hart Benton of Missouri that he did not think Jackson would really hang anyone, Benton, who knew Jackson better, replied, "I tell you, Hayne, when Jackson begins to talk about hanging, they can begin to look out for ropes!" Jackson also lobbied to ensure no other southern state supported South Carolina and pushed Congress to keep the tariffs low.

In the end, no shots were fired. On March 1, 1833, Congress passed a compromise tariff that Henry Clay had crafted based on Adams's proposals and gave the president the authority to put down the rebellion. Wiser heads in South Carolina decided to compromise. The state convention reconvened and declared victory based on the new Clay tariff. For spite they also nullified the congressional vote of new military authority, which they called the "Force Bill," but that action was now meaningless since South Carolina was no longer resisting federal authority.

Jackson won the nullification battle, but it was an incomplete victory. He made it clear, in words and actions, which Abraham Lincoln would use as precedent, that no state could nullify federal law and that the U.S. government would use force to assert its authority. He was treated as a hero in many parts of the country and even

THINKING HISTORICALLY
The Nullification Crisis

The 1832 South Carolina convention that passed the Ordinance of Nullification said:

Whereas the Congress of the United States, by various acts, purporting to be acts laying duties and imposts [taxes] on foreign imports, but in reality intended for the protection of domestic manufacturers, and giving the bounties to classes and individuals engaged in particular employments, at the expense and to the injury and oppression of other classes and individuals…hath exceeded it just powers under the Constitution…

We, therefore, the people of the State of South Carolina in Convention assembled, do declare and ordain…That the several acts and parts of acts of the Congress of the United States, purporting to be laws for the imposing of duties and imposts on the importation of foreign commodities…are unauthorized by the Constitution of the United States, and violate the true meaning and intent thereof, and are null, void, and no law, nor binding upon this state, its officers or citizens.

This declaration was not the first time in U.S. history that a state had taken such a stand. The Kentucky and Virginia resolves

of 1798 and 1799, written by Thomas Jefferson and James Madison, had said the same thing about the Alien and Sedition Acts. The Hartford Convention that met in 1814 said the much the same thing about Congress having declared war on Great Britain in 1812. Yet unlike the response to earlier challenges, President Jackson declared the South Carolina ordinance "incompatible with the existence of the Union" and prepared for a military response.

Source: Statues at Large of South Carolina, Vol. I, pp. 329ff. (Columbia, South Carolina: A. S. Johnston, 1836).

Thinking Critically

1. Documentary Analysis
Why did the authors of the Ordinance of Nullification believe that the Tariffs of 1828 and 1832 were unconstitutional?

2. Craft an Argument
Defend or refute the following statement: "As the Nullification Crisis demonstrates, the ratification of the Constitution in 1788 was only a first, tentative step towards defining the relationship between the federal government and the states." What events and developments between 1788 and 1832 support your position?

given an honorary degree by Harvard University. Even so, neither Calhoun nor the South Carolina legislature admitted defeat. In fact, that legislature passed a new law in 1834 requiring anyone holding state office to swear primary loyalty to South Carolina and only conditional loyalty to the federal government. This law effectively barred Unionists, those moderates who disagreed with nullification, perhaps a third of the state's voters, from state office for the next 30 years.

Alexis de Tocqueville was in the United States during the Nullification Crisis. He took a dim view of the compromise on the tariff and the decision of South Carolina to nullify the "Force Bill":

> Either I am mistaken or the federal government of the Unites States is daily losing its power; it is gradually withdrawing from public affairs and is increasingly narrowing its sphere of action.…I think I have seen a more lively feeling of independence and a more evident affection for regional government developing in the individual states of the Union.

The outcome of this movement, Tocqueville said, was "hidden in the future and I do not claim the ability to lift the veil." But he remained worried for the future of the country.

10.1 **Quick Review** Was Andrew Jackson's presidency democratic? Which of his actions and policies support your argument?

DEMOCRATIZED RELIGION: THE SECOND GREAT AWAKENING

10.2 Analyze the diversity of American religious experience and how the freedom of the era gave rise to diverse religious expressions.

Most Americans had strong opinions about Andrew Jackson. They might love or hate him, but they followed his career. However, politics was far from the only interest of most people. Many things closer to home, and sometimes closer to their own souls, mattered more. For many Americans in the 1820s and 1830s, the growth of a more popular democracy and popular social movements led by ordinary citizens was far more important than President's Jackson's policies or opinions.

No popular movement was more powerful than the upsurge in religious activity that took place in Jacksonian America. Once again de Tocqueville understood the country well: "There is no country in the whole world in which the Christian religion retains a greater influence over the souls of men than in America." He described the Christianity he saw as "a democratic and republican religion." When de Tocqueville wrote these words in the early 1830s, the Second Great Awakening was in full swing. It had begun around 1800 (see Chapter 8), but gathered new strength in Jacksonian America. Contrary to what Tocqueville implied, not all Americans were Protestant Christians, and many of those who were Christians did not fit into traditional Protestantism. But for a large number of those who lived from the 1820s to the 1840s, religion was important, even if formal membership in a specific religious congregation was not.

Charles G. Finney and New York's "Burned-Over District"

In 1821, Charles Grandison Finney, a 29-year-old lawyer in Adams, New York, not far from the Erie Canal, was struggling with the question of whether true religious belief was consistent with his legal career. He decided to leave his law practice, and began to preach in churches in upstate New York, eventually becoming one of the most influential preachers in the United States.

In July 1824, Finney was ordained a Presbyterian minister in spite of his lack of formal training. In 1826, the spirit of revivalism hit upstate New York, and in 1830, Finney led the largest religious revival ever seen in Rochester, New York. Six hundred people joined one of the town's three Presbyterian Churches, and the other denominations were also strengthened.

Finney did not seek an emotional catharsis from his congregants but, like an attorney, argued his case logically using wit and wisdom. Nevertheless, in his preaching, the rigid religious orthodoxy that dominated Congregational and Presbyterian churches gave way to a more egalitarian spirit. Finney called people to change their lives, not necessarily to agreement with specific creeds. Because of his preaching, hundreds, then thousands took religion more seriously, joined churches, participated in reform movements, and changed New York and American society.

By the late 1830s, the area along the Erie Canal where Finney preached had become known as "the burned-over district" because of the fires of religious enthusiasm that rolled over the region. Finney was far from the only revivalist in New York. However, he gave the New York revivals a distinct tone—different not only from the emotionalism of frontier revivals but also from the staid life of many established churches. The Erie Canal also made communications easier and faster than before, so word of the revivals traveled fast.

Lyman Beecher and the Growth of Voluntary Societies

As a young minister, Lyman Beecher had been one of the staunchest defenders of state support for the Congregational churches in Connecticut (see Chapter 8). Once the Connecticut churches lost their government support, Beecher embraced the new situation and supported revivals and voluntary associations for moral reform in New England and the nation. Beecher described his goal:

> A Bible for every family, a school for every district, and a pastor for every 1000 souls, must be the motto upon the standard, round which the millions who enjoy these blessings must rally for the purpose of extending them to those who do not.

As the Second Great Awakening grew in force in the 1820s and 1830s, a series of voluntary societies or interdenominational organizations that Beecher helped launch grew in their influence. These societies were not owned by any one religious body but, rather, depended on the voluntary contributions of members of several different religious bodies. They represented a new form of cooperation across traditional religious lines in the service of a larger goal to change the culture of the United States. The American Bible Society distributed Bibles, the American Sunday School Union provided curriculum materials for church-based Sunday schools, and the American Education Society supported the education of ministers. In addition, the American Board of Commissioners for Foreign Missions sent missionaries around the world, including Adoniram Judson and his wife Ann Hasseltine Judson, whose efforts in Burma became role models for generations of foreign missionaries to convert the world to Christianity. Beecher included prominent members of the Congregational, Presbyterian, and Episcopal churches in the leadership of these societies. The underlying mission of all of these societies was moral reform—the creation of a sober, God-fearing, American public.

By the early 1830s, Beecher had become convinced that the key to transforming the nation lay in the Mississippi Valley. He became president of Lane Theological Seminary in Cincinnati to

Lyman Beecher, one of the leaders of the Second Great Awakening, is shown here with his numerous children including petitioner and educator Catharine (to the left of her father), Harriet Beecher Stowe (far right), and one of the most famous ministers of the next generation, Henry Ward Beecher (standing on the right).

fulfill this goal. Beecher helped prepare future ministers, strengthened religious colleges, and placed Protestant pastors in hundreds of Midwestern churches. He also helped create the public school system of Ohio and supported schools and teachers across the Midwest.

The goal of all of this activity was to strengthen the moral sway of Congregational-Presbyterian Protestantism against the individualism of Jacksonian Democrats, Catholics, and other Protestants who disagreed with them. In the world that Beecher and his fellow Protestant evangelists were creating, the separating of church and state meant that specific denominations would not wield political power, but together, these Protestants would help build a culture in which the churches, voluntary societies, and public schools would reinforce common beliefs and practices.

Revivalism and Moral Reform Movements

Most converts in the revivals that preachers like Finney and Beecher led, perhaps three-fourths of them, were women who then prayed and lobbied for their husbands and families to convert. Finney and his closest lieutenant, Theodore Dwight Weld, encouraged women to be active in their religious communities. Where New England churches had urged women to keep silent except at home, the new generation of revivalists welcomed them as prayer leaders and preachers. Such speaking in "promiscuous assemblies," may have been familiar in Baptist and even Methodist churches, but it was new in the more middle-class Presbyterian and Congregational churches. Women who became religious leaders in the revivals often also became leaders in their communities. The movement demanding women's rights that swept the United States in the 1840s sprang from the same areas of upstate New York that revivalists called the burned-over district (see Chapter 12). The link was not surprising.

For Finney, conversion meant that one needed to show one's new faith in ethical behavior, and no ethical behavior was more important to him than opposing slavery. Upstate New York's churches sent revivalist preachers into the rest of the country to preach for the abolition of slavery. For the next 30 years, the Finney-Weld brand of revivalism spread across the country and was one of the streams of abolitionism that inspired Northerners to fight a war to end slavery.

The rights of women and opposition to slavery were not the only reform causes to spring from the revivalism of the Second Great Awakening. Other reformers, inspired by the same forces, began to advocate for important changes in the way prisoners were treated. Too often, they said, overcrowded prisons were simply schools for crime, and the focus on punishment, whatever the original crime, did little to redeem or reclaim prisoners to reenter society. At first, reformers advocated the building of prisons in which each prisoner would be confined to a solitary cell where they would have time to reflect on their past, be taught new habits, and prepare to reenter society. But too often, the solitary confinement led to insanity rather than reform. In response, prison reformers built a new kind of prison in which each prisoner had a separate cell, but also had access to common dining quarters, workshops, and a chapel. In all of these spaces, the authorities sought to teach prisoners a new way of behaving as preparation for reclaiming them. In the 1830s, the New York state penitentiary at Auburn was redesigned to foster the new approach, and soon thereafter, a large new penitentiary at Sing Sing on the Hudson River was built with 1,000 cells plus the common areas. Reformers hoped that the new, more humane approach would change lives and ultimately society. Other states quickly followed in adopting the new models.

Many mentally ill people were treated very much like prisoners before the reforms, and they often found themselves in similar circumstances. Reformers quickly took up the cause of those they said were insane. Perhaps no one equaled Dorothea Dix as a reformer in the treatment of the mentally ill. In 1843, Dix told the Massachusetts legislature that she was calling their attention "to the present state of Insane Persons confined within this Commonwealth, in cages, closets, cellars, stalls, pens! Chained, naked, beaten with rods, and lashed into obedience!" Moreover, she had the facts to

This illustration from an anti-alcohol publication makes the claim that drunkenness was the cause of many problems in society, especially the abuse of women.

prove her point. The result, beginning in Massachusetts, was that a system of state hospitals for the insane replaced the earlier prisons.

Many other reforms also blossomed. Although the campaign against alcohol would reach its peek many decades later, it began during the Second Great Awakening. Lyman Beecher preached temperance sermons that were widely reprinted, including one in which he said, "What then is this universal, natural, and national remedy for intemperance? It is the banishment of ardent spirits from the list of lawful objects of commerce…" Many, including members of Congress took the pledge to stop drinking, the U.S. Army stopped the old tradition of a ration of alcohol, and refusing to drink became a mark of religious observance in many circles. At the same time, the American Peace Society advocated an end to all wars. The American Sunday School Union distributed not only Bible stories, but also basic reading books in places where there were no schools. Schools were opened for those who were deaf and blind. Efforts were made to rescue prostitutes. Countless reforms designed to create a better, more humane, and sometimes more tightly controlled society emerged from the enthusiasm of the awakening.

Utopian Religious Communities

The religious enthusiasm of the early 1800s also inspired untraditional ways of thinking about religious matters. Large American spaces that allowed people to develop their own communities relatively undisturbed and the American emphasis on liberty, even the liberty to be eccentric, made the United States fertile ground for radical experiments and utopian religious communities. Some of these religious experiments were short lived. Others lasted for generations. A few, most of all the Mormons, have continued to the present.

MOTHER ANN LEE AND THE SHAKERS   The founder of the United Society of Believers in Christ's Second Appearing, or the Shakers, was Ann Lee—known as Mother Ann Lee—who before the American Revolution gathered a few supporters in England and came to America in 1774. Lee was convinced that she was receiving a special revelation from God that human sexuality was the basis of all sin and celibacy was the only way to live a godly life.

Lee inspired Shaker communities in New York and New England. Shaker worship reflected Lee's spirituality and, according to observers, included, "shaking and singing, hopping and turning, smoking and running, groaning and laughing." Shaker communities at New Lebanon, New Hampshire; Sabbath Day Lake, Maine; and elsewhere thrived, and the Shakers became one of the largest and most successful of the pre-Civil communitarian movements.

In Shaker worship and community life, women and men were kept separate, but all participated in lively music and dance designed to shake sin out of their bodies.

Shaker theology placed Ann Lee on a par with Jesus and committed the society to the equal leadership of women with men. But Shakers were united by their community life more than by theology. They demanded celibacy, a requirement that limited the community's appeal and prevented increasing membership by means of childbirth. Instead, all new members had to be converts who were attracted to Shaker life. The revivals produced many such converts who sought a deeper spiritual life than they found in traditional churches. Shaker beliefs were reflected in their commitment to making things of beauty, and Shaker furniture remains a reminder of their beliefs.

American Voices

The Shaker Community, "Tis the Gift to be Simple," 1830s

The simplicity and joyfulness of the Shakers have infiltrated American culture in many ways. Shaker furniture, now so popular, was not just a product for them. Mildred Barker, leader of a Shaker Community in Maine, who died in 1990, once reflected, "I almost expect to be remembered as a chair or a table." But Barker reminded those who came to interview her that behind all of the Shakers' physical artifacts, "There's the religion." And while many of their complex theological ideas have largely been forgotten, the basic joy, humility, and playfulness of the Shakers continue to be remembered in this familiar hymn that dates to the 1830s:

'Tis the gift to be simple, 'tis the gift to be free;
'Tis the gift to come down where we ought to be;
And when we find ourselves in the place just right,
'Twill be in the valley of love and delight.

When true simplicity is gaind,
To bow and to bend we shan't be asham'd
To turn, turn will be our delight,
'Till by turning, turning we come round right.

Source: Stephen J. Stein, *The Shaker Experience in America* (New Haven: Yale University Press, 1992), p. 191.

Thinking Critically

1. Documentary Analysis
What values and priorities are extolled in the hymn?

2. Historical Interpretation
Why might simplicity, certainty, and humility have been particularly appealing to 1830s Americans? What aspects of the larger society might Shakers have found most disturbing and unwelcome?

The things they created, whether furniture, houses, or art, were owned in common, not individually, a requirement that some found as difficult to accept as celibacy.

JOHN HUMPHREY NOYES AND THE ONEIDA COMMUNITY   The Oneida Community also had its roots in the Second Great Awakening and flourished in Oneida, New York, between 1848 and 1879. Its founder and spiritual guide was John Humphrey Noyes, who was born in Vermont in 1811. As a student for the ministry, he became convinced that repentance from sin was not enough and that people should simply stop sinning. Noyes became convinced that all Christians could achieve a state "in which all the affections of the heart are given to God, and in which there is no sin."

Gathering a small community in Putney, Vermont, he expanded his definition of Christian perfectionism to include what he called "complex marriage," an arrangement in which monogamy was replaced with many sexual companions. Noyes argued that sexual pleasure was a gift from God and that Christianity demanded the sharing of that gift without any exclusive or jealous reservations.

Vermont authorities, however, took a dim view of these sexual practices and beliefs, and Noyes and his followers moved to Oneida, New York, where the community thrived for decades, supported ultimately by producing and selling silverware. Oneida eventually fell victim to Victorian morality and to its dependence on Noyes as its single charismatic leader. Between 1875 and 1879, Oneida was torn by debates as New York authorities began threatening arrests for Oneida's flouting of the marriage laws. Noyes fled to Canada and the community dissolved although the silver business supported former members for generations.

ROBERT OWEN AND THE NEW HARMONY COMMUNITY   After making a fortune in London, Robert Owen founded a model factory town at New Lanark, Scotland, in which he sought to put the spirit of universal welfare into practice. In the early 1820s, Owen decided to relocate his utopian vision of a community designed to benefit all of it members and establish it in the United States.

In early 1825, 900 people arrived at New Harmony, Indiana, where Owen had purchased land. But New Harmony failed within a year. The community could not attract enough skilled workers to make it economically successful. There was tension between those who ran New Harmony and the rest of the community. As one disaffected resident recalled, the "aristocrats" quarreled, and the fields went to ruin. Owen lost most of his fortune, which he had invested in New Harmony, but returned to England to continue to advocate his version of social reform.

JOSEPH SMITH AND THE CHURCH OF JESUS CHRIST OF THE LATTER-DAY SAINTS   Joseph Smith (1805–1844) was as much a product of New York's burned-over district as Charles G. Finney. Smith was born in 1805 and moved with his family to a farm in Palmyra, New York, when he was age 11. In 1827, word spread along the Erie Canal that Smith had found a treasure that would unlock the Indian history of the area. He had, he said, found golden plates and magical stones known as Urim and Thummim with which to read and translate what was written on the plates by an ancient prophet-historian named Mormon. He published the result, the *Book of Mormon*, in 1830. With that book, a uniquely American religious tradition was born, one that its followers believed represented a rebirth of true Christianity.

Smith, however, did much more than publish a new book; he organized a community. Within a month of the book's publication, the first Mormon community began to form near Palmyra, New York, with Smith as its leader. Some responded with hostility to his efforts, even tarring and feathering Smith at one point. But converts seeking religious truth poured in, a temple was built, and the community grew.

In response to the hostility, Smith and the Mormon community moved first to Missouri and then in the late 1830s, to Nauvoo, Illinois, which became the largest and fastest growing city in Illinois because of Mormonism. The city's 15,000 residents became a virtually autonomous state, and their militia was recognized by state law. But Smith's political involvements and religious teaching, especially his suggestion that all members participate in marriages involving one husband and multiple wives, brought renewed hostility. On June 27, 1844, a mob killed Smith and his brother Hyrum.

Mormons, like those shown in this wagon train, crossed the plains and mountains to get to new homes in Utah.

With Smith's death, Brigham Young became the new leader of the Mormons in 1847 and led them on a cross-continent trek to the shores of the Great Salt Lake in what is now Utah. Salt Lake was then on the northern edge of the Republic of Mexico, which was soon to be annexed by the United States. There, far from any governmental authority, they set up settlements in a tight, church-regulated community. They also embraced Smith's revelation that a man could take as many wives as he could support.

But the Treaty of Guadalupe Hildago, which marked the end of the U.S. War with Mexico from 1846 to 1848, brought Salt Lake City and the Mormon community under the control of the U.S. government. For a while, the U.S. government left the Mormons alone, but in 1857, President James Buchanan replaced Young with a non-Mormon territorial governor, and the Mormon War broke out as federal authorities tried to enforce monogamy on the Mormons and the Mormons fought back. In one well-publicized incident, Mormons massacred a group of non-Mormon settlers. Only in 1890, after an intense time of prayer and a new revelation, did the Mormon leadership abandon plural marriage. Relations with the government improved, and Utah became a state in 1896. Of all the new religious communities spawned during the Second Great Awakening, the Church of Jesus Christ of the Latter-Day Saints has been the most successful.

Transcendentalism

In 1838, far from Salt Lake City or the revivals of New York, Ralph Waldo Emerson gave a speech at Harvard Divinity School in Cambridge, Massachusetts, that had as much impact as any revival sermon. Emerson had been ordained as a Unitarian minister but had resigned when he came to believe that the Lord's Supper and public prayer were barriers to direct experience of the divine.

In the *Divinity School Address*, Emerson told an audience of future Unitarian ministers that too often in formal worship, "The soul is not preached." And he said, "The true preacher can be known by this, that he deals out to the people his life,—life passed through the fire of thought." Emerson's call to preach "throbs of desire and hope" rather than formal theology offended most of his audience and he was never invited back to the Divinity School, but the speech represented a new approach to religious life that was developing in America in the 1830s.

While Emerson continued to develop his ideas for another 40 years, the Transcendentalist movement with which he is most associated blossomed in the 1830s. In 1836, a group that came to call themselves the Transcendental Club met at the Boston home of George Ripley, another Unitarian minister, to discuss ideas. The members of the club created a theology that reflected a powerful personal experience of life.

In 1841, under Ripley's leadership, members of the Transcendental Club founded Brook Farm, a utopian community in West Roxbury, Massachusetts, where the residents sought to support themselves through manual labor. Women and men shared work equally, and an effort was made at true gender equity. But few of the residents of Brook Farm actually knew much about farming, the farm did not prosper, and the community disbanded in 1847. Nevertheless, Emerson's writings and the Transcendental movement he helped launch reflected an impatience with "old ways" and a desire for direct and immediate experience of the divine that continued to impact American religious life.

10.2 **Quick Review** How did the increasing diversity of religion in America reflect other political and social changes in the nation?

DEMOCRATIZED EDUCATION: THE BIRTH OF THE COMMON SCHOOL

10.1
10.2
10.3

10.3 Explain the development of public education as a result of, and in response to, the cultural currents of the 1820s and 1830s.

The years during which Andrew Jackson dominated American politics were also years in which the nation's public school system was radically transformed, though the transformation was mostly the work of Jackson's staunch opponents. Many of the most prominent education reformers were Whigs who did not share Jackson's vision for American society. They often sought to change the ways schools were organized and conducted for the same reasons they opposed Jackson politically. Schools, Whig educators believed, could build a new American culture more to their liking than the Jacksonian brand of democracy that most school reformers found too individualistic and unlikely to transmit the kind of moral code they thought was essential to a well-regulated national life.

Various individuals with their own agendas contributed to what came to be known as the Common School Crusade. Catherine Beecher sought to empower women by opening the doors for them to become school teachers. Horace Mann, a Whig Party leader, helped launch a new and more tightly organized school system in Massachusetts—a system that came to serve as a model for much of the nation. The transformation of the nation's schools in this period was a key dynamic of the changing culture of the United States between the 1820s and the 1840s.

Women Become Teachers

In 1835, Catharine Beecher, daughter of the religious leader Lyman Beecher, was already well known for founding the Hartford Female Seminary to help educate women and for her petitions seeking to stop Jackson's Indian Removal. In her *Essay on the Education of Female Teachers* published in that year, Beecher argued that women were much better equipped than men to be teachers, but she also wanted to educate them for the work. She saw teaching as an extension of motherhood, a nurturing role: "What is the most important and peculiar duty of the female sex? It is the physical,

Women, mostly very young women, taught school, most often in one-room schools like this one where children of all ages learned to read, write, count, and then advance through more complex assignments. Not all the schools were as comfortable as the one shown here and not all the children were as well behaved.

intellectual, and moral education of children." She continued, "Woman, whatever are her relations in life, is necessarily the guardian of the nursery, the companion of childhood, and the constant model of imitation. It is her hand that first stamps impressions on the immortal spirit, that must remain forever." At a time when most teachers were still men, Beecher argued not only that women actually made better teachers than men, but also that including women as teachers would expand the supply of teachers for the country and open the door to a professional life for middle-class women who had few employment options.

Beecher's impassioned views reflected those of Emma Willard, who had founded the Troy Female Seminary in 1821 in upstate New York to prepare women to be teachers. Like Beecher, Willard had argued, "There are many females of ability, to whom the business of instructing children is highly acceptable." She also believed that women should get the same education as men and modeled the curriculum at Troy on what men studied at college, though she added courses on how to teach. In 1837, Mary Lyon founded Mount Holyoke Female Seminary in Massachusetts to give future female teachers a college education.

New Structures for Schooling

While Catharine Beecher and her colleagues were transforming the gender of the teaching profession, other reformers sought to transform the structure of schools. None of these leaders was more important than Horace Mann. In 1836, Mann, a rising star in the Massachusetts Whig Party, helped shepherd a bill through the Massachusetts legislature that created a state Board of Education. He then became the board's full-time, paid secretary. Mann spent the next 12 years advocating tighter state standards for education, more money for schools and teacher salaries, and a better education for children. He became the best-known spokesperson for public education of his generation.

Mann believed in state standards for the schools. He described the schools of Massachusetts as, "so many distinct, independent communities." Mann meant to change that. He also believed that it was the responsibility of all citizens to pay taxes to support schools; looking at the conditions of the state's schools when he took office, he did not think that they paid nearly enough at the time in such taxes. Like Beecher and Willard, Mann wanted educated teachers and created a system of state-sponsored teacher preparation schools, called "normal schools," that offered 1 year of state-funded preparation to any young woman or man who wanted to be a teacher. Mann's greatest concern, however, was the moral education of the state's citizens. He believed that there needed to be a public guardian of morality, and since the United States had no state church, that guardian had to be the public school.

While Mann was the best-known educational reformer, almost all Whigs also came to advocate the same changes he did: state systems of education, state support for teacher preparation, and state efforts to ensure a common morality. Like many reformers, Mann and his allies could not understand why anyone would oppose them. Yet even in Massachusetts, there was opposition. Jacksonian Democrats in the legislature tried to abolish the Board of Education and the office of secretary. They saw the state control that Mann advocated as expensive, unnecessary, and an unwarranted interference by the state in local affairs, which would undermine local support for each town's school.

Roman Catholics were especially unhappy with the growing influence and cost of the public school system. Catholics saw the public schools as essentially a Protestant venture, something Protestants like Mann could never understand. Mann advocated teaching the Protestant Bible in school "without note or comment," leaving it to churches or parents to interpret it. But Catholics believed that the Bible should be read in light of the teachings of the Church and not left to individual interpretation.

They found anti-Catholic bias in many of the textbooks the public schools used. To pay taxes only to have their children read such material outraged them. Citing examples from textbooks that spoke of "deceitful Catholics," Catholics in New York City wrote that they could not "in conscience, and consistently with their sense of duty to God, and to their offspring" send them to the city's public schools and requested public funds so that they could operate their own schools. When such funds were denied, Catholics in New York and around the country started their own parochial system at their own expense.

The Nation's Textbook: *McGuffey's Reader*

In 1836, the small Cincinnati publishing house of Truman and Smith brought out a new textbook for schools. The first *McGuffey's Reader* became part of a series, the *McGuffey's Primer*, *McGuffey's Speller*, and the *First* through the *Sixth McGuffey's Eclectic Readers*. By 1920, when most school districts had turned to other materials, 122 million copies of the books had been sold.

The *McGuffey Reader* offered lessons in reading and public speaking designed to create a unified, literate, and patriotic society. The *Readers* reflected the same morality that Mann and Beecher wanted the schools to teach. They included patriotic speeches by Patrick Henry and stories of George Washington as well as tales of the poor boy and his faithful dog or the poor boy who worked hard and made good. The texts also included ethical instruction, for example, don't steal apples from someone else's tree, and instruction in how to speak and present oneself. The goal was a citizenry that could speak well, participate in a common democratic dialogue, and use a common national language instead of regional dialects.

A story in the *Second Eclectic Reader* is illustrative of the McGuffey approach. "Henry, the Bootblack," begins with the story of Henry, "a kind good boy." Henry's "father was dead, and his mother was very poor. He had a little sister about two years old." One day, Henry found a pocketbook. He could have kept all the money in it, but he found the owner and returned it. The owner then gave him a dollar for doing so. Henry used the dollar to set himself up as a bootblack and he was "so polite that gentlemen soon began to notice him, and to let him black their boots." When Henry brought home his first fifty cents in earnings his mother responded, "You are a dear, good boy, Henry. I did not know how I could earn enough to buy bread with, but now I think we can manage to get along quite well." This account is not the kind of success story that would appear fifty years later. In the story, Henry does not go on to own a factory or make a fortune. He is simply a dutiful child who makes his mother happy. The students who read the McGuffey texts were urged to do the same. They were also urged to learn the correct pronunciation and spelling for *support, boots, notice, money,* and other words in the story. McGuffey was teaching a common morality but also a common American English to all students.

The United States that the *Readers* portrayed was white, middle class, hard working, and willing to sacrifice for the common good. The *Readers* also demanded a high standard of reading ability and moved students step by step to attain it. In one-room schoolhouses, often staffed by teachers with little training, which was the national norm throughout the 1800s, a teacher could encourage different students to move from *Reader* to *Reader* in careful order and be confident that, by the time the student had mastered the *Sixth Eclectic Reader,* he or she would be fluent in the English language and in the nation's

The *McGuffey Readers* were filled with patriotic speeches and stories like the one shown here, designed to teach morality, in addition to instruction on common ways of pronouncing key terms.

ethical norms. Not everyone agreed with the specific values the *Readers* taught, and reformers were often tone-deaf to complaints, but the public schools and their teachers shaped American culture as significantly as any of the religious, political, or commercial ventures of the Age of Jackson.

10.3 | **Quick Review** Why might education be increasingly important in an expanding country?

CONCLUSION

Andrew Jackson was like no other president before him. He had no connection to the Founding Fathers, either by blood, class, or any similar privilege. Jackson was determined to make the presidency the center of American government, believing that the government should be an expression of his agenda and of his party. In his two terms as president, Jackson successfully prodded Congress to bend to his will or used executive power to realize his goals, despite fierce opposition. A complex American leader with a long-standing distrust of centralized government, his views were reflected in his actions: an Indian Removal policy that forced thousands of Native Americans out of their ancestral homes in Illinois, Georgia, Mississippi, Alabama, and Florida and on to new lands in present-day Oklahoma; opposition to the Second Bank of the United States because he thought the federal government should have no role in banking, issuing paper currency, or expanding credit; and the Nullification Crisis in which Jackson successfully challenged South Carolina's efforts to declare federal law null and void in that state. Those actions would have long-lasting effects on the nation.

For many Americans in the decades between 1820 and 1850, the growth of a more popular democracy and popular social movements led by ordinary citizens were far more important than President Jackson's policies or opinions. Along with the market revolution that was transforming the physical, commercial, and political landscapes of the United States, the Age of Jackson, as his years in the White House were called, was also a period of social and religious revival and reform. It was the peak of a long-running series of religious revivals known as the Second Great Awakening. This upsurge in religious activity resulted in greater rights for women, stronger opposition to slavery, and radical transformation of the nation's public schools, whose teachers and moral teachings shaped American culture as significantly as any of the religious, political, or commercial ventures of the Age of Jackson.

CHAPTER REVIEW | Considering the political, economic, and social aspects of the "Age of Jackson," to what extent was the United States in that period different from the beginning of the 1800s?

Chapter 10   Chapter Review

JACKSONIAN DEMOCRACY

10.1 Analyze Jackson's advocacy for Indian Removal, his opposition to the Bank of the United States, his support for a tariff, and the impact of these policies on other Americans.

Review Questions

1. Comparison
How did Jackson's vision of the presidency differ from that of his predecessors?

2. Crafting Arguments
What were Jackson's most important political priorities? What connections can you make between his policies and his vision of the presidency?

3. Historical Interpretation
What does the debate over Indian Removal tell you about political divisions in the United States in the 1830s? What groups were most likely to support removal? What groups were most likely to oppose it?

4. Synthesis
In what ways was the Nullification Crisis part of a long-standing disagreement about the nature of American government that went at least as far back as the debate over ratification of the Constitution?

DEMOCRATIZED RELIGION: THE SECOND GREAT AWAKENING

10.2 Analyze the diversity of American religious experience and how the freedom of the era gave rise to diverse religious expressions.

Review Questions

5. Synthesis
How did the role of religion in American society and culture change between 1800 and 1840? What explains the changes you note?

6. Historical Interpretation
What might explain the close connection between calls for religious revival and campaigns for social reform in the 1830s and 1840s?

7. Comparison
Compare and contrast the various utopian religious communities of the early 1800s. What common features did they share? What common forces might have contributed to their emergence?

DEMOCRATIZED EDUCATION: THE BIRTH OF THE COMMON SCHOOL

10.3 Explain the development of public education as a result of, and in response to, the cultural currents of the 1820s and 1830s.

Review Questions

8. Contextualization
Why did reformers like Catherine Beecher believe women had a natural aptitude for teaching? In what ways did Beecher see teaching as a natural extension of women's role in the home?

9. Crafting Arguments
Is it fair to describe Mann's system of public education, as some of his opponents did, as nothing more than a vehicle for imposing mainstream Protestantism on all Americans? Why or why not?

10. Historical Interpretation
How did textbooks in *The McGuffey Reader* series shape the society and culture of the United States in the first half of the 1800s?

Manifest Destiny: Expanding the Nation

In this painting, *Emigrants at Kanesville* by William Henry Jackson, a backlog of wagons waits to be ferried across the Missouri River at Council Bluffs, Iowa.

I n the summer of 1845, the *Democratic Review*, a New York City paper edited by John L. O'Sullivan, urged the nation to annex the independent Republic of Texas: "It is time now for opposition to the annexation of Texas to cease," Sullivan wrote. Texas was a hot topic, and many newspapers were taking the same position. But the *Review* claimed that including Texas in the United States was an essential part of the "fulfillment of our manifest destiny to overspread the continent allotted by Providence for the free development of our yearly multiplying millions." **Manifest Destiny** quickly became a core American belief. It was a mindset that justified the Louisiana Purchase of 1803, the hoped-for U.S. acquisition of the Oregon Territory along with the northern half of Mexico including Texas and California, and a significant influence across the Pacific Ocean.

Manifest Destiny gave a new name to an old idea. Even before the American Revolution and in growing numbers in the 1790s, white Americans had crossed the Allegheny Mountains in spite of government prohibitions and had established colonies in Kentucky and in the Ohio River Valley. Soon after 1800, others were crossing into Florida and Missouri, both then under Spanish control. In both cases, the settlers were confident that the American army and American government would soon follow. While the first Americans to cross into Texas spoke of loyalty to the

CHAPTER OBJECTIVE

Demonstrate an understanding of how the idea of Manifest Destiny and the policies of the Polk administration almost doubled the size of the United States in 12 years in spite of opposition from many people in the country.

LEARNING OBJECTIVES

MANIFEST DESTINY—THE IMPORTANCE OF AN IDEA

Explain what Manifest Destiny meant and how it led the United States to involvement in Texas, California, and Oregon.	**11.1**

THE U.S. WAR WITH MEXICO, 1846–1848

Analyze the causes, strategies, and outcomes of the U.S. War with Mexico.	**11.2**

WEST TO THE PACIFIC

Analyze the causes and outcomes of U.S. expansion in California and into the Pacific region, including establishing new relationships with Hawaii, China, and Japan.	**11.3**

Manifest Destiny

The doctrine, first expressed in 1845, that the expansion of white Americans across the continent was inevitable and ordained by God and was a means to spread Protestant Christianity and Jacksonian Democracy to more people.

Republic of Mexico, by 1830, they too were seeking protection from the American government. In all these cases, many in the government were happy to oblige, seeing the movement of colonists as a first step in expanding the nation. Being aware of the nation's long-term expansion, the power of the idea of Manifest Destiny, and the political and military actions that the nation's leaders took in the name of that idea is essential to understanding how the nation expanded into the shape it has today. This chapter will explore the political, diplomatic, and military issues involved in turning the idea of Manifest Destiny into a geographic reality.

It is also important to understand how the acquisition of so much new territory in the 1830s and 1840s, as well as other developments in people's thinking, changed the lives of those who lived in the United States. The population of the country was expanding as dramatically as its geographical borders. Migrants from around the world especially flocked to California to find their fortunes in the gold. Citizens of the Republic of Mexico suddenly found themselves living in the United States because the border had moved, as did American Indians, who rejected the claims of all nations to their lands. Other immigrants came to the already established parts of the nation. In addition, amid the many changes, slaves, supporters and opponents of slavery, and women became increasingly vocal about the issue of freedom and equality. These issues will be explored in Chapter 12. The great territorial expansion of these years and dramatic changes in the makeup and the thinking of people in the United States during the same time period transformed the country and its future.

MANIFEST DESTINY—THE IMPORTANCE OF AN IDEA

11.1 Explain what Manifest Destiny meant and how it led the United States to involvement in Texas, California, and Oregon.

The idea that the United States had a "manifest destiny" led to more than simply acquiring land, though between 1845 and 1848, the United States would almost double in size, from 1.8 million square miles to almost 3 million. Advocates of Manifest Destiny claimed that the United States—with God's blessing—should rule the heart of North America from the Atlantic Ocean to the Pacific and from a still-to-be-defined border with British Canada to an even more undefined border with the Republic of Mexico. For O'Sullivan and other supporters of Manifest Destiny, it was the nation's appointed role to spread not only democracy—in its Jacksonian form—but also to spread Protestant Christianity in place of the Catholicism of Mexico or the native beliefs of American Indians. The same year that O'Sullivan coined the term *Manifest Destiny*, Illinois Representative John Wentworth told Congress that he "did not believe the God of Heaven…designed that the original States should be the only abode of liberty on earth. On the contrary, he only designed them as the great center from which civilization, religion, and liberty should radiate and radiate until the whole continent shall bask in their blessing." That belief, held by many beyond Wentworth, that the United States was specially chosen by divine will to bring liberty and democracy to the planet—and especially North America—was a driving force in the push for new lands in the 1840s.

Many Americans supported versions of Manifest Destiny for their own reasons. Land speculators and those promoting the extension of the nation's railroads wanted to exploit the vast lands in the West. Farmers dreamed of starting over in rich—and cheap—new lands. Workers believed that rapid national expansion would guarantee industrial profits and thus their jobs, or give them a chance to start over if necessary. Protestant leaders and missionaries saw U.S. control of the new lands as an opportunity to ensure that a Protestant United States, not a Catholic Mexico, controlled the continent. Manifest Destiny also referred to a patriotic belief that the nation had a divine mission to become a world power.

At the mythical level, Manifest Destiny was seen as the spirit hovering over the westward movement of white settlers, leading them and urging them on whether they came by foot, covered wagon, or stage coach.

In contrast, many other Americans opposed the whole idea of a "manifest destiny." Democrats tended to support expansion, but most Whigs, led by Henry Clay, had grave reservations. Clay's goal was not necessarily a larger country but a better developed one with roads, canals, railroads, and industries knitting it together and ensuring its prosperity. Antislavery advocates opposed the acquisition of more land, especially Texas, since they were certain that new lands meant new slave states. However, some proslavery advocates, notably South Carolina Senator John C. Calhoun, wanted Texas but worried that other incorporated lands, especially California and Oregon, might become free states peopled by darker-skinned citizens, which would shift power away from the white slaveholding regions.

Some Americans also saw the violence associated with expansion as simply wrong. Many residents of the lands from Texas to California did not want to become part of the United States at all. Antonio Maria Osio spoke for those who did not want to become U.S. residents when he described himself as "a *californio* who loves his country and a Mexican on all four sides and in my heart." He opposed the annexation of California to the United States, and when it happened, he left, eventually settling in Baja California so that he could to remain a citizen of Mexico.

californio
Person of Spanish descent—and after 1821, citizen of Mexico—living in California.

While many Americans debated Manifest Destiny in the Congress, the press, and the pulpits, other Americans, especially trappers and farmers, moved into the regions, just as a generation before the same types of people had expanded beyond the Mississippi. Regardless of whether the United States, Mexico, or Britain claimed the land, these frontiersmen and women were confident that, in time, their government would follow them. Most of all, they moved into Texas (see Map 11-1).

The Birth of the Texas Republic

The tensions between Americans living in Texas and the Mexican government that governed it had been building even before Mexico gained its independence from Spain in 1821. When the United States purchased Louisiana from France in 1803, the western

MAP 11-1 **Trade networks between Mexico, Texas, and the United States.** Mexico (and before it, Spain) had established settlements and trade networks throughout its sparsely populated northern territories. Texas trade ran not only south from San Antonio and Goliad in Texas to Monterrey and other trading centers in Mexico but also east into the United States. Separate networks connected the heartland of Mexico with its settlements in Santa Fe and Taos in New Mexico, with Tucson in the future Arizona, and with the missions and presidios along the coast of California.

border of the territory was disputed. Spain insisted it was the Sabine River (the current border between Louisiana and Texas), but French officials hinted that the United States might claim territory further west. Jefferson had wanted Louisiana to include all of the land from modern-day Texas to the Rio Grande River, but he was not prepared to fight Spain over it. In the Adams-Onís Treaty of 1819, Spain ceded Florida to the United States, along with Spanish claims to Oregon, in exchange for U.S. recognition of the Sabine River as the border between U.S. Louisiana and Spanish Texas, though some in Congress criticized the treaty for that reason. Despite treaties, however, Americans still crossed the Sabine in the early 19th century settling in Texas.

Soon after the Adams-Onís Treaty was signed, a revolutionary uprising began in Mexico. Like the people of the United States, most Mexican citizens wanted to be free of control by a European power. The Mexican revolution against Spanish rule, which lasted from 1810 to 1821, was long and bloody and decimated the Mexican economy. In Texas, the Mexican population, people known as **Tejanos**, fell from 4,000 in 1800 to 2,500 in 1821. Comanche and Apache tribes dominated large parts of Texas, and much of the desert was vacant of any human habitation. Nevertheless, after 1821, Mexico had won its independence.

Tejanos
People of Spanish or Mexican descent born in Texas.

With the establishment of the Republic of Mexico, two independent republics—the English-speaking, overwhelmingly Protestant United States in the north and the Spanish-speaking and mostly Catholic Republic of Mexico to the south—bordered each other at the Sabine River, with settlers from one living in the territory of the other.

Even before Mexican independence, the Spanish government had given Missouri merchant Moses Austin permission to start a colony in Texas, believing that more settlers—whatever their origin—would help stabilize a border area that was far from the population centers of either Mexico or the United States. In 1821, Moses's son Stephen F. Austin, along with Erasmo Seguín, a Tejano with liberal political views, rode into Texas to build the new settlement. A month later, Austin and his party learned that Mexico had won its independence. Austin then went to Mexico City where he met with Mexico's new leader Agustín de Iturbide and announced, "I make a tender of my services, my loyalty, and my fidelity to the Constitutional Emperor of Mexico." Austin's physical presence in Mexico City and willingness to make an oath of allegiance to the new nation impressed the new government. In April 1823, Austin received confirmation of his claims to a huge swath of land in Texas and his right to act as an *empresario*, or colonizing agent, for this land. He was the only American to get such rights.

At first, the new American colony grew slowly, but Austin continued to recruit settlers. The Mexican government, aware that it could do little to stop settlement and anxious for a buffer against Indian tribes and the United States, hoped that settlers in Texas would create a stable population of loyal citizens.

Few Europeans and even fewer Mexicans moved into Texas, but Americans came in large numbers. The Tejano community was overwhelmed by the newly arrived Americans. By 1830, 20,000 American colonists had arrived and had brought 2,000 slaves with them. The Americans generally ignored the requirement that they convert to Catholicism, though they did not build Protestant churches, and most absolutely refused to free their slaves in spite of the fact that Mexico had abolished slavery in 1829 and expected the residents of Texas to obey that decree. One American visitor to Texas, Amos Parker, wrote, "A person may travel all day; and day after day, and find Americans only." Those in the Tejano community were also divided. Many Tejanos profited from trade with the Americans and identified with their independent streak. Others clung to their connection to Mexico. Distance, difficult travel conditions, and an unstable government in Mexico City with more pressing concerns closer to home allowed an American community to develop in Texas that was officially governed by one set of laws but lived by its own rules (see Map 11-2).

The Mexican government's benign neglect of the American community in Texas ended in 1830 when the Mexican Congress closed Texas to further American immigration and the importation of slaves. Mexico also insisted that trade be routed through established ports further south in Mexico rather than directly between Texas and the United States. The government stationed more soldiers in Texas to enforce the new rules. Austin was stunned, and revolts broke out in the English-speaking colonies, a few of which drew Tejano support.

In 1832 Mexican troops defeated an American effort to take control of an army garrison, but in October, American colonists met at San Felipe and called for autonomy for Texas within the Republic of Mexico. In 1833, they organized an army under the command of Sam Houston and sent Austin to Mexico City to negotiate for them. Tejanos were not represented in these meetings, and most of the 5,000 Tejanos probably opposed these actions. But by now, there were 30,000 Americans in Texas, and the Tejanos were greatly outnumbered. Austin had little success in Mexico City. He was arrested in the fall of 1833 and at the time of his release from jail in the summer of 1835 he wrote, "War is our only recourse. There is no other remedy." Most Americans in Texas seemed to agree.

empresario
An agent who received a land grant from the Spanish or Mexican government in return for organizing settlements.

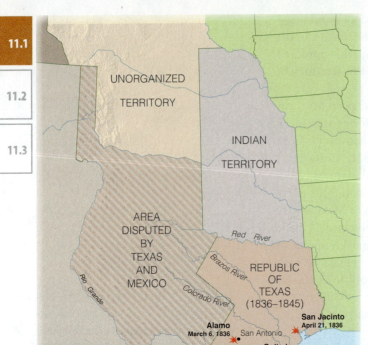

MAP 11-2 Contested boundaries between Texas and Mexico. The borders of Texas were highly contested in the 1830s and 1840s. The Adams-Onís Treaty of 1819 had fixed the border between the two nations as the Sabine River—the border between modern Louisiana and Texas. Austin's land grant from the Mexican government allowed him to settle to the west of that line. Most people considered the Nueces River to be the western border of the Republic of Texas in the 1830s and 1840s, but at President Polk's insistence, the Rio Grande River became the border as a result of the Treaty of Guadalupe Hidalgo in 1848, which tripled the total size of Texas.

Alamo

A Franciscan mission at San Antonio, Texas, that was the site in 1836 of a siege and massacre of Texans by Mexican troops.

Although revolt had been brewing since 1830, the campaign for the independence of Texas became a full-fledged war late in 1835 when American volunteers captured the Alamo fortress at San Antonio de Bexar from its Mexican garrison. In January and February 1836, James Bowie and William Travis took joint command of the Alamo, while another Texian (as the Americans in Texas were called) force remained in the town of Goliad under the command of James Fannin. Austin went to Washington, D.C., to try to secure American support for the insurrection while Sam Houston took command of a volunteer army based at the Texian's temporary capital of Washington-on-the-Brazos.

In response to these military actions, Mexican president Santa Anna ordered the Mexican army north, capturing the Alamo and killing its defenders in March 1836. After a furious fight, the nearly 200 defenders of the Alamo, including former Tennessee Congressman Davy Crockett, adventurer Jim Bowie, and the garrison's commander William B. Travis, were killed. It is estimated that 600 Mexican soldiers were also killed in the assault. The defeat and grisly deaths of the Alamo's outnumbered defenders entered Texas—and American—legend. "Remember the Alamo!" became a rallying cry for the independence of Texas and later in the war with Mexico.

After his victory at the Alamo, Santa Anna marched his army to the second Texan garrison at Goliad, which surrendered in late March. Santa Anna ordered his soldiers to execute all of the Goliad troops and some 341, including the garrison's commander James Fannin, died on the spot. For some, the phrase quickly became "Remember the Alamo and Goliad."

While Texian volunteers fought against the Mexican army, political leaders in the American colony met in convention at Washington-on-the-Brazos and on March 2, 1836, declared the independence of the Republic of Texas and adopted a constitution. Having defeated the insurgent forces at the Alamo and at Goliad, Santa Anna had little use for the Texas declaration. He turned on Sam Houston's army, the only remaining defenders of the Republic of Texas and its new constitution. Houston, mindful of Santa Anna's strength, began a slow retreat. Then, after Santa Anna's troops had been marching for days with an increasingly thin supply line, Houston suddenly turned on them. On April 21, 1836, Houston defeated Santa Anna at the Battle of San Jacinto. Houston's troops showed no more mercy than Santa Anna had and executed hundreds of Mexican prisoners. The next day, Santa Anna himself was captured and forced to sign the Treaty of Velasco, promising to withdraw all Mexican troops from Texas, end the war, and recognize the independence of Texas. The Mexican Congress refused to recognize the treaty, but neither the Mexican government nor the Texians were in the mood for more fighting.

In the early fall of 1836, Sam Houston, the hero of the Battle of San Jacinto, was elected president of the new republic, defeating Austin, who became secretary of state. Both men, and most of their followers, did not want long-term independence but rather annexation by the United States. However, the United States was a reluctant partner. Texas would be a new huge slave state, and many in Washington worried about the destabilizing impact on the nation of having such a powerful addition to the slave states in the U.S. Senate. In addition, U.S. trade with Mexico was too important to trifle with. Even Andrew Jackson did not want to risk the political cost of annexing Texas, especially in 1836 when Martin Van Buren, his handpicked successor, was in the midst of the presidential election. After the election, Jackson, a good friend of

Sam Houston, officially recognized the Republic of Texas, but that was as far as its neighbor to the north would go. The Texas Republic would stand on its own for the immediate future.

Distant California

While Texas was declaring its independence from Mexico, Alta California, as it was known to distinguish it from Baja California to the south, was a sleepy and distant outpost of the Republic of Mexico, and most people in Mexico and the United States were content to leave it that way. California had wonderful harbors, large and prosperous rancheros, and a string of missions, but it was a long way from the heart of either nation. In the 1830s, the population there included not only Mexicans, most of whom valued self-government in local matters and cared little for the authorities in Mexico City, but also a much smaller number of Americans. Neither group was thinking seriously about independence. A majority among the declining number of American Indians in California were doing their best to maintain their tribal ways and keep their distance from both Mexican and American settlers, though some of them were living under the supervision of the missions.

Although Spanish explorers had sailed the coast of California and claimed the lands in the 16th century, meaningful European settlements in California began only in the mid-18th century, just before the American Revolution. In 1769, a Franciscan priest, Father Junípero Serra, was sent to Alta California with instructions to found a chain of missions that would aid in converting the California Indians to Catholic Christianity, put them to work for the Spanish, and establish a stronger Spanish presence to protect against possible Russian expansion.

Father Serra and his Franciscan successors succeeded in establishing a chain of missions stretching from San Diego to San Francisco. The Franciscan friars meant to save the Indian souls and bring them the gifts of Spanish culture, but they also worked them hard to ensure a good economic return for the missions, maintaining tight control and a tough discipline. One of the Franciscan friars noted, however, that the Indians "live well free but as soon as we reduce them to a Christian and community life…they fatten, sicken, and die." When Serra arrived in California, there were probably 300,000 Indians in the area, but by the time Spanish rule ended in 1821, that number had been reduced to 200,000. From the Spanish government's perspective, however, the missions were significant in asserting sovereignty as they controlled the Indian work force and managed the colony's cattle, grain, and trade.

The Franciscans administered the California missions until 1833 when the Mexican government, which had seized power from Spain in 1821, transferred ownership of the missions from church to state and eventually to private hands. Mexico's revolution was partly a rejection not only of Spanish royal authority but also of the power of the Catholic Church, and seizing the missions was a means to that end. Missions were sold off or awarded to powerful ranchers.

As late as 1821, California's total Mexican population was about 3,000, though it grew to between 10,000 and 15,000 by 1846. The majority lived on large ranches spread along the coast. Some few immigrants from the United States also moved to California in these years. Most of the Americans arriving before 1840 learned Spanish, converted to Catholicism, took on Mexican citizenship, and became part of the local culture of Alta California.

Beginning in the 1840s, however, a different group of immigrants from the United States began to arrive who were more interested in making California part of the United States. Even before the war with Mexico began, President Polk, well aware of the interests of these recent immigrants to California, told Congress that California's harbors "would afford shelter for our navy, for our numerous whale ships, and other merchant vessels employed in the Pacific Ocean, and would in a short period become the marts of an extensive and profitable commerce with China, and other countries of

An early photograph of a young Mexican American woman illustrates some of the comfort and confidence that the Californios had before their homes became part of the United States.

American Voices

Eulalia Perez, Memories of Mexican California, ca. 1830s

Eulalia Perez was born about 1768 in Baja California. She and her husband first moved to the Alta California mission of San Diego and then to San Gabriel near Los Angeles. At San Gabriel, the priests selected her as cook for the mission where she also served as a midwife and eventually "keeper of the keys" or mayordoma—head of the mission household. Perez lived a long life, and in 1877, a historian at the University of California interviewed her on her memories of a much earlier era in California history. Her account provides a rare glimpse of mission life in California before that area's acquisition by the United States.

When we arrived here, Father Jose Sanchez lodged me and my family temporarily in a small house until work could be found for me.…He, as well as his companion Father Jose Maria Zalvidea, treated the Indians very well, and the two were much loved by the Spanish-speaking people and by the neophytes [Indians recently converted to Christianity] and other Indians.

Father Zalvidea introduced many improvements in the Mission of San Gabriel and made it progress a very great deal in every way. Not content with providing abundantly for the neophytes, he planted [fruit] trees in the mountains, far away from the mission, in order that the untamed Indians might have food when they passed by those spots.…

In the morning the girls were let out. First they went to Father Zalvidea's Mass, for he spoke the Indian language; afterwards they went to the mess hut to have breakfast, which sometimes consisted of corn gruel with chocolate, and on holidays with sweets and bread. On other days, ordinarily they had boiled barley and beans and meat. After breakfast each girl began the task that had been assigned to her beforehand—sometimes it was at the looms, or unloading, or sewing, or whatever there was to be done.…

The Indians were taught the various jobs for which they showed an aptitude. Others worked in the fields, or took care of the horses, cattle, etc. Still others were carters, oxherds, etc.… The Indians also were taught to pray. A few of the more intelligent ones were taught to read and write. Father Zalvidea taught the Indians to pray in their Indian tongue; some Indians learned music and played instruments and sang at Mass. The sextons and pages who helped with Mass were Indians of the mission.

The punishments that were meted out were the stocks and confinement. When the misdemeanor was serious, the delinquent was taken to the guard, where they tied him to a pipe or a post and gave him twenty-five or more lashes, depending on his crime. Sometimes they put them in the head-stocks; other times they passed a musket from one leg to the other and fastened it there, and also they tied their hands. That punishment, called "the Law of Bayone," was very painful. But Fathers Sanchez and Zalvidea were always very considerate with the Indians. I would not want to say what others did because they did not live in the mission.

Source: Eulalia Perez, from an original manuscript in Spanish in the Bancroft Library, University of California, Berkeley originally written in 1877 and published in Nancy F. Cott, et al, *Roots of Bitterness: Documents of the Social History of American Women* (Boston: Northeastern University Press, 1996), pp. 185–192.

Thinking Critically

1. Documentary Analysis

How would you characterize Perez's view of the mission system? How did she respond to its coercive elements?

2. Historical Interpretation

What assumptions about Indian peoples underlie Perez's account? What to her were the signs of progress in California?

---

the East." Polk's Secretary of the Navy George Bancroft anticipated the coming of war with Mexico and ordered Commodore John D. Sloat, commander of the U.S. Pacific squadron, based in the nation of Hawaii, to land in San Francisco if war came. At the same time, U.S. Army Captain John C. Frémont led what he claimed was a military map-making expedition overland from St. Louis, arriving in Monterey, California, in late December 1845. Frémont told the Mexican authorities he was simply exploring. They had their doubts that he was just making maps—doubts that later turned out to be well founded—but allowed him to remain. Then in April 1846, a U.S. warship arrived at Monterey, with orders for Frémont and the U.S. counsel in California, Thomas Oliver Larkin, to stir up a pro-American revolt in California. The once distant outpost was quickly becoming an important focus of attention in the growing tensions between the United States and Mexico.

Manifest Destiny and American Presidential Politics

The creation of the Democratic Party as a vehicle to continue his political philosophy and support his handpicked successors was one of Jackson's most significant achievements. The twin pillars on which the party rested were a small federal government and the idea of

Manifest Destiny. The political parties that had emerged from the John Adams-Thomas Jefferson presidential election—the Federalists and the Democratic-Republicans—were long gone. America's founding generation, including all presidents up to John Quincy Adams, disliked "party spirit," even if they accepted that spirit when it helped them. Martin Van Buren, who had built on the base of the older Democratic-Republican organizations to create the new Democratic Party that elected Jackson and who followed him as its candidate, had no such reservations. He thought it best "to deal with the subject of Political Parties in a sincerer and wiser spirit—to recognize their necessity [and] to give them the credit they deserve."

As part of their effort to build a strong political party, Jackson and Van Buren called the first national political convention to be held by a major party. The event was held in Baltimore in 1835, a year before the presidential election. (The small Anti-Masonic Party actually held the first national political convention, modeled on a religious revival in 1831, but it won only seven electoral votes in the 1832 election and faded from national prominence thereafter.) The Democrats borrowed the idea of a national convention as part of their preparation for the 1836 election, and their tight political organization allowed the Democrats to win most presidential contests until the Civil War when the party splintered. At the 1835 convention, Jackson stage-managed Van Buren's nomination as the Democratic party's candidate for what some said was basically a third term for Jackson. The outgoing president also managed to ensure the nomination of his hand-picked candidate for vice president, Richard Mentor Johnson of Kentucky, in spite of an effort by Virginia's delegates to derail his nomination.

The core principle of the emerging Whig Party was opposition to Jackson, though it also wanted a larger federal government that could manage internal improvements. The Whigs continued to support a Bank of the United States. But the Whigs disliked Van Buren's ideas of political parties and continued to distrust the growing sense of party spirit, or at least said that they did. Given this distrust, the Whigs were not well enough organized to have a national convention in preparation for the 1836 election relying instead on state conventions. They reasoned that, even if the various states did not nominate the same candidate for president, they might use a number of popular candidates to gain enough electoral votes to throw the election into the House of Representatives where they were confident they could control the outcome. Having lost decisively with Henry Clay in 1832, most Whig leaders wanted a different candidate. One choice, popular in the North and West, was William Henry Harrison, who had won as many battles as Jackson during the War of 1812. Some states duly nominated Harrison, and Clay reluctantly supported him. Southern Whigs nominated Hugh Lawson White of Tennessee, who agreed with Jackson on many issues but had broken with him over what he saw as Jackson's abuse of power. Whigs in Massachusetts went their own way with Senator Daniel Webster. The Whig effort to appeal to diverse constituencies with different candidates failed. In November 1836, the Jackson magic stuck to Van Buren and he received 50.79 percent of the popular vote and 170 electoral votes against 124 votes scattered among the three Whig candidates.

Van Buren faced several challenges as he began to govern. He pledged to continue Jackson's policies and did so, in particular, presiding over the final removal of the Cherokees to Oklahoma and a long and bloody war against Seminoles in Florida. Given his difficulties with the Seminoles, Van Buren decided against removing Iroquois tribes from New York. He avoided a war with Britain when rebels in Canada recruited volunteers along the American side of the Great Lakes. In spite of his ties to the party of Manifest Destiny, he had no inclination to deal with Texas or Oregon.

In addition, issues of nullification and abolitionism continued, unresolved. Like Jackson, Van Buren opposed nullification or any effort to disrupt the Union. He also opposed abolitionism, which, despite his northern roots, he saw as another attack on the Union along with nullification. Southerners supported Van Buren, and he repaid them by supporting a **gag rule** in Congress. The Constitution gave all citizens the

gag rule
A procedural rule passed in the House of Representatives that prevented discussion of antislavery petitions from 1836 to 1844.

right to "petition the government for a redress of grievances," and abolitionists had begun flooding the House and Senate with antislavery petitions. The gag rule was a promise by congressional leaders in the House of Representatives to ignore the abolitionist petitions. In the end, the gag rule only highlighted the divisions over slavery. As a member of the House, John Quincy Adams took it upon himself to undermine the rule in every possible way. He saw it as a limitation on the constitutional rights of abolitionists, and they came to view him as "Old Man Eloquent." Through the 1830s and 1840s, Adams and a handful of like-minded Whigs began to introduce antislavery petitions at each session of Congress before the House adopted its rules, including the gag rule. Then, during sessions, he regularly interrupted other debates to ask the Speaker whether this or that petition ran afoul of the gag rule while knowing full well that it did but using the occasion to describe both the petition and the gag rule. Perhaps more effectively than if there had been no rule, Adams used these manipulations of the gag rule to change public opinion on slavery, even if he could not get the votes he wanted from the House.

Most challenging for Van Buren's political fortunes, however, was the fact that some of the economic policies Jackson had advocated had their greatest impact during Van Buren's term and it was not a good one. Only 2 months after Van Buren's inauguration, the **Panic of 1837** hit the country. The initial cause of the panic was a sudden drying up of credit. Without the ability to borrow money, cotton brokers failed, banks failed, and the great New York mercantile house of Arthur Tappan and Company failed. In his hatred of banks and distrust of debt, Jackson had paid off the national debt—sending a great deal of U.S. currency to bond holders in Britain and reducing the currency available in the United States. Jackson also had closed the Second Bank of the United States, which had held the ability to expand credit when it was needed. In addition, he had issued a **Specie Circular** in 1836, requiring speculators to pay for federal land in silver or gold coinage, not bank notes. The Specie Circular reflected Jackson's distrust of banks, but once the economy began to decline in 1837, many Americans started to think that if the U.S. government would not trust bank notes, then they should not either. There was a run on banks, and few banks had sufficient reserves of silver and gold to redeem all of the bank notes they had issued. Banks failed, and credit became even scarcer, crippling the economy.

Panic of 1837

A major economic downturn brought on by temporary excesses in international trade and the inability of the United States to control the currency or make credit available after the closing of the Second Bank of the United States.

Specie Circular

A proclamation issued by President Andrew Jackson in 1836 stipulating that only gold or silver could be used as payment for public land.

Soon after Jackson left office, the Panic of 1837, which many blamed on him, wracked the nation. In this political cartoon, the results of Jackson's economic policies are shown as drunkenness, women begging a rich banker for money, and long lines of the unemployed.

A second panic hit in 1839, this one the result of overspeculation in cotton and cotton-producing land. When British investments and international trade stalled, the value of cotton, land, and slaves all plummeted. The sale of public lands, and federal revenue from these sales, virtually stopped. Northern textile and shoe industries laid off thousands of workers. More banks closed. The panic lasted until 1843 and was arguably as severe as any economic downturn before the Great Depression of the 1930s.

Given his Jacksonian commitment to small government, there was little that Van Buren could or would do about the economy. His position enabled the Whigs in the 1840 election to describe him as "cold and heartless." The Whigs had also learned from the Democrats. In 1840, they held a single national convention that unified them behind one candidate. For a second time, they pinned their hopes on the aging war hero William Henry Harrison, despite Clay's effort to secure the nomination for himself. They nominated John Tyler of Virginia, who had served as governor and senator, for vice president, an ill-fated choice. Tyler brought balance to the ticket—he was from the South while Harrison was from the North, and at age 50, he was much younger than the 68-year-old Harrison. But Tyler was a Whig only because he found Jackson "high handed," not because he disagreed with most of his policies. The 1840 political campaign pitted Martin Van Buren, running for a second term, against "Tippecanoe and Tyler Too," a reference to Harrison's victory at the Battle of Tippecanoe in 1811. This time, the Whigs won with 52.8 percent of the popular votes and 234 electoral votes against only 60 for Van Buren. But the high expectations for the Whig presidency would not last long.

At his inauguration in March 1841, Harrison delivered a long address laying out the Whig agenda; in fact, it was the longest inaugural address in American presidential history. The day was cold and blustery, and Harrison did not wear a coat. He caught a bad cold that turned to pneumonia. A month later, President Harrison was dead and Tyler was president. This instance marked the first time a president had died in office, and Tyler made it clear that he was not just an "acting president" but that he had inherited the presidency for the full term. A worse disaster for the Whig Party was hard to imagine. The election of 1840 was the only time when the country elected a Whig president and Whig majorities in both houses of Congress. After only a month into the new administration, "Tyler Too," who shared little of the Whig agenda beyond an intense dislike of Andrew Jackson and an interest in holding office, was president.

Before he became seriously ill, President Harrison had called a special session of Congress to deal with the economic crisis. When the Whig-dominated Congress convened, it re-created the Bank of the United States so that there could be federal control of the currency and credit, thus easing economic conditions that had been created when the bank had been abolished. President Tyler, a believer in small government every bit as much as Jackson or Van Buren, vetoed the bill. Congress then created a "fiscal corporation" that would have more limited powers. Tyler vetoed that, too. Tyler did sign the Land Act of 1841, which made it much easier for homesteaders to buy federal land or keep land on which they were squatters, and he signed the first federal Bankruptcy Act. But the Whigs were furious at Tyler. In September 1841, the entire cabinet except for Secretary of State Daniel Webster resigned in protest over the veto of the bank bills, and the Whig congressional caucus expelled Tyler from the party, marking the only time in U.S. history that a president was expelled from his own political party.

Expanding the size of the United States remained an issue throughout the Tyler presidency. Webster had refused to resign as secretary of state primarily because he was negotiating with Britain to resolve a dispute that came dangerously close to war over where to locate the border between Maine and Canada. The **Webster-Ashburton Treaty** of 1842 resolved the border with Canada as far west as Minnesota. Tyler supported Webster because he did not want problems with Britain when he turned to his real priority—Texas.

Webster-Ashburton Treaty
The treaty signed by the United States and Britain in 1842 that settled a boundary dispute between the United States and Canada and provided for closer cooperation in suppressing the African slave trade.

Tyler had two paramount goals—the annexation of Texas and his own reelection. He failed at the latter but not the former. In September 1843, Tyler began secret negotiations with Texas over annexation. In April 1844, Tyler's new Secretary of State John C. Calhoun, who was also a Whig only because of his hatred for Jackson over the nullification issue, presented a treaty to the Senate for the annexation of Texas. Calhoun justified the treaty in explicitly proslavery terms, insisting that if the United States did not annex Texas as a slave state, Britain would take it over and end slavery there, blocking the expansion of U.S. slavery. But the nation's leading Whig, Henry Clay, and former Democratic President Martin Van Buren both announced their opposition to annexation largely because of slavery. The Senate rejected the treaty by an overwhelming vote of 35 to 16.

The link between Texas and slavery doomed the presidential hopes of both Tyler and Calhoun since both were seen as using a political gimmick to gain their way. The Whigs nominated their old hero Henry Clay. Having been expelled by the Whigs, Tyler tried for the Democratic nomination, but the party spurned him. Jackson still dominated the Democratic Party. He would not allow Tyler to be their candidate, and Jackson was furious at Van Buren over Van Buren's opposition to the annexation of Texas. As a result, the Democrats ended up nominating Jackson's choice, a political unknown, James K. Polk of Tennessee, instead of their own former president Martin Van Buren.

James K. Polk was a true "dark horse" in American presidential politics. He had served as speaker of the house from 1835 to 1839 but had twice been defeated for governor of Tennessee. Few besides Jackson thought he would be president. His Whig opponent, Henry Clay, was one of the best-known political leaders in the United States. If Van Buren had been the Democratic nominee, the election would have been fought over Clay's support for federally financed internal improvements and his advocacy for the Bank of the United States, both of which Van Buren opposed. Polk's nomination changed everything. The Democratic Party platform called for "the reoccupation of Oregon and the reannexation of Texas." With Polk as their nominee, the Democrats planned to focus the election on Manifest Destiny, claiming that they were the party of national expansion while painting the Whigs as timid defenders of the status quo. This focus on Manifest Destiny, especially as it applied to Texas, assured Polk the support not only of Jackson but also of President Tyler and of Calhoun's pro-slavery partners who included both Whigs and Democrats in the South. Many Catholics also saw the Whigs as a Protestant party, while the Democrats courted Catholic voters, especially recent immigrants. Most of the country's Catholics voted Democratic, especially in Pennsylvania and New York. In the end, Polk won 170 electoral votes to 105 for Clay. Expansion in Oregon and Texas was going to be at the top of Polk's agenda.

Because the new president would not take office until March 4 (the practice from the country's beginning until passage of the Twentieth Amendment in 1933), Tyler still had 4 months to serve in office. He did not waste them. When the Senate had rejected the annexation of Texas in 1844, it had rejected a treaty with the Republic of Texas. But the Constitution provided that while treaties had to be ratified by two-thirds of the Senate, a new state could be admitted by a majority vote in each house of Congress. Up to this point, all new states had been U.S. territories, not separate sovereign countries. There was no precedent for incorporating another country into the United States. Now Tyler, with Jackson's advice and Polk's support, tried a new approach: simply admit Texas as a state. The idea worked. Instead of a treaty with Texas, which required a two-thirds vote in the Senate that Tyler could not get, both houses of Congress passed a resolution admitting Texas as a state in February 1845, leaving it to the president to negotiate the Texas border with Mexico (see Map 11-2). Five senators, led by Missouri's Thomas Hart Benton, who had opposed annexation, now supported the statehood resolution based on a promise that President Polk would conduct the negotiations about the Texas border. Tyler did not feel bound by the promise. On March 1, 1845, with 4 days left in office, Tyler signed the resolution admitting Texas, sent envoys to Texas offering immediate statehood without any negotiations, and held a gala White House party to celebrate the admission of the new state to the union. Benton was furious, and most Whigs were equally distraught. Three days later on March 4, 1845, James K. Polk was inaugurated as president of a nation that considered Texas to be one of its states, even if Mexico did not agree.

54° 40′ or Fight—The United States and Oregon

Until the mid-1830s, few Americans had followed the route of the Lewis and Clark expedition and explored or settled in Oregon. The Canadian Hudson's Bay Company dominated the fur business in Oregon, and Indian tribes traded furs to the company for rifles and other goods. While American political debates seemed fixated on Texas, Oregon was generally ignored by the press or in Congress. The lack of interest in Oregon began to change in July 1836 when some 70 people traveled through a pass in the Rocky Mountains into what is now Wyoming. Some of the group, including four Protestant missionaries, settled in the fertile farming areas of the Willamette Valley south of the Columbia River in present-day Oregon. Two of those missionaries, Marcus and Narcissa Whitman, also became first-rate publicists for beauties of the Oregon Territory (see Map 11-3).

MAP 11-3 Westward Trails. Beginning at places like St. Louis or Independence, Missouri, or Council Bluffs, Iowa, a variety of trails were used by early American migrants seeking new homes in not only Oregon but also territory claimed by the Republic of Mexico from Texas to California.

American Voices

The Letters of Narcissa Whitman, 1836–1847

Narcissa Whitman and her physician husband Marcus were sent by the American Board of Commissioners for Foreign Missions to establish a mission to the Cayuse Indians near what is now Walla Walla, Washington, in 1836. The mission converted few Cayuse. But Narcissa's letters home and her husband's speaking tours encouraged white settlement in the Oregon territory, settlement that alienated Indians but led to a strong American presence in the area. Although the letters were filled with descriptions of the hardships of the journey across the Rocky Mountains and the difficulty of life in Oregon, Narcissa's praise of the beauty and fertility of the land made the greatest impact.

September 12. [1836] What a delightful place this is; what a contrast to the rough, barren sand plains, through which we had so recently passed. Here we find fruit of every description, apples, peaches, grapes, pears, plums, and fig trees in abundance; also cucumbers, melons, beans, peas, beets, cabbage, tomatoes and every kind of vegetable too numerous to be mentioned. Every part is very neat and tastefully arranged, with fine walks, lined on each side with strawberry vines. At the opposite end of the garden is a good summer house covered with grape vines.

Dec. 26th. [1836] It is indeed, a lovely situation. We are on a beautiful level—a peninsula formed by the branches of the Walla Walla river, upon the base of which our house stands, on the southeast corner, near the shore of the main river. To run a fence across to the opposite river, on the north from our house—this, with the river, would enclose 300 acres of good land for cultivation, all directly under the eye. The rivers are barely skirted with timber. This is all the woodland we can see; beyond them, as far as the eye can reach, plains and mountains appear. On the east, a few rods from the house, is a range of small hills, covered with bunchgrass—a very excellent food for animals, and upon which they subsist during winter, even digging it from under the snow.

Waiilatpu, Oregon Territory [The Whitman Mission near Walla Walla]

August 23. [1847] For the last two weeks immigrants have been passing, probably 80 or 100 wagons have already passed and 1,000 are said to be on the road, besides the Mormons…The poor Indians are amazed at the overwhelming numbers of Americans coming into the country. They seem not to know what to make of it. Very many of the principal ones are dying, and…[t]he remaining ones seem attached to us, and cling to us the closer; cultivate their farms quite extensively, and do not wish to see any Sniapus (Americans) settle among them here.

The Cayuse Indians, who were the focus of the Whitman Mission, were indeed "amazed at the overwhelming numbers of Americans coming into the country." When, as a result of the immigration, a measles epidemic struck in 1847, the amazement turned to anger. The Whitmans provided medical care to Indian and white children, but many Cayuse still died. In November 1847, the Cayuse Chief Tiloukaikt led a party that killed both Whitmans and burned the mission. In response, a white militia attacked the Cayuse. Two years later, Tiloukaikt was executed for the murder of the Whitmans. From the gallows he said, "Did not your missionaries teach us that Christ died to save his people? So we die to save our people." Disease and white raids so weakened the Cayuse that they could not continue as an independent nation, and they merged into the Nez Perce and Yakima tribes.

Source: www.pbs.org/weta/thewest/program/resources/archives/two/whitman1.htm#120536 www.pbs.org/weta/thewest/program/resources/archives/twowhitman2.htm#040447 *The Letters of Narcissa Whitman, 1836–1847* (Fairfield, WA: YeGalleon Press, 1986).

Thinking Critically

1. **Documentary Analysis**

   On what aspects of the land did Narcissa focus? Why?

2. **Comparison**

   How might the Cayuse Indians have seen the land? How might their view have differed from that of Narcissa?

The Whitmans' letters about Oregon did much to attract further American settlement, but the claim to the Oregon Territory had been shared by the United States and Britain since a series of treaties negotiated by then Secretary of State John Quincy Adams between 1818 and 1824 created the joint American-British governance of Oregon (see Chapter 8). The Oregon Territory stretched along the Pacific coast from the northern border of Spanish-Mexican California to the southern border of what was then Russian America, (now Alaska) and included the present U.S. states of Oregon, Washington, and Idaho as well as the Canadian province of British Columbia and the Yukon Territory. By the 1840s, both governments wanted to resolve the border and end the joint ownership of the territory.

In the Webster-Ashburton Treaty of 1842, the United States and Britain had already negotiated a U.S.-Canadian border at the 49th parallel from the Great Lakes west to the beginning of Oregon. Continuing that border west would split the Oregon Territory

Fort Vancouver on the north shore of the Columbia River in present day Washington state was a beautiful site, shown in this 1848 lithograph, after an 1845 drawing by Lieutenant Henry J. Warre of Native Americans gathered in front of the fort. Pictures like this, along with Narcissa Whitman's letters did much to popularize the Oregon-Washington region.

between the two countries. Tyler's ambassador in London proposed making the 49th parallel the boundary all the way to the Pacific but giving the British the southern tip of Vancouver Island, sliced by the 49th parallel, and giving both countries the right to navigate the Juan de Fuca Strait between Vancouver and the mainland. It seemed like a straightforward compromise. Polk, however, wanted more, or pretended to.

In his 1844 campaign, Polk promised to win all of Oregon up to the Alaskan border, or 54°40′ in terms of latitude. But Polk needed his army for the war that he expected to have with Mexico and did not want to fight Britain, too. The coalition that elected him was divided about Oregon. Calhoun and the southern planters would have happily given all of Oregon to Britain. They did not want a war or even tension to interrupt the cotton trade with Britain that was making the South wealthy. In addition, from Calhoun's perspective, any future states carved out of the Oregon Territory would most likely be free states, tipping the balance in the Senate against southern interests. But Missouri's powerful Senator Thomas Hart Benton was growing fond of Oregon because the trail from Independence, Missouri, to Oregon was adding wealth to his state. Polk had promised 54°40′, and Benton meant to hold him to it. John Quincy Adams, now a power in the House of Representatives, agreed with Benton. Although he was opposed to annexing Texas because of slavery, Adams was still an American expansionist, he liked the region for all the reasons Calhoun disliked it, and he wanted Oregon in the Union.

The British government, led by Prime Minister Sir Robert Peel, also wanted a compromise that would support the Hudson's Bay Company but guarantee an uninterrupted flow of American cotton to British mills and avoid war with the United States. Peel also faced other issues that were more pressing than Oregon. But others in London wanted more of Oregon and insisted that the southern border of British Oregon should be the Columbia River, which created the so-called "disputed triangle" of land that both nations claimed.

The Peel and Polk administrations eventually compromised along the 49th parallel (the current border) in spring 1846. The agreement was an obvious compromise, particularly for the United States, but it meant that the United States was free to pursue actions that Polk considered more important. As the Democratic *New York Herald* said, "We can now thrash Mexico into decency at our leisure."

> **11.1** **Quick Review** Why was annexing Texas more controversial than dividing the Oregon Territory? Discuss at least two major factors.

THE U.S. WAR WITH MEXICO, 1846–1848

> **11.2** Analyze the causes, strategies, and outcomes of the U.S. War with Mexico.

Two years before Presidents Tyler and Polk had managed the U.S. annexation of Texas, Mexico had warned the United States that such a move would mean war because Mexico still claimed the territory. One week after Tyler signed the annexation legislation, the Mexican ambassador in Washington declared the move "an act of aggression," and Mexico severed diplomatic relations with the United States.

Although the vote to make Texas a state of the United States was passed and celebrated in Washington in March of 1845, Texas did not ratify the agreement until July 1845, and Congress did not ratify the Texas decision until December. Meanwhile, Mexican President José Joaquín Herrera, a political moderate, agreed to negotiate with the United States. He knew his country did not have the resources to fight a war, but he also knew that public opinion in his country would never accept the loss of Texas, particularly the larger area of Texas going all the way to the Rio Grande that the United States now claimed. Polk sent former Louisiana Congressman John Slidell to Mexico City to negotiate.

Fighting the War in Texas and Mexico, Responding to Resistance

Although there were tensions between Americans and the government of Mexico from Texas to California, the heart of the concerns in 1846 had to do with Texas. While leaders in both countries negotiated about whether the United States could annex Texas, another question loomed: just what constituted Texas? The Republic of Texas had never governed any land west of the Nueces River. Many in the United States and Mexico considered that river to be the western boundary of Texas. But Polk and many Texans claimed that the Rio Grande was the border, a claim that made Texas a much bigger state (see Map 11-2). Herrera would never accept that claim. Moreover, Polk really wanted not only Texas as far as the Rio Grande but also New Mexico and California. He would purchase it if he could, but he also considered a war as a viable way to secure that land.

While the negotiations continued, Polk ordered General Zachary Taylor to cross the Louisiana-Texas border at the Sabine River in June 1845 and from there continue to "approach as near the boundary line, the Rio Grande, as prudence will dictate." Taylor was indeed a prudent general, and he initially moved only as far as the Nueces where he halted at Corpus Christi to train his 4,000 troops. But his orders were clear: any Mexican movement across the Rio Grande would be considered an act of war. It took almost a year for Polk to get his war, but in April 1846, Taylor's army moved to the northern edge of the Rio Grande. On April 25, 1846, 11 Americans were killed in a battle with Mexican troops who had crossed the Rio Grande. Polk was delighted when Taylor reported that "hostilities may now be considered as commenced." In his war message to Congress on May 11, 1846, Polk said, "Mexico…has invaded our territory and shed American blood upon the American soil.…War exists…by the act of Mexico herself."

Not everyone in Congress agreed. Most Whigs opposed war, though they wanted to support the American troops who might be in harm's way and worried about being seen as unpatriotic. Kentucky Whig Garrett David said, "It is our own President who began this war. He has been carrying it on for months." The key vote on the war passed the House 123 to 67, though many Democrats did not want to be seen as opposing their party's president and a subsequent vote formalizing the declaration of war carried the House by 174 to 14 with 35 abstentions. In the Senate, the key test of strength carried only by 26 to 20, but a subsequent vote that included funds financing the war carried 40 to 2 with 3 abstentions. President Polk declared that a state of war existed between the United States and Mexico on May 13, 1846.

The war that a divided Congress declared was fought by a divided nation. Polk and his supporters expected a quick victory. Senator Thomas Hart Benton wrote that the president wanted "a small war, just large enough to require a treaty of peace, and not large enough to make military reputations dangerous for the presidency." Polk got a longer and more costly war than he bargained for—one that also produced more military heroes.

The war provoked strong opposition. A decade before it began, John Quincy Adams warned Congress that the annexation of Texas would bring on a war in which the United States would be in the wrong, saying: "Sirs, the banners of freedom will be the banners of Mexico; and your banners, I blush to speak the word, will be the banners of slavery." A decade later, Adams voted against the war in the House of Representatives.

The artist Richard Caton Woodville's painting *War News from Mexico* captured the interest and, in some cases, surprise that came as news of the war reached people in most parts of the United States much more quickly than ever before, thanks primarily to the spread of telegraph lines that transmitted information faster than ever previously possible.

Once the war began, others, including Congressman Abraham Lincoln of Illinois, joined Adams in opposition. An aspiring Whig politician from Illinois, Lincoln voiced his suspicions about the war. He thought that President Polk "is deeply conscious of being in the wrong…that he ordered General Taylor into the midst of a peaceful Mexican settlement, purposely to bring on a war." Some of those in the field agreed. In Texas, a young Lieutenant Colonel Ethan Hitchcock noted in his diary that "It looks as if the government sent a small force on purpose to bring on a war, so as to have a pretext fort taking California and as much of this country as it chooses."

Perhaps the most influential response to the war with Mexico came from a poet rather than a politician. While he is remembered today mostly for his reflective stay at Walden Pond, Henry David Thoreau also believed that the war with Mexico was immoral. In a pamphlet titled *Civil Disobedience*, Thoreau wrote, "I meet this American government, or its representative the State government, directly, and face to face, once a year, no more, in the person of its tax-gatherer." Thoreau saw the demand for his tax money as the opportunity to resist what he saw as the government's injustice and refused to pay his tax, a portion of which would go to support what he considered to be an unjust and immoral war. He was arrested and spent a night in the town jail in Concord before someone, to his frustration, paid the tax for him. But his willingness to face arrest for his convictions and the pamphlet that he wrote explaining his actions made Thoreau not only one of the most famous opponents of the War with Mexico but a model of civil disobedience for generations to come, in the United States and elsewhere.

In the first battles of the war, Taylor defeated a larger Mexican force and occupied the Mexican town of Matamoros in May 1846. The Mexican army fought bravely, but the Americans had superior technology—rifles that shot farther and better artillery. The U.S. Navy blockaded Mexican ports on the Gulf and Pacific coasts, so Mexico could not import supplies from abroad. Taylor's army moved slowly into Mexico, but heat and disease took a heavier toll than battles. One in eight U.S. soldiers died in a 6-week encampment in the Mexican city of Camargo even though no battles took place there. If the troops, especially the volunteers, had learned to fill canteens upstream from where horses were washed, the death toll would have been far lower. Then in

THINKING HISTORICALLY

Considering Henry David Thoreau

Henry David Thoreau (1817–1862) published "On the Duty of Civil Disobedience" in 1849. The essay has at least two themes: Thoreau's opposition to most, if not all, government and his belief that civil disobedience—in this case breaking an immoral law—was the right thing to do. Thoreau's belief in civil disobedience—refusing to obey an unjust law and a willingness to face the consequences—have made Thoreau a model for others who advocated civil disobedience, including Martin Luther King, Jr. (1929–1968) in the United States and Mohandas Gandhi (1869–1948), who led the nonviolent protests that eventually won India independence from Great Britain, both of whom cited Thoreau.

But Thoreau's arguments are complex and many who may agree with some of what he might say would reject other aspects of his essay. In the essay he begins by arguing:

> I heartily accept the motto, "That government is best which governs least"; and I should like to see it acted up to more rapidly and systematically. Carried out, it finally amounts to this, which also I believe—"That government is best which governs not at all"; and when men are prepared for it, that will be the kind of government which they will have. Government is at best but an expedient; but most governments are usually, and all governments are sometimes, inexpedient. The objections which have been brought against a standing army, and they are many and weighty, and deserve to prevail, may also at last be brought against a standing government.

He then moves on to his specific critique of the war with Mexico and his appeal for resistance:

> How does it become a man to behave toward the American government today? I answer, that he cannot without disgrace be associated with it. I cannot for an instant recognize that political organization as my government which is the slave's government also....Under a government which imprisons unjustly, the true place for a just man is also a prison. The proper place today, the only place which Massachusetts has provided for her freer and less despondent spirits, is in her prisons, to be put out and locked out of the State by her own act, as they have already put themselves out by their principles. It is there that the fugitive slave, and the Mexican prisoner on parole, and the Indian come to plead the wrongs of his race should find them; on that separate but more

> free and honorable ground, where the State places those who are not with her, but against her—the only house in a slave State in which a free man can abide with honor.

Finally, he says he is not willing to be like "the thousands who are in opinion opposed to slavery and to the war, who yet in effect do nothing." Thoreau refused to pay taxes to support the war and was jailed for his crime of conscience.

While Thoreau's words and actions were widely praised by some and condemned by others, the arguments also involved significant internal differences:

- Some who agreed with Thoreau in his opposition to the war were not willing to risk jail as he was and did not think it was necessary to do so or indeed proper to break the law as he did.

- Some who agreed with Thoreau in his opposition to the war also disagreed with his critique of all government and would never echo Thoreau's words, "The objections which have been brought against a standing army, and they are many and weighty, and deserve to prevail, may also at last be brought against a standing government." Indeed, many have criticized Thoreau for being a philosopher of excessive individualism—advocating the moral worth of the individual over the state or a social group—a stance that observers from Tocqueville to the present have criticized the United States for representing.

Source: Henry David Thoreau, *On the Duty of Civil Disobedience* (New York: Houghton Mifflin, 1893).

Thinking Critically

1. **Contextualization**

   How would you explain Thoreau's decision to use a fugitive slave, a Mexican prisoner, and an Indian as examples of those wronged by his government? What connections might he make between the plight of all three? What was happening in the United States that might lead an author to link these different groups of people in 1849?

2. **Chronological Reasoning**

   What are the implications of his rejection of all government when he says, "That government is best which governs not at all." Is it necessary to agree with Thoreau in his rejection of government to agree with his critique of the War with Mexico or his decision to go to jail as a matter of conscience rather than pay taxes to support the war?

September 1846, Taylor defeated another larger Mexican force and captured the crucial Mexican town of Monterrey. With both armies now exhausted, Taylor allowed the Mexicans to withdraw peacefully and declared a truce, which infuriated Polk.

After the victory at Monterrey, Polk tried to open peace negotiations, but the Mexican government was not interested. This lack of interest came as a surprise because the United States had secretly helped the former Mexican dictator Santa Anna

MAP 11-4 Battles in the U.S. War with Mexico. Once war was declared between the United States and Mexico, General Taylor led his armies into the disputed territory and further south to battles in Monterrey and Buena Vista in Northern Mexico, while General Kearney led forces across the continent to take control of Santa Fe, New Mexico, and then parts of California. The Navy played a major role in the takeover of California but also blockaded Pacific and Gulf ports in Mexico while General Winfield Scott landed at Veracruz and soon thereafter won control of Mexico City itself.

seize power in Mexico City, based on his promise to U.S. negotiators that he would conclude a peace treaty. But once in office, Santa Anna shifted his position and prepared to fight rather than bargain (see Map 11-4).

Santa Anna marched north to engage Taylor, whom he knew was now short of troops. In February 1847, the two armies met at what Americans called the Battle of Buena Vista. It was the largest single engagement of the war, and it was a draw, which meant that Santa Anna had failed to defeat the Americans on Mexican soil. Taylor's army remained intact.

Many of Taylor's best troops had been moved further south. As Polk realized he was in for a long fight, he also knew that Taylor could not march across the deserts to Mexico City. The distance was too long to supply an invading army. Polk also worried

✳ Explore the War with Mexico on MyHistoryLab

WHAT DID THE TEXAS REVOLUTION AND MEXICAN-AMERICAN WAR MEAN FOR AMERICAN EXPANSION?

In the 1830s, the Mexican government faced problems in its northern state of Texas. The area was home to many Anglo-American settlers, and they were growing increasingly unhappy under Mexican governance. Texans successfully rebelled, forming the independent Republic of Texas in 1836. During the next decade, the United States annexed Texas as a new state, but disputed land claims quickly led to war between the United States and Mexico in 1846. The U.S. victory over the Mexican forces in 1848, after a series of consecutive U.S. battle successes, led to huge territorial losses for its southern neighbor as the United States acquired the territory that today is the modern Southwest.

U.S. General Winfield Scott led his troops into Mexico City to accept the official Mexican surrender in 1847. This popular picture shows the clean ending of the war but not the bloody battles that led to it.

MAJOR BATTLES OF THE MEXICAN-AMERICAN WAR

Battle	Date	Victor
Battle of Palo Alto	May 8, 1846	U.S.
Battle of Resaca de la Palma	May 9, 1846	U.S.
Battle of Monterrey	Sept. 21–24, 1846	U.S.
Battle of San Pasqual	Dec. 6, 1846	Mexico
Battle of Rio San Gabriel	Jan. 8, 1847	U.S.
Battle of Buena Vista	Feb. 22–23, 1847	U.S.
Battle of Sacramento Rier	Feb. 27, 1847	U.S.
Battle of Veracruz	March 29, 1847	U.S.
Battle of Cerro Gordo	April 18, 1847	U.S.

KEY QUESTIONS   Use MyHistoryLab *Explorer* to answer these questions:

Context ▶▶▶ *What was the political situation in Mexico leading up to its war with the United States?*

Map the nation's transformations between the 1820s and 1840s.

Response ▶▶▶ *How did the Texas Revolution unfold?*

Understand the progress, troop movements, and major battles.

Consequence ▶▶▶ *What did the acquisition of Mexican territory mean for the slavery in the United States?*

Consider the potential implications for the extension of slavery.

about making Taylor a war hero and political rival. So he turned to the experienced professional soldier Winfield Scott to plan an invasion of the Mexican heartland. In March 1847, after careful planning, Scott landed troops at the port of Veracruz. (It was the largest amphibious operation of U.S. troops before D-Day during World War II.) Scott's army then marched to Mexico City, taking the same invasion route that Hernán Cortés had used against the Aztecs 328 years before (see Chapter 2). After hard fighting, Mexico City surrendered in September 1847. Polk, still worried about military heroes, then removed Scott from command in early 1848. The United States had lost 12,518 soldiers and spent almost $100 million in the war. Mexico had lost many more lives—soldiers and civilians—and its economy was devastated.

From New Mexico to Alta California and the Bear Flag Revolt

While the major focus of the fighting in the U.S. war with Mexico took place on the Texas border and in the heartland of Mexico, New Mexico and California were not exempt from battles, though they were of smaller scale than anything seen elsewhere. The initial U.S. conquest of New Mexico was easy. In the summer of 1846, General Stephen Watts Kearny marched 850 miles from Fort Leavenworth, Kansas, to Santa Fe. The Mexican governor had already fled, and Kearny took silence and sullenness among the people for support or at least acceptance of the American takeover. He raised the U.S. flag in Santa Fe and promised that the government would respect the residents' property and religious freedom as well as protect them from Indian raids. Kearny appointed Charles Bent, an American already living in Taos, as territorial governor. Then in September 1846, a month after he had arrived, Kearny marched most of his troops off to secure the U.S. victory in California. Although a bloody rebellion against U.S. rule by Hispanics and Indians broke out later that year, and Bent himself was killed by the rebels, U.S. troops soon suppressed it, and most armed resistance to annexation ended.

Emboldened by this show of support, a group of armed American immigrants in the inland town of Sonoma arrested General Mariano Vallejo, the man they considered the symbol of Mexican authority in Sonoma, and jailed him at Fort Sutter near Sacramento. Vallejo had retired from active duty with the Mexican government and was quite friendly to a possible American takeover. But to the Americans, Vallejo symbolized Mexican authority. With no other Mexican leader in sight, the rebels organized what they called the **Bear Flag Revolt** by declaring California to be an independent Republic. They also designed a flag and raised it in the town square in Sonoma. The flag displayed a large star next to a grizzly bear atop a bottom border stripe and the words "California Republic." To the Mexicans like Vallejo, the Bear Flag was a symbol that these new immigrants were the bears who came as a thief to take their cattle and their land. Soon after Vallejo's arrest, Sloat's U.S. Navy squadron sailed into Monterey Bay and proclaimed U.S. conquest of California as a victory in the War with Mexico. The independent California Republic was a short-lived convenience. The rebels replaced the Bear Flag (now the state flag of California) with the Stars and Stripes.

The American conquest of California was much easier than the war along the Rio Grande in Texas. The Mexican government was much less interested in California than in Texas, a reality that had allowed a unique Californian culture to develop in the early decades of the 19th century. Mexican citizens of California, the products of this culture, had a decidedly ambivalent attitude toward annexation by the United States. Nevertheless, some native Californians opposed the American takeover and fought against the Bear Flag rebels and the American forces led by Navy Commodore Robert Stockton, who had replaced Sloat, and Captain Frémont. Those Californians saw themselves as citizens of the Republic of Mexico, even if sometimes disgruntled citizens, and they saw the Americans as an invading army. In a series of skirmishes between 1846 and 1847, 35 of those fighting on the American side died in battle while an estimated eight Californios (those fighting for the Mexican cause) were killed. Later, the Californios suffered much greater losses in property and, indeed, their way of life.

Bear Flag Revolt

A revolt led by recent American immigrants who temporarily declared California to be an independent Republic until U.S. forces took control of the territory.

There were many reasons for the limited nature of the warfare in California. The total non-Indian population of California was very small, and most of the regular Mexican forces had abandoned the region before hostilities began. Probably even more significant, most of the Mexican leaders in California were really hoping for an American takeover to replace the distant and inept Mexican administration and the lawlessness of the American Bear Flag frontiersmen. In 1847, the final skirmishes between Californio defenders under Andrés Pico and the American troops took place in southern California. As it became increasingly clear that no support could be expected from Mexico, Pico negotiated the terms of what he saw as an honorable surrender. In January 1847, Pico's troops marched into Los Angeles and disbanded. The American control of the region was complete.

Negotiating the Peace, Defining the Borders

In April 1847, Polk had sent Nicholas Trist, an experienced diplomat, to accompany Scott and negotiate a treaty with the Mexican government. After the fighting in Mexico City had ended, Trist began serious negotiations. With Mexico City, New Mexico, and California already in the hands of the U.S. Army, however, Polk decided that Trist was not being tough enough and recalled him. Instead of returning to Washington, Trist warned the Mexican authorities that he had been recalled and that his replacement would demand much more. Perhaps they might want to conclude a treaty quickly with him. The Mexicans were anxious to end the U.S. occupation of Mexico City and the country's key ports, and Trist was right: after the conquest of Mexico City, Polk wanted even more Mexican territory. On February 2, 1848, Trist and the Mexican commissioners signed the **Treaty of Guadalupe Hidalgo**. Trist told his wife that he had asked Mexico for the minimum that Polk would accept because he was ashamed of "the iniquity of the war, as an abuse of power on our part." But his minimum included all of Polk's original demands—all of Texas to the Rio Grande and land further west to California as far south as San Diego. Mexico was paid $15 million, which went to its creditors. The treaty may have been for less land than Polk wanted, but it reshaped both the United States and Mexico.

A furious President Polk, realizing that he was stuck with the treaty that Trist had negotiated, submitted it to the Senate, which ratified it. But Polk refused to pay Trist for his services. (Trist was not paid until 1871.) The Whig-affiliated editor Horace Greeley wrote in his *New York Tribune*, "Let us have peace, no matter if the adjuncts are revolting." The abolitionist Frederick Douglass was harsher: "They have succeeded in robbing Mexico of her territory, and are rejoicing over their success under the hypocritical pretense of a regard for peace." Nevertheless, with the Treaty of Guadalupe Hidalgo, peace had come. The United States was much larger as a result of the war, now including 90,000 new citizens who had been citizens of Mexico and even more Indians who preferred to stay independent of both countries. It was a different country from when Polk took office.

In 1853, one of Polk's successors, President Franklin Pierce, sent James Gadsden to Mexico City with instructions to buy a strip of land south of Arizona and New Mexico for a southern transcontinental railroad from New Orleans to El Paso to Los Angeles, which needed to be located south of the Rocky Mountains. Gadsden was also told to purchase as much additional land as possible, including perhaps all of Baja California. Mexican authorities suspected that the United States was after much more than a railroad route. In the end, Mexico sold only the minimum that the United States wanted. For $10 million, money its government badly needed, Mexico ceded 39,000 sparsely populated square miles to the United States. This area, known as the **Gadsden Purchase**, was the final extension of U.S. territory within what would be the contiguous 48 states (see Map 11-5).

In his own eyes, Polk had an amazingly successful term. He had made the United States a continental nation. He had completed the job he had promised to do and did not seek a second term. For the election of 1848, Polk's Democrats nominated Lewis

Treaty of Guadalupe Hidalgo
The treaty, signed in 1848, ended the U.S. War with Mexico and granted the United States control of all of Texas, New Mexico, and California.

Gadsden Purchase
The final acquisition of land in the continental United States was completed in 1853 when the United States paid Mexico $10 million for a strip of land in what is now southern New Mexico and Arizona.

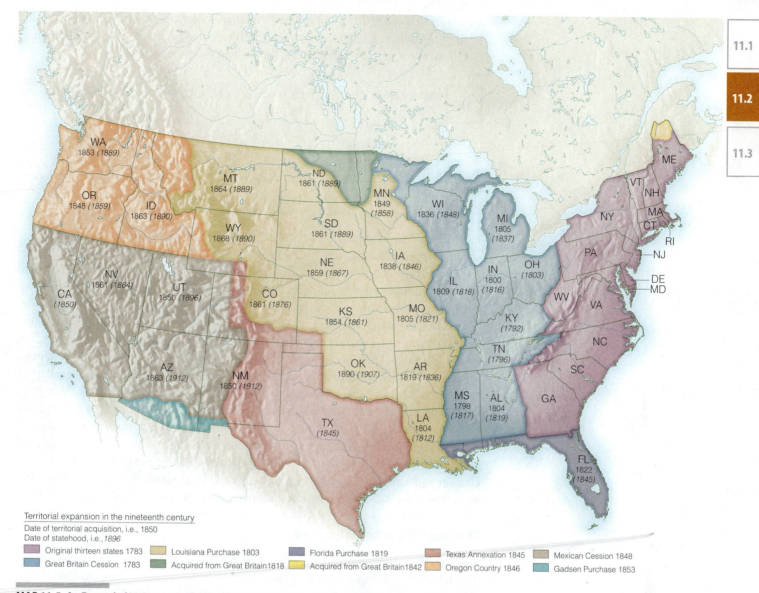

Territorial expansion in the nineteenth century

Date of territorial acquisition, i.e., 1850
Date of statehood, i.e., *1896*

- Original thirteen states 1783
- Great Britain Cession 1783
- Louisiana Purchase 1803
- Acquired from Great Britain 1818
- Florida Purchase 1819
- Acquired from Great Britain 1842
- Texas Annexation 1845
- Oregon Country 1846
- Mexican Cession 1848
- Gadsden Purchase 1853

MAP 11-5 An Expanded Union. With the treaty setting the Oregon border in 1846 and the Treaty of Guadalupe Hidalgo in 1848, the territory of the continental United States was almost set. The small Gadsden Purchase in 1853 made it easier to build a railroad south of the Rocky Mountains.

Cass of Michigan. The Whigs, having won once with a general and having lost three times with their hero Henry Clay, turned to a new war hero and nominated General Zachary Taylor, known as "Old Rough and Ready," and former Congressman Millard Fillmore from New York as Taylor's running mate. While Taylor was as strong a nationalist as Jackson, he was also a slaveholder, and Cass, like Polk, was an expansionist. Northerners opposed to slavery could not stomach either of them and some created the Free Soil Party, which was committed to ensuring that all new territories would be free of slavery. The Free Soilers did not propose abolishing slavery where it already existed but did oppose any extension of slavery into any new territories. Using that platform, they nominated former President Van Buren as their candidate. In the three-way race, Taylor won a solid victory. It was an ironic outcome for President Polk. The Whigs had opposed Polk throughout his term, especially on the issue of the War with Mexico, and the president feared creating military heroes throughout the war. In the end, a Whig war hero succeeded him. A little over a year into his term, on a hot July 4th of 1850, Taylor suddenly died and Vice President Fillmore ascended to the presidency. This time, however, unlike Tyler's accession with the death of Harrison, there were no major policy shifts when Fillmore took office.

11.2 **Quick Review** Considering U.S. actions in Texas and California, was the Mexican-American War a "land grab"? Why or why not?

WEST INTO THE PACIFIC

11.3 Describe the causes and outcomes of U.S. expansion in California and into the Pacific region, including establishing new relationships with Hawaii, China, and Japan.

Early in his term of office, President Polk had told Congress that he was interested in acquiring California's harbors from Mexico because, he said, these ports would shelter American ships and allow the Pacific Ocean to provide the basis for "an extensive and profitable commerce with China, and other countries of the East." He had no idea how quickly his dream would come true. Even before the negotiations with Mexico were complete, gold was discovered in California, and the resulting Gold Rush made into thriving commercial centers not only the gold camps but also the cities around harbors that Polk wanted. These same Pacific coast harbors quickly became home to American ships that had been dominating much of the Pacific Ocean for a decade before Polk spoke. In the 1840s, American whaling ships led all other nations in the whale trade in the Pacific, and the U.S. Navy led the way to American negotiations for a role in trade with Hawaii and China. After the acquisition of California, the Navy also established a trading relationship with Japan. After 1848, the profits of the Pacific trade poured into the United States through the newly acquired Pacific ports. The acquisition of Oregon and California not only expanded the United States to the Pacific coast but also allowed the nation to become a dominant player all across the Pacific Ocean.

The Gold Rush to California

Another 1848 development was perhaps even more important to California's history than the shift in political authority from Mexico to the United States. On January 24, 1848, while American and Mexican negotiators were still meeting in the Mexican town of Guadalupe Hidalgo, James Marshall, a carpenter at the fort and mill owned by Swiss native Johann Sutter on the American River in northern California, was deepening the channel going into the mill's water wheel when he noticed some odd material in the water. He reported, "Boys, I believe I have found a gold mine." His was the first discovery of gold that would quickly lead to the **California Gold Rush**.

Sutter and Marshall tried to keep the discovery a secret, but word spread all too quickly. By May 1848, everyone in San Francisco seemed to know that gold had been discovered. And while communications were still slow, prospective miners from all over California—Indians, long time Mexican residents, and American settlers—as well as immigrants from Oregon, Hawaii, Mexico, and as far away as Chile, Peru, Australia, France, and parts of China moved into the gold fields of the Sierra Nevada mountains. The rush was on. Two-thirds of the white men in Oregon came south to California. Recently discharged soldiers from the Mexican and American armies joined them there. In the earliest days, California Indians who knew the land best made excellent gold prospectors. Newcomers expressed surprise that in the first year of the gold rush Miwok Indian women panned for gold alongside of Miwok men and the newcomers from around the globe. The diversity in the fields did not last.

In August 1848, an article in the *New York Herald* included a brief mention that "gold, worth in value $30, was picked up in the bed of a stream of the Sacramento." President Polk, determined to show the value of the newly acquired territory,

California Gold Rush
The rush to find gold that brought thousands of new residents to California and produced millions of dollars in new wealth for the region and the United States.

included a mention in his Annual Message to Congress. Ten million dollars in gold was produced in California in 1848, and within 3 years, the revenue had grown to $220 million. So much gold changed the economic calculations of the United States and much of the world from China to South America to Europe. Suddenly, there was a great deal of gold in circulation everywhere.

Thousands of people wanted to get rich quickly by coming to California to find the gold. California's non-Indian population was around 7,000 in 1845. It had grown to almost 93,000 in the first U.S. census of 1850. While the first prospectors had come from the south—Mexico and South America—and the east—from Pacific whaling ships, Hawaii, and China—by 1849, the largest numbers were coming from the eastern United States and Europe. Getting to California from other parts of the United States or Europe could mean a long, slow, and expensive trip by ocean around the southern tip of South America. It could also involve a shorter sea voyage to Nicaragua, then an overland trek by pack mule across the isthmus, and another voyage from there up to San Francisco. Still for others, it could mean traveling overland by walking and on ox-drawn wagons across the continent. Sea travel around South America was certainly the most comfortable and perhaps safest, but it cost a lot, from $300 to $700, and it was slow, taking 4 to 8 months. The trip via Nicaragua or Panama was almost as expensive, perhaps $600, and dangerous, but it was certainly the fastest, taking 5 to 8 weeks. Coming by land across the continent was by far the cheapest, costing not more than $200, but it also took at least 3 months and had to be timed just right to avoid winter on the Rocky Mountains. The majority opted for the cheapest way. Small numbers of people had been coming west for decades, but in 1849–50, many thousands of prospective Californians traveled along the Platte and Humboldt Rivers and then the Oregon and California Trails into the gold fields (see Map 11-3).

The gold camps themselves were harsh places. Fortunes were made and lost not only in the fields but also at gambling tables and through theft and intimidation. White Americans, some of them very recent Americans, resented the competition of miners from South America and elsewhere, especially those who came from China or who were Indians or Californios. Within a short time, most Chinese and Indians miners had been driven from the gold fields through violence and intimidation, though some Indians were retained to work for subsistence wages mining gold for others while the Chinese found other kinds of work, eventually building the western railroads and developing service industries for miners and others.

The incredible jump in California's immigrant population came at a terrible cost for the California Indians. Their population, already declining in the face of the missions, declined much more rapidly after the beginnings of the Gold Rush because of disease and outright murder, decreasing by almost 85 percent between 1848 and 1880 to 23,000. African slaves were rare both because slave owners knew it was all too easy for a slave to escape in California and because other miners hated all competition.

Few women were able to succeed as miners; indeed, far fewer women than men even came to California in the gold rush. Mining camps were overwhelmingly male communities. Some women who did come to California were forced or tricked into prostitution to pay for their passage from Europe, China, and Latin America.

The most freewheeling era of the gold camps was very short lived. By 1851, the chances of finding gold by simply looking in a stream bed, as Marshall and Sutter had done in 1848, or even finding gold with a pan had pretty much ended except in the more southerly Tuolumne and Merced gold regions. Some miners began using a "rocker" or "cradle" that washed dirt out more quickly. Soon enough, gold mining was transformed into large-scale hydraulic mining, which required large corporate investments and reduced most miners to hired labor. Even for hired laborers, though mining paid much better than most East Coast jobs, the possibility of making a fortune evaporated. Gold mining continued and fortunes were still made in the gold fields, but the Gold Rush was over.

Whaling in the Pacific Ocean

In February 1849, the owners of the whaling ship *Minerva* from New Bedford, Massachusetts, received a letter from its captain. The communication reported that, after hunting whales in the Pacific, he had stopped in San Francisco for supplies and to recruit more sailors, "but the excitement there in relation to the discovery of gold made it impossible to prevent the crew from running away. Three of the crew in attempting to swim ashore were drowned, and the ship's company soon became too much reduced to continue the whaling voyage." The *Minerva* thus joined dozens of other whaling ships abandoned in San Francisco harbor while their crews sought wealth in the California gold fields.

Some sailors no doubt found fortunes in the gold fields that had eluded them at sea, and some ship owners lost substantial sums when their ships were abandoned, but in general, the whaling industry was a source of wealth to some Americans while supporting many others and contributing to the growth of the American economy. The golden age of the American whaling industry began after the War of 1812 and continued until the outbreak of the Civil War in 1861. During these years, hundreds of American ships moved from their earlier and safer whale hunts in the Atlantic to 2-, 3-, and 4-year voyages to the Pacific Ocean. Whale oil, which burned brighter than any other fuel available at the time, was used for lamps across the globe. Whale products provided oil for the industrial revolution as well as the bone for the hoop dresses and corsets that were the height of women's fashion. Despite British efforts to launch their own whaling fleets, by the 1830s four-fifths of all the whaling ships in the world were American.

The owners and captains of most American whaling ships were mostly men of old New England English stock, many of them Quakers, but there were exceptions. A few African-Americans, including Paul Cuffee and Absalom F. Boston, became captains,

Clipper ships like the famous *Flying Cloud* made the trip from New York to San Francisco in record speed—89 days in one case—while slower whaling ships traveling from New Bedford and other Atlantic ports into the Pacific often took 2 or 3 years. During the 1830s and 1840s, American sailing ships projected American influence into the Pacific Ocean region as never before.

and Cuffee became a ship owner. The crews, white and black, came from almost every corner of the globe—Pacific Islanders, West Indians, South Americans, or Portuguese. Whaling was one of the few occupations in which blacks were paid the same as whites. Even a runaway slave could admit, as John Thompson did in 1840, "I am a fugitive slave from Maryland….I thought I would go on a whaling voyage, as being a place where I stood least chance of being arrested by slave hunters." By some estimates, 10 percent of those who worked on whaling ships were black. Nevertheless, most sailors in the whaling business were white men, like Ishmael, the fictional narrator of Herman Melville's 1851 novel *Moby-Dick,* though like the fictional Ishmael, the real-world whites served as part of racially diverse crews.

Few women served on whaling ships. There were occasional stories of women who hid their gender and embarked with the crew, not easy in the close quarters of a small ship on a long voyage. Some captains also took along their wives and children, and some crew members said they appreciated having a woman on board who might know more medicine than the men and who could soothe an angry captain.

Whaling ships also explored parts of the world unknown to previous generations of Americans. The first Americans to enter Japan were whaling sailors. Almost a decade before Commodore Perry's famous voyage to "open up" Japan in 1853–54, the *Manhattan* entered Tokyo harbor in 1845 to return shipwrecked Japanese sailors. The *Superior* was the first whaling ship to enter the Arctic Ocean off the coast of Alaska in 1848. U.S. whaling ships explored much of the South Pacific, sailed off the coast of Australia, and explored Antarctica. As a result of the many whaling ships that anchored there, Honolulu and San Francisco became major American ports, rivaling New Bedford, Boston, and Nantucket.

The Navy and Diplomacy Across the Pacific

While many American whaling ships had been sailing the Pacific since 1815, the 1848 Treaty of Guadalupe Hidalgo added a string of Pacific ports, especially San Francisco, to the United States. Indeed, the push for Pacific Ocean ports had been part of the driving force behind President Polk's push for war. The acquisition of those ports expanded U.S. interest in the Pacific and beyond. By 1851, Daniel Webster, who had become secretary of state again under President Fillmore, proclaimed that the United States should "command the oceans, both oceans, all the oceans."

Central to the "command" of the Pacific Ocean was securing U.S. influence in Hawaii. In 1778, the British explorer Captain James Cook was the first European to reach the Hawaiian Islands, but by the mid-19th century, the United States had a much larger presence in Hawaii. Many Protestant missionaries and merchants began arriving in Hawaii in the 1820s where they built churches, schools, and businesses. Missionaries, merchants, and whalers boosted the Hawaiian economy, but they also brought alcohol, gambling, prostitution, and disease, including venereal diseases that killed many Hawaiians and reduced the islanders' ability to maintain their independence.

On occasion, the United States did protect the native Hawaiians. An American missionary, William Richards, advised King Kamehameha II (r. 1819–1824) on ways to maneuver among the great powers and play the United States, Britain, and France against each other. In 1842, Secretary of State Daniel Webster added Hawaii to the protections of the Monroe Doctrine and made it clear that the United States would not tolerate a British or French takeover. In 1851, Webster negotiated a secret treaty with King Kamehameha III that, in the event of war, Hawaii would become a U.S. protectorate. Webster's priority was securing trading rights and the use of Honolulu as a coaling station for U.S. steamships—merchant vessels and warships—on their way to trade with China and Japan.

Just as the United States gained San Francisco and influence in Hawaii, Britain was forcing China to open to the West. China saw itself as the center of the world. Foreigners were barbarians who might be allowed to trade in a limited way through

A Japanese artist captured a U.S. Navy commanded by Commodore Mathew Perry landing in Tokyo and demanding that Japan open itself to trade with the United States.

the port of Guangzhou but would never be treated as equals. Despite the restrictions, American merchants wanted access to more trade with China, and American missionaries wanted access to its people. Regardless, both were mostly shut out. Losing patience with the Chinese, the British turned to violence. In the so-called Opium War (1839–1842), the British forced China to open its ports to British products, including opium from British India, and cede Hong Kong Island as a British colony. Following in the footsteps of the British, U.S. Ambassador Caleb Cushing negotiated the Treaty of Wang-hsia in 1844, which gained the United States the same trade rights as the British.

While Britain took the lead in China, the United States forced the even more isolated Empire of Japan to open to the West. The United States wanted Japan as another coaling station beyond Hawaii on the route to China and wanted to trade with Japan for its own sake. President Fillmore sent Commodore Mathew Perry to "open up" Japan and force a "weak and semi-barbarous people" to deal with the United States. In July 1853, Perry led four large warships with nearly 1,000 sailors into Tokyo Bay and began negotiations. He returned in March 1854 with an even larger fleet. Perry did everything he could to impress the Japanese, providing Japanese officials with champagne, Kentucky bourbon, and a history of the war with Mexico to let them know what happened to those who opposed United States might. In return, the Japanese grudgingly agreed to the **Kanagawa Treaty** that opened two relatively isolated ports to the United States. Only in 1858 did Japan open more ports and establish formal diplomatic relations with other countries. Britain quickly became a larger economic and military force in Japan than the United States. Nevertheless, the United States had established a solid presence in Japan and China by the late 1850s.

As a result of expansion in the 1840s, the nation's border was extended to the Pacific, and U.S. ships sailed everywhere on that ocean. The Pacific and every nation on its shores including China, Japan, and Russian Siberia were in much closer contact with the United States than they had been a short time before. After 1848, the United States was an emerging force in the world.

Kanagawa Treaty
An 1854 agreement–the first between the United States and Japan–it opened two Japanese ports to American commerce, protected shipwrecked American sailors, and ended Japan's 200 years of isolation.

11.3 **Quick Review** Was expansion to other nations (Hawaii, China, Japan) a logical extension of Manifest Destiny? How were U.S. intentions across the Pacific different than U.S. goals in North America?

CONCLUSION

From the late 1830s through the 1840s, the United States became a continental power whose territory spanned from the Atlantic to the Pacific oceans. A strong belief in the Manifest Destiny of the United States justified the Louisiana Purchase of 1803 (though the term was not yet in use) and supported hoped-for territory acquisitions from Oregon to Texas to California. Manifest Destiny reflected the larger belief that the United States was specially chosen by divine will to bring liberty and democracy—usually in its Jacksonian form—to the planet.

While Americans discussed Manifest Destiny, the nation experienced hard times in the 1830s. The financial Panic of 1837, brought on by a worldwide glut in trade, created economic uncertainty in the cotton-growing South and the industrial North. It took several years for the nation's economy to recover.

Many Americans supported versions of Manifest Destiny for varied political or economic reasons, while others had grave reservations. Whether one supported or opposed slavery played directly into views about expansion, which new territories one wanted, and how new territories would be used. Military actions that leaders took in the name of Manifest Destiny led to territorial expansion that spanned the continent to the Pacific coast.

During the presidency of James Polk, Texas entered the Union as a slave state, and after a bloody war from 1846 to 1848, Mexico ceded much of what became the American West to the United States, including New Mexico and—aided by the local Bear Flag Revolt—California. While many Americans, from politicians like John Quincy Adams to philosophers like Henry David Thoreau, opposed the War with Mexico, many other Americans celebrated the victory and the acquisition of so much new territory. The United States also ended the joint ownership of the Oregon Territory with Britain, and both countries resolved borders that allowed each country to have full control of its share. The Gold Rush accelerated the settlement of California with diverse people, and it produced enormous amounts of gold but decimated the American Indian population in the far west.

Winning California from Mexico dramatically changed the U.S. economy not only in terms of gold but also in terms of increased ventures throughout the Pacific involving whaling and trade. The United States now projected Manifest Destiny across an ocean where it had few rivals. The United States became the world leader in the production of whale oil, established a relationship with Hawaii, increased its trade with China, and forced Japan to open itself up to the West. The intensification of American interest in Asia in the 1840s and 1850s reflected the desire of American policy makers to successfully compete with Europe for new markets and coincided with the realization of the long-standing desire among many Americans to create a continental nation that could become a world power.

CHAPTER REVIEW How did U.S. reliance on the idea of Manifest Destiny permanently alter the geographical, social, and political complexion of the United States?

Chapter 11   Chapter Review

MANIFEST DESTINY—THE IMPORTANCE OF AN IDEA

11.1 Explain what Manifest Destiny meant and how it led the United States to involvement in Texas, California, and Oregon.

Review Questions

1. **Crafting Arguments**
   Was the war that broke out in 1835 between the Mexican government and American settlers in Texas inevitable? Why or why not?

2. **Contextualization**
   Why was the status of Texas such a divisive political issue in the early 1840s?

3. **Historical Interpretation**
   What light do the letters of Narcissa Whitman (see the American Voice feature on page 312) shed on the motives behind American settlement in the Oregon Territory in the 1830s?

THE U.S. WAR WITH MEXICO, 1846–1848

11.2 Analyze the causes, strategies, and outcomes of the U.S. War with Mexico.

Review Questions

4. **Crafting Arguments**
   Is it fair to describe the U.S. War with Mexico as a war of conquest? Why or why not?

5. **Contextualization**
   What connections did opponents of the U.S. War with Mexico make between the war and slavery?

6. **Historical Interpretation**
   What changes did incorporation into the United States bring to the society and economy of the former Mexican provinces of New Mexico and California?

WEST INTO THE PACIFIC

11.3 Analyze the causes and outcomes of U.S. expansion into the Pacific region, including establishing new relationships with Hawaii, China, and Japan.

Review Questions

7. **Historical Interpretation**
   What role did the whaling industry play in American expansion in the Pacific in the first half of the 19th century?

8. **Crafting Arguments**
   How would you explain the intensification of American interest in Asia in the 1840s and 1850s?

Expansion, Separation, and a New Union

1844–1877

Living in a Nation of Changing Lands, Changing Faces, Changing Expectations

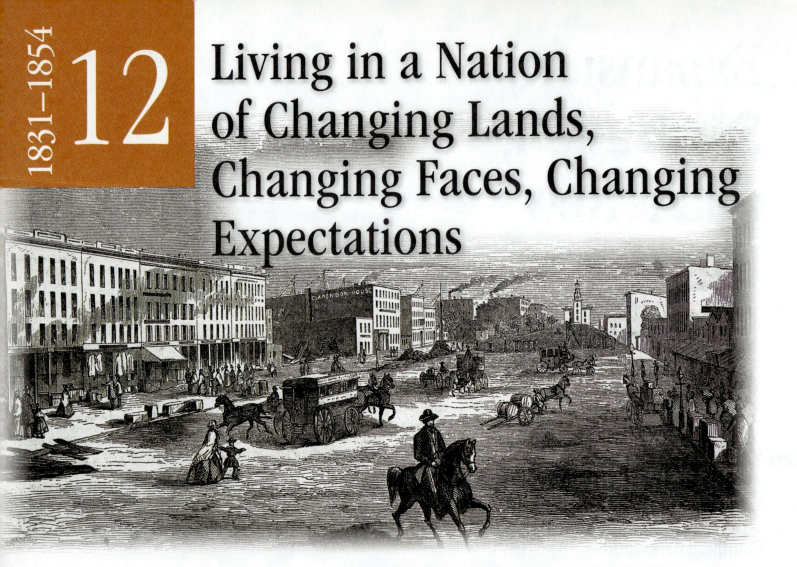

In the 1830s, 1840s, and 1850s, the United States became increasingly divided as immigrants and native-born Americans flocked to industrial cities of the North, while in the South, cotton-generated wealth created a life of ease for a few based on misery for the many.

CHAPTER OBJECTIVE

Demonstrate an understanding of how immigration, new debates over slavery, and an activist generation of women shaped the lives of Americans.

LEARNING OBJECTIVES

THE CHANGING FACE OF THE AMERICAN PEOPLE IN THE 1840s AND 1850s

12.1 Analyze how immigration from China, Ireland, and Germany, as well as the incorporation of Mexican citizens in the Southwest, changed the United States.

SLAVERY IN THE UNITED STATES, 1840s AND 1850s

12.2 Explain how the lives of slaves, slaveholders, and abolitionists evolved in the decades before the Civil War.

NEW STRENGTH FOR AMERICAN WOMEN

12.3 Describe how the women's rights movement developed in the United States in the 1830s and 1840s.

In 1848, as word of the discovery of gold in California traveled across the Pacific, a young man in Canton, the capital of Guangdong province in China, wrote, "Good many Americans speak of California….They find gold very quickly, so I hear.…I think I shall go to California next summer." Halfway around the world in a thatched roof cottage in Ireland, a mother was facing the crisis caused by the rotting potato crop and a typhus epidemic that had claimed one of her daughters. She told her two remaining daughters, "There's a curse on ould [old] green Ireland and we'll get out of it." She saved enough money to send one girl, Tilly, to America and, as her sister remembered, "She came to Philadelphia and got a place for general housework at Mrs. Bent's." Tilly saved her money, sent for her sister, and eventually, they were able to bring the rest of their family from Ireland. Both sisters worked as housekeepers for decades before retiring comfortably after a lifetime of scrimping and saving. The wave of immigration that brought people of diverse ethnic backgrounds changed the face of the United States dramatically in the 1840s and 1850s.

During the same years, many who had lived in the United States for generations were also going through their own significant changes. Residents of the newly expanded country in the Southwest became U.S. citizens as a result of the Treaty of Guadalupe Hidalgo without moving at all. Slaves and abolitionists were challenging the institution of slavery with a vehemence not seen before. Slaves rebelled and ran away. Abolitionists—white and black—became more determined to end slavery, not just stop its expansion. In response, slaveholders became more defiant and defensive than ever before. When Abraham Lincoln looked at a nation that was "half slave and half free" and wondered if it could survive, he was not alone. Women, who had struggled for rights since the Revolutionary Era, found new voice in the 1830s and 1840s. The Seneca Falls Women's Rights Convention of 1848 helped to launch a new political movement for women's rights, including the right to vote. While the right to vote was a key demand of the growing women's right movement, other women also demanded a broader equality in all aspects of society, insisting that "whatever it is morally right for a man to do, it is morally right for a woman to do." This chapter takes a look at the changing nature of the country's racial and ethnic makeup and the thinking of its people, especially about slavery and women's rights, that took place during the 1840s and 1850s.

THE CHANGING FACE OF THE AMERICAN PEOPLE IN THE 1840s AND 1850s

12.1 Analyze how immigration from China, Ireland, and Germany, as well as the incorporation of Mexican citizens in the Southwest, changed the United States.

Immigration and the nation's expanding borders increased the population of the United States in the 1830s, 1840s, and 1850s. A nation of a little fewer than 13 million people in 1830 included 17 million people in 1840, and the United States had 23 million inhabitants in 1850. Births to native-born Americans accounted for the largest part of this increase, but many people also crossed oceans to come to the United States, especially from Ireland, Germany, and China. By 1860, the United States had about 1.5 million Irish-born inhabitants, about 1 million German-born inhabitants, and perhaps 35,000 Chinese-born inhabitants—a number that would grow dramatically in the next few years as more immigrants from China arrived, especially to build the railroads. Desperately poor people in Europe and China fled famines in their home countries. The California Gold Rush and growing U.S. industrialization beckoned with new economic opportunities. Both the push of hunger and oppression and the pull of a better future brought many to the United States.

The extraordinary increase in the area of the United States also incorporated many people who did not move at all. In 1840, the United States included 1.8 million square miles. Less than 10 years later, the country included almost 3 million square miles. Some of the land acquired through the war with Mexico was sparsely populated. However, many people—Mexican Americans in Texas, New Mexico, and California; Mormons in Utah; and the many tribes of Plains and Pueblo Indians—found themselves residing within the United States. As a result, the nature of the U.S. population shifted significantly in the late 1840s.

The United States of 1840 could accurately be described as including three major ethnic groups—Europeans mostly of English stock, Africans of different backgrounds, and American Indians of diverse tribes. Most of the Europeans and many of the Africans were Protestants. By 1850, the nation was much more ethnically diverse with many Asians (mostly Chinese), Irish, Germans, and Mexican-Americans (of mixed European and Indian ancestry). With the growth of these immigrant groups, the United States was also a more Catholic country, and with the coming of so many white immigrants, the percentage of African-Americans in the population shrank even though their actual number grew. While the governing elite was still of European Protestant background, the people who made up the country were more diverse than ever before and increasingly making their presence felt. Political and military changes traced in the previous chapter changed the borders of the United States in the 1830s and 1840s. This chapter traces the parallel changes in the lives of many people who were, by 1850, residents of the United States, whether or not they had been so 20 years before.

1831	William Lloyd Garrison launches *The Liberator*
	Nat Turner leads slave revolt in Virginia
1833	American Anti-Slavery Society founded in Boston
1836	American Anti-Slavery Society launches campaign to send antislavery agents to every state of the union
1838	Sarah Grimké's *Letters on the Equality of the Sexes and the Condition of Women*
1843	Henry Highland Garnet's "Address to the Slaves of the United States of America"
1845–1850	The Great Famine in Ireland
1847	Rebellion against American authorities in Taos, New Mexico
1848	Discovery of gold in California lures immigrants from around the world, including China
	Women's Rights Convention at Seneca Falls, New York
1849	Harriett Tubman escapes from slavery
1851	Sojourner Truth's "Ain't I a Woman?" speech
1854	William Lloyd Garrison burns a copy of the Constitution as "source and parent of the other atrocities" of slavery in the United States

Chinese Immigration Across the Pacific

Many young people in China were fascinated by the stories from across the Pacific. Lee Chew described his neighbor's return to China from the "country of the American wizards," explaining that the man had earned enough in a short stay in the United States to build a magnificent house and invite his fellow villagers, who lived mostly on rice, to a grand feast with roast pig, chicken, and duck. Soon after, Lee was on his way to California, which became known as *Gam Saan* (Gold Mountain) on both sides of the Pacific.

Before 1840, only a few hundred Chinese lived in the United States, but in the 1840s and 1850s, Chinese immigrants came to California and to the then-independent Kingdom of Hawaii because of a push from China and also a pull from the United States and Hawaii. Those years were hard in China, especially in Guangdong province where most immigrants originated. Under Chinese law, it was illegal for anyone to leave China, but in desperate times, thousands did. California was one of many destinations. The Opium Wars that began in 1839 spawned great violence as British and Chinese forces battled and as violent feuds erupted between Chinese communities. One Chinese migrant remembered the results of a revolt: "We were left with nothing, and in disillusion we went to Hong Kong to sell ourselves as contract laborers." The government of the Qing Dynasty, in Beijing, was rapidly losing control of events. It was not strong enough to suppress the civil wars or to prevent the British imposition of the opium trade on China.

In addition, the population of China had also grown from some 200 million in 1762 to 421 million in 1846. With this huge population, land became scarce, rents soared, and many peasants could not maintain their meager land holdings. For all its ancient expertise in rice cultivation, China simply did not have enough land to grow rice for 421 million people. Beginning in 1810, there were terrible famines in China, with some of the worst coming in the 1840s. In those four decades, 45 million people may have starved to death. Poor people begged for admission to soup kitchens or simply died on the doorsteps of the rich. As one immigrant from Guangdong remembered, "Sometimes we went hungry for days....We had only salt and water to eat with the rice." Under such conditions, a fresh start in a new place—temporary or permanent—was appealing.

Americans in Hawaii and California saw Chinese laborers as a key to solving a shortage of workers to toil on sugar plantations on Maui or to clear and cultivate land in California. The poorest Chinese peasant workers had long been known as *k'u-li*, literally "hard strength," and the western term for Chinese laborers quickly came to be "coolie." Immediately after the conclusion of the U.S. War with Mexico, a long-time presidential advisor, Aaron H. Palmer, reported to Congress that "No people in all of the East are so well adapted for clearing wild lands and raising every species of agricultural product...as the Chinese." At first, Chinese immigrants were warmly welcomed in California. An 1852 article in the *Daily Alta California* noted, "Scarcely a ship arrives that does not bring an increase to this worthy integer of our population." As a result, the Chinese population in the west grew rapidly. The initial Chinese response to the Gold Rush was relatively small: 325 immigrants from China arrived in California in 1849 and 450 more in 1850. Then the numbers grew rapidly: 2,716 in 1851 and 20,026 in 1852. By 1870, Chinese immigrants represented nine percent of the population of California (but 25 percent of the work force since most Chinese immigrants were men of working age) and larger percentages in Oregon and Washington. The Chinese also made up 29 percent of the much smaller population of Idaho and 10 percent in Montana.

Nearly 95 percent of Chinese immigrants to California before 1870 were male. They tended to see their voyage across the Pacific—a harsh 8-week trip—as a temporary separation from their families in China. United States law dating from 1790 prohibited nonwhite immigrants from achieving citizenship, and most Chinese expected to return home after a few years. In the early years, most male Chinese immigrants joined other newcomers in the search for gold. Chinese gold miners could be seen all along the rivers of California in their blue cotton blouses and wide-brimmed hats, shoveling sand into pans or rockers. These men left wives, fiancées, children, and parents behind to find ways to support them. Chinese culture dictated that a woman should stay with her family, especially her husband's parents, while the man found the means of support. Cultural practices such as these and the cost of travel made immigration difficult for women, though Hawaii was much more welcoming of families than was the United States. Of the few Chinese women who avoided the cultural prohibitions and came to California before 1870, many were forced to work as prostitutes, either lured into the work by false promises or forced into the work by the absence of other ways to survive. In 1870, 2,157 of the 3,536 Chinese women in California reported their profession as "prostitute." Only later did other options open for Chinese women.

As more Chinese entered the gold fields, they encountered growing resistance from white miners. The cry "California for Americans" began in the gold fields and was picked up by many, including the political leaders of the state. In 1852, the California legislature adopted a foreign miners license tax of $3 per month, which was aimed specifically at the Chinese. It provided between a quarter and a half of state revenue before 1870. The tax, and the growing anti-Chinese sentiment that it represented, slowed but did not stop Chinese immigration. As the gold fields became less productive, many Chinese went to work building the railroads. Immediately after the Civil War, 12,000 Chinese laborers laid the tracks of the Central Pacific Railroad. Chinese workers also moved into agriculture, mining, fishing, and later into urban businesses. Men from China often found work at the least desirable jobs or jobs that other men considered to be "women's work," including starting the ubiquitous Chinese laundries that were solely a Chinese-American development. Although many individual Chinese immigrants returned home after a few years, other Chinese immigrants stayed in the United States, creating permanent communities in the American West.

Miners of many nationalities competed for gold in the California gold fields, but the tensions, especially between miners of European origin and Chinese miners, were severe, and most Chinese miners were driven from the gold fields before long.

Irish and German Immigration of the 1840s and 1850s

The Irish who came to the United States as a result of the Great Famine of the late 1840s were not the first Irish to come to America, but they came from a different part of Ireland than their predecessors and for different reasons. Most Irish who had come before or immediately after the Revolution were Irish Protestants, mainly Presbyterians whose ancestors had emigrated from Scotland to Ireland. The Protestant Irish, who became known as Scots Irish, settled in all the colonies, but especially along the rural frontier from Pennsylvania to the Carolinas. After the American Revolution, and especially after the failure of an Irish rebellion of 1798 against the British, more Irish immigrants, both Catholic and Protestant, arrived.

Great Famine of 1845–1850
The potato blight in Ireland that caused mass starvation and immigration to the United States.

The roots of the **Great Famine of 1845–1850** go deep in Irish history—anchored in a rapidly growing population of poor people; in policies that made most people almost totally dependent on a single, easy-to-raise crop rather than a diversified agriculture; and in British policies that forced Irish Catholics to labor for Protestant landowners. But its immediate cause was a plant fungus of unknown sources that devastated potatoes. A potato disease, which had already affected parts of continental Europe, came to Ireland with surprising rapidity. August 1845 was unusually wet with heavy rains, and the early spread of the disease left potatoes, as one observer said, "blighted and mildewed" and inedible. In 1846, the blight struck with full force, and up to 90 percent of the fall potato crop was lost. For many landless Catholics, there was no other substantial food source. The result was widespread starvation. Potato crops continued to be blighted each year through 1850, and cholera struck in 1848 and 1849. Out of a total Irish population of approximately 8 million, more than 1 million people died from disease or starvation in the 5 years of the Great Famine. During the decade that followed the start of the famine, over 2 million people left Ireland, most of them for the United States.

One observer described the suffering of the Great Famine:

> They died in their mountain glens, they died along the sea-coast, they died on the roads, and they died in the fields; they wandered into the towns, and died in the streets; they closed their cabin doors, and lay down upon their beds, and died of actual starvation in their own homes.

And when they could, they left. The cost of the trip to America was about 3 British pounds, about the same as the cost of a new cow or the annual rent on a farm. As the historian Cormac Ó Gráda noted, "In the hierarchy of suffering the poorest of the poor emigrated to the next world; those who emigrated to the New World had the resources to escape." Somehow, many found the funds to make the trip. Even when a family could scrape together enough funds to get only one family member off to America, there was a good chance that, if the rest could survive another winter or two, then they too would immigrate. In 1848, Irish immigrants to America sent 500,000 British pounds, a significant amount of money, back to Ireland to feed relatives and pay for their transport out of the country (see Map 12-1).

In the 1840s, the voyage from Ireland across the Atlantic was terrible. The ships, which took 5–6 weeks to make the crossing, became known as "coffin ships" because of the high death toll due to poor nutrition, unsanitary conditions, and overcrowding.

Once in the United States, the new Irish immigrants, overwhelmingly Catholic and poor, were seen as another race by Americans of English and especially Scotch-Irish origin. Centuries of deep hostility toward the Irish among English Protestants had been continued by their American descendants, who viewed Catholicism as a degrading religion and, thus, the Irish, particularly the throngs of devastatingly poor Irish, as an inferior race. Nevertheless, though many Irish immigrants lived in terrible poverty, they came at a good time to get a foothold in the American economy. Women immigrants got work as household domestic help for native-born middle-class Americans. Irish women and men also labored in the factories where their willingness to work hard made them prized employees. In addition, Irish men did the backbreaking work of building the nation's fastest-growing cities, most of all New York, which became the center of the country's Irish population. Irish immigrants also moved to Boston, Philadelphia, Chicago, and smaller cities from New Jersey to California. Few of the Irish moved to farms; it was too expensive to start a farm, and farming had little appeal to those who remembered the famine that had sparked their journey. After the Civil War, Irish laborers built the eastern end of the Transcontinental Railroad just as Chinese laborers built the western end.

Wherever the Irish Catholic immigrants settled, they created their own communities, including a Catholic church usually led by an Irish priest. By 1850, the Catholic Church had become the largest single denomination in the United States.

While Irish immigration was especially dramatic and rapid because of the famine, many other Europeans, including more than 1 million Germans, also came to the United States in the 1840s and 1850s. On average, German immigrants came with slightly more financial resources than the Irish, and many settled on farms or in cities in what was becoming the Midwest. In new and growing cities like Milwaukee, St. Louis, and Chicago, the majority of residents were foreign-born, mostly from Germany.

German immigrant communities often kept to themselves as opposed to the Irish who took jobs in the households of native-born families or the factories of native-born owners. German-dominated immigrant farm towns and German neighborhoods were recognized and sometimes distrusted by the native-born elite, but German immigrants provoked less distrust than Irish immigrants. German immigrants introduced many traditions into American culture—from the Christmas tree to beer, both of which were relatively unknown in the United States until the Germans introduced them. One American observer described his surprise at visiting an isolated German community in the Southwest where people drank "coffee in tin cups," while listening to "a Beethoven symphony on the grand piano." Along religious lines, the Germans were a diverse group. Many were Catholics, but there were also many Protestants, including Lutherans and the Amish.

Even though the Irish and German immigrants played a crucial role in expanding the American economy, the rapid growth of these new European groups also frightened many native-born Americans. The Irish were particularly vulnerable to prejudice because there was a long history of discrimination against the Irish, especially Irish Catholics, even before the Great Famine. In August 1834, a Protestant mob burned the convent and school of the Ursuline nuns in Boston. Boston's Catholic bishop Benedict Fenwick wrote, "No law or justice is to be expected in this land where Catholics are constantly calumniated and the strongest prejudices exist against them. Shame!" Perhaps because of their relative isolation, the Germans provoked somewhat less hostility, but many native-born Americans expressed their anger at German immigrants who created communities where English was not the primary language.

With the growth of the Irish Catholic and German populations in the late 1840s, the prejudice grew. An anti-immigrant group called the Native American Association was founded in 1837, and by 1845, it had become a political party known as the **Know Nothing Party** because when members were asked about the party, they were

the sidebar tabs 12.1, 12.2, 12.3

Population Change in Ireland, 1841–1851

Percentage of change per county

- +9
- 0
- -13
- -20
- -25

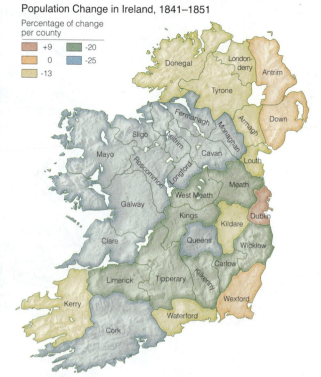

Pauperism in Ireland, 1847–1851

Over 50% of people living in such poverty as to be declared paupers

MAP 12-1 Depopulating Ireland. The Great Famine led to a significant decline in the population of Ireland, especially in the western part, where some counties never recovered from the population loss of those years.

Know Nothing Party

Anti-immigrant party formed from the wreckage of the Whig Party and some disaffected Northern Democrats in 1854.

Native-born Americans, especially those in the Know Nothing Party, reacted with fear and anger to the surge in immigration to the United States during the 1830s and 1840s. Some of the stereotypes included images of whiskey-drinking Irish and beer-drinking Germans in a country that was turning its back on its own hard drinking ways.

told to say "I know nothing." In the 1850s, the Know-Nothings elected eight governors, more than 100 members of Congress, mayors in several major cities, and many state legislators. The Know-Nothing Party's platform was anti-Catholic and anti-immigrant, including plans to limit Catholic political power, in part, by banning immigrants from holding office and requiring them to wait 21 years to become citizens.

Moderate reformers like Horace Mann were horrified by the burning of the Ursuline convent in Boston and the political platform of the Know-Nothings but still sought to ensure that the public school system was used to make all future citizens, especially immigrants, into good "Americans" as they understood the term. Massachusetts Governor Edward Everett told the state's school board to "save society not with the cannon and the rifle, but with the spelling book, the grammar, and the Bible." Nevertheless, despite hostility and their own poverty, Irish and German immigrants eventually gained political and economic power in the nation's major cities.

The Mexican Experience in the Southwest

In 1847, as immigrants to America were trying to fit in to the new culture, Father Antonio Jose Martinez was trying to keep peace in his own community of Taos, New Mexico, where Mexican and Pueblo Indian residents had rebelled against the new American authorities, killing the American appointed governor, Charles Bent. Father Martinez tried to convince rebels that killing Americans was wrong and futile while trying to convince the Americans to give due process to insurgents. He was not fully successful in either effort, but by the end of 1847, the rebellion had ended after a group of rebels were defeated by U.S. soldiers. Like the rebels he was seeking to defend, Father Martinez had suddenly become an American citizen, no longer a citizen of the Republic of Mexico, not because he moved, but because the American border had moved hundreds of miles south and his home was now in a different country.

Under the Treaty of Guadalupe Hidalgo, territory that was home to Pueblo, Navajo, Comanche, Apache, Ute, and Cheyenne tribes as well as Spanish settlements, some dating back 300 years, was now part of the United States. While in the short run, the treaty had little impact on Native Americans, it almost immediately had a huge impact on people who were now Mexican Americans. The 1848 treaty gave every Mexican citizen within the new boundary of the United States the right to American citizenship or the right to keep Mexican citizenship. Mexico urged its citizens who lived to the north of the new border to move to Mexico, and some 4,000 people from New Mexico and smaller groups from Texas, California, and Arizona did move south, back in to Mexico. But most former Mexican citizens chose to stay in their homes and make new lives as citizens of the United States. Their choice turned out to be a difficult experience for them, however.

Many within the Mexican community in California were initially optimistic about their new country. Indeed, quite a few of the Mexican leaders in California, men such as Mariano Vallejo and Juan Bandini, had been hoping for an American takeover of their territory even before the War with Mexico because they saw the United States as a vibrant democracy that could replace the distant and inept Mexican administration. When the constitutional convention met in Monterey in August 1849 to prepare California for statehood, eight of the 48 voting delegates were Californios (as former Mexican citizens were called). On most matters, they did not vote as a separate bloc, assuming that their interests and those of newer American residents were the same. The huge population surge of the gold rush, however, meant that the Californios quickly became a small minority in California. By the time that statehood came in 1850, they numbered only about 13,000 out of a non-Indian population of over 100,000.

Ultimately, the sheer numbers of those newly arrived from the United States destroyed the economic base for the culture that Mexican citizens like Vallejo represented. Looking back, Vallejo described the impact of statehood and the gold rush on California when "legal thieves, clothed in the robes of the law, took from us our lands and our houses, and without the least scruple, enthroned themselves in our homes like so many powerful kings." Vallejo's dreams of being an equal citizen of the United States never materialized.

The vehicle by which the "legal thieves" stole the land of the Californians was established even before statehood was granted: the United States Land Commission was set up specifically to challenge the Mexican land grants on which Vallejo's and his compatriot's fortunes rested. Although the Treaty of Guadalupe Hidalgo had promised that all residents of these lands "shall be maintained and protected in the free enjoyment of their liberty and property," the Land Commission treated every grant as invalid until documented and proven. The result was that many of the old families lost their land. Being of Mexican descent in California meant second-class citizenship for a long time to come.

In Texas, the Mexican, or Tejano, population was also small. Like their counterparts in California, the Tejanos did not fare well after Texas joined the United States. Juan Seguin, one of the heroes on the Texas and American side of the decisive battle of San Jacinto and mayor of San Antonio, eventually joined the exodus to Mexico. In San Antonio, the city with the largest Tejano population, the number of Tejanos elected to office, which had been high under the Republic of Texas, declined sharply once statehood was achieved. New migrants from the United States took over the political and economic control of the state.

The Mexican or Hispano elite in New Mexico fared better because American newcomers remained a minority in New Mexico throughout the 19th century. The Hispano elite were a majority in the first American territorial assembly held in 1851, and they published its proceedings in both Spanish and English. Merchants from the United States had played a significant role in New Mexico since the 1820s when the Santa Fe Trail connected St. Louis with Santa Fe.

Despite the revolts in northern New Mexico after U.S. annexation, many in the territory made their peace with the new government, and some made fortunes in the new economy. Gertrudis Barcelo achieved both fame and fortune for the elegant

Committees of Vigilance
Also known as vigilantes, groups of people who took on extralegal means to assert law and order.

saloon and gambling house she controlled in Santa Fe. Barcelo's saloon was a fixture for Santa Fe Trail traders from the 1820s to the 1850s and a business of sufficient success to allow her to make significant bequests to charity and leave three houses and other wealth to her heirs when she died in 1852. Barcelo was not alone in attending to her own interests whether the flag of Spain, Mexico, or the United States flew on the plaza near her establishment.

For many poor people in the Southwest, however, the transfer of authority from Mexico to the United States meant increased poverty and far less opportunity for justice in a court system that was operated in a strange language by people who were often filled with racial and ethnic prejudices. Not surprisingly, the term *vigilante* (meaning people who take justice into their own hands rather than rely on lawful authorities) came from the **Committees of Vigilance** in the California mining camps. Vigilante groups made up of private citizens took the administration of justice into their own hands when they thought that the official government authorities were absent or, too often, when they did not like their decisions. Members of these groups delivered public whippings and lynched people they did not like, whether or not a crime had been committed. California mobs lynched at least 163 Mexicans between 1848 and 1860. In southern California, a white gang known as the El Monte boys used the hysteria around a short-lived Mexican rebellion to settle old scores and attack Mexican families regardless of whether they had been involved in the rebellion. Similar outrages happened across the West. Still, in Texas, New Mexico, and Arizona, the Latino presence remained strong.

The Mexican American community fought back as it could. One Californio, Joaquin Murrieta, became a California legend—feared in the white community, honored in the Mexican community—because of his vengeance on those who had stolen his gold claim, raped his wife Rosa, and hung his brother. Murrieta stole horses and gold and killed those who had raped and murdered his loved ones before he, in turn, was discovered and killed by the California Rangers in 1853. Kangaroo courts (unauthorized and obviously biased courts) and lynchings were all too common within and across all ethnic lines as traditional community relationships were destroyed by distance and greed.

12.1 **Quick Review** How did native-born Americans react to immigrants in the 1840s and 1850s? How did immigrants react to their new American surroundings?

SLAVERY IN THE UNITED STATES, 1840s AND 1850s

12.2 Explain how the lives of slaves, slaveholders, and abolitionists evolved in the decades before the Civil War.

The institution of slavery had existed in the United States from the nation's beginning, but slavery, which had never been a static institution, changed significantly yet again after 1820 (see Chapter 9). For enslaved people and those who claimed to own them, life in a slave society was a different experience at different points in history. Slavery was always harsh and dehumanizing, but it was harsh in different ways at different times.

After the end of the War of 1812, Southern planters experienced new economic benefits from slavery, benefits that grew with each decade as the world's cotton market exploded and slave labor, as well as developments in technology and transportation, made it possible and profitable for American slave-grown cotton to satisfy the market. Since most cotton was produced by slave labor, the new demand for cotton greatly increased the value of individual slaves. Thus, just as slavery was dying out in the North—for both economic and ethical reasons—the new cotton economy of the South made slavery far more profitable than ever before. The result was a kind of industrialized agriculture that by the 1840s produced 60 percent of the world's cotton and made the South, and particularly some elite Southerners, extremely wealthy. With the increase in profits and wealth, many slaveholders developed what they claimed was a new ethical rationale for slavery and challenged their critics head on (see Map 12-2).

Slaves and Slave Masters

As cotton prices kept increasing in the 1830s, and especially in the 1840s and 1850s, close to a million slaves were moved from the coast, where many had cultivated tobacco, indigo, and other crops, to new cotton states, where they had to learn the different and difficult work of tending cotton. Yet even as slavery was becoming more profitable, Northern public opinion was turning against it. More people were joining what had been a small group of abolitionists in viewing human bondage as a terrible wrong and a stain on the honor of a nation dedicated to human freedom. With slavery disappearing in the North, Northern abolitionists got an increasingly responsive hearing from their neighbors. Other Northerners who had fewer moral qualms about slavery saw slaves as competitors for scarce jobs, and they too joined the opposition to slavery. In 1840, antislavery forces created the Liberty Party and nominated James G. Birney for president, and in 1848, the short-lived antislavery Free Soil Party nominated former President Martin Van Buren as its candidate. Neither party campaigned for outright abolition, only for an end to extending slavery to new areas of the country. Nor did either party win any electoral votes, though

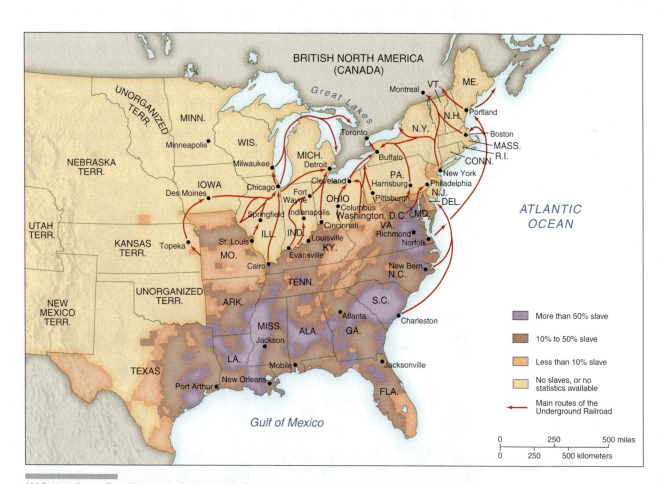

MAP 12-2 Expanding Slavery. In the 30 years before the Civil War, slavery became strongest in the cotton belt states of the Deep South. For an individual slave, the further north one was, the better one's chances were to connect to the Underground Railroad, but slaves from every part of the South made their way north to freedom.

Van Buren did win some 10 percent of the popular vote in 1848. Nevertheless, abolitionist rhetoric and political muscle were frightening an increasingly defensive slaveholding South.

Slaveholders and their political and intellectual allies responded to both the increased profit and the increased criticism. In the past, most slaveholders, including all of those from the South who attended the Constitutional Convention, had defended slavery as a "necessary evil." Somehow, they argued, slavery had become an economic and social necessity that was, at best, unfortunate. However, after 1830, a new generation of slaveholders began to describe slavery as a positive good, an institution that Christianized "heathen" Africans while providing them with food, shelter, and an ordered life. These new defenders of slavery also contrasted it with work in Northern factories and noted that slaves, unlike factory workers, were not fired when work got slow or they grew old, but rather, were provided for throughout their lives. Southern apologists also became increasingly angry with Northern critics of slavery.

One example of the new proslavery ideology was the changing views of Roger B. Taney, who served as Chief Justice of the United States from 1836 to 1864. As a young attorney in Maryland in 1819, Taney defended a Methodist preacher, Jacob Gruber, who had warned it was inevitable that slaves would "rise up and kill your children, their oppressors...." When Maryland charged Gruber with breaking the peace and inciting rebellion, Taney asserted Gruber's legal right to free speech and said that slavery was, "a blot on our national character, and every real lover of freedom, confidently hopes that it will be ...wiped away."

In 1857, however, almost 40 years after the Gruber trial and 20 years after Taney's appointment to lead the Supreme Court, he wrote in reference to the Dred Scott decision (see Chapter 13) that blacks were "altogether unfit to associate with the white race, either in social or political relations; and so far inferior, that they had no rights which the white man was bound to respect." The Chief Justice, like many other Southerners, had come to see slavery as simply the inevitable result of black inferiority. Taney was far from alone.

As every able-bodied slave and every new-born slave child became more valuable from 1800 to the outbreak of the Civil War in 1861, any thought of abolishing slavery disappeared among slaveholders. After 1830, Southern states also made it more difficult to set any slaves free and for free blacks to stay in the South.

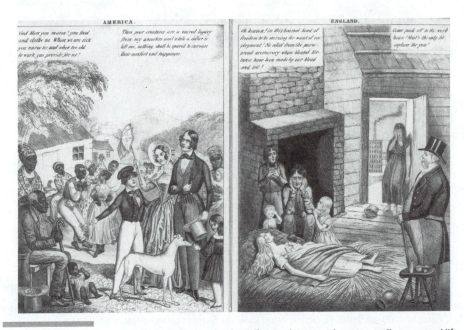

The apologists for slavery never tired of pointing out the difference between the supposedly contented life of Southern slaves and the harsh lives of factory workers in the Northern states and Great Britain.

American Voices

Edmund Ruffin, *Slavery and Free Labor Described and Compared*, ca. 1860

Edmund Ruffin (1794–1865) was a Southern agronomist who in the 1850s turned from improving the productivity of Southern soil to defending Southern slavery. He published several proslavery articles and pamphlets (this one probably in 1860 or 1861), advocated succession of the Southern states after Lincoln's election, and fought in the first battles of the Civil War. At the end of the Civil War, he committed suicide rather than live under what he called "Yankee rule."

The privilege of the English laborer to choose his employment and his master, even when such choice legally exists, does not prevent his service being truly slavery. For he has no choice but to toil incessantly for wages barely affording a scant and wretched support, or to starve—and no change of pursuit, or of service, can make that condition better....[I]n comparison to the English pauper, and even to his earlier condition as the over-worked, under-fed and suffering hireling laborer, supporting a family on regular wages, the general condition of our negro slaves is one of comfort, ease and happiness....

Until recent investigation and discussion had elicited more truth, it had been claimed by the people of the North and by all the opposers of slavery, and even was generally admitted by the people of the Southern States, that the free-labour States of New England were greatly superior to the old Southern States in obtaining the fruits of industry and capital....Southern capital and industry were almost exclusively devoted to agriculture—northern capital was much more vested in commerce and manufactures, which are deemed much more profitable than agricultural investments....It has also been especially and loudly claimed, for and by the people of the New England States...that such difference was the necessary result of the blighting and demoralizing effects of negro slavery in the South, and of its absence in the North....

Instead of our labors and investments in slave-labor being less profitable than northern operations, it is manifest that the slaveholding States are much richer than the free States, and to make this result the more striking, even if counting every slave as if free, and supposing the whole property to be divided among all the population, (slaves included,) still on this general average, the individual share of every one, bond or free, would be considerably larger than in the free States.

Source: Edmund Ruffin, "Slavery and Free Labor, Described and Compared," Library of Congress, American memory, From Slavery to Freedom: the African-American Pamphlet Collection, 1824–1909, http://memory.loc.gov.

Thinking Critically

1. **Documentary Analysis**
   According to Ruffin, in what ways was the life of a poor white worker worse than that of a black slave in the South?

2. **Historical Interpretation**
   In what ways did Ruffin argue slavery was a "positive good"?

The growing value of individual slaves also led—ironically—to somewhat better treatment for them. A slave life was now of too much economic value to be lost easily. The same states that made it difficult to free slaves passed new laws against their murder or mistreatment. In many instances, the nutrition and medical care provided for slaves also improved.

A healthy, relatively well-fed slave could work harder than a sickly or starving slave. A pregnant slave could produce a valuable new slave who could, in time, also work or be sold. However, a slave who died of mistreatment was a lost investment. There is evidence that the actual treatment of slaves, while never approaching anything that could be called humane, did improve throughout the 19th century. Where multiple slave families had been crammed into cramped quarters, more plantation owners built—or had their slaves build—individual family cabins with board floors instead of dirt. More meat was added to slave diets, and slaves were allowed to grow their own vegetable gardens as well as hunt and fish to supplement their diet. Slave hours of work were controlled by custom and unspoken agreement; most slaves had Sunday as a day of rest, and except in harvest time, few were expected to work after dark. A new generation of slave children was allowed to play relatively freely until put to work at age 10 to 12. Former slave Harriet Jacobs wrote, "I was born a slave; but I never knew it till six years of happy childhood has passed away." For defenders of slavery like Edmund Ruffin, such improvements in the lives of slaves became proof that slave life was better than the lives of some Northern or European workers and peasants.

Slave quarters, like these shown on a South Carolina plantation, provided better living conditions than what was provided to previous generations of slaves, though hardly anything that could be called comfortable. The houses built close together also fostered a sense of community life that helped enslaved people survive.

The slave population of the United States grew from 1.5 million slaves in 1820 to 4 million slaves in 1860. After 1808, it was illegal and difficult to bring new slaves into the country, so much of this growth reflected reproduction among existing slaves. Many saw this growth as a sign of the new and better treatment that slaves were receiving. In the United States slaves were surviving, reproducing, and providing significant profits to others.

Although some improvements in slave life occurred, there were limits to those developments. The slave cabins were hot and stuffy in summer and inflammable in winter. The meals were monotonous. The work for adults was backbreaking, being called out to work at 4:00 or 5:00 a.m., and then working in hot fields, hoeing or picking cotton, with little break until sunset. Slaves were whipped routinely for falling behind in their work or for infractions of the plantation rules. While some Southern reformers talked of honoring slave marriages, the separation of spouses continued without interruption. Slave women could not protect their own bodies. Harriet Jacobs also remembered that once she came of age, "It was deemed a crime in her to wish to be virtuous." And she spent considerable time avoiding the constant advances of the owner of her plantation and the jealous anger of his wife. Many slave women were not so fortunate, and the rape of slave women by white men was a commonly acknowledged reality. Mary Boykin Chestnut, wife of a plantation owner, described the treatment of slave women as a "monstrous system," and noted that "Any lady is ready to tell you who is the father of all the mulatto children in everybody's household but her own. Those, she seems to think, drop from the clouds." Even laws that were being passed against murdering a slave could be enforced only if there was a white witness because slaves were not allowed to testify in court. Most of all, nothing could change the fact that slavery was still slavery. No amount of reform or improvement could change that reality.

In the midst of appalling conditions, slaves created lives for themselves and developed the psychological strength to withstand the horrors they faced. Historians have argued whether slave life was better on the small family farms that included only a few slaves or on large plantations with many. In reality, it probably depended on the conditions and the owner of an individual farm or plantation. Slaves on small farms

American Voices

Susan Merritt, Memories of Slavery in the 1850s

In the late 1930s, Susan Merritt was interviewed near Marshall, Texas, not far from where she had once been a slave, by historians working for the Federal Writers' Project. She estimated herself to be 87 years old but still remembered slavery all too well.

I couldn't tell how old I is, but does you think I'se ever forget them slave days?…I'se born right down in Rusk County [Texas], not a long way from Henderson, and Massa Andrew Watt am my owner. My pappy, Hob Rollins, he come from North Carolina and belonged to Dave Blakely and Mammy come from Mississippi. Mammy have eleven of us chillen, but four dies when they babies. Albert, Hob, John, Emma, Anna, Lula, and me lives to be grown and married.

Massa Watt lived in a big log house what set on a hill so you could see it round for miles, and us lived over in the field in little log huts, all huddled along together. They have homemade beds nailed to the wall and baling sack mattresses, and us call them bunks. Us never had no money but plenty clothes and grub, and wear the same clothes all the year 'round. Massa Watt made our shoes for winter hisself. He made furniture and saddles and harness, and run a grist mill and a whiskey still there on the place. That man had everything.

The hands was woke with the bit bell…They was in that field before day and stay till dusk dark. They work up till Saturday night and then washes their clothes, and sometimes they gets through and has time for the party and plays ring plays.…

When the hands come in from the field at dusk dark, they has to tote water from the spring and cook and eat; and be in bed when that old bell rings at nine o'clock. About dusk they calls the chillen and gives 'em a piece of corn pone about the size my hand and a tin cup milk and puts them to bed. But the growed folks et fat pork and greens and beans and such like and have plenty milk. Every Sunday Massa give 'em some flour and butter and a chicken. Lots…caught a good cowhiding for slippin' round and stealin' a chicken 'fore Sunday. Massa Watt didn't have no overseer…He carry a long whip round the neck and I's seed him tie [slaves] to a tree and cowhide 'em till the blood run down onto the ground.…

Lots of times Massa Watt give us a pass to go over to George Petro's place or Dick Gregg's place. Massa Petro run a slave market and he have big, high scaffold with steps where he sells slaves. They was stripped off to the waist to show their strength.

Our white folks have a church and a place for us in the back. Sometimes at night us gather 'round the fireplace and pray and sing and cry, but us darn't 'low our white folks know it. Thank the Lord us can worship where we wants nowadays.

Source: Susan Merritt, interview, in Norman R. Yetman, editor, *Voices From Slavery: 100 Authentic Slave Narratives* (Mineola, NY: Dover Publications, 2000), pp. 224–226.

Thinking Critically

1. Documentary Analysis
On what aspects of slavery did Merritt focus? How would you characterize her relationship with her master?

2. Comparison
How might Merritt's life have compared to that of poor Southern whites? How were they similar? How were they different?

---

worked alongside the owners and often shared the same meals. But if the owner was cruel, there was little respite from the suffering, and it was hard to maintain connections with other slaves. If the owner ran short of funds, and many did, it was all too easy to cut the food and clothing of the slaves. Working conditions on a large plantation with several hundred slaves could be much harsher, but slaves had more opportunity to create a community and cultural identity of their own, and often, the routines and expectations were more regularized.

On large plantations, the work life of slaves was usually controlled by an overseer, often a poor white whom the plantation owner hired to get as much work—and profit—from the slaves as possible. Slaves and overseers had to develop a working relationship of sorts, however tense it might be. An overseer who was too lax would not produce the profits an owner expected; one who was too cruel could also be unproductive. The owner of one of Alabama's larger plantations, A. H. Arrington, wrote in his diary, "I have this day discharged my overseer, Mr. Brewer. I found so much dissatisfaction amongst the negroes that I placed under his charge that I could not feel satisfied to continue him in my employment." Such decisions were not uncommon. While overseers had total legal control over the slaves, slaves also knew that for any work to get done at all, an accommodation had to be reached between their white masters and themselves. Slaves knew how to make the most of what power they had. It was risky to complain about an overseer, but it was less risky to feign illness, even pregnancy, and more slaves did that. Some slaves feigned clumsiness and broke tools that then had to be repaired; others pretended laziness and attempted to slow the pace of work. Resistance took many ingenious forms, and it helped slaves survive.

Especially on larger plantations, slave families were also essential to the emotional, and often physical, survival of their members. While slaves were not allowed legally recognized marriages, many slave partnerships lasted for a long time while others were disrupted by the sale of one partner or the tensions that drive people apart in any circumstance. Slave parents, especially mothers, had a difficult task, loving children while also preparing them for the rigors of slavery. Many former slaves recalled parents being especially tough in ways that, as adults, they recognized as the most loving thing slave parents could do. After all, to allow a slave child to grow to adulthood without proper preparation for a world in which submission (at least outward signs of submission) was key to survival was to give that child a death sentence. Some slave mothers simply could not endure the thought of children they loved being raised to be slaves. One former slave told the story of a mother who, after seeing three children sold away from her, gave her fourth child "something out of a bottle" and soon it was dead: "'Couse didn't nobody tell on her or he'd [the owner] of beat her nearly to death."

Resisting Slavery

Enslaved people found many different ways to resist their enslavement. For those with no other options, they could pretend illness, laziness, or stupidity to resist their circumstances. Slave labor could be notoriously slow when slaves actively tried to subvert the work of a plantation, doing just enough work to avoid punishment. But passive resistance was not the only kind of resistance. Newspaper advertisements for runaway slaves give solid evidence that thousands and thousands of slaves tried to run away from the places where they were held. While many runaways were caught, many tried again and again to find shelter in free states of the North or in Canada, and quite a few succeeded. And finally, in every generation, there were full-scale slave revolts, some small and some large, in which enslaved people attacked their oppressors and sought to claim their freedom.

RUNAWAY SLAVES   In 1837, Joseph Taper and his family ran away from their lives as slaves on a Virginia plantation. It was a dangerous decision to do so. The chances of being caught were great and the punishments harsh—perhaps flogging, perhaps having the family separated and sold into the Deep South, farther from the opportunity for a second escape, perhaps being killed.

At first, the Tapers made their way to Pennsylvania where Joseph Taper found work. But when he read the offer of a reward for his return, the family moved further north and eventually left the United States for Canada in 1839. Britain had abolished slavery in all its dominions in 1833, making it illegal for slave hunters to seek former slaves there. In November 1840, a year after their arrival in Canada, Joseph Taper wrote of his journey "that I am in a land of liberty, in good health….My wife and self are sitting by a good comfortable fire happy, knowing that there are none to molest or make afraid."

As happy as the Taper story was, the long and dangerous journey north was frightening for any slave who sought to escape. Harriet Jacobs escaped from slavery by boat in 1843. She remembered that even after she was safely on the boat,

> "We were filled with constant apprehensions that the constables would come on board. Neither could I feel quite at ease with the captain…might he not be tempted to make more money by giving us up to those who claimed us as property?"

But she was relieved when, "the next morning I was on deck as soon as the day dawned…for the first time in our lives, on free soil." Nevertheless, though she had successfully escaped from slavery, Jacobs remembered the next days as difficult ones. She was lonely, having "left dear ties behind us; ties cruelly sundered by the demon Slavery."

The Taper and Jacobs stories are unusual. Most slaves who ran away were quickly caught. The route to freedom in the North was known as the **Underground Railroad**, a highly secret system of safe havens and supporters that guided slaves toward a new, free life. It was a symbol for many but a reality for only a few. Nevertheless, every year more and more slaves were aided by "conductors" who were either former slaves who had run away or free people, black and white, who hated slavery and were willing to take enormous risks to help new people on the road to freedom. Conductors on the Underground Railroad knew the hidden paths and the safe houses where sympathetic owners were willing to hide runaway slaves as they journeyed ever further north, either to cities in the United States or, increasingly, out of the United States to Canada. Both Taper and Jacobs were among the few slaves who were literate, which helped them elude the authorities and prosper. But they were not nearly so unusual in deciding to run away from slavery.

Advertisements that appeared in Southern newspapers in the 19th century offered considerable detail about runaway slaves. One 1850 issue of the *New Orleans Daily Picayune* reported the offer of rewards for Jack, Sam, Zip or Harry, Edward, Daniel, Henrietta, Mary Mackendish, William, and Tom. By 1860, some 50,000 slaves ran away every year out of a total slave population of 4 million who were held by 385,000 slave owners, which meant that one in seven slaveholders could expect someone to run away each year.

Runaway slaves became abolitionists and, later, national leaders during Reconstruction. Henry Highland Garnet, whose adult writing inspired fear in the hearts of many slaveholders, was born a slave in Maryland. While he was a child, his

Underground Railroad

Support system set up by antislavery groups in the upper South and the North to assist fugitive slaves in escaping the South.

By far the most famous conductor on the Underground Railroad, Harriet Tubman, shown here with a few of the perhaps 300 people she led north out of slavery, ran away from slavery and then returned to the South again and again to lead others to freedom.

family set out on the pretext of going to the funeral of a slave on a nearby plantation but went instead to the home of a Quaker Underground Railroad conductor in Delaware who started them on the road to freedom in New York City where each member of the family took a new name in a ceremony of "baptism to Liberty."

Frederick Douglass was born a slave in Maryland around 1817. Douglass remembered visits from his mother who lived on another plantation 12 miles away and made the journey on foot at night before returning for the next day's work: "She was a field hand, and a whipping is the penalty for not being in the field at sunrise…I do not recollect of ever seeing my mother by the light of day."

Douglass made his first attempt to run away in 1835 but was caught and sent to a former master in Baltimore. Instead of giving in to the fear of capture, Douglass tried again 3 years later and succeeded in running away to freedom in New York in 1838.

Harriet Tubman became famous as a slave who not only ran away but also returned to the South and guided between 200 and 300 others along the Underground Railroad to freedom. By most reckonings, she was responsible for freeing more slaves than any other person in the institution's long history.

Tubman was born about 1820. Two of her older sisters were sold to a plantation farther south, and Tubman never shook her own fears of a similar fate. She almost died at the age of 14 from a severe head injury when an overseer threw a 2-pound weight at another slave but hit Tubman instead. In 1844, she married John Tubman, a free black who lived nearby. (Marriages of slaves and free blacks were uncommon, but not unknown.) The free husband thought his wife worried too much about being a slave. In 1849, Tubman made her way north to Philadelphia without her husband or other help and found work as a domestic. She recalled, "I was free; but there was no one to welcome me to the land of freedom." Everyone she knew and cared for was "down in the old cabin quarters, with the old folks and my brothers and sisters."

THINKING HISTORICALLY

Understanding Advertisements for Runaway Slaves

On December 22, 1848, the following advertisement appeared in the *Baltimore Sun*:

> FIFTY DOLLARS REWARD—Ran away from the subscriber, on the 10th inst [this month], a MAN named Celus, calls himself Celus Dorsey, about 23 years old, slender made, about 5 feet, 7 or 8 inches high, dark complexion, rather thick lip; he has a large scar on one of his hands from a burn. It is probable he is lurking about Baltimore. I will give the above reward if taken out of the State, and $30 if taken in the State, and secured so I get him again.
>
> SAML C. HUNT, 10 miles from Baltimore, on Baltimore and Susquehanna Railroad

Historians have found hundreds of similar advertisements in newspapers in slaveholding states from the American Revolution to the middle of the Civil War. Each advertisement tells a small part of the story of someone who had the opportunity and the courage to run away from slavery and the slaveholder's determination to see him or her returned.

Source: *Baltimore Sun*, December 22, 1848.

Thinking Critically

1. **Contextualization**

   What does Hunt's location tell us? What opportunity would a slave living further from a city have to run away? Why might Hunt have thought that Dorsey was "lurking around Baltimore"? Was there something about a city, even in a slaveholding state, that might attract a slave?

2. **Historical Interpretation**

   Why were slaveholders so willing to advertise about runaway slaves and let others know that enslaved people were running away as often as the advertisements imply? What might be lost and what might be gained for a slave owner by posting such advertisements?

Tubman decided that the best solution was to bring the rest of her family to freedom, though she never rejoined her free husband.

Having successfully brought most of her family north, Tubman developed a pattern that she would continue until the Civil War. She worked for a while, raised some money, and then made a trip south to free a group of slaves. Between 1850 and 1861, Tubman made trip after trip, helping slaves escape and taking them north. As the full impact of the 1850 Fugitive Slave Law took effect, she did not stop in Pennsylvania but accompanied each group to Canada. As Tubman's fame grew, it earned her the support of Northern abolitionists and the hatred of many slaveholders. The reward for her capture grew steadily, but she kept returning south to free more people. Northern abolitionists supported her work, and in 1859, the Unitarian minister Thomas Wentworth Higginson took up a collection at the Massachusetts Anti-Slavery Society so that Tubman could "resume the practice of her profession!"

REBELS AND SLAVE REVOLTS   Although slaveholders typically claimed that their slaves were happy and content, the number of slaves who ran away undermined those claims. On some level, slaveholders were aware of the reality because, as much as they sought to catch runaway slaves, they most intensely feared the possibility of a slave revolt. Slave revolts were relatively rare, but they did happen. Historians have documented over 200 slave revolts in the United States in the 60 years before the Civil War. Some were little more than small-scale events on a single plantation; others were much larger. On August 30, 1800, Gabriel Prosser led over 1,000 slaves in a planned attack on Richmond, Virginia (see Chapter 7). In 1810, plans for a revolt were discovered in Lexington, Kentucky. In 1811, 400 slaves revolted in New Orleans. And in 1815, a white man named George Boxley attempted to lead a slave revolt in Virginia.

In 1822, Denmark Vesey and his supporters planned to burn the military and financial center of Charleston, South Carolina, murder the white residents, and then seize the city's caches of weapons and gold. They would then set sail for a new life of freedom in Haiti. Vesey, who had purchased his own freedom in 1800, had been plotting his revolt for years. He led a Bible class in Charlestown for the African Methodist Episcopal Church, and he spoke of the biblical stories of moving from slavery to freedom with the passion of a latter-day Moses. He also spoke fluent French and was clearly influenced by the success of the Haitian slave revolt. No one really knows how close Vesey came to success before his plot was betrayed. Some estimated that his co-conspirators numbered in the thousands, making it one of the largest slave revolts. In stories whispered behind closed doors, Vesey and his followers represented the ultimate terror to the white community.

In 1831, Nat Turner led a revolt that was more successful than Vesey's. Terror spread throughout the South when Turner's forces killed over 60 slave-owning whites before the revolt was defeated by state and federal troops. Over 100 slaves were killed in the fighting or executed after capture. Turner himself was captured and interviewed by his white, court-appointed attorney, Thomas Gray, before he was executed. Gray subsequently published an account of the conversation as *The Confessions of Nat Turner*.

Turner reported having been a religious man from his earliest years. His prayers and meditations convinced him of three things: "that I was ordained for some great purpose in the hands of the Almighty," that the Almighty's purpose included freedom for American slaves, and that "the great day of judgment was at hand."

It was some time after the revolt before Nat Turner was captured. In spite of his capture, his actions had already sent fear through the slaveholding South.

In the aftermath of the Turner revolt, Southern fears increased, and repressive laws were passed across the South, including laws making it illegal to teach a slave to read and write to prevent others like Turner from studying the Bible and other information on their own. In the slave quarters, however, Turner became a legend, and stories of his exploits were told and retold. Despite the consequences, the revolts continued.

Some Northern blacks also called for slave uprisings. David Walker, who was born free in Ohio, published his *Appeal to the Colored Citizens of the World* in Boston in 1829. Walker's goal was "To awaken in the breasts of my afflicted, degraded and slumbering brethren, a spirit of inquiry and investigation respecting our miseries and wretchedness in this Republican Land of Liberty!!!!!!" Walker also asked white Americans, will God "let the oppressors rest comfortably and happy always?" But the primary audience for Walker's *Appeal* was among his fellow African-Americans to whom he said, "The whites want slaves, and want us for their slaves, but some of them will curse the day they ever saw us."

In his 1843 "Address to the Slaves of the United States of America," Henry Highland Garnet also did not mince words. He said to the slaves of the South,

> Brethren, arise, arise! Strike for your lives and liberties. Now is the day and the hour....Let your motto be resistance! Resistance! RESISTANCE!

For Garnet and Walker, the time was long past for aiding individual escapes or agitating for a constitutional end to slavery; they were ready for direct action.

White Abolitionists

The Liberator
A newspaper dedicated to the antislavery cause launched by William Lloyd Garrison in 1831.

In the first issue of his newspaper **The Liberator**, published in 1831, William Lloyd Garrison declared, "I am in earnest—I will not equivocate—I will not excuse—I will not retreat a single inch. –AND I WILL BE HEARD." Over the next 35 years until the passage of the Thirteenth Amendment ending slavery in the United States in 1865, Garrison never backed down. He was a loner who alienated most people who tried to work with him. Nevertheless, in 1833 he was one of the key members in launching the **American Anti-Slavery Society** in Boston, which, like *The Liberator*, was committed to the total abolition of slavery everywhere in the United States, and for a third of a century, he kept the issue of slavery in front of a white society that often did not want to hear about it. Garrison's role in the abolitionist movement can hardly be overstated.

American Anti-Slavery Society
Founded in Boston in 1833, the society was dedicated to the abolition of slavery.

In the 1830s, Garrison was already a believer in the "free labor" doctrine that the Republican Party would adopt in the 1850s. He contrasted Northern free labor, which provided opportunities for anyone to gain the economic independence so important to freedom, and Southern slavery, which created a rigid hierarchy of wealthy elites, poor whites, and enslaved blacks.

Garrison was not a church member, but he modeled himself on the image of an Old Testament prophet, and he saw the considerable abuse that was heaped on him over many years as proof of his own righteousness. Other abolitionists, white and black, also were subject to considerable abuse. In 1835, Garrison himself was almost lynched in Boston. In New York City, Lewis and Arthur Tappan, highly successful merchants, were also shunned for their abolitionist activity. And in Alton, Illinois, on the Mississippi River opposite the slaveholding state of Missouri, Elijah Lovejoy was killed by a mob in 1837 after he had set up a small printing press to publish antislavery literature. Despite his status as a loner, Garrison did befriend other abolitionists and runaway slaves. He helped launch Frederick Douglass on his remarkable career as an abolitionist leader, though the two differed on many issues.

On the fourth of July in 1854, at a sunny afternoon picnic of the Massachusetts Anti-Slavery Society in Framingham, Massachusetts, Garrison burned a copy of the hated Fugitive Slave Act of 1850 that required all citizens to help return escaped slaves to those who claimed them. As it burned, Garrison shouted, "And let all the people say, 'Amen.'" It was not a surprising action at an antislavery rally, but when the crowd roared its response, Garrison also held up a copy of the United States Constitution—a sacred document to many—and called it "the source and parent of the other atrocities" because of its clauses that protected slavery and set it on fire, too. And again the crowd responded to his call for an "Amen." For all his radicalism, Garrison was also a pacifist. He always insisted that his goal was "to accomplish the great work of national redemption through the agency of moral power," not force. While he argued that events like Nat Turner's bloody rebellion were inevitable, he could never condone violence, even the violence of the Civil War, to end slavery.

Garrison may have crusaded independently, but many other white Americans were joining forces as abolitionists in the 1830s and 1840s, and especially after the passage of the Fugitive Slave Act in 1850. What came to be known as "Oberlin abolitionism" emerged from the revivals that Charles Grandison Finney led in upstate New York in the 1820s. In May 1836, the American Anti-Slavery Society began a campaign to evangelize the nation for abolitionism. What was needed, the society's leaders decided, were antislavery revivalists who modeled their activities on the work of religious revivalists. Funds would be raised to send out at least 70 organizers to preach the sin of slavery and the need for the repentance of abolitionism. Theodore Dwight Weld, who had begun his career working with Finney, was commissioned to choose the agents.

This banner announced the publication of a new journal, *The Liberator*, dedicated entirely to the complete abolition of slavery in all parts of the United States.

Weld turned to his old classmates from theology school, especially now that many of them were seeking their first appointments as ministers. Eventually, 30 of the 54 students who had been part of Weld's class at Lane Seminary in the early 1830s became antislavery agents. They carried revivalism and activism to all the free states of the union.

In the 1840s and 1850s, 12 to 15 percent of all Americans were slaves like Susan Merritt or former slaves like John Taper. Most Americans held some opinion about the condition of slaves, and increasingly, activists on both sides of the issue were taking strong stands. Some, including Edmund Ruffin, were defenders of slavery; others such as William Lloyd Garrison, David Walker, and Sarah Grimké were its opponents. But almost no Americans were completely free of economic ties to slavery or were able to ignore its impact on American culture and politics. Slaves produced cotton, which clothed most Americans and fueled the nation's economy. By the 1850s, the issue of slavery also dominated American politics. Whatever one's place in society and one's point of view, slavery was a central issue and topic of debate. It would not go away.

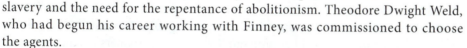

12.2 **Quick Review** In what different ways did enslaved people and their free allies, white and black, resist the institution of slavery and help individuals escape from it? How did apologists for slavery respond to the growing criticism of the institution that emerged in the 1830s and 1840s? What do the numbers of slaves who ran away say about the defense of slavery?

NEW STRENGTH FOR AMERICAN WOMEN

12.3 Describe how the women's rights movement developed in the United States in the 1830s and 1840s.

Declaration of Sentiments and Resolutions

The resolutions passed at the Woman's Rights Convention at Seneca Falls in 1848 calling for full equality, including the right to vote, for women.

On July 20, 1848, 68 women and 32 men signed a **Declaration of Sentiments and Resolutions** at the end of their 2-day meeting in Seneca Falls, New York. The document—which followed the form of the Declaration of Independence—is often viewed as the opening statement of the women's rights movement in the United States. This declaration stated,

> We hold these truths to be self-evident; that all men and women are created equal; that they are endowed by their Creator with certain inalienable rights; that among these are life, liberty, and the pursuit of happiness.

Then, just as Jefferson listed grievances against George III, those who gathered in upstate New York offered their grievances against the male-dominated culture in which they lived. Their document made history and achieved far more recognition than its authors ever imagined. But the Seneca Falls convention would likely not have happened without the work of others who began to question women's roles in the decades before the convention, and the work of the those at the convention still depended on the continued efforts of supporters to fight for change.

New Ideas about Women's Rights

The 1848 convention of women at Seneca Falls was not the first time women in the United States began to lobby for their rights. Although hardly a feminist in today's terms, Abigail Adams had reminded her husband, John, that the framers of a new government in 1776 should "remember the ladies." In 1838, the abolitionist and feminist Sarah Grimké published *Letters on the Equality of the Sexes and the Condition of Women*, portions of which she first published in Garrison's *The Liberator* and which she originally addressed to the Boston Female Anti-Slavery Society. In the 1838 book she argued that in the present "condition of women in my own country," well-off women were "taught to regard marriage as the one thing needful, the only avenue to distinction," while "in those employments which are peculiar to women, their time is estimated at only half the value of that of men." Grimké also argued that men suffered from the assumption that they alone needed to support families while she believed they would ultimately find greater happiness in seeing women "as their equal" even if that view did not come easily to them.

Few women symbolized the strong links between feminism and abolitionism as did Sarah and Angelina Grimké, sisters from South Carolina. Born to a prosperous South Carolina slaveholding family, both women broke with their family over the issue of slavery. By 1836, the sisters had become the first female representatives of the American Anti-Slavery Society, based in New York City. They had also become ardent feminists. In 1838, Angelina married another abolitionist, Theodore Dwight Weld. For most of the rest of their lives, Weld and the two sisters lived together and campaigned to end slavery, racism, and sexism in society.

Sarah Grimké wrote *Letters on the Equality of the Sexes* after she and her sister were criticized for giving public lectures on the antislavery cause. The ministers and others who criticized the sisters might have been sympathetic to the women's antislavery views, but they thought women had no place speaking in public to a group that included women and men. Sarah had no intention of backing down on either topic. She began her *Letters*, "Here I plant myself. God created us equal:" Then, focusing on women's rights, she continued:

> All history attests that man has subjected woman to his will, used her as a means to promote his selfish gratification, to minister to his sensual pleasures, to be instrumental in promoting his comfort; but never has he desired

to elevate her to that rank she was created to fill. He has done all he could to debase and enslave her mind; and now he looks triumphantly on the ruin he has wrought, and says, the being he has thus deeply injured is his inferior…. To me it is perfectly clear that WHATEVER IT IS MORALLY RIGHT FOR A MAN TO DO, IT IS MORALLY RIGHT FOR A WOMAN TO DO. . . she is clothed by her Maker with the *same rights*, and…the *same duties*.

Grimké's *Letters* were in circulation a decade before the meeting at Seneca Falls, but that gathering brought the cause of women's rights to a much larger audience. Because it brought together such powerful women as Elizabeth Cady Stanton, Lucretia Mott, and many others—soon joined by others including Susan B. Anthony and Matilda Gage—Seneca Falls provided the foundation for a half-century long campaign for women's rights and specifically women's suffrage.

The Seneca Falls Convention Shapes a Movement

Elizabeth Cady Stanton and Lucretia Mott were the organizers of the 1848 **Seneca Falls Women's Rights Convention** that brought the cause of women's rights to the attention of many. Stanton and her family had come to rural Seneca Falls, New York, only the previous year. They missed life in their former home in Boston but thought Seneca Falls would provide a rest. However, Elizabeth found life in Seneca Falls difficult and lonely.

In the summer of 1848, Lucretia Mott, already a well-known Quaker abolitionist and reformer, and her husband James were visiting Seneca Falls as part of a trip to the nearby Seneca Indian tribe and to former slaves now living as free people across the border in Canada. Stanton visited Mott and poured out her frustration. Mott had similar grievances. Both women had long been active in the antislavery cause. Henry B. Stanton, Elizabeth's husband, was a well-known abolitionist, and he and Elizabeth had traveled widely in the service of the cause. Stanton and Mott had both attended the World Anti-Slavery Convention in London in 1840 with their husbands. At that gathering, all of the women were excluded from any speaking role. As they talked about it in 1848, Stanton and Mott decided, "then and there, to call a 'Woman's Rights Convention'" for the following week.

The Woman's Rights Convention at Seneca Falls generated far more attention—most of it negative—than the organizers expected. Stanton remembered, "All the journals from Maine to Texas seemed to strive with each other to see which could make our movement appear most ridiculous." Looking back on the hostility that the convention generated, Stanton said, "If I had had the slightest premonition of all that was to follow that convention, I fear I should not have had the courage to risk it."

Not all the responses were hostile, however. The abolitionist Frederick Douglass attended the Seneca Falls gathering and spoke in favor of, and signed, the declaration. Abolitionists were used to hostility, and much of the abolitionist press supported the Seneca Falls statement, launching an important alliance between abolitionists and advocates for women's rights. Stanton, Mott, and many like them were abolitionists first who then added women's rights to their concerns, in part, because of their exclusion from leadership positions in the abolitionist movements and, in part, because they saw the rights of enslaved people and new freedoms for women as part of the same reform effort. Douglass and many male abolitionists were also among the strongest supporters of women's rights. And many of the most determined opponents of one movement also opposed the other.

Reports of the Woman's Rights Convention at Seneca Falls caught the attention of other women and subsequent conventions were held across New York state and in Massachusetts, Ohio, Indiana, and Pennsylvania. Among those who heard the news of the Seneca Falls convention were Susan B. Anthony and Matilda Joslyn Gage. Anthony was a teacher in Rochester, New York, and active in temperance and antislavery reforms.

Seneca Falls Women's Rights Convention
A significant convention demanding women's equality in legal rights, held in upstate New York in 1848.

Gage gave birth to a son just before the Seneca Falls meeting and could not attend. Both of these women quickly became friends with Stanton and fellow leaders of the women's rights movement for over half a century. They also joined as editors of the first three volumes of *History of Woman Suffrage* published between 1881 and 1886. The gathering at Seneca Falls, the declaration that the convention issued, and the movement that followed became far more than the small band of organizers dared hope for when they gathered on those hot summer days.

A Growing Women's Rights Movement

Women continued to lead campaigns to open other doors to women during the years after the convention at Seneca Falls. Some collaborated with the Seneca Falls leaders and some worked on their own. When Lucy Stone graduated from Oberlin College in 1847—Oberlin and Antioch were among the first American colleges to admit women as students—she was chosen as the commencement speaker but was told that a man would have to read her speech because it was not appropriate for women to speak to mixed audiences. In response, she refused to write one. In 1855, when she married Henry B. Blackwell, Stone insisted on keeping her own name, a huge break with tradition. Stone's Oberlin friend and sister-in-law Antoinette Brown Blackwell was the first woman ordained as a Protestant minister in 1851. In 1849, Elizabeth Blackwell, sister-in-law to both women, became the first woman awarded an M.D. degree.

Another reformer, Amelia Bloomer, who had participated in the Seneca Falls convention and served as a temperance lecturer, embraced a different kind of freedom for women when in 1851 she popularized a kind of trousers that women might wear instead of the cumbersome hoop skirts that were expected of all middle-class women.

Elizabeth Cady Stanton and Susan B. Anthony became lifelong friends soon after the Woman's Rights Convention at Seneca Falls and, in spite of occasional disagreements, worked together for almost half a century to fight for women's right to vote.

Other women demanded other kinds of rights. One of the most important issues for many women was the right to control their own property. In nearly all the states before the 1830s, a married woman's husband controlled all of the couple's property. Women fought such rules, and after the Panic of 1837, in which many women saw their life savings disappear because of a husband's bankruptcy, their voices began to be heard. Mississippi was the first state to pass laws specifically allowing women to keep the property they brought into their marriages. The 1839 law said that property that women had before a marriage or inherited during a marriage—including slaves—could not be controlled by their husbands. Michigan passed a law in 1844 that protected a women's property from a husband's creditors, and in the 1840s and 1850s, other states followed. In Texas and other states that had once belonged to Mexico, Spanish-era laws had long given women the rights to control their own property, and those rights were incorporated into the new American legal systems.

In the 1830s, other women formed antiprostitution societies to protect women from being forced into such work. Additional reformers of the 1830s became advocates for dietary reform, including Mary Gove Nichols, who along with Sylvester Graham (of Graham crackers) advocated a healthier diet free of alcohol, coffee, meat, sugar, and spices.

Advocates for the rights of women also had their differences with one another. Some of the most intense differences came over the issue of divorce. Frances (Fanny) Wright, who had been influenced by Robert Owen's ideas about an ideal community (see Chapter 10), represented an extreme view of the topic. Wright tried to create her own utopian community at Nashoba, Tennessee, where she advocated that the best way to end slavery and the racial prejudice that maintained it was to promote interracial unions that would produce a new breed of Americans. Even after the failure of Nashoba, Wright continued to argue that the institution of marriage was a barrier to women's equality. More moderate women, including Elizabeth Cady Stanton, argued that marriage was a simple legal contract, not a sacred institution, and that at least in the case of a husband who was a drunkard or abusive, divorce should be easy. Others disagreed, not only those hostile to women's rights but also leaders of the women's movement such as Antoinette Brown Blackwell.

The links between the women's rights and antislavery efforts, important as they were, were not without their tensions. Some African-American women felt those tensions especially deeply. As early as 1832, the first female antislavery society in the United States was created by African-American women in Salem, Massachusetts. White women soon followed with their own societies in a number of large cities, but black women were often reluctant to join the integrated societies in which white women nearly always claimed all of the leadership roles. At a women's rights convention in Akron, Ohio, in 1851, Sojourner Truth asked, "May I say a few words?" Truth was already a nationally recognized figure. She had been born a slave in New York State in 1799 but was freed by the New York Emancipation Act of 1827. She took the name Sojourner Truth and traveled across the nation demanding freedom for her fellow Americans of African origin. She told the convention:

> I have as much muscle as any man, and can do as much work as any man. I have plowed and reaped and husked and chopped and mowed, and can any man do more than that? I have heard much about the sexes being equal. I can carry as much as any man, and can eat as much too, if I can get it. I am as strong as any man.…But man is in a tight place, the poor slave is on him, woman is coming on him, he is surely between a hawk and a buzzard.

Versions of the speech published later added the famous refrain "And ain't I a woman?" In that speech, Truth linked the antislavery and women's rights campaigns, telling those who opposed that link that they would indeed be caught "between a hawk and a buzzard" if she had anything to do with it.

THE BLOOMER COSTUME.

The "bloomers" that Amelia Bloomer popularized were much more than a fashion statement. They essentially meant that women could wear pants, liberating them from the long hoop skirts that were virtually required wear for middle-class women and that made any sort of activity, from walking upstairs to physical activity out of doors, extremely difficult.

12.3 Quick Review What did the women's and abolitionist movements have in common? How did the two movements build on each other?

CONCLUSION

In the decades leading up to the Civil War, the United States grew in area and in population. From 1830 to 1850, the number of people living in the United States almost doubled, from fewer than 13 million to more than 23 million. Rising birth rates among native-born Americans fueled the largest proportion of this growth, but other forces also sent U.S. population statistics upward. Immigrants, particularly from China, Ireland, and Germany, contributed to the rise as did the multitudes of new residents acquired when the United States gained new territory after its war with Mexico. Responding to a variety of push-and-pull factors, immigrants flocked to America to escape hardships at home and to pursue economic opportunity on American soil as domestics, farmers, miners, railroad workers, builders, and factory laborers. In many cases, native-born Americans did not take well to immigrants, seeing them as a threat to their own jobs and quality of life. The country's growing diversity brought new tensions.

Large territorial gains, ceded to the United States under the terms of the Treaty of Guadalupe Hidalgo in 1848 and purchased from Mexico by U.S. diplomat James Gadsden in 1853, stretched the nation's borders farther south and west, bringing many Spanish-speaking people, as well as Plains and Pueblo Indians, into the country. Although the treaties had promised that these residents would be respected and allowed to continue living in the areas, Americans who flocked into those regions generally pushed out those who were already there, leaving them in much more marginal positions.

Changes in fashion, technology, and transportation led to cotton's becoming a highly profitable crop in the 19th century, more profitable with each succeeding decade. Its cultivation spread across the lower South, transforming the Southern economy and the dynamics of slavery. The slave population also surged during this time, increasing from 1.5 million to 4 million between 1820 and 1860. By 1840, the American South was the leading producer of cotton in the world, and plantation owners, eager to exploit the rising demand for the crop, moved slaves into new cotton-growing regions to work in the fields from dawn to dusk. This new cotton economy made slavery in the South far more profitable than ever before. Slave owners justified the institution of slavery as a "positive good" wherein slaves were thought to be better off being provided for on plantations than left to fend for themselves. Slaves, through open revolt, escape, and other less dramatic means, resisted their enslavement. Abolitionists in the North—white and black—also resisted slavery, campaigning against the institution with renewed vehemence that heightened sectional tensions.

Women, who were also struggling for full rights as citizens, launched a suffrage movement at Seneca Falls, New York, in 1848 and a campaign for full rights in all areas of society. Many women and some men saw a link between freedom from slavery and the emancipation of women, and they agitated tirelessly for both causes, even though others of both sexes renounced their efforts.

CHAPTER REVIEW Which changes in the United States had the greatest impact on emerging social movements in the 1840s and 1850s? You may want to consider immigration, the growth of both antislavery and proslavery propaganda, and the campaign for equal rights for women in your answer.

THE CHANGING FACE OF THE AMERICAN PEOPLE IN THE 1840s AND 1850s

12.1 Analyze how immigration from China, Ireland, and Germany, as well as the incorporation of Mexican citizens in the Southwest, changed the United States.

Review Questions

1. **Historical Interpretation**
   What forces pushed Chinese immigrants to leave their homeland? What forces pulled them toward California?

2. **Comparison**
   Compare and contrast the place of Irish immigrants in American society before and after the Great Famine of 1845–1850. How would you explain the differences you note?

3. **Chronological Reasoning**
   How did life change for Hispanic elites living in California, Texas, and New Mexico after the absorption of those territories into the United States? What explains the changes you note?

SLAVERY IN THE UNITED STATES, 1840s AND 1850s

12.2 Explain how the lives of slaves, slaveholders, and abolitionists evolved in the decades before the Civil War.

Review Questions

4. **Chronological Reasoning**
   How did the nature of slavery change between 1800 and 1850? How would you explain the changes you note?

5. **Contextualization**
   How did slaves build lives and communities of their own within the institution of slavery?

6. **Historical Interpretation**
   How would you explain the growth of antislavery sentiment in the North after 1830? What connections do you see between the rise of the abolitionist movement and the changing nature of the Southern defense of slavery?

NEW STRENGTH FOR AMERICAN WOMEN

12.3 Describe how the women's rights movement developed in the United States in the 1830s and 1840s.

Review Questions

7. **Historical Interpretation**
   What links were there between the abolitionist and women's rights movements of the 1840s and 1850s? How would you explain the connections you note?

8. **Chronological Reasoning**
   Why was the Seneca Falls convention such an important turning point in the history of the struggle for women's rights?

13 The Politics of Separation

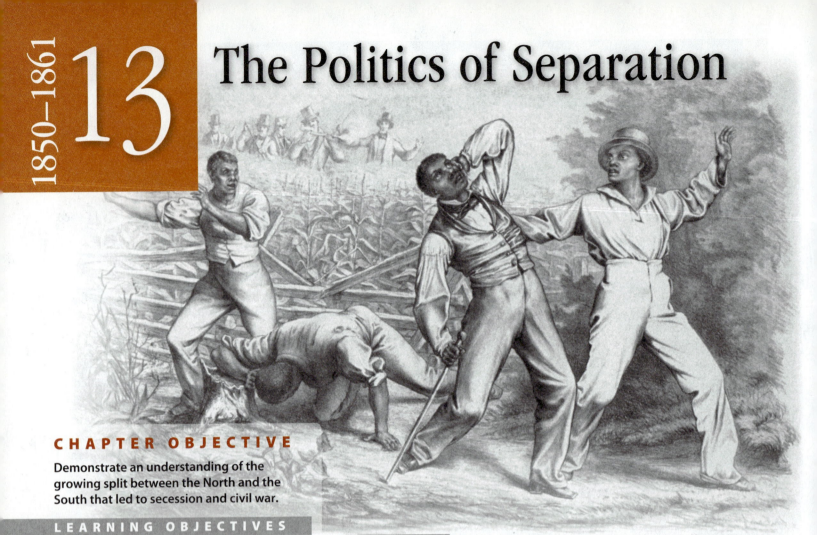

CHAPTER OBJECTIVE

Demonstrate an understanding of the growing split between the North and the South that led to secession and civil war.

LEARNING OBJECTIVES

FROM UNION TO DISUNION

13.1 Analyze the political jockeying in Congress and how reaction to the Fugitive Slave Act and the publication of *Uncle Tom's Cabin*, changed the opinions of many Americans—South and the North—making a break between them hard to avoid.

BLEEDING KANSAS AND *DRED SCOTT V. SANDFORD*

13.2 Analyze the causes and consequences of the battle over slavery in Kansas and the Supreme Court's decision in the Dred Scott case and the impact of those events on public opinion.

THE ECONOMY, THE PANIC OF 1857, AND THE LINCOLN-DOUGLAS DEBATES

13.3 Explain how the economic crisis of 1857 and the growing political crises of the decade impacted each other and led the nation to divide.

FROM JOHN BROWN TO THE SECESSION OF THE SOUTH

13.4 Analyze the political impact of John Brown's raid and why Lincoln won the presidential election of 1860 and the southern states then voted to leave.

Leaflets like this reflected the outrage many northerners felt in response to the capture and reenslavement of African Americans that resulted from the passage of a tougher fugitive slave law.

While thousands of Americans, along with Asians and Europeans, were pouring into California in search of gold, other Americans were attacking or defending slavery. These two seemingly separate issues came to a head in Congress in 1850. Because of its rapid gold-rush-inspired growth, President Taylor advocated statehood for California from the time that he took office in 1848, and in 1849, Californians adopted a state constitution and applied for statehood only 1 year after the United States acquired it from Mexico. The territory far exceeded the minimum population threshold for statehood, but there was a problem: although the admission of California as a free state would once again restore the carefully crafted balance of free and slave states, evening out the numbers after the balance in the Senate had been disrupted by admitting Texas as a slave state, other future free states might follow, which threatened those in the South. Contrary to some expectations, the U.S. War with Mexico had not produced another slave state for the Union after Texas. Admitting California as a free state would restore the balance in the Senate that had been the rule since the Missouri Compromise of 1820 and that the admission of Texas had disrupted in 1846, leading to 15 slaves states represented, but only 14 free states. Many in the North and South thought a balance was essential to maintaining the Union. But Southern senators, both Whig and Democrat, agreed that if California were admitted as a free state, then other free states might quickly follow, especially because there were virtually no slaves in either Oregon or New Mexico territories, the other land acquired by the United States in the 1840s that might logically soon be divided into states. The young senator from Mississippi, Jefferson Davis, concerned about that possibility, warned his colleagues that "we are about permanently to destroy the balance of power between the sections." The South's ill and aging champion John C. Calhoun wrote in his diary, "As things now stand, the South cannot with safety remain in the Union." Much had happened to lead Davis and Calhoun to their conclusions. In the 1850s, more Southerners would come to believe that they could not remain in the Union, and hostility to the South and its "peculiar institution" of slavery would increase in the North. Although a new generation in Congress tried again to enact the kinds of compromises that had held the country together since the adoption of the Constitution in 1789, those efforts no longer worked. The tensions that led Southern states to feel compelled to secede from the United States in 1861 are the focus of this chapter.

FROM UNION TO DISUNION

13.1 Analyze the political jockeying in Congress and how reaction to the Fugitive Slave Act and the publication of *Uncle Tom's Cabin* changed the opinions of many Americans—South and the North—making a break between them hard to avoid.

The Congress that met in 1849 and 1850 and debated whether and how to admit California was one of the most contentious ever seated. The same three men, Daniel Webster of Massachusetts, John C. Calhoun of South Carolina, and Henry Clay of Kentucky, who had dominated the Senate as young men in 1820 now, as old men, played the central role in 1850. The dramatic debates of 1850 would be the last time the three would appear on the Senate floor. A new generation of senators would also play crucial roles in the coming years: Stephen A. Douglas of Illinois (who would contest the presidency with Abraham Lincoln in 1860), William H. Seward of New York and Salmon P. Chase of Ohio (who would both seek the Republican nomination for president in 1860 and then serve in Lincoln's Cabinet), and Jefferson Davis of Mississippi (who would be elected president of the Confederacy in 1861).

Proslavery senators like Calhoun and Davis were worried about California, but they were even more worried about abolitionism in the North, which had been a growing force since the 1840s. Throughout the 1840s and 1850s there were many different kinds of abolitionists with differing levels of commitment to their cause, but Southerners tended to view all abolitionists as extremists. At the core of the movement were those known as the radical abolitionists for whom slavery was the greatest evil in the nation, an evil that needed to end immediately and completely. A larger group of Northerners were sympathetic with the radicals, but not willing to move as quickly or do as much to oppose slavery. Many of these moderates fell into the free-soil category, willing to let slavery stay where it already existed but adamantly opposing any extension of slavery to new territories where it did not yet exist by law. Finally, there were others for whom ending slavery was perhaps a good thing but not the highest priority. All of these Northerners, however, were committed to "free labor," the belief that slavery undermined the value and dignity of hard work and that many white people were also marginalized in places where slave labor was predominant. In the 1850s, this sentiment would lead voters in the new Republican Party to cheer for "Free Soil, Free Speech, Free Labor, and Free Men."

Many of the tensions that exploded in Congress in 1850 dated to the U.S. War with Mexico in the 1840s. In 1846, Democratic Congressman David Wilmot of Pennsylvania proposed an amendment to a military appropriations bill, prohibiting slavery in any territory acquired from Mexico. This so-called **Wilmot Proviso** sprang from growing anger among Northern Democrats at what they saw as the pro-Southern tilt of the Polk administration. With support from northern Whigs, the amendment

| 13.1 |
| 13.2 |
| 13.3 |
| 13.4 |

Wilmot Proviso

The amendment offered by Pennsylvania Democrat David Wilmot in 1846, which stipulated that "as an express and fundamental condition to the acquisition of any territory from the Republic of Mexico...neither slavery nor involuntary servitude shall ever exist in any part of said territory."

passed the House, but died in the Senate where Southern Senators were able to block all such measures in 1846 and 1847. A Boston newspaper said of the Proviso, "As if by magic, it brought to a head the great question that is about to divide the American people." By 1850, the question of slavery created divisions that cut across party lines, whether Democrat or Whig.

California, the Compromise of 1850, and the Fugitive Slave Act

A new Congress, elected just after the end of the War with Mexico, and a new president, war-hero Zachery Taylor, tackled the complex question of California's statehood. Taylor was a political unknown. Southerners tended to trust him because he owned slaves and a Louisiana plantation, but 40 years as an officer in the U.S. Army had led Taylor to value the Union. He hated the threat of secession. In 1849, Taylor proposed admitting not only California but New Mexico as new states. California would certainly be a free state, but Taylor's proposal left the future status of New Mexico uncertain, though there were virtually no slaves there. By the time Congress convened in December 1849, much of the country was in an uproar, with many in the South threatening secession if two free states were admitted and many in the North willing to call their bluff.

In that charged situation, Senator Henry Clay of Kentucky, long known as the "Great Compromiser" for his role in crafting the Compromise of 1820, tried again. Clay offered a series of proposals that he hoped would pass Congress and avert a sectional crisis by defusing tension in a number of areas. The first compromise would admit California as a state but organize New Mexico under a territorial government with no "restriction or condition on the subject of slavery." As a territory, New Mexico would have no votes in the Senate, a key concern of slaveholders in Congress since they were certain—probably rightly—that New Mexico would opt to enter the union as a free state. The second compromise Clay proposed would resolve the contested question of the Texas–New Mexico border by giving more land to New Mexico and giving Texas $10 million to pay off the debts of the former Republic of Texas. Since many Southerners held Republic of Texas bonds, this proposal had great appeal in the South. The third proposal abolished the slave trade but not slavery itself in the District of Columbia. Finally, to ensure Southern support, Clay proposed a fourth compromise: a law enhancing slaveholders' right to reclaim slaves who fled north. The whole package may have seemed to Clay like a careful balance that would appeal to both sections. In fact, most members of Congress from each section disliked it, claiming that it did not go nearly far enough in the direction they wanted.

In the debate that followed Clay's proposals, John C. Calhoun warned that if California were admitted as a free state, it would "destroy irretrievably the equilibrium between the two sections," and that Southerners could not remain in the Union. The threat of secession was clear. Three days later, Daniel Webster spoke in favor of the compromise. Webster began, "I wish to speak to-day, not as a Massachusetts man, nor as a Northern man, but as an American....I speak to-day for the preservation of the Union." It was an impressive speech and one memorized by generations of school children. But it virtually destroyed Webster's reputation in an increasingly abolitionist Massachusetts where many of his constituents were no longer willing to compromise with slaveholders.

In the long hot summer of 1850, first Calhoun and then President Taylor both died in office. The new President Millard Fillmore, from New York, favored compromise, perhaps more than Taylor had. In addition, a new generation of senators, of whom Stephen A. Douglas was the leader, managed to forge a final compromise close to Clay's proposal. In a series of separate resolutions, California was admitted as a free state; New Mexico and Utah were organized as territories with no votes in Congress, thus maintaining the balance in the Senate; the slave trade but not slavery was prohibited in the District of Columbia; and Texas happily accepted the $10 million in exchange for a less expansive border with New Mexico. Most fatefully, Congress also

Henry Clay, John C. Calhoun, and Daniel Webster, three men who had dominated the Senate since 1820, debated for the last time in Congress as they tried to resolve the complex issues raised by the admission of California as a state.

passed the **Fugitive Slave Act**, which was designed to please the South by giving them the right not only to reclaim runaway slaves but also to demand federal and local Northern help in the process.

There was great rejoicing in Washington in the fall of 1850 when the package passed. President Fillmore called it "a final settlement," but not everyone agreed. A convention of delegates from Southern states condemned the compromise and affirmed the right of secession. In the North, Charles Francis Adams, son and grandson of moderately antislavery presidents, called the compromise "the consummation of the iniquities of the most disgraceful session of Congress." Horace Mann, the former Massachusetts education leader who had succeeded John Quincy Adams as a representative from Massachusetts in the congressional seat that was, because of Adams's long efforts, considered *the* abolitionist seat, said that the compromise meant the Declaration of Independence applied only to white men. For Northerners, the vigorous enforcement of the Fugitive Slave Act would soon become intolerable, and many Southern leaders became convinced that the abolitionists wanted to end slavery not only in the territories but also in the states where it was strong and that the only solution was to leave the Union. No one knew what the next decade would hold, but the most perceptive among them thought the celebrations of 1850 were premature.

Enforcing the Fugitive Slave Act

When Henry Clay proposed a new Fugitive Slave Act as part of the Compromise of 1850 and Stephen A. Douglas persuaded Congress to adopt it, or when Presidents Fillmore (1850–1853) and Franklin Pierce (1853–1857) vigorously enforced that law, none of them expected the firestorm that resulted. The core of the new law was not new. The Constitution said

> No person held to service or labor (i.e., a slave) in one State under the laws thereof, escaping into another, shall in consequence of any law or regulation therein, be discharged from such service or labor, but shall be delivered up on claim of the party to whom such service or labor may be due.

Fugitive Slave Act
A law that was part of the Compromise of 1850. It created a new set of federal agents to help track runaway slaves and required authorities in the North to assist Southern slave catchers and return runaway slaves to their owners.

CAUTION!!

COLORED PEOPLE
OF BOSTON, ONE & ALL,

You are hereby respectfully CAUTIONED and
advised, to avoid conversing with the

**Watchmen and Police Officers
of Boston,**

For since the recent ORDER OF THE MAYOR &
ALDERMEN, they are empowered to act as

KIDNAPPERS
AND
Slave Catchers,

And they have already been actually employed in
KIDNAPPING, CATCHING, AND KEEPING
SLAVES. Therefore, if you value your LIBERTY,
and the *Welfare of the Fugitives* among you, *Shun*
them in every possible manner, as so many *HOUNDS*
on the track of the most unfortunate of your race.

**Keep a Sharp Look Out for
KIDNAPPERS, and have
TOP EYE open.**

APRIL 24, 1851.

After enforcement of the Fugitive Slave Act became common, abolitionists posted warnings to African-Americans that whether born free or escaping from slavery, they were no longer safe in Northern cities like Boston.

Even though Northern states had passed "personal liberty laws" in the 1830s that made it harder to recapture a former slave, the Supreme Court in 1842 had affirmed that slaveholders had a constitutional right to capture slaves who had escaped to a free state. Given the number of runaway slaves, slave catching was a growth industry in the United States before 1850.

Nevertheless, the new Fugitive Slave Act went much further than any previous law. It created a new corps of federal agents to help capture runaway slaves. Court-appointed federal commissioners would determine whether a person claimed by a slave catcher was truly a slave or actually a free person. Commissioners were paid a double fee every time they found that a person was a fugitive slave as opposed to a free person, and there was no appeal from their decisions. Finally, the law provided for a $1,000 fine and up to a year in jail for anyone who helped a fugitive slave. Across the North, free blacks were worried, and many, knowing that it would be difficult to prove that they had been born free, moved to Canada before trouble arrived. But the slave catchers, now supported by federal agents, fanned out across the North, seeking escaped slaves, and in town after town, people saw the results. It was an ugly spectacle.

Anthony Burns escaped from slavery in Virginia, went to Boston, and found work in a clothing store. But his former owner discovered his whereabouts, and under the Fugitive Slave Act, a federal marshal arrested Burns on May 24, 1854. Bostonians were incensed. White and black abolitionists attacked the courthouse where Burns was held, and a federal marshal was killed in the melee. President Pierce ordered marines, cavalry, and artillery to Boston to ensure that the Fugitive Slave Act was enforced. On June 2, 1854, federal troops marched Burns in chains through the streets of Boston to a Coast Guard ship that was waiting in Boston harbor to take him back to slavery in Virginia. Huge crowds watched the spectacle, church bells tolled, and flags flew upside down. Pierce had upheld the law, but he had lost the respect of many of the nation's citizens. Amos A. Lawrence, one of the richest men in Massachusetts and a conservative Whig, was a changed man after watching the Burns affair. He said that he and many of his friends "went to bed one night old fashioned, conservative, Compromise Union Whigs & waked up stark mad Abolitionists." Lawrence was far from alone. Happily for Burns, his Boston supporters eventually purchased his freedom. Nevertheless, the sight of this man being marched by U.S. troops back to slavery on the streets of Boston was indelible for many who saw and heard about it.

Similar incidents happened across the North. In Ohio, Margaret Garner, an escaped slave who had crossed the Ohio River from Kentucky, discovered slave catchers at her door, and she tried to kill her children rather than allow them to be returned to slavery. One of the children died. Garner was sold back to slavery in New Orleans. For Northerners, these sorts of events undermined the notion that they were living in free states. Many concluded that freedom could not exist in a nation that allowed slavery anywhere.

Southern defenders of slavery and even their nonslaveholding neighbors were similarly coming to the conclusion that slave states and free states could not remain in the same country. The divisive issue could not be contained by compromise. Federal law had banned the international slave trade since 1808, but smugglers found ways to flout that ban and bring new slaves directly from Africa. Northerners likewise flouted the Fugitive Slave Act. When the best known of the Southern slave smugglers, Charles A. L. Lamar, was tried in federal court for smuggling slaves into the United States, a Southern newspaper asked, "What is the difference between a Yankee violating the fugitive slave law in the North and a Southern man violating…the law against the

African slave trade in the South?" In the 1850s, the vigorous enforcement of some laws and the flouting of others angered many Americans, but they differed greatly on which laws they wanted enforced and which flouted.

Uncle Tom's Cabin

Anger at the Fugitive Slave Act also convinced Harriet Beecher Stowe, already a well-known author, to do something for the antislavery cause. As the Fugitive Slave Act took effect, Stowe wrote "that the time is come when even a woman or a child who can speak a word for freedom and humanity is bound to speak." And speak she did.

Although she was living in Brunswick, Maine, at the time, Stowe had spent many years in Cincinnati, Ohio, and had herself seen slavery directly across the Ohio River in Kentucky. Cincinnati—a city that faced the Ohio River and from which one could see the slave state of Kentucky on the far shore—was itself home to many fugitives from slavery. She began writing what would become *Uncle Tom's Cabin*. It was first published in serial form in the *National Era* in 1851 and 1852 and then as a book. Within a year, 310,000 copies were in print, making it the bestselling book of the century, other than the Bible. What seems to modern readers to be an unrealistic and sentimental story of Uncle Tom, the ever-patient and kind slave, his evil owner Simon Legree, and heroic Eliza Harris, the slave mother who jumps on ice floes in

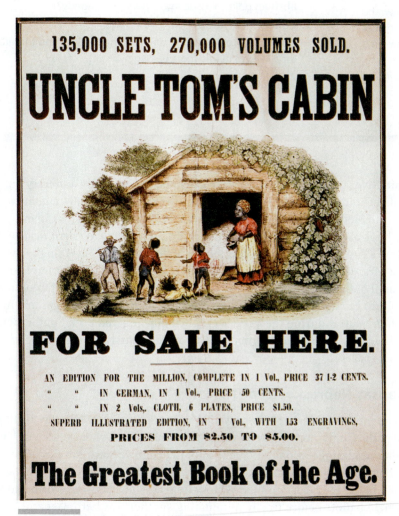

Selling 300,000 copies, *Uncle Tom's Cabin* was one of the best selling books of the century and helped to galvanize Northern opinion against slavery.

THINKING HISTORICALLY

Uncle Tom's Cabin

Early in *Uncle Tom's Cabin*, Stowe described her heroine Eliza's decision to run away from a Kentucky plantation after hearing that her young son was about to be sold away from her and the family to a new owner:

> It is impossible to conceive of a human creature more wholly desolate and forlorn than Eliza, when she turned her footsteps from Uncle Tom's cabin.
>
> Her husband's suffering and dangers, and the danger of her child, all blended in her mind, with a confused and stunning sense of the risk she was running, in leaving the only home she had ever known, and cutting loose from the protection of a friend whom she loved and revered. Then there was the parting from every familiar object.…But stronger than all was maternal love, wrought into a paroxysm of frenzy by the near approach of a fearful danger. Her boy was old enough to have walked by her side, and, in an indifferent case, she would only have led him by the hand; but now the bare thought of putting him out of her arms made her shudder, and she strained him to her bosom with a convulsive grasp, as she went rapidly forward.…

If it were *your* Harry, mother, or your Willie, that were going to be torn from you by a brutal trader, tomorrow morning,—if you had seen the man, and heard that the papers were signed and delivered, and you had only from twelve o'clock till morning to make good your escape,—how fast could *you* walk?

For many Americans, Eliza's fear and determination made the reality of slavery come alive in ways that decades of antislavery publications and true-life stories had not. What a modern reader reads as melodrama, readers of the time found compelling.

Source: Harriet Beecher Stowe, *Uncle Tom's Cabin, or, Life among the lowly* (Boston: J.P. Jewett, 1852).

Thinking Critically

1. **Historical Interpretation**
   How does Stowe transform the slavery question from an abstract political issue into a personal tragedy?

2. **Contextualization**
   How does Stowe build understanding for Eliza and therefore for all slaves in this short passage.

the Ohio River to escape pursuing slave catchers, was not only a literary but also a political phenomenon in the 1850s and 1860s. If any one book brought home a picture of slavery to moderate or ambivalent Northerners it was *Uncle Tom's Cabin.*

The book also enraged the South. *De Bow's Southern and Western Review*, one of the nation's largest proslavery publications, said the novel was "insulting to the South, because Mrs. Stowe wants the world to believe that all she has written is true!" In the turmoil of the 1850s, however, the book galvanized antislavery opinion not only in the North but also in England where it was credited with playing a role in keeping Britain neutral during the Civil War. The book angered both Southerners who rationalized slavery and Northerners, many of whom first saw the nature of slavery through its pages.

The Kansas-Nebraska Act of 1854

Developments in the early 1850s proved how wrong President Fillmore had been to think that the Compromise of 1850 was a "final settlement" of North–South tensions. The Fillmore administration's enforcement of the Fugitive Slave Act exacerbated antislavery opinion across the North and probably cost Fillmore the Whig nomination for president. In the 1852 elections, the Whigs, deeply divided between North and South, voted on 53 ballots before finally nominating another war hero, General Winfield Scott. An almost equally divided Democratic Party nominated Franklin Pierce of New Hampshire, whom many in the South considered "as reliable as Calhoun himself" on the issue of slavery because, they thought, he would win the White House for them by sweeping the South. The Democrats' gamble paid off; Pierce won and enforced the Fugitive Slave Act as actively as Fillmore.

Despite that highly tense political atmosphere, Senator Stephen A. Douglas of Illinois hoped to get federal support for a transcontinental railroad from Chicago to the Pacific Coast. A railroad did not seem to be something that would immediately stir up the tensions swirling around slavery, but it soon did. As one step toward organizing the railroad, Douglas and Congressman William A. Richardson, a fellow Illinois Democrat, introduced bills into Congress in 1853 that would organize the remaining land in the Louisiana Purchase north of the Arkansas River into what they called the Nebraska Territory to facilitate awarding a right-of-way for the railroad (see Map 13-1).

Southern senators feared an effort to create another free state out of Nebraska and blocked the bill. After several failed efforts at compromise, Douglas proposed to split Nebraska into two territories—Nebraska and Kansas—and allow each territory to decide whether to allow slavery. He called this approach "**popular sovereignty**"— letting each state or territory decide for itself whether to allow or ban slavery in its jurisdiction. Others had used the term before him, but Douglas became its most prominent proponent. The term sounded democratic—as least for white voters—but

popular sovereignty
A solution to the slavery crisis suggested by Senator Lewis Cass of Michigan by which territorial residents, not Congress, would decide slavery's fate in any proposed new state.

MAP 13-1 The Compromise of 1850 and the Kansas-NebraskaAct. The Compromise of 1850 admitted California as a free state and set the borders for the New Mexico and Utah Territories. Three years later, Senator Stephen A. Douglas proposed a plan for the Unorganized Territory between Minnesota and Oregon that set off a firestorm in Congress and the country about whether the territory might eventually become slave or free states.

it explicitly repealed the Missouri Compromise of 1820, which banned slavery north of Missouri no matter what local residents said. The proposal to split the Nebraska Territory and allow popular sovereignty to overrule the Missouri Compromise got Douglas the support he needed from Southern senators, but it also raised "a hell of a storm," as Douglas knew it would. For many moderates, even for President Pierce, the Missouri Compromise had held the Union together for 34 years, almost half the nation's lifetime. Tampering with it seemed dangerous. Douglas was offering to repeal it to be able to organize the new territories that he thought were essential to his plans for a railroad. The risk was that repealing the Missouri Compromise could allow slavery, if the local voters supported it, in territory where it had been banned since 1820. While defenders of slavery were delighted, Northern abolitionists and moderates saw taking this risk as another step toward spreading slavery throughout the Union, something they found unacceptable.

Northern outrage was intense. The most moderate free-soil advocates who opposed extending slavery united with the most radical abolitionists in opposition. Five state legislatures and hundreds of meetings and conventions sent petitions to Congress declaring, "This crime shall not be consummated." Whig Senator William Pitt Fessenden of Maine called the Kansas-Nebraska bill "a terrible outrage." On the other hand, Southerners of both parties strongly supported the **Kansas-Nebraska Act**. In the end, the bill passed in 1854, Pierce signed it, and Douglas got his territory, but he also virtually destroyed the Whig Party.

The Congressional Elections of 1854 and the Birth of the Republican Party

The Kansas-Nebraska Act became the defining issue in the 1854 elections for Congress. Battles between antislavery and proslavery factions within Kansas dominated the national news for the next several years. In 1854, northern Whigs, led by Senator William H. Seward of New York, along with members of the declining Free Soil Party came together to create the **Republican Party**. Many former Whigs and members of smaller parties campaigned for office as Republicans—members of a brand new party—in the 1854 congressional elections, and the Republicans, not the Whigs, would nominate candidates for president in 1856 and 1860. Southern and proslavery Whigs tried to maintain their party for a few years, but what had been a major political party in the United States since it was organized to oppose Andrew Jackson disappeared during the 1850s.

In Illinois, a former one-term Whig Congressman, Abraham Lincoln, was "aroused...as he had never been before" by the Kansas-Nebraska Act and began a campaign for a seat in the U.S. Senate that would allow him to oppose the act on the national stage. Stephen A. Douglas, in the middle of his own 6-year term as the other senator from Illinois (since all states elect two senators for 6-year terms at different times), opposed Lincoln, hoping instead for a fellow Democrat to join him in the Senate. Since U.S. Senators were elected by state legislatures at that time, not by popular votes, the 1854 senatorial campaign was actually a race among candidates for the Illinois legislature, who would then elect the new U.S. Senator. Everyone understood that, if the Democrats won a majority of the state legislature, they would elect a Democrat to join Douglas, but if the winning majority was the emerging Republican Party, supported by the remnants of the Whig Party, they would, many expected, elect Lincoln.

In the fall of 1854, Lincoln and Douglas campaigned throughout the state to support the candidates they favored for the Illinois legislature. Lincoln was a moderate, far too moderate for many abolitionists, and he remained a Whig throughout the 1854 campaign, choosing at that time not to join the new Republican Party; however, his opposition to the spread of slavery was growing stronger. He argued that while the Constitution protected slavery in the states where it existed, it "furnishes no more

Kansas-Nebraska Act
A law passed in 1854 creating the Kansas and Nebraska Territories but leaving the question of slavery open to local residents.

Republican Party
A new political party created in 1854 that was dedicated to stopping the spread of slavery in any place in the nation where it did not exist.

excuse for permitting slavery to go into our own free territory, than it would for reviving the African slave trade." When Douglas defended his long-standing policy of "popular sovereignty" and the "sacred right of self-government," Lincoln responded, "when the white man governs himself that is self-government; but when he governs himself and also governs another man…that is despotism." Lincoln said that he understood that ending slavery where it existed was difficult, but he also insisted that there could be no moral right for anyone to enslave any other person.

Lincoln's coalition won the majority of the Illinois legislature, but the coalition included former Democrats who would not vote for a Whig like Lincoln. In the end, Lincoln backed Lyman Trumbull, a former Democrat turned Republican, for the Senate rather than allow a Democrat to win. But during the 1854 campaign, Lincoln had established himself as a national actor on the political stage. The speeches that both Lincoln and Douglas made were a preview of the more formal debates that would take place between them 4 years later when Lincoln campaigned directly against Douglas in an effort to win his seat in the Senate.

Across the North, the 1854 election led to victories by anti-Kansas-Nebraska Act coalitions in state after state. Democrats lost control of most Northern state legislatures. The majority of the members of the Senate were not up for election in 1854 but the state of Wisconsin elected the first Republican to serve in that body. More significant changes came in the House of Representatives—the members of which are elected for 2-year terms directly by the voters, not by state legislatures. Northern Democrats dropped from 93 to 23 seats in the House of Representatives while Southern Democrats held 58 seats. But 150 members of Congress were now committed to stopping slavery in the territories, some as Whigs, some as Republicans, and some as members of minor parties. Since the formation of the Jacksonian Democrats and Whig opposition in the 1830s, leaders had changed party affiliations on occasion in response to strong issues, but never as often as they did in the 1850s as the old parties weakened. After 1854, voters—South and North—cared mostly about whether candidates were anti- or proslavery and whether they were moderate or radical in their views. The Kansas-Nebraska Act had unified Northern political opinion against the spread of slavery as nothing before it had done. A new political party, the Republican Party, was forming to speak for that point of view. Unlike the Whigs or the Democrats, both of which included Northern and Southern members, the Republican Party represented only one section of the nation and one political perspective. The party had virtually no Southerners and no one who spoke for popular sovereignty or any other plan to allow the growth of slavery. When the new Congress assembled in late 1855, the House eventually elected as its new Speaker, Nathaniel P. Banks of Massachusetts, a former Know Nothing who had recently switched his political allegiance to the Republican Party. A representative of a political party that had not existed 2 years earlier now held the gavel in the House of Representatives.

13.1 **Quick Review** How did the escalation of hostility over slavery indicate the issue could not be settled peacefully?

BLEEDING KANSAS AND *DRED SCOTT V. SANDFORD*

13.2 Analyze the causes and consequences of the battle over slavery in Kansas and the Supreme Court's decision in the Dred Scott case and the impact of those events on public opinion.

The Kansas-Nebraska Act, however, was still the law of the land in spite of the outcome of the 1854 elections. The act essentially split the former unorganized territory in half (see Map 13-1). The southern portion was the modern state of Kansas and the northern, called Nebraska, included the modern states of Nebraska,

South Dakota, and North Dakota. Kansas and Nebraska each now had to decide whether to apply for admission to the Union as slave or free states. No one was sure when elections would be held or who would vote, though many wanted to control the outcome. While Nebraska stayed relatively calm, Kansas, with its proximity to the slave state of Missouri but also within easy travel of the free states of Illinois and Iowa was easier for Southerners and Northerners to move to. It quickly became a dangerous and violent place.

Even before President Pierce appointed Andrew Reeder, a Pennsylvania Democrat, as territorial governor, hundreds of proslavery "border ruffians" from Missouri and abolitionists from the North began pouring into Kansas. The Missourians got there first and when the first elections were held for the territorial representative to Congress in November 1854, they won easily. They also gained a majority of the territorial legislature that was elected in March 1855. The proslavery faction could probably have won these early elections fairly, but the votes were accompanied by widespread cheating, fraudulent vote counting, votes by people who still resided in Missouri, and voter intimidation. So the results were challenged even as more anti-slavery voters began arriving in larger numbers and quickly came to outnumber the proslavery advocates.

In response to the first elections, the settlers who supported admitting Kansas as a free state called a convention in December 1855 in which they declared the territorial legislature elected in March to be illegitimately elected. They then held their own election, established their own legislature to meet at Topeka, adopted a state constitution (the Topeka Constitution), and elected their own governor. Thus by January 1856, Kansas had two legislatures and two governors as well as sent two different territorial representatives to Congress. For the most part, each faction voted in its own elections and boycotted the elections called by the other.

In 1856, U.S. troops under orders from President Pierce, dispersed the Topeka legislature since it lacked any legal mandate to meet, and the "official" legislature called a convention to write a state constitution. A new federal governor, Robert Walker, finally began to establish order in the territory and convinced both sides that an honest election could be held. In the October 1857 elections—probably the most honest in the territory—in which both factions voted for the first time, the free-state faction won a sizeable majority. But while the free-state majority now controlled the legislature, the constitutional convention, which had been appointed by the previous proslavery legislature, continued to write a constitution. The situation in Kansas then got even more complicated.

The proslavery convention at Lecompton, Kansas, that wrote what came to be known as the **Lecompton Constitution** finished its work in the fall of 1857, and a vote on the constitution was called for December. However, the convention decreed that the vote was only on the clause that would decide whether Kansas would be a slave or a free state. Free-state residents were convinced that the whole Lecompton document was a fatally flawed defense of slavery: even if voters made Kansas a free state, the Lecompton document said that slaves already in the territory were bound to remain slaves. They boycotted the election, and the proslavery clause won by a vote of 6,226 to 569. Then the new legislature called for a vote on the whole constitution in January 1858. Proslavery residents boycotted this election, and the constitution was defeated by a vote of 10,226 to 162. Both votes were then sent forward to Congress to sort out.

Lecompton Constitution
Proslavery draft written in 1857 by Kansas territorial delegates elected under questionable circumstances; it what was decisively defeated by Congress.

In 1854 and 1855, thousands of "Missouri Ruffians" as their opponents called them arrived in Kansas, well armed and determined to control the territory. Before long, equally well-armed abolitionists from the North began arriving in the territory. Given the presence of so many guns and such anger, it was not surprising that bloodshed quickly followed.

After another long and bitter debate on Kansas in the late spring of 1858—this time with Douglas in opposition to admitting Kansas as a slave state because of the "trickery and juggling"—Congress called for a new vote in Kansas on the Lecompton Constitution. The legislation said that if the constitution passed, Kansas would gain immediate statehood, but if it did not, statehood would be delayed significantly. In August 1858, Kansas voters defeated the Lecompton Constitution and the offer of immediate statehood by a vote of 11,300 to 1,788. Kansas would remain a territory until 1861.

The 4-year battle from 1854 to 1858 gave the territory the name of **Bleeding Kansas** and hardened public opinion North and South. The battle in Kansas not only was confusing but also was violent. Missouri "border ruffians" and Missouri militia intimidated and killed free-state voters. But the violence was not all on one side. Samuel Jones, the country sheriff for Lawrence, Kansas, was shot while trying to serve warrants on the free-state leaders. He survived and led the militia back to town to take prisoners and demolish a hotel, a newspaper office, and the home of the free-state governor. His successor threatened the free-state legislature in 1857 and was killed.

Bleeding Kansas
Violence between pro- and antislavery forces in Kansas Territory after the passage of the Kansas-Nebraska Act in 1854.

John Brown came to Kansas to "strike terror in the hearts of the proslavery people." Brown attacked a small proslavery community near Pottawatomie Creek and killed and mutilated five settlers. The battles continued in 1856 and 1857. Missourians boarded steamboats on the Missouri River to search for antislavery immigrants. Both sides claimed their martyrs. In most parts of the territory, the U.S. Army slowly asserted control, but just before the final resolution in May 1858, proslavery guerrillas shot nine unarmed free-state farmers, and five of them died.

The violence was not limited to Kansas. In Washington, Congressman Preston Brooks of South Carolina, who believed that protecting the status of Kansas as a slave state was a "point of honor," badly beat Massachusetts Senator Charles Sumner in the Senate chamber after Sumner delivered his "Crime Against Kansas" speech favoring a free-state Kansas. In Brooklyn, New York, the nation's most famous

SOUTHERN CHIVALRY — ARGUMENT VERSUS CLUB'S.

Congressman Preston Brooks of South Carolina was enraged by Massachusetts Senator Charles Sumner's antislavery arguments during the debates about Kansas, which Brooks took as an attack on the honor of his family and the South. In May 1856, Brooks came into the Senate chamber and beat Sumner with a cane while he sat at his desk. Sumner never fully recovered from his injuries but remained in the Senate as a staunch Republican through the Civil War and Reconstruction until he died in 1874.

Dred Scott v. Sandford
A Supreme Court case brought by Dred Scott, a slave demanding his freedom based on his residence in a free state and a free territory with his master.

preacher, Henry Ward Beecher, warned of the need to "stand firm," and collected funds for "Beecher's Bibles," which were Springfield rifles to be sent to Kansas. Even after the nation turned to other matters, few Americans forgot the intense emotions Kansas aroused.

The Supreme Court and Dred Scott

While the battle for Kansas transfixed the nation, a court case was making its way through the nation's slow judicial process. The case, ***Dred Scott v. Sandford***, resulted in one of the most far-reaching decisions in the history of the Supreme Court. It began in state courts in St. Louis, Missouri, in 1846 when abolitionists urged Dred Scott, a slave, to sue for his freedom because his owner, an army surgeon, had taken him to Illinois and then on to Fort Snelling in what is now Minnesota (then simply the northern tip of the Louisiana Purchase where the Missouri Compromise banned slavery). After living for years in free territory, his lawyers claimed, Scott had won his freedom.

In a series of trials and appeals, Scott's case went back and forth. Scott lost the first time, but on retrial in state court in St. Louis, he won his freedom. The Missouri Supreme Court then overturned the decision on appeal in 1852 and returned Scott to slavery. Although the Missouri high court had previously found in favor of slaves who had lived in free territory, ideas were hardening across the South, and the court concluded that Missouri law governed the case even though Scott had been in federally controlled free territory for years. Scott's lawyers appealed to the federal courts, and when the district court in Missouri decided against Scott, his lawyers appealed to the U.S. Supreme Court where the case was heard in 1856.

The Supreme Court also decided against Scott. The justices could have based their ruling on fairly narrow grounds. Instead, the majority used the case to make a larger legal point. Considerable (though behind the scenes) pressure was apparently brought to bear on the justices. Chief Justice Roger Taney, however, did not need pressure to speak his mind. On March 6, 1857, he spoke for a majority of the court. In a long and complex decision, Taney made two key points. First, as a black man (presumably even a free black man), Taney said that Scott had no rights that the United States needed to honor. Based on his reading of the Constitution, Taney said that black people "had no rights which a white man was bound to respect." When two dissenting justices noted that blacks had actually been voters in five of the states that had ratified the Constitution in 1789, Taney countered that they might, indeed, "have all the rights and privileges of the citizen of a State," but that they were "not entitled to the rights and privileges of a citizen in any other state." This opinion seemed to directly contradict Article IV, Section 2, of the Constitution, which said, "The citizens of each state shall be entitled to all privileges and immunities of citizens in the several states," but Taney ignored the clause and previous case law.

Second, Taney broadened the ruling. Scott had no standing to bring the case, the Chief Justice said, and even if he did have standing, he did not have a case. Fort Snelling was not actually free territory because the Missouri Compromise was unconstitutional. Congress did not have the right to bar slavery in any federal territories. Depriving slave owners of their slaves, he said, violated the Fifth Amendment that said no one could be deprived of life, liberty, or property without due process of law, and slaves were the private property of their owners. He did not say anything about the lives or liberties of enslaved people. But he did say that Congress "could not authorize a territorial government to exercise" any power to prohibit slavery.

After the Supreme Court's decision on the Dred Scott case, many Americans, North and South, concluded that slavery had to be banned everywhere or nowhere.

The Court not only returned Scott to slavery but also ruled that Congress could not prohibit slavery in any federal territory under any circumstances. Abolitionists soon purchased Scott and set him and his wife free. But the decision seemed to lock millions of their fellow African-Americans either in slavery or in second-class status even if they were free.

The outcome thrilled Southern leaders. The proslavery *Constitutionalist* in Augusta, Georgia, editorialized that "Southern opinion upon the subject of Slavery… is now the supreme law of the land." At the same time, many Northern Democrats were also delighted, seeing the decision as "the funeral sermon" of the new Republican Party. Many moderate Northerners, however, were outraged. William Cullen Bryant, editor of the *New York Evening Post,* wrote that Taney's decision was a "willful perversion" of the Constitution. Republican leaders, especially Seward of New York and Lincoln of Illinois, attacked the decision as the result of a secret negotiation between the Chief Justice and President-elect James Buchanan. Lincoln also said that if the Taney policy stood, then the advocates of slavery would soon make it "lawful in *all* the States…*North* as well as *South*." He promised that, if a Republican were elected president in 1860, he would find a way to undo the decision. The lines between the pro- and antislavery camps were hardening, not only in Congress but also in the country as a whole.

Quick Review Why was the Dred Scott case a significant turning point in public opinion—North and South—in the years leading up to the Civil War?

THE ECONOMY, THE PANIC OF 1857, AND THE LINCOLN-DOUGLAS DEBATES

13.3 Explain how the economic crisis of 1857 and the growing political crises of the decade impacted each other and led the nation to divide.

Historians have long debated the degree to which economic issues, rather than arguments over slavery, caused the Civil War. The disagreements are nearly always ones of emphasis, but most agree that both issues—economic factors in the nation and debates over the morality of slavery—were factors.

The growth of the cotton economy between 1815 and 1860 tied the nation together, creating common interests among Southern slave-owning producers of cotton, Northern mill owners, and owners of ships that transported cotton to Britain. Abolitionist Senator Charles Sumner of Massachusetts despaired of a country dominated by the "lords of the lash and the lords of the loom."

Other economic forces, however, were dividing the country. The opening of the Erie Canal in 1825 created an east–west trade axis from New England through New York and into the Midwestern states of Ohio, Indiana, and Illinois with connections through the Great Lakes to Michigan, Wisconsin, and even Minnesota. This trade network rivaled and then exceeded the trade down Mississippi River. In 1835, 95 percent of the trade in the Ohio Valley flowed south through New Orleans and only 5 percent through New York. But by 1850, more trade went from the Midwest to New York than to New Orleans. Midwesterners who before the mid-1830s saw their economic lives connected to the states that bordered the Mississippi were now much more connected to New York and New England and had little reason to care about the Southern states that had once been so important to them.

As the railroads were built, slowly in the 1820s and 1830s but much more rapidly in the 1840s and 1850s, they also followed the newer trade routes, linking the Midwest to the Northeast while other rail networks linked the interior of the South to Charleston and New Orleans. New settlement followed the trade routes. More and more of the growing population of the upper Midwest came from New York and New England, the most antislavery regions of the country. In the 1850s, the new Republican Party reflected the interests of this fast-growing swath of the nation that stretched from New England into all of the Ohio River Valley and beyond to Indiana, Illinois, and Iowa. Most people in the region tended to be opposed to slavery, even if few were serious abolitionists. In addition, the Republican Party also spoke for their economic interests. John Sherman (brother of Civil War General William Tecumseh Sherman) began his political career as a Whig, but by 1854, he was elected to Congress as a Republican from an Ohio district on the shores of Lake Erie. Sherman said that while the Republican Party was born with "the immediate purpose and aim" of stopping the spread of slavery into the territories, it also supported an increase in the tariff to strengthen American industries; a homestead bill to encourage settlement of the new territories by people who wanted to build small family farms and who had no intention, or money, to bring slaves with them; land grant colleges that would serve agriculture and industry; and a transcontinental railroad that would link California to the East Coast. It was a good summary of what would become the Republicans' economic program in the 1860s and 1870s, and it played well across the region.

However, neither that same economic program nor the Republicans' opposition to the spread of slavery was seen as a benefit in the South, especially the Deep South. The pre–Civil War South was not an economic backwater. Indeed, it was the most prosperous part of the nation in the 1850s, but the prosperity could not be separated from cotton growing and slavery. As much as Southern cotton served as the raw material for New England mills, far more of it was shipped across the Atlantic to the larger mills in England. As much as the South was building railroads—often with slave labor—its rivers and extended coastline meant that water transport served the South better than the North. The Southern planter elite saw far less reason than most Northerners to support federal spending on canals

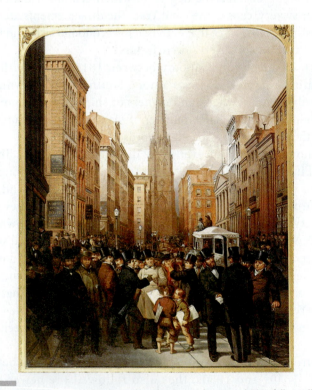

As the price of Midwestern wheat and goods produced in Pennsylvania and Ohio fell rapidly in 1857, panic hit the nation's financial center of New York's Wall Street. Newsboys sold extra editions of newspapers with news brought by telegraph from around the country, and the papers were snapped up by fearful investors.

or a federal tariff that protected Northern industries. Southern-leaning presidents from Polk in the 1840s to Pierce in the 1850s vetoed bills for internal improvement that most Northerners, regardless of political party, badly wanted.

The **Panic of 1857** exacerbated the economic split between the regions. It was much more severe in the North than in the South. Overproduction of Northern wheat helped precipitate the panic. When the Crimean War, which had pitted Britain and France against Russia, ended in 1856, European farmers resumed full-scale wheat production, and prices for American wheat fell sharply. But the English mills continued to need Southern cotton, and the price of cotton held steady. Moreover, in the iron- and coal-producing areas of the country, Pennsylvania and Ohio, demand for steel fell, people lost their jobs, banks failed, and panic ensued. Not surprisingly the Republican platform of 1860 supported a tariff both to provide revenue for the government and to protect Northern industry. The platform solidified support for the Republicans, especially in Pennsylvania and New Jersey. It also showed how deeply these states were cut off from the interests of the South where the tariff raised the cost of manufactured goods but did nothing to keep the price of cotton high.

Panic of 1857
A banking crisis that caused a credit crunch in the North; it was less severe in the South, where high cotton prices spurred a quick recovery.

The Lincoln-Douglas Debates Define the Political Parties

On June 16, 1858, Abraham Lincoln spoke to the Republican State Convention in Springfield, Illinois, that had just nominated him as their candidate against Stephen A. Douglas for the U.S. Senate. Reflecting on the Fugitive Slave Act, the Kansas-Nebraska crisis, and the Dred Scott decision, Lincoln quoted the Bible—well known to all of the convention delegates—and told them: "A house divided against itself cannot stand." He continued:

> I believe this government cannot endure, permanently half *slave* and half *free*.
> I do not expect the Union to be *dissolved*—I do not expect the house to *fall*—
> but I *do* expect it will cease to be divided.
> It will become all one thing, or all the other.
> Either the *opponents* of slavery, will arrest the further spread of it, and place it where the public mind shall rest in the belief that it is in the course of ultimate extinction; or its *advocates* will push it forward, till it should become alike lawful in *all* the States, old as well as new—*North* as well as *South*.

With all that had happened since 1850, Lincoln could see no other option. He begged his fellow Republicans to be sure the outcome was what they wanted. "The result is not doubtful," he concluded. "We shall not fail—if we stand firm, we shall not fail." Some of the delegates who had just nominated Lincoln thought the speech was too radical and would hurt Lincoln in the fall elections but by 1858 he was prepared to stand firm on his ideas.

Later that summer, on August 21, 1858, Democratic Senator Stephan A. Douglas met Lincoln in Ottawa, Illinois, for the first of seven debates they held across Illinois in that election season. Douglas and Lincoln were campaigning to be elected by the Illinois legislature to represent the state in the U.S. Senate. They were also seeking to define the philosophy of their respective political parties. Hundreds attended their debates, and newspapers in every part of the country took their words to thousands of Americans. The debates were long and closely argued. Each sometimes spoke for 2 hours at a time. The speeches and the responses were not sound bites, but carefully reasoned arguments that forced each leader to refine his views and the audience to follow them closely.

At the Ottawa debate, Douglas spoke first. He painted Lincoln and the Republican Party (Black Republicans Douglas called them) as allies of the most radical abolitionists. He attacked Lincoln's "a house divided against itself" speech. "Why can it not exist divided into Free and Slave States?" Douglas asked. "Washington, Jefferson, Franklin, Madison, Hamilton, Jay, and the great men of that day, made this government divided into Free States and Slave States, and left each State perfectly free to do as it pleased on the subject of slavery."

In the 1850s, Frederick Douglass, who had grown up in slavery, became one of the nation's best known abolitionist speakers. Even many who disagreed with, or were frightened by, his words admired his public speakving ability and his capacity to win many to the abolitionist cause.

Douglas also criticized Lincoln's attack on the Dred Scott decision. Douglas said that he agreed with the decision and told his audience that Lincoln's approach would fill Illinois with blacks who would "become citizens and voters, on an equality with yourselves." He warned that Lincoln was trying to "array all the Northern States in one body against the South, to excite a sectional war between the Free States and the Slave States." He and the Democrats, Douglas said, were the party of unity while Lincoln and the Republicans promised only civil war. In response, Lincoln declared that he was no abolitionist and that he had "no prejudice against Southern people." He also said that he would not himself know how to quickly abolish slavery where it already existed and, indeed, would honor all of the South's "constitutional rights," to protect slavery. He would even support the Fugitive Slave Act if it "should not, in its stringency, be more likely to carry a free man into slavery." But the issue for him, Lincoln said, was the spread of slavery in the territories. Lincoln said that he had no interest in "perfect social and political equality with the negro." Douglas's efforts to say that he did were a "fantastic arrangement of words, by which a man can prove a horse-chestnut to be a chestnut horse." Lincoln also attacked Douglas's belief in "popular sovereignty": "When he invites any people, willing to have slavery, to establish it, he is blowing out the moral lights around us."

The Republicans lost the campaign for the legislature, and therefore Lincoln lost the senatorial election of 1858 to Douglas. But the 1858 debates helped shape the core philosophies of the nation's political parties. They also put in the spotlight two political rivals who would meet again in 1860.

13.3   **Quick Review** How did the various expressions about slavery—written, spoken, and acted—deepen the already profound split in the Union?

FROM JOHN BROWN TO THE SECESSION OF THE SOUTH

13.4   Analyze the political impact of John Brown's raid and why Lincoln won the presidential election of 1860 and the southern states then voted to leave.

Mason-Dixon Line
A line surveyed by Charles Mason and Jeremiah Dixon between 1763 and 1767 that settled the border between the then colonies of Pennsylvania and Maryland.

The year 1859 was an off year in American electoral politics. Regardless, in August, not far north of the **Mason-Dixon Line** that divided Pennsylvania from Maryland and thus free states from slave states, people in the small town of Chambersburg, Pennsylvania, suddenly turned their attention to the issue of slavery and abolition. One of the nation's best-known abolitionists, Frederick Douglass, who had escaped from slavery on a Maryland plantation when he was a young adult and began his abolitionist career with William Lloyd Garrison, gave a speech in the Franklin County town. Both the town's Democratic and Republican newspapers gave Douglass high marks as a speaker even though both said they disagreed with his views. But the speech was a cover for the real reason for Douglass being there. He had been summoned for a secret meeting with his old friend John Brown, who was a fugitive for his role in the violence in Kansas and who was living in Chambersburg under the name of Dr. Isaac Smith.

John Brown at Harper's Ferry

Douglass knew that Brown harbored dreams of sparking a slave uprising across the South. Until he met with him that August day in 1859, however, he had no idea how close Brown was to implementing his ideas. Years later, Douglass recounted their meeting while the two went fishing at an old quarry: "The taking of Harper's Ferry, of which

American Voices

Lydia Maria Child and Governor Henry A. Wise, Letters Regarding John Brown, 1859

When she heard of John Brown's raid and trial, Lydia Maria Child, a well-known Massachusetts abolitionist, defender of women's rights and the rights of American Indians, who was also a popular children's author, deplored the violence of Brown's effort but offered to go to Virginia to support him while he recovered from his wounds and awaited execution. Virginia Governor Henry A. Wise, known as a moderate, responded, offering Child protection in Virginia but also making it clear he held her and her fellow abolitionists guilty of inspiring Brown's violence. Their correspondence was published in Garrison's Liberator.

Wayland, Mass., Oct. 26th, 1859.

Governor Wise! …Enclosed is a letter to Capt. John Brown. Will you have the kindness, after reading it yourself, to transmit it to the prisoner?

I and all my large circle of abolition acquaintances were taken by surprise when news came of Capt. Brown's recent attempt; nor do I know of a single person who would have approved of it had they been apprised of his intention. But I and thousands of others feel a natural impulse of sympathy for the brave and suffering man. Perhaps God, who sees the inmost of our souls, perceives some such sentiment in your heart also. He needs a mother or sister to dress his wounds, and speak soothingly to him. Will you allow me to perform that mission of humanity?...

I have been for years an uncompromising abolitionist, and I should scorn to deny it or apologize for it as much as John Brown himself would do. Believing in peace principles, I deeply regret the step that the old veteran has taken…. But…I will also say that if I believed our religion justified men in fighting for freedom, I should consider the enslaved everywhere as best entitled to that right. Such an avowal is a simple, frank expression of my sense of natural justice.

Yours, respectfully,   L. MARIA CHILD.

Richmond, Va., Oct. 29th, 1859.

Madam: …I will forward the letter for John Brown, a prisoner under our laws…for the crimes of murder, robbery and treason, which you ask me to transmit to him....

You ask me, further, to allow you to perform the mission "of mother or sister, to dress his wounds and speak soothingly to him." By this, of course, you mean to be allowed to visit him in his cell, and to minister to him in the offices of humanity. Why should you not be so allowed, Madam? Virginia and Massachusetts are involved in no civil war, and the Constitution "which unites them in one confederacy" guarantees to you privileges and immunities of a citizen of the United States in the State of Virginia. That Constitution I am sworn to support, and am, therefore, bound to protect your privileges and immunities as a citizen of Massachusetts coming into Virginia for any lawful and peaceful purpose.

Coming, as you propose, to minister to the captive in prison, you will be met, doubtless, by all our people, not only in a chivalrous, but in a Christian spirit…your mission being merciful and humane, will not only be allowed, but respected, if not welcomed….

I could not permit an insult even to a woman in her walk of charity among us, though it be to one who whetted knives of butchery for our mothers, sisters, daughters and babes. We have no sympathy with your sentiments of sympathy with Brown....His attempt was a natural consequence of your sympathy, and the errors of that sympathy ought to make you doubt its virtue from the defect on his conduct. But it is not of this I should speak. When you arrive at Charlestown, if you go there, it will be for the Court and its officers, the Commonwealth's attorney, sheriff and jailer, to say whether you may see and wait on the prisoner. But, whether you are thus permitted or not, (and you will be, if my advice can prevail,) you may rest assured that he will be humanely, lawfully and mercifully dealt by us in prison and on trial.

Respectfully,   HENRY A. WISE

Source: Anti-Slavery Tracts, No. 1. New Series (Boston: American Anti-Slavery Society, 1860).

Thinking Critically

1. Documentary Analysis

How would you describe the tone of the two letters? What might explain the authors' strenuous efforts to demonstrate respect for one another?

2. Historical Interpretation

What light do these letters shed on regional tensions in the years before the Civil War? What values and beliefs do the authors appear to share? On what points are they divided?

Captain Brown had merely hinted before was now declared as his settled purpose." Douglass thought Brown's idea was crazy, would result in immediate defeat, and as "an attack upon the Federal government…would array the whole country against us." Brown was not persuaded. Douglass left Chambersburg dejected and fearful, perhaps doubly so because the former slave Shields Green who had accompanied Douglass to the meeting had decided to stay with Brown. As he told Douglass, "I b'leve I'll go wid de ole man."

All that summer, Brown had been planning for his raid. In the fall, he moved from Chambersburg to a farmhouse in Maryland not far from Harper's Ferry, where a lightly guarded federal arsenal stood at the junction of the Potomac and Shenandoah rivers. Brown and his army of 16 white and five black men began their attack on the evening of October 16, 1859. They were confident that the slaves of the region would rise up to join them. As they entered Harper's Ferry, they cut telegraph lines and took hostages, but they were also quickly attacked. They were encircled by angry townspeople, and within hours, federal troops under the command of Robert E. Lee arrived in Harper's Ferry. When Brown refused to surrender, the troops attacked, killing or capturing most of the rebels. Only a few escaped. Brown was wounded. He and the other captured fighters were tried on charges of insurrection and treason against the state of Virginia. The jury took less than an hour to find them all guilty, and they were sentenced to hang on December 2, 1859.

Brown used the 6 weeks between his arrest and execution effectively. His calm words and actions after the raid, much more than the raid itself, made him a hero in much of the North and a frightening figure in the South. At his trial, Brown told the court:

> Now, if it is deemed necessary that I should forfeit my life for the further-ance of the ends of justice, and mingle my blood further with the blood of my children and with the blood of millions in this slave country whose rights are disregarded by wicked, cruel, and unjust enactments, I say, let it be done.

While in prison, Brown also managed to conduct interviews and write letters that were widely circulated. He told a reporter from the *New York Herald*, "You may dispose of me very easily…but this question is still to be settled—this negro question I mean—the end of that is not yet."

This famous painting of John Brown on his way to the gallows, stopping to kiss a slave child, shows Brown as the hero to the antislavery cause, which is the way that many in the North were beginning to see him.

Immediately after the October raid, virtually everyone—Democrats, Republicans, even many abolitionists—condemned Brown as an insane fanatic. Soon, however, public opinion started to shift. In the North, Brown's words and actions began to galvanize a wide spectrum of public opinion. People who initially dismissed him as insane started, much to their own surprise, to be swayed by his condemnation of slavery and—even more surprising to themselves—to consider his claim that violence might be needed to end it.

Henry David Thoreau's "Plea for Captain John Brown" argued that Brown's violence could not be compared with the violence of slavery. The pacifist William Lloyd Garrison criticized the raid but came to view it as "a desperate self-sacrifice for the purpose of giving an earthquake shock to the slave system." Many Northerners concluded that Brown was a hero.

Northern sympathy for Brown sent a chill through the white South. With the emergence of the telegraph and faster printing presses, news traveled fast. Many Southerners became convinced that most Northerners were in league with radical abolitionists like Brown and with those slaves who harbored thoughts of revolt. Many in the South started to think that abolitionists really did want to promote a slave uprising. In response, much of the South quickly became an armed camp, and doubts about remaining in the Union began to grow.

The Election of 1860

The Republican Party that nominated Lincoln for the Senate in 1858 was still very new on a fast-changing political landscape. The first election that the new Republican Party contested had been in 1854 and resulted in a Republican Speaker of the House of Representatives. The Republicans, it seemed, were the party of the future. In contrast, the Democrat and the Whig parties had struggled with opposing members that included antislavery Northerners and proslavery Southerners. The Kansas situation had split both parties and was the death knell of the Whigs. They never again nominated a candidate for president.

By the 1856 presidential elections, the nation had three political parties, two of them new. The Democrats managed to continue as an uneasy coalition. The Republicans consolidated their strength in the North but were virtually nonexistent in the South. A third party, the American Party, more commonly known as the Know Nothing Party, gained strength as anti-immigrant hysteria swept the country. The Democrats nominated James Buchanan from Pennsylvania whose prime strength seemed to be an exceeding vagueness about slavery and who had been seeking the presidency since serving as Polk's secretary of state in the 1840s. The Republicans nominated war hero and adventurer John C. Frémont. And the Know-Nothings nominated former president Millard Fillmore. Fillmore carried only Maryland where anti-immigrant feelings were especially strong, while Frémont carried most of the most Northern states and Buchanan carried the South, including the more moderate parts of the South, plus Illinois, Indiana, and California, winning easily. If Buchanan entered the White House with any mandate in 1857, it was to avoid the issue of slavery. It was one the new president could not possibly fulfill, try though he did.

After 1856, the Know Nothing Party faded rapidly. Opposition to immigration did not have staying power as a political issue, especially when new immigrants provided the swing votes in key states like New York. Most Know-Nothings became Republicans in an uneasy alliance with the proimmigrant faction of the party. Republicans were also divided on just how far to go in embracing the abolitionists among them. As late as June 1859, Lincoln had begged Ohio Senator Salmon P. Chase to be sure that the Ohio Republican Party's demand for "a repeal of the atrocious Fugitive Slave Law" not become an issue in the national Republican convention because "it will explode it." But after 1857, it was the Democrats' turn to divide as it became impossible for Northern moderates like Douglas and Southern extremists like Jefferson Davis to stay in the same political organization. Everyone knew that the elections of 1860 were going to involve tough political contests. No one knew they would lead to war.

While the Lincoln-Douglas debates of 1858 established Abraham Lincoln as a national political leader, it was by no means certain that he would be the Republican nominee for president in 1860. Lincoln himself had mixed feelings about a presidential nomination since he had hopes of a career in the U.S. Senate. The frontrunner for nomination was New York Senator William Henry Seward, a former Whig and a founder of the Republican Party. But Seward also had many enemies, people who thought he was too radical or who just did not trust him. Many, including Lincoln, thought that if Seward did not get the nomination on the first ballot, his support would melt away. Two other prominent Republicans were also in the field—Governor Salmon Chase of Ohio, one of the party's staunchest opponents of slavery, and Judge Edward Bates of Missouri, the candidate of the more moderate Republicans. And then there was Lincoln, respected by everyone, an extraordinary speaker, and more moderate than either Seward or Chase.

Lincoln's convention manager, Judge David Davis, reported to Lincoln, "We are laboring to make you the second choice of all the Delegations we can, where we can't make you first choice." The strategy worked. While Seward took the lead on the first ballot, Lincoln—not Chase or Bates—came in second. By the third ballot, it was all over as delegates made Lincoln's nomination unanimous. Of course, being the nominee of a new political party did not guarantee victory. Seward, Chase, and Bates all campaigned hard for Lincoln, and after the election, he appointed all three to his Cabinet as secretaries of state and treasury as well as attorney general. But in between the nomination and the victorious election, there was a hard-fought presidential campaign.

Given the tensions in the country in the summer of 1860, it is not surprising that traditional political parties splintered. A faction of the old Whig Party reemerged as the Constitutional Union Party. It nominated slaveholder John Bell of Tennessee for president and Edward Everett of Massachusetts for vice president on a vague platform of "the Constitution, the Union, and the Enforcement of the Laws" (presumably a reference to the Fugitive Slave Act). Some saw this small party as the best hope to hold the country together through new compromises. Others ridiculed them as the "Old Gentlemen's Party," since most of those who campaigned for Bell were well past age 60.

The Democrats, who had elected the last two presidents, met in Charleston, South Carolina, in April 1860. They were deeply divided. Stephen A. Douglas was the frontrunner for the nomination, but although Douglas had once been popular in the South, after his opposition to admitting Kansas as a slave state, most Southern political leaders now considered him to be a traitor to their cause. Mississippi Senator Jefferson Davis insisted on a platform that pledged the party to protect "the constitutional right of any citizen of the United States to take his slave property into the common territories." But Douglas's supporters could not stomach abandoning their candidate's long-held commitment to "popular sovereignty" and would not support a platform that opened all the territories to slavery regardless of what the voters said. After 57 ballots, the convention could not agree on any nominee and adjourned to meet again in Baltimore in 6 weeks to try again.

When the Democrats convened again in Baltimore, however, the same splits were evident. One-third of the delegates—nearly all of the Southerners and a few proslavery Northerners—walked out of the convention. The remaining Democrats nominated Douglas and adopted a popular sovereignty platform. The delegates who had walked out of the convention organized their own convention and nominated John C. Breckinridge of Kentucky, who was Buchanan's vice president, adopting the platform advocated by Jefferson Davis. Southern Democrats understood that the split in the party would benefit the Republicans, but they were so angry with Douglas that they were willing to accept that result. Some also believed that a Republican victory would build support for their real goal, which was secession. A Democratic Party leader and former congressman, William Lowndes Yancey, told a crowd in Charleston that it was time for "a new revolution," and "an Independent Southern Republic."

This political cartoon published during the 1860 presidential election depicts Lincoln and Douglas, on the left, fighting over much of the country while, in the center, Breckinridge tries to tear off the South and, on the right, Bell, with glue pot in hand, tries to put the whole thing back together.

The Republican ticket did not even appear on ballots in most of the South, and Republican candidates would have risked their lives campaigning in the region. Lincoln campaigned against Douglas in the North. Breckinridge campaigned against Bell in the South. No one had ever seen a presidential election quite like it. Despite the crazy split, the North, with its larger population, was going to settle the election. Douglas had a chance to win the election if he and the Northern Democrats could carry enough Northern states and some of the slave states known as "border states" where Northern influence was strongest and the attachment to slavery was weakest (see Map 13-2). Douglas claimed to be the only candidate who could unite the nation. He continued to paint Lincoln as a radical and tried to frighten Northern voters by saying that Lincoln would bring blacks into the North as the social equals of whites who would also compete with whites for jobs.

The Republicans had a lot going for them. They were new. They attracted young, first-time voters. They were united. Their economic policies appealed to many in the North. Even so, some abolitionists did not trust the Republicans. William Lloyd Garrison said that "the Republican party means to do nothing, can do nothing, for the abolition of slavery in the slave states." Frederick Douglass, perhaps more of a realist, countered, saying that a Republican victory "must and will be hailed as an anti-slavery triumph."

On Election Day in November 1860, the breadth of the Republican victory was clear. Breckenridge carried most of the South. Bell won Virginia, Kentucky, and Tennessee. Although Douglas received far more votes than either Breckenridge or Bell, he carried only Missouri and half the electoral votes of New Jersey. Lincoln received only 40 percent of the national popular vote, but it was the most of any single candidate, and his 180 electoral votes were a solid majority. As cheering crowds in his hometown of Springfield, Illinois, celebrated, Abraham Lincoln, who had served one term in Congress and had never held an executive position, became the president-elect of the United States. What his election would mean for him and for the country only time would tell. Few thought it would lead to a long and bloody war.

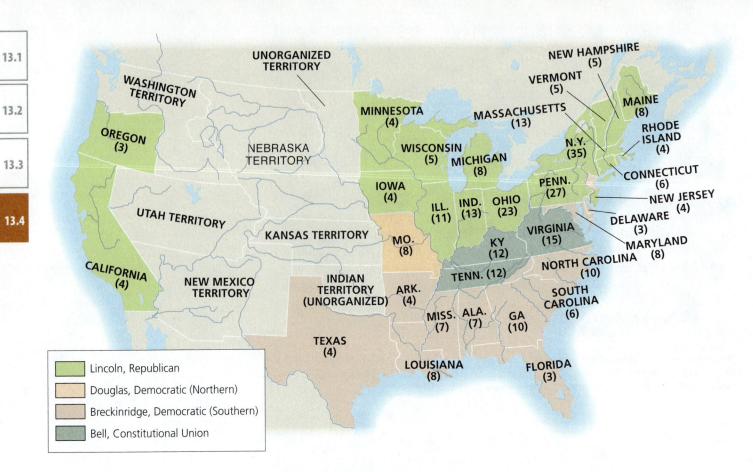

MAP 13-2 The Election of 1860. This map, indicating the electoral vote of each state, illustrates the regional nature of the final vote in the 1860 presidential election. Lincoln carried all of the North as well as California and Oregon. Breckinridge, the southern Democrat, carried all of the Deep South and beyond. Bell, the candidate who called for glossing over all the differences, carried the key border states of Virginia, Kentucky, and Tennessee that Douglas had been counting on. In the end, Douglas carried only the slave state of Missouri and split the electoral votes of New Jersey with Lincoln.

As Alexander McClure, a prominent Pennsylvania attorney, wrote 40 years after the Civil War, "The North believed that the South was more bombastic than earnest in the threat of provoking civil war for the protection of slavery, and the South believed that Northern people were mere money-getters, ready to yield anything rather than accept fratricidal conflict."

The Secession of the South

As some had predicted, Lincoln's election provided Southern secessionists with just the rationale they needed. Many Southerners, including moderates, were furious about Lincoln's election. They saw the breadth of Northern support for a committed free-soil candidate as one more effort to exclude slavery from the territories. They also saw it as part of a larger pattern that included Northern failure to enforce the Fugitive Slave Act and Northern support for John Brown. The *Charleston Courier* editorialized that Lincoln's election meant it was time for "a Southern Confederacy," something "desired by all true hearted Southerners."

The night after the election, a huge crowd of demonstrators in Charleston demanded action, and the South Carolina legislature called a special convention to consider secession. On December 20, 1860, the convention voted 169–0 in favor of dissolving "the union now subsisting between South Carolina and other states." Other states in the Deep South followed. In January 1861, Mississippi, Florida, Alabama, Georgia, and Louisiana all voted to leave the Union, followed by Texas on February 1. None of the other states after South Carolina were unanimous in their votes, but over 80 percent of the delegates in each of these states voted for secession, which was probably a fairly accurate reflection of the opinions of the white male population. Nevertheless, a minority in most Southern states, even in the Deep South, preferred to wait and see what Lincoln would actually do, but as Louisiana Senator Judah P. Benjamin wrote, the "prudent and conservative men" of the South were not able "to stem the wild torrent of passion which is carrying everything before it."

The reality was, however, that the demands of these "prudent and conservative men" of the South were for things to which Lincoln would not agree. When Kentucky Senator John Crittenden proposed the **Crittenden Compromise** to preserve the Union by extending the Missouri Compromise line to the Pacific and thus protect slavery in the New Mexico Territory and California, Lincoln refused to consider the compromise even though his close ally William Seward urged him to do so. As he had made clear in his various campaigns, he did not intend to abolish slavery where it existed, but he did not want to spread slavery any further. Lincoln had also come to believe that any effort at appeasement would do nothing to control slavery but would simply open the door for continuing demands. The pressing question in February and March of 1861 was about the slave states that had not yet voted to secede, the so-called border states that were closer to the North, less militant in their defense of slavery, and perhaps most likely to stay with the Union: Maryland, Arkansas, North Carolina, Delaware, Missouri and, most of all, the strategically placed states of Kentucky, Tennessee, and Virginia—the largest and most industrialized state in the South. Lincoln did not want to lose them, at least not all of them.

In the face of the secession crisis, the wait from November 1860 to the presidential inauguration in March 1861 seemed especially long. The outgoing Buchanan administration, never decisive, seemed more unsure of itself than ever. Rumors of a Southern invasion or an internal coup filled the capital. Many senators joined Seward and Crittenden in seeking a compromise that would avoid secession or war. Others in and out of Congress proposed all sorts of solutions, including even abolishing the office of president. The senators and representatives of the seven states that had voted to secede by February 1 packed their belongings, gave their farewell speeches, and left town to organize the government of the Confederate States of America—a project they accomplished with amazing speed at a 6-day convention in Montgomery, Alabama, where they drafted a temporary constitution and selected a provisional president and vice president. In the meantime, the rest of the country seemed frozen.

Although the states of the Deep South voted to leave the Union, conventions in Virginia, Arkansas, and Missouri did not vote on secession. North Carolina and Tennessee did not even hold conventions. But leaders in all of these states warned that any violence by the federal government against those states that had voted to leave the Union would force them to depart also. Some in the North seemed happy to see part of the South depart. The *Chicago Tribune* said that if South Carolina wanted to leave, "let her go, and like a limb lopped from a healthy trunk wilt and rot where she falls." In New York, Horace Greeley's *Tribune* said, "If the Cotton States shall become satisfied that they can do better out of the Union than in it, we insist on letting them go." However, secession angered others in the North.

One resident of Illinois wrote to Congress saying, "We elected Lincoln, and are just as willing, if necessity requires, to fight for him." A resident of Ohio wrote that Lincoln "must enforce the laws of the U.S. states against all rebellion, no matter what the consequences." Even Senator Seward's wife criticized her husband's efforts at compromise, telling him, "Compromise based on the idea that the preservation of the Union is more important than the liberty of nearly 4,000,000 human beings cannot be right." While it is likely that many Northern white voters would have been willing to preserve the Union at the cost of 4 million people remaining in slavery, a good

Crittenden Compromise
A last-ditch effort at a compromise to amend the Constitution to protect slavery in states where it existed.

portion of Northerners—though far from all—seemed to be ready to fight rather than let the Union be dissolved. In that tense and uncertain situation, after months of waiting, Lincoln made his way from Springfield to Washington.

Abraham Lincoln was inaugurated as the 16th president of the United States on March 4, 1861. His inaugural address broke little new ground. He said that he considered secession illegal and that he would assert federal authority, especially over forts and other federal installations in the South. He insisted that he had no interest in interfering with slavery in the states where it existed. And he promised to enforce the Fugitive Slave Act while also asserting that he wanted stronger protection against free people being kidnapped in the name of enforcing the law. In closing, he made a poetic plea that the Union must be preserved:

> We are not enemies, but friends. We must not be enemies. Though passion may have strained, it must not break our bonds of affection. The mystic chords of memory, stretching from every battle-field, and patriot grave, to every living heart and hearthstone, all over this broad land, will yet swell the chorus of the Union, when again touched, as surely they will be, by the better angels of our nature.

Northern response to the speech was mixed. Garrison's *Liberator* noted that Lincoln's insistence that free blacks needed protection from the Fugitive Slave Act represented the first time any president had spoken of citizenship rights for blacks—a direct contradiction of the Dred Scott decision. Other abolitionists were disappointed. Many moderates agreed with the Jersey City newspaper that said, "it was hardly possible for Mr. Lincoln to speak with more mildness."

Confederate leaders did not see the speech as mild. Lincoln's refusal to recognize the right of secession and his claim on the federal property in the South seemed to them to be a prelude to war. Two days after the speech, the Confederate Congress authorized a call for 100,000 troops. Lincoln did not respond by making any similar call of his own. One of his advisors, Orville H. Browning, had written to the president that it was "very important that the traitors shall be the aggressors.…[T]hen the government will stand justified, before the entire country, in repelling that aggression." That policy was exactly the one Lincoln planned to follow.

Conflict seemed most likely to begin at Fort Sumter, a new federal installation guarding the harbor of Charleston, South Carolina. Sitting within view of the city where secession had begun, Fort Sumter was a dramatic symbol of federal authority in the heart of the Confederacy. The 80-man garrison was commanded by Major Robert Anderson, a former slaveholder from Kentucky, whose decades in the army had made him a devoted supporter of federal authority. Soon after their vote to secede from the Union in December 1860, South Carolina authorities demanded that outgoing President Buchanan remove the federal garrison and hand the fort over to them. In an uncharacteristic show of strength, Buchanan refused and tried to reinforce the fort in January 1861. South Carolina fired on the supply ship—but not the fort—and the ship turned back. By the time Lincoln came to office in March, Anderson was running low on supplies and knew he would have to either surrender or evacuate soon.

On April 6, after some hesitation, the new president announced that he was sending a supply ship with food and medicine, but not arms, to Fort Sumter. Jefferson Davis was not willing to allow the federal presence in what Davis now considered an independent country and ordered Pierre G. T. Beauregard, the officer in charge of Confederate troops in Charleston, to attack the fort. On April 12, 1861, at 4:30 a.m., shore batteries in Charleston began to shell Fort Sumter and continued to do so for the next day and a half. On April 13, out of food and ammunition, Major Anderson surrendered. Anderson and the defending troops were allowed to leave, and they sailed to New York where they were greeted as heroes, but the Confederates had control of the fort. The Confederates had won the battle, but they had fired on the American flag and started a war.

This popular illustration of the firing on Fort Sumter adds drama to the scene. Confederate guns did fire on the fort almost nonstop on April 12 and 13, and the fort's defenders, with very little ammunition, fired back on occasion before finally, out of food and ammunition, they surrendered on April 13.

President Lincoln declared that a state of insurrection existed and called on the state governors for 75,000 volunteers while also ordering the expansion of the regular army and navy and recalling some troops from the West. The attack and Lincoln's response brought unity—even if temporary—to most of the North. Stephen A. Douglas, though seriously ill, came to the White House to promise his support and then returned to Illinois to tell Democrats and Republicans that they owed undivided loyalty to the Union.

As the president focused on preserving the Union, some African-Americans and their supporters called the looming war "a White Man's war." Lincoln had made it clear, they said, that the fighting was to "save the union" not necessarily to free the enslaved. Nevertheless, some abolitionists saw an opportunity. Senator Charles Sumner of Massachusetts reminded Lincoln that "under the war power the right had come to him to emancipate the slaves." The black-owned *Weekly Anglo-African* told readers that the slaves "have a clear and decided idea of what they want—Liberty." It would take time before the president or Northern public opinion would agree, but some supported the goal of emancipation from the first days of the war, especially slaves who followed the news closely.

Lincoln's call for federal troops united the South. Tennessee's governor announced that his state "will not furnish a single man for the purpose of coercion, but fifty thousand if necessary for the defense of our rights and those of our Southern brothers." Within days of the firing on Fort Sumter and Lincoln's call for troops, every border state had begun to consider secession and four—Virginia, North Carolina, Tennessee, and Arkansas—voted to join the Confederacy. The 88 to 55 vote to secede in Virginia was far from South Carolina's unanimity, and the western counties of Virginia later declared their loyalty to the Union. Representatives from that area took Virginia's seats in Congress until West Virginia could be organized as a separate state in 1863.

Missouri had its own civil war that started with mob violence in St. Louis where most German immigrants favored the Union cause while recent arrivals from the South supported the Confederacy. The Confederate government admitted Missouri as its 12th state, but Union loyalists also organized their own state government. Two opposing Missouri state governments sent representatives to both Washington and Richmond while lawlessness reigned in most of the state throughout the war.

Kentucky declared neutrality. Since there was probably more proslavery and pro-Confederacy sentiment in Kentucky than in any other slave state that remained in the Union, Lincoln courted the state carefully. If Kentucky seceded, the border between the United States and the Confederacy would be the Ohio River, dangerously far north. If Kentucky stayed in the Union, then Lincoln and his generals would have much easier access to multiple points of attack on the heartland of the Confederacy. Given its strategic importance, Lincoln was reported to have said that "he hoped to have God on his side, but he must have Kentucky." He got Kentucky. The state did not secede, and sentiment for preserving the Union was strong in that state, though Kentucky sent soldiers to both sides. Perhaps more than anywhere else, the Civil War in Kentucky was a war of brother against brother. Four of Henry Clay's grandsons fought for the Confederacy and three for the Union.

The other two border states also remained loyal to the Union: Delaware's northerly location and the few slaves there made the decision almost inevitable. Maryland's loyalty to the Union was assured by the influx of federal troops and Lincoln's arrest of some pro-Confederacy members of the state legislature. If Maryland had joined the Confederacy, Washington would have been cut off from the rest of the country, and Lincoln was not going to let that happen. Thus Maryland, Delaware, and Kentucky remained as slave states within the Union throughout the duration of the war while Virginia and Missouri were represented in both the Union and Confederate congresses. After Union victories in Louisiana and Arkansas, those states were also represented in the U.S. Congress by one set of people while others represented them in the Confederate Congress.

Despite Lincoln's success in retaining some of the border states, the loss of others, especially Virginia, was a severe blow to the Union. Over half of all those who fought in the Confederate Army came from border states, including several of the South's most prominent generals. On the day Virginia voted to secede, Robert E. Lee was offered command of the Union army but responded, "I cannot raise my hand against my birthplace, my home, my children." Lee resigned from the U.S. Army and eventually commanded the Confederate Army of Northern Virginia. Almost as important, Virginia included the Tredegar Iron Works in Richmond, the only factory in the South capable of making heavy shells and armor, and the federal arsenal at Harper's Ferry and the Gosport Navy Yard. All of these facilities were in Confederate hands by the end of April.

Even after the attack on Fort Sumter and the secession of the border states, many doubted that a real war would take place. People in the North were confident that the South would come to its senses, perhaps after an easy Union conquest of Richmond, Virginia. People in the South were confident that the North was not really up for a fight, certainly not a fight to end slavery where it had existed for over 200 years and probably not a fight to save the Union either. Both sides were terribly wrong.

 Quick Review How did Lincoln's election impact the thinking of people in the South and, therefore, the course of U.S. history?

CONCLUSION

Throughout the 1850s, divisions between the North and the slaveholding South intensified despite efforts of some politicians on both sides to keep growing tensions in check. The burning question that continually threatened to divide the nation—would slavery be permitted to expand into new territories and states—could not be amicably decided.

Attempts by Southerners to defend the institution of slavery, and to ensure that slavery could expand into new states in the West, were met by growing choruses of antislavery sentiment in the North. Once-moderate opponents of slavery hardened their positions against the South as the events of the decade unfolded. Abolitionism, whose adherents saw slavery as an evil that had to be destroyed, continued to grow in force, and many in the North, regardless of their opinions about racial equality, simply did not want the future of the country to be defined by slave labor. Slave labor, if it were allowed to exceed the confines of the South, would undermine the value of the "free labor" ideology of the North.

California's application for statehood endangered the balance of power in the Senate between the North and the South. In an effort to find a new middle ground, the Compromise of 1850, originally planned by the aging Senator Henry Clay of Kentucky, admitted California to the Union as a free state but gave Southerners several incentives for resisting secession, including a new, strengthened Fugitive Slave Act. But the Fugitive Slave Act infuriated many in the North, and Northern reluctance to enforce the law infuriated many in the South, even people who themselves did not hold slaves.

The Compromise of 1850 did not save the Union for long. Harriet Beecher Stowe's 1852 novel, *Uncle Tom's Cabin*, written in response to her own anger about the Fugitive Slave Act, may have seemed to be a romanticized version of events to some, but it brought the reality of the pain of slavery home to many in the North. It quickly became a best seller and inflamed public opinion. When Congress passed the Kansas-Nebraska Act in 1854 in an effort to organize a government for the previously Unorganized Territory between Minnesota and Oregon, the legislation provided new opportunities for slavery to spread, even in regions north of the geographical divide between free and slave that had been established by the Missouri Compromise in 1820. The result was not only national tension but a civil war in Kansas so bloody that the territory came to be known as "Bleeding Kansas." In 1857, the Supreme Court's landmark decision in *Dred Scott v. Sandford* triggered further outrage in the North when it declared that the federal government had no authority to regulate the spread of slavery in any of the territories. In that same year, the Panic of 1857, which hit the North far more than the South, illustrated how distinct the two regions had become in their economies. Later, Southerners were outraged by Northern sympathy for the radical actions of John Brown when he attacked the federal arsenal at Harper's Ferry, Virginia (now in West Virginia but then part of the state of Virginia), in 1859. These events deepened sectional tensions and rivalries. As the nation responded, a new political party, the Republican Party, emerged, and an established political party, the Whigs, dissolved. At the same time, Abraham Lincoln gained national prominence as he campaigned first for a U.S. Senate seat and then for the presidency. With Lincoln's election to the presidency in 1860, tensions came to a head: a majority of Southern states seceded from the Union and civil war, which many hoped and expected would be short, began.

CHAPTER REVIEW What areas of conflict between North and South led to the Civil War? What do most historians consider to be the single most important cause of the war? Why?

Chapter 13   Chapter Review

FROM UNION TO DISUNION

13.1 Analyze the political jockeying in Congress and how reaction to the Fugitive Slave Act and the publication of *Uncle Tom's Cabin*, changed the opinions of many Americans—South and the North—making a break between them hard to avoid.

Review Questions

1. **Historical Interpretation**
   What light does the debate over the admission of territories acquired by the United States at the conclusion of the War with Mexico shed on the root issues dividing the North and South in the decades before the Civil War?

2. **Crafting Arguments**
   How did passage of the Kansas-Nebraska Act contribute to the rise of the Republican Party and the demise of the Whigs?

3. **Crafting Arguments**
   How did the Fugitive Slave Act of 1850 affect public opinion about slavery in the North? How would you explain the impact of the law?

BLEEDING KANSAS AND *DRED SCOTT V. SANDFORD*

13.2 Analyze the causes and consequences of the battle over slavery in Kansas and the Supreme Court's decision in the Dred Scott case and the impact of those events on public opinion.

Review Questions

4. **Contextualization**
   Why did both pro- and antislavery forces believe that victory in Kansas was critical to their cause?

5. **Crafting Arguments**
   Why did the Supreme Court ruling in the Dred Scott case make a peaceful resolution of the conflict between the North and the South over slavery less likely?

THE ECONOMY, THE PANIC OF 1857, AND THE LINCOLN-DOUGLAS DEBATES

13.3 Explain how the economic crisis of 1857 and the growing political crises of the decade impacted each other and led the nation to divide.

Review Question

6. **Contextualization**
   What light do the Lincoln-Douglas debates shed on Lincoln's views on slavery and race in 1858?

FROM JOHN BROWN TO THE SECESSION OF THE SOUTH

13.4 Analyze the political impact of John Brown's raid and why Lincoln won the presidential election of 1860 and southern states then vote to leave the Union?

Review Questions

7. **Historical Interpretation**
   How did John Brown's 1859 raid on Harper's Ferry help radicalize public opinion in both the North and the South?

8. **Crafting Arguments**
   Defend or refute the following statement: "After Lincoln's election in November 1860, war between the North and the South was inevitable."

And the War Came: The Civil War

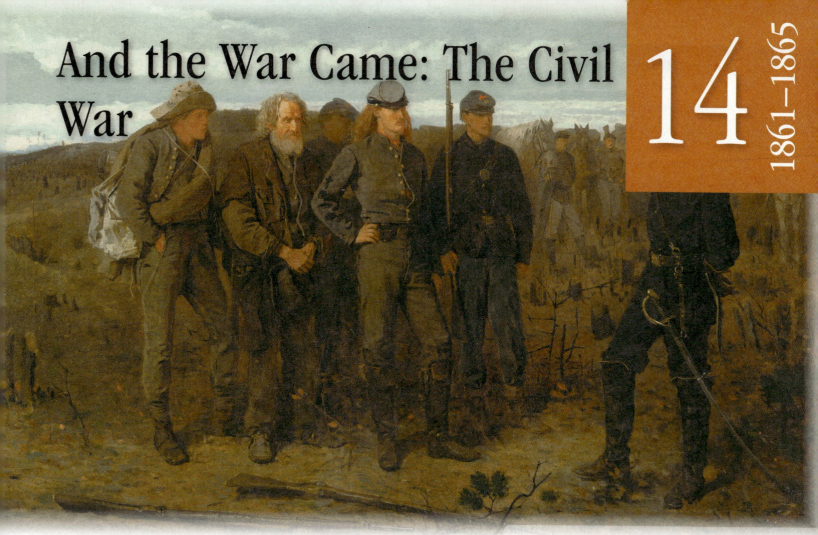

North and South, men volunteered with enthusiasm to serve in their respective armies. These new Confederate soldiers, like their Northern counterparts, reflect a commitment that did not always last as the long years of fighting the war continued. Homer, Winslow (1836-1910.) Prisoners form the Front. 1866. Oil on canvas, 24x38 in. (61 x 96.5 cm). Gift of Mrs. Frank B, Porter, 1922 (22.207). Metropolitan Museum of Art, New York, NY, U.S.A. Image copyright © The Metropolitan Museum of Art. Image source: Art Resource, NY

Once Fort Sumter had been fired on, large patriotic rallies were held North and South. Of course, what it meant to be patriotic varied depending on where one lived. Calls for volunteers by Confederate and Union authorities were quickly oversubscribed. Young men did not want to miss out on the fun and glory of what everyone thought would be a short war and an easy victory. A Confederate volunteer from Mississippi wrote home in June 1861 that he was ready "to fight the Yankees—all fun and frolic." On the Union side a New York volunteer wrote "I and the rest of the boys are in fine spirits…feeling like larks."

Letters from new recruits also showed seriousness of purpose. A New Jersey soldier wrote that he joined the army because "Our glorious institutions are likely to be destroyed," while a Midwestern recruit said that his service was "a duty I owe to my country and to my children to do what I can to preserve this government." Sentiment among soldiers in the Confederacy was equally patriotic. Mississippi's Lucius Lamar, who would achieve high rank in the Confederate army, said, "Thank God! We have a country at last to live for, to pray for, to fight for, and if necessary to die for." An enlisted man in the Confederate army gave a simple answer when he was asked after his capture why he, a nonslaveholder, fought for the South, "I'm fighting because you're down here." Soldiers were sent off in new uniforms with cheering parades. The war did not long remain so lighthearted.

CHAPTER OBJECTIVE

Demonstrate an understanding of the strategies involved in fighting a civil war and the impact of the war on American life—North and South.

LEARNING OBJECTIVES

FORT SUMTER TO ANTIETAM, 1861–1862

Explain how the early battles of the war shaped future events.

14.1

THE ROAD TO EMANCIPATION

Analyze how the war influenced attitudes toward slavery in white and black communities, leading to the Emancipation Proclamation and to black soldiers in the Union army.

14.2

THE HOME FRONT—SHORTAGES, OPPOSITION, RIOTS, AND BATTLES

Explain how the war's death toll and civilian shortages affected life—North and South—during the war.

14.3

FROM GETTYSBURG TO APPOMATTOX AND BEYOND

Analyze the strategies and costs of fighting a long and terrible war.

14.4

This chapter traces life in the United States through the 4 years of the Civil War. The battles that were fought over those 4 long years determined the war's outcome. But the fighting also helped shape public opinion. No one, North or South, was prepared for the terrible death toll of the war, and the fear of being killed or losing loved ones haunted almost everyone in the United States during the Civil War. Ideas were also changing throughout the nation as the war continued. Many in the North who started fighting a war to save the Union went through periods of wondering whether it might be better to just let the South go and then ended up fighting to end slavery. Many in the South—slaveholders and nonslaveholders alike—who started out fighting to preserve their independence from Northern influence slowly became resigned to a different fate even if they never stopped resenting the reality that the war created. And many who began the war as enslaved people, officially "owned" by other human beings, ended the war as free citizens, many of them veterans of the Union army that had won their freedom. The Civil War changed all of subsequent U.S. history, and its impact is important to understand.

FORT SUMTER TO ANTIETAM, 1861–1862

14.1   Explain how the early battles of the war shaped future events.

After Fort Sumter surrendered in mid-April, no further serious battles occurred for the next 2 months as each side sought to understand the other's goals and strategy. Both governments raised and positioned their armies. The Confederates had only to fight a defensive war to protect their territory. They did not need to win victories in the North, only protect their lands to win what they wanted. The North, however, needed to defeat the Confederate army to reunite the nation. As the war began, the commander of the Union armies was the aging hero of the War with Mexico, General Winfield Scott. He proposed what came to be known as the Anaconda Plan to blockade the South by sea, take control of the Mississippi River, and slowly squeeze the Confederacy into submission—as an anaconda snake squeezed its victim—without a full-scale invasion of the region that he thought would be too bloody and lead to generations of hatred no matter what the outcome. But many Northerners believed that the North needed to defeat the Confederates on Confederate turf.

Union generals wanted a lot of time to prepare supplies and train recruits. In Lincoln's opinion, his generals always wanted more time—until Grant took command much later in the war. When General Irvin McDowell, commander of the Union forces in 1861, complained that he had only green recruits, the president responded, "[Y]ou are green, it is true, but they are green, also; you are all green alike." For Lincoln, a quick attack on the Confederacy, especially if Richmond could be taken, would mean victory. No one was yet thinking of a long war.

Early Inconclusive Battles

The first serious battle of the war took place on July 21, 1861 (see Map 14-1). At Lincoln's prodding, McDowell, with 18,000 troops, finally advanced from Washington across the Potomac River into Virginia. The army was accompanied by Northern reporters, members of Congress, and others who thought it would be the one time they would see a battle. Confederate commander Pierre Beauregard was alerted to the Union army's movement by Confederate spies in Washington. The armies met at the small town of Manassas, Virginia, on Bull Run Creek. (Northerners called it the First Battle of Bull Run, Southerners the Battle of Manassas.) Union troops, tired from the long march from Washington, started to surround the Confederate forces, but the Confederates held their ground. In an afternoon charge, Confederates let out the scream that came to be known as the **rebel yell**. One Northerner said "There is nothing

rebel yell
A frightening yell that Confederate soldiers gave when entering battle. Many Northern troops commented on how unnerving it could be.

Soldiers on both sides, like these Union soldiers in camp, spent most of the first months of the war either in training or sitting in camp and waiting. Note the one African-American off to the side. This early in the war, African-Americans were not yet in uniform, but that would soon change.

like it on this side of the infernal region." The Union troops began to flee, merging with panic-stricken civilians who ran back to the relative safety of Washington, DC.

The Battle of Manassas, or First Bull Run, was a clear Confederate victory. It gave the Confederates great, perhaps even dangerously high, levels of confidence. Confederate newspapers asked why their generals had not gone on to capture Washington, though in fact McDowell had done a good job of developing the defense of the capital. Northerners were despairing. Horace Greeley, who had done much to stir up support for the war, now wrote to Lincoln, "If it is best for the country and for mankind that we make peace with the rebels, and on their own terms, do not shrink even from that." Lincoln had no intention of taking that action, but the president now realized that it would take more than a few easy battles to win the war. Perhaps Mary Boykin Chesnut, the plantation wife who was deeply devoted to the Southern cause but never blind to reality, best understood the impact of the first battle when she wrote that she feared this early victory "lulls us into a fool's paradise of conceit."

Lincoln responded to the loss at Bull Run by calling for 1 million new volunteers. He fired several Union generals, including the unlucky McDowell, reorganized the army on the Maryland–Virginia line as the **Army of the Potomac**—which would remain the prime Union army throughout the war—and appointed George B. McClellan to command it. He tightened federal control in Washington and Maryland. In addition, he reorganized federal troops in the West as a separate army, with orders to proceed down the Mississippi River and try to divide the Confederacy. The country was in for a long war.

Although some in the South were clamoring for Confederate troops to march north and defeat the "damn Yankees," Jefferson Davis believed that the key to Confederate victory was doing what George Washington had done in the Revolution: simply survive. In time, he hoped, Northern opinion would tire of war and foreign governments would recognize the South.

Many in the South were confident that Britain would support them because of British need for Southern cotton. But they underestimated abolitionist opinion in Britain—which had abolished slavery in its own colonies in the 1830s—and the

Army of the Potomac
The main Union army led by a series of generals until Ulysses S. Grant took command in 1863 and led it to the final victory in 1865.

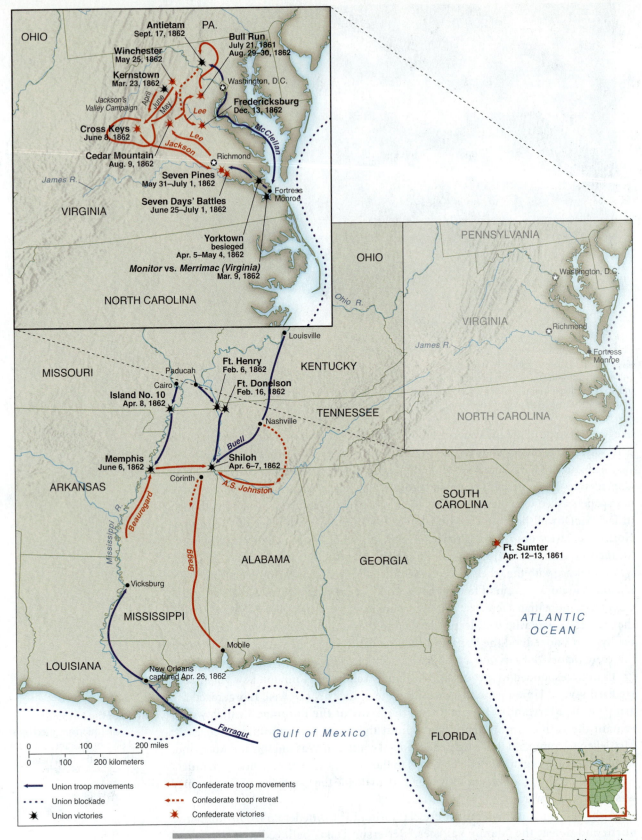

MAP 14-1 Major Civil War Battles, 1861–1862. As this map shows, during the first 2 years of the war, the major battles took place in northern Virginia, where the Confederacy tried to defend its capital of Richmond and Union forces defended Washington, DC, and in the Mississippi River valley.

caution of the British government, which wanted to "keep quite clear of the conflict." Some owners and workers in the cotton mills in Manchester and Liverpool wanted a Confederate victory, but overall, British opinion was opposed to slavery. In the end, Britain stayed neutral.

General McClellan was a first-rate organizer, and he trained the Union army well. The Army of the Potomac became a strong fighting force. Nevertheless, McClellan was never quite ready to fight. In one meeting with Lincoln, the general made but one request, "Just don't let them hurry me, is all I ask." By October 1861, McClellan was in command of 120,000 soldiers. The Confederate Army in Virginia was about 45,000 strong, but McClellan was sure it included at least 150,000 soldiers. Considering the possibilities for terrible loss of life, McClellan's caution is understandable. For Lincoln, however, that kind of caution would result only in the end of the Union.

By December 1861, there had been no major land battle since Bull Run. The cost of maintaining and supplying an army was still high, however, much higher than the expenditures of any previous peacetime government had been. Secretary of the Treasury Salmon Chase reported difficulty balancing the federal budget. The *London Times* reported "the independence of the South virtually established." Then McClellan got sick. In January 1862, a discouraged Lincoln said, "The people are impatient; Chase has no money;…The General of the Army has typhoid fever. The bottom is out of the tub. What shall I do?"

The U.S. Navy Takes Control of Southern Rivers and Ports

The Union cause was not as bleak as Lincoln feared. Although the North and South began the war with more or less equal size armies, the North had a much stronger navy. As early as August 1861, the U.S. Navy attacked Confederate fortifications on the Atlantic and Gulf coasts. By November, the Union controlled the sea islands off South Carolina and, not incidentally, some 10,000 slaves who had been left behind by fleeing plantation owners. With the U.S. Navy attacking Southern coastal fortifications and beginning a blockade of Southern ports early in the war, the South was losing access to the Atlantic. By April 1862, only the ports of Charleston, South Carolina; Wilmington, North Carolina; and Savannah, Georgia, were still open. From these ports, the South sent fast blockade-running ships to maintain contact with the rest of the world, getting supplies from the Bahamas, Bermuda, and Cuba as well as from Britain and France, but at high cost.

The closing of its ports by the U.S. Navy also led the Confederacy to build a new kind of ship. At the Tredegar Iron Works in Virginia, armor plates were placed on a salvaged ship that had been the U.S.S. *Merrimack* but was renamed the C.S.S. *Virginia*. The *Virginia* also had 10 well-protected guns and an iron ram that could sink wooden ships. While the North celebrated the early naval victories, word of a new Southern ironclad led the U.S. Navy to plan for a similar ship. An eccentric designer, John Ericsson, proposed a strange but potentially powerful design for an ironclad that looked like a floating raft that had a revolving gun turret with two 11-inch guns. His ship was named the *Monitor*. When the C.S.S. *Virginia* sank two Union ships off the mouth of the James River, the Navy ordered the *Monitor* to proceed south from the Brooklyn Navy Yard without even time for a test run. On March 9, 1862, the crew of the *Virginia* saw something they thought "was a raft" taking one of the Navy ships boilers "to shore for repairs," but then the boiler started firing at them. After hours of firing and maneuvering, the *Virginia* returned to port, and each side declared victory. The two ships never fought again—the crew of the *Virginia* blew up their ship rather than let it fall into Northern hands when the Union army invaded Virginia in May 1862, and the *Monitor* sank in a gale. But naval warfare had changed forever as the two ships showed that ironclads could easily defeat a wooden-hulled navy. For the remainder of the Civil War, however, fast wooden ships continued as best they could to keep the Confederacy supplied with war material by outrunning the U.S. Navy, and the U.S. Navy blockaded most Southern commerce.

The seagoing ironclad ships, the *Virginia* (formerly the *Merrimack*) and the *Monitor* fought one battle in March 1862, but the Union Navy's smaller ironclad riverboats, like the one shown here, did more to turn the tide of the war as they attacked Confederate fortifications all along the Mississippi River and its tributaries.

In early 1862, the U.S. Navy also won important battles on the Mississippi River. Cairo, Illinois, where the Ohio River flows into the Mississippi, was the southernmost city under Union control. South of Cairo, the Confederacy controlled the Mississippi as well as the Cumberland and Tennessee Rivers that flowed into it. The navy commander at Cairo was Andrew H. Foote, a sober abolitionist, while the army commander was the hard-drinking Ulysses S. Grant, who had given little thought to abolition before the war. Together, they attacked the South's rivers. On February 6, 1862, Union forces overwhelmed Confederate Fort Henry, and Union gunboats turned the Tennessee River into a Union thoroughfare. Grant became a hero. The Union controlled most of Kentucky and Tennessee. Southern optimism disappeared.

In April 1862, a fleet commanded by David G. Farragut got past a string of Confederate forts and took New Orleans, the largest city in the South, which remained in Union hands for the duration of the war. Farragut's ships moved up the Mississippi, capturing Baton Rouge and Natchez by the end of June. Only Vicksburg on high bluffs over the Mississippi River prevented complete Union control of the river, which would have cut the Confederacy in half.

The Beginning of a Long War

While the Union navy won battles, General Grant led 40,000 troops in an attack on Corinth, Mississippi. Corinth was where the South's major north-south and east-west rail lines crossed, and Grant meant to disrupt the network. Before Grant's forces got to Corinth, however, Southern forces attacked the Union army near Shiloh Church in Tennessee on April 6. In 2 days of terrible fighting, Grant won, but at a high cost of killed or wounded troops—13,047 for the Union and 10,699 for the Confederates.

Shiloh undermined morale in both armies. A Confederate private wrote, "I never realized the 'pomp and circumstance' of the thing called glorious war until I saw this….Men… lying in every conceivable position; the dead…with their eyes wide open, the wounded begging piteously for help." Union General William T. Sherman said, "The scenes on this field would have cured anybody of war." The cost of the Union victory at Shiloh convinced many that it would be a long and terrible war. Mary Boykin Chesnut wrote in her diary, "I have nothing to chronicle but disasters." Nevertheless, by May 1862, Union forces had won control of several Southern rivers and cities, disrupted the Southern rail system, and taken many prisoners. Grant, however, would spend the next year stalled at Vicksburg.

With Union victories in the west, Lincoln urged McClellan to attack the Confederate forces in the east. The Confederate **Army of Northern Virginia** was the South's elite force, assigned to protect the capital of Richmond, Virginia, and the essential supply sources nearby. McClellan landed troops on the Virginia coast to march up the peninsula—hence the name the **Peninsular Campaign of 1862**—to capture Richmond. With 135,000 troops, he seemed poised for victory. But McClellan moved slowly, with great caution, driving Lincoln to distraction.

In May and June 1862, Confederate General Stonewall Jackson defeated Northern forces in the Shenandoah Valley and kept Knoxville and much of east Tennessee in Confederate hands. It was an area filled with Northern sympathizers. But Jackson kept winning. Northern troops had had to be diverted from the attack on Richmond to deal with Jackson, whose troops had captured badly needed food and medical supplies.

At the end of May, Union and Confederate forces fought a series of inconclusive engagements at the Chickahominy River only a few miles from Richmond. Jefferson Davis made Robert E. Lee commander of the Army of Northern Virginia, a move that almost turned the tide of war. Lee forced McClellan to pull back from Richmond to the James River. The costs of the war were getting higher. General D. H. Hill, whose unit Lee had ordered to attack Union forces at Malvern Hill on July 1, said of the result, it "was not war—it was murder." Some 20,000 Confederates had been killed or wounded, twice as many as in the Union army, but Lee kept up the pace.

At the end of August 1862, Union and Confederate armies met again at Manassas on Bull Run Creek where the South had won its first victory a year before. The Confederates, led by Lee and Jackson, again defeated the Union army, which pulled back into northern Virginia. At the beginning of the summer, Union soldiers could hear the church bells of Richmond. By the end of August, Richmond was safe, and the Confederate army was within 20 miles of Washington, DC. It was a major reversal of fortunes.

Army of Northern Virginia
The main Confederate army led for most of the war by Robert E. Lee, it fought in Virginia, Maryland, and Pennsylvania before surrendering at Appomattox Court House in April 1865.

President Lincoln meeting with General McClellan at an army camp.

By the fall of 1862, Lee and Jefferson Davis wanted a decisive win as badly as Lincoln had. The Confederate army planned to encircle Washington, DC. At Antietam Creek near Sharpsburg, Maryland, McClellan attacked Lee's army on September 17, 1862. The result was the single bloodiest day of the war with approximately 23,000 soldiers killed or wounded—four times the number of U.S. soldiers killed or wounded on D-Day in World War II. Neither side could claim victory at Antietam, but neither side was defeated. The next day, Lee withdrew his army to the relative safety of the Shenandoah Valley in Virginia, but McClellan did not pursue Lee's retreating forces, which was the last straw for Lincoln. When a month later McClellan still had not moved and reported that he needed to rest his horses before any attack, Lincoln telegraphed, "Will you pardon me for asking what the horses of your army have done since the battle of Antietam that fatigue anything?" It was the end of the president's patience, and he relieved McClellan of command.

14.1 **Quick Review** Why were early Union Army generals so reluctant to fight as hard as Lincoln wanted? Why was the Navy so important to the North's ultimate victory?

THE ROAD TO EMANCIPATION

14.2 Analyze how the war influenced attitudes toward slavery in white and black communities, leading to the Emancipation Proclamation and to black soldiers in the Union army.

Lincoln had long insisted that although he personally thought slavery evil, it was not the role of the national government to interfere with the settled institutions of states. Soon after his election, he wrote to former Congressman Alexander Stephens of Georgia, who was trying to convince his state not to secede:

> Do the people of the South really entertain fears that a Republican adminis-
> tration would, *directly, or indirectly*, interfere with their slaves, or with them,
> about their slaves? If they do, I wish to assure you, as once a friend, and still,
> I hope, not an enemy, that there is no cause for such fears.

After he had assumed office, and even after the fighting began, Lincoln kept restating the same position.

Once the Southern states began to secede, his top priority was to hold the Union together with or without slavery. As late as August 1862, Lincoln wrote to Horace Greeley, knowing that his words would be published in the *New York Tribune,* insisting, "My paramount object in this struggle is to save the Union, and is not either to save or destroy slavery." He closed the letter noting that this was his *official* position but that he also intended "no modification of my oft-expressed *personal* wish that all men everywhere could be free." But his official position was evolving, and some historians would argue so were his personal views.

Contraband of War

While Lincoln's views were evolving, slaves and former slaves were clear on what they wanted from the war. Only a month into the Civil War, on May 23, 1861, three slaves found their way to the Union-held Fortress Monroe in Virginia and asked the fort's commander, General Benjamin F. Butler, for his protection. Butler, needing workers, put them to work. He also coined a term for escaped slaves who came behind Union lines: "contraband of war."

Since American law then defined slaves as private property, and since interna-
tional law allowed belligerent nations to seize goods and property meant to help the other side wage war, there was logic to Butler's new term. If slaves were property that the Confederacy planned to use against the Union, then the Union had a right to seize that property. Throughout much of the war, slaves who fled to the Union army were

known as **contrabands**. There were "contraband camps" and "contraband schools." Word of Butler's decision spread rapidly. More slaves started coming to Fortress Monroe, which some now called "freedom fort." Lincoln was not yet ready to set firm policy, but Butler's policy was "approved," and Fortress Monroe continued to be a haven for escaping slaves.

Nevertheless, federal authorities—including new officials appointed by Lincoln—continued to enforce the Fugitive Slave Act in the District of Columbia, and some generals returned slaves to their "rightful" owners. With no national policy to guide him, General John C. Frémont, the head of the U.S. Army in Missouri, announced that his troops would emancipate any slave belonging to a Confederate supporter. This announcement infuriated Lincoln because he believed that he—and not one of his generals—should decide an issue as weighty as emancipation.

Lincoln pressed for compensated emancipation in which the government would pay to free slaves in the areas loyal to the Union. Slaveholders in Kentucky, however, had no interest in giving up their slaves with or without payment, and the idea went nowhere. Lincoln also pursued the possibility of **colonization** in which freed slaves could leave the United States for Central America or even Africa. No nation showed much interest in the project, and freed slaves showed even less interest. Lincoln continued to be more interested in keeping Kentucky loyal to the Union than in the fate of any slaves. A Northern reporter noted, "In all attempts to soothe southern wrath, the negro is thrown in as the offering." Well into 1862, there was little cause for optimism for those who wanted the war to end slavery. Former slave and abolitionist leader Frederick Douglass wrote of his disappointment: "In dealing with the causes of our present troubles, we find in quarter high and low, the most painful evidences of dishonesty." For Douglass, the problem was obvious, "We have attempted to maintain our Union in utter defiance of the moral chemistry of the universe….We have sought to bind the chains of slavery on the limbs of the black man, without thinking that at last we should find the other end of that hateful chain about our own necks." Regardless, in 1862, most of Northern white public opinion was not ready to agree with Douglass.

contrabands
Also known as contraband of war, the name Union generals gave to former slaves who escaped to the Union lines and worked in support of Union troops.

colonization
A plan, popular in the 1830s and briefly considered by President Lincoln, to create colonies in Africa to which former slaves might return. It was never popular with slaves or former slaves themselves.

In the summer of 1862, a group of former slaves, now officially contraband of war, waited for their next assignment. Before long many such former slaves would be fighting as full-fledged soldiers in the Union army.

As the Union army marched deeper into the Confederacy, however, commanders realized that slaves could be of great value to them. Slaves knew the country, they knew hidden roadways, and they knew what white Southerners were thinking. George E. Stephens, one of the few black newspaper reporters accompanying Union troops, wrote that "when the Union soldier meets the negro in the enemy's country, he knows him as a friend." For many Union soldiers, meeting slaves firsthand began to change their minds. Future president James A. Garfield, commanding an Ohio unit in Tennessee, said that he found "the rank and file of the army steadily and surely becoming imbued with sympathy for the slaves and hatred for slavery."

With or without authorization, some blacks began to fight in the Union army. In Indian Territory (Oklahoma), blacks who lived with Creeks and Seminoles joined them in attacking other tribal members who had signed a treaty with the Confederates. Union officers in Kansas and on the coast of South Carolina began to recruit black troops. Secretary of War Edward M. Stanton approved the move, though he asked his officers to keep it quiet because it was "so much in advance of public opinion." But the government needed more soldiers, and many blacks wanted to fight—if the fighting was for their freedom.

Issuing the Emancipation Proclamation

President Lincoln also began to change his mind. Lincoln was far too wise a politician to reveal all of his thinking. He had long said that although he thought slavery a terrible evil, the Constitution protected slavery where it already existed, and his only goal was stopping its spread into new territories. In 1861 and early 1862, his priority was securing the loyalty of Kentucky and other border states, which meant protecting slavery there. He understood that many Northerners feared free blacks almost as much as they disliked slavery. Public opinion would support a fight to save the Union, but not necessarily a fight to end slavery.

But by 1862, Northern opinion was changing. Generally, the Northern thinking was that the slaveholding South was waging war against the United States because it wanted to defend the institution of slavery, and it was using slaves to support the war effort while its young white men went off to war. Abolitionists were getting an audience where they had previously been shunned. Blacks were willing to fight in the Union army when many whites were not. And many slaves were fleeing to the Union lines. In July 1862, the Republican-dominated Congress declared that anyone convicted of assisting the rebellion against the U.S. government was liable to seizure and sale of all property and that all rebel-owned slaves who escaped to the Union army were "forever free of their servitude." Lincoln then began discussing emancipation with his cabinet in July. Secretary of State Seward among others urged caution until a Northern victory would make talk of emancipation look less like a desperate measure.

On September 22, 1862, Lincoln told his cabinet that he had promised God that if Lee's army was forced out of Maryland where they were then trying to encircle Washington, DC, then he would act. The Battle of Antietam enabled him to do so. Senator Sumner had told him more than a year before that the South's rebellion gave the president war powers, including the right to seize property, even the kind of private property known as slaves. The proclamation that Lincoln was planning to issue was, he said, a matter of military strategy. It was also directed at building Northern support for the war, especially black and abolitionist support. His proposed emancipation would apply only to those areas of the country that were in a state of rebellion as of January 1, 1863. Lincoln hoped that, as a result, at least some areas would vote to shift sides and support the Union, and in an ironic twist, voters in Tennessee and southern Louisiana around New Orleans—both areas where the Union army was in control—did just that, thus exempting themselves from the impact of the proclamation.

The **Emancipation Proclamation** did not free a single slave when it was first issued. It did not apply in areas loyal to the Union, including slave states, and though it technically freed all of the slaves in the Confederate areas, the government had no

Emancipation Proclamation
Decree announced by President Abraham Lincoln formally issued on January 1, 1863, freeing slaves in all Confederate states still in rebellion.

power as of yet in areas that were not under Union control. However, the proclamation did resolve the issue of contraband slaves, made abolishing slavery a military goal, and fundamentally changed the Civil War.

Northern Democrats immediately attacked the proclamation. While the Democratic minority in Congress supported the war effort to save the Union, they opposed any widening of the war's goals. By 1862, some in Congress known as **Peace Democrats** advocated letting the Confederacy go rather than endure further bloodshed. In the November 1862 congressional elections, Peace Democrats attacked Republicans because, they said, the Emancipation Proclamation was widening the purpose of war and therefore making it longer and more bloody. The New York Democratic platform called the Emancipation Proclamation "a proposal for the butchery of women and children, for scenes of lust and rapine, and arson and murder." For governor, New York's Democrats nominated Horatio Seymour who said that "the people of the South should be allowed to withdraw themselves from the government." Seymour won, as did a Democrat in New Jersey, Joel Parker, who, although a "war Democrat" because he supported the war effort, was highly critical of the Emancipation Proclamation. Democrats gained control of the state legislatures in Illinois and Indiana. Northern Democrats opposed to emancipation also won 34 more seats in the House of Representatives. Since few Southerners remained in Congress, this number was not enough to win a majority, but it expanded the influence of those who wanted to challenge the president's new war goals.

The November 1862 Democratic gains seem to have hardened the views of Lincoln and his cabinet. Just after the election, Attorney General Edward Bates, usually one of the cabinet's more cautious members, ruled that free blacks had all the rights of citizens and that the Dred Scott decision held "no authority" except in the specific circumstances of the case. Bates's ruling did not include voting rights; free blacks were considered like women and children, who were citizens but could not vote. Nevertheless, they were now citizens.

On January 1, 1863, Lincoln signed the Emancipation Proclamation, declaring that all slaves in areas then in rebellion—about 3 million of the nation's 4 million slaves—"are and henceforth shall be free," and that the military should "recognize and maintain" their freedom. The proclamation also said that black soldiers and sailors could be organized in the "armed service" of the United States. There was no stirring rhetoric about human rights, only a claim of "military necessity," but the Civil War was now a war to end slavery.

While Northerners debated and voted, slaves in the South voted with their feet. Slaves came to understand that their freedom was one of the issues the war would settle. Early in the war, many Virginia plantations lost all their slaves, and by August 1862, as Confederate troops had to be diverted from fighting to ensure that slaves did not escape, a North Carolina resident wrote that "our Negroes are beginning to show that they understand the state of affairs, and insolence and insubordination are quite common."

Black Soldiers in the Union Army

In January 1863, just after Lincoln signed the Emancipation Proclamation, the *Weekly Anglo-African* said, "A century may elapse before another opportunity shall be afforded of reclaiming and holding our withheld rights." Blacks, both slave and free, joined the military in great numbers. More than 180,000 black soldiers—one-fifth of the nation's adult black male population under age 45 and about 10 percent of the total Union force—eventually fought for the Union.

Former slaves quickly signed up for service, especially in the west where Grant encouraged full inclusion of blacks in the army. In Massachusetts, Governor John Andrew, with Lincoln's support, authorized the organization of what became the Fifty-fourth and Fifty-fifth Massachusetts regiments. Civil War regiments were typically organized by states, but the Fifty-fourth and Fifty-fifth, although they were Massachusetts regiments, recruited free blacks from across the North—though with

Peace Democrats
Also known as Copperheads, a large faction within the Democratic Party that advocated immediate peace with the Confederacy on terms that would allow it to leave the Union.

American Voices

Susie King Taylor, "Reminiscences of My Life in Camp," 1862

Susie King Taylor (1848–1912) published her autobiography long after the Civil War, but her memories of the war and the rumors of freedom that arrived in advance of the reality remained vivid. Taylor was born in rural Georgia but lived in Savannah as a child where she attended a secret—and illegal—school for slaves and learned to read and write. Soon after her trip to St. Simon's Island and freedom with the Union army, she opened a school for other newly freed slaves and later taught black troops to read and write while also serving as a nurse.

I WAS born under the slave law in Georgia, in 1848, and was brought up by my grandmother in Savannah. There were three of us with her, my younger sister and brother. My brother and I being the two eldest, we were sent to a friend of my grandmother, Mrs. Woodhouse, a widow, to learn to read and write. She was a free woman and lived on Bay Lane, between Habersham and Price streets, about half a mile from my house. We went every day about nine o'clock, with our books wrapped in paper to prevent the police or white persons from seeing them. We went in, one at a time, through the gate, into the yard to the L kitchen, which was the schoolroom. She had twenty-five or thirty children whom she taught, assisted by her daughter, Mary Jane.…

About this time I had been reading so much about the "Yankees" I was very anxious to see them. The whites would tell their colored people not to go to the Yankees, for they would harness them to carts and make them pull the carts around, in place of horses. I asked grandmother, one day, if this was true. She replied, "Certainly not!" that the white people did not want slaves

to go over to the Yankees, and told them these things to frighten them. "Don't you see those signs pasted about the streets? one reading, 'I am a rattlesnake; if you touch me I will strike!' Another reads, 'I am a wild-cat! Beware,' etc. These are warnings to the North; so don't mind what the white people say." I wanted to see these wonderful "Yankees" so much, as I heard my parents say the Yankee was going to set all the slaves free.…

On April 1, 1862, about the time the Union soldiers were firing on Fort Pulaski, I was sent out into the country to my mother. I remember what a roar and din the guns made. They jarred the earth for miles. The fort was at last taken by them. Two days after the taking of Fort Pulaski, my uncle took his family of seven and myself to St. Catherine Island. We landed under the protection of the Union fleet, and remained there two weeks, when about thirty of us were taken aboard the gunboat P—, to be transferred to St. Simon's Island; and at last, to my unbounded joy, I saw the "Yankee."

Source: Susie King Taylor, Reminiscences of My Life in Camp with the 33D United States Colored Troops Late 1st S.C. Volunteers (Boston: Published by the Author, 1902), pp. 10–12.

Thinking Critically

1. **Documentary Analysis**

   What steps did Taylor's family take to prepare her for freedom?

2. **Historical Interpretation**

   What does this document tell you about the priorities of enslaved African-Americans as freedom approached? What might explain the importance they attached to education?

white officers. In rural Franklin Country, Pennsylvania, not far from the Mason-Dixon Line, 45 free black men signed up for the Fifty-fourth regiment and more joined the Fifty-fifth. Most free blacks who volunteered for service were from the lowest rungs of the economy, including Thomas Burgess, a carpenter; Joseph Christy, a woodcutter; and Hezekiah Watson and Thomas Cuff, quarrymen. The bounties paid to all soldiers for joining and the subsequent pay mattered to poor families—black or white. The opportunity to fight for freedom mattered even more to black soldiers.

In spring 1863, black soldiers in Louisiana fought hard and rescued white troops who faced defeat, turning what could have been defeat into a victory. At Fort Wagner, South Carolina, the Fifty-fourth Massachusetts regiment lost half its number, including its white commander Robert Gould Shaw, after requesting the right to be first in the assault. After those encounters, many shared Secretary of War Stanton's view that these troops were "among the bravest of the brave in fighting for the Union." Their bravery convinced some, including Lincoln, that they were as deserving as any whites not only of their freedom but also of the right to vote and participate equally in the political process.

Black soldiers also demanded, and eventually got, equal treatment within the army. Officers were told that any soldier, whatever his rank, who mistreated freedmen would be dismissed. The Militia Act of 1862 set the pay of black soldiers at the level of military laborers on the assumption that their work would be behind the lines. As their role changed, black soldiers demanded equal pay. Soldiers in the Massachusetts Fifty-fourth and Fifty-fifth regiments refused to accept any pay until it was raised to that of

Even before, and especially after, the Emancipation Proclamation formalized their place in the Union army, thousands of African-Americans joined the army to fight for the Union cause and for freedom.

white soldiers. In June 1864, Congress provided equal pay and enlistment bounties for blacks and whites. In the army, blacks also had equal rights in military courts and rights to testify in trials, something they could not do as civilians in most of the country. Finally, during the last months of the war, blacks were promoted to the officer ranks.

The presence of black troops in the Union army enraged many in the Confederacy. In May 1863, the South refused to include black troops in prisoner of war exchanges since they had declared all such troops to be runaway slaves who should be returned to slavery. In response, and despite pressure, Lincoln suspended the exchange of prisoners until early 1865 when the Confederacy agreed to resume exchanges. Black prisoners of war were treated more harshly than white prisoners. In April 1864, when the Union garrison at Fort Pillow, Tennessee, surrendered to Confederate General Nathan B. Forest, he ordered the massacre of black soldiers. Blacks who fought knew what danger they faced, and they fought anyway.

14.2 **Quick Review** How did the battles fought at the beginning of the Civil War change people's attitudes about the war in the North and the South?

THE HOME FRONT—SHORTAGES, OPPOSITION, RIOTS, AND BATTLES

14.3 Explain how the war's death toll and civilian shortages affected life—North and South—during the war.

After the initial euphoria wore off, and as the reports of casualties began to circulate, support for the war dropped in both the North and the South. Even those supporting the war had second thoughts. It was not only the terrible toll from the battlefields, though nearly every family was touched by those losses, but also the war's effects on the home front, which had not been expected when it began.

Inflation and Bread Riots in the South

The war's heaviest toll was in the South. The Confederate government never succeeded in placing its financial house in order. Southern politicians had long objected to federal tariffs and other taxes. It was hard now that independence was claimed to turn to these taxes. Although there were modest tax increases, the Confederate government was always short of money. To finance the war, the Confederates issued war bonds. It was fair, many argued, for future generations to pay the cost of the war. But buying war bonds that paid 8 percent per year in interest when inflation was running at 12 percent per month was not a good investment. And even rich Southerners often did not have much cash to invest. Southern wealth was invested in land and slaves, and neither could be easily converted to cash, especially in wartime. So the Confederate government sought to solve its financial problems by simply printing more money—$20 million in May 1861, $100 million in August. Creating more currency, however, caused terrible inflation that undermined the sale of war bonds and drove the price of goods out of sight. In 1862, Southern workers saw their wages increase by about 55 percent while the cost of living increased by 300 percent. The price of salt, essential to preserving meat, rose from $2 a bag before the war to $60 by the fall of 1862. In addition, the disruption of southern transportation, especially after the loss of the rail terminals in Memphis in June 1862, meant that though one area might have ample supplies of food, other areas were literally starving.

Managing the home front in the South fell primarily to women. During the war, three out of four white men of military age—ultimately defined by the Confederate government as ages 17 to 50—served in the army, and one out of five of this age range were killed in the war. Margaret Junkin Preston of Lexington, Virginia, described a world in which there were "no men left." In New Bern, North Carolina, women wrote to the governor to say that of 250 whites remaining in their town, only 20 were male, and of these 11 were old and three about to join the army. And in Carrollton, Alabama, a woman wrote to her governor in 1862 to say that the latest call for soldiers "almost literally depopulates the country of men." For white women, this situation meant taking on new roles, including managing slaves. In 1863, Lizzie Neblett of Texas wrote to her husband that she was "doing my best," as a manager and overseer, but by 1863, she realized that the news of the Emancipation Proclamation spreading in the slave quarter had changed everything: "I don't think we have one who will stay with us." Letters to distant husbands reflected how terribly their wives missed them and how these long separations were changing women's role in a society that had prided itself on male dominance and female fragility. As the *Montgomery Daily Advertiser* wrote in July 1864, "The surface of society, like a great ocean, is upheaved, and all the relations of life are disturbed and out of joint."

In spring 1863, food shortages led to bread riots across the South from Richmond, Virginia, to Mobile, Alabama. Women, often wives whose husbands were off fighting and who were trying desperately to sustain themselves and their children, attacked shops and warehouses.

By March 1863, the Army of Northern Virginia was subsisting on half rations, but the women of Richmond had far less. In April, a mob of over 1,000 women shouting "Bread, Bread" and "Our children are starving," began looting shops in Richmond—first for bread and then for clothing. When President Davis threatened to shoot rioters, they dispersed, but the anger did not subside. The government tried to distribute food and to stop hoarding in warehouses. Nevertheless, as the war continued, it created streams of refugees, inflation, and starvation across the South. As many as 50,000 civilians died in the South during the war, in addition to the 260,000 Confederate war dead.

Taxes, Mourning, and Resistance in the North

Life was easier in the North. Most of the fighting took place on Southern soil, and the Northern economy was more stable. The North also had an established Treasury Department and tax system when the war began, though revenue that had been sufficient for the 1850s was not even close to meeting

Bread riots by women in Richmond reflected the hardship of civilian life, especially in the South where food and supplies were in short supply throughout the war.

the needs of a war economy. The financier Jay Cooke, one of the richest and most reviled bankers of his day, advised the Treasury Department and created new federal bonds in amounts that allowed not only banks but also individuals to buy war bonds. Cooke made a significant profit on these transactions, but the bonds kept the government solvent.

Congress also created the **Internal Revenue Service** and began a federal income tax in August 1861. Most people were exempt from the tax since income under $800 per year was not taxed, and only a minority made more than that. Finally, the federal government began issuing federal notes that were secured not by gold or silver but simply by the government's promise to redeem them. Congress not only authorized such bank notes, which came to be known as "**greenbacks**" for their green ink, but also declared that they were legal tender, which meant that no one could refuse them as payment for goods or debts. The result was the creation of a solid monetary system that lasted long after the war.

Although there was little fighting in the North, families saw sons march off to war and often received the terrible news that they were never coming home. Death on the scale of the Civil War had never been known before—and has not been known since—in the United States. After major battles, newspapers and telegraph offices posted casualty lists. Close comrades or hospital nurses caring for those who died wrote letters to their families, and the awful news changed life for those waiting at home.

In many parts of the North, as in the South, communities were virtually depopulated of military-aged men during the war, and women took on roles that they had never before considered. Although the prewar North had less rigidly defined gender roles than the South, changes were significant for many.

Many Northerners never supported the war effort, and their numbers increased after the Emancipation Proclamation. By 1863, as the death toll rose and the prospects of defeating the Confederacy dimmed, the peace faction within the Northern Democratic Party grew rapidly, though the party always included not only Peace Democrats but also War Democrats who supported the war to save the union, if not the Emancipation Proclamation. Peace Democrats came to be known as Copperheads, after Republicans had coined the term, comparing antiwar Democrats to venomous snakes. But by 1863, Peace Democrats proudly took up the term and continued to call for peace while hoping to make more gains in the state elections of 1863.

By 1863, Ohio Congressman Clement L. Vallandigham had emerged as the leader of the Peace Democrats. For Vallandigham, the result of the war was "defeat, debt, taxation, sepulchers." Vallandigham strongly disapproved of the Emancipation Proclamation, declaring that the government should, "look only to the welfare, peace, and safety of the white race." His words touched a nerve in Northern public opinion but did not win over a majority. In a May 1863 speech, he said that "King Lincoln" had widened the war from one to save the Union to one to free the slaves and must be stopped. General Ambrose Burnside, the Union military commander in Ohio, had issued an order that "declaring sympathy for the enemy" was against the law. Vallandigham was arrested and convicted. After briefly being jailed, he was exiled to the Confederacy. He met with Confederate officials in Richmond, then made his way to Canada where, from exile, he ran as a Peace Democrat for governor of Ohio in November 1863. Although he lost the election, Vallandigham did win 40 percent of the votes.

New York City was a center of opposition to the war. Its large Irish Catholic population had little interest in fighting for the rights of African-Americans. More free blacks, they thought, meant more competitors on the streets and docks of New York, and they did not like it. After Lincoln issued the Emancipation Proclamation, New York's Catholic Archbishop John Hughes wrote that "we Catholics…have not the slightest idea of carrying on a war that costs so much blood and treasure just to gratify a clique of Abolitionists."

While Northern support for the abolition of slavery was growing as the war progressed, especially among troops in the army, Northern opinion was divided.

Internal Revenue Service
An agency created by Congress during the Civil War to collect federal taxes in support of the war effort.

greenbacks
Paper currency printed on order of Congress based on the federal government's promise to pay rather than backed by actual gold or silver as security.

New York Draft Riot
A mostly Irish-immigrant protest against conscription in New York City that escalated into class and racial warfare.

Irish Catholics were far from the only people in the North to dislike free blacks and have little interest in freeing slaves. As word of the Emancipation Proclamation spread in 1862, antiblack riots broke out in several cities, including Cincinnati where a strike by Irish dockworkers was defeated with the use of black strikebreakers. In Brooklyn, a mob attacked a tobacco factory where blacks were working.

As opposition grew in the North to the war itself, especially expanding the war goals to include emancipation, voluntary enlistment in the army declined. In July 1863, the government began to enforce a military draft, and the antiblack, anti-Abolitionist, antiwar fervor broke into violence. In New York City on July 13, mobs attacked the draft offices and then turned on black neighborhoods, Republican newspapers, and government offices. Blacks were beaten, lynched, and shot. Before it was over, 105 people, most of them black, were killed. The **New York Draft Riot** was the worst riot in American history up to that time. Only the arrival of federal troops on July 15, fresh from the Battle of Gettysburg, ended the violence.

Warfare in the North and West

Although the Civil War was fought primarily in the South, battles took place in distant areas of the nation. A victory at Glorieta Pass near Santa Fe kept New Mexico in Union hands. In Missouri, bands loyal to each side fought battles throughout the war that spilled over into neighboring states and often were fueled by earlier disputes. William Clarke Quantrill, who had been among the Missouri "border ruffians" in the 1850s, led attacks on Union troops and sympathizers in Missouri, and in 1863, Quantrill led a band of 450 Southern sympathizers in a raid on Lawrence, Kansas. In retaliation for events in "Bleeding Kansas," Quantrill ordered, "Kill every male and burn every house." The band followed orders, killing 183 men and boys and burning 185 buildings in Lawrence, eluding capture by Union troops. Quantrill was eventually killed by Union soldiers, but many of his followers, including Jesse and Frank James, became famous outlaws and continued to terrorize parts of the West long after the war was over. Confederate agents also tried to arrange attacks on the Union from Canada and planned an uprising in Chicago during the Democratic convention of 1864, but nothing came of that effort.

Those involved in the New York Draft Riot of July 1863 attacked Union draft officials, Republican newspapers and supporters, and, most of all, African-Americans.

Confederate and Union leaders both sought allies among the tribes in Indian Territory. Cherokee, Creeks, and Seminoles were all divided between some who thought the Confederacy would offer better terms than the United States had done, and others who sided with the United States. Even without Confederate influence, some Northern tribes were angry at the U.S. government over the loss of supplies that had been diverted to the war effort and over Lincoln's withdrawal of troops that were protecting the tribes from expanding white settlements, as promised in various treaties. In Minnesota in August 1862, Santee Sioux under Little Crow killed hundreds of white settlers and U.S. troops but were soon defeated. Little Crow along with 37 other Santee leaders were executed in the largest public hanging in U.S. history. Many from the tribe moved to Canada. In early 1863, the Shoshoni under Chief Bear Hunter, angry at the growing presence of white settlers and migrants in the tribe's region, attacked white settlements in the Utah and Idaho Territories. Union troops retaliated, massacring most of the Shoshoni warriors along with women and children in an attack on January 29, 1863. As Indian–white relationships degenerated during the war, Union troops were diverted from the war with the Confederacy to fight Indians. Indians suffered no matter which side they took, and most whites looked the other way.

14.3 **Quick Review** How did political opposition, popular opposition (especially where violent), and economic upheaval threaten the war effort in the North and South?

FROM GETTYSBURG TO APPOMATTOX AND BEYOND

14.4 Analyze the strategies and costs of fighting a long and terrible war.

As both its proponents and opponents understood, the Emancipation Proclamation widened the purpose of the Civil War. Military tactics also changed in 1863. Early in the war, generals hoped for a short and limited war. McClellan was far from the only general, North or South, who tried to avoid large losses of fighting troops. By the time the war entered its third year, however, military and civilian leaders on both sides had concluded that only a much more sustained offensive would end the war.

Lincoln relieved several cautious generals—McClellan, Hooker, and Meade—before he promoted Grant to overall command. Davis, on the other hand, promoted Lee to be the top military commander early in the war. In Grant and Lee, each president had selected a general who was willing to fight a large-scale offensive war and absorb large troop losses to win.

Gettysburg and the War in Pennsylvania and Virginia

In spring of 1863, Hooker, while he was still in command, marched Union troops into Virginia, and the two armies fought for 7 days at Chancellorsville. When Stonewall Jackson led his troops around the end of the Union lines, Hooker lost his nerve and ordered a retreat. Chancellorsville was a major Confederate victory, though it came at the high cost of 10,000 Confederate dead and wounded and 14,000 Union losses. In the battle, Jackson was accidentally shot by his own troops and died a week later. Lincoln relieved Hooker of command and appointed General George Meade to replace Hooker. Meanwhile, Lee convinced Davis that the time had come to invade the North, cut Washington, DC, off from the rest of the country, and end the war.

June 1863 was the high point of Confederate confidence and Confederate advances. As Lee led the South's largest army through rural Pennsylvania, many in the North—not just the unfortunate inhabitants of the towns through which the army marched—grew fearful. If the Confederate army could control the Pennsylvania countryside, they could attack Philadelphia or Washington as a well-fed, well-organized army of conquest. The North could not continue the war if its capital and major cities were under rebel control.

Long before any battles took place, Pennsylvania residents knew one was coming. While people living in many parts of the South had already experienced 2 years of war, such fears were new north of the Mason-Dixon line. Philip Schaff, a theologian and historian teaching at Mercersburg Seminary in Pennsylvania, remembered that trying times did not bring out the best in frightened and confused people. They turned on their neighbors because of pro- or antiwar politics or over squabbles about what to hide and where to hide it.

When the rebel army did arrive, Mercersburg was luckier than some towns, at least for its white citizens. General Lee ordered that "no private property shall be injured or destroyed." Schaff described the first Confederate officer he met as "intelligent and courteous, but full of hatred for the Yankees." Not all the Confederates who followed were as polite.

Mercersburg had a large free black population, and they suffered far worse than whites. Schaff said that some of the troops went "on a regular slave-hunt, which presented the worst spectacle I ever saw in this war." When white households hid black friends, the invading troops "proclaimed, first, that they would burn down every house which harbored a fugitive slave." And they considered all blacks to be fugitive slaves. Schaff was terrified that his servant Eliza and her son would be found. They escaped, but other blacks in the town were caught and sold into slavery. For blacks and whites, southern Pennsylvania in 1863 was every bit as much a war zone as Virginia or the Mississippi River valley had been in 1862.

Lincoln and Meade ordered the Army of the Potomac to stop Lee's advance at all cost. The Northern and Southern armies found each other near the town of Gettysburg, Pennsylvania. On July 1, Confederate forces drove Union troops out of the town and onto Cemetery Hill. The next morning, Lee ordered a major attack, but the Union army held its ground. After another major charge directly at the heart of the Union lines on July 3—known as Pickett's Charge for the officer commanding the lead unit—it became clear to Lee that, despite terrible losses, the Union forces, now reinforced, could not be dislodged. Of the 14,000 soldiers that Pickett led in the assault, only half returned. Confederate General Longstreet spoke of the Battle of Gettysburg as "hopeless slaughter…one of the saddest [days] of my life." In the 3 days at Gettysburg,

In the days after the Battle of Gettysburg, bodies littered the battlefield. Photographs brought the high cost of war home to people, North and South.

51,000 soldiers were killed or wounded, 23,000 from the North and 28,000 from the South. On July 4, Lee began a painful retreat back to Virginia. The Confederate army would never again be a major presence in the North. Lincoln, however, was furious that Meade, like McClellan, did not pursue the retreating Confederates.

While news was arriving in Washington that the Confederate forces had been turned back, word also came of a second Northern victory. Unable to defeat the Confederate garrison at Vicksburg in 1862, Grant surrounded the city and starved it. After holding on for a year, on July 4, 1863, the Confederate forces at Vicksburg surrendered. Watching the Union army march into Vicksburg, a local resident wrote, "What a contrast [these] stalwart, well-fed men…[were to]…the worn men in gray, who were being blindly dashed against this embodiment of modern power." The entire Mississippi River was now under Union control. The Confederacy had been cut in half. Lincoln made Grant General-in-Chief of all Union armies. But it would be another hard year before there was another Northern victory like Gettysburg or Vicksburg and 2 years before the war ended.

The Terrible Cost of War

In early 1864, Grant took direct command in the East and marched into Virginia to attack Lee. He quickly stalled. In early May 1864 at the Battle of the Wilderness, Southern forces mounted a furious attack with high casualties. Neither side won the Battle of the Wilderness, but unlike his predecessors, Grant pursued the Confederate forces

American Voices

Cornelia Hancock, "Letters of Cornelia Hancock," July 7, 1863

As a young woman from a Quaker family in New Jersey, Cornelia Hancock was originally rejected for service by the Union army's Superintendent of Female Nurses, Dorothea Dix. Hancock responded by making her way, on her own, to the field hospital set up in the days immediately after the Battle of Gettysburg and, once there, was quickly put to work. Her letter home was written just 3 days after the battle ended.

Gettysburg, Pa., July 7th, 1863 Wall Street, Half Past Two O'Clock, October 13, 1857 by James H. Cafferty and Charles G. Rosenberg
    Dear Cousin
        I am very tired tonight; have been on the field all day— went to the 3rd Division 2nd Army Corps. I suppose there are about five hundred wounded belonging to it….There are no words in the English language to express the sufferings I witnessed today. The men lie on the ground; their clothes have been cut off them to dress their wounds; they are half naked, have nothing but hardtack to eat only as Sanitary Commissions, Christian Associations, and so forth give them. I was the first woman who reached the 2nd Corps after the three days fight at Gettysburg. I was in the Corps all day, not another woman within a half mile….To give you some idea of the extent and numbers of the sounds, four surgeons, none of whom were idle fifteen minutes of time, were busy all day amputating legs and arms. I gave to every man that had a leg or arm off a gill of wine, to every wounded in the Third Division, one glass of lemonade, some bread and preserves and tobacco.

I feel very thankful that this was a successful battle; the spirit of the men is so high that many of the poor fellows said today, "What is an arm or leg to whipping Lee out of Penn." I would get on first rate if they would not ask me to write to their wives; that I cannot do without crying, which is not pleasant to either party. I do not mind the sight of blood, have seen limbs taken off and was not sick at all.

It is a very beautiful, rolling country here; under favorable circumstances I should think healthy, but now for five miles around, there is an awful smell of putrefaction. Women are needed here very badly, anyone who is willing to go to field hospitals.
    Cornelia

Source: Henrietta Stratton Jaquette, editor, South after Gettysburg, Letters of Cornelia Hancock, 1863–1868 (New York: Crowell, 1956), pp. 16–19; reprinted in p. 288.] Robert D. Marcus, David Burner, Anthony Marcus, *America Firsthand: Readings from Settlement to Reconstruction*, Sixth Edition, Volume One (Boston: Bedford/St. Martin's, 2004), p. 288.

Thinking Critically

1. **Documentary Analysis**
   What language does Hancock use to make the hospital come alive for those who are reading her letter?

2. **Historical Interpretation**
   What assumptions about women of the Civil War era is Hancock challenging? What assumptions might she be reinforcing?

after the battle. At the end of May, Union forces took control of the crossroads town of Cold Harbor, Virginia, but Confederate forces attacked, and Grant ordered a counterattack. The armies fought along a line from Cold Harbor to the Chickahominy River. In this case, even Grant thought the cost too high. Wounded soldiers could not escape fires that roared through the thick undergrowth, and the suffering was terrible. He wrote in his *Memoirs* that this attack was the only one he wished he had never ordered. The Union lost 13,000 troops to the Confederate 2,500. In spite of the terrible losses, Grant still did not retreat.

In June 1864, Grant attacked Petersburg, then the second largest city in Virginia, and settled down for a siege. Grant telegraphed Lincoln, "I propose to fight it out on this line if it takes all summer." It was what Lincoln wanted from a general. But while Grant was not retreating, he was not making much progress either. Some newspapers began to call Grant a "butcher." Others just wondered if the war would ever end.

At least three factors now caused the Civil War's high death toll. Lee and Grant had shifted tactics from a limited war to a war of attrition. Each army meant to destroy the other, killing and wounding as many soldiers as possible. After 1863, there were no more limited engagements. Weapons were also deadlier than anything used in previous wars. Finally, medicine was still in its infancy. The wounded often died from infections that only a few years later a new generation knew how to treat. Given all three factors, grieving became part of life, for troops and for families at home.

Before the Civil War, armies fought with muskets, which took time to load and were not that accurate. Most military authorities in prior wars agreed that the best way to attack was in a close-order formation in which a well-trained army marched forward shooting, reloading, and shooting again. If both sides had muskets, the inaccuracy and short range of the weapons reduced the danger to any one soldier. That strategy was what had been taught at West Point where most senior officers of both the North and the South had been trained.

But the close-order formation was a virtual death sentence to troops facing an army with rifles. The new rifles, developed in France and by the American James H. Burton at the federal armory at Harper's Ferry in the 1850s, increased the distance that a soldier could shoot four-fold, and the spin a rifle gave to a bullet meant that it did a lot more damage to the human body. By 1863, Union factories developed repeating rifles that made the firepower of these weapons much faster and more deadly. The accuracy of rifles also meant that opponents could identify officers and shoot them, a reason why so many generals were killed in the war and why generals, like Grant, began wearing private's uniforms. The South never matched the North in weapons production, and many of its new weapons were either captured or came from blockade runners. The South's slow production of rifles was one reason it suffered more casualties than the North.

Artillery also became a key defensive weapon in the Civil War. New cannons that fired grapeshot and canister, rather than old fashioned cannon balls, were like giant shotguns. Defending armies in the Civil War could shoot down row after row of attackers.

A Union cavalry officer described the results of these new weapons in combat. In July 1862, the morning after Confederate army units attacked Union placements at Malvern Hill, Virginia, he said, "Our eyes saw an appalling spectacle upon the slopes down to the woodlands half a mile away. Over five thousand dead and wounded men were on the ground…enough were alive and moving to give the field a singular crawling effect." That result is what the new weapons of war did to people.

Medicine, Nursing, and a New Role for Women

Many of those wounded in the Civil War died because of a lack of effective medical treatment. Indeed, more soldiers died of diseases during the war than died in combat. It was just after the war that European researchers Louis Pasteur and Joseph Lister developed modern bacteriology. No Civil War doctor, North or South, knew that microbes in contaminated water or on hands or unsterilized instruments caused infection, or that mosquitoes could be as dangerous to troops as enemy bullets. Antiseptics did not exist. Medical education was primitive.

Military camps, where large numbers of men lived in close and often unsanitary quarters, were breeding grounds for disease. Many soldiers thought that it was better to avoid a physician than get close to one. Soldiers North and South agreed with the Alabama soldier who wrote that "I believe the Doctors kill more than they cour [cure]" and with the Massachusetts officer who said that the regimental surgeon was "a jackass."

To fill gaps in medical care, women began to nurse the wounded and the sick. Before the war, nursing had been almost exclusively men's work. But now the men were fighting, and the women were determined to aid the cause for which sons, husbands, and lovers were risking their lives. In the North, the United States Sanitary Commission became a powerful voluntary women's organization that was able to brush aside the army Medical Bureau and take on everything from raising money for medical supplies to providing nurses in field hospitals.

Elizabeth Blackwell, the first American woman M.D., began organizing the **Sanitary Commission** in 1861 and with widespread support, most of all from the troops whom its nurses aided, it flourished despite hostility from male army physicians. The reformer and social worker Dorothea Dix was named "Superintendent of Female Nurses." By the end of the war, Dix had organized 3,000 Northern women volunteers to serve as army nurses in addition to others who were paid directly by the Sanitary Commission. Still other women, most notably Clara Barton, who later helped create the American Red Cross, became free-agent nurses, helping wherever they could. Mary Ann Bickerdyke began serving as a nurse at Cairo, Illinois, and followed Grant's and Sherman's armies across the South. Mother Bickerdyke, as the troops called her, was the only woman Sherman authorized to serve in his advanced base hospitals.

Women in the South took up similar duties, often despite greater hostility. Southern culture, even more than Northern, treated middle-class white women as in need of constant protection. Moving into a hospital as a nurse was hardly protected work, and it brought women into close contact with male bodies, something

Sanitary Commission
Created in 1861 to improve the medical services and treatment for sick and wounded Union soldiers during the course of the war.

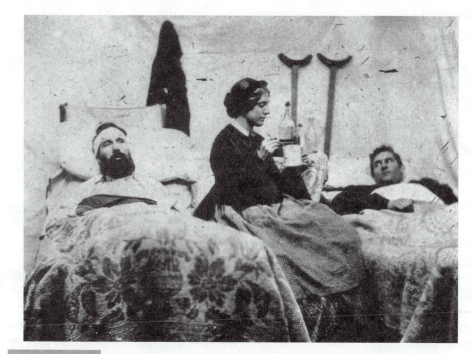

Ann Bell, a young nurse with the U.S Sanitary Commission, treats wounded Union soldiers.

previously thought improper. But the sick were there, and the women were determined to help. The *Confederate Baptist* offered religious sanction for this new role for women saying that "they are most valuable auxiliaries." In spite of concerns about "delicacy," "modesty," and "refinement," women went to work as nurses in the South.

Sara Agnes Pryor, who had lived in comfort before the war, volunteered to help in Virginia hospitals. When she saw a nurse kneeling to hold the stump of an amputated arm she fainted and thought she was wholly "unfit for the work." But Pryor overcame her "fine-lady faintness" and became a serious professional. Mary Rutledge Fogg was from one of the South's grand families in Nashville, and she used her status to pressure Jefferson Davis to allow her to start military hospitals in Nashville, Memphis, and Knoxville after seeing "50 brave soldiers" die "for the want of proper nurses." Phoebe Yates Levy Pember, a 40-year-old widow, was named matron of the Confederate hospital in Richmond where she and her sisters provided for the hundreds of wounded soldiers who streamed into the Confederate capital.

Women nurses, North and South, looked to their hero Florence Nightingale, the English woman who had virtually invented modern nursing while serving British troops in the 1853–1856 Crimean War. And, like Nightingale, the nurses of the Civil War sought to bring healing to wounded soldiers as well as comfort to the dying and those who were recovering.

Presidential Politics and Sherman's March to the Sea, Then North

While women like Pryor and Barton tried to comfort the wounded, soldiers fought, and Grant held his line in Virginia, it was not clear whether Lincoln could hold his office. Continuing losses, lack of progress at Petersburg, and hostility to emancipation all combined to strengthen the chances of the Copperhead antiwar Democrats in the 1864 presidential election. None were more aware of this situation than the leaders of the Confederacy. Lee knew he could not hold Petersburg forever, but he was confident that all he needed to do was hold the city until the November elections. If Grant made no progress, and casualties remained high, Lee and Davis thought that the Copperhead Democrats would win the election and make peace.

While the Democrats grew stronger, many Republicans were losing heart by 1864. Congressman Martin F. Conway, a Republican from Kansas who had once criticized Lincoln for pursuing the war too slowly, now asked the president, "For god's sake try and arrange [peace] with the South…. The war-spirit is gone." When in August 1864 the Democrats nominated General McClellan, whom Lincoln had fired for being too cautious, Lincoln expected to be a one-term president. His only hope, he wrote, was "to save the Union between the election and the inauguration" that would take place in March 1865. Then, the picture on the battlefield changed dramatically (see Map 14-2).

When Grant had come east to fight in Virginia, he left his closest subordinate William T. Sherman in charge in the west. Sherman began a march across the heart of the Confederacy. Just as the Mississippi River campaign had cut the Confederacy in half from north to south, Sherman aimed to cut it in half from west to east. Slowly, avoiding major confrontations and keeping a careful eye on his supply trains, Sherman led his army, moving from Tennessee across Mississippi, Alabama, and into Georgia. Sherman saw little value or glory in winning battles. He said that glory in war, "is all moonshine; even success the most brilliant is over dead and mangled bodies, with the anguish and lamentation of distant families." Sherman just kept maneuvering and kept marching, fighting when necessary.

Confederate General John Bell Hood tried to stop Sherman before he reached Atlanta, an important railroad center. In August 1864, Sherman changed course, and the Confederate general thought Sherman was retreating, but Sherman won the next battle on August 30. The Confederates then evacuated Atlanta and burned most of

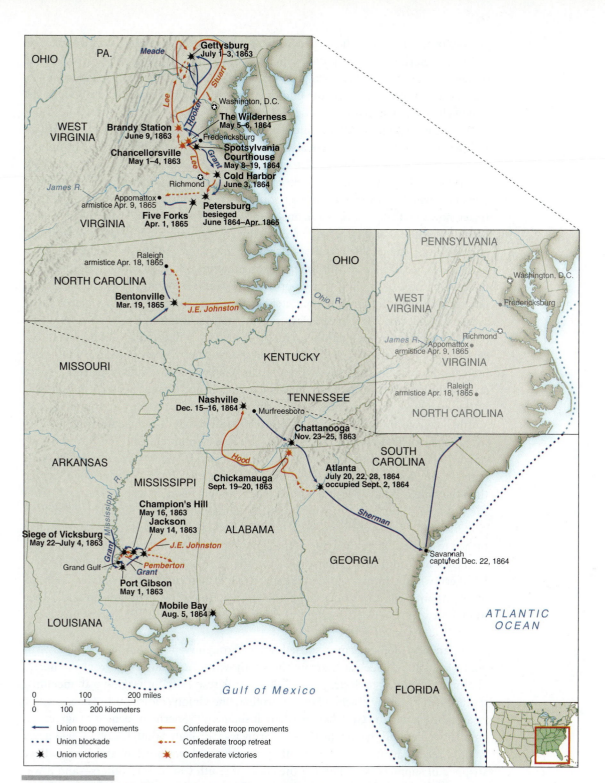

MAP 14-2 Major Civil War Battles, 1863–1865. While armies fought in Pennsylvania, Maryland, and Virginia all through 1863, 1864, and 1865, a Union force led by William T. Sherman marched through the Confederate states from Tennessee to Georgia and the Carolinas.

the city. On September 1, Sherman led his troops into Atlanta. Mary Boykin Chesnut wrote in her diary, "Since Atlanta I have felt as if all were dead within me, forever. We are going to be wiped off the earth."

As Sherman was taking Atlanta, Admiral Farragut led a daring raid on Mobile Bay, Alabama. Confederate forts guarded the harbor and well-placed mines (known then as torpedoes) blocked the entrance. When the lead ship in Farragut's fleet was sunk by an exploding mine, the fleet stopped. Farragut, in one of the war's immortal phrases ordered, "Damn the torpedoes! Full speed ahead." Farragut's fleet won control of Mobile's harbor. While Mobile, which was more inland, remained in Confederate hands, the port, which had been an essential base for Confederate blockade runners, was under Union control by the end of August 1864, adding one more link in the Union chain encircling the Confederacy.

Sherman's taking of Atlanta and Farragut's victory at Mobile Bay were important military victories, but they were also political victories for Lincoln and psychological victories for the North. Lincoln grew optimistic. Secretary of State Seward said, "Sherman and Farragut have knocked the bottom out of the" Democrats. Frederick Douglass, who had wanted a stronger abolitionist at the head of the 1864 Republican ticket, now said that "all hesitation ought to cease" regarding support for the president. Lincoln insisted that if he were reelected, the government must be based on "liberty and equality…an open field and a fair chance…in the race of life." Even the Democrat nominee McClellan shifted his tone, insisting that negotiations with the South be "on the basis of the Union," angering Copperhead/Peace Democrats who wanted peace on any terms. In November, Lincoln defeated McClellan by 2,220,846 popular votes to 1,809,445, ensuring Lincoln 212 electoral votes to McClellan's 21.

After the capture of Atlanta, no one was sure what Sherman would do next. His supply lines were stretched to the limit. In response, Sherman proposed to cut his army loose from supply lines entirely, live off the land, and march his 62,000 toughened troops straight through the heart of the Confederacy. Lincoln and Grant agreed. There would be little armed resistance, Sherman argued, since the Confederate army was fighting in the North, not protecting the Confederate heartland, which they presumed was safe.

Sherman believed that "[w]ar is cruelty and you cannot refine it." On November 15, he started his "march to the sea," destroying every farm, factory, and railroad in his path. Troops destroyed all that the army could not eat or use. In Milledgeville, Georgia, then the state capital, Sherman's troops met Union prisoners who had escaped from the notorious Southern prison camp at Andersonville. Some Union prisoners at Andersonville had spent years with only the barest rations, and their uniforms had turned to shreds. Many died there. The sight of these emaciated soldiers wearing rags "sickened and infuriated" the Northern soldiers. Along the way, escaping slaves and Southern white Unionists joined the march. Sherman captured Savannah, Georgia, on the Atlantic coast in late December. His telegram to President Lincoln said, "I beg to present you, as a Christmas gift, the city of Savannah, with 150 heavy guns and… about 25,000 bales of cotton."

In January 1865, Sherman started north through Georgia and the Carolinas. His goal was to attack Lee's army from the south while Grant attacked from the north. Sherman continued to destroy any of the South's resources for waging war, including food. When the army reached South Carolina, one Union soldier said, "Here is where treason began and, by God, here is where it shall end!" Sherman seemed to agree, and another soldier said that by the time the army was through, South Carolina "will never want to secede again." Every house they encountered was burned, and every village stripped of supplies. Sherman left the coast of South Carolina to others—and it was probably the good fortune of Charleston to be occupied by troops from the Union's Department of the South, including many black units, who saved the city. Sherman's army then marched inland to the state's capitol of Columbia, which was burned to the ground. When the army reached the North Carolina border, the burning stopped. But in South Carolina, the march left a trail of anger and resentment that lasted for generations as it demoralized a population that was already losing faith in the war.

The Road to Appomattox and Peace

Before Sherman could finish his march through North Carolina and into Virginia, other events began turning in Grant's favor. As news of Lincoln's November reelection, the capture of Savannah, and the destruction in South Carolina began to sink in, many

TABLE 14.1 Major Battles of the Civil War

Battle	Significance
Fort Sumter Charleston, South Carolina April 12–13, 1861	The firing on the federal garrison by Confederate forces was the opening of the war.
Bull Run or First Manassas Fairfax and Prince William Counties, Virginia July 21, 1861	Union forces marching south from Washington, DC, were met by Confederates at Bull Run Creek. Many Northerners expected a short skirmish and then a march to Richmond, but the Confederates turned the tide, and Union soldiers retreated back to Washington, DC.
New Orleans, Louisiana April 23–28, 1862	U.S. Navy ships under David G. Farragut took New Orleans, the largest city in the South, which remained in Union hands for the duration of the war.
Second Battle of Bull Run or Second Manassas August 28–30, 1862	The battle was a major Confederate victory and ended Northern hopes for an easy attack on the Confederate capital.
Antietam or Sharpsburg Washington County, Maryland September 16–18, 1862	Lee marched into Maryland but was stopped in a fierce battle at Antietam. Lincoln was furious that McClellan did not pursue Lee on his retreat into Virginia.
Fredericksburg, Virginia December 13, 1862	Union General Ambrose Burnside led an attack on the town as a first step toward attacking the Confederate capital of Richmond but was defeated by a well-defended force commanded by Robert E. Lee. The U.S. Army lost 13,000 troops, mostly in ill-conceived direct attacks while the Confederates lost 5,000. Northern morale sank.
Chancellorsville Spotsylvania County, Virginia April 30–May 6, 1863	A Union army led by General Joseph Hooker was defeated by a Confederate force, leading to a major incursion north of the Mason-Dixon line that threatened Washington, DC.
Gettysburg, Pennsylvania July 1–3, 1863	The bloodiest battle of the war led to Lee's withdrawal back to Virginia, ending the threat to Washington, DC.
Vicksburg, Mississippi May 18–July 4, 1863	Union troops commanded by Ulysses S. Grant finally took control of the Mississippi River from St. Louis to New Orleans and thus cut the Confederacy in half while securing easy access into the interior of the Confederacy.
Wilderness Spotsylvania County, Virginia May 5–7, 1864	Lincoln placed Grant in charge of all U.S. forces, and Grant led a bloody drive into Virginia. The first battle took place in deep woods (hence the Wilderness), and Grant—unlike previous Union generals—simply kept going.
Cold Harbor, Virginia May 31–June 12, 1864	Grant attacked the Confederate army and took horrible casualties. In his *Memoirs*, Grant wrote that this was the one attack he wished he had never ordered.
Atlanta, Georgia September 2, 1864	William T. Sherman led 62,000 troops into Georgia, defeating Confederate forces and taking Atlanta. Sherman's army then began its "march to the sea" taking Savannah on December 21 before running north and attacking Confederate forces in South and North Carolina.
Mobile Bay, Alabama August 2–23, 1864	U.S. Admiral David G. Farragut effectively ended blockade running out of Mobile, depriving the South of badly needed supplies.
Appomattox Court House, Virginia April 9, 1865	Lee surrendered to Grant.

14.1

14.2

14.3

14.4

in the South began to lose hope. In early 1865, Lee even began recruiting black soldiers with the promise of freedom for them, though not the end of slavery for others. By March 1865, Lee knew his army could not stay at Petersburg.

The retreat of the remaining Army of Northern Virginia out of Petersburg left Richmond open to attack. On April 2, while Jefferson Davis sat in Sunday morning services in Richmond, a messenger gave him a telegram. Many in the congregation thought they knew what it meant when Davis slipped out. All Sunday afternoon, the leaders of the Confederate government moved out of Richmond, taking what records, gold, and materials they could and burning the rest. By evening, mobs had replaced the government. The next morning, the Union army marched into Richmond, not to burn the city but to put out the fires that the retreating Confederates had started. The day after that, President Lincoln, with only a small guard of sailors, came to Richmond, sat at Davis's old desk, and greeted former slaves who were shouting "Glory to God!" and "Bless the Lord!" When one former slave knelt at Lincoln's feet the president said, "Don't kneel to me. That is not right."

Davis fled south from Richmond to Danville where he announced that "nothing is now needed to render our triumph certain, but…our own unquenchable resolve." But resolve was melting. Lee's troops were weak from lack of food. He tried one last attack on April 9, and when that failed, sent word to Grant that he was ready to surrender. The two generals—Grant and Lee—met in Wilmer McLean's living room in Appomattox, Virginia, that afternoon. Grant remembered the encounter. "We soon fell into a conversation about old army times.…Our conversation grew so pleasant that I almost forgot the object of our meeting." But when Lee turned back to the matter at hand, Grant wrote out the terms of surrender. He allowed the Confederate soldiers to keep their horses and mules with them to help in planting crops for the year ahead, and Lee noted that "this would have a happy effect."

The first Union troops to arrive in Richmond on April 4, 1865 looked on a city in ruins.

Explore the Civil War on MyHistoryLab

WHAT BROUGHT THE UNITED STATES TO THE CIVIL WAR?

By 1860, the United States was divided between North and South, a divergence centered on the issue of slavery. Other elements, however, also separated the two sides. The South was mostly agricultural and rural compared to the far more urbanized and industrialized North. By 1861, the two sides were in the Civil War as 11 southern states had seceded as the Confederacy. A bloody conflict ensued that lasted until 1865 and cost more American lives than any other U.S. war before or since. The Union eventually won, bolstered by its economic advantages, but only after the deaths of 752,000 men.

Union soldiers pose with a captured Confederate cannon.

RESOURCES OF THE UNION AND THE CONFEDERACY, 1861

	Industrial Workers	Factories	Railroad Tracks (miles)
Union	1,300,000	110,000	22,000
Confederacy	110,000	1,800	9,000

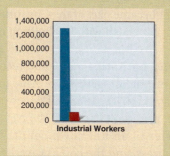

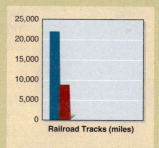

SOURCE: Multiple sources: Inter-University Consortium for Political and Social Research - http://www.icpsr.umich.edu/icpsrweb/ICPSR/studies/2896? archive=ICPSR&q=historical+economic+data+united+states]; Railroads and the Making of Modern America Digital History Project, University of Nebraska-Lincoln. [http://railroads.unl.edu/shared/resources/1861_Railroad.kml]; Inter-University Consortium for Political and Social Research - http://www.icpsr.umich.edu/icpsrweb/ICPSR/studies/2896?archive=ICPSR&q=historical+economic+data+united+states]

KEY QUESTIONS
Use **MyHistoryLab** *Explorer* to **answer** these **questions:**

Comparison ▶▶▶ *How did the South's population density contrast to that of the North?*

Map area data based on census information.

Response ▶▶▶ *Where were the major Civil War battles fought?*

Consider different regional strategies that affected military campaigns.

Analysis ▶▶▶ *How did the North win the Battle of Gettysburg?*

Examine the course of this decisive battle.

Grant arranged for Lee's starving army to receive military rations. At 4:30 p.m., Grant telegraphed Secretary of War Stanton, that "General Lee surrendered the Army of Northern Virginia this afternoon." The long and terrible war essentially over. Grant wrote of a sense of sadness "at the downfall of a foe who had fought so long and valiantly, and had suffered so much for a cause, though that cause was, I believe, one of the worst for which a people ever fought."

Lee's surrender did not quite end the war. Jefferson Davis fled south, hoping to regroup his government, perhaps in Texas, until he was captured in Georgia on May 10. He was held in custody for 2 years at Fortress Monroe before being released on bail. Davis was indicted for treason, but the charges were never pressed, although he was barred from ever holding a federal office again. During the next 2 decades, he tried various business ventures and wrote his defense of the cause he had led. Isolated Confederate units carried on the fight in remote areas, especially Texas, until May. But after the April 9 surrender at Appomattox, almost everyone knew that the war was over. Washington, DC, was draped with flags, people fired salutes, embraced, and sang. Soldiers on both sides found their weary way home. Those in the North were welcomed with grand parades; most of those in the South simply made it home.

Lincoln's Legacy

On January 31, 1865, even before Lee's surrender, the House of Representatives voted 119 to 56 to add a Thirteenth Amendment to the Constitution:

> Neither slavery nor involuntary servitude, except as a punishment for a crime whereof the party shall have been duly convicted, shall exist within the United States, or any place subject to their jurisdiction.

The floor of the House and visitors watching in the gallery erupted into cheers and applause. Many of those in the gallery were African-Americans; people who had not been even admitted to the House gallery until 1864. The Senate and the states quickly followed, and the amendment became part of the Constitution on December 18, 1865. The war that began over slavery ended with its abolition in every part of the United States.

After visiting Richmond, Virginia, on April 4 and 5 and receiving the news of Lee's surrender on April 9, President Lincoln gave what came to be known as his "last speech" at the White House on April 11, 1865. Of course, he did not know it was to be his last. Reviewing the president's speech, the *New York World* said, "Mr. Lincoln gropes…like a traveler in an unknown country without a map." In fact, the administration, the Congress, and the country were all groping to find their way through several extraordinarily difficult issues as the Civil War ended. Among the most contentious were those related to defining the rights of newly freed slaves: Did they have the right to vote? Did they have other political rights? Did they have a right to some of the land they had worked for so long? There were equally contentious arguments about the rights of the former Confederate states: Had they actually left the Union, in which case, did they needed to be readmitted, perhaps after a time as territories? Or had they never left the Union, in which case, could they could simply renew their place in the country and make their own laws? No one really knew the answers or how to get answers. As Lincoln said on April 11, "Unlike a case of a war between independent nations, there is no authorized organ for us to treat with. No one man has authority to give up the rebellion for any other man. We simply must begin with, and mold from, disorganized and discordant elements."

Lincoln also called the question of whether the Confederate states had left the Union a "pernicious abstraction." He did not want to debate whether the

THINKING HISTORICALLY
Abraham Lincoln, Second Inaugural Address, 1865

As Lincoln took the oath of office for the second time, everyone knew that the Civil War was about to end. No one, of course, knew that the president had only weeks to live. But it was the occasion of one of the most memorable speeches in American history. Lincoln said:

On the occasion corresponding to this four years ago, all thoughts were anxiously directed to an impending civil war. All dreaded it—all sought to avert it.…Both parties deprecated war; but one of them would *make* war rather than let the nation survive; and the other would accept war rather than let it perish. And the war came.

One eighth of the whole population were colored slaves, not distributed generally over the Union, but localized in the Southern part of it. These slaves constituted a peculiar and powerful interest. All knew that this interest was, somehow, the cause of the war. To strengthen, perpetuate, and extend this interest was the object for which the insurgents would rend the Union, even by war; while the government claimed no right to do more than to restrict the territorial enlargement of it. Neither party expected for the war, the magnitude, or the duration, which it has already attained. Neither anticipated that the *cause* of the conflict might cease with, or even before, the conflict itself should cease. Each looked for an easier triumph, and a result less fundamental and astounding. Both read the same Bible, and pray to the same God; and each invokes His aid against the other. It may seem strange that any men should dare to ask a just God's assistance in wringing their bread from the sweat of other men's faces; but let us judge not that we be not judged.

The prayers of both could not be answered; that of neither has been answered fully.…Fondly do we hope—fervently do we pray—that this mighty scourge of war may speedily pass away. Yet, if God wills that it continue, until all the wealth piled by the bond-man's two hundred and fifty years of unrequited toil shall be sunk, and until every drop of blood drawn with the lash, shall be paid by another drawn with the sword, as was said three thousand years ago, so still it must be said "the judgments of the Lord, are true and righteous altogether."

With malice toward none; with charity for all; with firmness in the right, as God gives us to see the right, let us strive on to finish the work we are in; to bind up the nation's wounds; to care for him who shall have borne the battle, and for his widow, and his orphan—to do all which may achieve and cherish a just and lasting peace, among ourselves, and with all nations.

Source: *Congressional Globe*, March 4, 1865, Senate, 39th Congress, 4th Session, pp. 1424–1440.

Thinking Critically

1. **Historical Interpretation**
   What does this speech tell you about Lincoln's views on the root causes of the war? Was his interpretation universally accepted?

2. **Historical Interpretation**
   What sort of postwar Reconstruction do you think Lincoln had in mind with his "with malice toward none; with charity for all; with firmness in the right" statement? Does it offer any hint of the possible nature of Reconstruction under Lincoln?

states had really left the Union and therefore needed to be readmitted or whether they had simply been "in rebellion" and therefore, with the end of the rebellion, were back in their old places. The issue for him, he said, was much simpler: "We all agree that the seceded States, so called, are out of their proper practical relation with the Union; and that the sole object of the government, civil and military, in regard to those States is to again get them into that proper practical relation." In fact, the issue was not so simple. If the states had actually left the Union, then Congress could impose conditions on their readmission such as granting blacks the right to vote. If they had never left, then it was more difficult to impose such conditions.

In April 1865, Lincoln began to give more attention to the postwar era. Some thought he had decided that guaranteeing former slaves the right to vote should be a key element in the integration of the Confederate states back into the Union, but he did not announce his policy. On the morning of April 14, he met with the cabinet to discuss what he was now calling "reconstruction." He directed Secretary of War Stanton to develop military districts and temporary military governments across the South to avoid anarchy and supervise a return to civilian rule. Those at the meeting remembered that Lincoln said the agenda had shifted from the war to a new set of peacetime issues on which "we must soon begin to act." But Lincoln would not be the one doing the acting.

That same evening, the president and his wife attended a play at Ford's Theater. He was shot by John Wilkes Booth, who had become convinced that Lincoln was, indeed, going to give former slaves the right to vote. Early the next morning, Lincoln died. As April 1865 ended, the country was in mourning, and it was at peace—and no one knew what the future held.

14.4   **Quick Review** How was the violence of the Civil War different from other wars in which the United States was involved?

CONCLUSION

When the Civil War began in 1861, people North and South hoped for and expected a short and limited war, but it was not to be. Four years of terrible violence would follow.

When the first calls for troops were issued, enthusiastic young men signed up for service in the Union and Confederate armies, anxious not to miss out on the adventure and glory that they were sure would come in a short and easy war. But attitudes changed quickly. In the first significant battle of the war, at Bull Run Creek near Manassas, Virginia, in July 1861 tourists from Washington, DC, accompanied Union forces to watch what they were sure would be an easy victory. But in spite of early predictions, Confederate forces turned the tide and the Union army and their visitors were quickly driven back to the relative safety of the nation's capital.

In spite of early successes by the U.S. Navy in blockading many Southern ports and in opening up portions of the Mississippi River to Union forces, President Lincoln soon became convinced that the nation was in for a long and bloody war and began looking for a general who had the tenacity to lead troops to a convincing victory. But through 1861, 1862, and 1863, in spite of bloody battles— a second one at Bull Run in August 1862 followed by the bloodiest day of the war at Antietam, Maryland, that September; further battles at Fredericksburg, Virginia, in December; then Chancellorsville, Virginia, in April 1863; and Gettysburg, Pennsylvania, that July—the war seemed to have no conclusive end in sight. Battles took place as far away as Missouri, New Mexico, and Minnesota, some with western Indian tribes angry at expanding white settlement and some between Northern and Southern sympathizers. Many, North and South, began to lose hope.

In the North, Peace Democrats, soon calling themselves Copperheads, began to campaign for an end to the war and for letting the South go its own way. The New York Draft Riots of July 1863 illustrated the way many white immigrants in that city had little interest in fighting a war and, indeed, blamed local blacks—whom they attacked across the city—for causing their troubles. At the same time, in the South, starvation spread, and Southern cities, including the Confederate capital of Richmond, Virginia, were wracked with bread riots.

While others debated, however, black and white abolitionists knew exactly what they wanted from the war—an end to slavery everywhere in the United States. From the earliest days of the war, abolitionists had urged Lincoln to use his war powers to free all slaves, and some, like the former slave Frederick Douglass, insisted that the only terms on which the war could be won and the nation united was the complete abolition of the institution of slavery that had led to war in the first place. Finally, in the fall of 1862, after more than a year of caution, President Lincoln decided to act and on January 1, 1863, signed the Emancipation Proclamation, freeing all slaves in the rebellious states and calling on former slaves to enlist in the Union army. Former slaves who had been flocking to Union posts now joined the army and quickly attained equality with white soldiers as well as a reputation for valor that impressed many.

Still the war itself continued. Women, North and South, became nurses—a previously all-male profession—to help the wounded and suffering soldiers. In 1863, after the Union army's victory at Vicksburg on the Mississippi River, Lincoln selected Ulysses S. Grant after searching for a general who had the determination to do what had to be done to win the war. Grant began a series of attacks on Confederate forces in Virginia in an effort to both defeat the main body of the Confederate army and take the Confederate capital of Richmond. At the same time, Grant's former deputy, William T. Sherman, began a march across the South, from the Mississippi River to Atlanta, Georgia, and then a "march to the sea" that captured the port city of Savannah, Georgia, in December, 1864. As 1865 began, Sherman's army turned north, marching through the Carolinas to attack Virginia from the south while Grant's army had new victories in Virginia. Finally on April 9, 1865, the main Confederate army commanded by Robert E. Lee surrendered to Grant. The Civil War was over. Days later, President Lincoln, who was just beginning to turn his attention to what might come next, was assassinated. The rebuilding of the country would be in other hands.

| CHAPTER REVIEW | The Civil War became a "war of attrition." How did that style of waging war contribute to the Union victory? |

Chapter 14   Chapter Review

FORT SUMTER TO ANTIETAM, 1861–1862

14.1 Explain how the early battles of the war shaped future events.

Review Questions

1. **Contextualization**
   What lessons did each side take away from the First Battle of Bull Run?

2. **Comparison**
   Compare and contrast the strategies of the North and the South in the first 2 years of the war. How did each side's strategy reflect its strengths and weaknesses?

3. **Historical Interpretation**
   How important was Union naval supremacy to the North's eventual victory?

THE ROAD TO EMANCIPATION

14.2 Analyze how the war influenced attitudes toward slavery in white and black communities, leading to the Emancipation Proclamation and to black soldiers in the Union army.

Review Questions

4. **Contextualization**
   How would you explain Lincoln's initial reluctance to link the war to the abolition of slavery?

5. **Historical Interpretation**
   What light does the Union response to escaped slaves shed on the diversity of opinion about slavery in the North?

6. **Chronological Reasoning**
   How did Lincoln's views on emancipation evolve over the course of the war? How would you explain the changes you note?

THE HOME FRONT: SHORTAGES, OPPOSITION, RIOTS, AND BATTLES

14.3 Explain how the war's death toll and civilian shortages affected life—North and South—during the war.

Review Questions

7. **Cause and Effect**
   How did financial problems undermine the Southern war effort?

8. **Historical Interpretation**
   How did Southern women contribute to the war effort? How did the war change the role of women in Southern society?

9. **Comparison**
   Compare and contrast the Northern and Southern home fronts. How would explain the changes you note?

FROM GETTYSBURG TO APPOMATTOX AND BEYOND

14.4 Analyze the strategies and costs of fighting a long and terrible war.

Review Questions

10. **Constructing Arguments**
    Defend or refute the following statement: "After the Union victories at Gettysburg and Vicksburg in July, 1863, the eventual defeat of the Confederacy was all but certain." What evidence can you produce to support your position?

11. **Comparison**
    How did Union strategy change after Grant was given overall command?

12. **Recognizing Cause and Effect**
    What factors contributed to the extraordinarily high death toll during the Civil War?

13. **Historical Interpretation**
    Reread Lincoln's Second Inaugural Address. To what forces does Lincoln attribute the war?

14. **Contextualization**
    What did "freedom" mean to Frederick Douglass? What rights and responsibilities did it entail?

Reconstruction

This popular picture, drawn by A. H. Ward for *Harper's Weekly* in November 1867, illustrated the prime meaning of Reconstruction for many African-Americans, whether former slaves or former soldiers in the Union army. The end of slavery brought—for the moment—the right to vote.

For those who had been enslaved it was a day of freedom. They celebrated as others had done. Houston H. Holloway, a slave sold three times before his 20th birthday recalled the day emancipation came to Georgia: "I felt like a bird out of a cage....The week passed off in a blaze of glory." Six weeks later, Holloway and his wife celebrated the birth of a new baby and "received my free born son into the world." For some former slaves, nothing mattered more than getting away from their old plantations. They moved short distances to be with friends and family or great distances to Louisiana, Indian Territory, or the North. For others, the news that they could now be wage-earning employees on the same plantations where they had previously worked without pay was the best option available. Whatever their situation and regardless of their previous status, emancipation changed every aspect of life for all people of the United States.

CHAPTER OBJECTIVE

Demonstrate an understanding of the development and decline of Reconstruction.

LEARNING OBJECTIVES

FEDERAL RECONSTRUCTION POLICY

Explain the political development of federal Reconstruction policy.

15.1

THE IMPACT OF RECONSTRUCTION

Explain the impact of Reconstruction on African-American life in the South.

15.2

TERROR, APATHY, AND THE CREATION OF THE SEGREGATED SOUTH

Analyze the reasons Reconstruction ended and the impact of Redemption.

15.3

Radical Republicans
A shifting group of Republican congressmen, who favored abolishing slavery and advocated full rights for former slaves in the South.

After January 1863, the Emancipation Proclamation made the Union Army an army of liberation for slaves during the war itself. Many slaves did not wait for the Union army to arrive. When Joseph Davis fled the plantation that he and his brother Jefferson Davis owned at Davis Bend on the Mississippi River in 1862, slaves took over the property and began running it themselves, much to the surprise of General Grant who arrived at Davis Bend with the Union army in 1863. Even for those still in slavery throughout the war, word passed quickly. In Mississippi, while the war was still far away, one slave responded to a planter's greeting "Howdy, Uncle" with an angry "Call me Mister." Other slaves refused to work unless they were paid or simply left, often in search of family members, sometimes just because, for the first time in their lives, they could.

In the aftermath of the Civil War, women and men who had been considered the property of others found that they could buy property. They could refuse to work for people who only recently had coerced their labor. They could travel without the hated passes from white masters. Sometimes they were reunited with family members from whom they had long been separated. People for whom literacy had been illegal now learned to read and write. They became teachers, started their own schools, and opened colleges and universities. Slaves and free blacks who had never dreamed of voting became voters and officeholders, members of state legislatures, and members of the United States Congress. They passed laws creating a system of public education and dreamed of better days ahead. The story of the era known as Reconstruction, its high hopes and its violent and tragic ending, is the focus of this chapter.

FEDERAL RECONSTRUCTION POLICY

15.1 Explain the political development of federal Reconstruction policy.

In December 1864, Senator Charles Sumner of Massachusetts thought Lincoln had agreed that former Confederate states must grant all citizens the same right to vote as whites (which meant the right of males to vote) to be readmitted to the Union. But while Lincoln had come to believe that blacks who fought in the Union army had won the right to vote, he also believed that the Constitution gave states the right to determine who voted and he did not yet seem ready, as far as anyone knew, to interfere.

When Lincoln died in April 1865, his own party was divided on the question of the vote for African-Americans and on how best to handle the readmission of the Confederate states within the nation. With the war just ending, the majority of Republicans, in and out of Congress, were still moderates. Many had begun the Civil War with the intention only to save the Union and had been won over in the course of the war to believing that the end of the war had to mean the end of slavery. Still, that revised intention was just a single goal; they were not committed to voting rights or the award of land for newly freed African-Americans. Other Republicans who were coming to be known as **Radical Republicans**—often called simply "the radicals"—in Congress were determined that the North's victory in the Civil War meant that the country should give formerly enslaved people not only their freedom but also the right to vote and to hold office. In addition, they believed the country should provide land to those who had previously worked other people's land as their slaves. In other words, formerly enslaved people should be given all the rights of white Americans.

American Voices

Jourdon Anderson, Letter to Colonel P. H. Anderson, 1865

After Jourdon Anderson and his wife Mandy were freed from slavery on a Tennessee plantation belonging to Colonel P. H. Anderson, they moved north and settled in Dayton, Ohio. A year later, with the war over and the Confederate army disbanded, Colonel Anderson wrote to his former slaves asking them to return as employees. Jourdan Anderson responded to his former master:

As to my freedom, which you say I can have, there is nothing to be gained on that score, as I got my free-papers in 1864 from the Provost-Marshall-General of the Department at Nashville. Mandy says she would be afraid to go back without some proof that you are sincerely disposed to treat us fairly and justly—and we have concluded to test your sincerity by asking you to send us our wages for the time we served you. This will make us forget and forgive old scores, and rely on your justice and friendship in the future. I served you faithfully for thirty-two years and Mandy twenty years. At $25 a month for me, and $2 a week for Mandy, our earnings would amount to $11,680. Add to this the interest for the time our wages has been kept and deduct what you paid for our clothing and three doctors visits to me and pulling a tooth for Mandy, and the balance will show what we are in justice entitled to....If you fail to pay us for faithful labors in the past we can have little faith in your promises in the future. We trust the good Maker has opened your eyes to the wrongs which you and your fathers have done to me and my fathers, in making us toil for generations without recompense. Here I draw my wages every Saturday night, but in Tennessee there was never any pay day for the negroes any more than for the horses and cows. Surely there will be a day of reckoning for those who defraud the laborer of his hire.

Jourdon Anderson

P.S. –Say howdy to George Carter, and thank him for taking the pistol from you when you were shooting at me.

Source: John David Smith, *Black Voices From Reconstruction, 1865–1877* (Gainesville: University Press of Florida, 1997), pp. 43–44.

Thinking Critically

1. Documentary Analysis

What examples can you find in the document of Jourdon Anderson's sense of humor?

2. Historical Interpretation

Why would Colonel Anderson invite Jourdon Anderson back to work on the plantation where he had been a slave? How do you think the former slave owner responded to this letter from Jourdon Anderson?

A similar kind of split existed over the proper ways to readmit states to the Union. Lincoln and many other Republicans had argued throughout the war that the Southern states had never left the United States; after all, preserving the Union had been the initial reason that the North went to war in 1861. If the Southern states had never left, there was little to do at war's end but for them to conduct elections for local and national office and resume their place in the nation. Others, however, especially the Radical Republicans, argued that after 4 years of fighting against the Union, the states of the former Confederacy were effectively out of the country and could be readmitted only after some period in which the federal government sought to reconstruct state governments to ensure that those who led the rebellion—traitors, as the radicals always called them—would not lead the new state governments and that the full civil rights of African-Americans would be ensured. The difference of opinion was significant, and compromise was not easy.

While Lincoln pondered the question of the vote and argued that the debate over the term *readmission* was a distraction from the work at hand, he did take another step that would have far-reaching significance in what was to come. Lincoln proposed establishing a federal Bureau of Freedmen, Refugees and Abandoned Lands.

15.1

15.2

15.3

Freedmen's Bureau
Agency established by Congress in March 1865 to provide social, educational, and economic services as well as advice and protection to former slaves.

Presidential Reconstruction
Name given to the immediate post–Civil War era, 1865–1866, when President Andrew Johnson took the lead to return full rights to the former Confederate states.

Congressional Reconstruction
Name given to the period 1867–1870 when the Republican-dominated Congress controlled Reconstruction era policy. Sometimes it is also known as Radical Reconstruction.

The **Freedmen's Bureau**, as it came to be known, would last longer and do more than Lincoln ever imagined when he signed the legislation authorizing it in March 1865.

Lincoln placed great faith in the new government established in Louisiana after the Union victories there. The new legislature pledged loyalty to the Union, created a public school system, and after it was proposed ratified the Thirteenth Amendment abolishing slavery. It had not, however, granted former slaves the right to vote. Lincoln pondered the question of whether Louisiana could be brought into proper practical relation with the Union sooner by sustaining, or by discarding, her new state government. His own answer was clear: he believed that the Louisiana government could *eventually* extend the vote and would provide a model of transition back into the Union for other Confederate states. The more radical members of Congress did not want to give Louisiana full rights as a state until it had guaranteed that blacks would be given the right to vote. They blocked counting Louisiana's electoral votes in the 1864 election and the seating of the state's new senators. They would soon do more.

The post–Civil War era is often described as including three distinct time periods. The first period is referred to as **Presidential Reconstruction** in 1865–66, when President Johnson sought to return states to their prewar status with only the institution of slavery being abolished. The next period is known as the more radical **Congressional Reconstruction** (sometimes Radical Reconstruction), which began when Congress began to challenge Johnson in 1867 and generally continued through

This illustration from *Harper's Weekly* shows agents of the Freedmen's Bureau trying to settle a dispute between white and black Southerners. The Freedmen's Bureau took an active role in the lives of citizens in a way that the federal government had never done before, managing disputes, organizing schools, and ensuring political rights for recently enfranchised African-Americans.

the end of Grant's two terms in 1877. The last period, known as **"Redemption"** (by its defenders but not by those who lost rights in the process), began with the election of Rutherford B. Hayes in November 1876 and involved the withdrawal of federal troops from the South as well as the return of white-only governments. That last period culminated in the 1890s with the virtual disenfranchisement of all blacks in the South.

Although this typical chronology is far too simplistic, it does provide an accurate framework for the reconstruction process. The reality of the process was much more complex. Many factions battled from 1865 well into the 1880s and 1890s. Johnson was challenged even during his first years in office. Congressional Reconstruction had many ups and downs. Grant generally agreed with the Congressional radicals, those Congressional leaders and their black and white allies in the South who sought to transform the former Confederacy into a racially integrated region with equal rights. Nevertheless, in every year between 1867 and 1877, those who sought a radical Reconstruction of the South met resistance, often very effective resistance in the South and a growing inclination of Northerners to look the other way as they grew tired of the effort. Perhaps most important, the end of Reconstruction did not come all at once. It was a long process involving defeats and successes throughout the country.

The Presidential Reconstruction of Andrew Johnson, 1865–1866

When Andrew Johnson became president on April 15, 1865, he had served as vice president for only 6 weeks. Even so, he came to the presidency with far more experience than Lincoln had in 1861. Like Lincoln, Johnson grew up in poverty, but he had risen in Tennessee politics from city alderman to member of the state legislature, to Congress, to two terms as governor to the U.S. Senate. When Tennessee seceded from the Union in 1861, Johnson—apart from any other Senator from a Confederate State—stayed loyal to the Union and stayed in the Senate. He had long seen himself as a spokesman for the "honest yeomen" of Tennessee, and he hated what he called the state's "papered, bloated…slaveocracy." During the Civil War, Johnson served with distinction as military governor of Tennessee in those parts of the state where the Union army had taken control. When the Republicans met in 1864 to nominate Lincoln for a second term, incumbent Vice President Hannibal Hamlin offered little to the ticket; his home state of Maine was sure to go Republican and he had played virtually no role in the war. The choice of Johnson as Lincoln's running mate—a border state senator and governor—might add essential votes. Although two previous vice presidents had succeeded to the presidency, no one expected it to happen again.

When Johnson became president after Lincoln died, many of those known as the Radical Republicans in Congress embraced him. These so-called radicals wanted to be sure that the end of the Civil War did not bring merely a return to a version of the prewar status quo minus slavery but, instead, wanted the whole South to be "reconstructed" to assure economic, educational, and political equality for the former slaves. The radicals were often a minority in the Congress and the country, where many were willing to accept second-class status for former slaves, but the radicals

Redemption

A term used by opponents of Reconstruction for the era in which the federal government ended its involvement in Southern affairs, and southern whites took control of state governments and ended black political rights.

had the clearest agenda for what they wanted to see happen, and every act of postwar Southern resistance tended to strengthen their hand. In 1864, Johnson had said, "Treason must be made odious, and traitors must be punished and impoverished." And he repeated similar views to members of Congress who met with him right after Lincoln's assassination. Ohio Senator Benjamin F. Wade said, "By the Gods, there will be no trouble now in running the government." Another was overheard saying, "I believe, that the Almighty continued Mr. Lincoln in office as long as he was useful, and then substituted a better man to finish the work."

When Johnson announced his plans for Reconstruction on May 29, 1865, there was widespread disappointment. Johnson supported the Thirteenth Amendment, already passed by Congress and ratified by several states, and insisted that support for the amendment be a condition for the readmission of any Confederate state to the union. But Johnson refused to go beyond that. He made it clear that he had little interest in political rights for former slaves. In contrast to his earlier claims, Johnson declared a full amnesty and pardon for most of those who had taken part in the rebellion as long as they were willing to pledge loyalty to the Union and support the end of slavery. The amnesty included restoration of all land taken by the Union army. There were exceptions to Johnson's amnesty, however. Major Confederate officials and individuals who owned more than $20,000 in taxable property had to seek individual presidential pardons.

At first glance, the policy seemed tough on the South or at least on the former slaveholders of the South—perhaps tougher than Lincoln would have been—and consistent with Johnson's pledge to keep slaveholders "out in the cold." But soon, many wondered how many individual presidential pardons would be granted as they realized that Johnson was granting many more than they had expected. Blacks, though now free, seemed destined to be excluded from most of the rights of citizenship in the Johnson plan. If former slaveholders were to be given back their land, what land would there be for former slaves? Illinois Congressman Elihu B. Washburne said, "I have grounds to fear President Johnson may hold almost unconquerable prejudices against the African race."

While the Radical Republicans in Congress were terribly disappointed, many Southern whites were delighted at the opportunity to create a "white man's government," if they accepted the end of slavery. Under Johnson's plan, former Confederate states were readmitted as soon as they ratified the Thirteenth Amendment, and the new state governments that were quickly organized in the South were recognized by Johnson as the legitimate government of these states. (Since most Republicans continued to insist that the rebellious states had never left the Union, there was no official way or time for them to be *readmitted*.) Once recognized, these state governments, dominated by many of the same people who had been in power before the Civil War, began passing laws strictly limiting black rights, most of all, the right to vote. In addition, hunting, fishing, free grazing of livestock, which whites all assumed were their rights and which some slaves had enjoyed, were now declared illegal for blacks in a series of what were known as **Black Codes**, passed by states across the South, beginning with Mississippi's code passed in November 1865. One part of the Mississippi code said:

Black Codes
Laws passed by states and municipalities denying many rights of citizenship to free blacks and to control black labor, mobility, and employment.

> All freedmen, free negroes and mulattoes in the State, over the age of eighteen, found on the second Monday in January, 1866, or thereafter, with no lawful employment or business, or found unlawful assembling themselves together, either in the day or nit time, and all white persons assembling with freedmen, Free negroes or mulattoes, or unusually associating…on terms of equality… shall be deemed vagrants.

In many states, Black Codes either made it illegal for an African-American to own a gun or taxed guns at high rates. In cities, new urban police forces, like the one in Mississippi in 1865, were designed to "keep good order and discipline amongst the negro population." Police patrols not only enforced the law but also often terrorized blacks, especially those who refused to sign long-term labor contracts with former slave masters. Any former slave who ran away from a labor contract could be either arrested and returned to the plantation holding that contract or sentenced to a chain gang to pay off the fine for running away. African-Americans in Louisiana noted how similar the contracts were to slavery and how similar the new police were to the old slave patrols. They also asked "why men who but a few months since were in armed rebellion against the government should now have arms put in their hands." Johnson's amnesty, especially his expectation that these states would reassume all the rights of any other state, made these oppressive developments almost inevitable.

Congressional Radical Reconstruction, 1867–1869

The new Congress that was elected with Lincoln in November 1864 did not assemble until December 1865—8 months after his death. This Congress had an overwhelming Republican majority, including many who had become disillusioned with Johnson by the time they met, especially as they saw what was happening in the states that had so recently been at war with the Union. The new president, they thought, was clearly siding with the former slaveholders rather than the former slaves.

Those in Congress most unhappy with Johnson, the Radical Republicans, were led by Charles Sumner in the Senate and Thaddeus Stevens in the House. Stevens told the House, "The whole fabric of southern society *must* be changed, and never can it be done if this opportunity is lost." For Stevens, the core values of the Republican Party remained, as the party's campaign slogan said, "free labor" by "free men" who earned their livelihoods by the sweat of their own brows. But with Johnson moving quickly to recognize the new state governments in the old Confederacy and those governments passing rigid Black Codes, the moment seemed to be quickly slipping away. Johnson focused on the Constitutional clause giving each state the right to set up its own government and arrangements for voting. Stevens and the radicals focused on a different part of the Constitution, the clause guaranteeing each state a republican form of government.

Most of the Republicans in Congress were not as radical as Stevens or Sumner. In 1865, a majority probably still had reservations about black voting rights. Even so, nearly all were disappointed at Johnson's easy amnesty of so many former Confederate leaders and the way Southern states were coming back into the Union with their old leaders in power. They discredited Johnson's version of Reconstruction because the results resembled the antebellum South in far too many ways. In particular, the fact that 58 members of the Confederate Congress, six Confederate cabinet officers, and the vice president of the Confederacy were all elected to Congress in 1865 and 1866 symbolized the failure of Johnson's policy to bring about meaningful change. However, the Constitution also gave Congress its own specific ways of asserting its authority.

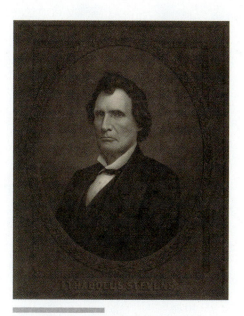

Pennsylvania Congressman Thaddeus Stevens wanted Reconstruction to mean a thorough reordering of Southern society in which former slaves would receive land and guaranteed voting rights from the federal government.

Soon after convening in December 1865, Congress created a Joint Committee on Reconstruction. Moderate Senator William Pitt Fessenden of Maine was appointed chair, and most of the radicals, including Stevens, were excluded. Nevertheless, Congress undermined presidential Reconstruction by refusing to seat the Congressional delegates from the former Confederate states, even though Johnson considered those states to be fully restored to the Union. (Johnson's use of "restoration" rather than "reconstruction" irked many in Congress who wanted to see at least some change rather than restoring states to the place they had held in 1860.) Despite Johnson's insistence that the states had a right to be represented in Congress, the reality was that the Constitution made each house of Congress sole judge of the qualifications of its members, and neither house was ready to seat former Confederate leaders. Senator Ben Wade demanded that no Southern state be given a vote in Congress until African-Americans had the right to vote in that state. Others called for the creation of territorial governments in the former Confederate states, which would be under the control of Congress so that both voting rights and land redistribution could be assured. But Congress itself was divided, and action beyond rejecting the delegates from the South was hard to come by. Even legislation to give blacks in the District of Columbia the right to vote—something Congress clearly had authority to do—could not make it through both houses, especially after a December 1865 referendum of white voters in the District rejected black voting rights 6,951 to 35.

Early in 1866, Illinois Senator Lyman Trumbull proposed two new pieces of legislation. Unlike the more radical Republicans, Trumbull still maintained a good working relationship with Johnson and worried about the federal government exceeding its authority. But given developments in the South, Trumbull felt Congress had the authority—even the duty—to protect the rights of newly freed African-Americans under the Thirteenth Amendment, which included language giving Congress the power to pass laws to enforce the amendment.

First, Trumbull proposed extending the life of the Freedmen's Bureau. When Lincoln signed the legislation creating the Bureau, it was envisioned as a 1-year transitional body. However, through late 1865 and early 1866, the Freedmen's Bureau was the key federal agency distributing food to former slaves, supporting the establishment of schools, and in some cases, even helping former slaves gain their own land. After consulting with the head of the bureau, General O. O. Howard, Trumbull became convinced that its work would take many years and proposed extending it to 1870. He also proposed giving it new authority to ensure that blacks had all "civil rights belonging to white persons" and giving bureau agents the authority to press charges against state officials who denied those rights.

Trumbull then proposed the far-reaching Civil Rights Bill of 1866 that defined all persons born in the United States (except Indians) as citizens, permanently ending the Dred Scott distinctions between whites and blacks. Although the bill was silent on the issue of voting, given that many of the citizens it referred to—women and children, for example—could not vote, it explicitly guaranteed rights to make contracts, bring lawsuits, and have the equal benefit of the laws without regard to race. The law declared that such provisions were "fundamental rights belonging to every man as a free man." It also authorized federal authorities to prosecute violations in federal courts, a significant provision since Southern state courts were quickly reverting to their white-dominated ways.

Both of Trumbull's bills would have appeared radical a year or two earlier, but in 1866, they were seen as moderate proposals from a moderate Senator, and everyone expected smooth sailing for them. Then, after they passed Congress easily, President Johnson vetoed both bills. He called the Freedmen's Bureau an "immense patronage" system that exceeded the constitutional authority of the federal government, and he characterized the civil rights bill an as unwarranted "concentration of all legislative powers in the national Government." In his veto of the Civil Rights bill, Johnson also went out of his way to say that giving blacks citizenship rights was wrong and that "the distinction of race and color is by the bill made to operate in favor of the colored and against the white race."

The vetoes ended congressional efforts to work with the president on Reconstruction. Trumbull attacked the president. Senator William Pitt Fessenden, up to then considered a moderate, predicted that Johnson would "veto every other bill we pass." Johnson was prepared to do just that. He wanted to court Northern Democrats and Southern whites in his bid for a second term. Congress passed both pieces of legislation over Johnson's vetoes and began to use a veto-proof two-thirds majority to pass similar legislation in spite of presidential opposition. The era of presidential-led Reconstruction was fast coming to an end.

After passing Trumbull's two major bills over the president's veto in the spring of 1866, Congress proposed another amendment to the U.S. Constitution. Amendments to the Constitution proposed in Congress are not subject to a presidential veto, although three-fourths of the state legislatures need to agree to them. So in 1866, Congress set out to put the Civil Rights law into the Constitution itself. Agreement to do so came quickly; however, agreement on the other provisions of the amendment came much more slowly. Congress was not yet ready to give all black males the same voting rights that all white males had, but Sumner and some other radicals would never support an amendment that did not guarantee such rights. When their opposition was combined with the Democratic minority who did not want any new rights inscribed in the Constitution, crafting the amendment became a major hurdle. Many members of Congress wanted to punish any state that withheld the vote from black males, but they did not want to punish those states—currently all of them—that withheld the vote from women or those states—including several in the North—that made it hard for recent immigrants to vote. All of these issues led to months of wrangling, but the compromise that emerged as the Fourteenth Amendment guaranteeing rights of citizenship to former slaves and others born or naturalized in the United States was nevertheless significant.

The key provision of the Fourteenth Amendment said:

> All persons born or naturalized in the United States, and subject to the jurisdiction thereof, are citizens of the United States and of the State wherein they reside. No State shall make or enforce any law which shall abridge the privileges or immunities of citizens of the United States; nor shall any State deprive any person of life, liberty, or property, without due process of law; nor deny to any person within its jurisdiction the equal protection of the laws.

Other clauses of the Fourteenth Amendment stated changes drastically different from the Three-Fifth's clause and other previously accepted parts of the Constitution. They included language saying that any state that limited the voting rights of male inhabitants of a state would have its representation in Congress reduced, that any person who had held federal office and then participated in rebellion against the government could not again hold office, and that Confederate debts were null and void as far as the federal government was concerned.

Both houses of Congress finally passed the amendment in June 1866 and sent it to the states for ratification. Just as Johnson had refused to recognize a state as having returned to the Union until it ratified the Thirteenth Amendment, Congress now refused to seat the members of the House or Senate elected by a state until the state had ratified the Fourteenth Amendment. The amendment was popular in the North and many in the South were anxious to return to Congress, so approval from the required three-quarters of the states came quickly and the amendment was ratified in July 1868.

When Congress reconvened in December 1866, the majority of Republicans had no interest in working with Johnson. While the president called for immediate restoration of the "now unrepresented States" to Congress, Congress decided that, in fact, the states of the former Confederacy needed to be governed directly from Washington until "some indefinite future time." Some said that Congress was raising the bar after earlier requiring only assent to the Fourteenth Amendment, but the majority in Congress were no longer in any mood to compromise.

In January 1867, Congress quickly passed a law—over presidential veto—giving black males in the District of Columbia the right to vote. Since the district was directly controlled by Congress, they could pass such a law even though the Fifteenth Amendment, giving all black males the same voting rights as white males, was not yet contemplated. Congressional leaders then turned to more far-reaching legislation. They passed the Reconstruction Act of 1867, which declared all Southern state governments—already recognized by Johnson—to be inoperative and divided the former Confederate states into five military districts, ordering the military to oversee the writing of new constitutions that would guarantee universal male suffrage (see Map 15-1). Only after these new constitutions were in place, and after a state had ratified the Fourteenth Amendment, would Congress admit its representatives to Congress.

The president protested that the Reconstruction Act was, "the death-knell of civil liberty." African-Americans in the South, however, embraced the opportunity to participate in the political process. In addition to registering to vote and participating in constitution writing, blacks struck for higher pay in Charleston, Savannah, Mobile, Richmond, and New Orleans. Blacks in Richmond demanded integrated horse-drawn streetcars. Across the South, they created **Union Leagues** that became a base for political action and mutual support. The leagues offered opportunities to gain experience in the political process or, as one former slave said, "We just went there, and we talked a little, made speeches on one question and another." Former slaves became political leaders. By 1867, James H. Jones, the former "body servant" to Jefferson Davis, was a featured speaker at Republican meetings across the South.

Union Leagues
In the South, a Republican Party organization led by African-Americans, which became an important organizing device after 1865.

The Final Break—Johnson's Impeachment

By 1867, President Johnson had become virtually irrelevant to federal Reconstruction policy. Congress passed laws, the president vetoed them, and Congress passed them over the president's veto. But the Freedman's Bureau was under the control of the president even if he vetoed the bill that kept it going. The creation of military districts in the South also gave the president significant powers as commander-in-chief, even though he had opposed creating them.

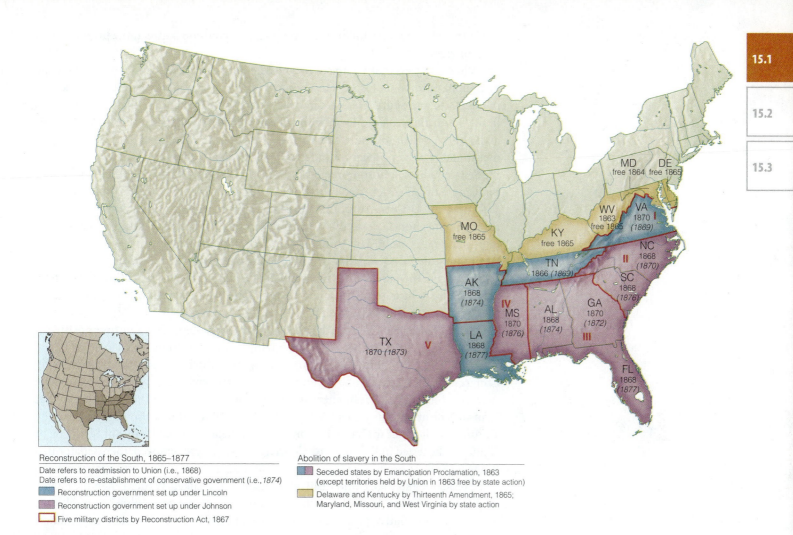

Reconstruction of the South, 1865–1877

Date refers to readmission to Union (i.e., 1868)
Date refers to re-establishment of conservative government (i.e., *1874*)

- Reconstruction government set up under Lincoln
- Reconstruction government set up under Johnson
- Five military districts by Reconstruction Act, 1867

Abolition of slavery in the South

- Seceded states by Emancipation Proclamation, 1863 (except territories held by Union in 1863 free by state action)
- Delaware and Kentucky by Thirteenth Amendment, 1865; Maryland, Missouri, and West Virginia by state action

MAP 15-1 Southern Military Districts. Having lost all faith in President Johnson's leadership, the Congress in 1867 created five military districts to govern the states of the former Confederacy until new state constitutions that guaranteed the rights, including voting rights, of African-Americans were put in place.

Some in Congress began to consider removing Johnson in early 1867, but they were in a minority. Instead, Congress passed a number of laws that most hoped would keep Reconstruction moving in spite of the president. One law required all presidential orders to the military to pass through the army chief, General Grant, before going to commanders in the field. Grant was known to side with Congress, and this strategy seemed like an important safeguard and a significant limitation of Johnson's power. Congress also passed the Tenure of Office Act, which said that any person whose appointment required the Senate's consent, namely, members of the cabinet and ambassadors, could be replaced only when the Senate approved a successor. The goal of the act was to ensure that Secretary of War Stanton, who had been appointed by Lincoln and who took a tough stance on Reconstruction, stayed in office.

These Congressional actions might have worked had Johnson been willing to play a passive role, but Johnson could be stubborn, proud, and self-focused. His loyal Secretary of the Navy Gideon Welles said, "He has no confidantes and seeks none." As a result, unlike Lincoln, Johnson was often out of touch with congressional thinking.

These traits set the stage for an even more serious collision between the president and the Congress.

While Congress took charge of Reconstruction, Johnson became convinced that he had public opinion on his side and began to encourage opponents of Reconstruction, in the North and South. He also removed several of the tougher military commanders in the South and replaced them with officers who were willing to let events take their own course, which meant letting former Confederates take control of local governments and use their power to undermine black rights. Then in February 1868, after the Senate refused Johnson's request to remove Stanton, the president, in violation of the Tenure of Office act, fired him. It was a clear challenge to congressional authority.

Under the U.S. Constitution, a president can be removed only for "high crimes and misdemeanors," terms the Constitution does not define. But the procedure for impeachment is clear. The House of Representatives is required to act as a sort of Grand Jury, deciding whether or not to bring charges, called impeachment, against the president. Then the Senate, with the Chief Justice of the Supreme Court presiding, acts as a jury to hear and vote on the charges. Only with a Senate vote to convict can a president be removed from office.

Led by Thaddeus Stevens, the House, with every Republican voting positively, agreed on a long list of charges, most having to do with Johnson's violation of the Tenure of Office Act but also a charge saying that the president had tried to bring Congress "into disgrace." However, the trial in the Senate did not go as well for the radicals. Removing a president was very serious business, and it was unclear that Johnson's obstructionism met the level of a "high crime." It was also not clear that the Tenure of Office Act was constitutional. Johnson claimed that he meant the firing of Stanton to be tested in the Supreme Court. If Johnson were removed, then Senator Ben Wade, president pro tem of the Senate, would become president since there was no vice president, and many who disliked Johnson also disliked Wade. When the Senate finally voted in mid-May of 1868, Johnson survived by one vote. Johnson could serve out his term in relative peace, although his chances for the Democratic nomination and reelection were slim.

The Right to Vote—Grant's Election and the Fifteenth Amendment

After Johnson's impeachment was resolved, both parties turned to selecting nominees for the presidential election in the fall of 1868. For the Republicans, the choice was easy. Ulysses S. Grant as commander of the army had supported the Republicans in Congress on the issues of Reconstruction; his own attitudes on race had been significantly reshaped by the courage shown by black troops during the Civil War, and he was the nation's war hero. The Republicans easily nominated him along with the Speaker of the House Schuyler Colfax of Indiana as his running mate. Grant ran on a cautious platform that nevertheless embraced extending voting rights to former slaves. His slogan was, "Let Us Have Peace."

Democrats were divided on issues of personality, on their opposition to Congressional Reconstruction, and on fiscal policies—whether to continue to authorize the printing of money, or "greenbacks," based on the federal promise to pay. After 21 ballots in which a number of candidates, including Andrew Johnson, failed to win the nomination, they chose former New York Governor Horatio Seymour, who had flirted with supporting the Confederacy during the war and who had called protesters in the New York Draft Riot "my friends." For vice president, they nominated a former Union general from Missouri, Francis Blair, who called for an end to Reconstruction, which he called the rule of "a semi-barbarous race of blacks."

While neither party articulated a fully developed economic policy, the lines between the parties were drawn on the issues of race. August Belmont, one of the nation's leading bankers, said that, in the 1868 election, financial matters paled in comparison with black voting rights. In November, Grant carried most of the North and the parts of the South under federal control, including North and South Carolina and Alabama. Seymour's home state of New York, along with New Jersey, Georgia, and Louisiana favored Seymour. The state governments in Florida, Mississippi, and Texas had not yet been recognized, and those states did not vote. Grant won 53 percent of the popular vote but an overwhelming 73 percent of the electoral vote for an easy victory.

With Grant about to become president, Republicans in Congress moved quickly on the issue of voting rights. In February 1869, Congress passed the Fifteenth Amendment, which stated:

> The right of citizens of the United States to vote shall not be denied or abridged by the United States or by any State on account of race, color, or previous condition of servitude.

Harper's Weekly carried many illustrations of the changes happening in the South to Northern audiences. This issue of July 1868 showed the enthusiasm with which African-Americans, many of whom had been slaves only a few years before, were taking to electoral politics.

In a little less than a year, by February 1870, the required three-fourths of the states ratified the amendment and the right of former slaves, and other citizens, including the children of Chinese immigrants—who were citizens but had also been denied the right to vote—had been inscribed in the Constitution.

As powerful as the language of the Fifteenth Amendment is, it lacked some wording that many had wanted to include. The radicals had wanted the amendment to state that neither the right to vote nor the right to hold office could be abridged. But others feared that several Northern states, including California with its large Chinese population, might reject the amendment if the right of nonwhite people to hold office were included. Many also had wanted wording to prohibit the many tricks that some Southern governments were already using to limit the black vote, including literacy tests that could be manipulated to exclude whoever the test giver wanted excluded, or tests related to property or education. Supporters of the amendment, however, worried that they would lose too much Northern support if they included such clauses. Massachusetts and Connecticut used literacy tests to limit voting by foreign-born citizens, while Pennsylvania and Rhode Island had property or tax qualifications for voting, and no one wanted to risk losing the support of those states. As a result, important safeguards were not included.

Many women, especially the most prominent leaders of the women's rights movement, were deeply disappointed and angered by the Fifteenth Amendment. Women like Susan B. Anthony, Elizabeth Cady Stanton, and Sojourner Truth had labored long and hard in support of abolition and the Union cause, and now they saw women's right to vote ignored. Frederick Douglass was an advocate of women's rights in addition to African-American rights, but in 1869, he precipitated a long and painful, though temporary, break with Anthony and Stanton over the Fifteenth Amendment. Douglass argued for one step at a time, guaranteeing black men the same rights as white men, and then guaranteeing women of all races the right to vote. Douglass said, "I hold that women, as well as men, have the right to vote, and my heart and my voice go with the movement to extend suffrage to women." These were not just words. In the decade before and after battles around the Fifteenth Amendment, Douglass actively campaigned for women's right to vote. But between 1865 and 1870, Douglass was willing to compromise to achieve his immediate goal.

The compromise that Douglass proposed brought a sharp rebuke from the former slave and abolitionist Sojourner Truth. In 1867, at the height of the debate, Truth gave her own passionate response to Douglass. She said that she, too, had been born a slave and rejoiced that "They have got their liberty—so much good luck to have slavery partly destroyed; not entirely. I want it root and branch destroyed." For Truth, root and branch meant the vote for all. Partial justice would not do, "and if colored men get their rights, and not colored women theirs, you see the colored men will be masters over the women, and it will be just as bad as it was before."

In spite of compromises and disappointments, many hailed the Fifteenth Amendment as completing the work of abolition. As late as 1868, free blacks could vote in only eight Northern states. In 1870, by law, black men could vote everywhere in the United States. William Lloyd Garrison celebrated "this wonderful, quite sudden transformation...from the auction-block to the ballot-box." While there was already clear evidence of the many steps—by law and by violence—that would be taken to deny most blacks the right to vote for most of the next century, in 1870, there was also grounds for very real optimism.

Quick Review Compare Presidential Reconstruction and Congressional Reconstruction. What are the most significant differences between the two plans? Given these differences, was the tension between them inevitable?

THE IMPACT OF RECONSTRUCTION

15.2 Explain the impact of Reconstruction on African-American life in the South.

In the early years of Reconstruction, many of the South's former leaders returned to power. Only one Southern official was tried for treason and executed—Henry Wirz, commander of the infamous Andersonville prison where so many Union soldiers died. Jefferson Davis was imprisoned for 2 years but then was freed and retired to write his memoirs. Many other Confederate leaders quickly declared their loyalty to the Union after the war's end, received a pardon from Johnson, and resumed leadership in their states. Within a year of announcing his plan to exclude the wealthy and the political leaders of the Confederacy from the original amnesty conditions, Johnson had granted 7,000 individual pardons. The prewar status quo seemed to be returning in the Southern states. Then Congress took over Reconstruction, and everything changed. In state legislatures, local sheriff's offices, and school boards, former slaves, Northern abolitionists, and Southern Unionists took power under the banner of the Republican Party or local Union Leagues. A radical remaking of the South began in the late 1860s and continued into the 1870s.

Voting in the South

In January 1870, the Mississippi state legislature elected Hiram R. Revels to the United States Senate. Revels was the first African-American ever elected to the Senate. The legislature that elected Revels included 40 blacks and 100 whites—hardly a black-dominated body. He was elected, ironically, to fill Jefferson Davis's former seat, left vacant since Davis departed in 1861.

Hiram Revels, the first African-American senator (left) sits with six of the first blacks elected to the House of Representatives representing Alabama, Florida, South Carolina (three representatives), and Georgia.

Revels was born free in Fayetteville, North Carolina, in 1827. Like many of the African-American political leaders during Reconstruction, he was a minister in the African Methodist Episcopal Church, serving as a pastor in Baltimore, Maryland, when the Civil War began. Revels organized two all-black regiments and served as their chaplain. At the war's end, Revels went with his unit to Vicksburg, Mississippi, and then moved to Natchez. He was not initially a candidate for the Senate, but his lack of ambition for the post made him a perfect compromise candidate.

Senator Garrett Davis of Kentucky challenged the right of an African-American to be seated in the Senate. But Revels's key defender, James Nye of Nevada, told his colleagues, "In 1861 from this hall departed two senators who were representing here the state of Mississippi; one of them who went defiantly was Jefferson Davis." For Nye, and eventually for a majority in the Senate, nothing was a more fitting symbol of the outcome of the Civil War than the seating of an African-American in the place of the former president of the Confederacy.

Mississippi later sent Blanche K. Bruce to the Senate in 1874. Bruce was born a slave, but he attended Oberlin College and established himself as a planter in Mississippi in 1868. Unlike Revels, he worked his way up the political ladder, serving as the sergeant-at-arms of the Mississippi state senate, assessor and sheriff of Bolivar County, and a member of the Board of Levee Commissioners of the Mississippi River. Navigation on the Mississippi was a major concern of his during his U.S. Senate tenure, as was opposition to Chinese exclusion. Bruce was the last African-American to serve in the Senate until Edward Brooke was elected from Massachusetts in 1966.

More African-Americans were elected to the House. Twenty-two blacks served in Congress during Reconstruction, including 13 who had been born slaves. Between 1871 and 1873, South Carolina had three African-Americans in the House—Joseph H. Rainey, Robert B. Elliott, and Robert G. DeLarge. In the same sessions, Benjamin S. Turner represented Alabama; Josiah T. Walls, Florida; and Joseph Long, Georgia. Rainey served three terms in the House during which time he played an important role in arguing for the first major federal aid to education bill that was considered, although defeated, in Congress.

Reconstruction state governments, with black and white leadership, expanded the right to vote, abolishing restrictions that had existed for black and poor white voters. In addition, newly formulated state constitutions created public school systems and internal improvements designed to bring the South into the modern world. It was a heady time, yet not an easy one.

Schools for Freedom

Northern whites who came to the South with the Union army were amazed by the thirst for literacy demonstrated by former slaves. A member of an education society in North Carolina said, "he thought a school-house would be the first proof of their *independence*." Booker T. Washington, a well-known African-American educator remembered the immediate aftermath of emancipation: "Few people who were not right in the midst of the scenes can form any exact idea of the intense desire which the people of my race showed for education. It was a whole race trying to go to school."

Realizing that blacks saw the schoolhouse as "proof of their independence" surprised white observers. It did not surprise former slaves who had grown up in a world where literacy, for them, was a crime. As a slave child of seven or eight,

Frederick Douglass had been taught the alphabet by a white woman, but the lessons did not last long. He remembered:

> Mr. Auld found out what was going on, and at once forbade Mrs. Auld to instruct me further, telling her, among other things, that it was unlawful, as well as unsafe, to teach a slave to read.…It would forever unfit him to be a slave."

Nothing appealed more to young Douglass than being made unfit for slavery. Douglass found secret ways to continue his studies, and by the time he made his escape to Massachusetts, Douglass had the literacy skills that would make him one of the great orators and writers of his day. Slave masters and slave-state legislatures who made it illegal to teach a slave to read or write, unwittingly also made literacy a powerful symbol of freedom.

While the majority of teachers who went South to teach were white women, an African-American, Charlotte Forten, began teaching in Port Royal, South Carolina, where she said, "The children are well-behaved and eager to learn. It will be a happiness

American Voices

John Roy Lynch, The Work of Reconstruction, 1869

John Roy Lynch was born a slave and elected as a Republican to the Mississippi legislature in 1869. In this essay, he described what Reconstruction meant to those who, like him, were trying to create a new political system, indeed a new culture, in the states that had been part of the Confederacy only a few years before.

The new administration had an important and difficult task before it. A state government had to be organized from top to bottom. A new judiciary had to be inaugurated, consisting of three justices of the state supreme court, fifteen judges of the circuit court, and twenty chancery court judges, all of whom had to be appointed by the governor, by and with the advice and consent of the [state] senate. In addition to this, a new public school system had to be organized and established. There was not a public school building anywhere in the state except in a few of the larger towns, and they, with possibly a few exceptions, were greatly in need of repair. To erect the necessary schoolhouses and to reconstruct and repair those already in existence so as to afford educational facilities for both races was by no means an easy task. It necessitated a very large outlay of cash in the beginning which resulted in a material increase in the rate of taxation for the time being, but the constitution called for the establishment of the system and, of course, the work had to be done. It was not only done, but it was done creditably and as economically as circumstances and conditions at that time made

possible. That system, though slightly changed, still stands as a creditable monument to the work of the first Republican state administration that was organized in the state of Mississippi under the Reconstruction Acts of the Congress.

It was also necessary to reorganize, reconstruct, and in many instances, rebuild some of the penal, charitable, and other public institutions of the state. A new code of laws also had to be adopted to take the place of the old one, and thus wipe out the black laws that had been passed by what was known as the Johnson legislature. Also it was necessary to change the statutes of the state to harmonize with the new order of things. This was no easy task, especially in view of the fact that a heavy increase in the rate of taxation was thus made necessary.

Source: John Hope Franklin, editor, *Reminiscences of an Active Life: The Autobiography of John Roy Lynch* (Chicago: The University of Chicago Press, 1970),

Thinking Critically

1. **Documentary Analysis**
   According to Lynch, what were the most important priorities of the new Republican governments?

2. **Historical Interpretation**
   What light does the document shed on the challenges faced by Republican governments during Reconstruction?

A school operated by the Freedman's Bureau in Richmond, Virginia, was shown in this September 1866 issue of *Frank Leslie's Illustrated Newspaper*.

to teach here." By 1870, several thousand teachers—whites and blacks, Northern immigrants, and veterans of the Confederate army—were teaching in schools for former slaves. Although a majority stayed for only a year or two, some found their life's work in these schools.

Many newly free African-Americans welcomed Northern white teachers for the long term, but they also wanted teachers from their own communities. The Freedmen's Bureau and Northern missionary groups helped in founding black colleges in the South, including Atlanta, Fisk, Hampton, and Tugaloo, which were specifically designed to train black teachers, often in a short course that lasted 1 or 2 years. The results of the new efforts at teacher preparation were impressive, and as early as 1869, the bureau reported that of the 3,000 teachers for the freedmen, the majority were now African-American.

The Reconstruction Act of 1867 also fostered the growth of Southern schooling. The 1867 act required states of the former Confederacy to call state conventions to rewrite their state constitutions, and the new constitutions were expected to include support for public education. Later, even as state after state returned to white rule, the public school system remained. In *Black Reconstruction in America*, W.E.B. Du Bois, a renowned African-American activist, wrote, "Public education for all at public expense was, in the South, a Negro idea."

The Reality of Sharecropping

For many newly freed slaves, another issue was as important as the vote or education—land. In Virginia, a freedman told a Union army officer that, if the army had a right to take away the master's slaves, then they "had the right to take master's land too."

In Alabama, a state convention delegate insisted, "the property which they hold was nearly all earned by the sweat of our brows." Those closest to the land, who had worked it for no pay, valued land and the promise of land ownership. Land provided independent economic opportunity on which freedom rested.

When Sherman's army arrived in Savannah, Georgia, in December 1864, the army of 60,000 troops was accompanied by some 20,000 former slaves. Sherman met with local blacks in Savannah. Garrison Frazier, a leader of that group, made it clear what they wanted: freedom and land, which meant "placing us where we could reap the fruit of our own labor." Four days later, Sherman's Special Field Order No. 15 provided for 40-acre parcels of land for black families, which was to be taken from the plantations of owners in active rebellion on the Sea Islands and coastal areas in Georgia and, later, in South Carolina (once his army got there). Sherman also offered army mules that were no longer needed. Thus, 40 acres and a mule became the symbol of freedom to many, and by June 1865, 40,000 newly freed people were settled on "Sherman land" in the former Confederacy. Sherman's order did not make it clear whether the land grant was temporary or permanent, but the link of freedom and land was permanent in the minds of many.

President Johnson wasted no time ending the redistribution of land after taking office. He ordered an end to the "40 acres and a mule" policy. As head of the Freedman's Bureau, General O. O. Howard had expanded Sherman's original South Carolina plan, instructing his agents to "set aside" 40-acre tracts for individual

THINKING HISTORICALLY

John W. Alvord's First Report to the Freedmen's Bureau, 1866

John W. Alvord was an unusually perceptive observer who was in charge of setting up schools for the Freedmen's Bureau. In his first report to the bureau in Washington, DC, in 1866, Alvord noted, somewhat to his surprise, that there were often black-initiated schools already in operation when he arrived to open schools. Thus, he wrote in his first report:

Throughout the entire South an effort is being made by the colored people to educate themselves.…In the absence of other teaching they are determined to be self-taught; and everywhere some elementary text-book, or the fragment of one, may be seen in the hands of negroes.…Native schools… are making their appearance through the *interior* of the entire country.

A more detailed reading of the report makes it clear that Alvord was surprised first by the commitment of the newly freed people to education, second by their sense of initiative in launching their own schools even before any federal or missionary teachers arrived, and third by the sense of self-respect and self-determination that those running the schools were maintaining.

Source: John W. Alvord, *Inspector's Report of Schools and Finances*. U.S. Bureau of Refugees, Freedmen and Abandoned Lands. Washington, D.C.: U.S. Government Printing Office, 1866, pp. 9–10, cited in James Anderson, *The Education of Blacks in the South, 1860–1935* (Chapel Hill: University of North Carolina Press, 1988), pp. 6–7.

Thinking Critically

1. **Documentary Analysis**
   What does Alvord's surprise at finding "Native schools" say about the way African-Americans were perceived?

2. **Historical Interpretation**
   How do you account for the determination to be self-taught and to develop their own schools by people who only a year before had been enslaved by others and who many portrayed as passive?

freedmen. Blacks across the South quickly began farming their own plots. Johnson overrode Howard's order, issued pardons to former plantation owners, and ordered Howard to restore the land to them, which meant taking it away from those who were currently using it. Once land had been returned to its former owners, there was very little chance that former slaves would regain their parcels.

In October 1865, General Howard made a painful journey to Edisto Island in South Carolina to announce the president's order. A committee of freedmen drafted their response:

> General, we want Homesteads…if the government having concluded to befriend its late enemies and to neglect to observe the principles of common faith between its self and us its allies in the war you said was over, now takes away from them all right to the soil they stand upon save such as they can get by again working for *your* late and their *all time* enemies….You will see this is not the condition of really freemen.

Redistribution of land, it seemed, was not going to be part of Reconstruction.

In a few places, however, former slaves were able to purchase or win government land. Having spent their lives in unpaid labor, few slaves had any resources to buy land, even when it was being sold very cheaply in the aftermath of the war. In South Carolina, which had an exceptionally strong Reconstruction government, the legislature established a state land commission that provided grants of land to some 14,000 black families—perhaps one-seventh of the state's black population—in various parts of the state. They also created the town of Promised Land, which continues as a black-led community to the present.

The primary economic opportunity open to slaves was to return to the plantations where they had worked in the past, but do so as paid employees. Neither former slaves nor former slave owners found the prospect encouraging. One Georgia planter complained that, "Once we had reliable labor controlled at will. Now…it is both uncertain and unreliable." When railroads or new enterprises offered jobs, blacks left the plantations to take other work.

During the Johnson-dominated Reconstruction, Southern landowners not only reclaimed their lands but also ensured the passage of vagrancy laws made it a crime to be without a job, which meant former slaves had to take whatever was offered or be jailed. Some landowners agreed to hire only their own former slaves, making it extremely difficult for newly free people to bargain for wages or move to better opportunities.

Many in Washington were pleased to see blacks become wage earners, paid for raising the cotton, sugar, rice, and tobacco they had previously raised without pay as slaves. But former slaves did not like working for wages, especially the low wages that were offered for work in the same places where they had once labored as slaves. Wage-earning blacks resented their status as what some called "wage slaves." They wanted land of their own, and if they could not get land—and in most parts of the South they could not—they wanted a share in the profits of their work.

Given the dissatisfaction that both white landowners and black workers felt, a new economic arrangement was born: **sharecropping**. Sharecropping meant just what the name implied. Instead of working for wages, former slaves worked as independent entrepreneurs who were guaranteed a share of the crop in return for their labor. At the same time, landowners, who provided the land, the seeds, and the loans to get through the year, also received a share of the crop.

As this agricultural economy developed after the Civil War, the owner of a large tract of land (almost always a former plantation owner who had the land returned

Sharecropping
Labor system that evolved during and after Reconstruction whereby landowners furnished laborers with a house, farm animals, tools, and advanced credit in exchange for a share of the laborers' crop.

Edisto Island, off the coast of South Carolina, was one of the first places where the government provided land and mules—and mule carts. Former slaves quickly used the opportunity to become independent farmers.

by the Johnson administration) agreed to provide crude housing, a short-term loan for living expenses (known as the "furnish" and usually provided at the beginning of the growing season in March), seed, fertilizer, tools, and the right to grow cotton on a specified piece of land 15 to 40 acres in area. Landless tenants (almost always former slaves) agreed to work the land, plant, weed or "chop" the cotton through the growing season, and bring in a crop. Landowner and sharecropper would then split the profits after the harvest.

Once the harvest was done, just before Christmas at "the settle," the landowner would provide the sharecropper with a statement of accounts showing the value of the cotton harvest, the cost of the "furnish," and any other loans or purchases at the commissary on the plantation (usually the only place the sharecropper could buy goods and often a place where prices were very high), and the difference or profit due to the sharecropper. Everyone knew that many planters cheated their often illiterate tenants. Asking for a detailed accounting meant risking one's home and perhaps one's life. Few took the risk, though many sharecroppers were privately furious when the end-of-year payments were finally made and, somehow, the results for those who had worked all year were so modest.

Sharecropping began on the sugar plantations of Louisiana and quickly spread to the rest of the agricultural South. With sharecropping, black workers had a significant new incentive to work since they retained a portion of the profits they created. Women and children, who had resisted work in the field for wages, now returned to the fields as families sought to make a living.

At first, landowners were far from enthusiastic about sharecropping. While it meant that they no longer needed to supervise employees, they did not like the sense

Homes for sharecroppers were not much different from the cabins that had been built in the old slave quarters.

of independence that sharecropping brought to former slaves. They also disliked the shift from having farm work done by gangs of laborers, as had been the case in slavery and wage-earning times, to having the work done by family units on smaller plots. One South Carolina planter complained about the black-led Union Leagues that fostered sharecropping saying, "Their leaders counsel them not to work for wages at all, but to insist upon setting up for themselves." Nevertheless, by the early 1870s, sharecropping had become the primary means of agricultural organization in much of the South, especially the region's great cotton-growing heartland (see Map 15-2).

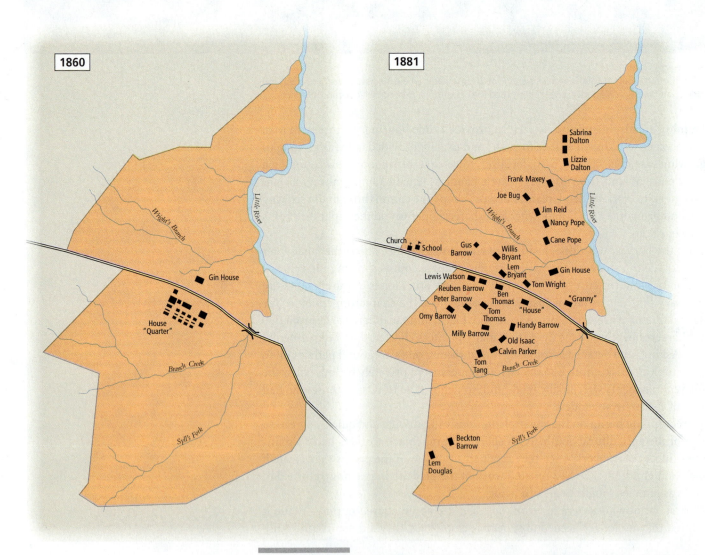

MAP 15-2 Sharecropping Reshapes a Plantation. These two maps show the changes in the living and work arrangements on the Barrow Plantation in Oglethorpe County, Georgia, between the last days of slavery in 1860 and the establishment of sharecropping in 1881. By the latter date, the old Slave Quarter had disappeared, replaced by dispersed cottages of the sharecropping families, each of whom worked a portion of the land.

Before long, plantation owners found ways to manipulate it for their own ends. Owners developed a credit system whereby a plantation-store sold everything from food to clothing on credit to the sharecroppers to be repaid when the crop was harvested. Many plantation owners made as much money with their stores as with their crops. With crops mortgaged before they were even planted, workers fell further and further into debt to the landowners. If sharecropping initially gave black families freedom that work for wages did not, it also tied them to the land in poverty for generations.

15.2 **Quick Review** Consider the early impacts of Reconstruction up to 1877. Would you consider it a success or a failure? Give at least three reasons to support your position.

TERROR, APATHY, AND THE CREATION OF THE SEGREGATED SOUTH

15.3 Analyze the reasons Reconstruction ended and the impact of Redemption.

During the first decade after the Civil War, Americans witnessed extraordinary changes. Slavery ended, and the Constitution was amended to give former slaves citizenship rights and the same right to vote as whites. Black males voted, held office, and served on juries, and black men, women, and children rode on integrated transit and attended school. Some even managed to own their own land. However, few of the advances of the first decade of Reconstruction lasted.

The rise and decline of black rights was an uneven process. Blacks were organizing and gaining new rights while the Civil War was still being fought. Many whites resisted black political and economic progress throughout Congressional Reconstruction. Although the withdrawal of federal troops in 1877 greatly hastened the process of undoing the gains of Reconstruction, what some white Southerners called "Redemption," that, too, was uneven. In some areas, white-only government had been reestablished well before 1877, while in other areas, blacks maintained political rights well into the 1880s and 1890s. Nevertheless, eventually, the high hopes of Reconstruction ended everywhere.

Opposition to Black Rights and the Roots of "Redemption"

Opponents of black rights were never completely excluded from power during Reconstruction. In September 1868, the white majority in the Georgia legislature voted to expel all 27 African-American representatives. Henry McNeal Turner, one of the 27, responded: "You may expel us, gentlemen, by your votes today; but while you do it, remember that there is a just God in Heaven." Two years later, in response to actions like the expulsion of the black legislators, President Grant reinstated military rule in Georgia. Black legislators returned to their seats along with white allies and opponents, and a majority in the legislature ratified the Fifteenth Amendment.

With Grant in the White House and Republican leaders in Congress who were willing to use federal troops if necessary to support the rights of former slaves and their allies, the Republican Party in the South was the party of black rights and racial equality. Blacks, often organized in Union Leagues, were at the heart of the party, but there were also large numbers of white Republicans in the South, including both Southern born and immigrants from the North. Southern whites who supported Republican and multiracial efforts were called **scalawags**, and they were a diverse lot. Some had

Scalawags
A disparaging term for southern whites who supported the Southern Republican Party during Reconstruction.

Carpetbaggers
Term used by white Southerners for Northern transplants who came to the South to help with Reconstruction.

opposed secession from 1861. Others, like Confederate General James Longstreet or army veteran Albert R. Parsons, embraced the Republican Party only after the war. Some, like Parsons, strongly supported equal rights for blacks. For others, support for black rights was secondary, but they saw the party as a place of personal opportunity.

Northern whites who came South were called **carpetbaggers** because, Southerners said, they could carry everything they owned in a single suitcase covered with carpet-like material. Resentful, Southerners claimed that carpetbaggers had come South to get rich. Carpetbaggers were on the whole younger and less prosperous than the scalawags. Some carpetbaggers were no doubt opportunists, coming to make their fortune, while others were abolitionists, coming South to implement policies they had long advocated. Many were veterans of the Union army, and some like Governor Adelbert Ames, the Republican Governor of Mississippi, had first been ordered South by the army and had stayed on.

In the 1860s and 1870s, there were virtually no black Democrats in the South. The post–Civil War Democratic Party was the party of "white only" government. Southern Democrats organized at every political level from small towns to state legislatures and governors' offices. Their twofold goal was to assure that, even if blacks were now free, they would have few rights and that whites committed to excluding blacks from power would dominate every aspect of society, politically, economically, and culturally. For these segregationist Democrats, African-Americans of the Union Leagues, scalawags, and carpetbaggers were all their enemies.

Lucius Quintus Cincinnatus Lamar of Mississippi, an example of the Southern Democratic Party leaders of his day, was from an old elite Southern family. He represented Mississippi in the U.S. Congress before the war and became a staunch secessionist. During the war, he was a general in the Confederate army. In the postwar period, he decided to enter politics again. Lamar wrote to a friend, "It does seem to me that if there ever was a time when the white people of this state…should rise & with one unanimous voice protest against the domination about to be piled upon them the present is that time." He proceeded to do everything he could to ensure white rule in Mississippi.

In November 1872, having long-since secured a presidential pardon, Lamar won a seat in the U.S. Congress. He also helped to organize the Democratic Party in Mississippi. In campaign speeches, Lamar attacked black voting rights. In Congress, he tried to ensure that the federal government did not enforce black rights. He helped defeat the Enforcement Act of 1875, which would have given President Grant more authority to implement the Fourteenth and Fifteenth Amendments in Mississippi. While he was engaged in partisan politics, Lamar also helped to develop another political organization outside of the Democratic Party—hidden from view but essential to his political victory—the Ku Klux Klan.

The Rise of Violence and the Ku Klux Klan

Ku Klux Klan
One of several vigilante groups that terrorized black people in the South during Reconstruction Era, founded by Confederate veterans in 1866.

The **Ku Klux Klan** was founded as a social club among Confederate veterans in Tennessee in 1866. It quickly turned into the largest of several secret and violent organizations bent on ensuring a reign of terror against not only Republican political leaders of either race but also teachers in black schools and blacks in general. The Klan was committed to ending Reconstruction and returning the South to white rule. The Klan assassinated Arkansas's Congressman James M. Hinds, members of the South Carolina legislature, and other members of state constitutional conventions. It had only just begun its work.

Similar organizations grew across the South. In Louisiana, the Knights of the White Camellia played a similar role, as did the White Line organizations in Mississippi. Although leaders like Lamar maintained a public distance, they secretly kept close ties to these violent extralegal organizations. By political organizing and sheer violence and intimidation, they were confident that they could return the South to its prewar ways.

Even before the emergence of the KKK, African-Americans and their white Republican allies faced violence. Just after the war's end in May 1866, a bloody riot in Memphis, Tennessee, which began when two carriages, one driven by a black and one by a white, collided. The riot resulted in the burning of black schools, churches, and over 90 black homes as well as the killing of at least 48 people; all but two of whom were black. A Memphis teacher was murdered, and others were told they would be killed if they did not leave the city immediately. The following fall, only 13 of the 40 teachers in the black schools of Memphis returned. A few weeks later, a similar riot in New Orleans, Louisiana, resulted in at least 100 injuries as well as the killing of 34 blacks and three of their white supporters.

By the spring of 1873, what could only be described as a civil war was going on in Louisiana. Tension mounted after the November 1872 elections in which one group of voters elected a Republican governor and another group, a Democratic one. When a federal judge ruled in favor of the Republican slate, President Grant sent troops to New Orleans to oust the Democratic governor and install the Republican administration. But in the small town of Colfax, Louisiana, two sheriffs had also been elected, and federal troops were a long way off. On Easter Sunday, April 13, 1873, tensions reached a boiling point. Several dozen black families along with William Ward, who was the Republican sheriff as well as a former slave and Union army veteran, barricaded themselves inside the town and sent urgent telegrams to the governor in New Orleans, asking for the army to rescue them. Help was too late in coming. Two to three hundred whites marched on the town, led by the Democratic sheriff, Confederate veteran Christopher Columbus Nash. Nash and his army attacked the town and killed everyone they could find. At least 60 blacks, perhaps many more, were killed. The next day, witnesses saw only piles of bodies everywhere. Colfax was far from an isolated incident.

Some of the greatest violence was in Mississippi. On July 4, 1874, as the Republican Party held a meeting in Vicksburg, Mississippi, armed whites arrived and shot and killed many of those, white and black, in attendance. Peter Crosby, the sheriff in Vicksburg, demanded federal intervention, but did not get help. On September 1, 1875, at a Republican meeting in Yazoo City, Henry Dixon began shooting at the mixed-race gathering. One person was killed instantly. Before long, those who were at the meeting scattered and a company of organized Mississippi White Liners—the Mississippi version of the Klan—took over the town and forced its elected government to flee.

On Election Day, the Democrats won statewide in Mississippi. In Port Gibson, black voters arriving at the polls were met by some 80 whites armed with Remington rifles, who started firing at them. One old man, John Morris, was killed, six others wounded, and none voted. At Peytona, not a single Republican vote was cast.

Klan members quickly adopted hoods and masks both to hide their identity and to frighten those who opposed them.

The Memphis riot was but one of many in which whites, enraged by new black rights, attacked homes, schools, and churches belonging to newly free blacks and any whites who supported them.

Democratic sentries on the Tombigbee River ensured that black voters could not cross the river to get to polling places. Governor Ames fled for his life before his term ended, while Democratic Party teams warned politically active Republicans, black and white, to leave the state before they were killed. Reconstruction ended in Mississippi with the 1875 elections.

Efforts to Defend Reconstruction

The antiblack, anti-Republican violence with which the South was slowly "redeemed" from Reconstruction met resistance at every step, sometimes very significant resistance. In March of 1870, just as the Fifteenth Amendment was ratified, Congress also passed the first Enforcement Act, making the denial of the right to vote because of race through force, fraud, bribery, or intimidation a federal crime. Up to that time, protecting voting rights had been completely a state issue, but in 1870, Congress had significant reasons not to trust that all the states would protect voting rights, especially for newly enfranchised African-Americans. Two further Enforcement Acts gave the federal government the right to intervene when elections were unfair. In addition, the Ku Klux Klan Act of April 1871 made conspiracies to deprive citizens of the right to vote a punishable federal offense. In June 1870, Congress also created the U.S. Department of Justice with a specific mandate to enforce Reconstruction. (Up until then, the U.S. Attorney General had been a kind of in-house lawyer and legal advisor to the president and cabinet but with no agency to lead.) All of these acts represented a major expansion of federal power. Because of the new legislation, crimes against individuals could, for the first time, be prosecuted by the federal government, especially if state governments did not step in and do their duty.

President Grant used this legislation forcefully. In October 1871, the president proclaimed nine counties of South Carolina to be in a "condition of lawlessness" and sent federal troops to restore order and arrest several hundred Klan leaders, some of whom ended up serving terms in federal prison. In addition, perhaps 2,000 Klan members left the state. Seven hundred leaders of the Klan were also arrested in Mississippi and several hundred more in North Carolina. By the end of 1872, the Klan, as an organization, had been destroyed.

The Klan would rise again, but not for many decades later. Nevertheless, despite its absence, violence against blacks and their white Republican allies continued in the 1870s. In the North, people were growing more and more willing to let the South settle its own affairs. When the Democrats nominated newspaper editor Horace Greeley for president in 1872, they adopted a platform attacking Republican corruption and calling for civil service reform while also promising a general amnesty for former Confederates and an end to federal intervention in the South. Grant was easily renominated by the Republicans and won the election handily, but Democrats gained power in Congress. As it turned out, Greeley died before the electoral votes were counted, which caused some confusion, but no one doubted that Grant had won the election. In his inaugural address at the beginning of his second term in March 1873, Grant told the nation, "The effects of the late civil strife have been to free the slave and make him a citizen. Yet he is not possessed of the civil rights which citizenship should carry with it. This is wrong, and should be corrected. To this correction I stand committed, so far as Executive influence can avail." Grant did his best, but it was not enough.

In 1875, Grant sent fellow Civil War General Philip Sheridan to Louisiana to investigate the political violence. Sheridan documented the killing of 2,141 blacks and the wounding of 2,115 more since the war had ended. All of these crimes remained unpunished. Another Civil War veteran, former slave Henry Adams, organized a committee of 500 blacks to "look into affairs and see the true condition of our race." In northern Louisiana around the Red River area alone, the committee documented 683 murders, including the following notations:

> Sam Maybury, whipped to death, December 1865
> Henry West, badly whipped, November 1874
> George, a colored man, killed by white men 1873
> Nancy Brooks, badly whipped by a white man, 1873

In most cases, the list included the name of the victim and the unpunished killer. The reality that Sheridan and Adams documented would not change for a very long time.

A Changing National Mood and the End of Reconstruction

A number of factors led to the growing national weariness with federal intervention in the South. Southern Reconstruction governments were regularly accused of corruption, and some office holders, black and white, certainly enriched themselves. P.B.S. Pinchback of Louisiana, the only black governor in the Reconstruction-era, admitted that he made considerable profit for himself in his political career. South Carolina's white Republican Governor Robert K. Scott speculated in state bonds, and North Carolina's Governor William Holden was aware of "damnable rascality." In truth, the Reconstruction governments were probably no more corrupt than those that came before or after, but the charges tarnished Reconstruction.

The Grant administration also faced one corruption scandal after another. During Grant's first year in office, Jay Gould and James Fisk, the nation's leading bankers, tried to corner the nation's gold supply and thus control the economy, with possible support from administration insiders including Julia Grant, the president's wife. One after another, cabinet officers resigned and were replaced after they were charged with taking bribes or other forms of corruption. In 1870, former Ohio Governor Jacob Cox resigned as secretary of the interior to protest the administration's failure to implement civil service reform. In perhaps the biggest scandal, a congressional investigation uncovered the workings of the so-called Whiskey Ring, a group including elected officials, government employees, and whiskey makers who defrauded the U.S. Treasury of excise taxes on whiskey. Over 200 distillers and revenue agents were indicted, and Grant's personal secretary, Orville E. Babcock, resigned. Grant directed the investigations to continue saying, "Let no guilty man escape if it can be avoided," and he ordered the Attorney General not to grant immunity to any suspects, but he was seriously tarnished by the widespread corruption.

The sheer size of the federal interventions in the South also undermined public support. In late 1874, White League militants ousted the Republican governor, William P. Kellogg, in Louisiana and took over the legislative hall. Since Louisiana was still under military supervision, Grant ordered General Sheridan to restore order. With 5,000 U.S. Army troops, Sheridan restored Kellogg to the governor's office and forcibly removed Democrats from the legislative hall. The spectacle of U.S. Army soldiers marching into a legislative chamber and removing people who claimed to have been elected created a huge backlash. Newspapers that had supported the Union cause now compared the White League to the founding fathers defending their freedom from the tyranny of the British.

Debates in Congress reflected the change in Northern public opinion and the increasing swagger of Southern leaders. Joseph R. Hawley, a Connecticut Republican who called himself a "radical abolitionist," nevertheless argued that the "social, and educational, and moral reconstruction," of the South could "never come from any legislative halls." The Democrats in Congress praised "local self-government," while insisting that black and white Republicans in the South should stop depending "upon external aid." In that context, it was difficult for the federal administration or the U.S. Army officers in the South to get support.

The U.S. Supreme Court was not sympathetic to Reconstruction. In the *Slaughterhouse Cases* of 1873, the court severely restricted the reach of the Fourteenth Amendment. A group of butchers in New Orleans had challenged the right of the Louisiana legislature to grant a monopoly to one meatpacking company because, they said, it violated their Fourteenth Amendment rights to due process of law and citizenship rights. But the court ruled that the Fourteenth Amendment did not include such rights, making it much harder to bring other suits about state infringement of citizen's rights.

In March 1876, the court's decision in *United States v. Cruikshank* struck a further blow to Reconstruction. William J. "Bill" Cruikshank was a white participant in the attack on Colfax, Louisiana, in 1873. He was indicted on federal charges for violating the civil rights of blacks who were killed in the attack. But 3 years later, the Supreme Court ruled that the charges were unconstitutional. Chief Justice Morrison R. Waite wrote that protecting the rights of individual citizens was a state, not a federal duty. *Cruikshank* took away one of the federal government's most important enforcement powers—the right to bring federal charges against those who attacked the basic rights of African-Americans.

Finally, in 1883, the court ruled that the Civil Rights Act of 1875 was unconstitutional because the Fourteenth Amendment gave Congress only the right to outlaw state government actions, not discrimination by individuals, which the court left to the states to deal with. The legal foundation of Reconstruction seemed to be crumbling or, perhaps, the court was simply following public opinion. Associate Justice Samuel Miller, a Grant appointee, wrote to a friend, describing what many Americans were also feeling, "I am losing interest in these matters."

As the country prepared for the 1876 presidential elections, the loss of interest in Reconstruction was evident. The Republicans nominated Ohio Governor Rutherford B. Hayes, who was on good terms with all factions in the party and especially popular with some because of his crackdown on nascent labor unions in Ohio. The platform said surprisingly little about Reconstruction. The Democrats nominated New York Governor Samuel Tilden, who had made a fortune as legal counsel for some of the country's richest bankers and railroads and gained fame for fighting corruption in government. Promising to continue the fight against corruption and foster prosperity, and never mentioning Reconstruction, Tilden was the strongest candidate the Democrats had nominated in some time.

The campaign was intense, especially in the South where violence and confusion reigned. In November, Tilden outpolled Hayes, winning the popular vote 4,286,808 to 4,034,142, but it was the electoral votes that counted. In three states, Florida, Louisiana, and South Carolina, Republican election boards discarded enough votes to declare Hayes the winner, which meant that he would also win the electoral count. Not surprisingly, the Democrats challenged these decisions.

The months between the election and the inauguration were as tense as any since the Jefferson–Adams contest of 1800. Some Democrats vowed "Tilden or War." Congress created an Electoral Commission of 10 congressional representatives, five from each party plus five Supreme Court justices, to determine the outcome since the Constitution gave no guidance beyond saying that the votes "shall be counted" in the Senate. After intense negotiations, the Electoral Commission ruled 8 to 7 for Hayes. But the Constitution specified that a president could not be declared elected until the Senate actually counted the votes cast by the presidential electors from the various states. Democrats refused to convene the Senate to count that vote, thus making it impossible to resolve the crisis. Finally on February 26, a group of Southern Democrats met with Ohio Republicans and negotiated a compromise. Hayes, who promised to treat the South with "kind consideration," agreed that, if he were made President, he would use his power to end Reconstruction, most of all by withdrawing the federal troops that were in the South protecting Republican governments. The Southern Democrats liked the offer and agreed to let the Senate meet and count the votes including—following the Electoral Commission's recommendation—the votes of the Republican electors from Florida. On Inauguration Day, March 4, 1877, Hayes became president and moved quickly to fulfill his promises.

Southern Republicans who had supported Hayes were outraged. A former slave from South Carolina commented angrily, "To think that Hayes could go back on us when we had to wade through blood to help place him where he is now." Little could now be done, however. Hayes did not immediately remove federal troops from the South, but he made it clear that the troops who remained would not intervene in the South's internal matters as Grant had ordered. The changes in federal policy had been coming for some time, but after March 1877, there was little reason to expect any federal support for Reconstruction anywhere.

After 1877, the direction was clear. John C. Calhoun, an Arkansas planter and grandson of the South Carolina senator of the same name, told Congress that "left to ourselves," the white South could settle "all questions" about the region's political arrangements. And they did. Blacks, carpetbaggers, and scalawags were slowly excluded from offices, though some stayed on into the 1890s. Many were forced to leave the South altogether if they wanted long lives. In addition, blacks were excluded from voting altogether, education budgets were slashed, and the regulation of sharecropping shifted further in favor of plantation owners. After 1877, white rule in the South was assured.

The Birth of the Segregated South

Disenfranchisement and segregation did not happen overnight. African-Americans were still being elected to office in the 1880s and 1890s. George H. White of North Carolina, who was described as "the last of the Negro congressmen," bade a final farewell to the House of Representatives in 1901 saying: "This, Mr. Chairman, this is perhaps the Negroes' temporary farewell to the American Congress. But let me say, phoenix-like, he will rise up someday and come again." The absence of blacks from Congress lasted for 28 years until Oscar De Priest was elected from Chicago. Only after another civil rights movement many decades later did African-Americans reach the number of representatives in Congress that they had in the 1870s.

Various forms of what came to be called **Jim Crow segregation** developed at a rapid pace. (Jim Crow was a derogatory character in a minstrel show designed to denigrate blacks, but his name has been applied to the whole era of rigid racial segregation that was the rule in many parts of the United States from the 1870s to the 1960s.) Schools, public facilities, transportation, and most every other aspect of life were segregated. In addition to losing the vote, blacks were marginalized economically so that sharecropping became virtually the only option for most. A vicious campaign of lynching controlled blacks through fear and intimidation. Perhaps the capstone of this segregation was the U.S. Supreme Court's 1896 *Plessy v. Ferguson* decision that "separate by equal" facilities were quite acceptable under the United States Constitution. By the time that decision was issued, the high hopes of Reconstruction were a dim memory and most Americans—white and black—were living in a very different world.

Jim Crow segregation
Segregation laws that became widespread in the South during the 1890s, named for a minstrel show character portrayed satirically by white actors in blackface.

15.3 **Quick Review** Considering the events and trends of the later years of Reconstruction, or Redemption as it was called, who were the winners and who were the losers? Who was most responsible for what happened?

CONCLUSION

During the 12 years after the Civil War, Americans grappled with what the future held for newly freed slaves and how best to return to the Union those states that had been in rebellion during the Civil War. The so-called Radical Republicans in Congress sought ways to protect the educational, political, and economic rights of the freedmen—as former slaves, male and female, were called. Andrew Johnson, who became president upon Lincoln's death in April 1865, seemed indifferent to African-American rights and soon alienated congressional radicals by restoring power to former rebels intent on limiting the freedoms of former slaves.

Congressional Republicans had their own plans for consolidating the Union victory, however, and eventually, the House of Representatives impeached Johnson for obstructing its plans to reconstruct the South. Although he was acquitted of "high crimes and misdemeanors" by the Senate, which allowed him to stay in office, Johnson's political career was over. But Congress passed a number of laws, including the 1866 Civil Rights Act and the Fourteenth and Fifteenth Amendments to the Constitution, designed to protect black rights as citizens and voters. Across the South, African-Americans and whites committed to Reconstruction were elected to local and national office in larger numbers and began to reshape their states. In 1868, Ulysses S. Grant, the Republican nominee, was elected president. Grant was committed to the Reconstruction of the South in ways that would protect black rights, especially black voting rights.

After the war, African-Americans pursued full citizenship rights, education, and economic independence. Terrorized by white supremacists and lacking money and credit, most African-Americans never achieved either true equality or independence. At the same time, white veterans of the Confederate army were organizing to deny those rights, not only legally through the Democratic Party but also illegally through the Ku Klux Klan and other similar organizations. As time passed, and as public support for federal intervention in the affairs of the South eroded, the promise of Reconstruction's early days evaporated. By 1877, a new president, Rutherford B. Hayes, began to bring Reconstruction to an end, assuring white rule in the South and the disenfranchisement and "Jim Crow segregation" of African-Americans for generations to come.

CHAPTER REVIEW Why might the historian Eric Foner call Reconstruction "America's Unfinished Revolution"?

Chapter 15   Chapter Review

FEDERAL RECONSTRUCTION POLICY

15.1 Explain the political development of federal Reconstruction policy.

Review Questions

1. **Historical Interpretation**
   What do Johnson's policies before his impeachment tell us about his vision of the post-Reconstruction South?

2. **Constructing Arguments**
   How would you explain the increasingly radical nature of Congressional Reconstruction? What factors pushed Congress toward more aggressive intervention in Southern society and politics?

3. **Comparison**
   Compare and contrast Presidential Reconstruction and Congressional Reconstruction. What were some of the ways that Congress forced the states of the former Confederacy to accept Reconstruction that Johnson opposed?

THE IMPACT OF RECONSTRUCTION

15.2 Explain the impact of Reconstruction on African-American life in the South.

Review Questions

4. **Historical Interpretation**
   What aspects of the history of the 1860s and 1870s would a historian report to emphasize the success of Congressional Reconstruction? What aspects of those years would a historian report to emphasize Congressional Reconstruction as a failure?

5. **Contextualization**
   Why did newly freed slaves place such a high priority on education?

6. **Constructing Arguments**
   Defend or refute the following statement. "By the end of the 1870s, from an economic perspective, most Southern blacks were almost as closely tied to the land and dependent on white landowners as they had been under slavery." What evidence can you produce to support your position?

TERROR, APATHY, AND THE CREATION OF THE SEGREGATED SOUTH

15.3 Analyze the reasons Reconstruction ended and the impact of Redemption.

Review Questions

7. **Contextualization**
   What groups made up the Republican coalition during Reconstruction? What did each group hope to gain from its support of the party?

8. **Historical Interpretation**
   Is it fair to describe the Democratic Party during Reconstruction as the party of white supremacy? Why or why not?

9. **Constructing Arguments**
   Defend or refute the following statement. "The Ku Klux Klan of the Reconstruction era was, at its essence, a terrorist organization."

Appendix

THE CONSTITUTION OF THE UNITED STATES OF AMERICA

We the people of the United States, in order to form a more perfect union, establish justice, insure domestic tranquillity, provide for the common defense, promote the general welfare, and secure the blessings of liberty to ourselves and our posterity, do ordain and establish this Constitution for the United States of America.

ARTICLE I

Section 1. All legislative powers herein granted shall be vested in a Congress of the United States, which shall consist of a Senate and House of Representatives.

Section 2.
1. The House of Representatives shall be composed of members chosen every second year by the people of the several States, and the electors in each State shall have the qualifications requisite for electors of the most numerous branch of the State legislature.
2. No person shall be a representative who shall not have attained to the age of twenty-five years, and been seven years a citizen of the United States, and who shall not, when elected, be an inhabitant of that State in which he shall be chosen.
3. Representatives and direct taxes[1] shall be apportioned among the several States which may be included within this Union, according to their respective numbers, which shall be determined by adding to the whole number of free persons, including those bound to service for a term of years, and excluding Indians not taxed, three fifths of all other persons.[2] The actual enumeration shall be made within three years after the first meeting of the Congress of the United States, and within every subsequent term of ten years, in such manner as they shall by law direct. The number of representatives shall not exceed one for every thirty thousand, but each State shall have at least one representative; and until such enumeration shall be made, the State of New Hampshire shall be entitled to choose three, Massachusetts eight, Rhode Island and Providence Plantations one, Connecticut five, New York six, New Jersey four, Pennsylvania eight, Delaware one, Maryland six, Virginia ten, North Carolina five, South Carolina five, and Georgia three.
4. When vacancies happen in the representation from any State, the executive authority thereof shall issue writs of election to fill such vacancies.
5. The House of Representatives shall choose their speaker and other officers; and shall have the sole power of impeachment.

Section 3.
1. The Senate of the United States shall be composed of two senators from each State, chosen by the legislature thereof,[3] for six years; and each senator shall have one vote.
2. Immediately after they shall be assembled in consequence of the first election, they shall be divided as equally as may be into three classes. The seats of the senators of the first class shall be vacated at the expiration of the second year, of the second class at the expiration of the fourth year, and of the third class at the expiration of the sixth year, so that one third may be chosen every second year; and if vacancies happen by resignation, or otherwise, during the recess of the legislature of any State, the executive thereof may make temporary appointments until the next meeting of the legislature, which shall then fill such vacancies.[4]
3. No person shall be a senator who shall not have attained to the age of thirty years, and been nine years a citizen of the United States, and who shall not, when elected, be an inhabitant of that State for which he shall be chosen.
4. The Vice President of the United States shall be President of the Senate, but shall have no vote, unless they be equally divided.
5. The Senate shall choose their other officers, and also a president pro tempore, in the absence of the Vice President, or when he shall exercise the office of the President of the United States.
6. The Senate shall have the sole power to try all impeachments. When sitting for that purpose, they shall be on oath or affirmation. When the President of the United States is tried, the chief justice shall preside: and no person shall be convicted without the concurrence of two thirds of the members present.
7. Judgment in cases of impeachment shall not extend further than to removal from office, and disqualification to hold and enjoy any office of honor, trust or profit under the United States: but the party convicted shall nevertheless be liable and subject to indictment, trial, judgment and punishment, according to law.

Section 4.
1. The times, places, and manner of holding elections for senators and representatives, shall be prescribed in each State by the legislature thereof; but the Congress may at any time by law make or alter such regulations, except as to the places of choosing senators.
2. The Congress shall assemble at least once in every year, and such meeting shall be on the first Monday in December, unless they shall by law appoint a different day.

Section 5.
1. Each House shall be the judge of the elections, returns and qualifications of its own members, and a majority of each shall constitute a quorum to do business; but a smaller number may adjourn from day to day, and may be authorized to compel the attendance of absent members, in such manner, and under such penalties as each House may provide.
2. Each House may determine the rules of its proceedings, punish its members for disorderly behavior, and, with the concurrence of two thirds, expel a member.

---

[1] See the Sixteenth Amendment.
[2] See the Fourteenth Amendment.
[3] See the Seventeenth Amendment.
[4] See the Seventeenth Amendment.

3. Each House shall keep a journal of its proceedings, and from time to time publish the same, excepting such parts as may in their judgment require secrecy; and the yeas and nays of the members of either House on any question shall, at the desire of one fifth of those present, be entered on the journal.
4. Neither House, during the session of Congress, shall, without the consent of the other, adjourn for more than three days, nor to any other place than that in which the two Houses shall be sitting.

Section 6.
1. The senators and representatives shall receive a compensation for their services, to be ascertained by law, and paid out of the Treasury of the United States. They shall in all cases, except treason, felony, and breach of the peace, be privileged from arrest during their attendance at the session of their respective Houses, and in going to and returning from the same; and for any speech or debate in either House, they shall not be questioned in any other place.
2. No senator or representative shall, during the time for which he was elected, be appointed to any civil office under the authority of the United States, which shall have been created, or the emoluments whereof shall have been increased, during such time; and no person holding any office under the United States shall be a member of either House during his continuance in office.

Section 7.
1. All bills for raising revenue shall originate in the House of Representatives; but the Senate may propose or concur with amendments as on other bills.
2. Every bill which shall have passed the House of Representatives and the Senate, shall, before it become a law, be presented to the President of the United States; If he approves he shall sign it, but if not he shall return it, with his objections, to that House in which it shall have originated, who shall enter the objections at large on their journal, and proceed to reconsider it. If after such reconsideration two thirds of that House shall agree to pass the bill, it shall be sent, together with the objections, to the other House, by which it shall likewise be reconsidered, and if approved by two thirds of that House, it shall become a law. But in all such cases the votes of both Houses shall be determined by yeas and nays, and the names of the persons voting for and against the bill shall be entered on the journal of each House respectively. If any bill shall not be returned by the President within ten days (Sundays excepted) after it shall have been presented to him, the same shall be a law, in like manner as if he had signed it, unless the Congress by their adjournment prevent its return, in which case it shall not be a law.
3. Every order, resolution, or vote to which the concurrence of the Senate and the House of Representatives may be necessary (except on a question of adjournment) shall be presented to the President of the United States; and before the same shall take effect, shall be approved by him, or being disapproved by him, shall be repassed by two thirds of the Senate and House of Representatives, according to the rules and limitations prescribed in the case of a bill.

Section 8.
1. The Congress shall have the power To lay and collect taxes, duties, imposts, and excises, to pay the debts and provide for the common defense and general welfare of the United States; but all duties, imposts, and excises shall be uniform throughout the United States.
2. To borrow money on the credit of the United States;
3. To regulate commerce with foreign nations, and among the several States, and with the Indian tribes;
4. To establish a uniform rule of naturalization, and uniform laws on the subject of bankruptcies throughout the United States;
5. To coin money, regulate the value thereof, and of foreign coin, and fix the standard of weights and measures;
6. To provide for the punishment of counterfeiting the securities and current coin of the United States;
7. To establish post offices and post roads;
8. To promote the progress of science and useful arts, by securing for limited times to authors and inventors the exclusive right to their respective writings and discoveries;
9. To constitute tribunals inferior to the Supreme Court;
10. To define and punish piracies and felonies committed on the high seas, and offenses against the law of nations;
11. To declare war, grant letters of marque and reprisal, and make rules concerning captures on land and water;
12. To raise and support armies, but no appropriation of money to that use shall be for a longer term than two years;
13. To provide and maintain a navy;
14. To make rules for the government and regulation of the land and naval forces;
15. To provide for calling forth the militia to execute the laws of the Union, suppress insurrections and repel invasions;
16. To provide for organizing, arming, and disciplining the militia, and for governing such part of them as may be employed in the service of the United States, reserving to the States respectively, the appointment of the officers, and the authority of training the militia according to the discipline prescribed by Congress;
17. To exercise exclusive legislation in all cases whatsoever, over such district (not exceeding ten miles square) as may, by cession of particular States, and the acceptance of Congress, become the seat of the government of the United States, and to exercise like authority over all places purchased by the consent of the legislature of the State in which the same shall be, for the erection of forts, magazines, arsenals, dockyards, and other needful buildings; and
18. To make all laws which shall be necessary and proper for carrying into execution the foregoing powers, and all other powers vested by this Constitution in the government of the United States, or any department or officer thereof.

Section 9. 1. The migration or importation of such persons as any of the States now existing shall think proper to admit, shall not be prohibited by the Congress prior to the year one thousand eight hundred and eight, but a tax or duty may be imposed on such importation, not exceeding ten dollars for each person.
2. The privilege of the writ of habeas corpus shall not be suspended, unless when in cases of rebellion or invasion the public safety may require it.
3. No bill of attainder or ex post facto law shall be passed.
4. No capitation, or other direct, tax shall be laid, unless in proportion to the census or enumeration herein-before directed to be taken.[5]
5. No tax or duty shall be laid on articles exported from any State.
6. No preference shall be given by any regulation of commerce or revenue to the ports of one State over those of another: nor shall vessels bound to, or from, one State be obliged to enter, clear, or pay duties in another.
7. No money shall be drawn from the treasury, but in consequence of appropriations made by law; and a regular statement and account of the receipts and expenditures of all public money shall be published from time to time.
8. No title of nobility shall be granted by the United States: and no person holding any office of profit or trust under them, shall, without the consent of the Congress, accept of any present, emolument, office, or title, of any kind whatever, from any king, prince, or foreign State.

Section 10. 1. No State shall enter into any treaty, alliance, or confederation; grant letters of marque and reprisal; coin money; emit bills of credit; make any thing but gold and silver coin a tender in payment of debts; pass any bill of attainder, ex post facto law, or law impairing the obligation of contracts, or grant, any title of nobility.
2. No State shall, without the consent of the Congress, lay any imposts or duties on imports or exports, except what may be absolutely necessary for executing its inspection laws: and the net produce of all duties and imposts laid by any State on imports or exports, shall be for the use of the treasury of the United States; and all such laws shall be subject to the revision and control of the Congress.
3. No State shall, without the consent of the Congress, lay any duty of tonnage, keep troops, or ships of war in time of peace, enter into any agreement or compact with another State, or with a foreign power, or engage in war, unless actually invaded, or in such imminent danger as will not admit of delay.

ARTICLE II

Section 1. 1. The executive power shall be vested in a President of the United States of America. He shall hold his office during the term of four years, and, together with the Vice President, chosen for the same term, be elected, as follows:
2. Each State shall appoint, in such manner as the legislature thereof may direct, a number of electors, equal to the whole number of senators and representatives to which the State may be entitled in the Congress: but no senator or representative, or person holding any office of trust or profit under the United States, shall be appointed an elector.

The electors shall meet in their respective States, and vote by ballot for two persons, of whom one at least shall not be an inhabitant of the same State with themselves. And they shall make a list of all the persons voted for, and of the number of votes for each; which list they shall sign and certify, and transmit sealed to the seat of the government of the United States, directed to the president of the Senate. The president of the Senate shall, in the presence of the Senate and House of Representatives, open all the certificates, and the votes shall then be counted. The person having the greatest number of votes shall be the President, if such number be a majority of the whole number of electors appointed; and if there be more than one who have such majority, and have an equal number of votes, then the House of Representatives shall immediately choose by ballot one of them for President; and if no person have a majority, then from the five highest on the list the said House shall in like manner choose the President. But in choosing the President, the votes shall be taken by States, the representation from each State having one vote; a quorum for this purpose shall consist of a member or members from two thirds of the States, and a majority of all the States shall be necessary to a choice. In every case after the choice of the President, the person having the greatest number of votes of the electors shall be the Vice President. But if there should remain two or more who have equal votes, the Senate shall choose from them by ballot the Vice President.[6]

3. The Congress may determine the time of choosing the electors, and the day on which they shall give their votes; which day shall be the same throughout the United States.
4. No person except a natural born citizen, or a citizen of the United States, at the time of the adoption of this Constitution, shall be eligible to the office of President; neither shall any person be eligible to the office who shall not have attained to the age of thirty-five years, and been fourteen years a resident within the United States.
5. In case of the removal of the President from office, or of his death, resignation, or inability to discharge the powers and duties of the said office, the same shall devolve on the Vice President, and the congress may by law provide for the case of removal, death, resignation or inability, both of the President and Vice President, declaring what officer shall then act as President, and such officer shall act accordingly until the disability be removed, or a President shall be elected.
6. The President shall, at stated times, receive for his services a compensation which shall neither be increased nor diminished during the period for which he shall have been elected, and he shall not receive within that period any other emolument from the United States, or any of them.
7. Before he enter on the execution of his office, he shall take the following oath or affirmation:—"I do solemnly swear (or affirm) that I will faithfully execute the office of President of the United States, and will to the best of my ability, preserve, protect and defend the Constitution of the United States."

[5] See the Sixteenth Amendment.

[6] Superseded by the Twelfth Amendment.

Section 2. 1. The President shall be commander in chief of the army and navy of the United States, and of the militia of the several States, when called into the actual service of the United States; he may require the opinion in writing, of the principal officer in each of the executive departments, upon any subject relating to the duties of their respective offices, and he shall have power to grant reprieves and pardons for offenses against the United States, except in cases of impeachment.
2. He shall have power, by and with the advice and consent of the Senate, to make treaties, provided two thirds of the senators present concur; and he shall nominate, and by and with the advice and consent of the Senate, shall appoint ambassadors, other public ministers and consuls, judges of the Supreme Court, and all other officers of the United States, whose appointments are not herein otherwise provided for, and which shall be established by law; but the Congress may by law vest the appointment of such inferior officers, as they think proper, in the President alone, in the courts of laws, or in the heads of departments.
3. The President shall have power to fill up all vacancies that may happen during the recess of the Senate, by granting commissions which shall expire at the end of their next session.

Section 3. He shall from time to time give to the Congress information of the state of the Union, and recommend to their consideration such measures as he shall judge necessary and expedient; he may, on extraordinary occasions, convene both Houses, or either of them, and in case of disagreement between them with respect to the time of adjournment, he may adjourn them to such time as he shall think proper; he shall receive ambassadors and other public ministers; he shall take care that the laws be faithfully executed, and shall commission all the officers of the United States.

Section 4. The President, Vice President, and all civil officers of the United States, shall be removed from office on impeachment for, and conviction of, treason, bribery, or other high crimes and misdemeanors.

ARTICLE III

Section 1. The judicial power of the United States shall be vested in one Supreme Court, and in such inferior courts as the Congress may from time to time ordain and establish. The judges, both of the Supreme and inferior courts, shall hold their offices during good behavior, and shall, at stated times, receive for their services, a compensation, which shall not be diminished during their continuance in office.

Section 2. 1. The judicial power shall extend to all cases, in law and equity, arising under this Constitution, the laws of the United States, and treaties made, or which shall be made, under their authority;—to all cases of admiralty and maritime jurisdiction;—to controversies to which the United States shall be a party;[7]—to controversies between two or more States;—between a State and citizens of another State;—between citizens of different States;—between citizens of the same State claiming lands under grants of different States, and between a State, or the citizens thereof, and foreign States, citizens or subjects.
2. In all cases affecting ambassadors, other public ministers and consuls, and those in which a State shall be party, the Supreme Court shall have original jurisdiction. In all the other cases before mentioned, the Supreme Court shall have appellate jurisdiction, both as to law and fact, with such exceptions, and under such regulations as the Congress shall make.
3. The trial of all crimes, except in cases of impeachment, shall be by jury; and such trial shall be held in the State where the said crimes shall have been committed; but when not committed within any State, the trial shall be such place or places as the congress may by law have directed.

Section 3. 1. Treason against the United States shall consist only in levying war against them, or in adhering to their enemies, giving them aid and comfort. No person shall be convicted of treason unless on the testimony of two witnesses to the same overt act, or on confession in open court.
2. The Congress shall have power to declare the punishment of treason, but no attainder of treason shall work corruption of blood, or forfeiture except during the life of the person attained.

ARTICLE IV

Section 1. Full faith and credit shall be given in each State to the public acts, records, and judicial proceedings of every other State. And the Congress may by general laws prescribe the manner in which such acts, records and proceedings shall be proved, and the effect thereof.

Section 2. 1. The citizens of each State shall be entitled to all privileges and immunities of citizens in the several States.[8]
2. A person charged in any State with treason, felony, or other crime, who shall flee from justice, and be found in another State, shall on demand of the executive authority of the State from which he fled, be delivered up to be removed to the State having jurisdiction of the crime.
3. No person held to service or labor in one State under the laws thereof, escaping into another, shall, in consequence of any law or regulation therein, be discharged from such service or labor, but shall be delivered up on claim of the party to whom such service or labor may be due.[9]

Section 3. 1. New States may be admitted by the Congress into this Union; but no new State shall be formed or erected within the jurisdiction of any other State, nor any State be formed by the junction of two or more States, or parts of States, without the consent of the legislatures of the States concerned as well as of the Congress.
2. The Congress shall have power to dispose of and make all needful rules and regulations respecting the territory or other property belonging to the United States; and nothing in this Constitution shall be so construed as to prejudice any claims of the United States, or of any particular State.

[7] See the Eleventh Amendment.

[8] See the Fourteenth Amendment, Sec. 1.

[9] See the Thirteenth Amendment.

Section 4. The United States shall guarantee to every State in this Union a republican form of government, and shall protect each of them against invasion; and on application of the legislature, or of the executive (when the legislature cannot be convened) against domestic violence.

ARTICLE V

The Congress, whenever two thirds of both Houses shall deem it necessary, shall propose amendments to this Constitution, or, on the application of the legislatures of two thirds of the several States, shall call a convention for proposing amendments, which in either case shall be valid to all intents and purposes, as part of this Constitution, when ratified by the legislatures of three fourths of the several States, or by conventions in three fourths thereof, as the one or the other mode of ratification may be proposed by the Congress; Provided that no amendment which may be made prior to the year one thousand eight hundred and eight shall in any manner affect the first and fourth clauses in the ninth section of the first article; and that no State, without its consent, shall be deprived of its equal suffrage in the Senate.

ARTICLE VI

1. All debts contracted and engagements entered into, before the adoption of this Constitution, shall be as valid against the United States under this Constitution, as under the Confederation.[10]
2. This Constitution, and the laws of the United States which shall be made in pursuance thereof; and all treaties made, or which shall be made, under the authority of the United States, shall be the supreme law of the land; and the judges in every State shall be bound thereby, any thing in the Constitution or laws of any State to the contrary notwithstanding.
3. The senators and representatives before mentioned, and the members of the several State legislatures, and all executive and judicial officers, both of the United States and of the several States, shall be bound by oath or affirmation to support this Constitution; but no religious test shall ever be required as a qualification to any office or public trust under the United States.

ARTICLE VII

The ratification of the conventions of nine States shall be sufficient for the establishment of this Constitution between the States so ratifying the same.

Done in Convention by the unanimous consent of the States present the seventeenth day of September in the year of our Lord one thousand seven hundred and eighty-seven, and of the independence of the United States of America the twelfth. In witness whereof we have hereunto subscribed our names.

[Signatories' names omitted]

Articles in addition to, and amendment of, the Constitution of the United States of America, proposed by Congress, and ratified by the legislatures of the several States, pursuant to the fifth article of the original Constitution.

AMENDMENT I

[First ten amendments ratified December 15, 1791]

Congress shall make no law respecting an establishment of religion, or prohibiting the free exercise thereof; or abridging the freedom of speech, or of the press; or the right of the people peaceably to assemble, and to petition the government for a redress of grievances.

AMENDMENT II

A well regulated militia, being necessary to the security of a free State, the right of the people to keep and bear arms, shall not be infringed.

AMENDMENT III

No soldier shall, in time of peace be quartered in any house, without the consent of the owner, nor in time of war, but in a manner to be prescribed by law.

AMENDMENT IV

The right of the people to be secure in their persons, houses, papers, and effects, against unreasonable searches and seizures, shall not be violated, and no warrants shall issue, but upon probable cause, supported by oath or affirmation, and particularly describing the place to be searched, and the persons or things to be seized.

AMENDMENT V

No person shall be held to answer for a capital or otherwise infamous crime, unless on a presentment or indictment of a grand jury, except in cases arising in the land or naval forces, or in the militia, when in actual service in time of war or public danger; nor shall any person be subject for the same offense to be twice put in jeopardy of life or limb; nor shall be compelled in any criminal case to be a witness against himself, nor be deprived of life, liberty, or property, without due process of law; nor shall private property be taken for public use, without just compensation.

AMENDMENT VI

In all criminal prosecutions, the accused shall enjoy the right to a speedy and public trial, by an impartial jury of the State and district wherein the crime shall have been committed, which district shall have been previously ascertained by law, and to be informed of the nature and cause of the accusation; to be confronted with the witnesses against him; to have compulsory process for obtaining witnesses in his favor, and to have the assistance of counsel for his defense.

AMENDMENT VII

In suits at common law, where the value in controversy shall exceed twenty dollars, the right of trial by jury shall be preserved, and no fact tried by a jury shall be otherwise reexamined in any court of the United States, than according to the rules of the common law.

AMENDMENT VIII

Excessive bail shall not be required, nor excessive fines imposed, nor cruel and unusual punishments inflicted.

AMENDMENT IX

The enumeration in the Constitution of certain rights shall not be construed to deny or disparage others retained by the people.

[10] See the Fourteenth Amendment, Sec. 4.

AMENDMENT X

The powers not delegated to the United States by the Constitution, nor prohibited by it to the States, are reserved to the States respectively, or to the people.

AMENDMENT XI [JANUARY 8, 1798]

The judicial power of the United States shall not be construed to extend to any suit in law or equity, commended or prosecuted against one of the United States by citizens of another State, or by citizens or subjects of any foreign State.

AMENDMENT XII [SEPTEMBER 25, 1804]

The electors shall meet in their respective States, and vote by ballot for President and Vice President, one of whom, at least, shall not be an inhabitant of the same State with themselves; they shall name in their ballots the person voted for as President, and in distinct ballots, the person voted for as Vice President, and they shall make distinct lists of all persons voted for as President and of all persons voted for as Vice President, and of the number of votes for each, which lists they shall sign and certify, and transmit sealed to the seat of the government of the United States, directed to the President of the Senate;—The President of the Senate shall, in the presence of the Senate and House of Representatives, open all the certificates and the votes shall then be counted;—The person having the greatest number of votes for President, shall be the President, if such number be a majority of the whole number of electors appointed; and if no person have such majority, then from the persons having the highest numbers not exceeding three on the list of those voted for as President, the House of Representatives shall choose immediately, by ballot, the President. But in choosing the President, the votes shall be taken by States, the representation from each State having one vote; a quorum for this purpose shall consist of a member or members from two thirds of the States, and a majority of all the States shall be necessary to a choice. And if the House of Representatives shall not choose a President whenever the right of choice shall devolve upon them, before the fourth day of March next following, then the Vice President shall act as President, as in the case of the death or other constitutional disability of the President. The person having the greatest number of votes as Vice President shall be the Vice President, if such number be a majority of the whole number of electors appointed, and if no person have a majority, then from the two highest numbers on the list, the Senate shall choose the Vice President; a quorum for the purpose shall consist of two thirds of the whole number of Senators, and a majority of the whole number shall be necessary to a choice. But no person constitutionally ineligible to the office of President shall be eligible to that of Vice President of the United States.

AMENDMENT XIII [DECEMBER 18, 1865]

Section 1. Neither slavery nor involuntary servitude, except as a punishment for crime whereof the party shall have been duly convicted, shall exist within the United States, or any place subject to their jurisdiction.

Section 2. Congress shall have power to enforce this article by appropriate legislation.

AMENDMENT XIV [JULY 28, 1868]

Section 1. All persons born or naturalized in the United States, and subject to the jurisdiction thereof, are citizens of the United States and of the State wherein they reside. No State shall make or enforce any law which shall abridge the privileges or immunities of citizens of the United States; nor shall any State deprive any person of life, liberty, or property, without due process of law; nor deny to any person within its jurisdiction the equal protection of the laws.

Section 2. Representatives shall be apportioned among the several States according to their respective numbers, counting the whole number of persons in each State, excluding Indians not taxed. But when the right to vote at any election for the choice of electors for President and Vice President of the United States, representatives in Congress, the executive and judicial officers of a State, or the members of the legislature thereof, is denied to any of the male inhabitants of such State, being twenty-one years of age, and citizens of the United States, or in any way abridged, except for participating in rebellion, or other crime, the basis of representation there shall be reduced in the proportion which the number of such male citizens shall bear to the whole number of male citizens twenty-one years of age in such State.

Section 3. No person shall be a senator or representative in Congress, or elector of President and Vice President, or hold any office, civil or military, under the United States, or under any State, who having previously taken an oath, as a member of Congress, or as an officer of the United States, or as a member of any State legislature, or as an executive or judicial officer of any State, to support the Constitution of the United States, shall have engaged in insurrection or rebellion against the same, or given aid or comfort to the enemies thereof. But Congress may by a vote of two thirds of each House, remove such disability.

Section 4. The validity of the public debt of the United States, authorized by law, including debts incurred for payment of pensions and bounties for services in suppressing insurrection or rebellion; shall not be questioned. But neither the United States nor any State shall assume or pay any debt or obligation incurred in aid of insurrection or rebellion against the United States, or any claim for the loss or emancipation of any slave; but all such debts, obligations, and claims shall be held illegal and void.

Section 5. The Congress shall have the power to enforce, by appropriate legislation, the provisions of this article.

AMENDMENT XV [MARCH 30, 1870]

Section 1. The right of citizens of the United States to vote shall not be denied or abridged by the United States or by any State on account of race, color, or previous condition of servitude.

Section 2. The Congress shall have power to enforce this article by appropriate legislation.

AMENDMENT XVI [FEBRUARY 25, 1913]

The Congress shall have power to lay and collect taxes on incomes, from whatever source derived, without apportionment among the several States, and without regard to any census or enumeration.

AMENDMENT XVII [MAY 31, 1913]

The Senate of the United States shall be composed of two senators from each State, elected by the people thereof, for six years; and each senator shall have one vote. The electors in each State shall have the qualifications requisite for electors of the most numerous branch of the State legislature.

When vacancies happen in the representation of any State in the Senate, the executive authority of such State shall issue writs of election to fill such vacancies: Provided, That the legislature of any State may empower the executive thereof to make temporary appointments until the people fill the vacancies by election as the legislature may direct.

This amendment shall not be so construed as to affect the election or term of any senator chosen before it becomes valid as part of the Constitution.

AMENDMENT XVIII[11] [JANUARY 29, 1919]

After one year from the ratification of this article, the manufacture, sale, or transportation of intoxicating liquors within, the importation thereof into, or the exportation thereof from the United States and all territory subject to the jurisdiction thereof for beverage purposes is thereby prohibited.

The Congress and the several States shall have concurrent power to enforce this article by appropriate legislation.

This article shall be inoperative unless it shall have been ratified as an amendment to the Constitution by the legislatures of the several States, as provided in the constitution, within seven years from the date of the submission hereof to the States by Congress.

AMENDMENT XIX [AUGUST 26, 1920]

The right of citizens of the United States to vote shall not be denied or abridged by the United States or by any State on account of sex.

Congress shall have the power to enforce this article by appropriate legislation.

AMENDMENT XX [JANUARY 23, 1933]

Section 1.   The terms of the President and Vice President shall end at noon on the 20th day of January and the terms of Senators and Representatives at noon on the 3d day of January, of the years in which such terms would have ended if this article had not been ratified; and the terms of their successors shall then begin.

Section 2.   The Congress shall assemble at least once in every year, and such meeting shall begin at noon on the 3d day of January, unless they shall by law appoint a different day.

Section 3.   If, at the time fixed for the beginning of the term of President, the President-elect shall have died, the Vice President-elect shall become President. If a President shall not have been chosen before the time fixed for the beginning of his term, or if the President-elect shall have failed to qualify, then the Vice President-elect shall act as President until a President shall have qualified; and the Congress may by law provide for the case wherein neither a President-elect nor a Vice President-elect shall have qualified, declaring who shall then act as President, or the manner in which one who is to act shall be selected, and such person shall act accordingly until a President or Vice President shall have qualified.

Section 4.   The Congress may by law provide for the case of the death of any of the persons from whom, the House of Representatives may choose a President whenever the right of choice shall have devolved upon them, and for the case of the death of any of the persons from whom the Senate may choose a Vice President whenever the right of choice shall have devolved upon them.

Section 5.   Sections 1 and 2 shall take effect on the 15th day of October following the ratification of this article.

Section 6.   This article shall be inoperative unless it shall have been ratified as an amendment to the Constitution by the legislatures of three-fourths of the several States within seven years from the date of its submission.

AMENDMENT XXI [DECEMBER 5, 1933]

Section 1.   The Eighteenth Article of amendment to the Constitution of the United States is hereby repealed.

Section 2.   The transportation or importation into any State, Territory, or possession of the United States for delivery or use therein of intoxicating liquors in violation of the laws thereof, is hereby prohibited.

Section 3.   This article shall be inoperative unless it shall have been ratified as an amendment to the Constitution by conventions in the several States, as provided in the Constitution, within seven years from the date of the submission thereof to the States by the Congress.

AMENDMENT XXII [MARCH 1, 1951]

No person shall be elected to the office of the President more than twice, and no person who has held the office of President, or acted as President, for more than two years of a term to which some other person was elected President shall be elected to the office of the President more than once.

But this article shall not apply to any person holding the office of President when this article was proposed by the Congress, and shall not prevent any person who may be holding the office of President, or acting as President, during the term within which this article becomes operative from holding the office of President or acting as President during the remainder of such term.

This article shall be inoperative unless it shall have been ratified as an amendment to the Constitution by the legislatures of three-fourths of the several States within seven years from the date of its submission to the States by the Congress.

[11] Repealed by the Twenty-first Amendment

AMENDMENT XXIII [MARCH 29, 1961]

Section 1.   The District constituting the seat of Government of the United States shall appoint in such manner as the Congress may direct.

A number of electors of President and Vice President equal to the whole number of Senators and Representatives in Congress to which the District would be entitled if it were a State, but in no event more than the least populous State; they shall be in addition to those appointed by the States, but they shall be considered, for the purposes of the election of President and Vice President, to be electors appointed by a State; and they shall meet in the District and perform such duties as provided by the twelfth article of amendment.

Section 2.   The Congress shall have power to enforce this article by appropriate legislation.

AMENDMENT XXIV [JANUARY 23, 1964]

Section 1.   The right of citizens of the United States to vote in any primary or other election for President or Vice President, for electors for President or Vice President, or for Senator or Representative in Congress, shall not be denied or abridged by the United States or any State by reason of failure to pay any poll tax or other tax.

Section 2.   The Congress shall have power to enforce this article by appropriate legislation.

AMENDMENT XXV [FEBRUARY 10, 1967]

Section 1.   In case of the removal of the President from office or of his death or resignation, the Vice President shall become President.

Section 2.   Whenever there is a vacancy in the office of the Vice President, the President shall nominate a Vice President who shall take office upon confirmation by a majority of both Houses of Congress.

Section 3.   Whenever the President transmits to the President pro tempore of the Senate and the Speaker of the House of Representatives his written declaration that he is unable to discharge the powers and duties of his office, and until he transmits to them a written declaration to the contrary, such powers and duties shall be discharged by the Vice President as Acting President.

Section 4.   Whenever the Vice President and a majority of either the principal officers of the executive departments or of such other body as Congress may by law provide, transmit to the President pro tempore of the Senate and the Speaker of the House of Representatives their written declaration that the President is unable to discharge the powers and duties of his office, the Vice President shall immediately assume the powers and duties of the office as Acting President.

Thereafter, when the President transmits to the President pro tempore of the Senate and the Speaker of the House of Representatives his written declaration that no inability exists, he shall resume the powers and duties of his office unless the Vice President and a majority of either the principal officers of the executive departments or of such other body as Congress may by law provide, transmit within four days to the President pro tempore of the Senate and the Speaker of the House of Representatives their written declaration that the President is unable to discharge the powers and duties of his office. Thereupon Congress shall decide the issue, assembling within forty-eight hours for that purpose if not in session. If the Congress, within twenty-one days after receipt of the latter written declaration, or, if Congress is not in session, within twenty-one days after Congress is required to assemble, determines by two-thirds vote of both Houses that the President is unable to discharge the powers and duties of his office, the Vice President shall continue to discharge the same as Acting President; otherwise, the President shall resume the powers and duties of his office.

AMENDMENT XXVI [JUNE 30, 1971]

Section 1.   The right of citizens of the United States who are eighteen years of age or older to vote shall not be denied or abridged by the United States or by any State on account of age.

Section 2.   The Congress shall have power to enforce this article by appropriate legislation.

AMENDMENT XXVII[12] [MAY 7, 1992]

No law, varying the compensation for services of the Senators and Representatives, shall take effect until an election of Representatives shall have intervened.

[12] James Madison proposed this amendment in 1789 together with the ten amendments that were adopted as the Bill of Rights, but it failed to win ratification at the time. Congress, however, had set no deadline for its ratification, and over the years—particularly in the 1980s and 1990s—many states voted to add it to the Constitution. With the ratification of Michigan in 1992 it passed the threshold of 3/4ths of the states required for adoption, but because the process took more than 200 years, its validity remains in doubt.

SOURCES

Chapter 1 The World Before 1492

The Peopling of North America

Daniel K. Richter, *Facing East from Indian Country: A Native History of Early America* (Cambridge; Harvard University Press, 2001) is an especially useful source for all early American Indian history. See also James Wilson, *The Earth Shall Weep: A History of Native America* (New York: Grove Press, 1998); and Elsie Clews Parsons, *Pueblo Indian Religion*, (Lincoln: University of Nebraska Press, 1939, 1996). Some have also argued that the Indians of the Americas were actually descendants of ancient travelers across the Atlantic from Africa or Europe or a mix of these with the earlier arrivals from Asia. See for example, Ivan van Sertima, *They Came before Columbus: The African Presence in Ancient America* (New York, 1976) and Vine Deloria, Jr., *Red Earth, White Lies: Native Americans and the Myth of Scientific Fact* (New York: Scribner, 1988). The debate, while important, involves scholars and time periods far beyond the scope of this book. For earlier North American communities see, George R. Milner, *The Moundbuilders: Ancient Peoples of Eastern North America* (London: Thames & Hudson, 2004); Sally A. Kitt Chappell, *Cahokia: Mirror of the Cosmos* (Chicago: University of Chicago Press, 2002); Timothy R. Pauketat, *Ancient Cahokia and the Mississippians* (Cambridge, England: Cambridge University Press, 2004); William C. Foster, *Historic Native Peoples of Texas* (Austin: University of Texas Press, 2009); and Stephen H. Lekson, *The Architecture of Chaco Canyon* (Salt Lake City: The University of Utah Press, 2007); Robert W. Patch, *Maya and Spaniard in Yucatan, 1648–1812* (Stanford: Stanford University Press, 1993); Leslie G. Cecil & Timothy W. Pugh, editors, *Maya Worldviews at Conquest* (Bounder: University Press of Colorado, 2009).

Diverse American Communities in the 1400s

Richter, *Facing East from Indian Country: A Native History of Early America* is a prime source for this material. See also James Wilson, The Earth Shall Weep: A History of Native America (New York: Grove Press, 1998); Ruth Underhill, Religion Among American Indians," in Roger C. Owen, James F. Deetz, and Anthony D. Fisher, editors, *The North American Indians: A Sourcebook* (New York: The Macmillan Company, 1967); William Prescott, *History of the Conquest of Mexico* (New York: Modern Library, no date, probably 1844); Carroll L. Riley, *The Kachina and the Cross: Indians and Spaniards in the Early Southwest* (Salt Lake City: University of Utah Press, 1999); George R. Milner, *The Moundbuilders: Ancient Peoples of Eastern North America* (London, England: Thames & Hudson, 2004); Charles C. Mann, *1491: New Revelations of the Americas Before* Columbus (New York: Alfred A. Knopf, 2005); Samuel Eliot Morison, *The European Discovery of America: The Northern Voyages, A. D. 500–1600* (New York: Oxford University Press, 1971).

A Changing Europe in the 1400s

For an excellent study of the philosophical and theological foundation of medieval Europe's economy, and the leaders who changed all of that, see Robert L. Heilbroner, *The Worldly Philosophers* (New York: Touchstone, 1999). For a useful discussion of the debates about Prince Henry's motivation, especially among Portuguese historians, see John Thornton, *Africa and Africans in the Making of the Atlantic World, 1400–1800* (Cambridge, England: Cambridge University Press, second edition, 1998); Carlos Fuentes, *The Buried Mirror: Reflections on Spain and the New World* (Boston: Houghton Mifflin, 1999); Matt S. Meier and Feliciano Ribera, *Mexican Americans/ American Mexicans: From Conquistadors to Chicanos* (New York: Hill and Wang, 1993), pp.17–18.

Africa in the 1400s

John Thornton, *Africa and Africans in the Making of the Atlantic World, 1400–1800* (Cambridge, England: Cambridge University Press, second edition, 1998); Basil Davidson, F. K. Buah, J. F. Ade Ajayi, *A History of West Africa, 1000–1800* (London: Longman, 1996); and Eric Wolfe, *Europe and the People without History* (Berkeley: University of California Press, 1982).

Asia in the 1400s

Louise Levathes, *When China Rules the Seas* (New York: Simon and Schuster, 1994); Jared Diamond, *Guns, Germs, and Steel* (New York: W. W. Norton, 1997, 2005); J. H. Elliott, *Empires of the Atlantic World: Britain and Spain in America, 1492–1830* (New Haven: Yale University Press, 2006).

Chapter 2 First Encounters, First Conquests, 1492–1607

Columbus and the Columbian Exchange, and Early Conquests

Carlos Fuentes, *The Buried Mirror: Reflections on Spain and the New World* (New York: Mariner Books, 1999); Irving Rouse, *The Tainos: Rise and Decline of the People Who Greeted Columbus* (New Haven: Yale University Press, 1992); Oliver Dunn and James E. Kelley, Jr., translators, *The Diario of Christopher Columbus's First Voyage to America, 1492–1493*, abstracted by Fray Bartolome de las Casas (Norman: University of Oklahoma Press, 1988); Jared Diamond, *Guns, Germs, and Steel: The Fates of Human Societies* (New York: W. W. Norton, 1997, 2005); Alfred W. Crosby, *Ecological Imperialism: The Biological Expansion of Europe, 900–1900* (Cambridge: Cambridge University Press, 1986); and Alfred W. Crosby, Jr., *The Columbian Exchange: Biological and Cultural Consequences of 1492* (Westport, Connecticut: Greenwood Press, 1972); E. T. Jones, "Alwyn Ruddock: 'John Cabot and the Discovery of America," *Historical Research* 81 (2008), pp. 224–254; downloaded February 26, 2012; Hugh Tomas, "The Conquest," in *Aztecs* (London: The Royal Academy, 2002); *Letters of Amerigo Vespucci, and Other Documents Illustrative of his Career* (Cambridge, England: Cambridge University Press, 2010); Thomas Bender, *A Nation Among the Nations: America's Place in World History* (New York: Hill and Wang, 2006); Bartolome de las Casas, *History of the Indies*, translated and edited by Andree Collard (New York: Harper & Row, 1971).

A Divided Europe—The Impact of the Protestant Reformation

For material on the Protestant Reformation see Diarmaid MacCulloch, *The Reformation: A History* (New York: Viking Penguin, 2004); and two earlier but still excellent sources Hans J. Hillerbrand, *The Protestant Reformation*, revised edition (New York: Harper Perennial, 2009);

Williston Walker, *A History of the Christian Church*, third edition, revised by Robert T. Handy (New York: Charles Scribner's Sons, 1970).

Exploration and Encounter in North America: The Spanish

Juan Ponce de Leon, fundador y primer gobernador del pueblo puertorriqueño, descubridor de la Florida y del Estrecho de las Bahamas (Barcelona, Espana, Editorial Universitaria, Universidad de Puerto Rico, 1971); "Ponce de Leon, Juan," Encyclopedia Britannica, from Encyclopedia Britannica Online. http://search.eb.com/eb/articles?tocid-9060663. See also Jane Landers, "Free and Slave," in Michael Gannon, The New History of Florida (Gainesville: University of Florida Press, 1996); Alex D. Krieger, *We Came Naked and Barefoot: The Journey of Cabeza de Vaca Across North America* (Austin: University of Texas Press, 2002); *The Journey of Alvar Nunez Cabeza de Vaca and His Companions from Florida to the Pacific, 1528–1536*, translated from his own narrative by Fanny Bandelier, edited with an introduction by Ad F. Bandelier (New York: Allerton Book Co., 1922); Robert Silverberg, *The Pueblo Revolt* (Lincoln: University of Nebraska Press, 1970); John L. Kessell, "To See Such Marvels with My Own Eyes: Spanish Exploration in the Western Borderlands," *The Coronado Expedition From the Distance of 460 Years*, edited by Richard Flint and Shirley Cushing Flint (Albuquerque: University of New Mexico Press, 2003); Gloria A. Young and Michael P. Hoffman, editors, *The Expedition of Hernando de Soto West of the Mississippi, 1541–1543* (Fayetteville, The University of Arkansas Press, 1993); Lawrence A. Clayton, Vernon James Knight, Jr., and Edward C. Moore, editors, *The De Soto Chronicles: the Expedition of Hernando De Soto to North America in 1539–1543* (Tuscaloosa: The University of Alabama Press, two volumes, 1993); James Wilson, *The Earth Shall Weep: A History of Native America* (New York: Grove Press, 1998); Harry Kelsey, *Juan Rodriquez Cabrillo* (San Marino, CA: Huntington Library, 1986); Albert Manucy, *Sixteenth Century St. Augustine: The People and Their Homes* (Gainesville: University Press of Florida, 1997); "Florida," Encyclopedia Britannica Online, http://search.eb.com/ebi/articles?tocld=200862; Eugene Lyon, "Settlement and Survival," in Michael Gannon, editor, *The New History of Florida* (Gainesville: University Press of Florida, 1996).

Exploration and Encounter in North America—The French

Samuel Eliot Morison, *The European Discovery of America: The Northern Voyages, A.D. 500–1600* (New York: Oxford University Press, 1971); Roger Riendeau, *A Brief History of Canada* (Markham, Ontario: Fitzhenry and Whiteside, 2000).

Exploration and Encounter in North America—The English

Karen Ordahl Kupperman, *The Jamestown Project* (Cambridge: Harvard University Press, 2007); Tony Horwitz, *A Voyage Long and Strange* (New York: Henry Holt, 2008).

Chapter 3 Settlement, Alliances, and Resistance, 1607–1718

The English Settle in North America

J.H. Elliott, *Empires of the Atlantic World: Britain and Spain in America, 1492–1830* (New Haven: Yale University Press, 2006) is an excellent source for early English settlement. See also Karen Ordahl Kupperman, The Jamestown Project (Cambridge: Harvard University Press, 2009); Nathaniel Philbrick, *Mayflower: A Story of Courage, Community, and War* (New York: Viking Penguin, 2006); Edmund S. Morgan, *American Slavery, American Freedom: The Ordeal of Colonial Virginia* (New York: W. W. Norton, 1975/2003); Samuel Eliot Morison, *Builders of the Bay Colony* (Boston: Houghton Mifflin, 1930, revised, 1958); John Winthrop, *History of New England from 1610 to 1649*, ed. James Savage (Boston: Little, Brown, 1853); Ira Berlin, *Many Thousands Gone: The First Two centuries of Slavery in North America* (Cambridge: Harvard University Press, 1998).

England's Wars, England's Colonies

The story of England's civil war has been told many times from many perspectives. For understanding the religious nature of the conflict I have turned to Williston Walker, *History of the Christian Church*, third edition (New York: Scribners, 1970); J. Franklin Jameson, *Narratives of New Netherlands, 1609–1664* (New York: Charles Scribner's Sons, 1909); Eric Homberger, *The Historical Atlas of New York City* (New York: Henry Holt, 2005.); Berlin, *Many Thousands Gone: The First Two Centuries of Slavery in North America*.

France Takes Control of the Heart of the Continent

Craig Brown, editor, *The Illustrated History of Canada* (Toronto, Key Porter, 2002). See also David Hackett Fischer, *Champlain's Dream* (New York: Simon & Schuster, 2008). Charles J. Balesi, *The Time of the French in the Heart of North America* (Chicago: Alliance Francaise, 2000), Olivia Mahoney, *Chicago: Crossroads of America* (Chicago: Chicago History Museum, 2006); Francis Parkman, *La Salle and the Discovery of the Great West*, two volumes, (Boston, 1902, reprinted New York: AMS Press, 1969); Reuben Gold Thwaites, editor, *Travels and Explorations of the Jesuit Missionaries in New France, 1610–1791*, Vol. LXV, *Lower Canada, Mississippi Valley, 1696–1702* (Cleveland: The Burrows Brothers, 1900); Ned Sublette, *The World That Made New Orleans* (Chicago: Lawrence Hill, 2008); Charles E. Champan, *A History of California: The Spanish Period* (New York: The Macmillan Company, 1930).

Developments in Spanish Colonies North of Mexico

J.H. Elliott, *Empires of the Atlantic World: Britain and Spain in America, 1492–1830* (New Haven: Yale University Press, 2006); Robert Silverberg, *The Pueblo Revolt* (New York,: 1970; reprint Lincoln: The University of Nebraska Press, 1994); Franklin Folsom, *Indian Uprising on the Rio Grande: The Pueblo Revolt of 1680* (Albuquerque: University of New Mexico Press, 1973, 2000,); Charles Wilson Hackett, *Revolt of the Pueblo Indians of New Mexico* (Albuquerque: University of New Mexico Press, 1942).

Chapter 4 Creating the Culture of British North America, 1689–1754

England's Glorious Revolution and the Rights of Englishmen, 1689

Elliott, *Empires of the Atlantic World*; John Locke, *Second Treatise on Government* (originally 1689; reprinted Arlington Heights, IL: Crofts Classics, 1982).

The Plantation World—From a Society with Slaves to a Slave Society

Ira Berlin, *Many Thousands Gone: The First Two centuries of Slavery in North America* (Cambridge: Harvard University Press, 1998); Edmund S. Morgan, *American Slavery, American Freedom: The Ordeal of Colonial Virginia* (New York: W. W. Norton, 1975/2003); John Barbot, "A Description of the Coasts of North and South Guinea," (1682) in Thomas Astley and John Churchill, editors, *Collection of Voyages and Travels* (London, 1732), cited in Steven Mintz, editor, *African American Voices: A Documentary Reader, 1619-1877* (Malden, MA: Wiley-Blackwell, 2009), pp. 42–45; Edwin G. Burrows and Mike Wallace, *Gotham: A History of New York City to 1898* (New York: Oxford University Press, 1999); Jill Lepore's *New York Burning: Liberty, Slavery, and Conspiracy in Eighteenth-Century Manhattan* (New York: Random House, 2005).

Stability and Instability in the American and British World

Mary Beth Norton, *In the Devil's Snare* (New York: Random House, 2002); Gordon S. Wood, *The Americanization of Benjamin Franklin* (New York: Penguin Books, 2004); Benjamin Franklin, *Autobiography*; Jane Kamensky, "The Colonial Mosaic, 1600-1760," in Nancy F. Cott, editor, *No Small Courage: A History of Women in the United States* (New York: Oxford University Press, 2000); Mari Jo Buhle, Teresa Murphy, Jame Gerhard, *Women and the Making of America* (Upper Saddle River, NJ: Pearson, 2009); "The Letterbook of Eliza Lucas Pinckney, 1742," in Paul G. E. Clemens, editor, *The Colonial Era: A Documentary Reader* (Malden, MA: Blackwell, 2008); Navigation Act of 1660 and Gottlieb Mittelberger, *Journey to Pennsylvania in the Year 1750 and Return to Germany in the Year 1754* in Louis B. Wright and Elaine W. Fowler, *English Colonization of North America* (New York: St. Martin's Press, 1968); Sydney E. Ahlstrom, *A Religious History of the American People* (New Haven: Yale University Press, 2004); Hasia R. Diner, *A New Promised Land: A History of Jews in America* (New York: Oxford University Press, 2000); Clarence H. Faust and Thomas H. Johnson, editors, *Jonathan Edwards* (New York: The American Writers Series, 1935), pp. 159–163; Jonathan Edwards, *A Treatise Concerning Religious Affections* (Boston: S. Kneeland and T. Green, 1746, reprinted and edited by John E. Smith, New Haven: Yale University Press, 1959); Thomas Bender, *A Nation Among the Nations* (New York: Hill and Wang, 2006); Elliott, *Empires of the Atlantic World*; Leonard Labaree, et al, editors, *The Papers of Benjamin Franklin* (New Haven: Yale University Press, 1959–).

The International Context

Thomas Bender, *A Nation Among the Nations* (New York: Hill and Wang, 2006); Elliott, *Empires of the Atlantic World*; Wood, *The Americanization of Benjamin Franklin*; Leonard Labaree, et al, editors, *The Papers of Benjamin Franklin* (New Haven: Yale University Press, 1959–); Wright and Fowler, *English Colonization of North America*.

Chapter 5 The Making of a Revolution, 1754–1783

Preludes to Revolution

Material on the French and Indian War is from William M. Fowler, Jr., *Empires At War: the French and Indian War and the Struggle for North America, 1754-1763* (New York: Walker & Company, 2005). See also Daniel K. Richter, *Facing East from Indian Country: A Native History of Early America* (Cambridge: Harvard University Press, 2001). Richter's perceptive interpretation of the experience of American Indians is a key resource for understanding this material.

"The Revolution Was in the Minds of the People"

Gary Nash, *The Unknown American Revolution: the Unruly Birth of Democracy and the Struggle to Create America* (New York: Viking, 2005) is especially helpful for understanding the diverse voices of the revolutionary era. For a different perspective see Gordon S. Wood, *The Radicalism of the American Revolution* (New York: Random House, 1991). See also Bernard Bailyn, *The Intellectual Origins of the American Revolution* (Cambridge: Harvard University Press, 1992). An excellent new source on urban street resistance to British authority can be found in Benjamin L. Carp, *Rebels Rising: Cities and the American Revolution* (New York: Oxford University Press, 2007). In order to explore these topics further see also Merrill Jensen, *Tracts of the American Revolution* (New York: Bobbs-Merrill, 1967), Jeremy Black, *Revolutions in the Western World 1775–1825* (Hants, England: Ashgate, 2006), Edwin S. Gaustad, *A Documentary History of Religion in America to the Civil War* (Grand Rapids, MI: William B. Eerdmans, 1993), Carl Bridenbaugh, *Mitre and Sceptre* (1962), Mari Jo Buhle, Teresa Murphy, Jane Gerhard, *Women and the Making of* America (Upper Saddle River, NJ: Pearson Prentice Hall, 2009), Alfred W. Blumrosen and Ruth G. Blumrose, *Slave Nation: How Slavery United the Colonies & Sparked the American Revolution* (Naperville, IL: Sourcebooks, 2005), Phillis Wheatley, "To the Right Honourable William, Earl of Dartmouth, His Majesty's Principal Secretary of State for North America," *The Poems of Phillis Wheatley*, and Lemuel Haynes, "Lexington, Massachusetts, 1775," both in Herb Boyd, *Autobiography of a People* (New York: Doubleday, 2000).

The War for Independence

Robert Middlekauff, *The Glorious Cause: The American Revolution, 1763-1789* (New York: Oxford University Press, 2005) is a thorough source on the Revolutionary War. See also David McCullough, *John Adams* (New York: Simon & Schuster, 2001); Joseph J. Ellis, *American Sphinx: The Character of Thomas Jefferson* (New York: Alfred A. Knopf, 1997), *Common Sense* is worth reading carefully. I have been guided in analysis here by my own reading of the pamphlet and by Gregory Tietjen's introduction to the 1995 edition, Thomas Paine, *Common Sense* (New York: Barnes & Noble, 1995); Richard Archer, *As if An Enemy's Country: The British Occupation of Boston and the Origins of Revolution* (New York: Oxford University Press, 2010); John Shy, *A People Numerous and Armed: Reflections on the Military Struggle for American Independence* (New York: Oxford University Press, 1976); Charles Royster, *A Revolutionary People at War: The Continental Army and American Character* (1979). Elizabeth F. Ellet, *The Women of the American Revolution* (New York: Charles Scribner, 1852) is a goldmine of material on the ways many different women experienced the revolution. For women's experience see also Marylynn Salmon, "The Limits of Independence: 1760-1800," in Nancy F. Cott, editor, *No Small Courage: A History of Women in the United States* (New York: Oxford University Press, 2000).

Chapter 6 Creating a Nation, 1783–1788

The State of the Nation at War's End

David McCullough's *John Adams* (New York: Simon & Schuster, 2001) was on the top of the bestseller charts, followed not far behind by Joseph J. Ellis' *Founding Brothers* (New York: Alfred A. Knopf, 2000). Also very helpful in understanding the "founding fathers" is Ellis' *American*

Sphinx. Philip S. Foner, ed., *The Complete Writings of Thomas Paine*, (New York: Citidal Press, 1945), Vol. II, pp. 243, 286–287. The description of the Newburgh Conspiracy is taken from Richard H. Kohn, *Eagle and Sword: the Federalists and the Creation of the Military Establishment in America, 1783-1802* (New York: The Free Press, 1975), pp. 17–39. Kohn's work remains the best study of this and several other military developments in the earliest years of the Republic. For Shay's Rebellion, see David P. Szatmary, *Shay's Rebellion: The Making of an Agrarian Insurrection* (Amherst: University of Massachusetts Press, 1980) and Leonard L. Richards, *Shay's Rebellion: the American Revolution's Final Battle* (Philadelphia: University of Pennsylvania Press, 2002). For an Indian perspective on the new U.S. government, see Daniel K. Richter, *Facing East from Indian Country: A Native History of Early* America (Cambridge: Harvard University Press, 2001), p. 164. Richter's perceptive interpretation of the experience of American Indians is a key resource for understanding this material and also William L. Stone, *Life of Joseph Brant—Thayendanegea*, (New York: Alexander V. Blake, 1838) two volumes, Vol. II, pp. 237–239. Ira Berlin, *The Making of African America: The Four Great Migrations* (New York: Viking, 2010) is a terrific source on the African American experience in the early Republic. See also Benjamin Banneker to Thomas Jefferson, August 19, 1791 in Herb Boyd, editor, *Autobiography of a People: Three Centuries of African American History Told by Those Who Lived It* (New York: Random House, 2000), pp. 52–55; Phyllis Wheatley to Rev. Samson Occom, New London, Connecticut, February 11, 1774, in Julia Reidhead, editor, *The Norton Anthology of American Literature*, Fifth Edition (New York: W.W. Norton, 1998), Vol. I, pp. 838–839; and *Memoirs of the Life of Boston King, a Black Preacher*, 1798. I have used multiple sources in seeking to understand women's experience during and after the Revolution including Mary Beth Norton, *Liberty's Daughters: The Revolutionary Experience of American Women, 1750–1800* (Boston: Little, Brown, 1980), pp. 209–242; Mary Beth Norton, *Founding Mothers & Fathers: Gendered Power and the Forming of American Society* (New York: Random House, 1996), pp. 404–405; Mari Jo Buhle, Teresa Murphy, and Jane Gerhard, *Women in the Making of America* (Upper Saddle River, NJ: Pearson, 2009), pp. 77–97; Marylynn Salmon, "The Limits of Independence, 1760–1800," in Nancy F. Cott, editor, *No Small Courage: A History of Women in the United States* (New York: Oxford University Press, 2000), pp. 116–126; see quote on p. 120; and Dorothy A. Mays, *Women in Early America: Struggle, Survival and Freedom in a New World* (Santa Barbara, CA: ABC-CLIO, 2004), p. 179.

Creating a Government: Writing the U.S. Constitution

I have used three main sources in telling the story of the writing and adoption of the Constitution: Richard Beeman, *Plain, Honest Men: the Making of the American Constitution* (New York: Random House, 2009), Woody Holton, *Unruly Americans and the Origins of the Constitution* (New York: Hill and Wang, 2007), and Max Ferrand, *The Framing of the Constitution of the United States* (New Haven: Yale University Press, 1913). Material on the state conventions can be found in Beeman pp. 386–411. See also Max Farrand, editor, *The Records of the Federal Convention of 1787*, 4 vols. (New Haven, 1911–1937) ; Merrill Jensen, editor, *The Documentary History of the Ratification of the Constitution* (Madison, WI: 1976), XIV.

Chapter 7 Practicing Democracy, 1789–1800

Convening a Congress, Inaugurating a President, Adopting a Bill of Rights

Richard Labunski, *James Madison and the Struggle for the Bill of Rights* (New York: Oxford University Press, 2006), pp. 178–185, 187–204;, 278–280; Richard Beeman, *Plain, Honest Men: the Making of the American Constitution* (New York: Random House, 2009), pp. 413–414; John Ferling, *The Ascent of George Washington: The Hidden Political Genius of an American* Icon (New York: Bloomsbury Press, 2009), pp. 278–307.

Creating an Economy: Alexander Hamilton and U.S. Economic System

Ron Chernow, *Alexander Hamilton* (New York: Penguin Books, 2004) is a valuable source of information on Hamilton's life and economic views. See especially pp. 286–295, 291–331, 344–361, 370–381.

Setting the Pace: The Washington Administration

Ron Chernow, *Washington: A Life* (New York: the Penguin Press, 2010) is a useful new biography of George Washington. Also very useful is John Ferling, *The Ascent of George Washington: The Hidden Political Genius of an American Icon* (New York: Bloomsbury Press, 2009), especially pp. 287–289, 317–323, 330. There are many sources on Washington's second term diplomatic maneuvers. I have relied especially on George C. Herring, *From Colony to Superpower: U.S. Foreign Relations Since 1776* (New York: Oxford University Press, 2008), pp. 56–92.

The Birth of Political Parties: Adams and Jefferson

There are many useful descriptions of the election of 1796 and Adams's inauguration. See especially Gordon S. Wood, *Empire of Liberty: A History of the Early Republic* (New York: Oxford University Press, 2009), pp. 206–216; David McCullough, *John Adams* (New York: Simon & Schuster, 2001), pp. 458–471; Ferling, pp. 347–350. For the Quasi-War with France, see George C. Herring, *From Colony to Superpower: U.S. Foreign Relations Since 1776* (New York: Oxford University Press, 2008), pp. 83–92; Wood, *Empire of Liberty*, pp. 209–275; McCullough, pp. 467–536. The best source on the election of 1800 is Edward J. Larson, *A Magnificent Catastrophe: the Tumultuous Election of 1800, America's First Presidential Campaign* (New York: The Free Press, 2007). As the subtitle indicates, this book is a study of just the topic of this section of the chapter. See also Wood, pp. 276–314; McCullough, pp. 535–559.

Chapter 8 Creating a New People, Expanding the Country, 1801–1823

Jefferson and the Republican Ideal

Gordon S. Wood, *Empire of Liberty: A History of the Early Republic, 1789–1815* (New York: Oxford University Press, 2009) is a first rate overview of the culture and political life of the U.S. in the Jeffersonian era and beyond. It has served as my prime source for much of this material. See especially, pp. 276–356 and 576–619. For Jefferson's relationship with Sally Hemings, see Annette Gordon-Reed, *The Hemingses of Monticello: An American Family* (New York: W. W. Norton, 2008).

The Ideal of Religious Freedom

For religious developments in the era an excellent place to start is Sydney E. Ahlstrom, *A Religious History of the American People*, Second Edition (New Haven: Yale University Press, 2004), pp. 429–454. See also Alice Felt Tyler, *Freedom's Ferment: Phases of American Social*

History from the Colonial Period to the Outbreak of the Civil War (New York: Harper & Row, 1944); Thomas L. Webber, *Deep Like the Rivers: Education in the Slave Quarter Community, 1831–1865* (New York: W. W. Norton, 1978), pp. 80–81, 191–206; Ira Berlin, *The Making of African America: The Four Great Migrations* (New York: Viking, 2010), p. 93; John Hope Franklin and Alfred A. Moss, Jr., *From Slavery to Freedom: A History of African Americans*, Seventh Edition (New York: Alfred A. Knopf, 1994), pp. 100–103; Hasia R. Diner, *A New Promised Land: A History of Jews in America* (New York: Oxford University Press, 2003), pp. 17–21.

Beyond the Mississippi: The Louisiana Purchase and the Expedition of Lewis and Clark

George C. Herring, *From Colony to Superpower: U.S. Foreign Relations Since 1776* (New York: Oxford University Press, 2008), pp. 101–109; Wood, *Empire of Liberty*, pp. 357–399; Ned Sublette, *The World That Made New Orleans: From Spanish Silver to Congo Square* (Chicago: Lawrence Hill Books, 2008), especially pp. 106–111 and 161–164; Mari Jo Buhle, Teresa Murphy, and Jane Gerhard, *Women and the Making of America* (Upper Saddle River, NJ: Pearson Prentice Hall, 2009), pp. 115–117. For the Lewis and Clark expedition's story, I have relied primarily on Frederick E. Hoxie and Jay T. Nelson, editors, *Lewis & Clark and the Indian Country: The Native American Perspective* (Urbana: University of Illinois Press, 2007) and the classic *Journals of Lewis and Clark*, edited by Bernard DeVoto (Boston: Houghton Mifflin, 1953). For two very different views of the expedition see also Alvin M. Josephy, Jr., *Lewis and Clark Through Indian Eyes* (New York: Vintage, 2006) and Stephen E. Ambrose, *Undaunted Courage: Meriwether Lewis, Thomas Jefferson, and the Opening of the American West* (New York: Simon & Schuster, 1996).

The War of 1812: "Mr. Madison's War"

The story of the War of 1812 is told in many places. I have drawn primarily on Herring, *From Colony to Superpower*, pp. 93–133; Wood, *Empire of Liberty*, pp. 659–700; Thomas Bender, *A Nation Among the Nations: America's Place in World History* (New York: Hill & Wang, 2006), pp. 106–115. The material on Tecumseh and the Prophet is from John Sugden, *Tecumseh: A Life* (New York: Henry Holt, 1997), by far the best of many biographies of the Indian leader.

Expanding American Territory and Influence

Herring, *From Colony to Superpower*, pp. 134–175; Wood, *Empire of Liberty*, p. 370; Daniel K. Richter, *Facing East from Indian Country: A Native History of Early America* (Cambridge: Harvard University Press, 2001), pp. 226–236; Sellers, pp. 181–185.

Chapter 9 New Industries, New Politics, 1815–1828

Creating the Cotton Economy

Daniel Walker Howe, *What Hath God Wrought: The Transformation of America, 1815–1848* (New York: Oxford University Press, 2007) and Gene Dattel, *Cotton and Race in the Making of America: the Human Costs of Economic Power* (Chicago: Ivan R. Dee, 2009) are essential reading for understanding the impact of cotton on the United States in the early 1800s. See also Henry Bibb, *Narrative of the Life and Adventures of Henry Bibb* (New York: Published by the Author, 1849), pp. 114–118, cited in Sean Patrick Adams, *The Early American Republic: A Documentary Reader* (Malden, MA: Wiley-Blackwell, 2009), pp. 99–101; "R" in the *Voice of Industry*, March 26, 1847, cited in Philip S. Foner, editor, *The Factory Girls* (Urbana: University of Illinois Press, 1977), pp. 87–88 as well as the rest of that volume; Phyllis Deane, *The First Industrial Revolution* (Cambridge: Cambridge University Press, 2nd edition, 1979); Angela Lakwete, *Inventing the Cotton Gin* (Baltimore: Johns Hopkins University Press, 2003); Constance McL. Green, *Eli Whitney and the Birth of American Technology* (Boston: Little, Brown, 1956);. Ira Berlin, *The Making of African America: The Four Great Migrations* (New York: Viking, 2010), pp. 99–130; Charles Ball, *Fifty Years in Chains; or, The Life of An American Slave* (New York: H. Dayton, 1860), pp. 28–31, 240–241, 280; Harriet H. Robinson, *Loom and Spindle: Or Life Among the Early Mill Girls* (New York, 1898; reprinted Kailua, HI: Press Pacifica, 1976); Alan J. Singer, *New York and Slavery: Time to Teach the Truth* (Albany: State University of New York press, 2008), pp. 89–93. For the story of the packet ships see Stephen Fox, *Transatlantic: Samuel Cunard, Isambard Brunel, and the Great Atlantic Steamships* (New York: Harper Collins, 2003), pp. 3–7.

Commerce, Technology, and Transportation

In addition to Howe, *What Hath God Wrought*, Charles Sellers, *The Market Revolution: Jacksonian America, 1815–1846* (New York: Oxford University Press, 1991) is essential reading for this material. See also Carol Sheriff, *The Artificial River: The Erie Canal and the Paradox of Progress, 1817–1862* (New York: Hill and Wang, 1996); Washington Irving, *The Sketch Book* (New York, 1819). Gordon Wood's Introduction to *Empire of Liberty* tells the Rip Van Winkle story and its implications for a changing America very well. For the story of Ichabod Washburn see Joyce Appleby, *Inheriting the Revolution: The First Generation of Americans* (Cambridge: Harvard University Press, 2000), p. 9. See also Sellers, pp. 152–157.

From the Era of Good Feeling to the Politics of Division

Howe, *What Hath God Wrought* and Sellers, *The Market Revolution* are also essential reading for understanding the politics of the 1820s. For further detail see Joseph J. Ellis, *American Sphinx: The Character of Thomas Jefferson* (New York: Random House, 1996), pp. 316–317; Jon Meacham, *American Lion: Andrew Jackson in the White House* (New York: Random House, 2008), pp. 41–49.

Chapter 10 Democracy in the Age of Jackson, 1828–1844

Jacksonian Democracy, Jacksonian Government

Jon Meacham, *American Lion: Andrew Jackson in the White House* (New York: Random House, 2008) is an excellent political biography of Jackson. To understand the opposition to Jackson it is useful to read David S. Heidler and Jeanne T. Heidler, *Henry Clay: The Essential American* (New York: Random House, 2010). For an overview of the Jacksonian era an excellent source is Daniel Walker Howe, *What Hath God Wrought: The Transformation of America, 1815–1848* (New York: Oxford University Press, 2007); William G. McLaughlin's *Cherokee Renascence in the New Republic* (Princeton: Princeton University Press, 1986).remains the best story of the Cherokee experience in the half century leading up to Removal. Also important is Theda Perdue, *Cherokee Women* (Lincoln: University of Nebraska Press, 1998); Howe, *What Hath God Wrought*, pp. 342–357 and 414–423 and Meacham, *American Lion: Andrew Jackson in the White House*, pp. 141–145. De

Tocqueville quote is from Alexis de Tocqueville, *Democracy in America* (originally 1835; reprinted New York: Penguin Books, 2003), p. 380, pp. 463–464; Charles Sellers, *The Market Revolution: Jacksonian America, 1815–1846* (New York: Oxford University Press, 1991).

Democratized Religion: The Second Great Awakening

Sydney E. Ahlstrom, *A Religious History of the American People* (New Haven: Yale University Press, 2004), pp. 385–647; Jon Butler, *Awash in a Sea of Faith: Christianizing the American People* (Cambridge: Harvard University Press, 1990), p. 289; Timothy L. Smith, "Protestant Schooling and American Nationality, 1800–1850," *Journal of American History*, Vol. 53 (1966–67), pp. 679–694; Whitney R. Cross, *The Burned-Over District: The Social and Intellectual History of Enthusiastic Religion in Western New York, 1800–1850* (Ithaca, NY: Cornell University Press, 1950), especially pp. 151–169; Charles G. Finney, *Memoirs* (New York, 1876), p. 24; Mari Jo Buhle, Teresa Murphy, Jane Gerhard, *Women in the Making of America* (Upper Saddle River, NJ: Pearson Prentice Hall, 2009), p. 199; James W. Fraser, *Pedagogue for God's Kingdom: Lyman Beecher And The Second Great Awakening* (Lanham, MD: University Press of America, 1985); Louis Menand, *The Metaphysical Club* (New York: Farrar, Straus and Giroux, 2001), pp. 16–22; Ralph Waldo Emerson, "An Address Delivered before the Senior Class in Divinity College, Cambridge, Sunday Evening 15 July, 1838," included in Nina Baym, *The Norton Anthology of American Literature*, Fifth Edition, Vol. I (New York: W. W. Norton, 1998), pp. 1114–1126. There have been several excellent accounts of America's nineteenth-century communitarian movements including Dolores Hayden, *Seven American Utopias: The Architecture of Communitarian Socialism, 1790–1975* (Cambridge: MIT Press, 1976); J. Stein, *The Shaker Experience in America* (New Haven: Yale University Press, 1992); Spencer Klaw, *Without Sin: The Life and Death of the Oneida Community* (New York: Penguin Press, 1993); John Humphrey Noyes, *History of American Socialisms*; (1870); Robert Owen, *The Life of Robert Owen by Himself* (1920; first published in 1857); Charles Nordhoff, *The Communistic Societies of the United States* (1875); and Alice Felt Tyler, *Freedom's Ferment* (Minneapolis: University of Minnesota Press, 1944).

Democratized Education: The Birth of the Common School

Catharine Beecher, "An Essay on the Education of Female Teachers (New York: Van Nostrand & Dwight, 1835); Margaret A. Nash, *Women's Education in the United States, 1780–1840* (New York: Palgrave Macmillan, 2005); Kathryn Kish Sklar, *Catharine Beecher: A Study in American Domesticity* (New York: W. W. Norton, 1973); Anne Firor Scott, "The Ever Widening Circle: The Diffusion of Feminist Values from Troy Female Seminary," *History of Education Quarterly* (Spring, 1979), 3–25; James W. Fraser, *Preparing America's Teachers: A History* (New York: Teachers College Press, 2007); Polly Welts Kaufman, *Women Teachers on the Frontier* (New Haven: Yale University Press, 1984) ; Carl F. Kaestle, *Pillars of the Republic: Common Schools and American Society, 1780–1860* (New York: Hill and Wang, 1983); Wayne Urban and Jennings Wagoner, *American Education: A History* (New York: Routledge, 2008); Michael Katz, *The Irony of Early School Reform* (Cambridge: Harvard University Press, 1968).

Chapter 11 Manifest Destiny—Expanding the Nation, 1830–1853

Manifest Destiny: The Importance of an Idea

Anders Stephanson, *Manifest Destiny: American Expansionism and the Empire of Right* (New York: Hill and Wang, 1995); Frederick Merk, *Manifest Destiny and Mission in American History: A Reinterpretation* (New York: Alfred A. Knopf, 1963); Robert W. Merry, *A Country of Vast Designs: James K. Polk, the Mexican War and the Conquest of the American Continent* (New York: Simon and Schuster, 2009); Daniel Walker Howe, *What Hath God Wrought: The Transformation of America, 1815–1848* (New York: Oxford University Press, 2007), pp. 702–722; George C. Herring, *From Colony to Superpower: U.S. Foreign Relations Since 1776* (New York: Oxford University Press, 2008), pp. 173–184. See also Antonio Maria Osio, *The History of California: A Memoir of Mexican California*, translated and edited by Rose Maria Beebe and Robert M. Senkewicz (Madison: University of Wisconsin Press, 1996), p. 247; William C. David, *Lone Star Rising: the Revolutionary Birth of the Texas Republic* (New York: Free Press, 2004), pp. 213–224, 1–27, 73; Gregg Cantrell, *Stephen F. Austin: Empresario of Texas* (New Haven: Yale University Press, 1999), pp. 104–201, 348–364; Rodolfo F. Acuna, *Occupied America: A History of Chicanos*, Seventh Edition (Boston: Longman, 2011), pp. 39–43. The web site www.uselectionsatlas.org/TESULTS/national is a very helpful resource for tracking the breakdown of votes in all presidential elections from 1789 to the present.

The U.S. War with Mexico, 1846–1848

For the U.S. War with Mexico, see especially Robert W. Merry, *A Country of Vast Designs: James K. Polk, the Mexican War and the Conquest of the American Continent* (New York: Simon and Schuster, 2009) and Daniel Walker Howe, *What Hath God Wrought: The Transformation of America, 1815–1848* (New York: Oxford University Press, 2007), pp. 731–791. See also John Quincy Adams cited in Nash Candelaria, *Not By The Sword* (Tempe, AZ: Bilingual Press, 1982), p. 1; Roy P. Basler, editor, *Abraham Lincoln: His Speeches and Writings* (Cleveland: World Publishing, 1946), p. 202; Henry David Thoreau, *On the Duty of Civil Disobedience* (1848, republished New York: Macmillan, 1962); Carlos R. Herrera, "New Mexico Resistance to U.S. Occupation," in Erlinda Gonzales-Berry and David R. Maciel, editors, The Contested Homeland: A Chicano History of New Mexico (Albuquerque: University of New Mexico Press, 2000); Ronald Takaki, *A Different Mirror: A History of Multicultural America* (Boston: Little, Brown, 1993), p. 168–171; Norman Graebner, *Empire on the Pacific: A Study of American Continental Expansion* (New York, 1955); Alan Rosenus, *General Vallejo and the Advent of the Americans* (Berkeley, CA: Heyday Books, 1999), pp. 105–119; Mariano G. Vallejo, "What the Gold Rush Brought to California," in Valeska Bari, *The Course of Empire, First Hand Accounts of California in the Days of the Gold Rush of '49* (New York: Coward-McCann, 1931), pp. 55–56; Leonard Pitt, *The Decline of the Californios: A Social History of the Spanish-Speaking Californians, 1846–1890* (Berkeley: University of California Press, 1966, 1998); Genaro M. Padilla, *My History, Not Yours: The Formation of Mexican American Autobiography* (Madison: University of Wisconsin Press, 1993); Douglas Monroy, *Thrown Among Strangers: the Making of Mexican Culture in Frontier California* (Berkeley: University of California Press, 1990); Lisbeth Haas, *Conquests and Historical Identities in California, 1769–1936* (Berkeley: University of California Press, 1995); and Ramon A. Gutierrez and Richard J. Orsi, editors, *Contested Eden: California Before the Gold Rush* (Berkeley: University of California Press, 1998); Susan Lee Johnson, *Roaring Camp: The Social World of the California Gold Rush* (New York: W. W. Norton, 2000).

West into the Pacific

Eric Jay Dolin, *Leviathan: A History of Whaling in America* (New York: W. W. Norton, 2007); Herman Melville, *Moby Dick* (New York: Harper and Brothers, 1851); Jim Murphy, *Gone A-Whaling: The Lure of the Sea and the Hunt for the Great Whale* (New York: Houghton Mifflin, 1998); George C. Herring, *From Colony to Superpower: U.S. Foreign Relations Since 1776* (New York: Oxford University Press, 2008). See also materials at the New Bedford Whaling Museum www.whalingmuseum.org.

Chapter 12 Living in a Nation of Changing Lands, Changing Faces, Changing Expectations, 1831–1854

A Different People—The Changing Face of the American People in the 1840s and 1850s

Ronald Takaki, Strangers *From A Different Shore: A History of Asian Americans* (New York: Little, Brown, 1989); Iris Chang, *The Chinese in America* (New York: Viking, 2003); Jay P. Dolan, *The Irish Americans: A History* (New York: Bloomsbury Press, 2008); Stanley K. Schultz, Culture Factory: Boston Public Schools, 1789–1860 (New York: Oxford University Press, 1973); Fray Angelico Chavez. *But Time and Chance: The Story of Padre Martinez of Taos, 1793–1867* (Santa Fe, New Mexico: Sunstone Press, 1981); Rodolfo F. Acuna, *Occupied America: A History of Chicanos*, Seventh Edition (Boston: Longman, 2011); Mari Jo Buhle, Teresa Murphy, Jane Gerhard, *Women and the Making of America* (New York: Pearson Prentice Hall, 2009); George C. Herring, *From Colony to Superpower: U.S. Foreign Relations Since 1776* (New York: Oxford University Press, 2008),

Slavery in the United States, 1840s and 1850s

David Brion Davis, *Inhuman Bondage: The Rise and Fall of Slavery in the New World* (New York: Oxford University Press, 2006); Ira Berlin, *The Making of African America: the Four Great Migrations*, Chapter Three, "The Passage to the Interior (New York: Viking, 2010); Eugene D. Genovese, *Roll, Jordan, Roll: The World the Slaves Made* (New York: Vintage, 1976); Harriet Jacobs, *Incidents in the Life of a Slave Girl* (original 1861; Mineola, NY: Dover Publications, 2001); Elizabeth Fox-Genovese, *Within the Plantation Household: Black and White Women of the Old South* (Chapel Hill: University of North Carolina Press, 1988); Timothy S. Huebner, "Roger B. Taney and the Slavery Issue: Looking beyond—and before—*Dred Scott*," *The Journal of American History* 97:1 (June 2010), pp. 17–38; Elizabeth Fox-Genovese and Eugene D. Genovese, *Slavery in White and Black* (New York: Cambridge University Press, 2008); John Hope Franklin and Loren Schweninger, *Runaway Slaves: Rebels on the Plantation* (New York: Oxford University Press, 1999); Harriet Jacobs, "Incidents in the Life of a Slave Girl," in Herb Boyd, editor, *Autobiography of a People* (New York: Doubleday, 2000) cited in pp. 90–92; David E. Swift, *Black Prophets of Justice: Activist Clergy Before the Civil War* (Baton Rouge: Louisiana State University Press, 1989); Frederick Douglass, *Narrative of the Life of Frederick Douglass: An American Slave* (1845; reprinted Cambridge: Harvard University Press, 1967);. Biographical information on Tubman is taken primarily from Nancy A. Davidson, "Harriet Tubman," in *Notable Black American Women*, edited by Jessie Carney Smith (Detroit: Gale Research, 1992), pp. 11151–1155 and Judith Nies, *Seven Women: Portraits from the American Radical Tradition* (New York: Viking, 1977), pp. 34–59. See also Sarah Bradford, *Harriet Tubman: the Moses of Her People* (1886; reprint New York: Corinth, 1961). For slave revolts, see Herbert Aptheker, *American Negro Slave Revolts* (New York, 1943); David Robertson, *Denmark Vesey: The Buried Stories of America's Largest Slave Rebellion and the Man Who Led It* (New York: Alfred A. Knopf, 1999); and Manning Marable and Leith Mullings, *Let Nobody Turn Us Around: Voices of Resistance, Reform, and Renewal: An African American Anthology* (Lanham, MD: Rowman & Littlefield, 2000), pp. 35–36 and "The Statement of Nat Turner, 1831," in Marable and Mullings, *Let Nobody Turn Us Around*, p. 37. David Walker, *David Walker's Appeal in Four Articles; Together with a Preamble, to the Coloured Citizens of the World, but in Particular and Very Expressly, to those of the United States of America* (Boston: Revised and published by David Walker, 3rd ed, 1830), reprinted in Marable and Mullings, *Let Nobody Turn Us Around*, pp. 23–35; Henry Highland Garnet, "An Address to the Slaves of the United States of America," 1843 reprinted in Marable and Mullings, Let Nobody Turn Us Around, pp. 58–63. The best current biography of William Lloyd Garrison is Henry Mayer, *All on Fire: William Lloyd Garrison and the Abolition of Slavery* (New York: St. Martin's Press, 1998). For evangelical abolitionists see Gilbert H. Barnes, *The Antislavery Impulse, 1830–1844* (New York: American Historical Association, 1933, reprinted 1964) and Gilbert H. Barnes and Dwight L. Dumond, eds., *Letters of Theodore Dwight Weld, Angelina Grimke Weld, and Sarah Grimke, 1822–1844*, 2 vols. (1934, reprint Gloucester, MA: Peter Smith, 1965).

New Strength for American Women

The best current account of the Seneca Falls Convention is Judith Wellman, *The Road to Seneca Falls: Elizabeth Cady Stanton and the First Woman's Rights Convention* (Urbana: University of Illinois Press, 2004). See also Elizabeth Cady Stanton, Susan B. Anthony, and Matilda Joslyn Gage, editors, *A History of Woman Suffrage*, vol. I (Rochester, NY, 1881); Elizabeth Cady Stanton, *Eighty Years & More: Reminiscences 1815–1897* (T. Fisher Unwin, 1898, republished Boston: Northeastern University Press, 1993); Sarah M. Grimke, *Letters on the Equality of the Sexes and the Condition of Women* (Boston: Isaac Knapp, 1838), reprinted in Nancy F. Cott, et al, editors, *Roots of Bitterness: Documents of the Social History of American Women* (Boston: Northeastern University Press, 1996), pp. 123–127. For an excellent recent overview of the work of both sisters see the preface to also Gerda Lerner, *The Feminist Thought of Sarah Grimke* (New York: Oxford University Press, 1998), pp. 3–46. For the classic study of the Grimke-Weld work, see Gilbert H. Barnes and Dwight L. Dumond, editors, *Letters of Theodore Dwight Weld, Angelina Grimke Weld and Sarah Grimke: 1822–1844*, 2 vols. (1934, reprint, Gloucester, MA: Peter Smith, 1965). See also Elizabeth Ann Bartlett, editor, *Sarah Grimke, Letters on the Equality of the Sexes and Other Essays* (New Haven: Yale University Press, 1988); Gerda Lerner, editor, *The Feminist Thought of Sarah Grimke* (New York: Oxford University Press, 1998) and Gerda Lerner's *The Grimke Sisters from South Carolina: Rebels against Slavery and for Woman's Rights* (Boston: Houghton Mifflin, 1967). My interpretation of the Grimkes rests primarily on Lerner's important biographical work on their lives. For Sojourner Truth see *The Anti-Slavery Bugle*, June 21, 1851, cited in Manning Marable and Leith Mullings, editors, *Let Nobody Turn Us Around* (Lanham, MD: Rowman & Littlefield, 2000), pp. 67–68. I think there is reason to doubt some later versions of the speech that were rendered in the dialect of southern blacks because Truth spoke all of her life with the Dutch accent of her native Hudson Valley.

Chapter 13 The Politics of Separation, 1850–1861

From Union to Disunion

James McPherson, *Battle Cry of Freedom: The Civil War Era* (New York: Oxford University Press, 1988) is an excellent source on the tensions leading up to the Civil War as it is on the war itself. For the compromises and tensions of the 1850s see also David S. Heidler and Jeanne T. Heidler, *Henry Clay: The Essential American* (New York: Random House, 2010); "The Compromise of 1850," The Library of Congress American Memory Historical Collection, www.loc.gov/rr/program/bib/ourdocs/Compromsie1850.html; Craig Miner, *Seeding Civil War: Kansas in the National News, 1854–1858* (Lawrence: University Press of Kansas, 2008).

Bleeding Kansas and Dred Scott v. Sanford

McPherson, *Battle Cry of Freedom;* Timothy S. Huebner, *The Taney Court: Justices, Rulings, and Legacy* (ABC-CLIO, 2003).

The Economy, the Panic of 1857, and the Lincoln-Douglas Debates

David Brion Davis, *Inhuman Bondage: The Rise and Fall of Slavery in the New World* (New York: Oxford University Press, 2006); Lisa Clayton Robinson, "Uncle Tom's Cabin," *Africana: The Encyclopedia of African and African American Experience, Second Edition*, edited by Kwame Anthony Appiah, edited by Henry Louis Gates Jr. Oxford African American Studies Center, http://www.oxfordaasc.com/article/opr/t0002/e3928 (accessed Sat Oct 9, 2010); Wendy Wagner, "Uncle Tom's Cabin," *The Oxford Companion to United States History*, edited by Paul S. Boyer, Oxford African American Studies Center, http://www.oxfordaasc.com/article/opr/t119/e1567 (accessed Sat Oct 9, 2010); Michael Winship, "Uncle Tom's Cabin: History of the Book in the 19thCentury United States," http://utc.iath.virginia.edu/interpret/exhibits/winship/winship.html (accessed Fri Oct 8, 2010); "Article XIV-Editorial Miscellany," De Bow's Southern and Western Review, March 1853 http://utc.iath.virginia.edu/saxon/servlet/SaxonServlet?source-utc/sml/responses/proslav/p (accessed Fri Oct 8, 2010); Marc Egnal, *Clash of Extremes: The Economic Origins of the Civil War* (New York: Hill and Wang, 2009); Aaron W. Marrs, Railroads in the Old South: Pursuing Progress in a Slave Society (Baltimore: The Johns Hopkins University Press, 2009); Abraham Lincoln, "Speech delivered at Springfield, Illinois, at the close of the Republican State Convention," June 16, 1858, "First Debate, at Ottawa, Illinois, August 21, 1858," "Letter to Doctor C. H. Ray, November 20, 1858," "Letter to Salmon Portland Chase, June 9, 1859," in Roy P. Basler, editor, *Abraham Lincoln: His Speeches and Writings* (Cleveland: World Publishing, 1946); Doris Kearns Goodwin, *Team of Rivals: the Political Genius of Abraham Lincoln* (New York: Simon & Schuster, 2005), pp. 140–210; Edward l. Ayers, *In the Presence of Mine Enemies: The Civil War in the Heart of America, 1859–1863* (New York: W. W. Norton, 2003).

From John Brown to the Secession of the South

Doris Kearns Goodwin, *Team of Rivals: The Political Genius of Abraham Lincoln* (New York: Simon & Schuster, 2005); McPherson, *Battle Cry of Freedom*; Alexander K. McClure, *Old Time Notes of Pennsylvania* (Philadelphia: J. C. Winston Company, 1905, pp. 360362 cited in Edward L. Ayers, *In the Presence of Mine Enemies: The Civil War in the Heart of America, 1859–1863* (New York: W. W. Norton, 2003); Eric Foner, *The Fiery Trial: Abraham Lincoln and American Slavery* (New York: W. W. Norton, 2010).

Chapter 14 And the War Came: The Civil War 1861–1865

Fort Sumter to Antietam, 1861–1862

These accounts of the Civil War are taken primarily from James McPherson, *Battle Cry of Freedom: The Civil War Era* (New York: Oxford University Press, 1988). See also the National Park Service Battle Summaries of every Civil War battle http://www.nps.gov/hps/abpp/civil.htm

The Road to Emancipation

The Most useful source on Lincoln's thinking and the Emancipation Proclamation is Eric Foner, *The Fiery Trial: Abraham Lincoln and American Slavery* (New York: W. W. Norton, 2010); See also Edward L. Ayers, *In the Presence of Mine Enemies: the Civil War in the Heart of America, 1859–1863* (New York: W. W. Norton, 2003); John Hope Franklin and Alfred A. Moss, Jr., *From Slavery to Freedom: A History of African Americans*, Seventh Edition (New York: Alfred A. Knopf, 1994).

The Home Front—Shortages, Opposition, Riots, and Battles

For the impact of the war on civilians, see Drew Gilpin Faust, *Mothers of Invention: Women of the Slaveholding South in the American Civil War* (Chapel Hill: University of North Carolina Press, 1996) as well as McPherson, *Battle Cry of Freedom* and Ayers, *In the Presence of Mine Enemies* and http://www.nps.gov/history/hps.abpp/civil.htm. For an excellent way the death toll of the Civil War changed American attitudes towards death, see Drew Gilpin Faust, *This Republic of Suffering: Death and the American Civil War* (New York: Vintage Books, 2008).

From Gettsburg to Appomattox and Beyond

James McPherson, *Battle Cry of Freedom;* Eric Foner, *The Fiery Trial;* Drew Gilpin Faust, *Mothers of Invention*; Drew Gilpin Faust, *This Republic of Suffering*; Kenneth M. Ludmerer, *Learning to Heal: The Development of American Medical Education* (Baltimore: Johns Hopkins University Press, 1985); Ulysses S. Grant, *Memoirs and Selected Letters* (originally 1885, republished New York: Library of America, 1990), pp. 739–741.

Chapter 15 Reconstruction, 1865–1877

Federal Reconstruction Policy

By far the best source on federal Reconstruction policy is Eric Foner, *Reconstruction: America's Unfinished Revolution, 1863–1877* (New York: Harper & Row, 1988); See also Eric Foner, *The Fiery Trial*; John David Smith, *Black Voices From Reconstruction, 1865–1877* (Gainesville: University Press of Florida, 1997); Francis E. Abernethy, Patrick B. Mullen, Alan B. Govenar, editors, *Juneteenth Texas: Essays in African American Folklore* (Denton; University of North Texas Press, 1996); Henry Mayer, *All on Fire: William Lloyd Garrison and the Abolition of Slavery* (New York: St. Martin's Press, 1998); F. Douglass, "What the Black Man Wants:' Sojourner Truth , 1867 speech in New York City, reprinted in Herb Boyd, editor, *Autobiography of a People* (New York: Anchor Books, 2000); and for election results www.uselectionatlas.org/RESULTS/national.php?year=1868&off=0&f=1 and www.uselectionatlas.org.

The Impact of Reconstruction

Foner, *Reconstruction*, remains a key work. See also William L. Clay, *Just Permanent Interests: Black Americans in Congress, 1870–1992* (New York: Amistad Press, 1993),; John David Smith, *Black Voices From Reconstruction, 1865–1877* (Gainesville: University Press of Florida, 1997); W. E. B. DuBois, *Black Reconstruction in America* (1903, reprinted Boston: Bedford Books, 1997); W. E. B. DuBois, *The Souls of Black Folk* (1903, reprint New York: Crest, 1961); Brenda Stevenson, editor, *The Journals of Charlotte Forten Grimke* (New York: Oxford University Press, 1988); James D. Anderson, *The Education of Blacks in the South, 1860–1935* (Chapel Hill: University of North Carolina Press, 1988); Frederick Douglass, *Narrative of the Life of Frederick Douglass: An American Slave* (1845; Cambridge: Harvard University Press, 1967); Maria S. Waterbury, *Seven Years Among the Freedmen*, cited in Nancy Hoffman, *Woman's "True" Profession: Voices from the History of Teaching* (New York: Feminist Press, 1981); Rupert Sargent Holland, editor, *Letters and Diary of Laura M. Towne* (1912; reprint New York: Negro Universities Press, 1969); and especially Ronald E. Butchart, *Schooling the Freed People: Teaching, Learning, and the Struggle for Black Freedom, 1861–1876* (Chapel Hill: University of North Carolina Press, 2010).

Terror, Apathy, and the Creation of the Segregated South

See Foner, *Reconstruction*; Nicholas Lemann, *Redemption: The Last Battle of the Civil War* (New York: Farrar, Straus and Giroux, 2006); Mary Drake McFeely and William S. McFeely, "Chronology" in Ulysses S. Grant, *Memoirs and Selected Letters* (New York: The Library of American, 1990); Charles Lane, *The Day Freedom Died: The Colfax Massacre, the Supreme Court, and the Betrayal of Reconstruction* (New York: Henry Holt, 2008); Frances Smith Foster, "Introduction" to Frances E. W. Harper, *Iola Leroy* (1892; reprinted New York: Oxford University Press, 1988); and C. Vann Woodward, *The Strange Career of Jim Crow* (New York: Oxford University Press, 1966). See also "Speech on September 3, 1868, before the Georgia State Legislature," and Frances Ellen Watkins Harper, "An Address Delivered at the Centennial Anniversary of the Pennsylvania Society for Promoting the Abolition of Slavery, 1875," reprinted in Manning Marable and Leith Mullings, editors, *Let Nobody Turn Us Around: An African American Anthology* (Lanham, MD: Rowman & Littlefield, 2000), pp. 131–134 and pp. 138–143.

Photo Credits

[LC-DIG-ppmsca-33122], 377; Library of Congress Prints and Photographs Division [LC-DIG-ppmsca-19520], 381.

CHAPTER 14
The Metropolitan Museum of Art. Image source/Art Resource, NY, 385; National Archives and Records Administration Washington, DC 20408, 387; Bettmann/CORBIS, 390; Library of Congress Prints and Photographs Division [LC-DIG-cwpb-01131], 391; Library of Congress Prints and Photographs Division [LC-DIG-cwpb-02004], 393; Library of Congress Prints and Photographs Division [LC-USZC2-6431], 397; Library of Congress Prints and Photographs Division [LC-USZ62-42028], 398; Draft Riots in New York, 'The mob lynching a negro in Clarkson Street', 1863 (litho), American School, (19th century)/ Private Collection/Peter Newark American Pictures/The Bridgeman Art Library, 400; Library of Congress Prints and Photographs Division [LC-B8184-7964-A], 402; CORBIS, 405; Library of Congress Prints and Photographs Division [LC-DIG-ppmsca-08231], 410; Library of Congress Prints and Photographs Division [LC-DIG-cwpb-02596], 411.

CHAPTER 15
North Wind Picture Archives/Alamy, 417; Library of Congress Prints and Photographs Division [LC-USZ62-22120], 420; Library of Congress Prints and Photographs Division [LC-DIG-pga-04115], 423; Library of Congress, Prints & Photographs Division [LC-USZ62-125422], 429; Library of Congress Prints & Photographs Division [LC-DIG-ppmsca-17564], 431; Library of Congress Prints and Photographs Division/Taylor, James E[LC-USZ62-37860], 434; Library of Congress Prints and Photographs Division [LC-DIG-ppmsca-11370], 437; Charles Phelps Cushing/ClassicStock/Corbis, 438; Library of Congress Prints and Photographs Division [LC-USZ62-119565], 441; Library of Congress Prints and Photographs Division [LC-USZ62-111152], 442.

Text Credits

CHAPTER 1
Joe S. Sando. Nee Hemish: A History of Jemez Pueblo (New Mexico: Clear Light Publishers, 2008): 4; Quote originally appeared in a book from 1758 written by Antoine Simon Le Page du Prate entitled The History of Louisiana: OR of the Western Parts of Virginia and Carolina: 6; Translated out of Latin into English by Richard Hacklvit. [82] p, ill. [New York] [J. Sabin & Sons] [1871]: 13.

CHAPTER 2
Oliver Dunn and James E. Kelley, Jr, translators, The Diario of Christopher Columbus's First Voyage to America, 1492–1493, abstracted by Fray Bartolome de las Casas (Norman: University of Oklahoma Press, 1988), pp. 17–19: 29; de las Casas, Bartolomé. Historia de las Indias. (Madrid: Imprenta de Miguel Ginesta, 1875-1876). Jay I. Kislak Collection Library of Congress; John Boyd Thacher Collection, Library of Congress. Alvar Núñez Cabeza de Vaca. Cabeza de Vaca's Adventures in the Unknown Interior of America (New Mexico: University of New Mexico Press, 1983): 41.

CHAPTER 3
William Bradford. History of Plymouth Plantation. (Massachusetts: Little Brown, 1856): 63; Adapted from Goldfield, David, Abbott, Carl E.; Anderson, Virginia Dejohn; Argersinger, Jo Ann E.; Argersinger, Peter H.; Barney, William M.; Weir, Robert M., The American Journey: Commbined 3rd Ed., © 2004, p. 49. Reprinted and Electronically reproduced by permission of Pearson Education, Upper Saddle River, New Jersey: 66; Selections from Mary Rowlandson, The Sovereignty and Goodness of God, 1682, in Nathaniel Philbrick and Thomas Philbrick, editors, The Mayflower Papers: Selected Writings of Colonial New England (New York; Penguin Books, 2007), pp. 166–211: 74; Louis B. Wright and Elaine W. Fowler. Documents of Modern History: English Colonization of North America (New York: St. Martin's Press, 1968), pp. 163–165: 76; Reuben Gold Thwaites, editor, Travels and Explorations of the Jesuit Missionaries in New France, 1610–1791, Vol. LXV, Lower Canada, Mississippi Valley, 1696–1702 (Cleveland: The Burrows Brothers, 1900), pp. 101–105, 127–129, 145–147, 159–161: 80.

CHAPTER 4
Benjamin Franklin, The Works of Benjamin Franklin, with Notes and a Life of the Author by Jared Sparks. (London: Benjamin Franklin Stevens, 1882): 102; Early Americans by Carl Bridenbaugh, 1981 (New York: Oxford University Press, 1981), chapter five, "'The Famous Infamous Vagrant' Tom Bell," in pp. 121–149 By permission of Oxford Press, USA: 104; Jonathan Edwards, A Treatise Concerning Religious Affections (Boston: S. Kneeland and T. Green, 1746): 109.

CHAPTER 5
Phillis Wheatley. To the Right Honourable William, Earl of Dartmouth. 1773: 133; Joseph Plumb Martin, A Narrative of the Adventures, Dangers, and Sufferings of a Revolutionary Soldier: 141.

CHAPTER 6
Prince Hall, "Thus Doth Ethiopia Stretch Forth Her Hand from Slavery, to Freedom and Equality," (1797) in Manning Marable and Leith Mullings, editors, Let Nobody Turn Us Around: Voices of Resistance, Reform, and Renewal (Lanham, MD: Rowman & Littlefield, 2000), pp. 16–18: 161; Judith Sargent Murray, "On the Equality of the Sexes," first published in the Massachusetts Magazine, April 1790: 164; James Madison, The Federalist No. 10, November 22, 1787: 173; Patrick Henry, "Against the Federal Constitution," June 5, 1788: 173.

CHAPTER 7
Moses Seixas. Letter to President Washington. 1770. Library of Congress: 189; Letter from G. Washington To the Hebrew Congregation in Newport Rhode Island: 189.

CHAPTER 8
Frederick E. Hoxie and Jay T. Nelson, editors, Lewis & Clark and the Indian Country: The Native American Perspective (Urbana: University of Illinois Press, 2007), pp. 136–141: 225; Frederick E. Hoxie and Jay T. Nelson, editors, Lewis & Clark and the Indian Country: The Native American Perspective © 2007 Caxton Press: 225; Tecumseh. Speech to Governor Harrison at Vincennes. 1810: 229.

CHAPTER 9
Charles Ball, Fifty Years in Chains; or, The Life of An American Slave (New York: H. Dayton, 1860), pp. 28–31, 240–241, 280: 247; Harriet H. Robinson, Loom and Spindle: Or Life Among the Early Mill Girls (New York, 1898; reprinted Kailua, HI: Press Pacifica, 1976), pp. 42, 48–49, 51–52: 250.

CHAPTER 10
Andrew Jackson, Message to Congress, December 8, 1829: 277; RESIDENTS OF THE STATE OF OHIO, Town of Steubenville: ; Cherokee Women's Petition, June 30, 1818: 277; Timothy Dwight and Julian Hawthorne. The World's Great Classics: Democracy in America, by A. de Tocqueville. (Boalsburg: Colonial Press, 1899): 277; Stephen J. Stein, The Shaker Experience in America (New Haven: Yale University Press, 1992), p. 191: 291.

CHAPTER 11
Root of Bitterness by Nancy Cott pp. 185–192. University of New England, Lebanon, NH. Reprinted with permissions pages 185–192: 306; Henry David Thoreau (1817–1862) published "On the Duty of Civil Disobedience" in 1849: 316.

CHAPTER 12
Edmund Ruffin, "Slavery and Free Labor, Described and Compared," Library of Congress, American memory, From Slavery to Freedom: the African-American Pamphlet Collection, 1824–1909, http://memory.loc.gov: 341; Norman R. Yetman, editor, Voices From Slavery: 100 Authentic Slave Narratives (Mineola, NY: Dover Publications, 2000): 343; Austin Steward, Twenty-two Years a Slave and Forty Years a Freeman (1856) in Herb Boyd, editor, Autobiography of a People: Three Centuries of African American History Told By Those Who Lived It (New York: Random House, 2000), pp. 70–75: 346.

CHAPTER 13
U.S. Supreme Court: 368; Letters of Lydia Maria Child 1859, Garrison's Liberator: 373; Letter Governor Henry A. Wise, in Garrison's Liberator: 373.

CHAPTER 14
Susie King Taylor, Reminiscences of My Life in Camp with the 33D United States Colored Troops Late 1st S.C. Volunteers (Boston: Published by the Author, 1902), pp. 10–12 downloaded October 25, 2010, University of North Carolina at Chapel Hill: 396.

CHAPTER 15
John David Smith, Black Voices From Reconstruction, 1865–1877 (Gainesville: University Press of Florida, 1997), pp. 43–44: 419; Frances Ellen Watkins Harper, "An Address Delivered at the Centennial Anniversary of the Pennsylvania Society for Promoting the Abolition of Slavery, 1875," in Manning Marable and Leith Mullings, editors, Let Nobody Turn Us Around: Voices of Resistance, Reform, and Renewal (Lanham, MD: Rowman & Littlefield, 2000), pp. 138–143: 429.

Index

Winslow, Edward, 72
Winslow, Josiah, 73
Winthrop, John, 63, 64
Wirz, Henry, 431
Wisconsin, 154, 192
Wise, Henry A., 373
Witch trials (Salem), 98–99
Wolcott, Oliver, 186
Wolfe, James, 121
Wollstonecraft, Mary, 163
Wolsey, Thomas, 49
Women
  See also Feminism
  after the American Revolution, 162–165
  and the American Revolution, 130–131, 139–140
  as business owners, 99, 338
  Cherokee, 277
  in colonial America, 98–100, 115
  in the Confederacy, 398
  as gold miners, 322, 323
  as healers, 100
  Irish, 334
  in New Orleans, 223
  as nurses, 404–406
  property rights of, 352
  as prostitutes, 333
  in the Quaker religion, 68
  in religious communities, 289, 291
  and the right to vote, 164–165, 430
  rights of, 289, 331, 350–353
  and the Salem witch trials, 99
  as slaves, 100, 162, 342
  support for Continental Army by, 144

as teachers, 294–295
violence toward, 214
on whaling ships, 325
Woodville, Richard Caton, 315
Worcester v. Georgia, 261, 278
World Anti-Slavery Convention, 351
Wright, Frances (Fanny), 352
Wyandot tribe, 123, 124

X

XYZ Affair, 200, 203

Y

Yale University, 108, 217
Yamasee tribe, 111–112
Yamasee Wars, 111–112
Yancey, William Lowndes, 376
Yokuts, 11
York (slave), 223
York family, 18
Young Ladies' Academy (Philadelphia), 163
Young, Brigham, 293
Young, Clara, 219
Young, Litt, 219

Z

Zenger, John Peter, 87–88
Zhu Di, 23, 25
Zhu Gaozhi, 24
Zunis, 4, 7, 42
Zutucapan, 47